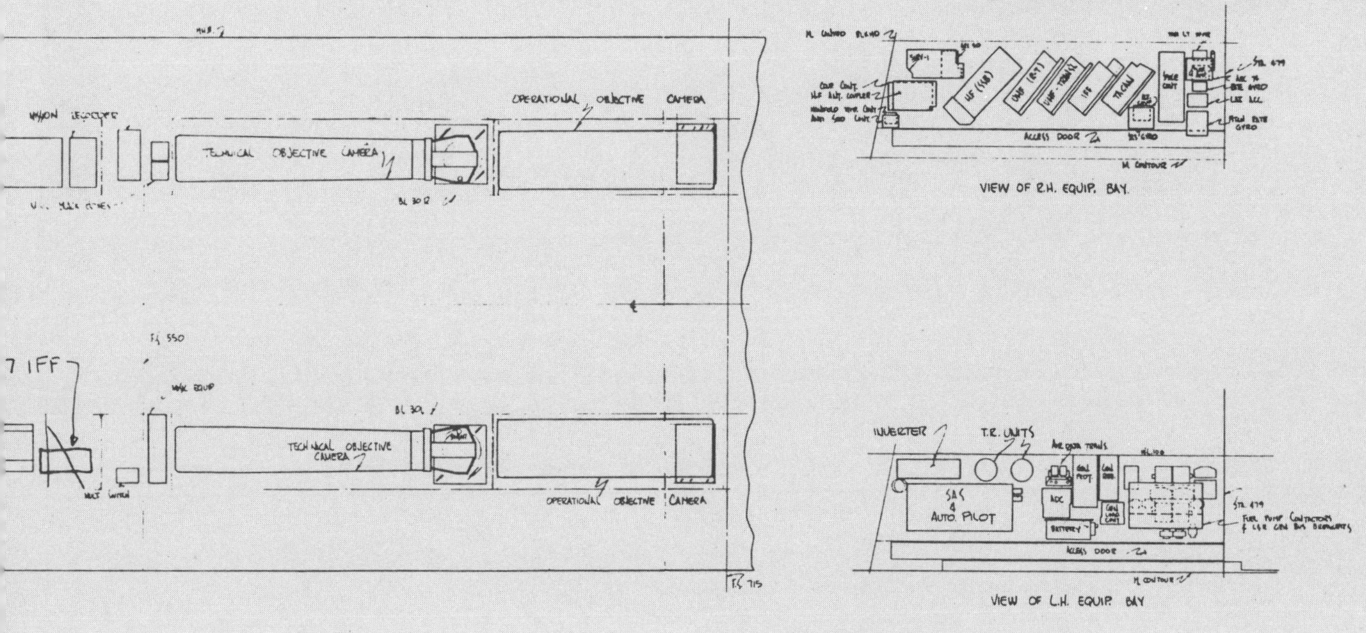

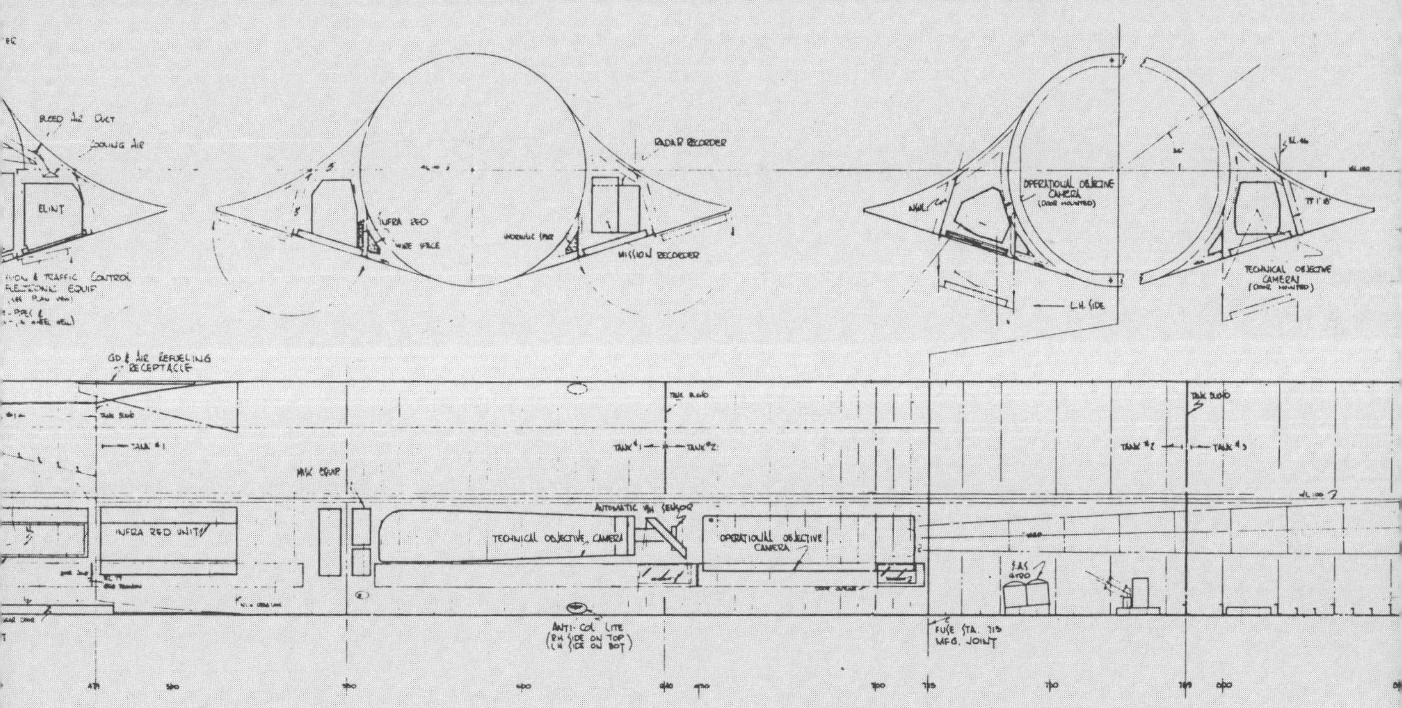

ADVANCED DEVELOPMENT PROJECTS LOCKHEED-CALIFORNIA COMPANY A DIVISION OF LOCKHEED AIRCRAFT CORPORATION		NO REQ	MODEL	NEXT ASSEM
		REQUIREMENTS PER SHIP		
MFG & FINISH PER LAC PROCESS SPEC. 100	INBOARD PROFILE R-12	DRAWN TAYLOR 5-27-63		
TOLERANCES EXCEPT AS NOTED .XX ± .03 .XXX = ± .010		APPD.		
SCALE 1/10		I.P. - R-12		

LOCKHEED
SR-71
THE SECRET MISSIONS EXPOSED

LOCKHEED SR-71

THE SECRET MISSIONS EXPOSED

Paul F Crickmore

For Nicola and Matthew

First published in Great Britain in spring 1993 by
Osprey Publishing, Elms Court,
Chapel Way, Botley, Oxford
OX2 9LP
E-mail: info@ospreypublishing.com

First reprint winter 1993
Second reprint autumn 1995
Revised edition spring 1997
Reprinted 2001

ISBN 1 85532 681 7

Editor Tony Holmes
1997 revision edited by Shaun Barrington
Designer Colin Paine
1997 jacket designed by the Black Spot
© Cutaway by Mike Badrocke/Aviagraphica
Typesetting by Servis Filmsetting Ltd, Manchester
Origination by Mandarin Offset, Hong Kong

Printed and bound in China through Bookbuilders, Hong Kong

Front jacket photograph by Paul F. Crickmore
Back jacket photograph, courtesy Blair Bozek, USAF

Contents

Foreword

Most people around Lockheed consider Paul Crickmore's first book about the SR-71 'the best book ever' about the world's most amazing flying machine. Paul's second volume is a superb collection of photographic essays in which the magnificent aeroplane speaks for itself. This third work reaches beyond the first two, bringing to the world the experiences of those who flew the early test flights and the important reconnaissance missions during the aircraft's quarter century of secret operations.

While working on his first book, Paul trod a tricky path through the thicket of high security classification to interview the pioneers of Mach 3 flight, who were naturally most reluctant to make statements for attribution. Paul's oral history research has now set the record straight and has blown away much of the myth and misinformation which has existed for years. Because of that shroud of secrecy, many people still say nothing, despite having helped in the great leap forward into the sustained high-speed flight brought about by Kelly's engineering genius.

Paul's new book faithfully documents the 'Habu's' achievements through the words of Lockheed, *Oxcart*, and SAC aircrewmembers. In his work we now share some of our exciting moments with the millions of SR-71 fans all over the world.

From my perspective in these brief comments, which are certain to be politically incorrect, two points should be made, although space constraints preclude elaboration. Firstly, it was a shocking error to have withdrawn this incomparable national asset. It was perfect for crisis management because of its ability to provide timely and accurate intelligence information to the President of the United States. And secondly, a unique opportunity was lost way back in the 1960s to provide America with pre-eminent military superiority for decades to come.

From the designer's standpoint, the hard part is designing an aerial platform that can go so high, so fast and so far, and that is what Kelly Johnson did. The relatively easy part, and this is where the opportunity was lost, is to modify that platform with missiles and call it an interceptor, with an H-Bomb and call it a strategic bomber, or, as was done with ELINT sensors and cameras, and call it a reconnaissance vehicle, whose mission was described as 'Global Strategic Reconnaissance'.

Speed and altitude would render such a

Copyright Bob Seidemann

vehicle virtually impregnable through the laws of physics, even though it would also possess ingenious stealth features. Kelly Johnson said, 'I have been involved in stealth since 1958', although the word itself was seldom mentioned until the 1980s.

Large-scale production efficiencies and commonality – an expression favoured by the then Secretary of Defense, Robert S McNamara – would have resulted in extremely low cost for such advanced capability. America could have had a lot more 'bang for the buck' that would be utilized even today. Thermal thicket? Metal fatigue? The airframe would be heat annealed and strengthened on every flight.

And what of the future? Back in the 1960s, Kelly Johnson confidently asserted, 'No airplane will exceed the performance of the SR-71 by the year 2000!' He knew better than anyone the attendant difficulties involved. When, and if, someone comes along and develops an efficient, long range, hypersonic air-breather, the entire world should stand back in awe and admiration. We all hope it happens.

Until then, we must salute the magnificent SR-71, which currently holds the official speed and altitude records, and all of those individuals who have contributed to its success, and especially to author Paul Crickmore, who now brings aviation fans everywhere the hitherto unknown comprehensive story.

Robert Gilliland
SR-71 Chief Test Pilot

Foreword

For the first time since the conception of the mysterious SR-71, you are about to learn its secrets, which were recently declassified. As you read of the places and events which shaped our national strategic reconnaissance efforts since the 1960s, appreciate that the missions we flew were integral to a very serious pursuit of truth in the international arena. Reconnaissance is critical – sorting an enemy's capability and intention fills the gap between what they say, and what they do. In the Soviet Union during the communist era, that gap was enormous. This book clearly etches in bold relief the central core of our mission – strategic reconnaissance.

The pursuit was fraught with danger; the more aggressive and technically advanced the adversary, the more dangerous our mission, but the reward was the isolation of totalitarian powers. We were convinced that for our freedom to thrive uncompromised, we had to be the best pilots and navigators, fly the best aircraft, operate the best intelligence-gathering sensors, be protected by the best defensive systems, and develop the best tactical doctrine against real and forseen threats. The word 'best' is not hollow, as the stark realization was clear – all of our adversaries (at one time or another Vietnam, China, North Korea, the Soviet Union, East Germany, Poland, Cuba, Libya, Syria, Nicaragua and Iran) would have, with lip-smacking delight, shot us down, captured or killed us and credited themselves with an international incident/victory over the 'great, imperialist, war-mongering United States'.

This story illustrates the dedication and sense of mission absolutely necessary if our civilization is to survive forever. There always will be enemies of freedom – the mighty blast of the twin-engined, afterburning SR-71, and its distinctive double sonic boom, are rightly described as 'the sounds of freedom'.

The SR-71 story is a proud record of a few individuals dedicated to that mission. It is illustrated by every person who created the most formidable aircraft ever flown, and by the maintenance crews who worked unceasingly and skilfully on an aircraft designed for speed but not for maintenance. Each crewmember who put his heart and soul into his work, willingly put his life on the line striving for excellence. Success in this programme was assured through a consistent and nurtured team effort, towards a shared and united objective.

The SR-71 was conceived from a serious deficiency in our reconnaissance capability

– the need to overfly armed, dangerously hostile territory. This spurred the creative talents of national authorities responsible for maintaining military pre-eminence. Private aircraft companies were challenged to develop an overflight reconnaissance system, and the genius Kelly Johnson, free enterprise, and channelled, talented, individualism, eagerly met that challenge in an awesome, unprecedented burst of accomplishment.

In the annals of technological development, there are few parallels to the story in this book – the concept, design, testing, and operational development of the SR-71. When discussing the 'Habu', and its sister aircraft, throw comparatives out of the window as superlatives invariably rule – the fastest, the highest flying, the most hostile flying environment, most highly classified.

Being an SR-71 crewmember is a privilege all of us cherish. To serve in such a unique capacity is truly an honour.

Paul F Crickmore, who has written two definitive volumes on the SR-71, is clearly the best author to reveal its secrets now that the aircraft is no longer classified. I am glad he has seized this opportunity to publish quickly the overall history of the programme. History is well served.

BC Thomas
'Habu'

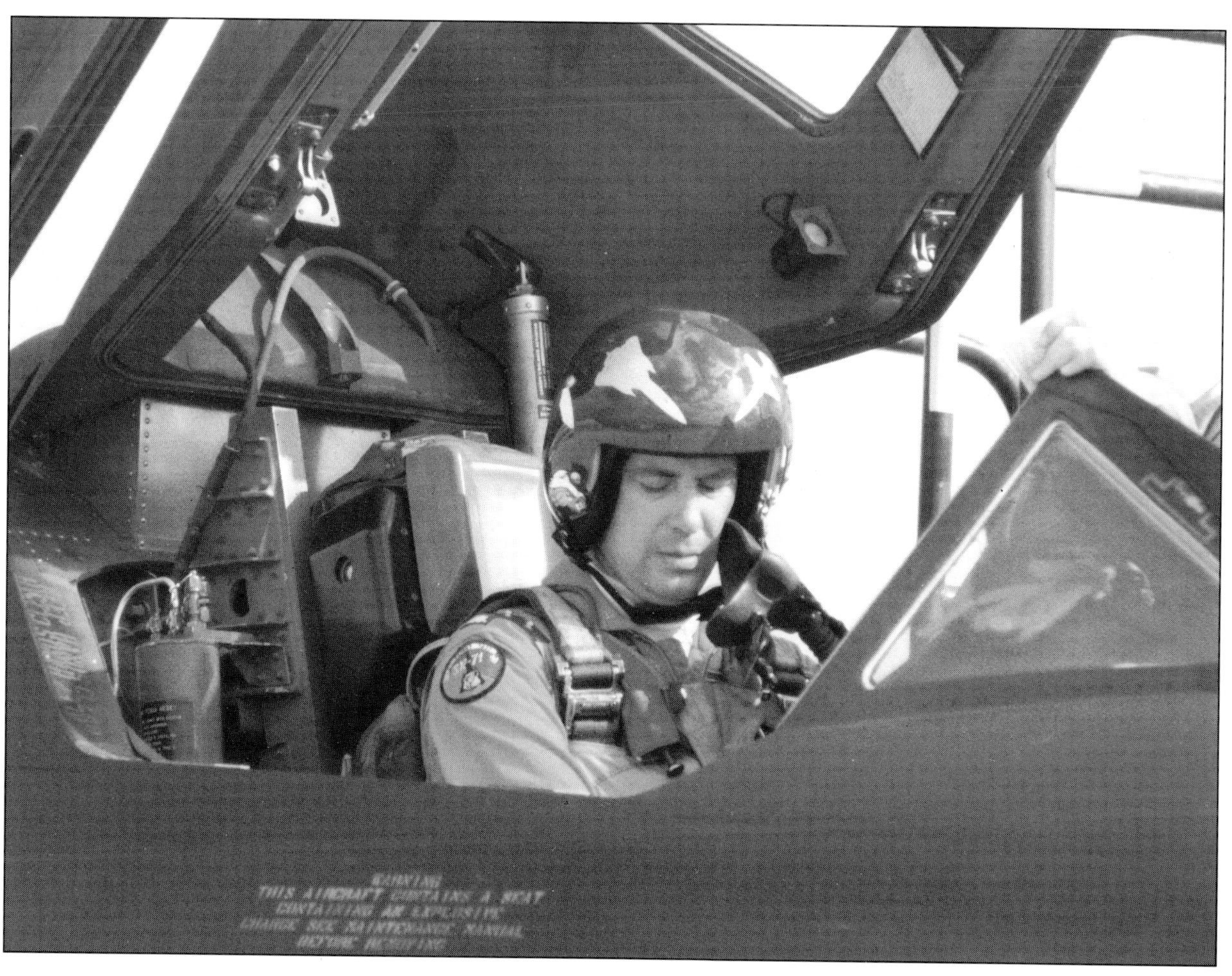

ACKNOWLEDGEMENTS

The material for this book came from two basic sources – open literature including books, newspapers, professional journals, various declassified reports and first-hand accounts from pilots and RSOs associated with the various programmes.

Most of the information contained within these pages was pieced together during the course of numerous interviews (most of which were taped), with those intimately connected with OXCART, TAGBOARD and the SENIOR CROWN programme. Several contributed information with the proviso that their anonymity be respected. Rest assured that those who so generously gave up their time, divulged no secrets that could compromise the interests of the United States, and its allies.

My deepest appreciation then goes to Col Don Walbrecht, who painstakingly edited the draft for technical accuracy, and as a friend and confidant, provided an often needed moderating perspective on the work.

My special thanks goes to Dave Adrian, Bob Gilliland, Cols Buddy Brown, Don Emmons, Frank Murray, Ed Payne, Tom Pugh, BC Thomas, Lt Cols Blair Bozek, Tom Veltri and Marta Bohn-Meyer, each of whom were particularly supportive.

I also wish to thank Maj Gens Doug Nelson, Pat Halloran and Mel Vojvodich; Brig Gens Dennis Sullivan, and Buck Adams; Cols Tony Bevacqua, Pat Bledsoe, Larry Boggess, George Bull, Gary Coleman, Ken Collins, Dr Roy Cross, Dave Dempster, Bruce Douglass, Carl Estes, Tom Estes, Rich Graham, RSM Colin Grice MBE, Ty Judkin, Joe Kinego, John Kraus, Jack Layton, Jay Murphy, Hugh Slater, Dewain Vick, Jim Watkins and Rich Young; Lt Cols Ben Bowles, Buzz Carpenter, Nevin Cunningham, Bill Flanagan, Jim Greenwood, Dan House, Tom Henichek, Bruce Leibman, 'GT' Morgan, Curt Osterheld, Bob Powell, Maury Rosenberg, Tom Tilden and Ed Yeilding; Majs Reg Blackwell, 'Stormy' Boudreaux, Brian Shul, Doug Soifer and Terry Pappas; and also James Bamford, Ellen Bendell, Keith Beswick, Kent Burn, William Burrows, Russ Daniell, Jim Eastham, Kevin Gothard, Mike Hirst, Graham Luxton, Berni Mearns, Lindsay Peacock, Chris Pocock, Bill Park, Lou Schalk, Jane Skliar, Betty Sprigg, Rich Stadler, Bill Weaver, Dave Wilton and Dan Zuck.

Thanks also go to my dear, longstanding friend Gill Turner who helped to type up the manuscript and my editors Tony Holmes and Shaun Barrington. for their continued support throughout. I wish to thank my parents, Neil and Pauline Jenkins and Alberto and Karen Policarpo.

Above all I would like to thank my wife Alison for her hard work and enthusiasm in readying this book and numerous articles and for always being there for me.

CHAPTER 1

To War

On the morning of Thursday 21 March 1968, Maj Jerry O'Malley and Capt Ed Payne were driven out to the Little Creek Hangar near the middle of Kadena Air Base on the island of Okinawa. Precisely 50 minutes before take-off, the rear doors of the white Physiological Support Division (PSD) van opened and the two USAF fliers emerged wearing full-pressure suits, 'space' helmets and 'moon-boots'. The two crewmen walked into the old hangar, which was filled with all manner of high-tech support gear surrounding one of the world's most unusual operational military aircraft.

After shaking hands with Col Charles Minter (the detachment commander), the four other SR-71 flight crewmembers present, key groundcrewmen and finally each other, O'Malley and Payne climbed the gantry-ladder that took them up to the cockpits of SR-71A number 976 (which now rests in the USAF Museum at Dayton, Ohio). Carefully lowering themselves into their respective cockpits, the crew were assisted by white-coveralled PSD specialists who swiftly connected them to their life-support gear, intercommunication leads and escape systems.

The exterior and interior preflight checks had already been completed by the 'buddy crew' who had 'cocked'[1] the aircraft while the 'prime' crew was suiting-up. Half an hour before the scheduled take-off time, Jerry turned his attention to the pre-start checklist, reviewing certain important switch-positions on his consoles and instrument panel. Those pre-start checks verified liquid oxygen and nitrogen quantities, and the positions of switches which controlled aircraft-specific systems such as the left and right aft bypass doors, the inlet centre-body spikes and forward bypass doors, suit-heat, face-heat and refrigeration for the cockpit and sensor bay environment control system. In addition, the moving-map projector was checked to ensure that it was loaded properly, the Stability Augmentation Systems (SAS) switched on and the TEB counters were each seen to display 16 units[2]. Although some of these checks were unique to the SR-71, many others were standard for conventional jet aircraft. Much of the challenge-and-reply system of formal checklist reading was carried out for the purpose of putting 'on record' (on the cockpit voice recorder) that the many standardised procedural steps had indeed been performed.

While Jerry was doing pilot tasks, Ed was also at work in his 'office' performing HF and UHF radio checks, Inertial Navigation System (INS) 'alignment' and aircraft Defensive Electronic Systems checkouts. Others embraced checkouts of the TACAN radio-navigation system, camera exposure control systems, Astro-Inertial Navigation System (ANS) and the forward-downlooking viewsight. Ed's final checks were concerned with the various reconnaissance sensors, the canopy seal, the Radar Correlator Display system, various camera controls and finally the Reconnaissance Systems Officer's (RSO) moving-map projector, which showed the entire pre-planned mission in considerable detail along a flight-sequenced photostrip of a standard jet-navigation chart.

During the aircrew's intercockpit checklist conversation, the crewchief was also plugged into the aircraft's interphone system (with head-set and microphone) through a phone jack-plug receptacle located in the nose-wheel bay. Through the use of this simple system he was able to monitor their checks and responses prior to them commencing the engine start sequence. 'Interphone' – 'Checked'; 'Bailout Light' – 'Checked'; 'Triple Display System' – 'Checked'; 'Fuel Quantity' – 'Checked'; 'CG Limits' – 'Checked'. As the clock ticked down to one minute before engine start, Ed called out the last four items. 'Oxygen Systems' – 'On and Checked'; 'Baylor Bar' – 'Latched and Locked'; 'Exterior Light

Switches' – 'On'; 'Brake Switch Setting' – 'Checked'.

The two Pratt & Whitney J58 engines were fired up by revving each powerplant up to 3000 rpm through the use of two Buick-powered start carts, which were spline-gear connected to a direct drive shaft in each engine's gear box. The cart's 400 bhp V8 Buicks (working in series) sound like racing cars when they were accelerated to high rpm during the J58's rapid 'spooling-up'.

At the designated moment, Jerry said 'crank number two chief' – a Buick roared to life with an ear-splitting din in the confines of the Little Creek Hangar. Cocooned within the sound-proofed protection of his helmet, Jerry smiled as the rpm increased on the right engine, the steady climb levelling out as he eased the throttle forward into the 'IDLE' position on the quadrant. The fuel flow into the engine was timed to meet with a 'thimble-full' of TEB, the successful use of which could be verified by a momentary flash of green flame in the tail-cone of the starting engine, and by a visible 'down-click' on the right TEB counter (indicating one shot of TEB-use) within the cockpit. Less than ten seconds after the Buick had begun cranking, the engine was idling smoothly at 3975 rpm. Once the other engine was 'turning and burning' after-start checks were performed. 'EGT, Fuel Flow and Hydraulic System Pressures – All Checked; Flight Controls – Checked'[3].

As their cockpit canopies closed minor problems appeared which threatened to jeopardise the mission. Firstly, Ed had no indication of cockpit pressurisation. That glitch was remedied by simply advancing the engine rpm, which duly inflated the canopy seals. As Ed searched through the GO-No GO checklist to determine the importance of the other minor discrepancies, Jerry said 'Well Ed, do you want to be the first guy to abort an operational sortie, or the first to fly one?' Ed's response was predictable. 'Kadena Tower, this is Beaver Five-Zero, radio check'. To which the tower operator answered,'Five-Zero you are loud and clear, and cleared to taxy'. Ed acknowledged with two unspoken clicks of his mic switch – a standard procedure used to minimise radio emissions on unguarded frequencies that could be monitored by Soviet 'fishing' trawlers which often lurked in international waters just a few miles off the coast.

Prior to the SR-71 moving out from the hangar, a ground technician released the scissor switch on the nose-wheel knee and hand-guided the aircraft backward via a nose wheel tow-bar. Slowly, 976 was towed by a tractor (back end first) out of the hangar under the control of a tug operator clad in an aluminised fire-protective 'fear naught' suit. As the groundcrew re-secured the nose-wheel scissor switch, Ed called out the last check-list items. The crewchief disconnected his intercom link, removed the wheel chocks and signalled Jerry that it was all clear to move out. The pilot then eased 976 forward and checked the brakes in the first few feet of the roll-out, after which he steered the jet down the taxyway to the hammmer-head run-up area adjacent to the end of the active runway.

Ed got a 'starlight' from the ANS, indicating that the system had already searched and successfully 'acquired' three stars for triangular position referencing. His Present-Position-Indicator confirmed that everything was working fine and that they were within 100 ft of track at runway end. In the pre-launch engine run-up position the wheels were tightly chocked, the brakes held firmly and engine trim checks completed. Once more, fuel sequencing, brake switches, pitot heat, battery and inverter switches were 'checked'. The INS's reference-altitude was updated, and the crew sat ready to taxy forward to the number one position on the active runway for an 'on-the-second' take-off roll.

All eyes on or around Kadena were fixed upon the 'black jet', which the Japanese Ryukan Islanders had already named 'Habu' after a highly respected island snake. A few minutes before take-off the 'mobile control' car was driven onto the runway by the spare crew, who then proceeded to conduct a runway-length 'foreign object' check for debris which might damage the tyres or engines during the launch. The groundcrew then sledge-hammered the chocks free from the wheels and stowed them in the back of their ground-support 'bread van', before sending 976 on its way with a crisp salute. As the final countdown moved towards brake release, Kadena Tower called 'Five-Zero, you are cleared for take-off'. Ed answered 'Click-Click', and Jerry, who had eased the throttles forward to 7200 rpm, released the brakes and said to Ed 'Military Power – Set; Tachometer, EGT, Nozzle

Bathed in the warm dusk light, a thirsty SR-71 eases ever closer towards a KC-135Q of the 100th Air Refueling Wing (*USAF*)

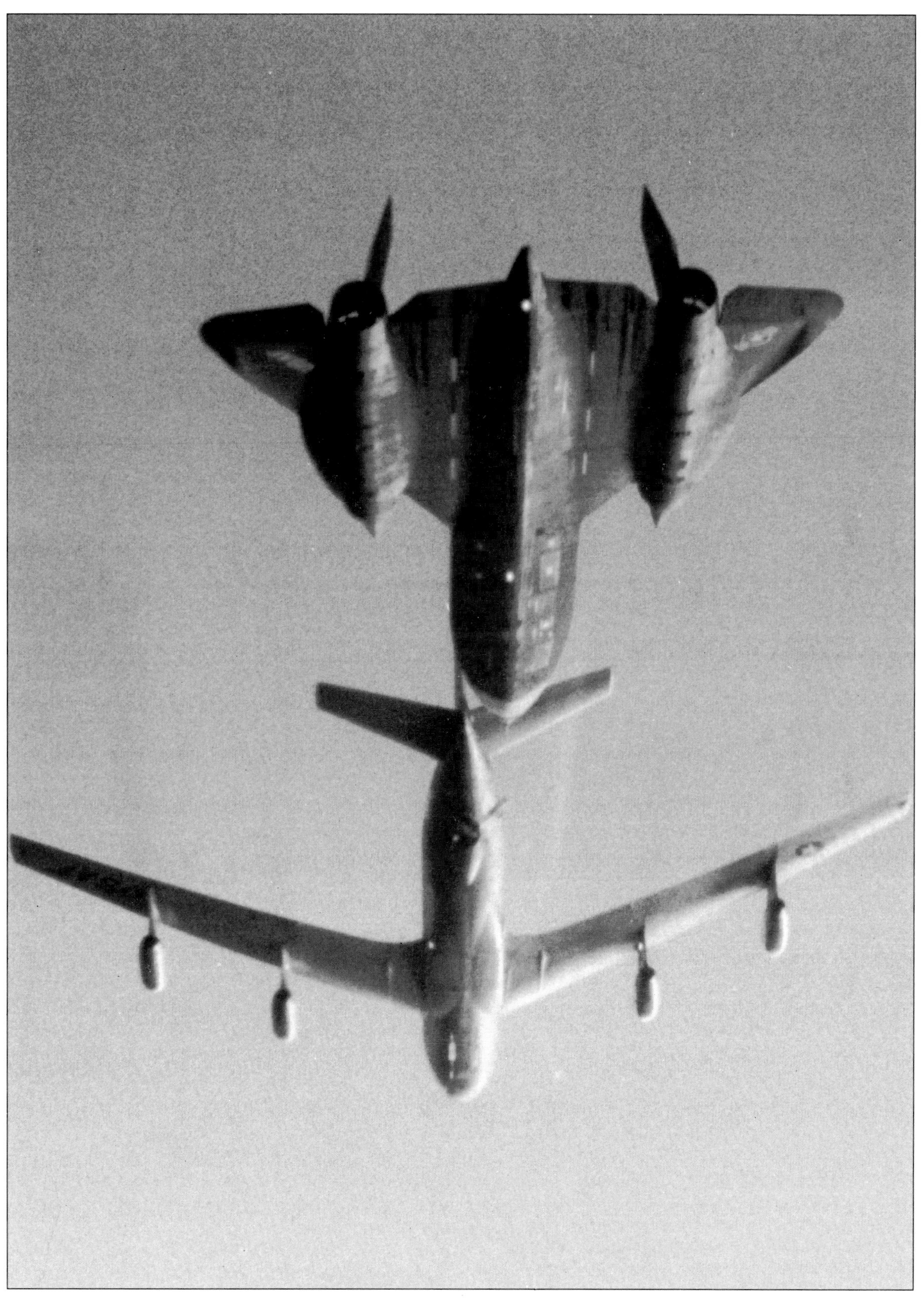

Position and Oil Pressure – All Checked. We're on our way Ed'.

The pilot then moved the throttles forward to the mid-afterburner position, which resulted in a left-right yaw movement as each afterburner lit, accompanied by a tongue of flame glinting from the rear of each engine. 'Throttles to Max A/B' Jerry said as the Habu's take-off roll accelerated, followed by 'Decision Speed – Looks Good. No Problems', ten seconds later. As 976 approached 180 kts, O'Malley gently pulled back on the stick, whereupon the nose rose smoothly to ten degrees above the horizontal. At 235 kts he murmured 'Lift-off' and 'Wheels up', and retracted the undercarriage immediately to ensure that the 300-kt gear-door limit was not exceeded. In less than 25 seconds Kelly Johnson's 'masterpiece' was airborne on its first operational mission.

Once airborne, Jerry reassured Ed that all systems were looking good, and that the engine instruments were checked. Almost immediately Kadena Tower called 'Beaver Five-Zero. Contact Kadena Radar'. Ed replied with two clicks on the mike, and selected Radar's frequency. 'Beaver Five-Zero, this is Kadena Radar. Squawk 2107'. Ed dialled the code on his IFF panel and pushed the 'Ident' button, whereupon the Kadena controller confirmed that the jet was cleared to proceed on track. Ed then selected an appropriate HF radio frequency for rendezvousing with the KC-135Q tankers.

At 0.5 Mach, Jerry engaged the control surface limiters and observed that the SURFACE LIMITER light on the tele-light panel extinguished. A cross-check between Jerry and Ed confirmed that both flight director platforms which powered their flight instruments were operational. Jerry selected the Astro-Inerital Platform Gyro for instrument power and reference, while Ed used the secondary gyro platform for back-up.

Automatic fuel tank sequencing was checked and the altimeter was set to 29.92 above 18,000 ft to insure that all aircraft would have a standard reference for altitude separation. On their way to the refuelling area, Jerry levelled 976 at FL 250 and maintained 0.90 Mach, taking up a heading toward the Air Rendezvous Control Point where the KC-135s were orbiting less than 15 minutes away. Ed, meanwhile, had activated his mission sensors.

For its first operational mission, the SR-71 carried a Goodyear Side-Looking Airborne Radar (SLAR) in the nose and a downward-looking, vertically-mounted Terrain Objective Camera in the centre of the fuselage, ahead of the nose gear and an AR 1700 radar recorder unit in the N bay within the right chine. Behind the cockpits in the P and Q bays were the left and right long focal-length 'Close-Look' Technical Objective 'TEOC', or 'Tech', cameras. Finally, bays S and T held two Operational Objective Cameras (OOCs).

At that point, Ed was waiting for the reconnaissance systems and sensors to warm up to verify their in-flight performance. It took six minutes for the radar to warm up, two minutes for the Recorder Correlator Display to function, two minutes for the Electromagnetic Recorder (EMR) to be ready and 20 seconds before the cameras were ready for testing. At that point, Ed pressed the Built-in Test (BIT) button for the radar, but it failed to work. Since it was not a primary sensor for this mission, they decided to proceed without it – they could rely totally on the ANS and Gyro Platform for navigation in any case. Ed then checked the DEF system jammers. First DEF A was turned on, and two minutes later, when the system had warmed up, the S (standby) light illuminated. This was followed by the other defensive systems, DEF B, C, E and finally DEF G, which was powered up and declared operational. At that point Ed told Jerry that the DEF System was ready – a definite 'Go' action on the GO-No GO checklist.

A special covert radio-ranging system known as the ARC-50 had been specially developed to allow the SR-71 to rendezvous discreetly with KC-135Q tankers by giving azimuth and distance information to both crews as they approached one another in total radio-silence. Linking up southwest of Okinawa, the KC-135Q started pumping the special JP7 fuel into the SR-71's tanks immediately after the jet had safely connected with the boom. With 70,000 lbs of fuel now in the tanks, Ed recomputed the aircraft's centre of gravity (CG). The final part of the refuelling was conducted in near-tropical air mass resulting in the SR-71 responding sluggishly to the military power settings on both engines as it cruised at 350 kts.

To overcome aerodynamic drag and the limited mil-power thrust, Jerry engaged 'MIN-Burner' on one engine and cross-controlled slightly to overcome the off-set thrust – the added thrust made it easy to take on the last 10,000 lbs of fuel. At a prearranged time and position, and with Beaver Five-

Zero full of JP7, the boom was disconnected. As the SR-71 dropped back and gently slipped clear of the tanker, Jerry lit both afterburners and pushed the throttles up to MAX, accelerating 976 to 0.90 Mach before climbing to FL 330.

At 33,000 ft Jerry eased the nose below the horizon into a 2500 ft per minute rate of descent to 'punch through the Mach'. The jet slid neatly through Mach I and the speed continued to build to 435 kts equivalent air speed (KEAS), at which point Jerry applied back pressure on the stick. At 30,000 ft the descent was changed into a climb and the Triple-Display-Indicator showed 450 KEAS, which was the standard speed for most of the climb to altitude. At that point Jerry re-engaged the autopilot and stabilised the climb angle to hold the 450 KEAS. On reaching Mach 1.25, EGT and Compressor Inlet Temperatures (CIT) were noted. At Mach 1.7, inlet parameters and CG trim positions were monitored, followed by the manual setting of the aft bypass door controls, and the locking out of the Inlet Guide Vane (IGV) switches. Finally, the DEF jammer systems were also rechecked.

At 60,000 ft, Ed switched off the IFF altitude read-out to ensure the security of the SR-71's altitude capabilities. Additionally, the aircraft's red-flashing anti-collision beacon was turned off and retracted to preclude heat damage to the lights, and to reduce the high-flying aircraft's visual signature. Reaching Mach 2.6 with the aft bypass door controls in the 'B' position, Jerry established a KEAS bleed, which resulted in the air speed being decreased by ten knots for the gain of each tenth of a whole Mach number[4].

Their high altitude route took them to the east of Taiwan, north of the Philippine Islands and out over the South China Sea. Skirting the east coast of China, and after passing Hainan Island, the autonavigation function of the ANS and autopilot turned 976 smoothly right in a 35 degree bank onto a northbound heading and the jet entered the Gulf of Tonkin. Continuing north, Ed peered through his view sight and located a large pier on the west side of Hainan that he had pre-planned as a visual-offset reference point to verify his track position. To his great satisfaction the pier was 'right on the money', the ANS flying the 'black line' within 50 ft of its centre. They had been travelling at Mach 3.0 up to that point at a height of 75,000 ft.

As they entered the Gulf Jerry started a cruise-climb to 78,000 ft and an acceleration to Mach 3.17, preparing for a 'front door' entry into North Vietnam. Through his viewsight, Ed could see ship wakes on the Gulf waters below, and they could both hear the excited chatter of US combat pilots in heavy action way below over Haiphong and Hanoi. With the tracking camera on for after-mission verification of their ground track, and with the ELINT and COMINT sensor-recorders already running, Ed switched the OOCs on ten miles prior to 'coasting in.'

Following a heading of 284 degrees, they crossed Haiphong at 78,000 ft, immune from any form of interception as they were travelling at the rate of a mile every two seconds. All the North Vietnamese could do was watch on their radars. The DEF systems aboard 976 indicated that they were being tracked from the moment they crossed the coast by *Fan-Song* radar units co-located with SA-2 *Guideline* Surface-to-Air Missile (SAM) batteries. Ed put out the correct ECM response and the radars failed to 'lock-on'. The weather below was perfect for a photo run, and as they flew over the harbour at Haiphong, Phu Kin Airfield, Busundi Airport and dozens of other targets in the vicinity of Hanoi, the exposure counters clicked down, indicating to Ed that the sensors were working 'as advertised' – it was going to be a perfect 'take'.

In just 12 minutes they had completed the first phase of the sortie as per the scheduled mission brief. Ed got ready to read the pre-descent checks to Jerry as they exited North Vietnam. Crossing the Red River (which is really brown), Jerry flicked the IGV switches to Lockout and Ed called out the checklist items. 'LN-2 quantity' – 'Checked'; 'Inlet Controls' – 'Auto and Closed'.

Jerry eased the throttles out of afterburner and set the EGT reading to 720 degrees Centigrade, the airspeed being allowed to decrease to 350 KEAS before starting the long gradual descent into Thailand. Carefully monitoring fuel tank pressure so as to avoid inflicting crush-damage on them as the jet descended into denser air, the crew reached 70,000 ft 100 miles after commencing their descent profile. Now at Mach 2.5, Jerry was able to further retard the throttles to 6000 rpm to hasten their descent.

The air-to-air TACAN's Distance Measuring Equipment, as well as the ARC-50's DME ranging element, rapidly 'clicked' down the distance between 976 and the ever-dependable tankers which were orbiting near Korat Air Base ready to 'pass gas' to their 'high and hot' receiver. Below Mach 1.7, Jerry turned the forward fuel transfer, pitot heat, and exterior anti-collision beacon light switches on. At 42,000 ft and slowing through Mach 1.3 he checked the inlet controls, clicked the IGV switches to Normal after making a slight throttle adjustment. Jerry then turned off the forward fuel transfer, and prepared for refuelling.

Craven 'Gibb' Givens, flying the lead tanker, timed his turn to perfection just as 976 arrived at 25,000 ft a few miles behind and 1000 ft below the two KC-135Qs. Sitting slightly to the right and a few hundred feet below in the pre-refuelling observation position, Jerry noted the boom was extended and the 'Boomer' was nodding it up and down to indicate that he was ready for a radio-silent contact. Jerry slipped smoothly in behind the trailing boom and stabilised in the pre-contact position, before moving forward. Once 'plugged in' a secure interphone link-up was established between the KC-135 and the SR-71, and while the much-needed fuel was being pumped into the thirsty receiver at the rate of 6000 lbs per minute, hearty words of congratulations were offered to the two 'Habu' crew members. Jerry took 40,000 lbs of fuel from the first tanker and topped off from a second; a third aircraft was standing by to act as an emergency 'spare' should either of the primary tankers be unable to offload their fuel.

After each refuelling, Jerry thanked the tanker crews. At the prescribed time and location, 976 left the KC-135s and headed out for another run to the north. Jerry repeated the climb and acceleration routine up to their prescribed altitude, on track for the second and final 'take' for the mission. This 'run' was to be flown over the Demilitarised Zone (DMZ) between North and South Vietnam, with a primary objective of finding the truck park that supported the transportation of supplies and troops down the north-south Ho Chi Minh Trail, and to the heavy guns that had been pounding the hell out of Khe Sanh. For this run the primary sensor was to have been the Side-Looking Radar (SLAR), which could penetrate the heavy jungle canopy. However, since the system had failed its BIT-test earlier, its serviceability was questionable. Ed concluded, however, that no damage could be done to the system if he positioned it manually and took some shots on the off-chance that it would find something. Soon after the jet exited the 'sensitive' area and they made their way back to Okinawa.

Feeling justifiably proud of how well their mission had gone up to that point, Jerry started his deceleration and descent back towards Kadena with the expectation of a 'proper' first-flight, mission-success party at the BOQ. On contact with Kadena Approach Control they were dismayed to find that the base was completely 'fogged in'. Jerry talked to the tower contoller and then to Col Charlie Minter, who agreed to allow them to attempt a low-visibility approach for a visual landing. Using Ground Controlled Approach (GCA) radar assistance, Jerry descended as low as was prudent into the fog, which the crews on the ground later reported was below the tops of the tanker tails only 30 ft above the ramp. Although the approach was good, Jerry never saw the runway and pushed the throttles forward to go back 'upstairs' to contemplate further options.

Low on fuel, he called for the standby tanker that had been launched earlier just in case the weather at Kadena turned nasty. After link-up, he took on 25,000 lbs of fuel while Ed copied a two-figure encoded number which told them their divert airfield location – Ku Kuan on the island of Taiwan. Two additional KC-135s were launched to accompany 976 to Nationalist China, the SR-71 adopting a tanker call sign as the number 'two' aircraft in a three-ship formation. This deception was undertaken to hide the inter-island diversion from SIGINT monitors on the Chinese mainland. As they made their way 'low and slow' with the tankers, the destination airfield's non-directional beacon returned the unexpected Morse Code identity signal of CCK. The tanker crew soon resolved this problem however. It turned out that Ku Kuan had recently been re-named Ching Chuan Kang!

Jerry asked the CCK tower for permission to land and made a straight-in visual approach at 175 kts before performing a smooth touch-down. After clearing the runway and lining up behind the lead tanker, Jerry sandwiched 976 between the two KC-135s as they taxied to the parking area. This unusual sight caused considerable confusion amongst the tower personnel, particularly when one controller asked for the call-sign of 'the little black aircraft between the two tankers, which had replied with a tanker call-sign'. While Ed was talking to the tower people, Jerry dialed up the radio frequency of the SAC Command Post which had recently opened on CCK. He asked for the aircraft to be 'hangared' (for security reasons).

Capt Ed Payne and Maj Jerry O'Malley strike a pose for the base photographer back at Beale, soon after returning to California following their inaugural OL-8 deployment (*USAF*)

Since CCK was a PACAF (US Pacific Air Force Command) joint-tenancy base with the Chinese Nationalists, most of its hangars were already filled with C-130 Hercules transports. To clear a secure spot for the SR-71, a C-130 up on jacks had to be rapidly lowered back onto its undercarriage and rolled out of a hangar. That action took 30 minutes to perform, which left the SR-71 standing in full public view close to the base perimeter fence, with its engines still running. A crowd of at least 500 Taiwanese gathered 10- to 15-deep along a 300-yard section of the fence, all of whom were fascinated to see such a futuristic jet standing on their airfield almost within touching distance.

Once 976 was safely hangared, and a security cordon thrown up around the area, the first order of business was to down-load the 'take' and get it to the various processing facilities so that the 'goods' could be fielded out to the intelligence community as quickly as possible. The next priority was to get the aircraft and its crew back to Kadena. To accomplish that, a recovery crew was sent over in a KC-135 from Okinawa the following day. Meanwhile, the raw intelligence data was dispatched to Yokota Air Force Base in Japan for processing by the 67th Reconnaissance Technical Squadron (RTS). The SLAR imagery was sent to Beale Air Force Base in California for processing by the 9th RTS, before being sent on to Washington DC for analysis by national-level agencies.

Meanwhile back in Taiwan, Jerry and Ed endured a night in CCK quarters which the RSO described as 'remedial at best'. Having no proper evening clothes other than 'moon suits', they borrowed ill-fitting flight 'grow bags' and went to dinner wearing their white 'moon boots'. Things took a turn for the better the following day however, with the arrival of their ever-resourceful Ops officer, Lt Col 'Beep-Beep' Harlon Hain, and his recovery team. He brought with him a full set of 'civvies' for both Jerry and Ed, and got them booked into a first-rate hotel near the base. After two nights at CCK, 976 was ready for a ferry flight back to Kadena. The unrefuelled 'hop' was uneventful, but the reception by their friends and colleagues back at the Little Creek Hangar was 'superb'.

The post-mission intelligence results were also quite stunning. The SLAR that Ed had manually programmed had indeed worked. Its 'take' revealed the location of the heavy artillery emplacements around Khe Sanh, and a huge truck park which was used in support of those guns; both sites had eluded US sensors on other recce aircraft up to that point in time. Within the next few days air strikes were mounted against both targets, reducing their effectiveness dramatically. After a 77-day siege, Khe Sanh was at last relieved on 7 April 1968 (two weeks after 976's 'discovery' sortie). As a result of their significant contribution to this highly successful mission, Maj Jerome F O'Malley and Capt Edward D Payne were each awarded the Distinguished Flying Cross. On its very first operational sortie, the aircraft had proven its value (as it would on thousands of other occasions), but this initial success had not come about overnight – years of hard work had preceeded this highly successful operational flight.

CHAPTER 2

'Gusto, Oxcart and Tagboard'

On 4 July 1956 a strange sailplane-like aircraft got airborne from Weisbaden and climbed steeply away from the West German base. Built by Lockheed, but funded and operated by the Central Intelligence Agency (CIA), this sortie was to mark the start of *Operation Overflight*. Despite attempts by the Soviet Air Force to intercept the high-flying jet, Harvey Stockman safely recovered CIA Article No 347 back at Weisbaden eight hours and forty-five minutes later. When the photographs were processed, the film was of breathtaking clarity, and revealed for the first time to Western intelligence analysts details of life behind the 'Iron Curtain'. The negatives covered everything from Soviet defences through to the East's industrial capability along a 2000-mile route from Berlin to Minsk, and then onward to Leningrad, Estonia, Latvia and Lithuania.

The very stable high-flying photo-platform (and its unique camera) was a remarkable technical achievement which would serve the intelligence community well for nearly four years until 1 May 1960 when Francis Gary Powers' U-2 was shot down by a SAM deep inside the Soviet Union near Sverdlovsk. That untimely incident catapulted the highly classified overflight operation into the world headlines, where it was politically manipulated by Soviet Premier Nikita Kruschev to embarrass President Eisenhower. Long before the May-Day incident, however, a design for the U-2's 'replacement' had already been decided upon.

A-12's Beginnings

In 1954, CIA Director Allen Dulles appointed Richard M Bissell (an economist and brilliant innovator) as his special assistant for planning and co-ordination to oversee the U-2 programme, codenamed *Project Aquatone*. Three years later Bissell commissioned an aerospace company to conduct an operational analysis to establish the relationship between an aircraft's speed, altitude and radar cross-section (RCS), and its probability of interception. The study concluded that supersonic speed, especially when combined with altitude and RCS, greatly reduced the chances of detection by radar.

Convair and Lockheed were then asked to conduct unfunded Concept Formulation Studies, which duly narrowed design concepts. Between April 1958 and September 1959, the boss of Lockheed's Advanced Development Projects (ADP) division, Clarence 'Kelly' Johnson, submitted a series of proposals designated A-1 through to A-11. Both the cost and the risks of such an ambitious programme were recognised from the outset by Dick Bissell, who set up a panel of two aerodynamicists, a physicist and the inventor EM Land of the Polaroid Corporation, who chaired the concept refinement meetings. These discussions took place on six occasions between 1957 and 1959 in Land's office in Cambridge, and were often attended by the designers from the two competing companies, along with the assistant secretaries for research and development of the Air Force and the Navy. During one meeting in November 1958, the members of the panel agreed that the project seemed feasible and recommended that President Eisenhower be asked to approve the concept, and to release funds for further studies and tests.

Following a meeting between the President, his scientific advisor Dr James Killian and officials from the CIA, approval was given to proceed with research and development. Lockheed and Convair were asked for design submissions, and funds were made available for a project codenamed *Gusto*. A further meeting with President Eisenhower on 20 July 1959 resulted in *Gusto* being funded in full. On 20 August 1959 Lockheed and Convair submitted

A-12 serial 933 is seen outside its 'barn' sporting the early black and bare titanium scheme (*CIA*)

their designs to a joint DOD, USAF and CIA evaluation panel. These design criteria revealed performance targets and aircraft dimensions:

	Lockheed	Convair
Speed	Mach 3.2	Mach 3.2
Range (total)	4120 nm	4000 nm
Range (at altitude)	3800 nm	3400 nm
Cruise Altitudes		
Start	84,500 ft	85,000 ft
Mid-Range	91,000 ft	88,000 ft
End	97,600 ft	94,000 ft
Dimensions		
Length	102 ft	79.5 ft
Span	57 ft	56 ft
Gross Weight	110,000 lbs	101,700 lbs
Fuel Weight	64,600 lbs	62,000 lbs
First Flight	22 months	22 months

On 3 September 1959 the CIA terminated project *Gusto*. The tripartite board had reached their decision; Lockheed would build a U-2 follow-on aircraft under a project code named *Oxcart*. The series of drawings that lead to the A-12 final shape involved a number of ADP designers. One of the leaders, Daniel Zuck, recalled an occasion when Kelly Johnson drew him a rough sketch of an aircraft sitting on its tail for take-off! Most of the other early drawings were quite conventional, but new shapes revealed important findings.

While working in Lockheed's anachoic chamber in Building Number 82, LD McDonald discovered that wedge shapes seemed to deflect radar waves over an aircraft's fuselage, thereby minimising its RCS. Although such shapes were a radical departure from contemporary aircraft design, McDonald approached Kelly with his findings. Kelly was

A-12 serial 928 was lost during a test sortie on 5 January 1967. Its CIA pilot, Walt Ray, was killed during the incident (*CIA*)

immediately interested in the potential of McDonald's concept and gave Dan Zuck details of the aircraft's wing loading, fuel load and general airframe layout, which featured three engines (one on each wing and one in the fuselage). The design was number A-7, and it included vertical stabilisers that were canted inward to help reduce RCS. Zuck recalled that no one in aerodynamics or structures liked the design, which 'clearly couldn't perform the mission'. The design evolution continued and eventually number A-11 yielded a clean-looking aeroplane with a single tail and engines slung beneath its high wing. It promised to have a superb altitude capability, and all of the engineers in weights, structures and aerodynamics were convinced that this model would be a winner.

The CIA, however, had other ideas and insisted that the aircraft should have a much smaller RCS. So it was that the A-12 evolved from a combination of the A-7 and the A-11. In November 1959, Lockheed built a full-sized mock-up of the aircraft and transported it in a special trailer to the secret test area at Groom Dry Lake, in Nevada. There it was hoisted to the top of a pylon and viewed from various angles by radar. By incorporating radar absorbing materials (RAM) along its edge, it was found that the profile could be reduced even further. In addition, the distinctive chine feature was added, which was later to prove invaluable for other reasons.

Oxcart received a shot in the arm on 30 January 1960 when the CIA gave ADP the go-ahead to manufacture and test a dozen A-12s, including one two-seat conversion trainer. Lockheed's chief test pilot, Louis W Schalk, joined the programme and set to work with Dan Zuck designing the cockpit layout. Dave Robertson was responsible for fuel systems, Henry Combs and Dick Bachme for structures, while Ed Martin supervised these experienced engineers, and many others, to bring the design into its final stages. Kelly's protégé, Ben Rich, was the chief thermodynamicist, and his area of specialization provided Lockheed with its greatest challenge.

Dick Fuller, Burt McMasters and Ben Rich made much use of the NASA computer facility at Naval Air Station (NAS) Moffett Field, California, which they occupied after office hours to preserve the security of their activities. Using the most advanced then available, the team discovered some variability in the design's speed parameters, as well as accruing detailed predictive data on the aircraft's flight characteristics. Some of this information enabled Lou Schalk to start writing the aircraft's flight manual.

As work continued on refining the aircraft's design, construction at the jet's secret test site in Nevada also commenced. Groom Dry Lake, referred to variously as 'the Ranch' or 'the Area', was initially built for the U-2 test programme in the mid 1950s. Located 100 miles northwest of Las Vegas (near Bald Mountain, Nevada), the site offered an expansive dry lake bed, exceptional remoteness, and good weather all year round. Its 5000 ft runway was too short however, and all other facilities were inadequate for such a significant flight-test programme, so an enormous amount of work was required to bring the base up to standard. Nevada law required that all contractor personnel staying in the state for more than 48 hours report to state authorities, but such large numbers would have attracted unwanted attention and breached the security of the project. The CIA's general counsel however, discovered that government employees were exempt from this requirement, so consequently all contractor personnel for the Nevada site received appointments as government consultants!

A new water well was drilled and new recreational facilities were provided for those workers who had to be billeted in trailer houses. In September 1960 work began in earnest and continued on double-shift schedules until mid-1964. A new 8500 ft runway was constructed using 25,000 cubic yards of concrete, 18 miles of off-base highway was resurfaced to allow half a million gallons of specially developed PF-1 fuel for the A-12 aircraft to be trucked in every month. Three Navy hangars and Navy housing units were disassembled at other locations and transported to the site for the people who would support aircraft number one which was expected to be delivered in May 1961. That date soon proved overly optimistic and slipped to late summer.

Problems in procuring and working with titanium, as well as the difficulties experienced by engine manufacturers, Pratt & Whitney, prompted Kelly to write to CIA officials in March 1961 explaining that schedules were in jeopardy because of the assembly of the wing and the slow development of the J58 engine. 'Our evaluation shows that each of these programmes is from three to four

In February 1963 Bill Skliar joined the *Oxcart* programme from the Armament Development Center, Eglin AFB, as the CIA's project test pilot. He later joined the *Senior Crown* programme, and is pictured seated in SR-71A serial 958 (*USAF via Jane Skliar*)

Before joining the *Oxcart* programme, Dennis Sullivan flew F-106 Delta Darts with the 318th Fighter Interceptor Squadron, based at McChord AFB, Washington. His 'Cygnus' call sign was 'Dutch 23' (*USAF*)

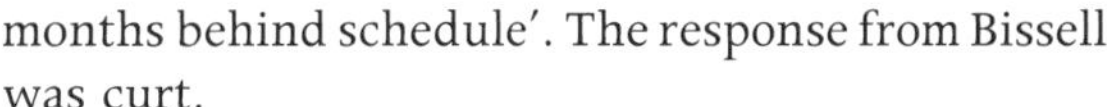

months behind schedule'. The response from Bissell was curt.

'I have learned of your expected additional delay in the first flight from 30 August to 1 December 1961. This news is extremely shocking on top of our previous slippage from May to August and my understanding as of our 19 December meeting was that the titanium extrusion problems were essentially overcome. I trust this is the last of such disappointments short of a severe earthquake in Burbank.'

The Agency then placed an aeronautical engineer in residence at Lockheed to monitor the programme and to submit regular progress reports in the hope that this step would avoid further delays and put the brake on rising costs. Nevertheless, delays persisted. In September Pratt & Whitney informed Lockheed that the J58 was experiencing weight and performance problems. Even with the completion date of the first aircraft put back to Christmas 1961 and its initial test flight postponed to late February 1962, the powerplant was still not ready. Pratt & Whitney would have to supply J75 engines in the interim to propel the A-12 to a 'half-way house' of only 50,000 ft and Mach 1.6. Meanwhile, Lou Schalk flew four flights in NACA's variable-stability F-100 Super Sabre to help prepare himself for the first flight in this new and unusual experimental aircraft. By running the F-100's centre of gravity well aft, the fighter could simulate the theoretical flight characteristics of the A-12.

Aircrew Selection

The selection process for operational pilots began in 1961 at the Pentagon, where Brig Gen Don Flickinger drew up the physical and experience criteria with the advice of Kelly Johnson and CIA representatives. The selection process soon involved the Pentagon's Special Activities Office representative (Col Houser Wilson) and the CIA's USAF liaison officer (Brig Gen Jack Ledford, who was later succeeded by Brig Gen Paul Bacalis). The most important requirement was that pilots be qualified in the latest high performance aircraft, and be expert in aerial refuelling. They were also required to be both emotionally stable and married, and be especially well motivated. Finally, they were to be between 25 and 40 years of age, weigh less than 175 lbs and be under six feet tall.

Pre-evaluation processing resulted in 16 potential nominees. Ken Collins, one of the first selected, recalled his experience:

'Walt Ray and I had not been at Shaw Air Force Base long, having spent four years in recce in Germany. I was approached and asked if I'd be interested in volunteering for a 'classified' program. I agreed and attended a week of psychological assessments in various hotel rooms in Washington DC. An intense medical examination followed at the Lovelace Clinic at Albuquerque, New Mexico (later known as the astronaut medical exam).'

The screening process was so secret that even the commanders of the candidates were not informed what their subordinates were up too. One day Capt Jack Layton's wing commander received a message stating that if Capt Layton needed an F-101 to go somewhere, the wing was to supply one and not to ask questions. Layton, from the 86th Fighter Squadron, recalled his immediate boss (Lt Col Marv Gibb) was quite angry with the sneaky procedure and called him into his office saying, 'Layton, if you don't tell me what the heck is going on around here, I'm going to get you'. Layton explained to his boss that he did not know himself. Layton later confided, 'I don't think Col Gibb ever believed me'.

On completion of the final screening, the first pilots were William Skliar, Kenneth Collins, Walter Ray, Alonzo Walter, Mele Vojvodich, Jack Weeks, Jack Layton, Dennis Sullivan, David Young, Francis Murray and Russ Scott (only six of the aforementioned were destined to fly operational missions). These ten began taking trips to the David Clark Company in Worcester, Massachusetts, to be outfitted with their own personal S-901 full-pressure suits just like those worn by the Mercury and Gemini astronauts.

Other Preparations

In late-1961 Col Robert Holbury was given the job of base commander at Groom Lake. The Director of Flight Operations was Col Doug Nelson, who had come from HQ 15th Air Force. His support aircraft began arriving in the the spring of 1962 – eight McDonnell F-101 Voodoos, to be used as companion trainers and pace-chase aircraft, two Lockheed T-33s for day-to-day flying proficiency for all the pilots and a Lockheed C-130 Hercules for cargo transport. In addition, a twin-engined Cessna U-3B utility aircraft was used for administrative support flights, a helicopter called 'Banjo' was flown for rescue purposes and a Lockheed F-104 was on hand for supersonic chase flights with the A-12 and Cessna 180 for liaison.

Early in 1962 an agreement was reached with the Federal Aviation Agency (FAA) that a large 'restricted airspace zone' would be secured to preserve

During stateside training sorties, *Oxcart* pilots used personalised call sign numbers. 'Dutch 21', Ken Collins, was the first pilot forced to eject from an A-12. The incident occured in aircraft serial 926 on 24 May 1963 (*CIA*)

A-12 serial 60-6027 was the only two-seat pilot trainer built for the *Oxcart* programme, and was powered throughout its life by the less impressive J75 engine, which was capable of taking the aircraft to a maximun speed of Mach 1.8 only (*CIA*)

Above This previously unpublished A-12 cockpit photograph was taken by Lockheed technicians on 8 November 1965 (*Lockheed*)

Below Taken during the same shoot as the above image, this photograph details the vital Stab Augmentation Systems and autopilot, as well as the uncluttered control column (*Lockheed*)

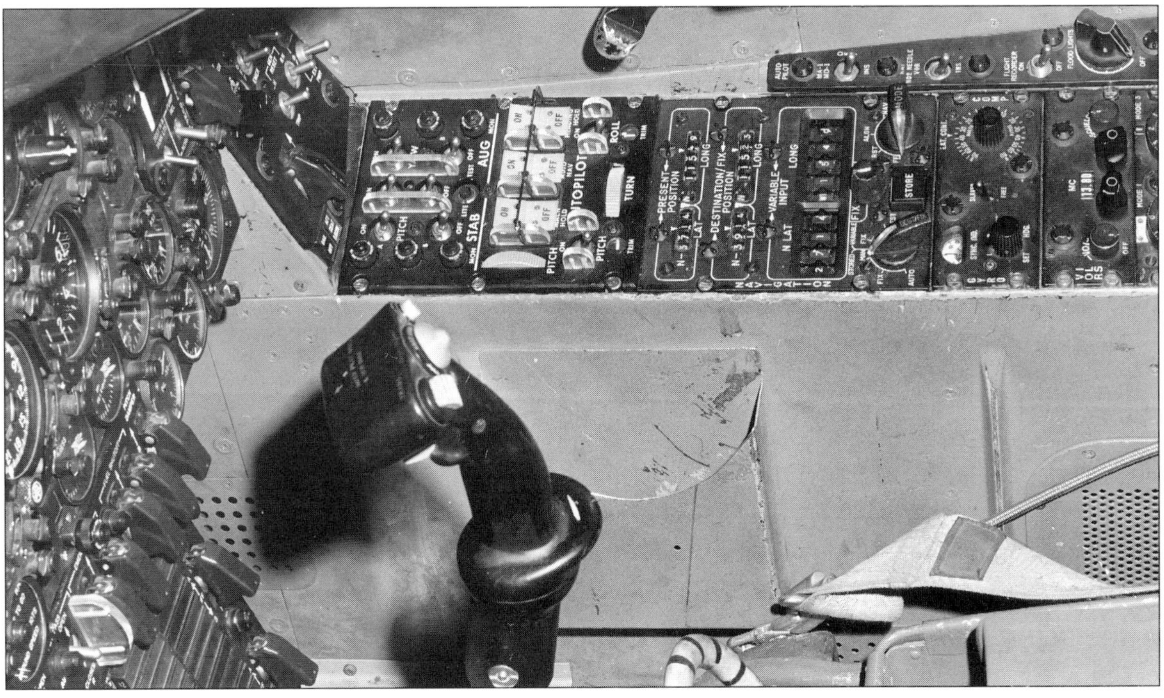

'enhanced security' around the test site. This security effort also required that a number of FAA air traffic contollers would also be cleared for *Oxcart* to ensure that they did not talk about what they had seen whilst at work. Similar procedures were also put in place within North American Air Defense (NORAD) to ensure that 'scope-watchers' in widespread radar stations did not report the very fast-moving targets on their screens.

New high-capacity 'tank farms' were constructed at bases in California, Alaska, Greenland, Okinawa and Turkey to provide worldwide storage of prepositioned special fuel for A-12 operations. Fuel storage facilities were also established at bases in Arkansas and Florida to support transcontinental training flights. The logistics preparations were underway not only to support the experimental, developmental and operational testing flights, but also the full-scale Air Force programme that would follow. Meanwhile, the 903rd Air Refueling Squadron at Beale AFB was equipped with KC-135Qs tankers which possessed separate 'clean' tankage and plumbing to isolate the A-12's fuel from the tanker's own JP4, and special ARC-50 distance-ranging radios for use in precision, long-distance, high-speed join-ups with the A-12s.

Final checks were carried out on aircraft number one (Article Number 121, Air Force Tail Number 60-6924) at ADP during January and February 1962. The airframe was dismantled for transportation to 'the Area' and loaded onto a custom-built trailer costing $100,000. On 26 February 1962, with help from the California and Nevada Highway Patrols, the slow-moving, wide-bodied trailer and convoy left Burbank at three o'clock in the morning and arrived late the next evening at its Groom Lake destination. Another delay occurred after the aircraft was reassembled. While preparing for the first flight it was discovered that the special sealing compounds had failed to adhere to the surfaces between the fuel tanks and the metal skin of the aircraft, causing the filled tanks to leak profusely. The defective tank sealant was removed and relined with new materials as a temporary fix.

The First Flight Test

By 24 April 1962, engine test runs were completed and low- and medium-speed taxy tests had been successfully carried out. Now it was time for chief test pilot Lou Schalk to take the aircraft on a high-speed taxy run that would culminate in a momentary lift-off and landing roll-out onto the salty lakebed. For this first 'hop' the stability augmentation system (SAS) was left uncoupled; it would be properly tested in flight. As 121 accelerated down the runway, Lou Schalk recalled:

> 'It all went like a dream until I lifted off. Immediately after lift-off, I really didn't think I was going to be able to put the aircraft back on the ground safely because of lateral, directional and longitudinal oscillations. The aircraft was very difficult to handle but I finally caught up with everything that was happening, got control back enough to set it back down, and to chop engine power. Touchdown was on the lake bed instead of the runway, creating a tremendous cloud of dust into which I disappeared entirely. The tower controllers were calling me to find out what was happening and I was answering, but the UHF antenna was located on the underside of the aircraft (for best transmission in flight) and no one could hear me. Finally, when I slowed down and started my turn on the lake bed and re-emerged from the dust cloud, everyone breathed a sigh of relief.'

That night Kelly asked Lou if the aircraft ought to fly again the next day. Lou (as chief test pilot) thought it should fly but added, 'I also think we ought to turn the SAS dampers on.'

The first real test flight was made two days later on 26 April 1962. This trouble-free sortie lasted 35 minutes, the aircraft's landing gear being extended throughout the flight to avoid 'historic first-flight gear retraction problems'. The SAS performed admirably, the aircraft failing to repeat the 'bucking bronco ride' of two days earlier even after each of the three SAS stability dampers (one for each axis) were switched off individually in proper test-flight sequencing. With all three dampers of the SAS re-engaged, Schalk terminated the first true A-12 flight with an 'absolutely uneventful' landing. He flew 121 on its second test flight four days later. The jet (at 72,000 lbs gross weight) lifted off at 170 kts and easily climbed to 30,000 ft where it attained a top speed of 340 kts. That smooth flight lasted 59 minutes and attained all second-flight test objectives. Four days later Lou broke Mach 1.

When word of these initial *Oxcart* successes was passed to Washington DC, John McCone, the new director of the CIA, telegrammed congratulations to Kelly – but the programme was a year behind schedule and much work remained to be done to prepare this new aircraft for its operational debut.

A-12 Build-Up

Over the next few months 121 was joined by more of its stable-mates. Article 122 arrived on 26 June, but was destined to spend three months conducting ground radar tests before taking to the air. Aircraft number three (Article 123) arrived in August and flew in October. In November the two-seat pilot trainer was delivered, which helped smooth transition training; the aircraft was to have been powered by J58 engines, but Pratt & Whitney was still having production problems. Since the Agency needed to get on with pilot training, it was decided to equip the two-seater with J75 engines and let the checked out pilots go on to high-Mach flight on their own. Once this decision was carried out, aircraft number four (the 'Titanium Goose') undertook its maiden flight in January 1963 fitted with the less powerful engines. Aircraft number five (Article 125) was delivered to the site on 17 December 1963.

Lou Schalk had been contracted to perform the first 12 experimental test flights in the A-12, and to thoroughly check out all important stability characteristics. An element of supersitition also led him to fly the 13th sortie on the aircraft. The burden of added test flying was shared with two other experienced test pilots, Bill Park and Jim Eastman, who began to build up flight time on the aircraft. Early trials proved the soundness of the overall design, and specific in-flight tests were performed on the cameras and sensors, the inertial navigation system and some of the more sensitive stability controls.

As time went by there was still no sign of the much vaunted J58 engines. The CIA became increasingly impatient to see some progress in return for the government's multi-million dollar investment in advanced propulsion. Senior Agency officials decided that the A-12 should be capable of Mach 2.0 with its J75 powerplants. Since the J75 could power the USAF's Convair F-106 Delta Dart interceptor to Mach 2.0, then the A-12 should certainly be able to match that speed. They did not understand that the A-12 had been designed to house a pair of J58s and that the J75s were mismatched with the inlet systems, which caused an inlet airflow vibration or 'duct-shudder' as Mach 2.0 was approached. Finally, in order to placate the directors who controlled the Agency's purse strings, Bill Park dived an A-12 to Mach 2.0, which relieved some of the high-level pressure on the design team.

World events were soon to provide the *Oxcart* project with a 'necessity' boost. Following Major Steve Heyser's historic U-2 overflight of Cuba on 14 October 1962, undeniable photographic evidence was obtained of the presence of Soviet SS-N-4 Medium Range Ballistic Missiles (MRBMs) and SS-N-5 Intermediate Range Ballistic Missiles (IRBMs) on the island. Consequently, U-2 overflight activities were increased to a peak level of five flights per day. On Saturday 27 October 1962, Maj Rudolph Anderson was shot down by an SA-2 SAM while he was flying a U-2 over Cuba. Just like the Gary Powers incident two and a half years earlier, the U-2's vulnerability had been demonstrated in a most spectacular fashion. Regrettably, Maj Anderson was killed in the Cuba overflight 'shootdown'. From that moment, the *Oxcart* programme assumed greater significance than ever and the achievement of 'operational status' became one of the highest national priorities.

When the *Oxcart* crews eventually saw an A-12 they were eager to confer a nickname upon Kelly's new 'Skunkworks' masterpiece. Being aware of Lockheed's penchant for christening their aircraft designs with names of celestial bodies, Jack Weeks came up with *Cygnus* (the Swan), which was the name of a constellation in the Northern Celestial Hemisphere, lying between Pegasus and Draco in the Milky Way. This was particularly apt for the secretive A-12 programme because research astronomers believe that Cygnus may contain one of the most mysterious of Nature's invisible bodies – a black hole.

J58s

In July 1962 the J58 finally completed its Pre-Flight Rating Test. An engine was taken to Groom Dry Lake and at last installed in article 121, which, until confidence levels in the new engine grew, would fly with a proven, but far less powerful J75 in the other nacelle. Even this arrangement had its usual crop of problems. One early 'hiccup' was ignition – the engine would not start no matter what procedure was tried by the Pratt & Whitney engineers! The small inlet wind tunnel model did not reveal that the engine's appetite for air was so great that instead of air flowing out of the compressor's fourth stage bleed ducts, flow reversal occurred and air was drawn into

This early Groom Dry Lake photograph shows to good effect the wedges of radar absorbing material (RAM) which completely skirted the aeroplane's outer edges. The shape was intended to trap any incident radar beam, causing it to reflect from one side of the wedge to the other. As it did so, its energy was gradually absorbed into the RAM, causing the A-12's radar signature to be much smaller than that of conventional aircraft (*CIA*)

the compressor from the back end. As a temporary fix, Lockheed removed an inlet access panel to facilitate ground starts. They subsequently cut holes into the rear section of the nacelle and installed two sets of suck-in doors, while Pratt & Whitney added an 'engine bleed' to the nacelle to improve airflow through the powerplant during ground starts.

On 15 January 1963, the first test flight of the A-12 powered by two new J58s occurred. By the end of the month, ten engines were available. Again, the Pratt & Whitney engineers and the Lockheed test pilots were faced with a multitude of problems that needed to be solved in order to attain Kelly's design goal of sustained high altitude flight at full Mach. The biggest hurdle remaining was to perfect airflow in the air induction system, which was designed to vastly augment engine thrust. To achieve this great thrust-boosting goal, the inlet spike's aft-movement schedule had to be programmed very accurately as speed was increased, and the same applied to the position of various bypass doors. When this fine-tuned control over high-speed inlet drag was finally achieved, the jet's thirst for fuel was notably reduced. In all, it took 66 flights to push the speed envelope from a marginal Mach 2.0 up to the full-scale design-speed of Mach 3.2.

Such repeated flights from Groom Dry Lake treaded a well-worn path across the emptiness of Nevada, northward over Wendover in Utah, high across southern Idaho and then turning east or west along a smooth 180 degree[1] arc just short of the Canadian border, before heading back south toward Arizona or California and finally down into the Groom Dry Lake 'roost', north of Las Vegas. Sonic booms were heard all over the western United States, and complaints were conveniently shifted toward the Arizona Air National Guard fighters at Phoenix, onward to the naval aviators at Fallon, Nevada, and then onward still toward any flying outfit capable of booming! This shifting of blame was conveniently ignored by the *Oxcarters* and the FAA controllers who knew the truth. During the return leg to Las Vegas, the A-12 would reach its test-point objectives above 72,000 ft, an altitude that would also allow the pilot to make a steep but safe recovery back to the 'Ranch' in the event of an in-flight emergency.

The cockpit workload for one person during A-12 test flying was extremely high since the turbine inlet temperature (TIT) tended to wander. This variation needed close monitoring if engine damage was to be avoided. At 7300 rpm, unstable

The same three A-12s remained at Kadena throughout the entire *Black Shield* deployment. Painted 'overall black', their only external markings were five-figure, dark red serial numbers sprayed on their twin fins. The completely bogus serials always began with the number '77'. One 'Agency' pilot recalls the same aeroplane, at various times, carrying the serials '858', '835' and '855'. Aircraft 932, pictured above, was lost with pilot Jack Weeks on 5 June 1968 (*CIA*)

'Dutch 30', Mel Vojvodich, deployed A-12 serial 937 to Kadena on 22 May 1967; he flew the same aircraft on *Black Shield*'s first operational mission nine days later (*CIA*)

temperatures caused thrust variations, so two toggle switches were introduced to allow the pilot to 'trim' the fuel flow in small increments without having to adjust the throttle positions to keep turbine temperatures within operable limits. Two rotating wafer switches controlled the inlet spike position (forward and aft), while a third set varied the bypass door positions (open to closed). The task of flying the aircraft, while manually operating those six control switches and determining the optimum inlet schedule of door and spike positions, created a situation where the pilot was saturated with switch movement activity during acceleration to high Mach. It was soon realised that it would be nearly impossible to fly the aircraft during unstable situations without the SAS operating; the gyro-stabilised system, coupled into the autopilot, made life in the cockpit more tolerable, despite the disheartening effect of using more than a third of the total fuel load accelerating to full speed due to poor inlet scheduling. The slow initial progression 'to full speed' was the result of a 'trial and error' positioning of door and spike inlet schedules.

During these early tests, the speed was gently increased by one tenth of a Mach number before the next spike progression increment was selected. If all worked well, that day's work was analysed in the labs and incorporated into the schedule. More often however, the spike position would not match the inlet duct requirements, and a hard 'unstart' (the violent and sudden expulsion of the normal shockwave from the internal throat of the inlet to the outside of the inlet) would cause a harsh yaw movement which swung the nose sharply in the direction of the 'unstarted' inlet, snapping the pilot's head quickly to one side in the process. To break a sustained unstart and to recapture the disturbed inlet shock wave, the pilot would have to open the bypass doors on the unstarted side and move the spike fully forward, before slowly returning them to the smooth-flowing, but less efficient, position that they were in just prior to the disturbance. Incessant problems in the air induction system caused Lockheed's propulsion engineers to change the inlet geometry and trim schedules. In addition, the manual trim schedule was speeded up to allow the aircraft to be accelerated more quickly, and to save fuel during the climb to high speed and altitude.

During that first year of developmental testing, the inlet control system was changed often, and on many flights the two inlets never seemed to work together. Pilot Walt Ray (wearing a Beatles' wig), after returning from a night training sortie filled with many unstarts, joked to the debriefing team at Groom Dry Lake, 'Man, that was a hairy flight'. Unstarts came to be expected on nearly all of the early A-12 flights. Ultimately the optimum pattern of door and spike sequencing was perfected and the inlet system was programmed to operate automatically with the assistance of inlet computers.

Thermodynamic considerations had minimised the number of electrical systems in the aircraft. Pneumatic pressure gauges were installed on the inlet systems to sense pressure variations of as little as one-quarter pound per square inch. Translating the position of the inlet spike was based on a schedule derived from pneumatic pressure readings. After a multitude of inlet malfunctions and unstarts, it became apparent that these pneumatic instruments were not sensitive enough for the job of accurately scheduling the spikes. Aircraft were coming off the production line with the pneumatic system installed, but Kelly decided that they should be replaced by an electrically controlled system. Although the Garrett Corporation's new system initially required far more maintenance per flight hour than the pneumatic system, its inflight performance was far superior to the old equipment. Despite the added cost, the electrical system was retrofitted to all aircraft already delivered and was incorporated in the remaining A-12s being produced at Burbank from number nine onwards.

Before the new spike control system was flight tested, many electromagnetic induction tests were carried out on the ground to ensure non-interfering operations. It was thought that 'all was well' with the EMI tests until a radio check made the inlet spikes retract. Clearly more work was still necessary before the inflight test. When Bill Park briefed the other pilots about the new system, he added that unstarts would soon be almost a thing of the past. None believed him, but the new system immediately began to prove its worth and the number of unstarts decreased dramatically. Fuel consumption also decreased significantly due to the tighter inlet spike and door scheduling.

The First Loss

Flying time was always at a premium, and consequently the operational pilots were also tasked to perform certain lesser flight tests while building up their own flying experience. On 24 May 1963, Ken Collins was flying a subsonic engine test sortie in aircraft number three (Article 123). Jack Weeks was 'pace-chasing' the A-12 in an F-101 Voodoo, and he was finding it difficult to stay with the aircraft, which was flying very slowly just above a solid overcast of clouds. Mindful of the notorious pitch-up problems associated with the Voodoo, Ken told Jack to continue on to the base without him. When Ken entered the clouds soon after, the A-12 suddenly pitched up and went completely out of control. Ken ejected safely from 123 which, it was subsequently determined, had entered an inverted flat spin before crashing approximately 50 miles west of the Great Salt Lake. As this was a low-altitude subsonic flight, Ken was wearing a standard-issue flight suit instead of his regular pressure suit. This simpler flying attire saved him from having to make a difficult series of explanations firstly to the truck driver who stopped to pick up the downed pilot along a main road, and then at the highway patrol office from where Ken contacted 'the boys back at the Ranch'.

The reason for this accident baffled flight safety investigators. To aid the analysis, Ken underwent hypnosis in order to relive the pre-bailout sequence of events, but this failed to work. He was then asked if he would allow the truth serum drug Sodium Pentatol to be used, which, since he was anxious to clear his name, he quickly agreed to. After the session, and still 'under the influence' of the narcosynthetic drug, Ken was driven to his home, where he was met on the doorstep by a less than understanding wife who thought the pilot had had far too much to drink – it was months before he was able to tell his wife the truth of the matter.

It was established that cloud vapour had collected in the aircraft's pitot system and formed ice which blocked the ram airflow into the pitot tube. The airspeed indicator showed an 'adequate but erroneous' airspeed reading which led to the stall and subsequent pitch-up from which there could be no recovery. The press was told that a Republic F-105 Thunderchief had crashed, a ruse which allowed A-12 security to remain intact.

Lou Schalk experienced what was perhaps the most 'thrilling' flight of his distinguished test flight career while flying 924 on an inlet schedule flight in 1963 with the electrically-controlled spike actuator installed.

'I was approaching Wendover, Utah, from the south and the aircraft was accelerating like it had never done before. It was apparent that I would be at Mach 3 before I left Utah (well before reaching the turn point short of the Canadian border) so I throttled back and started my turn early[1]. Emerging from the turn, I pushed the throttles to full burner and continued to climb. I got so far behind the aircraft that I didn't notice that the fuel flow fell off slightly which led to a loss in rpm on one engine. The next thing I knew I had an unstart, where upon I attempted to open the bypass doors to break the unstart but that action didn't seem to help. Then the other inlet unstarted and so it went on with terrific oscillations continuing, one after another. I made a single radio transmission saying that I was in real trouble. I thought I ought to bail out but stayed with the aircraft because it still seemed to be in one piece and still flying, although these violent oscillations continued all the way down to Mach 1.4. I then realised that I'd left the right engine in burner and that the left engine had flamed out. I was holding tremendous rudder pressure with one leg in an attempt to fly straight without even trimming out some of that pressure with the rudder trim switch. When I finally came out of afterburner it was much easier to handle so I restarted the flamed-out engine and headed back to base.

'At the debriefing I learned that the engineers had decided at their Monday morning maintenance planning briefing that the slow acceleration and high fuel consumption could be due to the bypass doors leaking air after they had been closed. They therefore decided to 'bolt' them closed but no one had told me about this decision and that's why the aircraft had taken off on me like 'a scorched dog'. It then became clear why I couldn't break the unstart and why when I tried to switch the bypass doors open nothing happened to change the inlet airflow. After that lesson in the lack of communication between engineers and pilots, I attended all the Monday morning maintenance planning briefings.'

Going Public

With the flight test programme now in full swing, and with a notable increase in *Cygnus* test and training sorties, questions were being raised as to how much longer the project could remain hidden from public attention, particularly if another accident should occur. To amplify such concerns, both Mel Vojvodich and Ken Collins were forced (under inflight emergency situations) to land at Kirtland Air Force Base, near Albuquerque, New Mexico, rather than their home base. In addition, the number of inflight sightings by airline pilots was on the increase and various aviation magazines were getting more and more leads on the secret project and were 'bursting' with the desire to 'blow *Oxcart*'s cover'.

On Friday 29 November 1963 (one week after the assassination of President Kennedy) the new president, Lyndon B Johnson, convened a meeting of the National Security Council (CIA Director John McCone, SecDef Robert McNamara, SecState Dean Rusk, Special Assistant McGeorge Bundy and FAA Chief Najeeb Halaby). The main question on the agenda was whether to, or how to, 'surface' the technological triumph of *Oxcart*. McCone counselled delay, but was in favour of some sort of press release in connection with the planned development of a Supersonic Airliner (SST); Halaby agreed. McNamara was in favour of total exposure because the *Oxcart* aeroplane would weaken the case for the B-70 programme, and other expensive Air Force projects which he did not like. At that point, Lyndon Johnson was informed by Bundy that Kennedy had been opposed to the early release of information pertaining to *Oxcart*, preferring instead to hold off its public debut until the following year

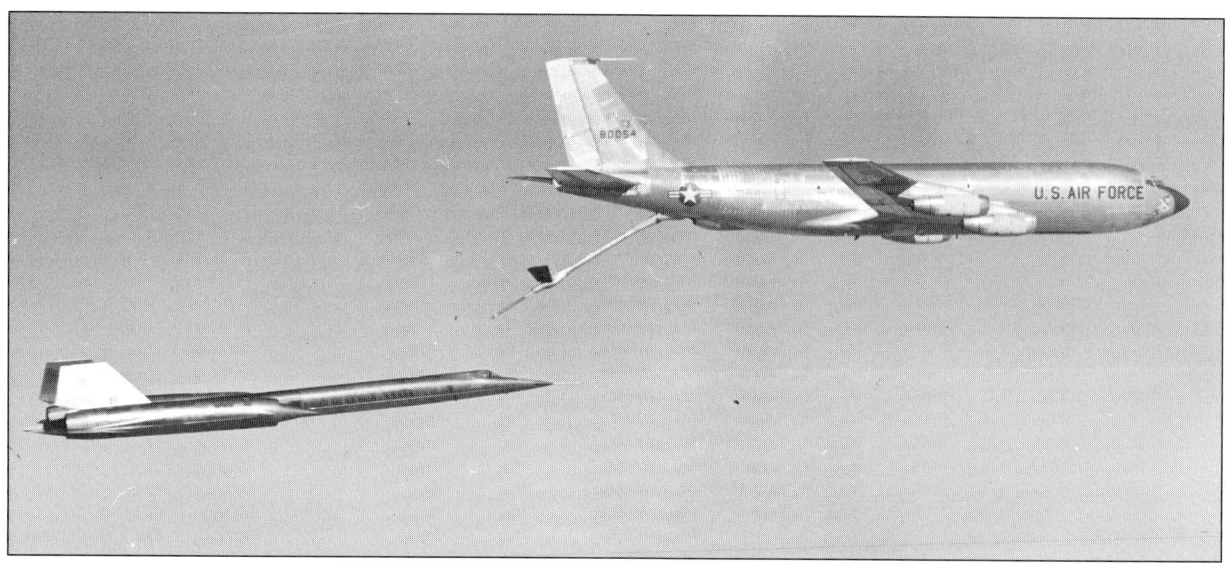

Slightly modified KC-135Qs of Beale's 903 Air Refueling Squadron provided the 'Road Runners' with invaluable AR support (*CIA*)

so as to strengthen his re-election campaign. Bundy was attuned to the politics of 'high tech' projects, and spoke against early release because of potential criticisms likely to be levelled at Johnson for attempting to make political 'capital' out of a great intelligence secret. Consequently, LBJ decided to 'keep his powder dry' until the run up to the 1964 presidential election. However, when Republican candidate Senator Barry Goldwater accused the Democrats of failing to sponsor new aircraft projects, President Johnson fired off the following announcement on 29 February 1964:

'The United States has successfully developed an advanced experimental jet aircraft, the A-11, which has been in sustained flight at more than 2000 mph and at altitudes in excess of 70,000 ft. The performance of the A-11 far exceeds that of any other aircraft in the world today. The development of this has been made possible by major advances in aircraft technology of great significance to both military and commercial applications. Several A-11 aircraft are now being flight-tested at Edwards Air Force Base in California. The existence of this programme is being disclosed to permit the orderly exploitation of this advanced technology in our military and commercial planes. This advanced experimental aircraft, capable of high speed and high altitude and long range performance at thousands of miles, consititutes the technological accomplishment that will facilitate the achievement of a number of important military and commercial requirements. The A-11 aircraft now at Edwards Air Force Base are undergoing extensive tests to determine their capabilities as long-range interceptors. The development of supersonic commercial transport aircraft will also be greatly assisted by the lessons learned from this A-11 program. For example, one of the most important technological achievements in this project has been the mastery of the metallurgy and fabrication of titanium metal which is required for the high temperatures experienced by aircraft travelling at more than three times the speed of sound. Arrangements are being made to make this and other important technical developments available under appropriate safeguards to those directly engaged in the supersonic transport program. This project was first started in 1959. Appropriate members of the Senate and House have been kept fully informed on the program since the day of its inception. Lockheed Aircraft Corporation, at Burbank, California, is the manufacturer of the aircraft. The aircraft engine, the J58 was designed and built by the Pratt & Whitney Aircraft Division, United Aircraft Corporation. The experimental fire-control and air-to-air missile system for the A-11 was developed by the Hughes Aircraft Corporation.'

The statement effectively split the programme in two, with three experimental YF-12 interceptor variants being transferred to Edwards AFB for an 'overt' programme, while *Oxcart* was left at Groom Dry Lake still very much in 'the black', hidden away from public scrutiny.

A bare titanium *Cygnus* comes home to roost at Groom Dry Lake (*CIA*)

Back at the 'Ranch'

All seemed to be progressing well until 9 July 1964 when Bill Parks experienced a complete lock-up of his flight controls in Article 133 as he descended for landing following a high Mach flight. Despite trying to save the aircraft from rolling under while turning on to final approach, Parks could not stop the bank angle from increasing. Realizing he was 'going in' he yanked the D-ring between his legs, which fired the rocket beneath his ejection seat, and succeeded in 'punching-out' at about 200 kts in a 45-degree bank, not more than 200 ft above the ground as the brand-new 133 exploded in a spectacular fire ball ahead of him. After just one quick swing under the quickly deployed canopy of his parachute, his feet were on the lake-bed! The 'Road Runners' were all certain that they had just witnessed their first fatality in the programme. To the great surprise of those hurrying to the scene, Bill was picked up walking toward the wreckage uninjured.

It is not uncommon for developmental flight testing to be punctuated by varying periods of stand-down to evaluate mistakes, or to make changes in hardware or procedures. When Mele Vojvodich came to the Site's main hangar two weeks later, number 126 (which he was to fly the following day) was lying about in bits and pieces across the hangar floor. He joked that this aircraft 'was never going to fly again', not knowing how prophetic his words would prove to be. On 28 December 1964, Mele taxied 126 out for a training flight and lit the burners for what he thought would be another run to altitude. As he reached rotate speed, he gently applied back pressure to the stick for rotation to lift-off attitude. Instead of 126's nose rising smoothly, it yawed viciously to one side, whereupon Mele stood on the rudder pedals to correct the yaw. Instead of rectifying the yaw, the rudder input made 126 pitch-up. The rash of instinctive responses which followed resulted in a series of counter movements opposite to those which an experienced pilot would expect to occur. It was indeed a pilot's nightmare. When the aircraft became airborne, it pulled itself toward the ground and back-stick pressure caused another hard yaw movement which could not be corrected by counter-rudder pressure without an increasingly sharp pitch movement. In the midst of this wild pitching and yawing, Mele pulled the ringed-loop D-ring between his legs and at an altitude of not more than a 100 ft, he blasted free of his unmanageable 'bronco' and rode his parachute to the only safe landing possible. Narrowly missing the flaming pyre that billowed up from yet another lost A-12, Mele landed safely after just six seconds of flight in a brand new aircraft – almost a new world record for the shortest test flight!

The subsequent accident board established that the SAS had been cross-wired, and that 'Murphy's Law' had claimed yet another jet[2]. The pitch SAS had been connected to the Yaw SAS actuators and vice-versa. With no cockpit warning lights available to warn the pilot of his predicament, and with no SAS effect felt until rotation, Mele had no opportunity to identify his potential problem until the Gyro-sensed SAS reacted to rotation as if it were a yaw input at the most critical moment of flight – lift-off. Through a series of tests in the new R-12 simulator then being installed at Beale AFB, it was determined that none of the trained A-12 pilots who repeatedly tried to fly out of such a situation could have saved 126. Indeed, it was considered 'miraculous' for Mele to have been able to escape with his life. From that experience, the SAS connectors were made 'Murphy-proof'.

Operations

The first attempt at a long-range, high-speed flight occurred on 27 January 1965 when a 3000-mile flight was made in one hour and forty minutes, with three-quarters of the time spent at Mach 3.1. In 1965 the A-12 was ready for operational testing and by late-1965, all of the Agency's pilots were Mach 3 qualified. Despite that near-state of readiness, the political sensitivities surrounding the Gary Powers shoot-down in May 1960 effectively ensured that the A-12 would never conduct sorties over the Soviet Union – the very country that it was originally built to overfly. Where then, was this multi-million dollar national security asset to earn its keep? The initial answer was Cuba. By early 1964, Project Headquarters had already begun planning for possible 'contingency overflights' under a programme code-named *Skylark*. On 5 August 1965, the Director of the National Security Agency, Gen Marshall S Carter, directed that *Skylark* was to achieve emergency operational readiness by 5 November. Should security considerations dictate, such contingency sorties would be executed below the optimum capability of the A-12 (nearer to Mach 2.8). To meet the tight time-frame, aircraft would have to deploy without their full ECM suite. Despite all the difficulties of the early programme, a limited *Skylark* capability was ready on the date prescribed by Gen Carter. A five-pilot, five-aircraft plan was accomplished for Cuban contingencies, but a more critical situation developed in South-East Asia which took priority. Consequently, *Skylark* missions were never flown over Cuban skies.

On 22 March 1965, Brig Gen Jack Ledford briefed Deputy SecDef Cyrus Vance on project *Black Shield*- the planned deployment of *Cygnus* to Okinawa, in response to the increased SA-2 threat that was facing U-2 and Firebee drone reconnaissance vehicles used over Communist China. Overflights of China would obviously have to be approved by the President himself, but Secretary Vance was willing to make $3.7 million available to provide support facilities at Kadena AFB, which were to be ready by the fall of 1965. On 3 June 1965, Secretary McNamara consulted with the Under Secretary of the Air Force on the build-up of SA-2 missile sites around Hanoi and the possibility of substituting A-12s for the vulnerable U-2s on recce flights over the North Vietnamese capital. He was informed that *Black Shield* could operate over Vietnam as soon as adequate aircraft performance was validated.

On 20 November 1965 the final stage of this validation process was completed when a maximum-endurance flight of six hours and twenty minutes was achieved, during which time the A-12 demonstrated sustained speeds above Mach 3.2 at altitudes approaching 90,000 ft. On 2 December 1965 the highly secretive '303 Committee' received a formal proposal to deploy *Oxcart* operations to the Far East. That proposal was quickly rejected, but the Committee agreed that all steps should be taken to develop a quick-reaction capability for deploying the A-12 reconnaissance system within a 21-day period anytime after 1 January 1966. Throughout 1966, numerous requests were made to the Committee to implement the *Black Shield* Operations Order, but all requests were turned down. A difference of opinion had arisen between two important governmental factions advising the Committee: the CIA, the Joint Services Committee (JSC), and the President's Foreign Intelligence Advisory Board who favoured the deployment; and Alexis Johnson of the State Department and Robert McNamara and Cyrus Vance of the Defense Department who opposed it.

Meanwhile, training and testing continued throughout 1966 while mission plans and tactics were prepared to ready the operational 'package' for deployment should the *Black Shield* decision be executed. Deployment timing was cut from 21 to 11 days, and the Okinawa-based maintenance facility was stocked with support equipment. To further underwrite the A-12's capability to carry out long-range reconnaissance missions, Bill Park flew a non-stop 10,200 mile flight in just over six hours on 21 December 1966.

Fifteen days after Park's proof-of-range flight, tragedy struck the programme with the crash of another jet, but this time with the loss of the first *Cygnus* pilot. Walt Ray was returning from a normal training flight when a faulty fuel gauge caused Article 125 (tail number 60-6928)[3] to run out of fuel some 70 miles short of Groom Dry Lake. After 'gliding' to a lower altitude and executing what appeared to be a controlled bailout, Walt could not separate his parachute from the ejection seat and was killed when he hit the ground.

The circumstances leading up to that loss were particularly ironic. Nearly a year earlier, on 25 January 1966, test-model SR-71 Number 952 was lost by a Lockheed test flight crew (Bill Weaver and Jim Zwayer) on a range-extension test in which Zwayer was killed. Post-accident investigations revealed that Zwayer had died from a broken neck sustained as the aircraft disintegrated following a Mach 3 pitch-up. The violent 'whiplash' that had resulted from the high-speed break-up of the aircraft, and the subsequent G-forces that slung Zwayer and Weaver about as they were forcibly torn from their non-ejected seats slammed Zwayer's head back against the seat's head rest. It was further determined, because of Zwayer's short stature, that his head-rest was farther back due to the thickness of the parachute's back-pack.

Subsequent to that accident, Lockheed undertook flight-safety modifications to the seat's head-rest cushion, tailoring it more closely to the contours of individual crew members to provide support and protection from future 'whiplash' injuries. Regrettably, Walt's extended head-rest had caused his parachute to become entrapped between the seat well and the head-rest to the degree that the 'butt-snapper' straps[4] (which had attempted to work as advertised) could not push Walt free from his seat. That accident was a bitter blow to the deployment timing of the programme, and came as a shock to all who knew Walt as an outstanding pilot. The *Los Angeles Times* reported the accident and identified the aircraft as an 'SR-71 Experimental Reconnaissance jet' and Walt Ray as a 'Lockheed test pilot'.

In May 1967, the National Security Council was briefed that North Vietnam was about to receive surface-to-surface ballistic missiles which could further escalate the conflict. Since the foundations for such beliefs remained unproven, it would be necessary to produce some hard evidence. When President Johnson was briefed on the missile issue, it was suggested that aerial reconnaissance might be able to certify the presence of that threat. Richard Helms of the CIA submitted a proposal to the '303 Committee' that the A-12 was ideally suited for the mission and that its camera was far superior to that fitted in either the U-2 or pilotless drone aircraft that were then being used in large numbers, and further that the A-12 was 'invulnerable to shoot-downs' by Soviet-made missiles. As a result, Helms proposed that they authorise the deployment of *Oxcart*'s A-12s, pilots, specialised support equipment and personnel to the Far East for Hanoi area surveillance. President Johnson approved the plan and a mid-May airlift was begun to establish *Black Shield* at Kadena Air Base on Okinawa.

Before that deployment, the fate of *Oxcart* seemed in doubt, resulting in serious morale problems setting in amongst 'project people' at all levels. A great deal of money had been spent since construction work had begun at Kadena 12 months earlier on a purpose-built four-bay hangar (with 'clean-room' workshops) and on three *Black Shield* dormitories. During 'dry run' exercises that were made from the Nevada site to Kadena in KC-135s to test the deployment of support personnel, it was revealed that the dormitories were already in use, crammed full of Vietnam-bound troops. Although the Agency had an agreement with the Air Force that the accommodation blocks would be vacated within 24 hours, it proved almost impossible to get the new tenants out because of the scale of SAC's operations in support of the war. When Gen Bacalis called Col Hugh 'Slip' Slater (the Air Force Commander of the 'Roadrunners') to enquire if the tight deployment time-frame could be met, Slater assured Bacalis that it would be possible 'provided that certain key people that had already left the program be re-recruited back'.

After the necessary 'clearing' action was taken,

Just visible are the twin fins of number 937 A-12, which was surrounded by other aircraft on Wake Island after it was forced to divert on 7 June 1968 (*P Crickmore collection*)

Forty-eight hours after the seizure of the USS *Pueblo*, Frank Murray conducted the first overflight of North Korea in an A-12 on 26 January 1968 (*CIA*)

Ken Collins finally made it to Hawaii after innumerable attempts to launch from Wake Island. He was attempting to ferry an A-12 back to Groom Dry Lake in 1968 following termination of the *Oxcart* programme (*P Crickmore collection*)

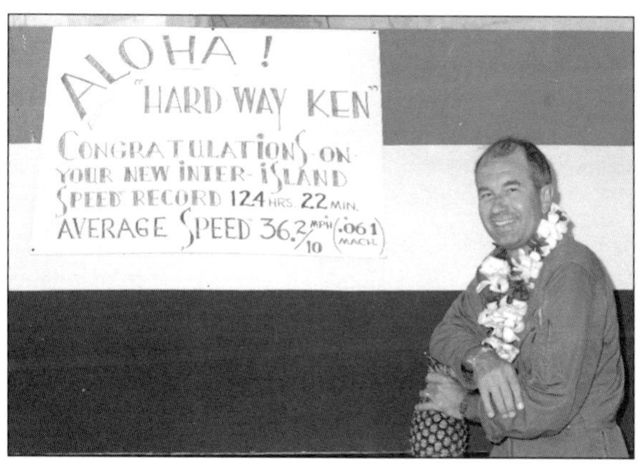

work to prepare Kadena for the new tenants 'shifted into overdrive'. Slip Slater's new deputy (an Agency civilian) made arrangements to take over a condemned quonset-hut housing area from the Air Force called 'Morgan Manor', and contracted for rennovation work which included extensive repair of the quonsets, adding air conditioning, and installing a complete messing facility brought in from the US. In a short time, all was ready for the *Oxcart* team.

At 0800 hours on 22 May 1967, Mele Vojvodich got airborne from 'the Area' in article number 131 and headed west across California for his first refuelling. After a top-off from a Beale tanker, he climbed and accelerated to high Mach toward the next refuelling control point near Hawaii. A third rendezvous took place near Wake Island to ensure that he had enough reserve fuel to divert from an intended landing at Kadena to either Kunsan Air Base in South Korea or Clark AFB in the Philippines (some 1200 miles beyond Kadena) should weather conditions over Okinawa deteriorate. When Mele arrived however, the weather was fine and he let down for landing after an uneventful flight of just over six hours in duration. Had it not been for the deployment's secrecy, the flight could have been recognised as a new transpacific speed record.

Two days later Jack Layton set out to repeat Mele's flight but aircraft 127 experienced an air data computer failure shortly after take-off. As a result, Jack lost important instrument readings on his Triple Display Indicator (KEAS, Mach Number and Altitude read-outs). Loss of the TDI instrument was 'an abort item' on his GO-No GO checklist but Jack (like all *Oxcart* team members) was acutely aware of the pressure on the programme to succeed. He therefore chose to continue the flight toward Okinawa by calculating bypass door and inlet spike position schedule changes by inlet temperature gauge indications. That careful action proved successful and Jack landed the second aircraft at Kadena in under six hours. Jack was met after engine shut-down by his old flying instructor, Slip Slater, who asked him if there were any maintenance write-ups, to which Jack replied, 'only the TDI'. 'When did you lose that?' enquired Slater. 'Away back', answered the A-12 driver. 'How far away back?' pressed the Colonel. 'Well, just after take-off, actually', Jack admitted. 'You crazy SOB', Slater laughed and never again mentioned the incident.

Jack Weeks left Groom Dry Lake according to plan in aircraft 129 on 26 May, but due to Inertial Navigation System and radio problems, he was forced to divert into Wake Island. An *Oxcart* maintenance recovery team arrived in a KC-135 from Okinawa the following day to prepare 129 for the final 'hop' to Kadena. After arriving at Kadena, Jack's aircraft was soon declared fit for operational service along with 127 and 131. As a result, the Detachment was declared ready for operations on 29 May, and following a weather reconnaissance flight on 30 May it was determined that 'seeing' conditions over North Vietnam were ideal for an A-12 photo-run.

Project Headquarters in Washington then placed *Black Shield* on alert for its first operational sortie, the highly skilled ground technicians preparing 131 and a backup aircraft for the first A-12 operational flight. Avionics specialists checked various systems and sensors, and at 1600 hours Mele Vojvodich and back-up pilot Jack Layton attended a mission alert briefing which included such details as projected take-off and landing times, routes to and from the target area, aerial refuelling areas, potential divert bases, and a full intelligence briefing of the area to be overflown. At 2200 hours (12 hours before planned take-off time) a review of the weather confirmed that the mission was still 'Go'. Shortly thereafter the pilots went to bed to ensure they got a full eight hours of 'crew rest'.

When they awoke on the morning of 31 May, torrential rain was pounding the island – a phenomenon new to the former 'desert-dwelling' A-12s. The two pilots ate breakfast, dressed and proceeded to prepare for the mission, despite local rain. Since the weather over the 'collection area' was good, Washington officials sent the final 'Go' message to Kadena at 0800 hours and the mission was definitely 'On'. The rain, however, continued without letup, casting serious doubts over the launch of the aircraft. The pilot had the final choice in the matter since conditions were within Air Force take-off limits. Mele (who was acutely aware of the pressure on the programme to 'deliver') chose to launch. After brief medical checks, Mele and Jack both donned their S-901 full pressure suits and breathed pure oxygen to purge potentially harmful body nitrogen. By taxy-time, the rain was falling so heavily that a staff car had to lead Mele from the hangar to the end of the main runway. After lining up for what would be the first instrument-guided take-off in an A-12, Mele engaged both afterburners and 131 accelerated rapidly down the runway to disappear completely into the rain, and then upward through the drenching clouds.

In a few moments Mele burst through the cloud tops and flew 131 up to 25,000 ft where he levelled off prior to approaching the first tanker just west of the Island. As soon as the A-12's tanks were topped up, Mele disengaged from the KC-135's boom and began to climb and accelerate. Since 131's inlet system performed well during acceleration to cruise Mach, Jack Layton's services as back-up would not be necessary. The Mach 3.0 trip down to Vietnam just off the East China Coast went smoothly and Mele prepared to penetrate hostile airspace at Mach 3.1 and 80,000 ft. A 'front door' entry would take the aircraft over Haiphong and Hanoi, and allow Mele to exit out of North Vietnam near Dien Bien Phu. Refuelling would take place over Thailand, followed by another climb to altitude and a second penetration of North Vietnamese airspace in the vicinity of the Demilitarised Zone, after which Mele would high-cruise 131 back to 'home-plate' at Kadena.

As 131 coasted-in by Haiphong its RHWR-gear (Radar Homing and Warning Receiver) alerted the pilot that 131 was being tracked by enemy fire-control radars. The apparent ease with which the North Vietnamese were able to track this new high-speed, high-flying aircraft would later cause considerable consternation back at Burbank, and Washington (especially after the time, effort and

Above Eight A-12s sat in long-term storage at Palmdale after their retirement in 1968. The two-seat 'Titanium Goose' (near the back of the hangar) still sports its two-tone paint scheme (*CIA*)

Below All nine surviving A-12s are seen outside the large storage hangar at Palmdale (*Lockheed*)

expense that had been devoted to reducing the aircraft's radar cross section image). As Mele approached Hanoi, the RHWR indicated that missiles were on their way up. He recalled observing numerous SAMs that had been launched many miles ahead. In desperation to score a kill on something so high and fast, the enemy SAM operators were firing salvos of missiles in the hope that they could get an SA-2 near enough for a lucky hit. Despite the number fired, none came anywhere near the A-12, all of them detonating above and well behind 131. The weather over the target area turned out to be almost clear and 131's cameras had successfully photographed ten priority target categories, including 70 of the 190 known SAM sites. After arriving back at Kadena only three hours and forty minutes after take-off, Mele was greeted by driving rain and very poor visibility, which required three instrument approaches before he could get the A-12 back on the ground safely. Later, after he had taxied 131 back to the hangar, the 'photo-take' was downloaded and sent by a special courier aircraft to the Eastman Kodak plant in Rochester, New York, for processing[5].

Later Missions

A total of seven of the fifteen sorties that were alerted between 31 May and 15 August were flown. One of those 'alerted' but subsequently aborted sorties was to be Jack Layton's first operational flight. All had gone well until Jack plugged into the KC-135 just southwest of Okinawa. The first thing that the boom operator said to Jack as his aircraft's fuel tanks began to top-off was, 'You don't want to go supersonic with this aircraft, Sir.' The puzzled A-12 pilot enquired why as there were no cockpit indications which would support such a remark, and the aircraft seemed to be handling well. 'I don't think you'll want to go fast, Sir', the Boomer replied, 'because the left side of your aircraft is missing'. After further consultation with him and other KC-135 crewmembers who viewed the most unusual sight, Jack decided that 'prudence dictated that he surely abort his important first mission.' As he turned back to Kadena, an F-102 interceptor was scrambled out of Naha Air Base, Okinawa, to serve as escort back to Kadena in the event of controllability problems. As the Delta Dagger drew alongside the crippled *Cygnus*, the F-102 pilot reported that the A-12 had lost practically all of its left Chine panels from nose to tail. In addition, large panels on top of the wing (which also covered the top side of the wheel well) had also disappeared, allowing the chase-pilot to see right through part of the aircraft's left wing. When these panels broke loose, at least one had impacted the top of the left rudder, causing even more damage.

As the two aircraft desended below 20,000 ft, they dipped into clouds and the A-12's cockpit fogged-up so badly that Jack was unable to see his hand in front of his face, let alone read his flight instruments. He quickly called for the F-102 pilot to report on the A-12's attitude since he became very concerned that it might depart its flight envelope by stalling or diving. Relieved that he had remained within normal flight parameters, Jack managed to climb back out of the clouds. By turning the cockpit temperature control to full-hot, he managed to eliminate the humidity that had caused the fogging, but the hotter-than-normal cockpit soon became extremely uncomfortable. Nevertheless, he was able to recover safely back at Kadena without further incident.

Twenty-six sorties were alerted between 16 August and 31 December of which fifteen were flown. One of Frank Murray's early sorties was to be a so-called 'double looper'[6]. Frank commenced his first photo run at an altitude above 80,000 ft on a track deep into North Vietnam with all systems functioning well. As he was about to turn off his cameras before heading south toward his air refuelling rendezvous, his left engine started vibrating and the left inlet unstarted. Frank recalled:

'I had my hands full for a while. In fact, I ended up having to shut the engine down. I increased the power on the good engine and flew it at maximum temperature for about an hour before I hooked up with the tanker. Because of the shut-down engine, I decided to divert into Takhli and the tanker crew relayed messages back to Kadena that I was diverting. Because I kept my radio calls to a minimum for security reasons, I didn't identify myself to the Takhli air traffic controllers until I was on final approach for landing. I landed without incident but inadvertantly screwed up a complete F-105 strike mission launch when I jettisoned the big brake chute on the main runway. I turned off the runway and sat there with the engine running and asked that the base commander come out to the aircraft as there were certain things I had to tell him. My presence was causing a pandemonium of curiousity; there was this most unusual

Palmdale, October 1980 – these A-12s were cocooned and tethered to protect them from the ravages of open storage (*John Andrews*)

black aircraft with no markings, the like of which nobody on that base had ever seen before, that had dropped in completely unannounced, disrupting a major operation, and its pilot insisting on the base commander coming out to see him. While this was going on guys on base with cameras were clicking away like mad. Eventually they sent out the Thai base commander which was no good because I wanted the US base commander. He eventually arrived and (despite all my disruptions to his war operations) was extremely helpful.'

After Frank's aircraft had been safely tucked away in an 'Agency' U-2 facility on the base, the Air Force Security Police had a 'field day' confiscating the opportunists' film. An inspection of the left engine revealed that most of its moving parts had been 'shucked like corn from a cob' and were laying in the tail pipe and the afterburner. A recovery crew flew in a spare engine, but the aircraft had also sustained notable damage to the nacelle and to some of its nearby electrical wiring. It was decided that the jet would have to be flown 'low and slow' back to Kadena on 9 October. Frank explained:

'I got airborne and headed off south over the Gulf of Thailand, where I picked up an F-105 escort that led me out over South Vietnam. There the escort was changed and F-4s covered me and my tanker out to sea before they broke off to return to their base. We then made our way via the Philippines, where I picked up another tanker which led me on back to Kadena.'

Whilst Frank was dealing with the inflight emergency over North Vietnam, his attention had been diverted away from switching off the photographic equipment to the more pressing priority of controlling the aircraft. As he turned south, his still-operating camera had taken a series of oblique shots into China. A close analysis of those photos revealed eight tarpaulin-covered objects among a mass of other material along the large main rail link between Hanoi and Nanking. Further photo interpretation ascertained that the 'tarps' were flung over rail flatcars in an attempt to hide 152 mm self-propelled heavy artillery pieces. A great mass of other war material in the rail yards had been assembled for

'Agency' pilots that flew the A-12 operationally were awarded the CIA Intelligence Star for Valour on 26 June 1968. From left to right are Mel Vojvodich (just in shot), Dennis Sullivan, Adm Rufus Taylor (Deputy Director of the CIA), Jack Layton, Ken Collins and Frank Murray (*P Crickmore collection*)

The coveted CIA Intelligence Star for Valour (*P Crickmore collection*)

movement to North Vietnam during the oncoming winter season when low clouds and poor visibility would hamper US bombing efforts to halt south-bound supply lines. A timely and highly valuable piece of strategic intelligence had been gained on Frank's troubled sortie, which allowed intelligence specialists a unique opportunity to track the further movement of those guns and supplies, obviously intended for use in future offensive actions.

During the next sortie on 28 October, Denny Sullivan had indications on his RHWR of almost continuous radar activity focused on his aircraft while he was inbound and outbound over North Vietnam, which also included the launch of a single SA-2 against him. Two days later he was again flying high over North Vietnam when two SAM sites tracked him on his first pass. During the second pass, he noted radar tracking as he approached Hanoi from the east. Over the next few seconds he counted eight SAM detonations in 'the general area, though none were particularly close'. After recovering back at Kadena without further incident, a post-flight inspection of the aircraft revealed that a tiny piece of shrapnel had penetrated the lower right wing fillet of his aircraft, and had become lodged against the support structure of the wing tank[7].

On a later mission, Jack Layton accidently violated Chinese airspace during a flight over North Vietnam when his Inertial Navigation System failed. Since the aircraft was flying on autopilot, Jack didn't notice that the INS glitch had resulted in a further failure of the autopilot to execute a pre-programmed turn, causing him to 'penetrate the bamboo curtain'. After turning south and getting back to an approximate course toward the air refuelling control point over Thailand, Jack had difficulty finding the tankers. He later recalled that the clouds were low and the visibility was poor:

'I got the aircraft up in a bank to search for the tankers but the visibility from an A-12 is very poor; you can look down and see the ground but you can't look inside the turn because of the canopy roof. I'd just about reached the point where I was about to divert into Takhli due to the lack of fuel when I finally saw the tankers. We got together and I was able to complete the mission even though the INS wasn't working.'

The *Pueblo* Affair

In an April 1965 intelligence planning meeting[8], it had been decided to establish a small seaborne fleet of Signal Intelligence vessels similar to the Soviet fleet of 40 such ships which operated near the United States and in many other strategic points around the world. That decision received prompt approval from Director of Defense Research and Engineering, Dr Harold Brown, and from Deputy Secretary of Defense Cyrus Vance for the implementation of a two-phase plan.

In Phase One, the USS *Banner* was transformed into AGER-1 (Auxilliary General Environmental Research Ship Number One), and duly steamed out of Washington State's Puget Sound Naval Shipyard on the first of its planned 16 sea patrols in the Western Pacific. Meanwhile, two Army supply ships, FS-344 and FS-389, were rechristened as the USS *Pueblo* (AGER-2) and USS *Palm Beach* (AGER-3). By 1 December 1967, the extensive modification programme was complete and the *Pueblo* joined its sister ship, the *Banner*, in Yokosuka Harbour in Japan. By then the *Banner* was a veteran on intelligence surveillance duties. While at Yokosuka, a six-month schedule was drafted covering nine separate missions, five of which were tasked by the National Security Agency (NSA).

The *Pueblo*'s first sortie was tasked by the US Navy and called for the ship to 'sample the electronic environment off the east coast of North Korea' and to 'intercept and conduct surveillance of Soviet naval units operating in the Tsushima Straits'. The risk estimate was assessed as 'minimal'. A request for final approval was contained in the 'Monthly Reconnaissance Schedule for January 1968', which is maintained by the Joint Chiefs of Staff's Joint Reconnaissance Center (JCS-JRC). On 29 December 1967, approval was received from the proper agencies (the JCS, the CIA, the NSA and the State Department) and from officials (Deputy Sec Def Paul Nitze and the NSC's '303 Committee').

On 5 January 1968 the unprotected *Pueblo* sailed as ordered on its maiden voyage for the east coast of a hostile-natured nation, North Korea. Just 18 days later during the night of 23 January, the ship's radio operator managed to get off an emergency signal. 'We Need Help! We Are Holding Emergency Destruction! We Need Support! SOS. SOS. SOS. Please Send Assistance! SOS. SOS. SOS. We Are Being Boarded!' The last sentence clearly stated what was happening aboard the vessel, and with one sailor dead and the rest of the crew captured, the year-long nightmare for Lt Cdr Lloyd Butcher and his crew was just beginning.

Two A-12 sorties were flown as a consequence of the capture of the *Pueblo*. The first was attempted by Jack Weeks on 25 January – just 24 hours after the ship was captured. A malfunction on the A-12 resulted in an abort shortly after take-off. The next day another attempt was made by Frank Murray, whose task was to overfly North Korea to ascertain where the *Pueblo* was being held, and if North Korea was about to embark on some form of large-scale follow-up ground action. Frank recalled:

'I left Kadena, topped-off, then entered northern airspace over the Sea of Japan via the Korean Straits. My first pass started off near Vladivostok, then with the camera on I flew down the east coast of North Korea where we

Above A-12s 940 and 941 were converted to M-12-specs to carry the (Tagboard) D-21 drone (*Lockheed ADP*)

Below The ceramic shells, covering the D-21's fixed inlet and exhaust, were ballistically removed prior to firing the Marquardt RJ-43-MA-11 ramjet (*Lockheed ADP*)

thought the boat was. As I approached Wonsan I could see the *Pueblo* through my view sight. The harbour was all iced up except at the very entrance and there she was, sitting off to the right of the main entrance. I continued to the border with South Korea, completed a 180 degree turn and flew back over North Korea. I made four passes, photographing the whole of North Korea from the DMZ to the Yalu border. As far as I knew, I was undetected throughout the flight but when I got back to Kadena some folks told me that the Chinese had detected me and told the North Koreans, but they never reacted.'

As usual 'the take' was immediately flown to the 67th RTS at Yokota for initial processing, where it was soon established that North Korea was not intending some form of follow-up action – at least, not immediately. US State Department officials were extremely wary of endorsing a second mission over North Korea after the *Pueblo* event. The diplomatic scars left by the 1960 Powers incident were still sensitive. It was not until Brig Gen Paul Baclais had briefed Secretary of State Dean Rusk on the specific mission objectives, and assured him that the aircraft would only be in North Korean airspace for just seven minutes, that State Department approval was finally given.

On 8 May 1968 Jack Layton launched and headed for North Korea. Unknown to him at the time, his mission was to be the final operational flight of an A-12. That sortie also experienced a moment of tension when Jack was on his way back to Kadena after a successful mission. After the high speed flight, 'milky white fingers' began slowly clawing their way across the front windshield. Having already experienced this 'white-out' phenomenon to a lesser degree during a stateside training sortie, Jack was aware of the problem, which was caused by frictional heating of the windscreen to the point that the glue between glass laminations became viscous and turned completely opaque. Proceeding on instruments all the way to landing, Jack completed a successful ground directed radar approach for a safe recovery back to Kadena.

Although the procurement of such intellignence information was not of direct benefit to Lt Cdr Butcher and his crew, who were beaten and not released by their North Korean captors until nearly a year had passed, such a 'hot-spot, quick-look' capability was considered an early and important achievement of the *Oxcart* programme, clearly demonstrating the ability of manned reconnaissance vehicles to respond with minimal lead times to international incidents of political and military importance. At the same time, the *Pueblo incident* ended the Navy's seaborne foray into the world of SIGINT trawling, the two remaining AGERs being scrapped soon after *Pueblo*'s seizure.

The Closedown of *Oxcart*

It seems almost unbelievable that during the very month *Oxcart* was finally declared operational (November 1965), and before the programme had had the opportunity of fully proving itself, moves were already afoot to close it down. It was during that month that a memorandum was circulated within the Bureau of the Budget (BoB) which expressed serious concerns at the costs of *Oxcart* and *Senior Crown* (the SR-71 programme). That BoB memo questioned the requirement for the overall number of high-performance aircraft and doubted the necessity for separate 'covert' CIA and 'overt' USAF operations. Its writer proposed several less costly alternatives, recommending that the A-12s be phased out by September 1966 and that all further procurement of SR-71s should stop. Copies of the memorandum were circulated in certain circles within the Defense Department and the CIA, together with the suggestion that they explore the alternatives set out in the paper. Since the SR-71 was not scheduled to become operational until September 1966, the Secretary of Defence quite rightly declined to consider the proposal. In July 1966, BoB officials proposed that a tri-agency study group be set up to again establish ways of reducing the costs of the two programmes[9]. After the study was completed, a meeting was convened on 12 December 1966 and a vote was taken on each of the three alternatives which had been proposed:

(1) To maintain the status quo and continue both fleets at current approval levels.

(2) To mothball all A-12 aircraft, but maintain the *Oxcart* capability by sharing the SR-71 between SAC and the CIA.

(3) To terminate the *Oxcart* fleet in January 1968 (Assuming an operational readiness date of September 1967 for the SR-71) and assign all missions to the SR-71 fleet.

Three out of four votes cast were in favour of option three. The BoB's memorandum was transmitted to President Johnson on 16 December despite protestations from the CIA's Helms, who was the sole dissenting voice in the vote. Twelve days later Johnson accepted the BoB's recommendations and directed that the *Oxcart* programme be terminated by 1 January 1968.

As the war in Vietnam escalated and the results of *Black Shield's* outstanding work became apparent to a privileged few, the wisdom of the earlier phase-out decision was called into question. As a result, the run-down lagged and the question was reopened. A new feasibility and cost study of *Oxcart* was completed in the spring of 1968, and despite the continuing objections raised by Richard Helms, the original decision to terminate the programme was reaffirmed on 16 May 1968 by the Secretary of Defense. This decision was further endorsed by President Johnson five days later during his weekly luncheon with his principal advisers.

Project officials decided that 8 June 1968 would be the earliest date to begin the redeployment from Kadena back to the States. During the intervening period, sorties would be restricted to those essential for maintaining flight safety and pilot proficiency. Those aircraft back at 'the Area' were to be flown to Palmdale and placed in storage by 7 June. Meanwhile at Kadena, preparations were being made for the A-12 ferry flights back to the United States. Mission sensors were down-loaded for the final time, and low-time/high-performance engines were replaced with the less highly-tuned units and test flights were being flown to confirm each aircraft's readiness for the transpacific ferry flights.

During one such test flight, Frank Murray got 129 airborne on 2 June 1968 and headed out south of Okinawa well away from unfriendly land-based radars. The well-worn test and training route was tear-drop shaped, pointing toward the Philippines at first where a long shallow 190 degree turn was initiated back toward Kadena. This high and fast cruise leg continued over the base, and was followed by a tighter let-down tear-drop pattern which brought the aircraft in towards final approach prior to landing. Having taken fuel from a tanker, the full route was flown but Frank recalled that the right engine would not go into bypass until it reached Mach 3, as opposed to the normal speed of Mach 2.6. The flight was continued without further incident until 129 passed over Kadena and Frank began what was to be a normal deceleration and descent. At that point, Frank discovered that the right engine would not come out of bypass. As deceleration continued, the inevitable happened. Since the bypass system continued to deliver most of the air to the afterburner section and very little to the combustion section, the engine flamed out. Once 129 was subsonic, Frank restarted the engine and recovered into Kadena without further incident. It was obvious that the right engine would have to be changed to solve this problem. Two days later Jack Weeks took 129 on another functional check flight (FCF) but he never returned. Despite an intense air and sea search lasting weeks, no trace of Weeks or article number 129 was ever found.

A rudimentary high frequency radio telemetry system had been installed on the A-12 fleet called 'Birdwatcher', which monitored various aircraft functions such as hydraulic pressure, fuel flow, throttle position, canopy opening, seat ejection, Mach number, compressor inlet temperature and other temperatures and pressures. Those signals were transmitted to a large ground monitoring console at Kadena. From this system's limited evidence it was ascertained that some kind of malfunction involving an overtemperature and low fuel flow on the right engine had contributed to what appeared to be a catastrophic failure and subsequent aircraft break-up. It was particularly ironic and an especially 'cruel twist of fate' to lose such a highly competent and professional pilot on one of the very last flights in the *Oxcart* programme.

The two remaining A-12s on Okinawa (article numbers 127 and 131[10]) were ferried back to Nevada before being sent to Palmdale. On 7 June 1968 Frank Murray boarded 131 for the flight back to the US. He topped-off his tanks near Iwo Jima and then flew a 'hot leg' to Wake Island, where he decelerated for another refuelling. Before 'plugging in', he noticed a high rate of fuel flow on the right engine. Through the small rear-view periscope, he saw that the right engine was leaving an unburnt trail of fuel behind the aircraft. He told the tanker crew that he had a fuel leak and that he would have to dump much of the remaining JP7 before landing at Wake Island. After the recovery team arrived, the A/B fuel line was replaced and the aircraft was flight tested. Next, Ken Collins flew 131 at subsonic speed into Hawaii's Hickam Air Force Base for a full service prior to flying the final leg home. It was found that the airframe-mounted gearbox was out of alignment and was vibrating so badly that it caused fuel lines to break. From Hickam, it took Frank Murray three more attempts before he was able to bring the reluctant *Cygnus-Bird* back to the

Above The M-12/D-21 pylon contained a cylinder of compressed air for blasting the drone away from the M-12 (*Lockheed ADP*)

Below 'Black paint' was used on the M-12/D-21 'combo' to help disguise composite radar absorbing material wedges (*Lockheed ADP*)

'Ranch'. Meanwhile, Denny Sullivan had flown the last remaining *Oxcart* aircraft back from Kadena to Nevada on 9 June in just five hours and twenty-nine minutes.

After it was all over, Maj Bill Wuest, the poetic weather officer at Groom Dry Lake, penned the following rhyming couplets in honour of those two record-breaking return trips

Congratulations from the Bard of Beatty – 19 June 1968

When Denny rushed across the Pond in 'Five-plus-Twenty-Nine',
All hopes had sunk for Ken and Frank to break that record time.
But nothing daunted, that slow pair conspired to save the day,
With greatest skill and cunning broke a record anyway.
Eleven days it took them both to make that ocean trip.
The Slowest 'Record', high-speed flight was now within their grip!
That Record time they'll surely keep until the Final Day.
For Beale's crews will never want to take their TIME away!

The final flight of an A-12 took place on 21 June 1968 when the last remaining *Cygnus*, number 131, was ferried from 'the Ranch' to Palmdale by Frank Murray (see map). On reaching the Lockheed plant, company maintenance technicians drained all fuel and hydraulic lines, and Mel Rushing skillfully 'interwove' all nine remaining *Oxcart* aircraft into a tightly-regimented, sardine-like parking array in a corner of one of the large hangars, where they remained for more than 20 years (awaiting recall or dispersal to museums).

On 26 June 1968, Deputy Director of the CIA, Vice-Adm Rufus Taylor, presided over a ceremony at the 'Area' where he presented the CIA *Intelligence Star for Valour* to Ken Collins, Jack Layton, Frank Murray, Denny Sullivan and Mele Vojvodich for their participation in *Black Shield*. The posthumous award to Jack Weeks was accepted by his widow. The *Legion of Merit* was presented to Col Slip Slater and to his deputy, Col Amundson. In addition, the *Air Force Outstanding Unit Award* was presented to members of the *Oxcart* Detachment, the 1129th Special Activities Squadron, also known as '*The Road Runners*'.

Tagboard

In 1963, Bob Murphy received a telephone call from his boss Ralph Poue, who informed him that he intended to promote 'Murph' to superintendent. Lockheed were carrying out modifications to Air Force U-2s which would enable them to utilise the more powerful J75 engine, and 'Murph' was to head-up the programme. Delighted by the news, he received yet another phone call from Kelly's secretary just minutes later requesting his presence. Kelly said, 'Murph I'm going to promote you to superintendent,' to which Bob replied, 'Yes, I know.' 'How do you know? I've only just told you.' – it was his second promotion that day!

What Kelly had in mind was something radically different from 'Murph's' earlier promotion. The ADP boss showed his newest superintendent some sketches of an altogether strange-looking beast, designated the D-21. Mindful of the Gary Powers 'aftershocks' and the inevitable political sensitivities concerning manned overflight of large expanses of 'denied territory', the 'Skunk works', under Kelly's direction, had designed a tri-sonic, air-launched, reconnaissance vehicle. Johnson instructed 'Murph' to 'find a building for housing the necessary engineering and build them.'

Programme manager for *Tagboard* (the code-name for this project) was Rus Daniel – when Rus became involved in the development of the RS-71, the D-21 was taken on by Art Bradley. Construction got underway in building 199 at Burbank and by June 1963 a D-21 had been mated to its mothership. The launch platform was to be the A-12. Two aircraft were retro-fitted to perform the task, serial numbers 60-6940 and 60-6941.

Built primarily from titanium, the D-21 had a range of 1250 nautical miles, cruised at Mach 3.3 and possessed an altitude capacity of 90,000 ft. It was powered by a Marquardt RJ-43-MA-11 ramjet, and once released from the modified A-12 by a Launch Control Officer (LCO) sitting in what was the aircraft's Q bay, the drone flew its sortie independently. The D-21 INS had programmed into it the desired track, flight profile, camera on and off points and bank angles, allowing it to satisfactorily execute the perfect photo-recce sortie. Having completed its camera run, the drones INS sent signals to the auto-pilot system to descend the vehicle to its 'feet wet' film collection point. The entire palletised camera unit was then ejected and

Above An F-104 Starfighter chase aircraft provides size comparison with the D-21 (*Lockheed ADP*)

Below Refuelling positioned the combination near its launch point (*Lockheed ADP*)

allowed to parachute towards the ground. As the drone continued its descent, it would be blown apart by a barametrically activated explosive charge. The camera unit containing its valuable film would be retrieved by a C-130 Hercules equipped with a Mid-Air Recovery System (MARS) and flown to a base for processing and analysis.

The maiden flight of this so-called 'Mother-Daughter' combination, took place at Groom Dry Lake on 22 December 1964. Take-off time slipped because of delays brought about by the late arrival of senior Lockheed executives, who had already attended the maiden flight of the SR-71 down at Palmdale earlier that day.

Lockheed test pilot Bill Park piloted all the M-12 / D-21 mated sorties. The monumental problems concerning platform and systems integration that *Tagboard* had to overcome cannot be overstated. By 1966 the programme had progressed to the point where vehicle separation was to be performed. The mission profile for this crucial stage called for Bill to fly the aircraft at Mach 3.2 and commence a slight pull up at 72,000 ft, then push over to maintain a steady 0.9 of a 'g' on the highly sensitive 'g' meter fitted in the M-12. With controllability checks on the D-21 completed, and its ram-jet 'burning', Keith Beswick in the LCO position initiated vehicle separation by throwing the switch that fired off a blast of compressed air from a cylinder fitted in the M-12's pylon.

This pioneering work achieved its first successful separation after five or six attempts on 3 July 1966. Keith Beswick had been the LCO on all previous launch attempts, and now Ray Torrick (the other ADP engineer on the flight test programme) would assist him, by alternating LCO duties.

The third launch was to take place on 31 July 1966. Bill and Ray left Groom Dry Lake in aircraft 941 and headed for the launch area, some 300 miles west of the naval air station of Point Magu in California. Accompanying them in chase M-12 940, was Art Peterson and Keith Beswick. The test card called for the M-12 to launch the D-21 at precisely 1g and at a slightly faster speed. This revised launch profile would hopefully be easier for the operational pilots to follow. In addition, the D-21 was also carrying a full fuel load for the first time.

Everything was progressing well, and a systems check of the drone revealed that its fixed inlet was feeding the Marquardt with the correct volume of air. At Mach 3.2+ and exactly 1g Ray effected drone separation, after which everything went horribly wrong. A combination of factors caused an unstart on the D-21, which slammed down onto the aft launch pylon of 941. The impact caused a violent pitch-up that was well beyond correction by the pilot through the manipulation of the aircraft's flight controls. The large underside chine area of the M-12 was subjected to the immense pressure of a Mach 3.2 airstream, which quickly ripped the fuselage forebody from the wing planform, trapping its two-man crew through the incredible g forces inside the shattered cockpit. With their life support pressure suits inflated, the crew were subjected to high levels of positive and negative g as the forebody tumbled through the sky. Although these forces loosened the seat harnesses, the pilot and LCO remained firmly stuck in their cockpits. Bill determined that despite their altitude and speed, their chances of survival were better outside. Both he and Ray ejected and made a 'feet wet' landing in the ocean. Soon after, Bill was picked up by a helicopter. Although both men incredibly survived the collision, Ray Torrick had tragically drowned before he could be brought aboard a US Navy vessel.

Kelly Johnson was desperately upset by the loss of one of his team, and cancelled the M-12/D-21 programme despite pleas from many of his engineers that the concept could be made to work.

Instead, the D-21s were modified to incorporate a less sensitive inlet and were launched from two B-52s of the 4200th Test Wing at Beale. This new operation, code-named *Senior Bowl*, produced its own array of problems. Launched from a slower, lower platform, the D-21 was accelerated to its operational Mach speed and altitude by a rocket booster fitted to the underside of the drone, which separated from the vehicle at cruising speed. The thermodynamic stresses on the D-21 were severe.

Fewer than five B-52/D-21 operational sorties took place. The 'collection areas' for these highly classified missions were targets in China. To maintain tight security, the B-52, hauling its unique payload, departed Beale at night and lumbered westwards to the Pacific island of Guam. Just before dawn the next day the flight resumed, the bomber departing Guam and heading for the launch point. Upon vehicle separation, the 'BUFF' made its way back to Guam, while the drone climbed and accelerated on course to China, ready to begin a day-time reconnaissance run.

Above Pictured on the wing pylons of a B-52H, the D-21 deployed operationally on reconnaissance sorties over China (*Lockheed ADP*)

Below A D-21 sits perched on its handling dolly at Davis-Monthan AFB in December 1979 (*Ben Knowles via Chris Pocock*)

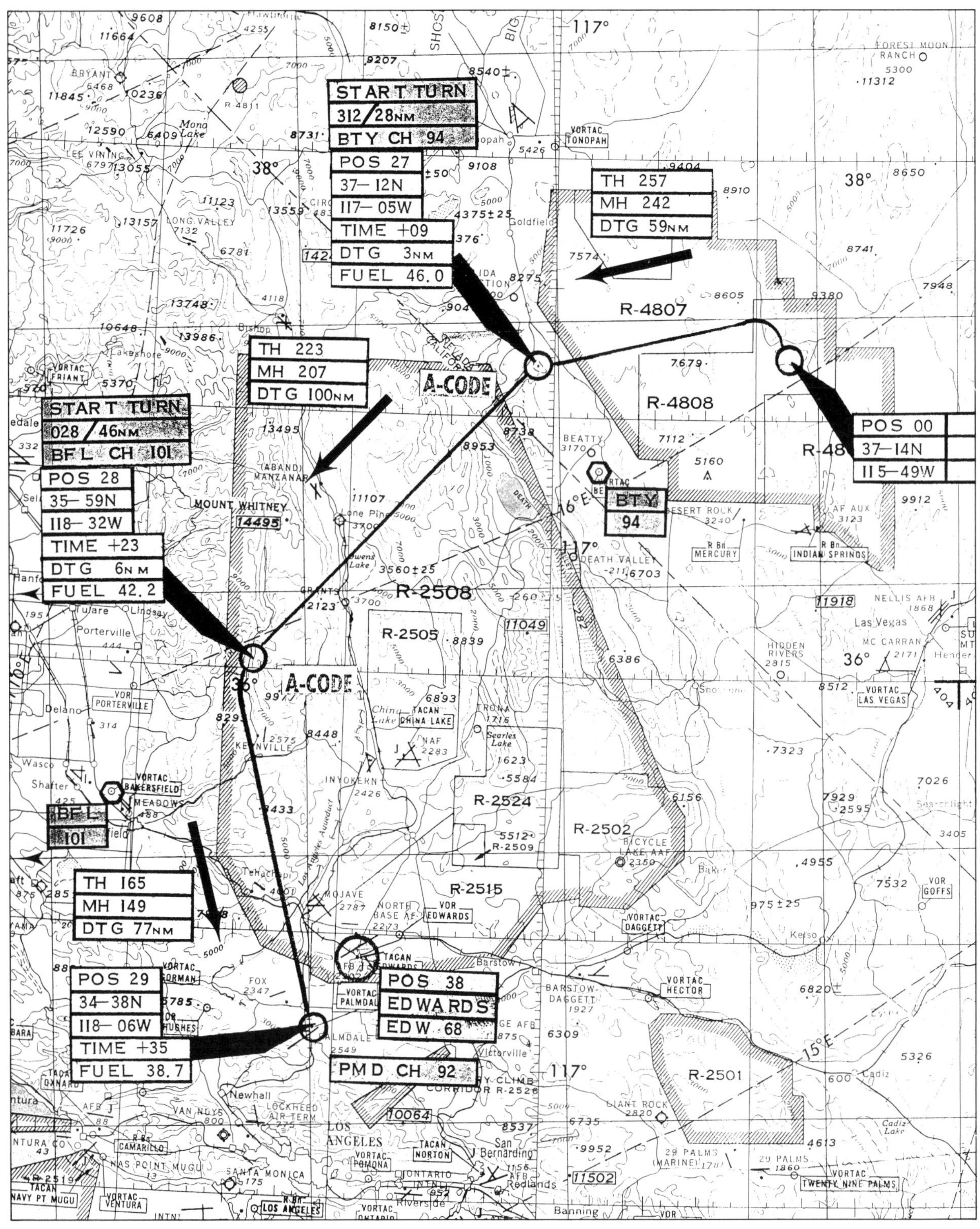

This pilot's card map was used by Frank Murray on the final A-12 flight (made in Article 131) to Palmdale's storage facility from 'The Ranch', which was performed on 21 June 1968

During the course of one such mission intelligence sources have stated that Chinese radar controllers tracked a D-21 over their territory, incorrectly identifying it as 'The Big One', their adopted term for the SR-71. During the course of this overflight however, the drone developed a malfunction and crashed in a remote mountainous region. The incident resulted in Peking protesting to Washington that SR-71s were violating their sovereign airspace, and this crash has been the basis of rumours that have persisted ever since. Indeed, President Richard Nixon perpetuated such rumours when, during the course of his state visit to China in February 1972, he promised that 'all SR-71' overflights of China would be halted.' During the closing stages of another China overflight by a D-21, problems arose during the recovery of the vital reconnaissance camera pallet ejected from the drone. Descending by parachute, the MARS-equipped recovery vehicle failed to capture the unit. In the subsequent water recovery attempt, a US Navy destroyer from the alternate recovery force snagged the floating parachute and keel-hauled the reconnaissance package.

Senior Bowl was prematurely cancelled due to operational difficulties, political considerations and the high cost of these limited-duration flights.

The unofficial emblem of the 1129th Special Activities Squadron was, rather appropriately, a 'hotted up' Cygnus

CHAPTER 3

Cabbage Slicers and Tailfeathers

The ambitious nature of *Project Gusto* cannot be overstated. At the time when E M Land of the Polaroid Corporation presided over the six historic meetings between 1957 and 1959 that led to the A-12, the best frontline fighter aircraft of the day were the early century-series jets like the F-100 Super Sabre and the F-101 Voodoo.

In a single bound, it was proposed that *Project Gusto*'s aircraft would operate routinely at double the altitudes and treble the operating speeds of contemporary fighters. Such an aircraft would be flying at heights where the ambient air temperature was minus 56 degrees Centigrade, and in atmospheric pressures that would be near a vacuum (0.4 of a pound per square inch at 80,000 ft). Additionally, the *Project Gusto* aircraft would be operating at a cruise speed of a mile every two seconds, which could generate external cockpit temperatures that would exceed 245 degrees Centigrade (well above the highest temperature setting of a standard household oven). Therefore, *Project Gusto*'s designers had to master not only the many daunting problems associated with sustained high-altitude and high-Mach flight, but they also had to employ the latest techniques and materials to reduce the A-12's RCS to produce what might now be regarded as the first operational 'stealth' aircraft.

General Layout

The A-12 and the SR-71 designs were characterised by an aft-body delta-wing with two large engine nacelles, each mounted at mid-semi-span. The two 'all-moving' vertical fins were fitted on top of each engine nacelle and canted inward 15 degrees from the vertical to reduce the aircraft's radar signature and to aid in controlling excess offset yaw-thrust during single engine flight. A large aft-moving inlet spike or centre-body protruded forward from each engine nacelle, which helped to regulate mass airflow to the two powerful Pratt & Whitney J58 engines at speeds above Mach 1.4. A variety of specialised sensors were housed in mission equipment bays located in the underside of the 'chine' (a boat-like hull-form) which extended along both sides of the long fuselage forebody. The two full-pressure-suited crew members sat in tandem behind a removable nose section which also carried various high-tech sensors.

Materials and Manufacture

To compensate for the extreme build-up of frictional heating in the A-12/SR-71 airframe at high Mach flight, the overall aircraft structure consisted of 93 per cent titanium (B-120 VCA: Ti-13V-11Cr-3Al) and the remaining seven per cent Teflon-like high-temperature-composite Radar Absorbing Materials (RAM). These composites framed the outer edges of the aircraft to significantly reduce radar-return signatures. The SR-71's titanium 'vertical' fins were later replaced by heavier composite units to further reduce RCS. The upper and lower wing surfaces were semi-corrugated with long longitudinal bulges that permitted the structure to accommodate differential rates of heating and cooling. To prevent the thin titanium outer skin from tearing when secured to heavier sub-structures, stand-off clips were used to insure structural continuity while creating a heat shield between adjacent components.

Kirchoff's law of thermal radiation states that a good absorber is a good emitter, and a good absorber (and emitter) is a black body. Since convective heating decreases with increasing altitudes (while radiation is independent of altitude) the SR-71 was to be painted black to give it a higher thermal emissivity when cruising at high Mach. For the A-12, it was calculated that the 60 lb coat of

The unmistakable planform of the SR-71 is characterised by its aft-body delta wing, two large nacelles and forward fuselage chine (*MoD*)

paint increased its emissivity value to 0.93 from 0.38 for bare titanium, thereby reducing internal temperatures as much as 30 degrees Centigrade. Further, the black paint contained tiny iron balls which dissipated electromagnetic radiation, making the aeroplane even more difficult to locate with radar. Although the aircraft was to be 'all-black', the Air Force had to comply with the rules of the 1907 Hague Convention which stipulated that military aircraft must bear conspicuously placed national insignia (which would necessitate using non-heat-resistant paint). Adding a touch of humour to a serious matter of international diplomacy, Ben Rich, who was chief thermodynamicist at the time, asked 'Who'll be up there to look at them?' Thereafter, an expensive red, white and blue paint was developed that would not tarnish after repeated 'heat-soaks'.

Powerplant

The Pratt & Whitney JT11D-20 engine (designated J58 by US military nomenclature) was chosen as the powerplant for the A-12, F-12 and SR-71 family of high-performance aircraft. This high-bypass ratio, afterburning engine was the result of two earlier programmes: *Project Suntan* and the PW JT9 engine. *Project Suntan* was to be a hydrogen-fuelled engine intended to power Lockheed's CL-400 aircraft, which was proposed to cruise at speeds of 2.7 Mach with a range of 2500 miles. Beating their old General Electric rivals, Pratt & Whitney signed a contract on 1 May 1956 to develop the engine for the CL-400, but three years later it was terminated when it was decided that the interceptor would be hard-pressed to execute its mission.

Meanwhile, Pratt & Whitney's JT9 single-spool, high pressure ratio engine that was already well developed for the original North American B-70, was considered for high Mach use. Using technological achievements learned from the previous programmes, Pratt & Whitney engineers developed the J58 engine as an 80 per cent scaled-down version of the JT9. Designed for an ill-fated US Navy attack aircraft, the new turbojet engine was rated at 26,000 lbs in afterburner, and was to have a dash capability of Mach 3 for several seconds. After spending what was thought to be too much money developing the aircraft and engine, the Navy axed the programme; nevertheless, its J58 engine had already completed 700 hours of full-scale engine testing and was indeed proving itself worthy of

The Bertia Company developed the high-temperature hydraulic actuators to power the all-moving fins (*P Crickmore collection*)

Five degrees of conical camber is applied to the outboard wing leading edge which reduces bending movement and applies most of its aerodynamic load to the rear of the nacelle. The nacelle then redistributes these loads to the forward and aft wing box sections (*P Crickmore collection*)

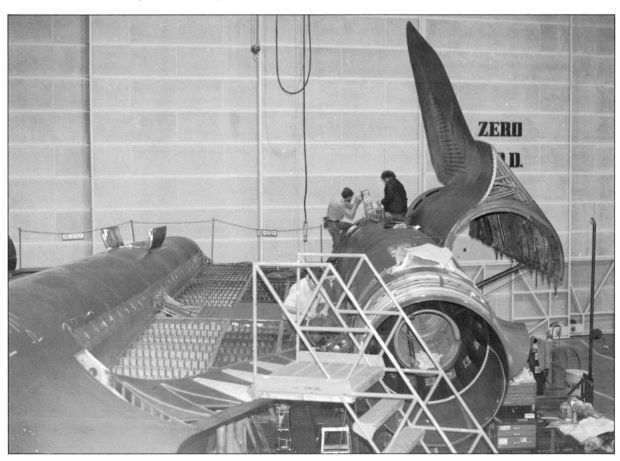

The inlet spike has been removed from this SR-71, which was undergoing depot maintenance at Palmdale. Also visible are Radar Absorbing Material (RAM) wedges from the inboard wing leading edge. The thin titanium skin has been removed revealing tanks 3, 6A and 6B (*Lockheed ADP*)

some other advanced aircraft project[1]. As with Lockheed, Pratt & Whitney would soon be taking a leap into the technical unknown with their engine.

The following table compares design requirements of the J58 with those of the J57 which powered the F-100 Super Sabre and the F-101 Voodoo, and the J75 which powered the F-105 Thunderchief and the F-106 Delta Dart (four of the best frontline fighters of the late-1950s):

	J57 and J75	*J58*
Mach Number	2.0 Mach for 15 minutes	3.2 Mach (continuous)
Corrected Airflow Turndown Ratio (cruise/maximum)	90 per cent	60 per cent
Altitude	55,000 ft	100,000 ft
Compressor Inlet Temperature	−40° to +250°F (J75 only)	−40° to +800°F
Combustor Exit Temperature	1750°F (take-off) 1550° F	2000°F (continuous)
Maximum Fuel Inlet Temperature	110° to 130°F	350°F
Maximum Lubricant Inlet Temperature	250°F	550°F
Thrust to Weight Ratio	4 to 1	5.2 to 1
Military Power Operation Limits Afterburner	30 minutes	continuous
Operation Limits	intermittent	continuous

As these factors were applied to the design criteria for Lockheed's Advanced Development Project (ADP) masterpiece, which followed *Gusto*, it was soon realized that the original J58 design would also be inadequate for the high temperatures to be encountered at Mach 3. Due to the incredibly hostile thermal conditions of sustained high Mach flight, only the basic airflow size (400 lbs per second of airflow) and the compressor and turbine aerodynamics of the original Navy J58 P2 engine could be retained (even these were modified at a later date). The stretched design criteria (particularly the increased Mach number and associated large airflow turn-down ratio) led to a variable cycle engine, later to be known as the bleed bypass engine – a concept conceived by Pratt & Whitney's Robert Abernathy.

At the high-Mach cruising speeds associated with high compressor inlet temperatures, a conventional turbojet suffers five major problems:

– a single-spool, fixed-geometry compressor runs out of surge margin.

– the combination of high inlet temperature and limited temperature gives lower cycle efficiency which reduces thrust and increases fuel consumption.

– compressor efficiency deteriorates because the front stages of the compressor are stalled which also reduces thrust and increases fuel consumption.

– compressor blades are subjected to high stresses from a combination of high rotational speeds causing the front stages to experience stall-flutter.

– the combination of high turbine temperatures and high ambient temperatures surrounding the engine results in cooling problems for the afterburner duct.

The J58's bleed-bypass system eliminated most of these problems by bleeding air from the fourth stage of the nine-stage, single-spool axial-flow compressor. This excess air passed throught six low-compression-ratio bypass ducts, which sharply reduced airflow pressures across the rear stages of the compressor assembly. This reduction of pressure prevented the rear stages from choking with high-velocity airflow, and the front stages from stalling due to low-mass airflow. The diverted air was then introduced to the turbine exhaust near the front of the afterburner at the same static pressure as the main flow, thereby reducing exhaust gas temperature and producing almost as much thrust per pound of air as the main flow which passed through the rear compressor, the burner section and the turbine. Scheduling of the bypass bleed was achieved by the main fuel control as a function of compressor inlet temperature and engine rpm. Bleed air injection occured at a compressor inlet temperature of between 85 and 115 degrees Centigrade (about Mach 1.9).

To further minimise stalling the front stage of the rotor blades at low engine speeds or 'off-design' speeds, the engine incorporated moveable inlet guide vanes (IGVs) to help guide airflow to the compressor. The angle of the trailing edges of the

Above Pratt & Whitney's J11D-20 engines (designated J58 by the Air Force) undergo maintenance at Palmdale. When the *Senior Crown* programme was cancelled by Gen Larry Welch on 22 November 1989, enough engines and spares had been built-up to keep the entire fleet running well into the next century (*Lockheed ADP*)

Below The chemical ignition system dispenses a shot of tri-ethyl borane (TEB) into the engines' combustion cans. The TEB ignites spontaneously, briefly giving out an emerald-green flash (*P Crickmore collection*)

guide vanes changed position from axial to cambered in response to the main fuel control which regulated most engine functions. The 'axial' position was used to provide more thrust during take-off and acceleration to intermediate supersonic speeds. A change to the 'cambered' position occured at compressor inlet temperatures between 85 and 115 degrees Centigrade (about Mach 1.9) and was mandatory above 150 degrees Centigrade (about Mach 2.0). At top speeds the maximum allowable compressor face temperature was 427 degrees Centigrade. Thereafter, the diffuser stage of the engine straightened the flow of air from the compressor section. This major structural unit supported the number two main bearing and accepted all the thrust and radial loads from the turbine shaft and also supplied high pressure air for other aircraft functions. The engine's eight cylindrical combustion cans were arranged in an annular configuration.

When operating at cruising speeds, the turbine inlet temperature rose to 1100 degrees Centigrade. To find materials that could withstand such awesome temperatures presented Pratt & Whitney's design team with one of its greatest challenges. Joseph Moore, a materials engineer at the Florida Research and Development Center, perfected 'Astralloy Discs' for the J58's first and second stage turbines.

Since the aircraft cruised in afterburner, fuel efficiency became an early issue of importance. As fluctuations in exhaust gas temperature caused notable thrust variations, engine exit temperatures had to be as uniform as possible for optimum efficiency. Newly-designed variable-area spraybars were able to give good fuel atomisation over a large area, resulting in a favourable turndown ratio by maintaining a high fuel spray velocity. Flameholders located downstream of the spraybars created turbulance that enabled combustion to occur before the fuel-air mixture left the exhaust nozzle. The blunt aft-end of the centrebody fairing also acted as a flameholder, which ensured that the afterburner did not vaporize and auto-ignite ahead of the flameholders. Engine efficiency is a function of temperature. It is widely recognised by propulsion engineers that every engine parameter is a function of inlet temperature. Consequently, the loss of a temperature sensor often results in the loss of engine control. Therefore, the J58 engine was equipped with dual temperature sensors, with 'select-high-pressure logic' offering a fail-safe operational capability.

Temperature-related problems in early J58s led to the development of a high-temperature combustion fuel, originally known as PF-1. It was discovered during the early A-12 flight test programme that the shock-diamonds produced by the afterburners were responsible for creating a large radar return. To enhance the A-12's 'stealth' characteristics, an expensive chemical known as A-50 (which contained cesium) was added to the fuel for operational flights. This additive had the desired effect and reduced the frequency response of the afterburner plume. Later known as JP7 (developed by Pratt & Whitney, Ashland Shell and Monsanto), the new fuel also contained fluorocarbons which increased lubricity, and Toluene and Mentyl Isobutylketone. These elements also helped to remove the risk of a flash fire through high skin temperatures being conducted into 'wet' fuel tanks. The fire risk had been further increased by the fact that the fuel was first used as a hydraulic fluid at 600 degrees Fahrenheit to control the afterburner's exit nozzle movements.

The engine main fuel controls were each mechanically linked to the pilot's throttle levers. Chandler Evans built the J58's unique steel-housed main fuel pump – so protected to operate in the very high temperature environment of the A-12's engines. In addition, the afterburner's fuel pump was driven by a gas turbine powered by compressor discharge air. Such a configuration avoided fuel overheating during descent from high-cruise when the afterburner was shut down. This same turbine pump was also used to drive the aircraft's environmental control system which cooled the cockpit and mission equipment bays.

Main and reduction gearboxes were mounted beneath the diffuser section of each engine and are mechanically linked to the engine's compressor section. The main gearbox was connected to an external driveshaft for starting the engine. The reduction gearbox provided mechanical power to the airframe-mounted Accessory Drive System (ADS), which included a constant-speed drive linked to a 60 KVA electrical generator, two hydraulic pumps and a fuel circulating pump.

The difficulty in producing the energy requirement to ignite JP7 (especially at the low pressures at high altitudes) required the use of a chemical ignition system (CIS) instead of a standard electrical system. Chemical ignition was achieved through the use of a highly volatile pyrophoric fluid known as tri-ethyl borane (TEB), which is extremely flash-sensitive when oxidised. A TEB injection system was developed to start-up or restart the main engines and afterburners on the ground or throughout the entire flight envelope. To ensure the system remained inert when not in use, gaseous nitrogen was used to pressurise the TEB tank and to power a piston that delivers a 'teaspoonful' of the chemical to the main engine burner or to the afterburner, regardless of engine operating conditions.

For ground starts of the J58, a turbine-driven or engine-driven system was used to propel a driveshaft connected to the engine's main gearbox. Below MIL power, engine speed varied with throttle position. At high throttle settings the main fuel control regulated engine speed as a function of compressor inlet temperature by modulating the variable-area exhaust nozzle to maintain a constant rpm. Should exhaust gas temperature reach 860 degrees Centigrade, a fuel de-rich system automatically reduced the fuel/air mixture ratio to prevent over-temperature damage to the engine.

Hydraulics

Four pressurised hydraulic reservoirs (each with its own engine-driven pump) supplied power to four independent hydraulic systems (designated A, B, L, and R). The A and L systems were driven by the left engine's accessory drive system (ADS), while the B and R devices relied on the right engine's ADS. Hydraulic fluid was cooled in oil/fuel heat exchangers that used the aircraft's JP7 fuel as a cooling agent. The A and B hydraulic systems operated in parallel to effect movement of the flight control surfaces. Each system provided the hydraulic power to half of the actuating cylinders at each servo assembly that moved the elevon and rudder flight control surfaces. The A system also provided hydraulic power to the stick pusher, which was part of the aircraft's stall prevention equipment as it was linked to the Automatic Pitch Warning System, which in turn was integrated within the Digital Automatic Flight and Inlet Control System (DAFICS).

Hydraulic system L powered the left engine's air inlet and air bypass controls, the normal brake system, landing gear extension and retraction, the normal nose wheel steering and the air refuelling equipment. Hydraulic system R motivated the right engine's air inlet and air bypass controls, the alternate brake and nose wheel steering systems and also provided back-up power to retract the gear if the L system failed prior to (or during) gear retraction. Hydraulic-actuated brakes were operated by toe-controlled flexion of the upper part of the pilot's rudder pedals. Finally, a large pilot-actuated landing drag chute was provided to assist in stopping the aircraft in approximately 4000 ft (compared to a 9000 ft 'brakes-only' roll-out).

The tricycle landing gear was electrically controlled and hydraulically actuated. The unique three-wheeled main gear retracted inboard into a wheel bay approximately one metre wide, which separated the forward and aft inboard wing sections. During retraction or extension, the normal transition time of the gear was approximately 14 seconds. The wheels were mounted on hollow axles which allowed any wheel to be changed without removing the other two. The two-wheeled nose gear retracted forward into a bay just aft of the cockpit, and was locked in the up position by an uplock which engaged the strut. A cable-controlled emergency gear release system permitted free fall of the undercarriage in the event of a hydraulic or electrical failure.

Fuel System

There were six fuel tanks on the SR-71 which occupied space within the fuselage and wings, outward to the engine nacelles. Tank 3 extended into the forward inboard section of the wing, while tanks 6A and B were located in the aft inboard wing section. The full internal fuel capacity of the SR-71 was 12,219 US gallons (80,280 lbs) compared to 9785 gallons (64,578 lbs) in the F-12. The fuel system not only provided JP7 to both engines, but also served as a 'heat sink' to cool the environmental control system; hydraulic systems oil; engine oil; the accessory drive system oil; the TEB tank; and the control lines that actuated the afterburner nozzle. The fuel system also helped to maintain the aircraft's centre of gravity by transferring fuel fore and aft from one tank to another.

Sixteen single-stage, centrifugal, fuel-cooled, AC-powered, electrical fuel boost pumps supplied JP7 to the engines and heat exchangers through left and right manifolds. Fuel movement (to maintain the proper centre-of-gravity limits) was normally

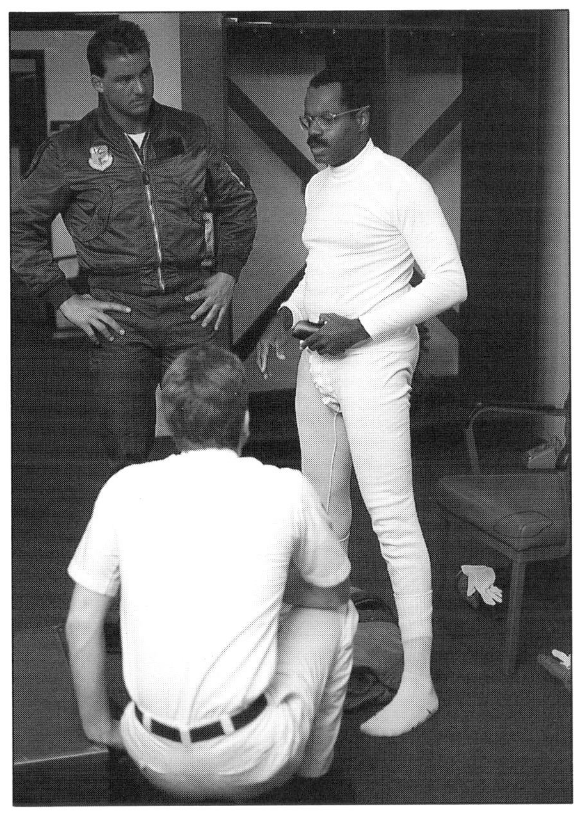

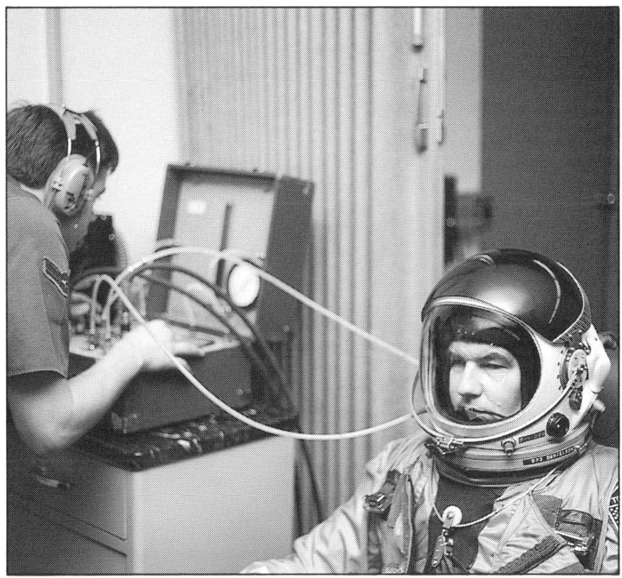

Above Maj Tom Danielson undertakes a helmet check to ensure no air leaks prior to an operational sortie from RAF Mildenhall (*P Crickmore collection*)

Left Maj Walt Watson wearing 'long-John' underwear prior to suit-up (*P Crickmore collection*)

effected by an automatic aft transfer system for supersonic flight. Forward fuel transfer was pilot-managed by a manual 'on-off' switch which allowed direct transfer of the right fuel manifold to tank 1 to move the aircraft's centre-of-gravity forward when returning to subsonic flight.

Nitrogen System

Liquid nitrogen was carried in two 105-litre and one 50-litre Dewar flasks to pressurise all fuel tanks. This positive 'head' of gaseous nitrogen pressure prevented ambient air loads from crushing emptying fuel tanks as the aircraft descended into the denser atmosphere from the near vacuum of high cruise altitudes. In addition, the gaseous nitrogen 'inerted' the space in the tank above the heated fuel to prevent fuel fuming and autogenous-ignition.

Environmental System

The Environmental Control System (ECS) consisted of three subsystems: an air distribution system; a temperature control system; and a pressurisation system. The two identical left and right air cycle systems each provided heating and cooling air for the cockpits and other aircraft systems. The hot air system provided air to various engine inlet components, while slightly cooler air was used for canopy seal pressurisation and de-fogging or de-icing of the pilot's windshield. Air from the cooling turbine was distributed via insulated ducts to the cockpits and equipment bays in the chine. By metering hot and cold air from the appropriate manifolds, the temperature control system circulated air at properly controlled temperatures to four subsystems: the hot air bypass system; the cockpit temperature system; the manifold temperature system; and the pressure suit ventilating air temperature system. The hot air bypass system functioned automatically, while the others were pilot-controlled. The cockpit pressurisation system automatically varied air pressure in both cockpits according to manually selected schedules, the optimum level being maintained through a pressure regulator which monitored both cockpit and exhaust air. A switch in each cockpit allowed a selection of either '10,000 ft' or '26,000 ft' pressure schedules. Canopy seal pressurisation was maintained at 20 lbs per square inch above cockpit pressure.

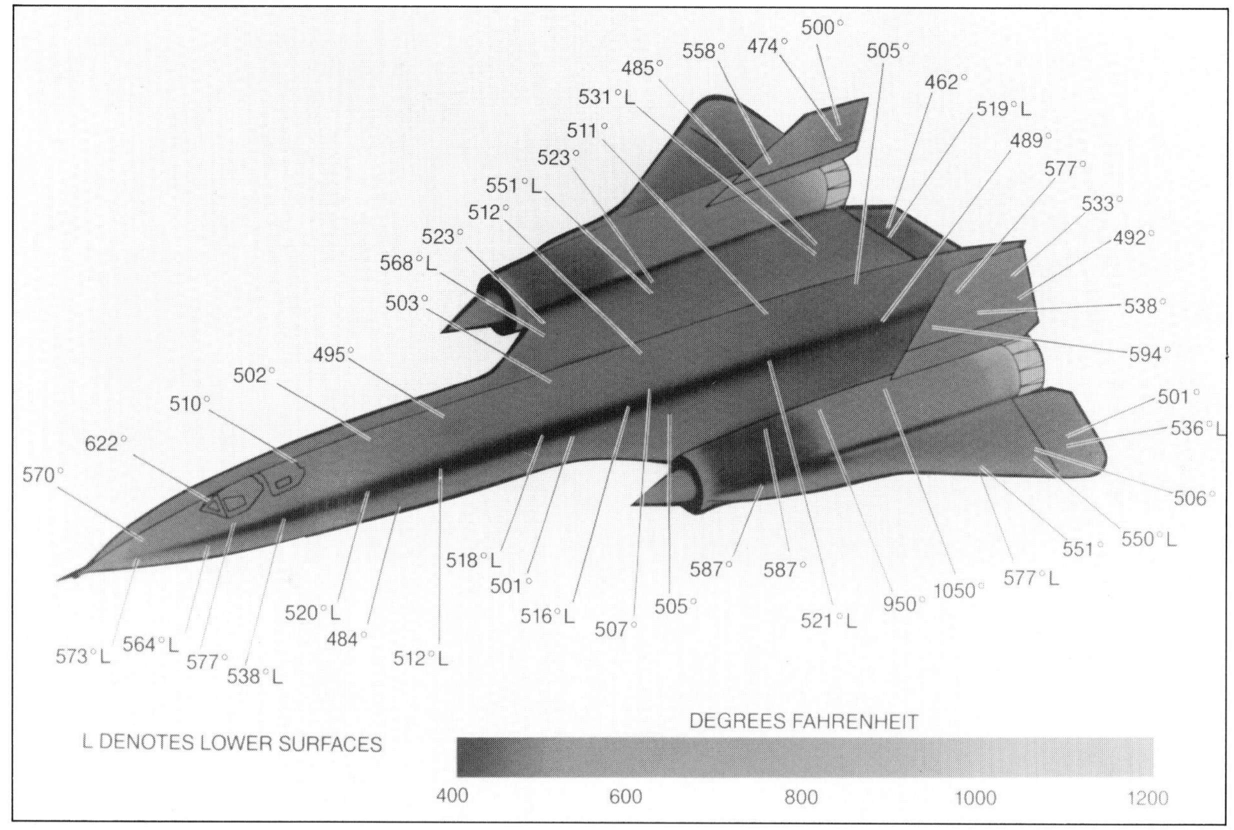

Incredible airframe temperatures are produced while cruising at one mile every two seconds at 82,000 ft. Such temperatures arise despite outside air temperatures and pressures of -56°C and 0.4 pounds per square inch respectively (*Lockheed*)

The Oxygen System

The SR-71 was equipped with two ten-litre liquid oxygen converters and one ten-litre standby converter to easily provide for aircrew oxygen consumption rates of approximately one litre per hour at a cockpit pressure altitude of 26,000 ft. Each converter produced gaseous oxygen at 65 to 100 lbs per square inch through a regulated evaporative process. An additional emergency oxygen supply (contained in each crew member's ejection seat survival kit) could be activated without seat ejection for emergency use should the primary and backup systems fail.

The Pressure Suit

The David Clark Company of Worcester, Massachusetts, were pioneers in the manufacture of life supporting 'full pressure' suits. Suit improvements evolved over a number of years, notably increasing suit durability and air crew comfort. An early version of the David Clark 'space suit', known later as the 'silver suit' (designated as the S-901), was worn by A-12 pilots. This suit was modified into the S-901J for the early SR-71 crew members. A few of the J-models were also produced in odd outer garment colours of olive-drab and chocolate-brown, but it eventually gave way to the S-970 'White-Suit', which was in turn replaced by the S-1030 'Gold-Suit'. The final variation worn by SR-71 personnel was the S-1031A 'Gold-Suit', which was nearly identical to the garb worn by U-2R and Space Shuttle crew members.

At high altitude many physiological problems might arise which, if left unchecked, could kill the crew in minutes or even seconds. Other problems might also arise in the near-vacuum flight-environment above 60,000 ft which could interfere with the crew's vision and spatial orientation. Hypoxia is one of the most serious physiological risks facing the crew. This condition results from the steady drop in the partial pressure of oxygen on ascent to higher altitudes. Flights at such heights produce some undesirable physiological effects. At 18,000 ft atmospheric pressure drops to half that of sea-level; this figure is halved again at 36,000 ft. The effect on the crew's performance is noticable above 20,000 ft unless they have been altitude adapted by living at very high elevations. At 25,000 ft, for example, there are progressive cardio-respiratory and neurological effects brought about by the sharp fall in partial pressure which assists the lungs in their function of absorbing oxygen into the blood stream. With more than 60 per cent loss of oxygen density and pressure at that height, individuals often suffer such uncontrollable symptons as euphoria, personality changes, loss of judgment and impaired memory. Unconsciousness normally follows, with death resulting sometime later by oxygen starvation. Above 45,000 ft the symptoms compress and overtake a crew member's consciousness in as little as 15 seconds, with death following less than four minutes later.

Decompression sickness usually develops above 25,000 ft, with its varied symptoms increasing rapidly at higher altitudes. Also known as 'divers sickness', it is caused by nitrogen gas bubbles escaping from body fluids and greatly expanding as the ambient pressure falls (much like the bubbles generated in a carbonated drink when the bottle cap is removed). Joint pain (commonly known as 'the bends'), chest pain, skin itching and other neurological manifestations may develop alone or together. Such combined effects can be fatal, and consequently flights above 50,000 ft mandatorily require the protection of a pressure suit.

The gas-contained cavities of the body (the lungs, the stomach, the middle ear and the sinuses) obey Boyle's law when subjected to pressure changes in the body. Thus, gas will increase in volume as outside pressure is decreased on ascent to altitude – in reverse, expanded gasses will contract on descent into denser air. Most of the problems associated with these changes are self-correcting via the body's orifices. When gas within the small intestine is not free to escape, its expansion can cause abdominal pain which can become disabling under extreme internal pressure.

This effect can be reduced by eflatus, or in advance by eating a controlled, low-residue diet which produces little intestinal gas. Considerable middle-ear pain can also occur during descent if previously-escaped air is unable to re-enter via the throat-to-middle-ear Eustachian tubes, which serve to equalise pressure in the middle-ear and sinus cavities. Crews undergo medical examinations before high altitude flights and are not allowed to fly when they have a throat infection or a cold which might block Eustachian-tube airflow.

Extreme temperatures also have to be dealt with at higher altitudes. Were the aircrew to be sub-

The heavy titanium cockpit canopy is somewhat reminisent of that fitted to the F-102 Delta Dagger (*P Crickmore collection*)

Above **The front cockpit of SR-71B serial 956. No CRTs or Multi Function Displays in this aircraft! (*P Crickmore collection*)**

Left **The instructor pilot's rear cockpit station on 956 (*P Crickmore collection*)**

jected to the ambient air temperature of minus 50 degrees Centigrade or lower, they would risk severe injury from frostbite or hypothermia. Consequently, they were doubly protected in warmed and pressurised cockpits, and in uninflated pressure suits (to provide an emergency atmosphere in the event of cockpit pressuration failure or bail-out). On initial climb-out to intermediate altitudes, the SR-71's cockpit pressurisation was free to decline from sea level to 8000 ft (pressure altitude) before pressurisation began to take effect. Thereafter, pressure would build to slow the loss of cockpit air density, stabilising at 26,000 ft even as the aircraft continued to ascend to very high altitudes. A maximum pressure differential of five pounds per square inch (PSI) between cockpit and ambient atmospheric pressures was then maintained by the aeroplane's pressurisation system

Left **The instructor's position in the new $50-million flight simulator – purchased just prior to the SR-71 programme's cancellation! (*P Crickmore collection*)**

Above **The back seat of the new flight simulator. Within NASA this crew space is known as the Research Systems Operator's position (*P Crickmore collection*)**

throughout its high altitude flight profile. The five PSI difference was chosen to ensure that the hull of the aircraft was not subjected to undue pressure gradients, and to keep aircraft construction weight down. SR-71 crewmembers would therefore need to wear full pressure suits to survive cockpit depressurisation[2].

The S1031A pressure suit is produced in 12 sizes and consists of four layers: an outer Dacron 'coverall' which is durable, tear- and fire-resistant and coloured 'Old Gold'; a 'restraint layer' which holds the suit together when inflated through expansion-limiting nets that serve as a 'pressure boundary'; a polyurethene 'bladder layer' which functions like an inner-tube in a tyre to contain inner pressure; and an inner layer of lightweight Dacron to protect the bladder from scuffing against 'long-john' underwear and the urine collection device (UCD), which was usually worn on long flights.

The suit was constructed to assume a seated position when pressurised; this posture aided cockpit mobility but limited standing manoeuvrability. Entry was accomplished through a rear, crotch to back-of-the-neck zipper which sealed and secured the four layers of the suit while leaving the front of the suit uncluttered for controls and parachute attachments. Special rubber-bladder pressure gloves completed the pressure seal, and were attached via snap-locking wrist ring-hinges. The Dacron-covered, leather-palmed gloves came in 13 sizes and had adjustable palm restraint straps running across the knuckles and the back of the hands to prevent the gloves from ballooning when pressurised. Heavy-duty zipper-closed leather boots were worn over the foot-extensions of the suit bladder, which also prevented ballooning. The boots featured strap-on heel-retraction spurs which were connected by cables to the ejection seat and attached when first entering the cockpit.

The original 'silver suits' cost more than $30,000 each in the mid-1960s, and lasted approximately 12 years. All suits underwent regular close inspection and maintenance, which included a thorough preflight and postflight check before and after each flight (including post-flight drying), a thorough inspection every 90 days or 150 flight hours, and a complete overhaul every five years. The newer 'gold suits' were much more costly, but will still continue to serve the U-2 reconnaissance pilots, as well as Edwards Air Force Based test pilots and student test pilots on flights above 50,000 ft.

Ejection Seats

The SR-71's ejection seat is a modified Lockheed C-2 device first designed in the late-1950s for the F-104. The original rocket-propelled escape system was designated by ADP as the SR-1 seat – later it was called the F-1 Stabilised Ejection Seat. It was a zero-speed/zero height system ('Zero-Zero' seat), which meant it could propel the occupant to a safe deployable parachute altitude from a stationary jet on the tarmac if necessary.

Flight Controls

The SR-71 used four elevons located along the trailing edge of its delta wing; two were located inboard and two outboard of the engine nacelles to provide control in the pitch and roll axes. The outboard units were slaved to the inboard units. Dual, central-pivoted, all-moving rudders provided control in the yaw axis. Elevon movement was limited to 35 degrees up-travel and 20 degrees down on the inboard elevons and 35 degrees down-only on the outboard elevons. Rudder travel was also limited to 20 degrees either side of the neutral position. Movement of the control surfaces was achieved via hydraulically-powered servos. Control inputs from the pilot were mechanically transmitted via control cables and linkages to the elevon and rudder servos. These servo linkages controlled actuators which moved the surfaces. Above Mach 0.5 the movement of both rudders was limited to approximately ten degrees either side of the neutral position. At the same time, differential elevon travel was also limited to about seven degrees by engaging a surface limiter to prevent excessive aerodynamic loads from being applied to the control surfaces.

Digital Automatic Flight and Inlet Control System (DAFICS)

During the mid-1970s mission requirements for the SR-71 increased significantly. Air Force Logistics Command determined that it was both impractical and uneconomical to maintain and repair the aircraft's original analogue automatic flight control and engine inlet control systems. To overcome this problem of obsolescence, a three-computer Digital Automatic Flight and Inlet Control System (DAFICS) was developed to replace both older systems, as well as the analogue air data computer, the autopilot and the automatic pitch warning system. Honeywell Corporation was awarded the replacement contract in mid-1978, whereafter conversions began in August 1980 and ended in November 1985. At the heart of DAFICS were three Honeywell HDP-5301 digital computers mounted in a single rack. The rack formed a 'Faraday Cage' around the computers protecting them against electromagnetic interference. Each computer had a 16 kilobyte memory (expanded to 32 KB in 1987) designated A and B. Both have identical software and provided 'back up redundancy' for stability augmentation in roll, autopilot, inlet control and pitch warning. The third computer, designated M for monitor, contained built-in-test (BIT) software. All three systems had software enabling them to carry out air data computations and stability augmentation in pitch and yaw.

A Pressure Transducer Assembly converted pressures from the pitot boom into digital signals, and transmitted this information to the three computers. In the cockpit, a control panel enabled the pilot to make inputs to the stability augmentation and autopilot functions. An onboard analyser interfaced with the M computer to enable maintenance personnel to recall previously stored faults detected by the built-in-tester to carry out checks, and adjust inlet schedules.

Stability Augmentation

The SR-71's centre of gravity (CG) was automatically moved aft during acceleration to high-Mach flight to reduce trim drag and to improve elevon authority in both the pitch and roll axes. The chine structure that extended along the forebody of the aircraft produced lift forward of the centre of gravity, which destabilised the aircraft in the pitch

Skilled engine technicians remove 976's J58 for maintenance. The hydraulically controlled 'dolly' is custom built for the purpose. In the early days it took about 16 hours to remove and replace an engine. By the end of the programme, technicians had cut that time in half (*P Crickmore collection*)

axis and reduced aft CG travel, resulting in low static margins of stability and safety. The aircraft was also less directionally stable during manoeuvres involving sideslip at cruise angles of attack (approximately six degrees of positive Alpha) because of the aerodynamic characteristics of the chine. Low aerodynamic damping (inherent at high altitudes) coupled with a low static margin of stability caused the SR-71 to be only marginally stable in both pitch and yaw at high Mach.

Controlling the aircraft in this delicate corner of the performance envelope was critical, and it was achieved by the elevons and rudders being worked through an Automatic Flight Control System (AFCS) controlled via the DAFICS computers. The AFCS consisted of three subsystems: a Stability Augmentation System (SAS); an autopilot; and a Mach trim system. The AFCS as a co-ordinating system provided pitch, roll and yaw stabilisation via the flight control surfaces. Eight rate-sensing gyros were employed to detect divergence from stable flight (three yaw-rate gyros, three pitch-rate gyros and two roll-rate gyros). These gyros, along with three lateral accelerometers, provided motion-sensing elements which were applied to the multi-redundant SAS circuits in the DAFICS. These signals were combined with pilot-selected astro-inertial navigation system (ANS), or inertial navigation system (INS) 'pitch, roll and heading' inputs, as base references to eliminate faulty rate-gyro signals in the event of a multi-gyro failure. The pilot turned on the AFCS on the right-console panel where the 'Pitch SAS', 'Roll SAS', and 'Yaw SAS' engagement switches were located. In addition to responding to signals from DAFICS, the servos could also be actuated by direct stick and rudder pedal inputs.

The autopilot featured separate pitch and roll autopilots. In pitch the pilot could select the basic attitude hold mode or Knots Equivalent Airspeed (KEAS) 'hold' or Mach 'hold'. In roll the pilot could select the basic roll attitude hold mode, heading-hold mode or an auto-steering 'AUTO NAV' mode, programmed to obey heading commands from the ANS. When the autopilot was engaged, the aircraft was held in the roll attitude established at the time of engagement. With 'AUTO NAV' selected, the autopilot controls rolled to ensure that the aircraft adhered to the predetermined navigation track which the ANS accurately maintained. During operational sorties the aircraft was almost always flown on autopilot in the 'AUTO NAV' mode to ensure that it remained stable and on an accurate track whilst the onboard sensors were activated.

A Mach trim system provided speed stability for the aircraft while accelerating or decelerating through mid-speed ranges up to 1.5 Mach when the autopilot was off. The trim system compensated via the pitch trim actuator for the aircraft's tendency to 'tuck' nose down while accelerating through the Mach, and rise nose-upward while decelerating.

Air Inlet Control System

The A-12's and SR-71's unique and highly efficient air inlet system was the product of no less than 250,000 wind tunnel tests conducted on a one-third scale model. Thrust was supplied by three distinct contributors: an axismetric mixed-compression, variable-geometry inlet; the Pratt & Whitney J58 engine; and a convergent-divergent blow-in-door ejector nozzle. The AICS regulated massive internal air flow throughout the aircraft's vast flight envelope, controlling and supplying air to the engines at the correct velocity and pressure.

The J58 required a voluminous supply of air, even while operating at ground-idle and during taxying and take-off. To satisfy this air-flow appetite, the centre-body spikes were positioned in the full-forward position allowing air to flow unimpeded to the engine's compressor. In addition, supplementary inflow air was provided through the spike exit-louvres and from six forward bypass exit-louvres.

Early tests revealed that the engine required an even greater supply of ground air when operating at low power settings. To solve this airflow deficiency, additional bypass doors were installed just forward of the compressor face. The size of the variable-area 'inlet ports' could be regulated by an external slotted-band, and could draw air in from two sets of doors. The task of opening or closing the doors was manually controlled by the pilot at first, control was later accomplished automatically by the DAFICS computer. The position of the electrically-operated, hydraulically-actuated spikes were also controlled by DAFICS. Together, the forward bypass doors and the centre-body spikes were used to control the position of the normal shockwave just aft of the inlet throat. To avoid the loss of inlet efficiency caused by an improperly positioned shock wave, the wave was captured and held inside the converging-diverging nozzle slightly behind

Above The Air Inlet Control System (*AICS*) is the key to regulating the correct flow of air to the J58 engine throughout the SR-71's vast flight envelope. Positioned fully forward, the inlet spike's centre-body bleed-slots are visible (*P Crickmore collection*)

Below The increased capture area is apparent at the aft limit of the inlet spike's 26-inch aft translation (*P Crickmore collection*)

The six main B F Goodrich tyres were 32 ply and filled with nitrogen at 415 psi. They cost $2300 each and were good for approximately 15 full-stop landings (*P Crickmore collection*)

A titanium shroud was fitted in each main gear to protect the tyres from heat damage during sustained Mach 3 flight. It also offered limited protection to hydraulic lines should a tyre explode inflight (*P Crickmore collection*)

the narrowest part of the 'throat', allowing the maximum pressure-rise across the normal shock.

Once the aircraft was airborne and the landing gear retracted, the forward bypass doors would close automatically. At Mach 1.4 the doors began to modulate automatically to obtain a programmed pressure ratio between 'dynamic' pressure at the inlet cowl on one side of the 'throat' and 'static' duct pressure on the other side. At 30,000 ft the inlet spike unlocked and started its rearward translation at Mach 1.6, achieving its full aft translation of 26 inches at Mach 3.2 (the inlet's most efficient speed). Spike scheduling was determined as a function of Mach number, with bias for abnormal angle of attack, angle of side slip, or rate of vertical acceleration. The rearward translation of the spike gradually repositioned the oblique shock wave, which extended back from the spike tip, and the normal shock wave, standing at right angles to the air flow, and increased the inlet contraction ratio (the ratio between the inlet area and the 'throat' area). At Mach 3.2, with the spike fully aft, the 'capture-airstream-tube-area' had increased 112 per cent (from 8.7 sq ft to 18.5 sq ft), while the 'throat' restriction had decreased to 46 per cent of its former size (from 7.7 sq ft to 4.16 sq ft).

A peripheral 'shock trap' bleed slot (positioned around the inside surface of the duct , just forward of the 'throat' and set at precisely two boundary layer displacement thicknesses) 'shaved' off seven per cent of the stagnant inlet airflow and stabilised the terminal (normal) shock. It was then rammed across the bypass plenum through 32 shock trap tubes spaced at regular intervals around the circumference of the shock trap. As the compressed air travelled through the secondary passage, it firmly closed the suck-in doors while cooling the exterior of the engine casing before it was exhausted through the ejector nozzle. Boundary layer air was removed from the surface of the centrebody spike at the point of its maximum diameter. This potentially turbulent boundary layer air was then ducted through the spike's hollow supporting struts and dumped overboard through nacelle exit louvres. The bypass system was thus able to match widely varying volumes of air entering the inlet system with an equal volume of air leaving the ejector nozzle throughout the entire speed range of the aircraft from low to high Mach.

The aft bypass doors were opened at mid Mach to minimise the aerodynamic drag which resulted from dumping air overboard through the forward bypass doors. The inlet system created internal pressures which reached 18 lbs per square inch when operating at Mach 3.2 at 80,000 ft, where the ambient air pressure is only 0.4 lbs per square inch.

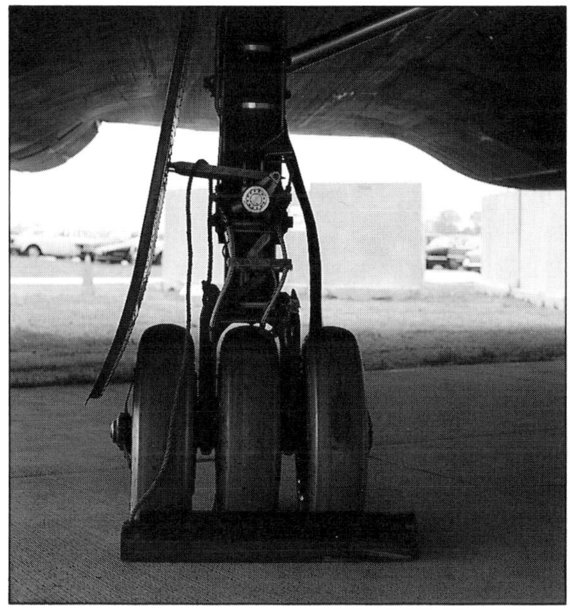

The SR-71's three-wheeled main gear has a hollow axle which enables any wheel to be changed without removing the other two. The side walls of the main tyres were impregnated with aluminium powder to dissipate airframe heat generated at high Mach cruise (*P Crickmore collection*)

The forward retracting nose gear is kept cool by the aircraft's environmental control system (ECS). Access to the two 105-litre liquid nitrogen Dewars is via the front nose gear well (a 50-litre Dewar is also located in left chine B2-bay). The offset main landing light is also clearly visible (*P Crickmore collection*)

This extremely large pressure differential produced a forward thrust vector which resulted in the forward inlet producing 54 per cent of the total thrust. A further 29 per cent was produced by the ejector, while the J58 engine contributed only 17 per cent of the total thrust at high Mach.

Inlet airflow disturbances resulted if the delicate balance of air flow conditions that maintained the shock wave in its normal position were upset. Such disturbances were called 'unstarts'. These disruptions occured when the normally-placed supersonic shock wave was 'belched' forward from a balanced position in the inlet throat, causing an instant drop in inlet pressure and thrust. This shock wave departure manifested itself in a vicious yaw toward the 'unstarted' inlet, sometimes lashing crewmembers about with such force that their helmets were knocked against the canopy framing – this violent shaking occurred even though the crews were firmly strapped in. When an unstart disturbance occurred, an automatic computer-sequenced inlet restart commenced. The spike was driven forward and the forward bypass doors opened to reposition the shockwave. The spike then returned to its proper position, followed by the forward bypass doors, which reconfigured the inlet to optimum performance.

The DAFICS A and B computers provided significantly improved automatic inlet controls over those employed by the analogue control system used during the first decade of SR-71 service. The main benefits of DAFICS was near-perfect inlet airflow control, especially after Lt Col Tom Tilden rescheduled the inlet with an ammended software programme which practically rid the jet of its unstarting problems[3].

The Electrical System

The SR-71 had an AC and a DC electrical power generation and distribution system. The AC equipment consisted of a 115/200 volt, three-phase, 400-Hertz system, supplied by two 60–KVA constant-

Sensor flexibility was enhanced by a changeable nose section (*P Crickmore collection*)

This shot depicts work being carried out on various wiring looms and hydraulic lines. Note sensor bay S in which the OOCs were housed during the early years of operation (*Lockheed*)

speed generators. Emergency back-up power was provided by a one-KVA solid-state inverter. The parallel-operating generators supply current to five AC electrical power buses[4]. A plug-in socket in the nose wheel well allowed an external ground power unit to be hitched up to the AC buses for maintenance and ground preflight activities before engine start. The 28 volt DC system was supplied by two 200-ampere transformer-rectifiers, independently powered from the left and right generator AC buses. These transformer-rectifiers supplied DC power to the AC-monitored DC bus and to the number 1 and number 2 essential DC buses. Excess capacity within the system ensured that all systems could work fully in the event of a single generator failure. If struck by a double generator failure, the electrial system could be operated in an unregulated emergency mode to supply power to the fuel boost pumps, while the hot bus would supply power for fuel transfer, pitch and yaw trim and for forward cockpit instrument lighting.

Instruments

Many aeronautical engineers were initially surprised to find that the Air Force had chosen to use the old-style, round-dial instruments in the cockpit of the SR-71. This was a direct result of Kelly Johnson's policy of using 'tried and tested' instruments and reliable systems in his radically new design – this philosophy also helped to keep development costs down. Finally, a manually-extendable, canopy-mounted, rear-view periscope was furnished to allow the pilot to view a 50 degree-wide aft 'patch of sky' by rotating the sighting optics from side to side. The high-altitude view could include the inlet nacelles, the rudders, contrails, SAM bursts and the afterburner plume, particularly at night. Little else of interest has ever been seen up at the SR-71's operational height.

Periperal Vision Display

The loss of two night-flying SR-71s in 1966 and 1967 led to the development of a laser-aided Peripheral Vision Display unit (PVD) which was later fitted to the remaining aircraft. For use in low-light and night-flight conditions, the PVD projected a laser-generated, thin red line on the pilot's instrument panel. The pitch- and roll-stabilised device aided the pilot in maintaining an horizon sense via a peripheral-vision stimulus. The laser-projected PVD signal enhanced pilot awareness of departures from level flight as they began to occur.

Map Projector

Each cockpit was equipped with a map projector which displayed a 'strip map' of the mission's entire pre-planned route. The aircraft's track over the ground was represented by a line running vertically down the middle of the display, and turnpoints were indicated by a small circle superimposed over the trackline. The film was transported through the 'moving-display' projector at a rate synchronized to match the aircraft's ground speed.

The middle of the screen represented a 'target' position over the earth directly beneath the SR-71 at any given moment.

Viewsight

The RSO's black and white video viewsight provided a visual position-update capability which enabled him to cross-check known gound positions against INS positions (particularly if the astro-inertial input was not available). The view sight had two selectable fields of view (114 degrees and 44 degrees), and was useful in either mode for observing forward activity below, such as SAM shots and cloud cover conditions which could obscure photo-reconnaissance.

The Velocity/Height System

A Velocity/Height System produced information scaled electrically to represent the angular rate of motion between the aircraft and the terrain below. Signal sources for the system were the ANS and the V/H indicator in the RSO's cockpit. System output signals were scaled at 0.2 volts DC per milliradian per second. This system produced reference information for the various reconnaissance sensors on the aircraft. Another device which aided in interpreting sensor material was the sensor event/frame count system. As an example, this system correlated time, position, altitude and heading when the 'close-look' cameras or TEOC's were in operation. The system used the ANS Mission Recorder System and a signal sensor processor to convert event input signals into six-millisecond-wide event-marker-pulses, which were monitored by the ANS. Upon receipt of an even-marker-pulse, the ANS activated a frame-count register associated with the particular sensor. This data (with precise location information) was continuously recorded by the Mission Recorder System.

Aircraft 967 shows off equipment bay Q in which the right palletised TEOC, or Technical Objective Camera, was housed (*P Crickmore collection*)

Reconnaissance System Controls

The RSO had the ability to manually operate and control all reconnaissance system sensors, despite the fact that they were normally fully-preprogrammed for automatic turn-on and turn-off, and for changing 'look angles' to many different points to focus on many hundreds of separate 'targets of interests'. A manual exposure control panel allowed the RSO to remotely control camera exposure settings. This set of controls was adjustable for lighting variants (brightness and reflectivity). The control was graduated in degrees of sun angle with reference indices for low, normal, high and very high terrain reflectivity. Such changes were made by regulating DC voltage between 10 and 38 volts for sun angle settings between five and ninety degrees.

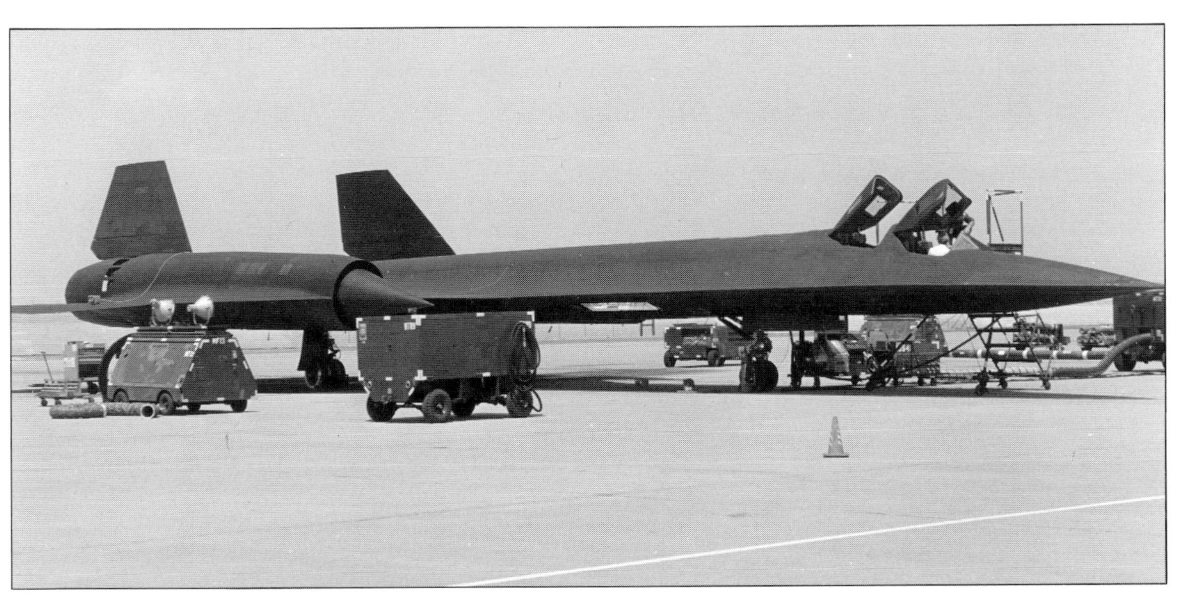

Communication and Navigation Equipment

All communication equipment was located in the R Bay and consisted of a COMNAV-50 UHF radio, an AN/ARA-48 Automatic Direction Finder, an AN/ARC-186(V) VHF radio and both 61BT and AN/ARC-190(V) HF radios, plus an aircrew intercommunication system. Radio navigation aids consisted of a TACAN receiver (with Distance Measuring Equipment which can range-measure distances to other similarly-equipped aircraft), an Instrument Landing System (ILS) and marker beacon equipment. An IFF identification transceiver for air traffic control use or 'friend or foe' identity was located in the D Bay, equipped with either a G or I band transponder, and was controlled by the RSO.

The Astro Inertial Navigation System

An SR-71 pilot once remarked, 'You've never been lost until you've been lost at Mach 3.0.' One begins to understand the significance of such a remark when realizing how far off course one can get by flying a wrong heading at 3000 ft per second. The statement becomes even more significant when one considers that SR-71 crews have flown operational sorties in the vicinity of some of the most sensitive areas in the world, while travelling at speeds of more than a mile every two seconds[5]. Accuracy, reliability and the capability to perform track-keeping tasks without recourse to external, ground-based navigation aids were the three key elements that led to the development of the Nortronics Division Astro Inertial Navigation System (ANS), designated NAS-14V2. Designed to ensure that SR-71 crew members were never 'lost', the ANS has clearly won the respect of users and intelligence analysts by controlling the aircraft's track within a few hundred feet of its programmed parameters by producing terminal error accuracy standards of less than a half mile after travelling equivalent distances of more than half way around the world.

The ANS combined data from an inertial platform with a time datum supplied from a chronometer which was accurate to within five milli-seconds. Position 'updating' was achieved automatically by astro-tracking some of the day-or-night visible stars from the 52 most permanently visible for navigational purposes. Those stars were computer-catalogued in an ephemeris memory which could be used for continuous cross-comparison for track position referencing. The ANS scanned at least three celestial bodies sequentially through a pre-programmed tracker-mechanism mounted on a gimballed platform on top of the nav unit to provide refined location information. When the autopilot was coupled to the ANS through the AUTONAV function switch, the aircraft could be flown automatically and precisely on a predetermined flight path. The preplanned route (worked out by highly experienced navigators) was electronically loaded into the ANS's computer memory a few hours before take-off. Inflight modifications could be made by the RSO via his Control and Display panel. During flight, the computer-sequenced plan directed the aircraft from one destination point (DP) to the next.

These DP's represented the end points of each leg on the mission. Apart from the final destination, these intermediate points were positions that the aircraft would never quite reach because the ANS and autopilot would initiate a back-set roll-in to a properly banked turn in order to prescribe an accurate track during the turn, and to roll-out precisely on course to the next DP. Turn radius was determined by the aircraft's true airspeed and angle of bank. During operational sorties, bank angles at Mach 3.2 were programmed up to a maximum of 42 degrees. This limit allowed for an extra margin of bank of three more degrees to make good an outbound leg without exceeding 45 degrees.

Two further features of the ANS included ground reference position updating through the forward-looking viewsight, and sensor monitoring by reference to Control Point (CP) actions. CPs were predetermined track points where the ANS would activate or deactivate reconnaissance sensor systems. These points would serve to alert the RSO that the system was about to turn on, that the system had functioned correctly, and that programmed activities were being automatically carried out.

Interial Navigation System

The Singer-Kearfott SKN-2417 INS was a very accurate back-up navigation system with a CEP of one nautical mile per hour. Used as the primary navigation system in early-series F-16s, the SKN-2417 replaced the earlier SR-71 gyro Flight Reference System (FRS) in June 1982. The earlier system

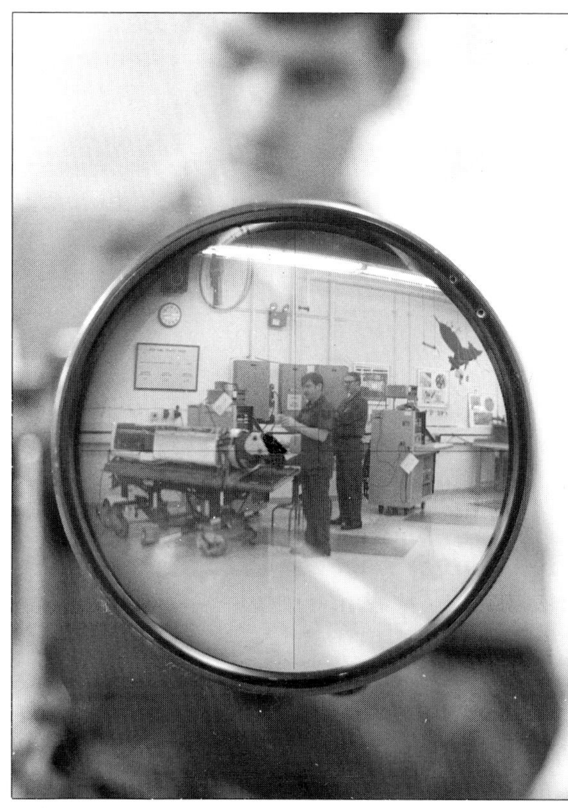

Viewed through a U-2 view-scope, technicians work on an Itek TEOC carried by the SR-71 (*USAF*)

had no navigation capacity and provided heading and attitude information only. The heart of the new unit was an inertially stabilised platform (four gimbals for all-attitude operation, vertical and azimuth gyros, and three sub-miniature pendulous linear acclerometers). Located in the 'R' Bay, the gyro-platform provided navigation data to a control panel located in the RSO's cockpit.

Mission Recorder System

The MRS was an airborne mission and maintenance data-recording system used to store up to 12 hours of monitored aircraft and system performance information. In addition, the MRS recorded the actions of the reconnaissance sensors and navigation systems, as well as all inter-cockpit and radio voice transmissions. The purpose of this 'crash-survivable' system was to identify failures, impending failures, and sub-standard system performances for maintenance purposes or accident analyses. Data collection was achieved through the use of multiplexing switches within the MRS, which sequentially shared analogue and digitalised signals at a sample rate of once every three seconds. Once activated, the system operated continuously and automatically. After a mission, the recorded data was copied from the unit-500 recorder-assembly on the aircraft using a Mobile Ground Formatter Unit (MGFU), which created a Computer-Compatible Tape (CCT) of non-voice data. A portable Tape-Copy-Unit (TCU) was used with the MGFU to copy the crew's voice audio recording. The table below summarises the number of signals monitored by the MRS within each aircraft system:

- engine – 16
- hydraulic system – 13
- DAFICS – 58
- electrical system – 24
- MRS – 18
- ANS – 100
- ECS – 16
- miscellaneous – 20

A-12 Sensors

The A-12 was designed as a photo platform to fulfil the demanding task of obtaining detailed telephoto images in 'high-threat' target areas beyond the reach of the low-speed U-2s, which were considered vulnerable to enemy action after two had been shot down by SAMs in 1960 and 1963. The A-12's large fuselage bay (which lay immediately behind the pilot's cockpit) was built to carry the bulky 'long focal length' optics of the late-1950s. The A-12 could carry either the Type H or KA-102A cameras, which produced very high quality photos. The Type H camera was built by Actron (now the imaging systems group of the McDonnell Douglas Corporation). The 60-inch focal-length camera was developed by the CIA and the USAF for use in the U-2 but was further adapted to the A-12. The first three cameras were delivered to the Air Force in April 1965. Imagery was focused onto Kodak 3414 film, which possessed a very low ASA rating of eight[6]. The film's square 4.5×4.5 inch format provided an image resolution as fine as two inches from 80,000 feet[7].

Both camera systems required image-stabilisation techniques to avoid target 'smearing'. The Technical Objective Cameras used on the SR-71s employed an active stabilisation system 'scan-head'

Encased within its own ECS 'jacket', an SR-71's OBC undergoes bench checks (*USAF*)

which provided stabilisation in both principal axes (azimuth and elevation), and minimised the effects of low frequency motion commonly associated with an aircraft in flight. The system permitted the optical axis of the camera to be stabilised inertially during an exposure, and the optical axis to be aimed precisely at specific targets (with on/off command signals supplied from the ANS). Finally, the aircraft's rapid speed was eliminated from the finished images by a Forward Motion Compensation mechanism (FMC).

The KA-102A camera was manufactured by the Itek Corporation under contract with the Atomic Energy Commission and the USAF. The early variants of the KA-102A were highly complex and sophisticated multi-million dollar systems which needed contract maintenance and field support by Itek's factory-trained technical representatives. Similar to the Type H, the KA-102A had a focal length of 48 inches and a maximum aperture of f.4. Its five inch-wide, 700 ft-long roll of film produced 1675 4.5 × 4.5 inch photographs. The KA-102A is still widely used today in exterior pods on fighter aircraft, its focal length having been increased to 60 inches. The cameras shot through distortion-free quartz glass windows which remained unaffected by heat generated at high frictional speeds. The three-year/$2 million development of the special transparencies ultimately involved an advanced process of fusing the quartz glass to its metal frame through the use of high frequency sound waves.

The largest sensor 'package' ever carried by the aircraft was the D-21 drone, which was mounted on a converted platform referred to as the M-12 due to its 'Motherly' role with the pilotless craft. The ramjet drone was attached to a pylon on the upper rear fuselage (see chapter two for details and mounting diagrams). Finally, the A-12 was equipped with signal sensors to monitor electronic and signal intelligence (ELINT and SIGINT). For self protection, the aircraft was provided with an AN/ALR-28 electronic countermeasure (ECM) package.

SR-71 Sensors

All sensors carried by the SR-71 were installed in either the nose or chine bays[8]. The nose section of all SR-71s were detachable to provide additional mission flexibility. Four different kinds of nose sections were developed: an Optical Bar Camera (OBC) nose; a lightweight training- or ferry-flight nose which contained no operational equipment or sensors; a radar nose which housed the Goodyear PIP and later the Loral CAPRE ground-mapping radar units; and a later-model radar nose which housed and Advanced Synthetic Aperture Radar unit (ASARS I) built by the Loral Company. This latter nose section was distinguishable from the earlier structure by its more bulbous, duck-bill-like appearance.

Equipment Bays

Bay E was known as the Electrical bay and Bay R the Radio bay. The diagram and table below show each of the SR-71 bays' dimensions and capabilities.

Bay	Volume (Cu Ft)	Payload Weight (lbs)	Maximum Dimensions (inches)
Nose	23	550	30 × 30 × 75
C	7.2	150	24 × 24 × 16
D	12	230	11 × 17 × 80
K and L	29.2	900	16 × 17 × 92
M and N	21.7	200	18 × 18 × 49
Q and P	32	340	18 × 18 × 90
T and S	22.7	400	18 × 18 × 62

All sensors carried by the SR-71 were continually improved upon by their manufacturers. Adding the RSO aircrew position to the SR-71 meant that the Q Bay which had carried the A-12's superb close-look camera, was no longer available. As a consequence, compressed-length cameras using cassegrainian optics were developed for the SR-71, allowing these new 'palletised' units to fit into the long narrow bays in the chines. It is interesting to note that until

Above This impressive view was photographed from the 'front office' of an SR-71 while cruising at 80,000 ft. The earth's curvature was exaggerated by the camera's wide-angle lens (*B C Thomas*)

Below A self-portrait of SR-71 driver BC Thomas who accrued 1217.3 hrs in this aircraft – more than any other 'Habu' pilot (*BC Thomas*)

Serial 963 returns to roost. Note vertical flow pattern generated at the root of the outboard wing section (*USAF*)

these cassegrainian units were improved, early photographs taken by SR-71s were inferior to those obtained by the long-axis A-12 camera which used a larger film format.

The Operational Objective Cameras (OOCs), made by Hycon, had a 13-inch focal length and used 9 × 9 inch film format. Unlike the Technical Objective Cameras (TEOCs), the OOCs were not programmable and had to be switched on and off by the RSO. The OOCs provided accurate images for interpreters to count aircraft on an airfield, and helped to establish reference points when analysing TEOC imagery. Most of the money available to improve optics was spent on the TEOCs; consequently, the OOCs were withdrawn from service in the early 1970s.

The TEOCs were made by the Itek Corporation with an initial focal length of approximately 36 inches. The camera was progressively improved to a focal length of 48 inches. This increase, coupled with improvements in film chemistry and film processing techniques, led to some spectacular results. Between 1978 and 1980, two SR-71s (numbers 955 and 975) both carried TEOCs made by CAI, the company having developed 'the magic' 66 inch focal length lens. Little information has been revealed about this advanced camera system since the SR-71 ceased operations.

In 1968 a nose-mounted 30-inch Optical Bar Camera (OBC), or Split-Scan Panoramic camera, was tested. Horizon-to-horizon panoramic scanning was accomplished by the full rotation of a prismatic optical barrel which swept above and below the aircraft's longitudinal axis. A frontally-stabilised, mirrored scanning head bent light rays through 90 degrees into the the lens, which focused ground-target images by way of a second mirror through an exposure slit and onto the film at the cylindrical focal surface. Image-film synchronisation was split between the film which was moved across the slit in one direction, and the exposure slit which travelled in the opposite direction – hence the term 'split-scan'. This system allowed the SR-71 to photograph 100,000 square miles of terrain per hour, from which selected target images could be enlarged up to 20 times for photographic analysis. Such a combination of wide-area coverage and high-resolution led to the progressive development of the superb-quality 48 inch focal length system.

Radios, SIGINT Receivers, and Defensive Jammers

The limited range of VHF and UHF radio reception, together with the great speed of the SR-71, conspired against the reconnaissance platform's ability to be particularly useful in signal intelligence collection. SIGINT radio recorders may well capture a ground controller giving a fighter pilot taxy instructions, but often the fast-moving SR-71 would be out of effective 'listening range' by the time the controller-directed aircraft was airborne. Therefore, the SR-71's importance in the SIGINT role lay in its ability to stimulate the overall defence environment, allowing stand-off receiver aircraft such as U-2s, RC-135s, or RAF Nimrods to monitor the triggered response from the various surveillanced command authorities.

Of more use was the SR-71's ability to gather electronic intelligence. A 'Habu' brought back the first electronic 'system signature' of the most advanced Soviet SAM – the SA-5. During co-ordinated sorties with RC-135s, the entire Soviet electronic order of battle was progressively revealed.

Without doubt, one of the most sensitive security issues was the SR-71's Defensive Electronic (DEF) systems. This equipment was especially effective, and was continually being evolved to counter further Soviet threats. Initially equipped with DEF A, B, C, E and G, these were later updated and became DEF A2, C2, H and M. By the time the SR-71 was retired a system using programmable software had been produced, known as DEF A2C, which was capable of defeating all known threats. Beyond the barest information, further comment on DEF systems is still restricted since other forms of this equipment are still in use on current USAF aircraft.

This wily skunk is the registed trade mark of Lockheed ADP (*Lockheed ADP*)

CHAPTER 4

The 1960s – Genesis

During the intitial stages of assembling the YF-12 in late 1960, it became apparent to ADP engineers that the basic interceptor airframe could be adapted to provide a strike bomber. Russ Daniel approached Kelly with the idea and asked to write a basic feasibility report. Kelly reviewed Daniel's B-12 proposal with Strategic Air Command's Commander-in-Chief (CINCSAC) General Curtis LeMay, who agreed to fund R & D studies provided that these projects would not be used to harm support for the XB-70 Valkyrie bomber programme. A copy of the engineering analysis was sent to the Special Projects Office at Wright Field, Ohio, where engineers confirmed that the proposed system would indeed make a highly effective strike-reconnaissance platform.

A refined proposal was briefed to the Secretary of the Air Force, Dr Joseph Charyk, in January 1961. The Pentagon staffing of the initiative became the province of the Chief of Special Activities, Col Leo Geary, and Lew Meyer, a Special Projects finance officer. The 'Skunk Works' proposal won further supporters, and funding was allocated to build two full-sized forward fuselage mock-ups. The USAF selected two competing teams (Westinghouse and Goodyear) to work in isolation to provide radar systems integration with the proposed Hughes nuclear-tipped missile.

The concept of operations called for B-12s to penetrate enemy airspace at Mach 3.2 at an altitude of 80,000 ft (immune from SA-2s), and use radar to search designated areas to locate, identify and strike selected targets. Each B-12 would carry four internal nuclear missiles which would be lowered for firing one at a time on a hydraulically-operated parallelogram-arm (similar to the mechanism planned for the F-12B).

The aircraft's radar and inertial guidance system would then transfer details of the target's relative position to the missile and the fired weapon would guide itself to the point of impact using either radar or an optical area correlation system[1]. This guidance concept was thought to be impractical by certain critics, but the team proved to Wright Field that the all-weather radar-guided missile was capable of hitting its target within a 50 ft circular error of probability (CEP), and 20 ft using an optical system, although it had been launched 50 miles away.

There remained important doubters, however. Secretary of Defense Harold Brown rather pompously proclaimed that the entire proposition was ridiculous and that 'finding a target along a 3000 mile track in a swath 20 miles wide was like quickly locating a single word in the *Encyclopaedia Britannica*. Viewed in such simplistic terms, target-finding and pin-point strike accuracy was certainly an ambitious undertaking, but to simplify matters the aircraft would look for certain en-route clues which would lead the proposed B-12 directly to specific targets. Even Kelly was sceptical. Russ Daniel recalled his conversation with the Lockheed chief designer during a flight from Washington to Burbank in the company Jetstar, which went along the lines of, 'Do you still think you can hit that garage door down there Russ?' Daniel replied in the affirmative, adding 'What you don't do is aim, shoot and forget. Like your car, you don't point it at your garage from the parking lot at work, close your eyes and drive'.

When Dr Joseph Charyk flew to Burbank to review 'progress to date', he was directed to one of the mock-ups into which a prepared mission tape had been installed. This demonstration consisted of experimental SLAR imagery taken from a B-58 Hustler as it flew 1200 miles at Mach 2 over six western states. The radar map was then transposed onto 35 mm film and moved through the back-seater's radar display at a speed that equated to

Mach 3. Charyk was briefed on how to work the cursor that would be placed over a target and then 'pickled' to feed information into the weapons system. He was then invited to 'fly' a mission and see at first-hand how, in the words of Secretary of Defense Harold Brown, 'a single word in the *Encyclopaedia Britannica*' could be located when you know how the system works. He emerged from the cockpit 40 minutes later beaming – he had located and 'pickled' all 20 designated targets! The feasibility argument was laid to rest once and for all.

On 4 June 1962 an Air Force evaluation team reviewed the B-12's design. Six months later Lockheed was contracted to build six pre-production airframes for static tests, and to produce 25 follow-on aircraft at a rate of one per month for 31 months. This production target was met and the entire static and flight test categories I, II and III were completed under budget at a cost of $146 million – a great achievement by any standards. Meanwhile, the Air Force assigned the so-called B-12 to a reconnaissance-strike role of post-ICBM 'look and clean-up', and incorporated the new aeroplane into SAC's nuclear war plan – the SIOP (Single Integrated Operational Plan). At this time, considerable doubt was being expressed in 'strategic think tanks' as to the long-term value of bombers as delivery platforms for nuclear weapons. The ballistic missile had come of age and more than 1500 B-47s were on their way out of SAC's inventory of weapon systems. The fall-out of such thinking within the Kennedy administration was that Secretary of Defense McNamara never ordered weapons for the B-12s. During this period of uncertainty, much re-titling of ADP drawings took place, which resulted in wide-spread confusion as to the new aircraft's exact designation.

B-12

It is interesting to note that the viability of the original 1961 B-12 proposal was demonstrated in practical terms just four years later by three YF-12s that achieved the following results firing AIM-47 missiles from high altitude, against much lower moving targets:

Date	*Number*	*YF-12*	*Speed*	*Altitude*	*Target*	*Target Altitude*
18 March 1965	G-11	935	M2.2	65K	Q-2C	40K
19 May 1965	G-13	935	M2.3	65K	Q-2C	20K
28 Sept 1965	G-15	934	M3.2	75K	Q-2C	20K
22 March 1966	G-18	936	M3.15	74.5K	Q-2C	1.5K
25 April 1966	G-19	934	M3.2	75K	QB-47	1.5K
13 May 1966	G-16	936	M3.17	74K	Q-2C	20K
21 Sept 1966	G-20	936	M3.2	74K	QB-47	Terrain

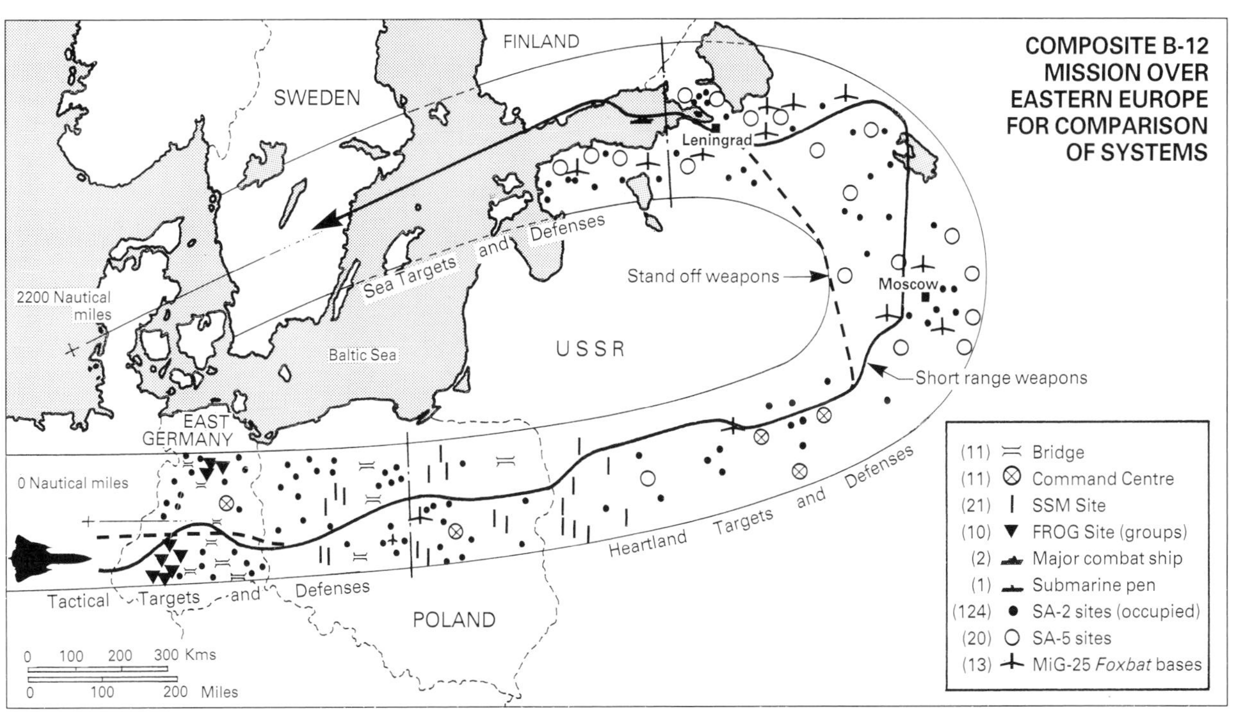

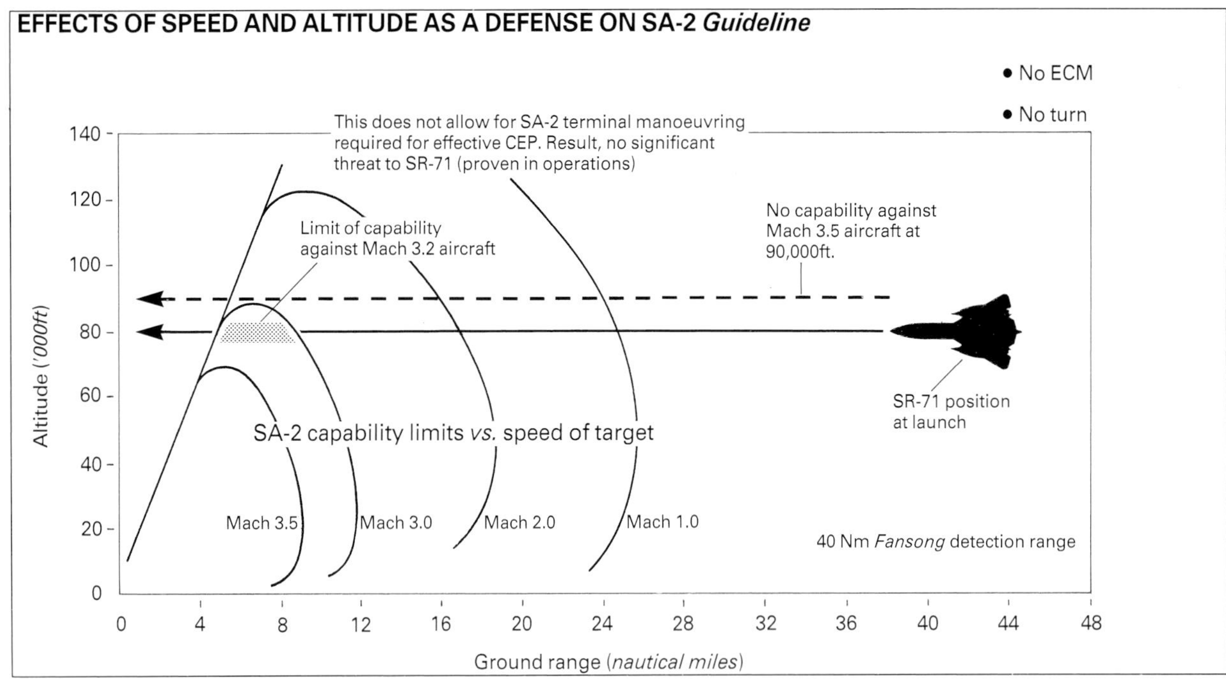

The secret of the aeroplane's adaptability to perform such varying tasks lay in its ability to have a re-engineered forebody, mated to the aft body at joint 715 (a point perpendicular to where the inboard wing leading edge met the fuselage chine). The weapons bay had the capability of housing either four AGM-69 SRAMS (when launched at Mach 3.2 their range increased dramatically to 514 NM downrange and crossrange up to 200 NM), or it could haul six strike missiles (each 113 inches long with a range of 360 NM), or 12 guided bombs (each 55 inches in length with a range of 40 NM).

In the late 1970s, Lockheed ADP continued to draft proposals to the USAF, outlining the platforms suitability as a bomber. One such proposal harnessed the SR-71's high cruise speed and altitude to impart greatly increased levels of kinetic and potential energy to inert weapons. Such weapons obviated the need for warheads, thus reducing the cost of the missiles appreciably. For example, a weapon weighing 1200 lbs launched at Mach 3.2 and 80,000 ft on an optimum −0.5 g trajectory had the ability to penetrate 23 ft of reinforced concrete. This high velocity projectile would cause virtually no collateral damage, but considerable damage to a subterranean target (like a bunker or missile silo), as the weapon's kinetic energy transfered to, and throughout, the structure. The same weapon could penetrate hard soil to a depth of about 120 ft. If combined with a small high explosive or nuclear warhead, it becomes a highly effective sub-surface weapon, as the explosion causes soil above to collapse, and thus contain fallout in a nuclear scenario. Despite the concept's feasibility and moderate cost, SAC showed little interest in it.

Sometime in 1966, the B-12 was christened the RS-71 (RS for Reconnaissance-Strike and the number '71' indicating a follow-on from the RS-70 Valkyrie, which was formerly the B-70). The lack of weapons procurement alarmed Lockheed, who produced drawings of a pure reconnaissance variant, designated the R-12. The 'R' series featured cameras and ELINT packages installed in the long, narrow weapons bays, together with a SLAR in the nose. This redesign was considered 'most innovative' since unlike the U-2 and A-12, it provided synergistic target coverage. The powerful cameras for the R-12 would have to be purpose-built to fit in the chine bays, which were formally narrow weapons spaces, yet retain their long-axis telephoto capability.

Despite the notable speed and altitude advantages of the RS-71 over the RS-70, Kelly stuck to the promise he made to LeMay and did not promote the Lockheed design over that of his North American-Rockwell competitors, even though Gen Bernard Schriever, then head of the Air Force Systems Division, was an ardent supporter of the superior survivability of the design. The R-12 was fully vindicated in May 1964 when McNamara cancelled the RS-70 programme. It was an election year in the United States and a time when political disagreements concerning national security were rife. The Republican candidate for president, Senator Barry Goldwater, was stridently critical of the Kennedy-Johnson track record on air power issues, contending that the Democrats had not initiated a single, significant advanced aircraft development programme and that they had neglected the defence needs of America. Predictably, the 'bullish' Lyndon Johnson reacted sharply to counter Goldwater's charge. On 25 July 1964, the White House press office released the following presidential statement:

'I would like to announce the successful development of a major new strategic manned aircraft system which will be employed by the Strategic Air Command. This system employs the new SR-71 aircraft and provides a long-range advanced strategic reconnaissance plane for military use, capable of worldwide reconnaissance for military operations. The Joint Chiefs of Staff, when reviewing the RS-70, emphasized the importance of the strategic reconnaissance mission. The SR-71 aircraft reconnaissance system is the most advanced in the world. The aircraft will fly at more than three times the speed of sound. It will operate at altitudes in excess of 80,000 ft. It will use the most advanced observation equipment of all kinds in the world. The aircraft will provide the strategic forces of the United States with an outstanding long-range reconnaissance capability. The system will be used during periods of military hostilities and in other situations in which the United States military forces may be confronting foreign military forces.

'The SR-71 uses the same J58 engines as on the experimental interceptor previously announced, but it is

At Kelly Johnson's request Bob Gilliland flew prototype SR-71A 950 on a fly-by for USAF officials during its maiden flight on 22 December 1964. Jim Eastham chased 950 in an F-104 Starfighter on that first flight (*Lockheed*)

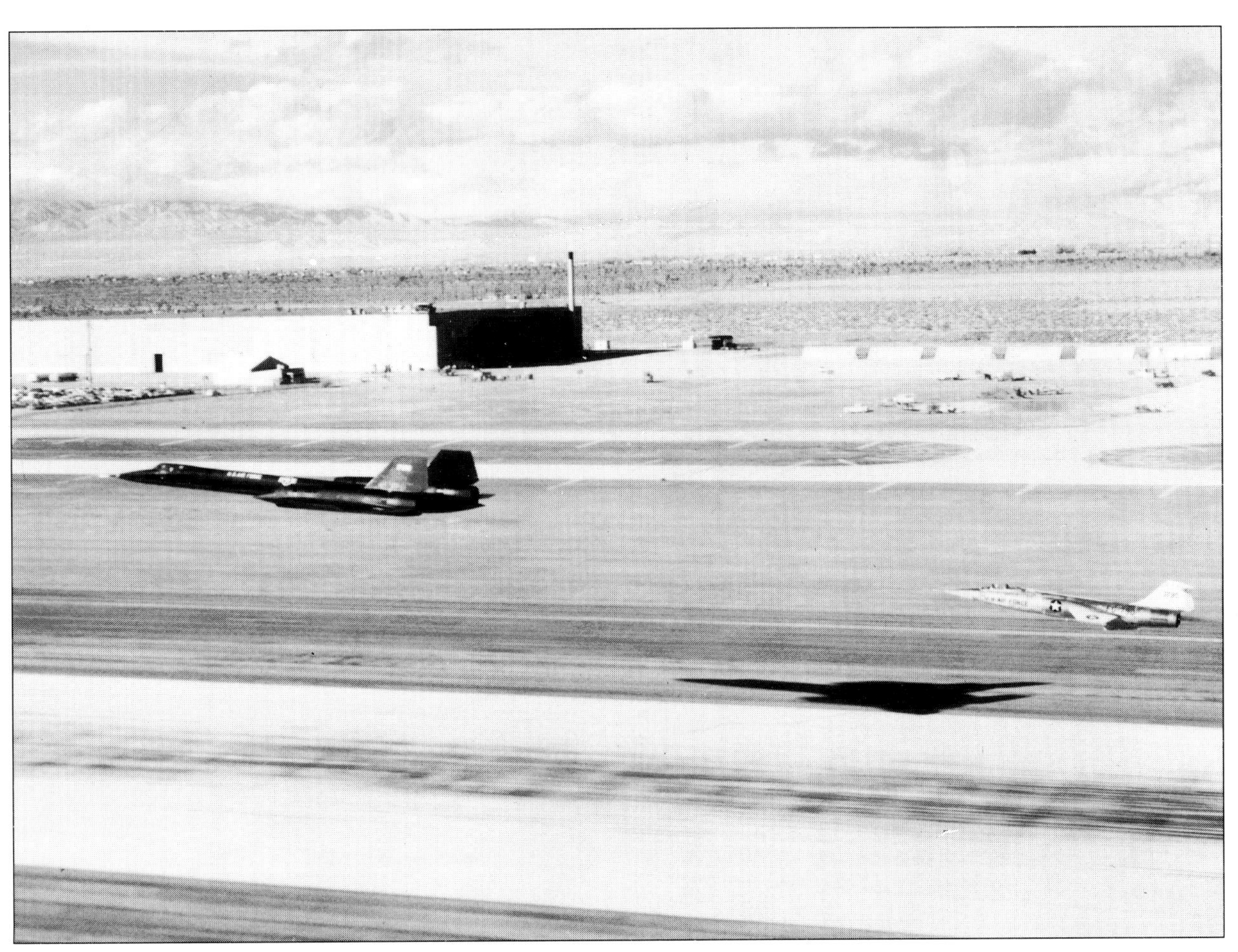

substantially heavier and it has a longer range. The considerably heavier gross weight permits it to accommodate the multiple reconnaissance sensors needed by the Strategic Air Command to accomplish their strategic reconnaissance mission in a military environment.

'The billion-dollar program was initiated in February of 1963. The first operational aircraft will begin flight testing in early 1965. Deployment of production units to the Strategic Air Command will begin shortly thereafter.

'Appropriate members of Congress have been kept fully informed on the nature of and the progress in this aircraft program. Further information on this major advanced aircraft system will be released from time to time at the appropriate military secret classification levels.'

Although the A-12 had flown before, such statements were political fodder for upcoming elections. The overall programme had been conceived during Eisenhower's Administration, but the SR-71 which Johnson announced had not yet undertaken its maiden flight. Although the political wrangling continued, the future of the R-12 was being assured by Goldwater's taunt. Johnson had conveniently (and politically) transposed 'Reconnaissance-Strike' into 'Strategic Reconnaissance' – hence 'SR-71', which was really Lockheed's R-12. Unfortunately the B-12 was lost to the McNamara era.

First Flight Preparations

In August 1964 Kelly phoned Bob Murphy and asked him if he wanted to work on the SR-71 programme. At the time, Murphy was a superintendent in charge of D-21 Drone production. Drone number one was undergoing final check-out while another nine were at various stages of assembly. Bob accepted his offer and was immediately briefed by Kelly who said, 'I want you to go to Palmdale and get Site 2 away from Rockwell. Hire the people you need. The pieces of the SR-71 will be up to you on November 1st and I want her flying before Christmas. Oh, I also want you to move up there because I don't want you to commute.' This was typical of the way Kelly operated. The next day,

Bob eases 'Dutch 51' into a left turn high over the Sierra Nevada Mountains north of Edwards (*Lockheed*)

Col Bill Hayes led highly skilled USAF maintenance technicians as they brought the SR-71 into operational service. He chose some of the best crew chiefs and maintenance supervisors in the entire Air Force (*USAF*)

Murphy went out to Palmdale and met the base commander, who arranged a meeting between the various parties affected by their activities. 'Murph' recalled:

'Rockwell controlled all three sites; they were using Site 1 and Site 3 for B-70 production. Site 2 housed various other facilities including a paint shop and a huge telephone exchange. The meeting got underway and I began negotiating for various parts of the building that would have to be vacated by specified dates to allow our people to move in. One of the Rockwell people said, "Well we don't have anything from the Air Force that says we need to be out of this building". At that point I bluffed a move to get out of my chair and said, "You don't? Well I'd better call Washington and find out what the heck is going on." The ruse worked and he said, "Wait a minute, we don't have to get Washington involved in this," and I was able to complete the arrangements without having any official orders to do so – although they were probably just around the corner.'

So it was that Lockheed inherited Site 2 at Palmdale. The prototype SR-71A (Article 2001; number 64–17950) was delivered in a disassembled form in two large trailers on 29 October 1964 to Site 2 (Air Force Plant 42, Building 210 at Palmdale, California). At that point Bob Murphy's team 'went into overdrive' in an attempt to fulfil the extremely tight deadline set by Kelly.

In the summer of 1964, Kelly had offered test pilot Robert J Gilliland the post of chief project pilot for the SR-71. It was a position that Bob was admirably qualified for having gained a great deal of experience as a member of the F-104 and A-12 test teams. In early December, Kelly and Bob flew from Burbank to Palmdale in Lockheed's corporate Jetstar to review the progress toward final assembly. Bob Murphy escorted them around Building 210, revealing that Article 2001 was spread all over the hangar floor in the process. During the return flight to Burbank, Bob (who was mindful that a number of Air Force generals from Omaha, Wright-Patterson and Washington were planning to be on hand at the 21 December maiden test flight) told Kelly, 'Maybe we'd better postpone this thing 'til after Christmas. It's likely to be a little embarrassing to you, me and the "Skunk Works" if we get them out here and don't go'. Kelly refused to budge, contending that if he postponed schedules everytime he was asked, the aeroplane would still be in the jigs.

Dick Miller led the flight test engineering effort for the entire contractor test programme. Once his brief had been decided upon and approved, he became responsible for the implementation of specific tests to be completed on individual flights. During those final weeks leading up to the first flight, Bob Gilliland recalled having to attend frequent meetings which he characterised as being 'tedious and in great danger of causing analysis-paralysis'. There was considerable discussion as to whether the first flight should be flown at subsonic speeds with the gear down, or whether the gear should be retracted and (if all went well) to fly supersonically. It was agreed that no dead-stick landing would be attempted if there was a serious problem on the first flight and it was also agreed that the aircraft would not be landed on its belly if the gear failed to extend. Ejection was the preferred option in either case. Kelly and Bob agreed that an attempt would be made to fully exercise Article 2001 on its first flight.

With two J58s installed, 950 conducted its first engine test run on 18 December 1964. Three days later, a 'non-flight' was conducted. All preflight checks were carried out as if the flight was really going to leave the ground. This checkout included firing up each engine, checking control movements, and a close scrutiny of all guages, lights, switches and indicators. External checks for hydraulic leaks or other abnormalities were also performed by ground crews. Finally, after testing the trim movement, centre-of-gravity and radio operations, Bob taxied out using the brakes and nose gear steering. He did full engine run-ups at the end of the runway and took the number one position for take-off as if he was really going to launch. 950 was lined up for take-off, and the test pilot eased the throttles to full military power, checked engines 'in the green' and released the brakes. As the aircraft lurched forward, Bob engaged 'min burner' to feel the asymmetric 'pulse-pulse' of light-up. Accelerating rapidly due to the light fuel load, he snapped the throttles back to idle upon reaching 120 knots. As he deployed the large 40-foot drag chute, the deceleration threw him almost as hard against the shoulder straps as a carrier landing. He jettisoned the chute at 50 knots, turned off the runway and taxied back to the hangar. There were very few write-ups and they knew that the aircraft was ready for its maiden flight.

On 22 December 1964, Gilliland (using his personal callsign 'Dutch 51') got airborne from runway 25 at Palmdale in the first SR-71 (64-17950). The back seat remained empty on this flight for safety reasons. Consequently, many of the functions that would have been carried out by an RSO or a Lockheed systems engineer were 'jury-rigged' onto a special instrument control panel mounted in the front cockpit. After take-off, Bob immediately retracted the landing gear, reduced afterburners to 'min', turned right and continued his climb northbound over the Edwards test range until he levelled off at 20,000 ft and 0.9 Mach. Lockheed's experienced A-12 test pilot, James Eastham (later to become the second pilot to fly the SR-71), flew one of three F-104s which 'chased' 950 to observe and assist if problems occurred. The two other Starfighters were flown by USAF test pilots Col Robert 'Fox' Stephens and Lt Col Walt Daniels – one of the jets was a two-seater and it carried a photographer in the rear.

Immediately after Bob's take-off, Eastham tucked into close formation position on 950's right wing, allowing the two pilots to compare and calibrate the SR-71's airspeed and altitude readings against the F-104's to verify accurate pitot-static system operations. The test flight instructions called for manoeuvrability and handling checks during 'static and dynamic' stability and contol tests. These checks were carried out with the SAS axes 'on' and 'off', both 'individually' and then 'collectively'. Performance comparisons of predicted values of speed versus thrust and fuel consumption were also recorded, followed by a climb to 30,000 ft where cabin pressure, oxygen flow and temperature control were checked. After passing Mojave, Bob turned left to fly on a heading west of NAS China Lake and then northward up the Owens Valley

This historic photograph, taken on 27 May 1967, depicts the initial cadre of the 9th SRW. They are from left to right, front rank; Sgt Dave Gallard, Jack Kennon (Ops Officer), Ray Haupt (1st SRS Commander), Hal Confer (DCO), Bill Hayes (9th SRW Commander), Charles Minter (9th SRW Vice Wing Commander), John Boynton (99th SRS Commander), Harlon Hain (Ops Officer), MSgt Loignon. The pilots in the second rank are paired with their RSO's, who stand behind them in the third rank as follows: Storrie/Mallozzi, Sowers/Sheffield, Hichew/Schmittou, Collins/Seagroves, Bill Campbell/Pennington, Halloran/Jarvis, Brown/Jensen, Dale Shelton/ Boggess, O'Malley/Payne, Walbrecht/Loignon, Boone/Vick, Bevacqua/Crew, Watkins/Dempster, DeVall/Shoemaker, Spencer/Branham, McCallum/Locke, St Martin/Carnochan, Bull/McNeer, Powell/Kendrick, Daubs/Roetcisoender, Bobby Campbell/Kraus, Kardong/Coleman, Maier/Casey, Fruehauf/unknown and Hudson/Ferrell (*USAF*)

between the Sierra Nevada Mountains to the west and the White Mountains to the east (all within the Edwards Special Operating Area). Just north of Bishop (near Mammoth and Yosemite National Parks) Bob completed a 180 degree turn to the left and rolled out on a southerly track over the spectacular high cordillera of the snow-covered Sierra Nevadas.

It was now time to do a supersonic dash since all systems were performing well. Just northwest of Bishop, and with Jim's F-104 sticking with the SR-71 like glue, Bob eased the throttles into 'min' burner', checked the engine parameters, and slid the throttle levers on up to 'max'. The light test jet accelerated very quickly to 400 knots in level flight and on to supersonic speeds quite easily. At Mach 1.2 the 'Master Caution' warning light flashed on which drew Bob's attention to the Annunciator Panel where he saw a 'read-out' light identifying the problem as 'CANOPY UNSAFE'. By visually checking the two canopy locking hooks on either side of the canopy, Bob verified that the canopy was really 'fully locked'. The pressure-sensitive micro-switches which transmitted the electrical 'unsafe' signal had been activated because an aerodynamic low pressure area above the aircraft had sucked the canopy up against the locking hooks. The canopy was really 'safe', but it had risen high enough to complete the electrical circuit which turned on the Annunciator and Master Caution Lights. Bob correctly analysed the situation as 'safe' and pressed on with the test flight. He advanced the throttles once again and continued to climb and accelerate while rigorously scanning his instruments. On reaching

50,000 ft and Mach 1.5, Bob eased the power out of burner into 'mil' and began a deceleration to 350 knots indicated airspeed, whereafter he descended to 20,000 ft to allow the engines to cool down.

As Bob approached Palmdale, he was advised by Test Ops that Kelly had requested a subsonic flyby down the runway. He and the accompanying F-104s streaked by to highlight the successful completion of the first flight. At the far end of the runway, Bob 'chandelled' 950 up onto the downwind leg where he dumped the gear and was most pleased to see the 'three little bright green lights' which indicated that all three of the landing struts were 'down and locked'. He turned onto a wide base leg and set-up a long final approach at 185 knots. After making a smooth touchdown on Palmdale's runway 25, he gently lowered the nose and deployed the drag 'chute. At 50 knots Bob jettisoned the 'chute, turned off the active runway and taxied back towards the crowd of USAF dignitaries and Lockheed engineers and technicians who awaited his debriefing.

After congratulations from Kelly and the others, the debriefing took place with more than two dozen engineers and subcontractor representatives present. Bob narrated details of his flight chronologically from start-up to shutdown, whereafter Dick Miller's Lockheed engineers and the other companies' technicians asked clarifying questions. Since the session was recorded, Bob's description was prepared in a typescript which was circulated to all concerned. After this 'first quick look' was satisfied, a further analysis was made of canopy-mounted camera recordings which had viewed the instrument panel throughout the flight. All of this data along with other 'automatic observer' panels enabled Bob Klinger's Data Reduction Group to 'reconstruct' the flight for engineering analysis. So ended Bob's 'pre-Christmas' historic and most successful maiden flight of an SR-71.

Following the first three experimental test sorties, Dick Miller flew as 'flight test engineer' on all of the development flights except the 'limited structural tests' which were 'pilot only' for safety reasons. Aeroplane numbers 951 and 952 were added to the test fleet for contractor development of payload systems and techniques. Shortly after the Phase II 'Developmental Test Program' was started, four other Lockheed test pilots were brought into the project: Jim Eastham, Bill Weaver, Art Peterson and Darrell Greenamyer.

The concentrated developmental test efforts were matched by those of HQ Air Force Systems Command (AFSC) at Wright-Patterson where Col Ben Bellis had been appointed System Project Officer (SPO) for the SR-71. His task was to structure a 'Development and Evaluation Program' that would 'sound out' the new aircraft for the Air Force. Implementation of this programme would be undertaken by the SR-71/YF-12 Test Force at the Air Force Flight Test Center at Edwards. AFSC pilots would work in parallel with their counterparts from Lockheed and ensure the successful development of systems and sensors. Both Phase I 'Experimental' and Phase II 'Developmental' test flying had moved to Edwards where 953, 954 and 955 were to be evaluated by the 'blue suiters'.

In 1965 the team began SR-71 air refuelling tests (supported by Beale's 903rd Air Refueling Squadron); the aircraft proved adequate for skilled pilots to refuel. The flight envelope expansion phase proceeded well, as did a host of other tests. On 2 November 1965, Bob Gilliland and Bill Weaver completed the maiden flights of the first two SR-71B pilot trainers (956 and 957). By the end of the year, Kelly Johnson could be justifiably pleased with the progress of his latest evolution of the A-12 family of black triple-sonic aircraft.

Aircrew Recruiting

US Army Camp Beale began its life as a military post in October 1942 when a vast site stretching over 80,000 acres was named in honour of Gen Edward Fitz-Gerald Beale (a mid-19th century Western explorer). Acquired by the newly formed US Air Force in early 1948, Camp Beale was used as a bombing and gunnery range during the Korean War. On 27 November 1951, General Order 77 reduced the bombing range by half and created Beale Air Force Base, which was later reduced to 23,000 acres (still more than all MoD acreage held in the United Kingdom by the US Air Force throughout the Cold War). Between April 1957 and August 1958, USAF engineers constructed a 12,000 ft strategic bomber runway at Beale, thus allowing the California base to become home to one of the first B-52 wings in SAC.

The 456th Bombardment Wing operated its B-52s and KC-135s from Beale, along with the 851st Strategic Missile Squadron's first-generation Titan ICBMs. After the 851st SMS was deactivated in

1964, the Air Force informed the Press in October that SR-71s would be stationed at Beale. Soon after an $8.4 million construction programme was initiated at the base, which included the installation of an array of specialised technical support facilities and 337 new Capehart houses for the newcomers.

The official announcement of the new SR-71 unit was made a week before the first test flight of the SR-71 when CINCSAC General John Ryan revealed that the 4200th Strategic Reconnaissance Wing would be activated at Beale on 1 January 1965. Three months after the activation of the 'parent wing', four permanent support squadrons were formed: the 4200th Headquarters Squadron; the 4200th Armament and Electronics Maintenance Squadron; the 4200th Field Maintenance Squadron; and the 4200th Organizational Maintenance Squadron.

Col John DesPortes was the commander of the new wing while construction works were being carried out at the base. This former U-2 wing Commander was soon promoted to Brigadier General and given command of the 14th Strategic Aerospace Division, after which Col Doug Nelson took over the SR-71 wing. Nelson was particularly well-suited to his new command, since he had been SAC's project officer for the deployment of the U-2 nine years earlier. In August 1961 he had been assigned Director of Operations for the *Oxcart* project. Three years later he received a telephone call from Lt Gen Archie Old (Commander of the 15th Air Force), who informed him that he was to be Director of Plans for the 14th Air Division at Beale, and to take over the new wing when DesPortes' promotion was announced.

Nelson's immediate task would be to select a small group of highly competent sub-commanders and SAC fliers to form the initial cadre of the SR-71 unit. Nelson began the necessary planning for the activation of the world's first triple-sonic flying wing. After being assured by General Thomas Power that he would have top priority for choosing the right people for the programme, Nelson believed that one of his first tasks was to find the best maintenance supervisors, flightline and shop personnel, and the best pilots and navigators. General Old agreed that Col William Hayes (later known as the 'White Tornado') 'had to be' deputy commander for Maintenance. Nelson recalled:

'Bill Hayes hit the ground running and immediately began selecting his team of maintenance supervisors, crew chiefs and system specialists. That Bill clearly realised our goal of putting together a top quality maintenance unit was evidenced by the outstanding results that his guys achieved within the first year.'

At the same time, Nelson was interviewing crew members for the flying squadron. He first recruited

'Dutch 51', Bob Gilliland (who was born in Memphis, Tennessee), was chief test pilot for the SR-71 programme (*Lockheed*)

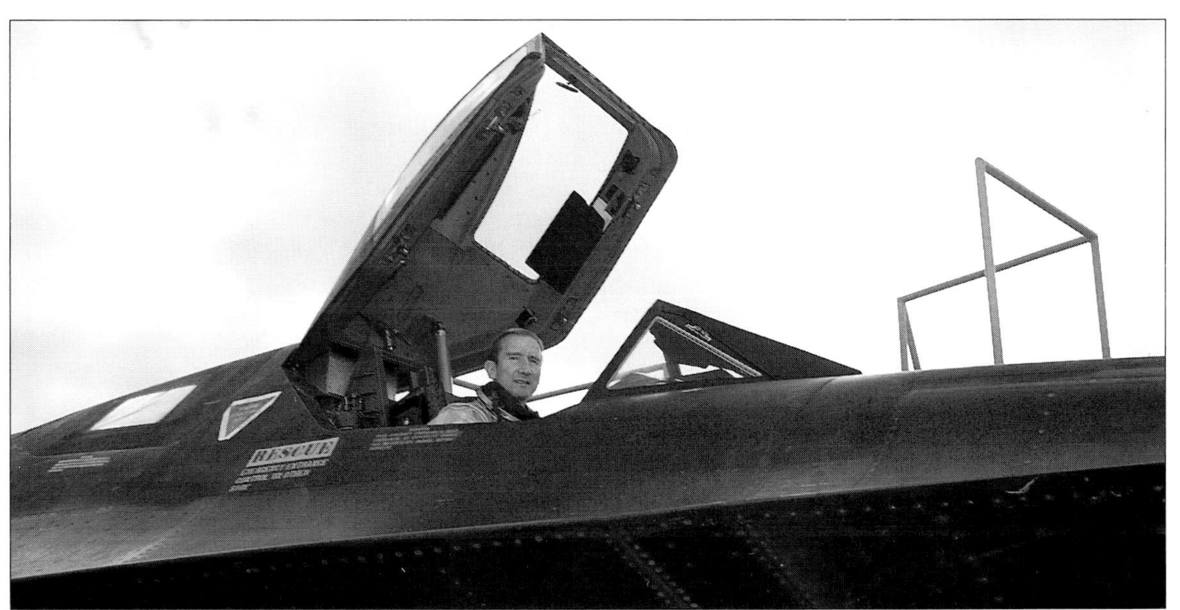

Lt Col Ray Haupt, a former U-2 pilot who was serving as Head Instructor and Standardisation Pilot at Groom Dry Lake. He joined the SR-71/YF-12 test force at Edwards AFB where he became the first Beale pilot to be fully qualified on the SR-71. Ray was to be Beale's Chief Instructor-pilot of all new SR-71 fliers.

Steadily, Nelson found the finest officers in SAC for his new hand-picked organizaton. The 4200th Medical Group was to be commanded by Col Walt Wright, the most outstanding flight surgeon and orthopedic surgeon in the Air Force. Col Clyde Denniston was chosen to supervise all the Category III flight test planning (to prove that the aeroplane could really do the mission for which it had been developed). Top-rated colonels and field grade officers were picked for unique staff positions and before the end of 1965 the wing had been 'fleshed-out' with the necessary talent 'to make it all happen'. Meanwhile, Nelson was busy visiting the two B-58 units, the U-2 organization, and HQ SAC to review the records of the best pilots and navigator-bombardiers among many highly qualified SAC aircrew members. Many of those whom Nelson considered were SAC's 'Select' crewmembers – those who had held spot promotions because of their proven status as SAC's best. Most who were considered were young enough to undertake another four years of new-generation flying.

From the start, SAC kept its *Senior Crown* programme its own 'exclusive preserve', restricting recruitment to 'select' crewmembers from bombers and U-2s. The only exceptions were graduates from the Air Force Test Pilot School at Edwards. Meanwhile, Nelson selected ten B-58 crewmembers: pilots Al Hichew, Robert 'Gray' Sowers, Charles 'Pete' Collins, Ben Bowles and John Storrie; and navigator-bombardiers Cosimo 'Coz' Mallozzi, Richard 'Butch' Sheffield, Jimmy Fagg, Tom Schmittou and Dave Dempster. They arrived at Beale to begin preliminary training after having successfully completed the tough 'astronaut's medical exam' at Brooks AFB near San Antonio, Texas. Since there were no aircraft at Beale, it was arranged that the ten would undertake a seven-week training course on the SR-71 at the Skunk Works. They would be able to spend their time with key Lockheed engineers including Kelly Johnson and Ben Rich, and would write up lesson plans for a Combat Crew Training School which they would later established at Beale. They would become the instructor cadre to train the other SR-71 crewmembers who would follow[2].

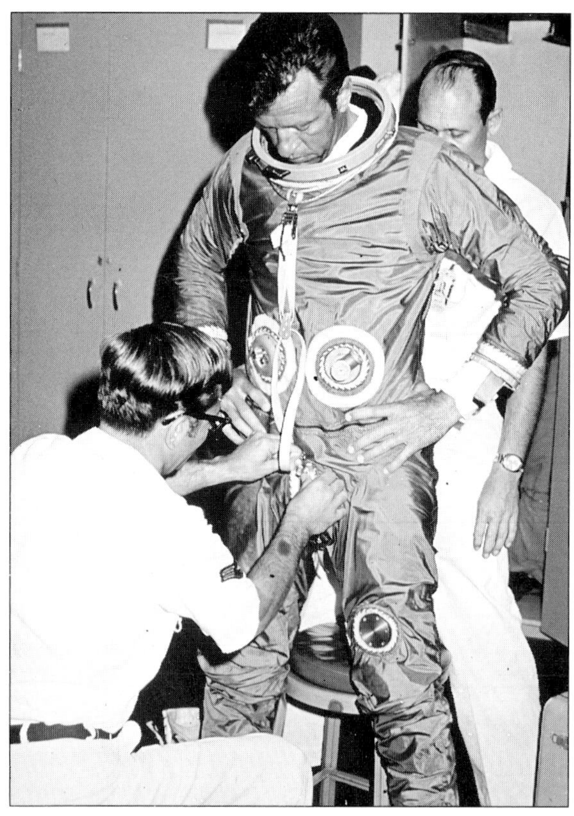

Buddy Brown, who piloted the first SR-71 to Kadena on 8 March 1968 is helped into the inner layer of the S-901J pressure suit (*USAF*)

At the end of the Burbank course, Doug Nelson (who had been monitoring the progress of all ten) called them together for some good and bad news. Some would go to the 'Ranch' for flying training in the 'Tin Goose' (the J75-equipped A-12 trainer) and another crew would go back to Beale to get the flight simulator's programme started and lessons planned for follow-on crew training. Further, he told them that as they were all on a par with one another academically and professionally, he would therefore have to make a purely arbitrary decision based on age. Since John Storrie and Dave Dempster were the youngest, they would return to Beale while the other four crews would get some preliminary flying time at Edwards and Groom Dry Lake prior to returning to Beale.

At the same time many others had applied to join the *Senior Crown* force. At Air Command and Staff College at Montgomery, Alabama, three former SAC

Maj Ben Bowles was among the first crewmembers selected by Col Doug Nelson for the *Senior Crown* programme. He later became the first pilot to log 900 hours on type on 12 April 1972 (*via Ben Bowles*)

select crewmembers who had flown B-47s and B-52s, and one general's aide who had flown B-47s, were selected on orders of CINSAC General Joseph Nazarro who instructed his Director of Personnel, Col Lester Miller to use SAC's best resources to man the new system. Consequently, Maj Jerry O'Malley, Don Walbrecht, Larry DeVall and Capt Connie Seagroves made the early cut without meeting Col Doug Nelson. Since there were no SR-71s at Beale, these early arrivals formed the flying squadron and managed the early activities at unit level (mobile control for T-38 flying, SR-71 simulator buddy-crew instructors, etc). As they had 'jumped the queue' and arrived ahead of all but a few of the B-58 selectees, General DesPortes interceded for his U-2 pilots and assigned them earlier check-out numbers than the B-47/B-52 inputs. As a result, U-2 pilots Pat Halloran and Buddy Brown got precedence as well as test pilots Bill Campbell and Russ Scott. When the final crew list shaped up between late 1965 and early 1966 it read as follows as Russ Scott had dropped out and others had arrived:

Crew 01 – Maj John Storrie (B-58) and Capt Cosimo Mallozzi (B-58)
Crew 02 – Maj Robert Sowers (B-58) and Maj 'Butch' Sheffield (B-58)
Crew 03 – Lt Col Al Hichew (B-58) and Maj Tom Schmittou (B-58)
Crew 04 – Capt Pete Collins (B-58) and Capt Connie Seagroves (B-52)
Crew 05 – Maj Jack Kennon (B-58) and Capt Cecil Braden (B-58)
Crew 06 – Capt Bill Campbell (Test Pilot School) and Capt Al Pennington (B-58)
Crew 07 – Maj Pat Halloran (U-2) and Capt Mort Jarvis (B-52)
Crew 08 – Maj Buddy Brown (U-2) and Capt Dave Jensen (B-52)
Crew 09 – Capt Dale Shelton (B-58) and Capt Larry Boggess (B-58)
Crew 10 – Maj Jerry O'Malley (B-47) and Capt Ed Payne (B-47)
Crew 11 – Maj Don Walbrecht (B-47) and Capt Phil Loignon (B-47)
Crew 12 – Capt Earle Boone (B-58) and Capt Dewain Vick (B-52)
Crew 13 – Capt Tony Bevacqua (U-2) and Capt Jerry Crew (B-52)

In addition, a number of other officers were on hand, or had been identified, for check out positions some time in the future but did not have crew identity until later. These pilots were Jim Watkins (KC-135), Larry DeVall (B-52), Bob Spencer (U-2), Roy St Martin (U-2), George Bull (U-2) and Bob Powell (U-2). The RSOs were Dave Dempster (B-58), Clyde Shoemaker (B-52), Keith Branham (B-52), Bob Locke (B-52), Jim Carnochan (B-58), Bill McNeer (B-52) and Bill Kendrick (B-52).

The first five crews were still at Edwards and 'The Ranch' getting some preliminary flying in T-38s and the A-12 trainer to become the first instructor pilots. Kennon, Braden, Bowles and Fagg stayed on at Edwards with the Test Force.

A typical RSO candidate was Spot Maj Ed Payne at Mountain Home AFB who had applied for the programme. His background was similar to that of most navigator-bombardier/RSO applicants at the time. He had joined the USAF only nine years before and had become a Radar-Bombardier on B-47

The second 9th SRW SR-71 to be lost was 965 which crashed on 25 October 1967 (*Lockheed*)

Stratojets. In 1962 as a 'spot-promoted' captain with the 303rd Bombardment Wing (BW) at Tucson, Arizona, he and his crew had won 10 of 22 trophies at SAC's annual bombing competition. In May of 1964 the 303rd BW deactivated, whereupon Ed was given orders to report to the 92nd BW at Spokane, Washington, which was equipped with B-52s.

'My squadron commander urged me to trade the assignment with another bombardier so we could retain our 'spot' promotions to major a year longer by transferring to Mountain Home, Idaho, where we could continue to fly B-47s. I accepted my bosses' advice and moved to Idaho with the rest of our crew.

'One day at the Standardization Board Office where our crew was assigned as flight evaluators, a young crewmember beamed "I know where I'm going, I know where I'm going!" I looked at a copy of the message which told of the qualifications for entry into a strange programme. I talked over such an assignment with my wife Millie and the next day I completed an application for duty as an RF-101 "pilot". Three weeks later I was notified that I'd been selected for an interview at Beale. The instructions informed me to travel in civilian clothes from Boise Idaho to Yuba City, California. On the final leg of the flight, another passenger asked me if I was Payne, Vick or Jarvis. I admitted my identity, whereupon Larry Boggess introduced himself. "How did you know who I was?", I inquired. "You're wearing a hack watch, Air Force sunglasses, and have a good haircut," replied Larry, "and those two guys up front must be Dewain Vick and Mort Jarvis", he continued.

'The interview at Beale was conducted in an old World War 2 building. A secretary in civilian clothes first called Dewain Vick into the office for the interview. He was followed by Mort Jarvis and me. Larry Boggess was last in that day. When I walked in and saluted I noted that Col Doug Nelson was wearing an orange-coloured flight suit complete with an RF-101 patch. As the tall, slim colonel read through my personal records, he said "welcome to Beale Capt Payne". Looking up he saw my gold majors leaves and apologized for the mistake, to which I replied, "Oh, well Sir, easy come, easy go," referring to the temporary nature of SAC's spot promotions. Col Nelson told me he was indeed hoping for an all-spot team. The interview was very short. Nelson asked a few personal questions, adding "were all RSO applicants 32 years old with five children, as the other two candidates had also been?" He then asked if I would be prepared to fly over enemy territory, to which I replied, "Of course." I was told that I had passed the interview and was "hired" pending passing the physical examination in Texas.'

Back at Mountain Home, Ed received orders to attend a ten-day medical exam at Brooks AFB, Texas in April. Prior to the medical exam he completed a 505-question paper asking all about his previous state of health. Ed recalled that the detail was 'incredible'. One question asked, 'Have you ever worked in or around a silo?' Since he had grown up on a Montana cattle ranch, he answered 'yes' and had to see a specialist at Brooks who checked him over for Silo Fever – a condition that a person working everyday in wheat dust might contract from the poor quality air one would breathe. Ed explained that during a summer vacation from school he had worked as a carpenter's helper repairing a silo, such was the detail of the examination, which was the same as that being used by NASA in their selections for the astronaut programme.

He was given a clean 'bill of health' and returned to Idaho. While he awaited further orders, it was announced that the 9th BW was to deactivate on 1 January 1966. On that date, Ed lost his spot promotion and returned to the rank of captain. He was in contact with Col Nelson at Beale who told Ed

Roy St Martin (below) and John Carnochan both safely ejected from 965 (*USAF*)

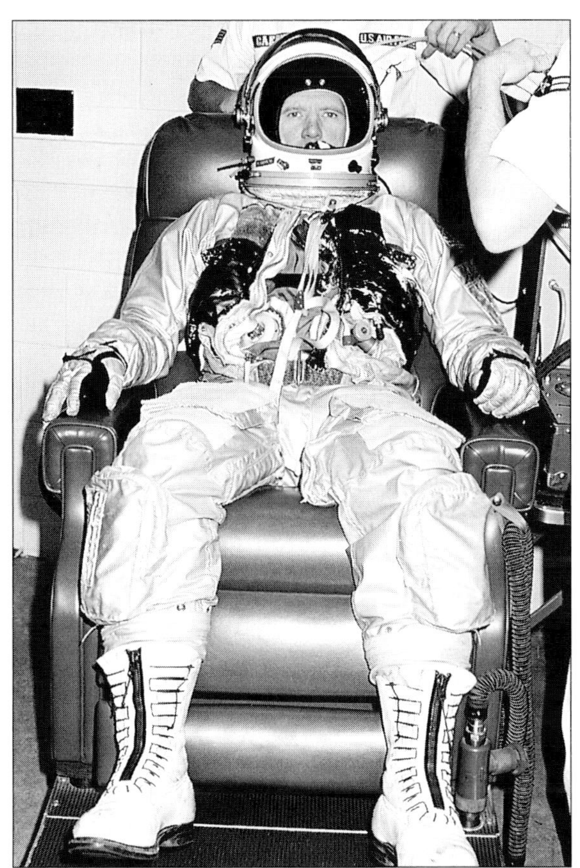

that they had no aircraft to commence the training programme, but that the 4200th SRW was inheriting the 9th BW's 'historical number', which dated from World War 1 and would be called the 9th Strategic Reconnaissance Wing (SRW) after 25 June 1966. On Nelson's instructions, Ed gathered up all of the 9th's heraldic items (pictures, trophies, battle flags, unit histories) and other paraphernalia relating to the wing and its squadrons, the 1st and the 99th, and packaged them for shipment. Another RSO (Capt Connie Seagroves) who was already at Beale came to Mountain Home in a DC-3 to collect the boxed treasures. Ed reported to Beale in April 1966 to team up with Maj Jerry O'Malley who had arrived from Maxwell AFB ten months earlier.

The first two of eight Northrop T-38 Talon trainers arrived at Beale on 7 July 1965. These small and agile white jets (widely used as basic pilot trainers in the Air Training Command) would be used as 'companion trainers' to maintain overall flying proficiency for the SR-71 crews at a fraction of the cost of flying the main aircraft. They were also to be used as 'pace-chase' aircraft to accompany every SR-71 flight during the first year of Beale operations to observe landing gear positions, and to give crew and staff pilots an opportunity to practice formation flying. Because of the T-38's size alongside the SR-71, one of the wives jokingly called the two aircraft 'the horse and the horsefly' when they first appeared together over Beale.

Doug Nelson recalled that the T-38s were obtained only after a long and traumatic battle with SAC headquarters over the companion trainer issue:

'Even though the need for such an aircraft to augment the SR-71 fleet had been clearly demonstrated in the A-12 programme in Nevada, I had some considerable difficulty convincing some of the senior staff people at HQ SAC and at HQ 15th Air Force. I think the argument that finally won them over had to do with the fact that some of these same people had already been expressing the view that I should consider selecting SAC B-52 bomber and KC-135 tanker pilots for entry into the programme, as well as supersonic B-58 pilots, test pilots, U-2 pilots and former fighter pilots. I agreed that this could probably be done, but was really only feasible if they could be put through a 'lead-in' training course conducted by us at Beale in an aircraft such as the T-38. Other alternatives I suggested included the F-5B, F-101F and F-104B. They settled on the T-38 as the obvious choice and went all out to obtain eight of them from Training Command.'

In December 1965, Maj Don Walbrecht flew Lt Col Ray Haupt to Palmdale where Haupt and Charlie Bock (USAF acceptance test pilot at Edwards) picked up SR-71B trainer (64-17957) from Plant 42 and test-delivered it a few miles away at Edwards, where it underwent further acceptance testing before it was ready for delivery to Beale. At 1400 hours on 6 January 1966, Col Nelson and instructor pilot Haupt made the first pass of an SR-71 over Beale to deliver the trainer to SAC's 9th SRW. Soon after, Storrie and Collins would be able to finish their pilot checkouts. Four months later Col Nelson and Maj Al Pennington took delivery of Beale's first SR-71A, number 64–17958. From then on, crew training and Category III Operational Testing could proceed in earnest.

SR-71 Losses

On 25 January 1966, Bill Weaver and Jim Zwayer took off from Edwards in SR-71A 952. Both were Lockheed test-flight employees[3]. The two main objectives of their flight were to evaluate navigation and reconnaissance systems, and to investigate procedures for improving high Mach cruise performance by reducing trim drag. This research required that the centre-of-gravity (CG) be moved further aft than normal to compensate for the rearward shift of the centre-of-pressure at high Mach. After in-flight refuelling, 'Dutch 64' climbed back to cruising altitude. While the aircraft was in a thirty degree bank to the right at approximately 80,000 ft and at a speed of Mach 3.1, an inlet scheduling malfunction occurred followed by an unstart of the right engine. The cumulative effect of the inlet malfunctions, CG configuration, speed, altitude and attitude resulted in pitching and yawing forces that exceeded the restorative authority of the flight controls and the SAS. This combination of rapid out-of-control actions led to the break-up of the aircraft, with the entire forebody becoming detached from the main body.

As soon as it became apparent that the situation was hopeless, Bill tried to tell Jim what was happening and to try to remain in the cockpit until they were down to a lower speed and altitude, since he did not think it would be possible to eject successfully under such stressful conditions. Unfortunately, as revealed upon subsequent recovery of the cockpit voice recorder, most of Bill's words were unintelligible due to the incredibly high G forces that both men were being subjected to at the time. At that point, Bill blacked out and to this day he still does not know how he escaped. Indeed, his ejector seat was found still inside the cockpit section of the wreckage.

During the break-up of the aircraft, the cockpit canopies were blown off and a combination of g forces and air loads had blown both men clear as Bill later explained:

'I thought I was having a bad dream and hoped that I would wake up and all this would go away. However, as I began to regain consciousness, I realized it was not a dream and that this had really happened. At that point, I thought I was dead because I was convinced that I could not have survived what had happened. I remember thinking that being dead wasn't so bad after all. I had a kind of a detached, euphoric feeling. As I became more conscious, I realized I wasn't dead after all, and that I had somehow became separated from the aircraft. I couldn't see anything as my visor had iced up.

'My pressure suit had inflated, so I knew the emergency oxygen supply in the seat kit attached to my parachute harness was functioning. This source provided breathing oxygen and pressurization essential at those altitudes, and physical protection against the intense buffeting and G forces I had been subjected to. It was like being in one's own life support capsule. After realizing that I wasn't dead and that I was free of the aircraft, I was concerned about stability and not tumbling at such high altitude. Centrifugal forces sufficient to cause physical damage can be generated if the body tumbles at high altitude where there is little air density to resist spinning motions. Fortunately, the small stabilization 'chute designed to prevent tumbling had worked fine.

'My next concern was the main 'chute – would the barometric automatic opening device work at 15,000 ft? I certainly hadn't made a proper exit – I knew I had not initiated the ejection procedure. How long had I been blacked out and how high was I? I was about to open the face plate so I could estimate my altitude above the terrain and locate my parachute's 'D' ring. At that moment, I felt the sharp, reassurring tug which indicated that the main 'chute had deployed. This action was a very reassuring feeling, believe me. I then managed to raise my face plate and noted that the visibility was just incredible. It was a clear winter's day at about three o'clock in the afternoon, and from my vantage point beneath the parachute canopy it appeared that I could see for a couple of hundred miles. But what made everything just perfect was that about a quarter of a mile away was Jim's 'chute. I

The 9th SRW lost half of its SR-71Bs when 'Gray' Sowers and Dave Fruehauf 'punched-out' of 957 on 11 January 1968 (*Appeal-Democrat*)

was delighted because I didn't believe either of us could have survived, and to think that Jim had also made it gave me an incredible lift.

'I couldn't manipulate the risers to steer my 'chute because my hands were frozen and I needed one hand to keep my iced-up visor raised (the up-latch was broken). As a result, I could only see in one direction and the terrain wasn't all that inviting. I was convinced we'd have to spend at least the night out there and I was trying to think of things I had been taught in survival training. I landed okay and was trying to undo my parachute harness when I heard a voice say, "Can I help you"? I looked up and there was a guy walking towards me wearing a cowboy hat and behind him was a helicopter. He turned out to be Albert Mitchell, whom I learned later owned a huge cattle ranch in Northeast New Mexico upon which I had landed. He helped me out of the 'chute, told me he had radioed the police, the Air Force, and the nearest hospital and then said, "I saw your buddy coming down, I'll go and help him".

'He climbed into his little helicopter and was back a few minutes later with the devastating news that Jim was dead. I asked him to take me over to see Jim and after verifying that there was nothing that could be done, other than have his ranch foreman watch over the body until authorities arrived, he flew me to Tucumcari hospital about 60 miles away to the south. I have vivid memories of that flight, as well. I didn't know much about helicopters, but I knew a lot about red lines, and the airspeed needle was above the red line all the way to Tucumcari. I thought about the possibility of that little thing shaking itself apart in flight and how ironic it would be to have miraculously survived the previous disaster only to be finished off in the helicopter that had come to my rescue! We made it without mishap and on reaching the hosptial I was able to phone Lockheed Flight Test at Edwards. They knew the aircraft had been lost, after loss of all radio and radar contact, and just didn't believe that I had survived.'

The solution to reducing the excessive trim drag problem was to move the centre of lift forward, thus reducing static margin and trim drag. This was achieved by Kelly inserting a 'wedge' between the aircraft's forward fuselage and its nose section. The result was the distinctive two-degree nose-up tilt.

During the closing stages of 1966 the SR-71 underwent a series of anti-skid brake trials. Bill Weaver conducted most of these tests and on 10 January 1967 was due to evaluate the system with the aircraft at maximum gross weight. By a twist of fate, he was unable to conduct this particular test because of the funeral of his friend Walt Ray who had been killed a few days earlier in an A-12 accident. Art Peterson was substituting and the RSO position remained empty. Entering a flooded test area of the Edwards runway at well over 200 knots, the brake 'chute failed to deploy properly.

Wheel brakes remained ineffective until the aircraft had cleared the test area. Once on a dry surface, the brakes locked the wheels and all six main tyres blew. As momentum carried the aircraft onward, the brakes burned out and the magnesium wheel hubs were consumed on the concrete runway which triggered an even greater fire. Peterson skilfully retained control of the stricken aircraft until he ran out of runway (although riding on the main gear stumps). On the overrun one of the main gear legs dug into the dry lake bed, causing side forces to rip the nosewheel leg off. This sudden breakage simultaneously stopped the aircraft and broke its back. Fire quickly spread to engulf the entire aircraft but Peterson managed to extract himself from the cockpit, sustaining back injuries which would ground him for several weeks in the process. It was the end of the line for the SR-71 prototype, Article 2001 (64-17950), which was written off as 'beyond repair'.

In mid-1966 Bill Skliar left the A-12 programme to become Chief of Operations for the SR-71 test force at Edwards. On 11 April 1969, Lt Col Skliar and Maj Noel Warner lined up SR-71A 64-17954 on runway 04 at Edwards and began a maximum gross weight take-off. 'Dutch 69' had just rotated when one of the left main gear tyres blew. Unable to support the additional weight on the two remaining tyres, they also deflated. Immediately Bill aborted the take-off, but the burning shrapnel from the disintegrating magnesium wheel hubs caused a fire which rapidly engulfed the entire aircraft. He managed to retain control of the aircraft and brought it to a halt on the runway. The worst of the fire was along the left side because a breeze kept the right side relatively clear; Skliar exited to the right and then assisted Warner from the rear cockpit as the fire began to billow all around them. Fortunately, both crew members survived but 954 never flew again. After this incident all SR-71s had their wheels replaced with less combustible aluminium units, and B F Goodrich beefed up the high-speed, 239 knot-rated tyres.

Pitch-Up Accident

On 18 December 1969, Director of the Test Force Lt Col Joe Rogers (an experienced test pilot with more than 200 hours on the SR-71) and RSO Lt Col Gary Heidelbaugh were scheduled to fly 64-17953 on a routine test sortie. The aircraft had been undergoing extensive modifications to install a new electronic countermeasures system, and this would be its first flight for many weeks. After completing air refuelling, Rogers initiated a pre-planned acceleration and climb. Soon after transitioning to supersonic flight, the crew of 'Dutch 68' experienced an explosion accompanied by a loss of power and severe control difficulties. As the aircraft decelerated, its angle of attack continued to increase despite Joe pushing the control stick 'hard against the firewall'. After slowing to a subsonic speed, the fully-fuelled aircraft was increasingly less controllable and both crewmembers realised that 953 had entered an irrecoverable corner of the flight envelope. Ten seconds after the explosion, Rogers knew it was time to go and ordered, 'Let's get out Gary!' Both men safely ejected while the aircraft (in a deep stall) entered 'pitch-up' from which it was impossible to regain controlled flight. Soon after, 953 made its crater-grave near the southern end of Death Valley. The cause of the explosion remains unknown.

Abe Kardong and Jim Kogler had a narrow escape when 977 had a wheel failure and spectacular take-off fire at Beale on 10 October 1968 (*Appeal-Democrat*)

Training and Category III Testing

Training techniques changed little over the 25 years of the SR-71's useful lifespan. The aircrew curriculum consisted of three phases of progressive activity which readied pilots and RSOs for the move from a variety of other jets into the highest performance aeroplane in the world. At first, crewmembers accumulated many hours in the flight simulator before beginning their inflight training[4]. The pilots, after completing the elongated simulator course, during which they had endured every conceivable emergency procedure and many T-38 flying hours, were then introduced to the SR-71B, which they all recognised as 'friendly'. The B-58 pilots found it particularly easy to fly. Most other aircrew also found that flying the SR-71B was simply an extension of their former jet flying, no matter what principal type they had flown. The new pilots (under the supervision of Haupt or Hichew) found that the first sortie flown in the SR-71B (957) was 'tame', and it proved both easy to fly and land.

The first training sortie was accomplished at

RESCUE
CANOPY JETTISON
1. PUSH BUTTON TO OPEN DOOR
2. PULL "T" HANDLE OUT 9FT
RESCUE
EMERGENCY
CANOPY ENTRANCE
1. FIRST USE CANOPY JETTISON
2. IF JETTISON FAILS
USE CANOPY LATCH UNLOCKER

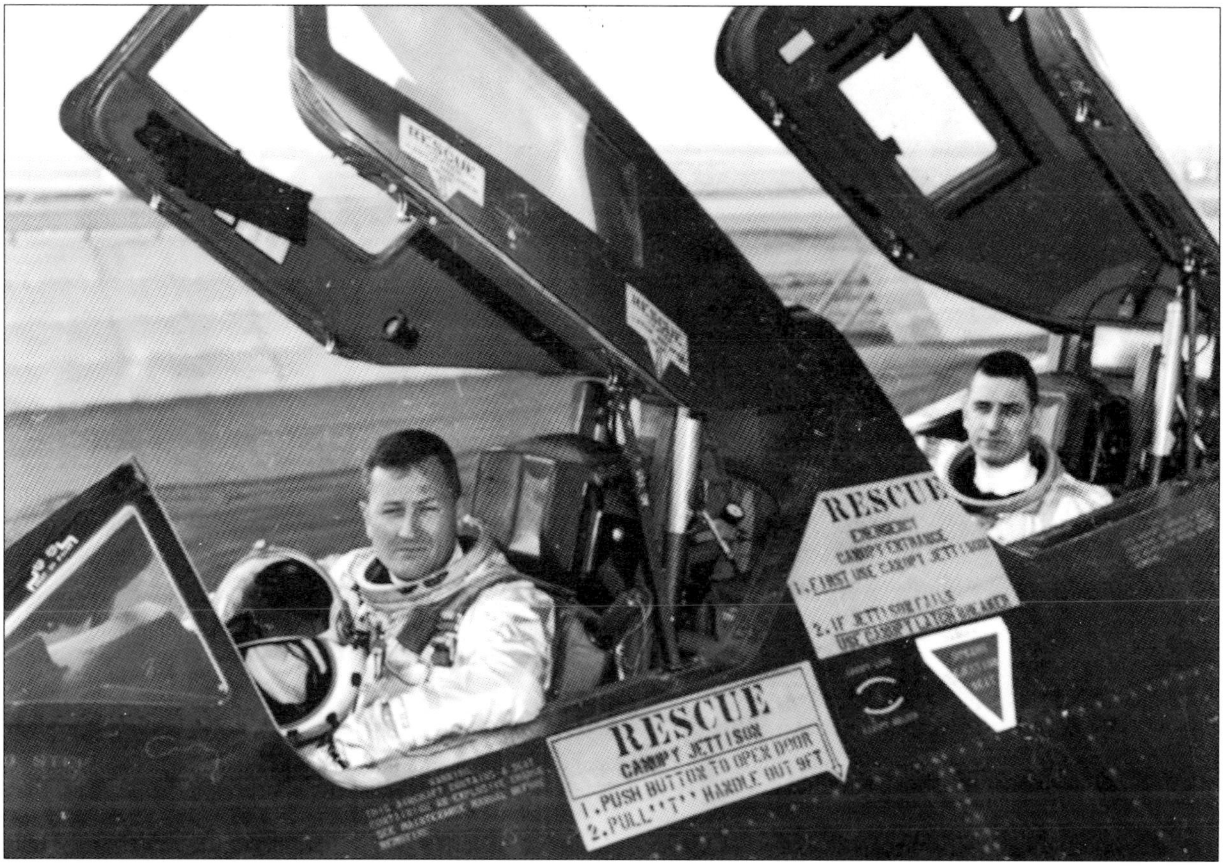

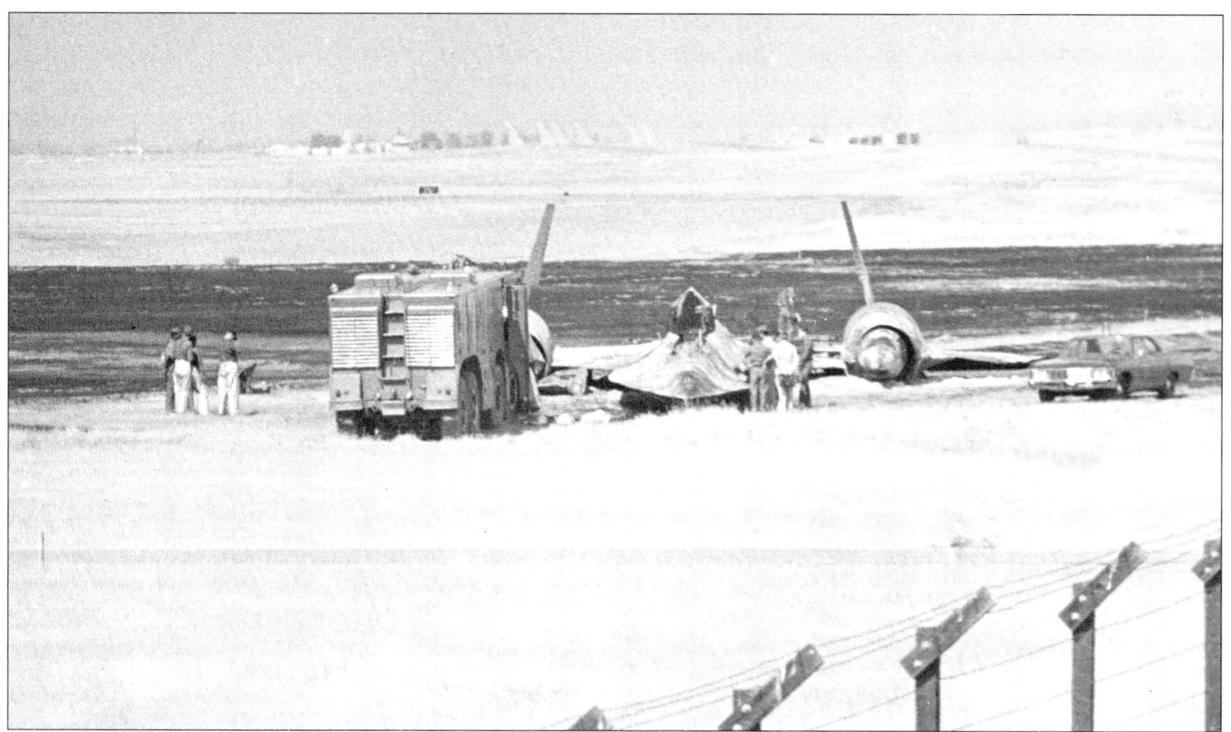

subsonic speeds under the supervision of an instructor pilot, who evaluated the new pilot's 'first performance'. Such a 'first flight' included 20 minutes of air refuelling practice as well as instrument approaches and landings. The indoctrination flight included additional touch-and-go landings and confidence-building manoeuvres which soon made the aircraft feel like an 'old friend'. Two other three-hour instructor-supervised sorties followed, which consisted of more air refuelling practice and an acceleration to Mach 3.0 and a descent and approach culminating in GCAs, ILSs and more landings. The fourth flight was a night sortie with air refuelling, acceleration to Mach 2.8 and four night landings. The fifth flight was a three-hour evaluation sortie which reviewed the students' total performance to assure that the pilots were ready to take their own simulator-trained RSOs on six more crew training sorties before both crewmembers could be declared 'qualified'[5]. Sorties lasted between three to five hours, and consisted of 'combat-oriented' missions which included emergency navigation legs at Mach 3.0 to demonstrate that large errors could develop unless headings were held for long distances.

The crew then undertook a simulator check ride. This 'no holds barred' evaluation tested the crew's ability to control serious inflight emergencies which involved flight judgment and crew co-ordination of high standards. A few days later, the crew flew a long inflight profile after which instructors reviewed every voice transmission made during the mission, and the MRS record of flight; their ability to fly a mission profile 'to the letter' was evaluated by the use of the latter device[6]. When the crews were declared 'combat ready', they then continued 'clocking-up' more hours by performing Category III (Operational) flight tests.

During operational testing, two major areas of concern were focused upon: the aircraft's inlet control system, and the effects of prolonged heat soaks during high-speed flight. The inlet control system was complex, and fault-free operation depended upon accurate sensing of many different parameters of air flow, shock wave position, spike position, bypass door position and aircraft attitude (pitch and yaw), and engine nozzle position. Due to the hydro-mechanical nature of the inlet control system, it became apparent that problems were arising with the analogue inlet sensor's inability to process data fast enough to trim or bias the signals responsible for triggering various actuators when in the normal automatic mode of inlet operation. Since the crews were often subjected to sharp and distracting unstarts, an immediate solution to the problem was to operate the inlet system in the manual mode, with the pilot controlling the spike and door positions with manual switches while reading their changing positions on cockpit indicator instruments. Such manual operations took up an undue amount of the pilot's attention at high speed and resulted in 'off-optimum' inlet operations. Though less effecient, this manual control often allowed new flyers to complete more training missions and accumulate data for the Phase III testing programme[7].

Sustained high-speed flight caused the airframe to undergo prolonged high-temperature heat soaks. Repeated expansion and shrinkage caused the silicone fuel tank sealant to diminish and crack, causing many leaks. This phenomenon was especially apparent when the aircraft was fully fuelled because most of the leaks appeared on the topside of the tanks, which became hotter and drier during high-Mach flight. As a consequence, it was necessary to perform routine resealing and extensive depot-level fuel tank maintenance when an SR-71 was returned to Palmdale (the old sealant was usually stripped away and replaced). It was a problem that remained with the aircraft throughout its operational life.

Heat was also responsible for electrical systems problems, especially in the high-output generators. Heat-related generator failures caused many air aborts during the first two years of training and Category III testing. After the loss of SR-71B 957 to a double-generator failure on 11 January 1968, a single generator failure was flagged as a mandatory abort item which meant 'land as soon as possible'. Over the next year, SR-71s with generator failures landed at bases across the US. Various modifications were tried before the problem was finally isolated.

SR-71s were not 'cleared' for top speeds during Cat III test flight training for most of 1966, an initial restriction speed of Mach 2.6 being applied. By mid-year the limit was raised to Mach 2.8, and by December Mach 3.0 was allowed. Finally, in early 1967 all aircraft were cleared to fly at the design limit of Mach 3.2. Since SAC allowed its wing commanders to be fully qualified in their unit's aircraft, Col Doug Nelson teamed up with senior staff RSO, Col Russ Lewis and formed 'Staff Crew

Number One'. They undertook the full aircrew course at Beale, completing their certification in September 1966. Soon after they flew SAC's first-ever Mach 3.0 flight.

As training began in earnest around the western US, the Air Force began receiving lots of sonic boom complaints. Most of the heavy booms were attributed to operations in the ascent and descent phases when the SR-71 accelerated or slowed. The 'nuisance factor', rather than real damage, caused Congress to instruct the USAF to modify its training routes to avoid flying over large urban areas. The township of Susanville situated just north of Beale on the 006 degree radial of the Sacramento VOR-TACAN, knew a great deal about sonic booms. During the first 18 months of flight operations, the SR-71s were cleared by the FAA flight controllers to accelerate and climb supersonically on that radial. On reaching FL 330 and Mach 0.90, the pilot would push the nose below the horizon to quickly accelerate beyond the Mach while descending to FL 270 before starting another climb at Mach 1.25. The intensity of a sonic boom is dependent upon the slant range from the aircraft to the ground along the shockwave – consequently, poor Susanville, which nestled high in the Sierra Nevada foothills, was taking a real hammering.

Prolonged flights in a full pressure suit could be uncomfortable, especially with a full bladder. For this reason a Urine Collection Device (UCD) was developed for a 'suit-dry' method of eliminating excess body fluids. The urine could be discharged into a condom-like receptacle that was tube-connected to a plastic collector bag which was donned prior to suiting-up. One crewmember described his pre-UCD inflight urination experience in the following terms: 'Wearing pressure-suit gloves, undoing several zippers and fighting through four inches of pressure suit wasn't easy'. Maj Dave Dempster was on a three-hour training sortie in April 1966 in 958 with Maj John Storrie when he was confronted with a full-bladder problem. His S-901J pressure suit had not yet arrived from the Clark Company and he had borrowed a suit from a similarly tall colleague. The demands of nature had become irresistable and Dave mentioned this unpleasant fact to John. Most crewmembers were very reluctant to use the 'jug' because (unlike the later UCD), suit integrity was not maintained and bloodstream re-nitrogenation was likely. John, after devoting some thought to Dave's problem, said 'Well, the way I see it, you can either hold it or let it go in your suit – by the way whose suit are you wearing?' Dave replied, 'Col Nelson's'. That thought provided him with all the encouragement he needed to wait until he landed!

Another wheel failure caused 954 to be lost following an aborted take-off from Edwards AFB. Lt Col Bill Skliar and his RSO Noel Warner both managed to escape from a fire which encircled the crippled aircraft (*Lockheed*)

The first two years of operating the SR-71 at Beale were crammed full of training and testing activity. More and more crews were building up flying time and testing the aircraft's ability to do its intended mission. In November 1966, Capts Earl Boone and Dewain Vick climbed into 966 for their first flight together. Their families were proudly witnessing the event from the PSD van. They had just cranked engines when one caught alight and fire engines converged on the 'hangar barn' from all points of the compass. The crew evacuated the aeroplane and the fire was quickly extinguished with minor damage to the aircraft, whereupon Earle and Dewain transferred to another SR-71 and were able to complete their sortie together. Similar aircraft switches allowed the crew members to get airborne on their day – other problems caused the loss of up to 20 per cent of the early training sorties.

Precautionary landings away from Beale were also frequent during this early period. Typical of many diversions were those of Jerry O'Malley and Ed Payne who landed at Hill AFB, Utah, with a generator problem, and then recovered the very same aircraft into Buckley Field, Colorado, a week later with the opposite generator inoperable. A few weeks later they lost a piece of the aircraft shortly after take-off. The fillet was found by a resident near Beale, who turned it over to the county sheriff, who in turn passed the nine-foot length of black aircraft skin back to the 9th SRW. Base officials identified the missing part as belonging to Jerry and Ed's aircraft. As Jerry prepared to refuel near Walton Beach, Florida, he was asked to pull farther forward so the KC-135 crew could look at the rear of his aircraft. The boomer had reported that 'the ass-end of the airplane was missing'. Since the aircraft had just transitted the US without the slightest indication of a problem, and the boomer had relayed to the crew that 'the panel appeared to merely cover some plumbing', Jerry refuelled with the intention of returning to Beale 'high and hot'. Ed reported the crews intentions via HF radio to the Beale Command Post, whose officer controller passed the information on to HQ 15th Air Force and SAC. In return, Ed got a return call from the 15th Air Force Command Post instructing him to divert into Barksdale AFB, Louisiana – this order was not queried as it came from Lt Gen P K Carlton, Commander of 15th Air Force, himself!

Jerry landed on the southern end of Barksdale's long runway, jettisoned the drag 'chute at 50 knots and switched off the anti-skid brakes, as per the checklist. At that point, the SR-71 entered a one-inch deep rain puddle and slewed into a sideways skid down the runway. As the aircraft exited the hydroplaning skid and touched dry runway, all six tyres blew. It was three days before Jerry and Ed could return to Beale. When they suited up for the flight home, PSD technicians accidentally inter-changed their 'moon suit' helmets, which in turn caused acute discomfort to Jerry on the four hour slow-flight back to northern California.

First Beale Accident

On 13 April 1967, Capts Earle Boone and Dewain Vick were scheduled to fly their ninth training sortie, a night flight which included air refuelling and a Mach 2.8 run over the Southern United States. During the preflight medical exam it was discovered that Vick had a cold which precluded him from clearing his middle ear pressure because of a swollen eustachian tube. As a consequence, the flight surgeon grounded Dewain, and 'Butch' Sheffield, the buddy-crew RSO, was substituted. It would turn out to be a very long night for the two fliers. After completing air refuelling near El Paso, Texas, Earle (an experienced B-58 pilot) decided to turn after leaving the tanker to avoid a thunderstorm which lay ahead on their planned track. Earle had started a subsonic climb to perform the 'dipsy-doodle' maneouvre to hasten the transonic breakthrough, but during the climb with a fully-fuelled aircraft, the airspeed fell below the desired 0.90 Mach profile. To regain lost momentum, Earle lowered the nose of the aircraft below level flight, but when he pulled the stick back, the heavy jet shuddered in an accelerated stall. He fought hard to regain control of 966 but its angle-of-attack became uncontrollable and it suddenly entered a pitch-up rotation from which there was no recovery. Both crew members ejected from the aircraft, which had broken in half and had spewed a great shroud of fuel around them. Since Butch ejected first, his ejection-seat rocket ignited the fuel-rich shroud into a fireball, through which Earle ejected a second behind the RSO.

The New Mexico surface winds were gusting at up to 40 knots when the pilot and RSO hit terrafirma, their wild ride across the desert floor eventually ending in a cattleman's barbed-wire fence more than a half a mile from initial touch-

Joe Rogers and Garry Heidlebaugh ejected from 953 following an inflight explosion on 18 December 1969. Both escaped uninjured (*Lockheed*)

down. Neither was seriously injured; although for the next few days Earle had blisters along the back of eight fingers[8], and both crew members suffered from considerable bruising and stiffness as a result of their night para-sail ride across a part of New Mexico not too far from the site of Bill Weaver's crash in 952.

A great deal was learnt from this accident, which was largely attributable to the pilot 'trying to do too much to soon' in an aircraft which was still being tested. Similar flight conditions were reflown in the SR-71 flight simulator by the other crews, and it was found that heavyweight accelerated stalls would be extremely difficult to recover from, and that secondary stalls could induced the dreaded pitch-up phenomenon, particularly at night or in clouds. SAC also began to realize that night training was being undertaken too early in SR-71 transition training. At the same time, it was decided that all flights, including subsonic movements, should be in pressure suits for improved aircrew protection. Eventually the Automatic Pitch Warning (APW) system was added. This device was far superior to the original system, and following its installation no further aircraft were lost through stalls.

A serious incident, which could very easily have resulted in an aircraft being lost was experienced by Maj Bob Spencer and Capt Keith Branham as they approached the Great Salt Lake on their return to Beale. Bob Spencer began feeling unwell, and before he was aware of the nature of his problem, he started to hyperventilate. In his reduced state of consciousness, Spencer realized that his oxygen supply had somehow been cut off so he yanked the 'green apple' oxygen flow-starter knob on his emergency oxygen supply in his parachute's survival seat pack, which unfortunately fed into the same supply lines through which the aircraft main oxygen flowed. Since he was 'hot and high' he realised that he was getting into deep trouble. The oxygen connections were located low on the right side of the ejection seat but were out of reach. Fortunately the SR-71's cockpit was pressured to 26,000 ft which left the major groggy and suffering from narrowed vision (at a pressure altitude higher than most mountains in the world). Suffering now from hypoxia, he told Keith that he was having some oxygen problems and might need some advice to better control a ragged descent. At that point, he reduced power and adjusted the pitch attitude on his autopilot. As the aircraft began to exceed the KEAS and Mach limits during descent, Bob grunted to open his 'gun-barrel' vision in an attempt to read the TDI instrument, which displayed Mach, KEAS and altitude. For the next ten minutes Keith shouted instructions to Bob to keep him from exceeding the dangerous low or high speed limits which could result in loss of control.

Fortunately, Bob and Keith brought the aircraft down to 15,000 ft, where Bob snapped out of his condition, or so he thought. He 'felt so good' from the raptures of hypoxia that he convinced Keith that there was no need to divert into Hill AFB at Ogden, Utah. After Keith computed that they had enough fuel to reach Beale at Mach 0.90, Bob headed for California. Halfway home the right engine flamed out. Bob looked at the fuel pressure warning light, which had not illuminated, indicating that the flameout was not due to fuel mis-management. He tried unsuccessfully to restart the engine, which left them in a less fuel-efficient condition since the rate of fuel use on one engine was much higher than normal. At that point they called the Beale Command Post, whose controller ordered a tanker to be scrambled to meet them over Nevada. Twenty-five minutes later, the tanker approached the rendezvous point, but initiated the 180 degree join-up turn much too late, and Bob and Keith saw their much-needed supply of JP7 fly straight past them. To rejoin with the tanker, which was now well in trail, would use even more of their precious fuel and they could not risk this. Luck was on their side however, and they recovered at Beale with little fuel left aboard.

The next day Bob and Keith listened to the voice recording and the 'read out' from their MRS. In his hypoxic state, Bob had been left incredulous to the predicament they faced, and he was stunned to hear his voice recordings. He realised how the lack of oxygen had made his responses sound absurd and he began to wonder if the flame-out had also been self-induced due to his mismanagement – that flight was a stark lesson in the dangers of hypoxia. The aeroplane's oxygen system was quickly modified so the primary and emergency oxygen supplies were independently routed to the crewmembers.

Russ Scott, a fighter pilot who had been an Air Force Test Pilot School graduate and a Gemini Astronaut candidate prior to being eliminated due to his excessive height, became impatient with the slow progression of SR-71 pilot checkouts, and requested a move to the remnant A-12/F-12 programme. After an *Oxcart* checkout, he flew the YF-12 briefly then joined Ling Tempco Vought as an A-7 production test pilot. Later he became 'Mister F-20 Tigershark' for Northrop. His departure from Beale in 1966 altered the crew line-up. John Storrie was then teamed up with 'Coz' Mallozzi since they had flown together in B-58s. Dave Dempster 'inherited' a pilot who had been recruited from the tanker squadron into the 1st Strategic Reconnaissance Squadrons staff as 'Ops Officer'. Jim Watkins[9] had been with Beale's 903rd ARS flying KC-135Qs, where he had received all the security clearances to deal with the Oxcart programme. Due to his progressing years, master joke-teller Jim took a lot of good-natured ribbing from his younger squadron colleagues, occasionally wearing a World War 2 leather flying helmet to reinforce the 'old pilot' image.

Jim Watkins and Dave Dempster flew their first SR-71 sortie together in 959 on 21 February 1967. As they progressed in their training, they flew weekly sorties including a 'Kitty Three' training sortie in 972 on 2 July 1967. The mission plan called for them to head east on a standard refuelling course across northern Nevada, accelerate east over Idaho and Wyoming and turn south to Texas, west over New Mexico to make a photo run on San Diego, and north past San Francisco before returning to Beale. On the eastbound leg over Wyoming, their ANS failed, and should have resulted in an abort of the 'high and hot' portion of the flight and a subsonic return to base via airway routes. Since they were aware that the *Senior Crown* reconnaissance programme would soon be moving to cover the Vietnam War, Jim and Dave were reluctant to lose an opportunity of flying a 'hot leg', especially when they had the chance to attempt emergency navigation training while being backed up by the stateside VORTAC radio navigation system, which told them where they were along the route. They reasoned that should their ANS failure occur when crossing the Pacific, they would have to continue 'at speed' because of fuel considerations.

Consequently, they continued to Mach 3.0 and cruise altitude using the aircraft's Attitude Heading Reference System, its compass systems and ground-

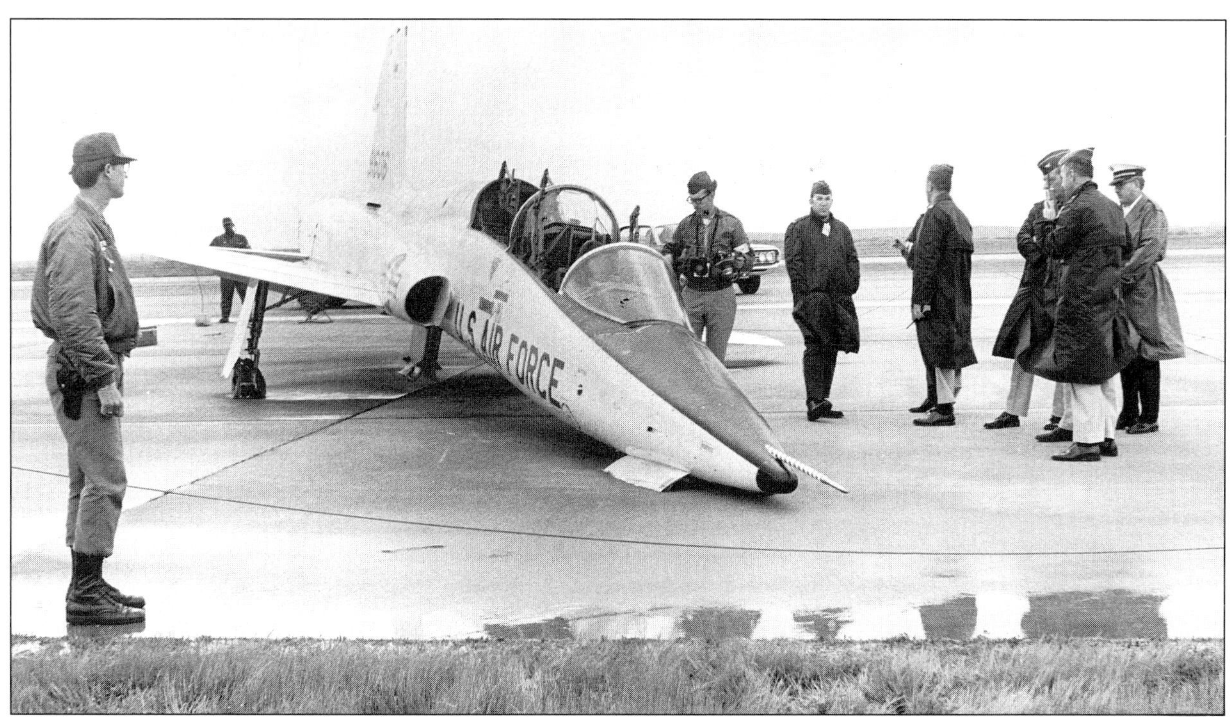

T-38 Talon 91606 was lost at Beale on 23 March 1971, when its elevator controls failed on take-off. Maj Jim Hudson, an SR-71 pilot, was killed when he ejected too low for his parachute to fully deploy. Lt Col Jack Thornton stayed with the uncontrollable aircraft, sustaining back injuries (*Appeal-Democrat*)

based TACAN transmissions for heading and location references. Whilst 'whistling along at Mach 3.0', they failed to note the precession in their magnetic compass, and when ATC at Tucson, Arizona, said: 'Aspen 21, you are now leaving the state', they did not understand the significance of the message. It was not until Dave checked their position using TACAN and the ground viewsight that he realized they had left Arizona, and violated Mexican airspace. Instead of their tracking camera showing images of San Diego's harbour, it featured photographs of Ensenada, Mexico. After a 'chewing out' by 9th SRW officials for violating the GO-No GO checklist, they joked that they were the first to fly an SR-71 on an 'international sortie'. Before long all crews were instructed to practice a transcontinental 'emergency navigation leg' when returning across the middle of the US.

Ten days later, Jim and Dave were airborne in 972 on a routine sortie that was typical of the flights being performed at that stage in the SR-71's development. They had climbed north from Beale into Washington and descended into Montana for refuelling. While climbing back to high altitude there was a loud bang as the left engine unstarted. The aircraft yawed hard into the 'dead' inlet but the SAS and autopilot 'kicked in' right rudder to maintain track. The unstart was so strong and the yaw angle so great that the right inlet unstarted and the engine compressor stalled. Jim fought to maintain control as 972 suffered repeated unstarts and began a descent which finally ended in stable flight at 29,000 ft. When 972 returned to Beale, inlet technicians found that the Linear Voltage Transducer within the left spike had suffered a 'hard-over' failure, and was not reacting to voltage signals from the analogue automatic inlet control system. At the time of the first unstart, the left spike had moved forward during the re-capture cycle and remained extended, rendering shock wave re-capture impossible. In the squadron's flight lounge such experiences were shared as 'things to watch-out for' when flying this still-to-be-proven aeroplane.

Another Loss

On the night of 25 October 1967, a black-tie dinner was being held at the Beale Officers' Club with Kelly

Johnson as the guest of honour. At the same time, Maj Roy St Martin and Capt John Carnochan were flying a night training sortie which included a Mach 2.8 run back towards Beale. As Roy eased 965 into the descent profile over central Nevada, the gyro-stabilised reference platform for the ANS drifted without a failure warning. Since that system provided attitude reference signals to the primary flight instruments and guidance signals to the autopilot, the aircraft entered an increasing right bank while the Flight Director and Attitude Director Indicator instruments showed no deviation from wings-level flight. There was no visible horizon at high altitude over Nevada at 2025 hours in the late fall, and the few scattered ground lights merged easily with the stars as night background. An emergency reference, the miniature standby artificial horizon instrument, which used an independent gyro, was working properly but was poorly located well down on the instrument panel, so the pilot did not note the increasing bank.

As the aircraft rolled over from its stable high-Mach run the nose began to fall far below a safe descent angle. The SR-71 quickly plunged below 60,000 ft. The crew first sensed that something was wrong when the speed increased despite the aircraft's supposedly wings-level, slightly nose down attitude as displayed on the flight instruments. At that point, Roy glanced at his standby horizon, which indicated a 'screaming dive and a roll-over toward inverted flight'. He quickly attempted a 'recovery from unusual positions maneouvre', which had been part of normal instrument training throughout his 12 years of flying, but the nose had progressed so low and the speed had built up to the point where the aircraft was unrecoverable, even though they were still 40,000 ft above Nevada.

Although Roy had pulled the throttles to idle and had rolled the wings level toward what would have been the nearest horizon, the aircraft was in a terminal dive well above the speed from which level flight could be achieved without straining 965 to the breaking point. With no options for recovery left, Roy gave the bailout order. The RSO ejected into the full force of a Mach 1.4 slipstream from which he suffered severe strains. Just before he pulled his between-the-knees bailout ring, Roy heard a warning horn blow which told him that he was below 10,000 ft (with the landing gear up) and descending at a very high speed.

Tugging on his ejection ring, the pilot escaped at a tremendous rate of descent. Exactly as programmed, his automatic escape sequence operated. The lap belt separated, the 'Butt-Snapper' strap in his seat tightened to fling him free of the seat, and the parachute's explosive slug fired it to full length, his canopy deploying just prior to landing at a terrain altitude above 5000 ft. While the ejection sequence was occurring, 965 plunged into the ground near Lovelock, Nevada, like a hypervelocity meteorite creating a ring crater at its point of impact. In a blinding flash almost all traces of the aircraft disappeared deep into the ground.

Luckily both crewmembers survived without permanent injuries, although John was grounded for a year as a result of severe head concussion. Roy remembered walking for what seemed like the rest of the night toward the crash site. Meanwhile, Beale's formal dinner had been disrupted with the discovery that Roy and John were missing somewhere over Nevada. Reports soon came in from Oakland Center and from Lovelock that an aeroplane had crashed. A search effort was quickly mounted and the crew were recovered at first light.

The accident board established that pilot error was not a factor in the loss of 965, and recommended the following design and procedural changes: (1) warning lights be provided to show ANS failure; (2) the standby attitude indicator instrument be enlarged and placed atop the pilot's instrument panel directly below the front windscreen; (3) the pilot and RSO's attitude instruments be powered by different sources[10], and (4) the training programme contain less night flying until crews had considerably more daytime experience in the SR-71.

Preparations for Operational Deployment

As the 9th SRW approached the time for overseas deployment, much talk in the crew lounge was devoted to anti-SAM tactics. The plan was to penetrate enemy airspace at Mach 3. If fired upon, the pilot would increase speed to Mach 3.2 and climb, thereby forcing the missile's guidance system to recalculate the intercept equation. Some crews considered other 'jinking' options, but such maneouvres were discounted as they would only disrupt effective intelligence gathering. One 'half-baked' consideration was to dump fuel to become lighter for a more rapid climb, but Watkins and

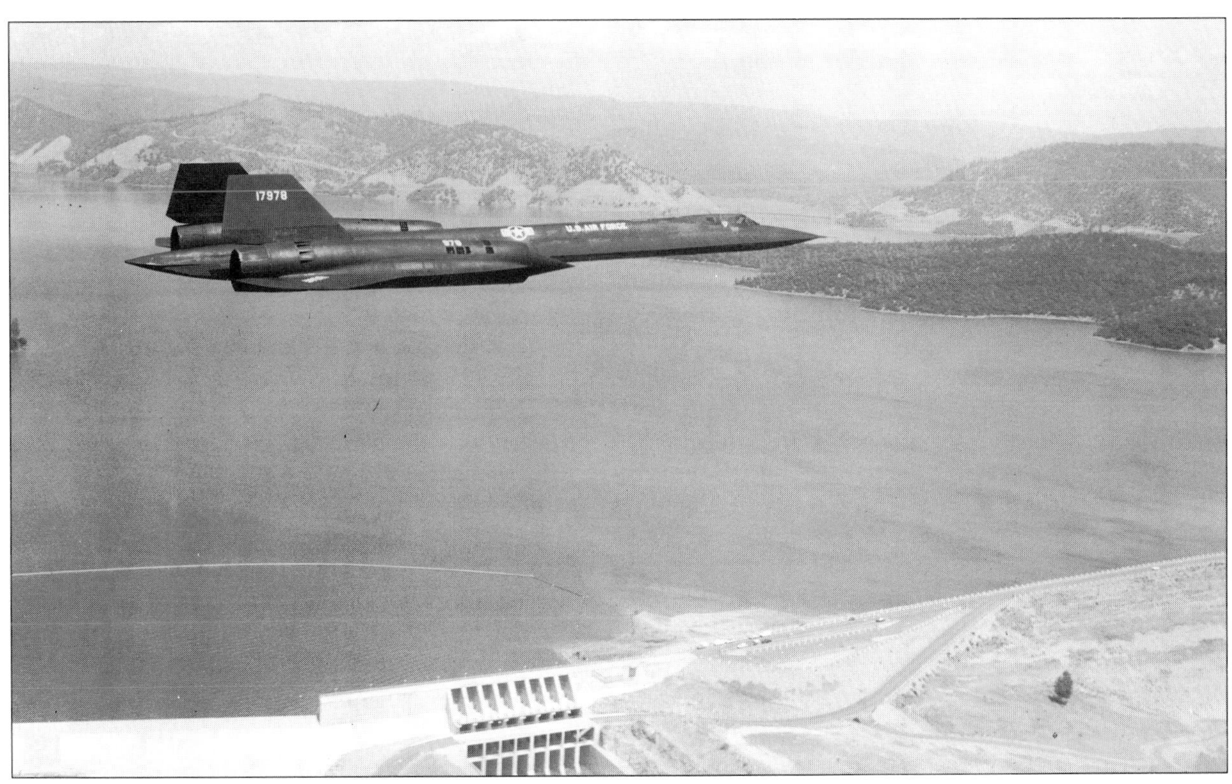

Aircraft 978 was written off in a landing accident at Kadena on 20 July 1972. At that point in its illustrious career 978 sported *Playboy* Bunny symbols on its tail surfaces and was known as 'Rapid Rabbit' (*Lockheed*)

Dempster ended that argument once and for all on a winter training sortie by dumping fuel for ten seconds high over Montana to see if the afterburner might ignite the fuel trail. The fuel instead turned into an instant ice cloud in the −55 degree stratosphere but left a five mile-long contrail-finger pointing directly to the aircraft. Jim reported that he could see that trail for hundreds of miles after they had turned back toward the west!

Yet another accident befell the 9th SRW on 11 January 1968. Lt Col 'Gray' Sowers (one of the most experienced instructor pilots and the commander of the 99th SRS) was airborne in SR-71B 957 with student pilot Capt Dave Fruehauf on his third training sortie. The aircraft experienced a generator failure near Spokane, Washington, followed by a second failure a few minutes later. They immediately switched off all non-essential electrically powered equipment to conserve battery power, and made repeated attempts to re-set both generators, which would come on briefly only to fail again. Since airfields directly under an SR-71 flying at altitude were as far away as 250 miles after the aircraft had descended, most Washington State bases were not considered suitable for a diversionary landing. Portland, Oregon, looked like the best bet, but it turned out to be overcast, so the crew pressed-on toward Beale which appeared within easy reach.

As they approached home on a long straight-in descent, the 175 knot airspeed placed the aircraft in its natural ten degree nose-up angle of attack. That positive attitude allowed some of the dry-tank fuel inlet ports to 'suck air', which in turn interrupted the gravity flow of fuel to the engine combustion chambers because the fuel boost pumps were inoperative. This caused cavitation, and both J58s to flame-out. Gray got each of the engines restarted intermittently, but they flamed-out again and again. Since 957 was rapidly losing its last feet of useful altitude, Gray ordered bail-out at 3000 ft above the ground. Both pilots watched 'good old' 957 'pancake' inverted only seven miles north of Beale's long runway as they rode their parachutes safely down.

Two months later, Maj Buddy Brown and Capt Dave Jensen departed from Beale in 978 to cross the

Pacific to Okinawa. The 9th SRW's long-awaited deployment to the war-zone had finally begun. Meanwhile, more and more new crews were being trained to reach SAC's desired operational strength of two full squadrons.

On 10 October 1968 a new pilot/RSO team began their take-off roll down runway 14 at Beale in the recently delivered 977. Maj Abe Kardong (an ex-B-58 pilot) neared his take-off GO-No GO decision point when a wheel failed throwing shrapnel up into the fuel cell. The afterburner's flames ignited the leaking fuel, starting a fire which was catching up with the fast-moving aircraft. The Buddy-Crew Mobile Control officers warned Abe that he had 'one helluva fire', whereupon he aborted the take-off at high speed. At that point the remaining tyres on the affected gear truck also burst. The brake 'chute blossomed to be quickly consumed by the fire. Abe steered the aircraft toward the arresting barrier at the far end of the runway. Since the aircraft crossed the roll-over sensors (which triggered the arresting cable's pop-up), off-centre and with one wing low, the cable snapped up in front of an inlet, whose sharp edge instantly knifed through the barrier cable, rendering it useless.

As they proceeded on a very hard ride into the rough, the helpless RSO, Maj Jim Kogler, decided to eject. A few moments later he descended safely under a fully deployed 'chute which had unfurlled a few hundred feet up. For a brief moment he thought that he would drift back into the blazing grass fire which 977 had caused. Meanwhile, Abe rode it out for a full half mile before the SR-71 finally ground to a halt, whereupon Mobile Control Crew members Willie Lawson and Gil Martinez dashed into the blaze and extricated the pilot from the wreckage. Jim was unhurt but Abe hobbled around for a few days from spinal compression bruising and other abrasions from his high-speed sleigh ride toward Beale's Main Gate. Yet another wheel failure (fortunately the last one), had resulted in the loss of an SR-71. Despite four 9th SRW aircraft losses between 13 April 1967 and 10 October 1968, Category III 'Operational' Testing ended in December 1968. The 9th SRW was awarded the Presidential Unit Citation for meeting the many great challenges that faced the unit as it brought the 'most advanced' reconnaissance system of its day to operational readiness.

Not all operational missions were flown over hostile territory, this graphic high altitude 'take' featuring the aftermath of a freight train explosion in Rosville, Sacramento, on 28 April 1973 (*USAF*)

CHAPTER 5

Beale Recon

On 17 June 1970, Majs Buddy Brown and Mort Jarvis were to fly a special test mission to check out a new type of defensive system and to verify some changes that had been made to another high-powered jammer. The test was to be conducted over the Gulf of Mexico in the Eglin AFB Test Range which was instrumented for tracking high altitude targets. The flight took them around the western US toward a second air refuelling near El Paso, Texas, before the planned 'high and hot' run across the Eglin Test Range. The flight, which began at 0730 hours from Beale, went well until the split-offload air refuelling from two tankers. Buddy described what happened next in the following passage:

'When we completed the rendezvous, I pulled up into the pre-contact position and waited for the 'cleared for contact' call from the boomer. After receiving the call, I flew to the contact position and waited for the boom to be inserted into 970's receptacle. I got the nozzle contact light and started taking on fuel. I remember commenting to Mort on how smooth the air was that morning; there wasn't any turbulence that one sometimes felt on the eastern side of the mountain range around the El Paso area in the summer time. During the refuelling, I was following the directional lights on the bottom of the tanker to keep position 'in the green' (the centre of the air refuelling envelope). After taking on about 35,000 lbs of fuel, a crewman called over the boom-linked interphone that I had taken the required amount of fuel and that they would initiate a disconnect on the count of three. At the end of the count I felt the disconnect, throttled back, dropped down and back slightly and spotted my second tanker which was to my right.

'I moved to the pre-contact position behind number two, reset my refuelling system for contact and called that I was ready to refuel. The second boomer acknowledged 'ready to refuel' and I pulled into the contact position and waited for boom contact. Shortly thereafter, the boom made contact, which I again verified by feel and the 'contact-made' light on my instrument console, and continued with what I expected to be a routine air refuelling. Two to three minutes into the second refuelling, the aircraft hit a sort of a bump and shook as if it had just flown through some turbulent air. I asked Mort "Did you feel that?", to which he emphatically answered, "Yes!" It felt quite unusual because the air had been so smooth that morning. It may have been another aircraft's jet-wash which was laid across our track by an airliner which had passed earlier. Again, there was a another disturbance which I corrected with a small stick input. Then it was quiet and smooth again.

'Out of nowhere, the nose gave a small pitch down and a hard pitch-up. I pushed the stick quickly forward but the nose and canopy struck the bottom of the tanker. The nose section was gone just forward of the cockpit and the canopy had caved in on me. I thought, "I'm inside the tanker; death is imminent!" My next thoughts were about bailing-out so I told Mort to bail-out and pulled the 'D' ring between my legs. I still thought I would eject up inside the tanker. There was a lot of noise and debris flying around as I was pushed down into my ejection seat by the rocket which was firing me free of the aircraft. Next, I was aware of free-falling in my ejection seat, whose little 'chute was stabilising my descent toward 14,000 ft where the butt-snapper lofted me out of my seat and my pretty parachute opened automatically. I opened my visor to look around the sky for my RSO, the "Habu" and the tanker. The tanker was making a turn overhead and Mort was about a thousand feet below in his 'chute. I didn't realize it at the time, but both my legs had been broken during the ejection. They were numb from the break and I couldn't feel a thing. During the descent, I looked at the ground and contemplated my landing. When I hit, I was dragged a few feet before I got one side of my parachute unhooked. I then unhooked the other side, crawled over to my seat kit and got the emergency radio out. I called the tanker and said that I was OK and

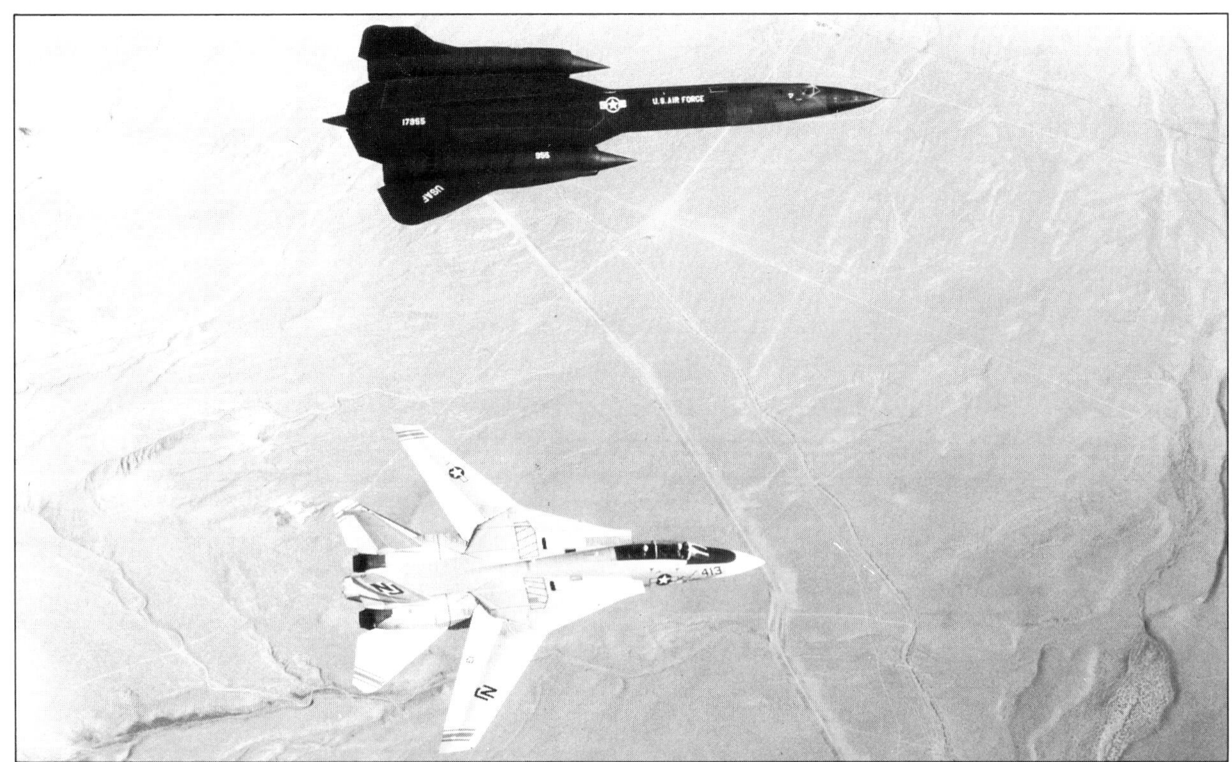

NAS Miramar F-14s took part in intercept trials against SR-71s off the coast of San Diego in the early 1970s. Code-named *Tom-Too-Hot*, they were enjoyable exercises that held none of the rivalry which tainted early USAF F-15 Eagle-Bait missions (*Grumman History Center*)

asked if they had contacted my RSO. The tanker crew responded affirmative to both questions and waited for us to be picked up by a chopper from the Fort Bliss Army Hospital at El Paso, where the doctors checked us over and splinted my legs.

'My aircraft had smashed into the ground approximately 20 miles east of El Paso at 0915 hours. The tanker flew back to Beale, did an inflight controllability check with an approach to landing speed and determined it was safe to make a landing. After it rolled to a stop off the Beale runway, it was encircled by fire trucks and Beale officials who were amazed at the amount of damage inflicted to the tail of the tanker, and how that tough old bird was able to continue flying with a severely damaged horizontal stabilizer.'

Buddy recovered from his broken legs, was cleared to return to crew duty later that year, and served a full career as a senior staff officer.

Eagle Bait

During the early 1970s, an evaluation programme began involving SAC's SR-71s and TAC's new F-15 fighters. Its purpose was to determine the interceptability of the SR-71 by the F-15 Eagle, which had speed and altitude characteristics similar to the MiG-25 *Foxbat*. Additionally, the very high altitude intercept training would be very useful for the 'Eagle-Drivers'. The programme initially got off to a bad start with inter-command rivalries coming into play, as Buddy Brown recalls:

'I was briefed on the particulars of one F-15 intercept training mission the day prior to the flight. The intercept was to take place in the Edwards Test Range area in California. We were to pass on our exact time, heading and altitude as to when we would be at a specific location over the range to assist the intercept as much as possible the day before the sortie. Additionally, we were to let down to 70,000 ft and slow to Mach 2.85, again to assist the F-15's intercept geometry. Just prior to our arrival at the 'start of intercept point', I was asked to dump fuel for approximately 15 seconds to mark my position in the sky. I was told that ground radar sites had got the F-15 lined up so that the pilot could make his pull-up at the right moment and 'acquire' my aircraft on his onboard radar. He called back a successful 'kill' on the SR-71. Immediately TAC Headquarters put out the word that they could shoot down an SR-71 because they had intercepted one.

'Well this did not go down at all well with the troops back at Beale because we had given the F-15 guys everything they needed to make the intercept. We had not even used our DEF system to jam them. Prior to the next mission, TAC asked for the usual information (position, altitude, speed and heading). We replied "we'll be in the Edwards Test Area tomorrow." An HQ TAC staff officer protested, "but we need the information to make the intercept". Our reply was, "Why? You claim you can intercept and shoot down an SR-71." For the next two missions the F-15 crews were unable to get anywhere near us; we didn't slow down or descend. They retracted the earlier claim, and from that point on we gave them the information they needed to ensure that the mutual training exercises were beneficial to both parties.'

Following their record-breaking long-distance flight of 26 April 1971, Tom Estes and Dewain Vick receive the 1972 Harmon International Trophy. The award was made on 20 September 1971 in a ceremony at the White House. (Left to right) Senator Barry Goldwater, Lt Col Tom Estes, President Richard Nixon, Lt Col Dewain Vick (*USAF*)

Supertankers and Long Flights

Gen P K Carlton, the commander of the 15th Air Force, became interested in extending SR-71 missions to fully encompass the concept of 'global reach'. In 1970 he initiated two actions which hastened very long range operations. The first idea was one covering nuclear war reconnaissance. One day he asked his Director of Reconnaissance, Lt Col Don Walbrecht, to concieve a post-SIOP coverage of the Soviet landmass with SR-71s assisted by advanced tankers which were not yet programmed into SAC's inventory. He said, 'Recce, you know that "Habu" well. I want a plan to help sell the Air Staff on the idea of big new tankers'. In the next few days, Don and his fellow 15th Air Force reconaissance officers drew up a plan whereby the existing SIOP was covered with lots of tankers and all of the SR-71s. After Don briefed the 'Boss' the first time, P K said 'back to the drawing boards Recce; you're not thinking big'. A few days later, a new plan was briefed which showed that a dozen prepositioned KC-747s and a dozen Beale-based 'Habus' could cover all probable targets less than five hours after the initial ICBM laydown. 'That's more like it!' he said. 'That'll help advocate the use of the Jumbos'. Soon after, newly-promoted Col Walbrecht found himself assigned to SAC Headquarters, where he was 'advocating new tankers and re-engined KC-

135s' as the Division Chief of Advanced Strategic Aircraft Systems.

To further the cause of an advanced tanker, General Carlton stimulated a test programme that mated Boeing's number one test 747 airframe with an SR-71. On 6 July 1972, Merv Evanson and Coz Mallozzi flew the Palmdale test airframe 955 on a three-hour sortie checking out the refuelling flight envelope and 'dry-boom' contact checks with the boom-equipped 747. The same day, B-52s and various fighters also took their turn in the 747 contact tests. Throughout the 1970s General Carlton used the 747/SR-71 recce concept, and the success of that test flight, to help promote SAC's advanced tanker programme, which eventually bore fruit in the 1980s with the purchase of 60 KC-10s.

The second P K Carlton initiative was proving that the SR-71 could fly longer than eight hours. In March 1971, he asked Don Walbrecht how long the 'Habu' could fly on a maximum effort mission. Don replied, 'about nine and a half to ten hours.' 'What's the limiting factor, TEB?' asked the general. 'No Sir,' replied Don. 'It's liquid nitrogen which is used to pressurize the hot fuel tanks while flying at high Mach'. After considering the answer briefly, P K instructed Don to 'Get with Hal Confer', who commanded the 9th SRW at the time, and have him set up the longest sortie possible. Go for ten hours!'

In compliance with those instructions, Col Confer said that he would pick a tight aircraft (one with new tank sealant to reduce nitrogen leaks) and get on with it the following week. On 26 April 1971, Majs Tom Estes and Dewain Vick established an endurance record for the SR-71 when they stayed aloft on multiple high-Mach legs for ten hours and thirty minutes, covering a distance of 15,000 miles. The mission involved five full-up aerial refuellings and five-and-a-half hours of Mach 3.0 time. The flight completely encircled the continental United States twice and ended with a high-Mach run around the western States. Three refuellings were done between Reno and Boise and two were done near Florida. The nitrogen dewars still had a bit of LN2 remaining after the long flight, and the aircraft had 'minimum maintenance writeups'.

Crew fatigue was a bit of a problem, but Tom and Dewain were greatly inspired to make the mission a full success. Dewain recalled taking along a packet of M&M chocolates. 'Each time Tom descended for a refuelling, I'd pop my visor and quickly take on my own refuelling (a few chocolates) and quickly reseal my visor. I guess I should have contacted the Mars Company for a product endorsement' Vick said. 'M&Ms really do melt in your mouth and not in your pressure suit glove!' After 13 hours in their pressure suits, both crewmembers recalled that the UCDs also worked 'as advertised'.

Col Pat Halloran headed the SR-71 detachment at Griffiss AFB, New York. Air Force Systems Command deployed 955 to New York, under the code-name *Black Knight*, to evaluate a new ECM suit. This exercise provided a cover story for the series of 11-hour transatlantic round-robin sorties over the Middle East (*Tom Pugh*)

In recognition of this outstanding flight achievement, Tom and Dewain won the 1971 *Mackay Trophy* for 'the most meritorious flight of the year', and the 1972 *Harmon International Trophy* for 'the most outstanding international achievement in the art and science of aeronautics'. The SR-71's 'long legs' were soon to be used in double-transatlantic sorties.

Yom Kippur War

After the disasterous 1967 Six Day War, President Sadat of Egypt decided that another conflict with Israel was necessary to re-establish Arab claims on former Egyptian lands beyond the Suez Canal. President Assad of Syria agreed to mount a simultaneous attack on the Jewish state from the north. At 1400 hours on 6 October 1973 (Yom Kippur Day – the Jewish day of Atonement), the Egyptians opened an hour-long barrage from 2000 artillery pieces along their western border. Simultaneously, 240 Egyptian aircraft hit three Israeli airfields, and other important targets in the Sinai.

Within 15 minutes the aggressors were advancing along a 130-mile front, employing five infantry divisions, supported by three mechanised and two armoured divisions. As Israeli soldiers prayed in their bunkers in celebration of Yom Kippur, the Egyptian war machine rumbled over ten pontoon bridges that had been thrown across the Suez Canal, stormed the supposedly impregnable 'Bar-Lev Line', and established bridgeheads on the East Bank. At the same moment, the Syrian phase of the attack opened in the north with another massive 30-minute artillery bombardment. This barrage presaged the advance of three Syrian Infantry divisions and two armoured divisions. To coincide with the advance, an independent attack was mounted by Syrian helicopter-borne commandos on the vital Israeli observation post at Mount Hermon in the Golan Heights.

The speed and ferocity of the Arab attack caught the Israelis off guard. Troops were mobilised from synagogues and Israeli Radio broke its traditional silence during Yom Kippur to broadcast instructions to its threatened population. Most Western intelligence agencies were equally surprised by the joint attack. Three days before the Arab onslaught, the Soviets launched the low-resolution camera-equipped Cosmos 596 satellite from Plesetsk in southwestern USSR. This device allowed them to watch the battle on behalf of their Arab allies.

The Israelis regrouped within two days and attacked the bridges over the Canal. In the north, the Syrians continued their push toward the River Jordan and the Sea of Galilee. The Soviet reconnaissance effort was strengthened on 8 October when they launched Cosmos 597; this satellite was able to change its orbit using rockets; despite the resultant increase in the satellite's speed, the perigee improved photographic resolution. Its path, inclined 65 degrees to the Equator, alligned it across both fronts. The next day Cosmos 596 was recovered but the ground situation had turned in favour of the Israelis. Syrian efforts in the north had ground to a standstill after a furious battle, and General Sheron's forces in the south had successfully attacked the Egyptians and retaken a second-line fortification that had fallen the day before.

The Soviets launched Cosmos 598 on 10 October to improve the surveillance of the war zone. Pitched slightly higher than the preceding Cosmos satellites, 598 was already in orbit when 597 returned its film cassettes to earth. The Soviets were also receiving real-time imagery from 598 via the Yevpatoriya tracking station in the Crimea. As a consequence of the Soviet advantage in reconnaissance, the US decided to step up its intelligence efforts. The SR-71 offered the best hot-spot reconnaissance capability, and plans were drafted to fly missions from Beale to Egypt and recover into Mildenhall. This long-range concept had been validated two years before by the Estes/Vick 15,000-mile test sortie.

CINCSAC General John Meyer ordered Col Pat Halloran to prepare for these missions. At that point, Pat knew that the sorties would attact wide attention within government circles, and that the success of those flights was central to the survival of the entire *Senior Crown* programme. Due to its importance, he asked the new 15th Air Force

Pictured in a hanger at Griffiss are 979 and 964. T-38 Talon 'Toxon 01' was used to chase 955 on its test flights (*Tom Pugh*)

'Toxon 01' chased Tom Pugh and Ron Selberg in 955 (*USAF*)

commander, Lt Gen Bill Pitts, for permission to 'run the show' himself. Col Halloran put together a maintenance recovery team and left Beale on a tanker for Mildenhall at midnight on the same day as their alert. He later recalled:

'I was scheduled to go straight to London to brief senior MoD officials on the plan, but upon my arrival at Mildenhall I was informed that the British government had had second thoughts and denied us authority to operate from the UK. I was then told that Griffiss AFB in New York State would be our operating location. Without rest, we turned the tanker around, and the full complement of planners and maintenance personnel were reloaded for a quick return trip to the US. Undoubtedly that was the shortest overseas TDY in the history of the 9th Wing!'

It appeared later that the Heath government had denied the Air Force use of Mildenhall so as to guarantee continued oil supplies from the Arabs – a move that would later produce heated exchanges between Europe and the US.

Palmdale's flight test SR-71 (955), had already been scheduled to conduct a series of evaluations on its new A-2 electronic defensive systems from Griffiss AFB from mid-October onwards, so by stationing Beale's detachment at Griffiss at the same time, Halloran would have additional support from Lockheed's technical field support personnel, and a cover story for their secret operations in the Middle East.

As Halloran's new operating location was firmed up and higher headquarters approved the overall transatlantic plan, crews began serious flight planning for the first mission. Lt Col Jim Shelton and Maj Gary Coleman got airborne from Beale in 979 at 2200 hours on 11 October and headed for Griffiss. They were met by an angry base commander and three Lockheed tech reps after laying 'a heavy late-night sonic boom track' across the US and down into New York state as they made their descent from altitude. A phone call from Jim Shelton to Al Joersz and John Fuller (who would fly a second SR-71 into Griffiss) advised them to make their descent profile over the Great Lakes to minimise the effects of the boom on the urban eastern states. Fortunately, there were no boom complaints when the second crew made their crossing. The next day's newspapers reported a strange phenomenon which was described by one scientist as a probable 'meteoric shock wave'.

The second aircraft developed a hydraulic problem that forced an engine change, leaving the new detachment down to one mission-ready aeroplane until specialised equipment could be flown in from Beale. An hour after the last SR-71 landed, the first tanker arrived carrying Tom Estes (the operations officer), three mission planners and a number of Beale's best intelligence and maintenance personnel. At 0600 hours a secure teleprinter clattered out the final details of the first sortie which was to be flown 22 hours later.

The first major question to arise when the aircrew met with the mission planners concerned diversionary fields, and no-one could offer a satisfactory answer. Later that morning, the Mildenhall tanker arrived, and the unit's technicians began preparing 979 for the longest operational sortie to date. By mid-afternoon someone suggested that the crew should get some sleep since they had been up for nearly 36 hours, and they would soon be airborne for another 16 hours during the sortie itself. They were directed to an old BOQ where their rooms were hot and the beds uncomfortable. Gary Coleman recalled, 'No one could snore like Jim Shelton and I got no sleep at all, but I consoled myself with the thought that my pilot was getting some solid rest!'

The attitude of America's allies had complicated the plans for the support of the forthcoming sorties. Tanker crews had to re-position great quantities of JP7 fuel from Mildenhall and Turkey to Zaragoza in Spain and emergency landing sites were still proving difficult to find. Nevertheless, Jim Shelton cranked 979's engines on cue and lifted off at 0200 hours to head eastward toward the first of his many refuellings. He flew toward the first cell of tankers which were holding just off the coast, and then accelerated toward the second refuelling point near the Azores. The inlets were not performing very well, but Jim was pleased that he had made it to altitude without any unstarts. The second air refuelling was just beyond the Azores followed by another high-Mach dash through the Straits of Gibraltar down to the third refuelling with Zaragoza-based tankers just beyond the heel of Italy. Due to the proximity of the air refuelling area with the war zone and Libya, the US Navy provided combat air patrols from carriers sailing in the region.

They then climbed and accelerated across the eastern Mediterranean to penetrate Egyptian airspace over Port Said. Gary Coleman recalled 'There was no indication of anything launched against us, but everyone was painting us on their radars as we made our turn inbound. The DEF panel lit up like a pin-ball machine and I said to Jim, "this should be interesting".' According to an official Egyptian communique released the next day, the aircraft spent 25 minutes in their airspace flying as far south as Nagaa Hammady (366 miles south of Cairo), before turning back north over the capital and then eastward towards Jordan and Syria, where it turned westward over the Mediterranean Sea. The commu-

The 1974 Palmdale Test crew; (left to right) Lt Col Tom Smith, Lt Col 'Coz' Mallozzi, Maj Tom Pugh and Maj Ron Selberg (*USAF*)

Photographed on 16 May 1975, Tom Pugh and John Carnochan fly 976 in formation with Tom Smith and Bill Frazier in 955 (*USAF*)

nique stated (incorrectly) that two SR-71s had entered Egyptian airspace at 1103 hours GMT and ended saying 'this was the first time that Egypt's airspace had been violated by this type of plane'.

The Egyptian mistake in identifying two SR-71s on this sortie may be attributed to the difficulty in tracking such high-performance targets with small radar cross sections, or could have arisen from the double-boom signature which the SR-71 throws down miles behind its position. Alternatively, such a mistake could have been a deliberate ploy on the Egyptians part to exaggerate their claims or mask radar weaknesses.

After leaving the war zone, Jim eased 979 down toward his fourth air refuelling, which was still being air-capped by the US Navy. Their next hot leg ended with a descent to the Azores for the fifth refuelling, but the tankers from Zaragoza had difficulty getting a clearance through the busy offshore airway which was filled with civilian airliners. They could not request a priority clearance because of the secrecy of their mission. When approval was at last received, the air traffic controllers hesitated clearing the tanker cell on their requested track because 'unidentified high-speed traffic, height unknown', was approaching from their 12 o'clock position. The tankers could not reveal that the 'traffic' was indeed their trade.

Soon after, Jim completed his mid-ocean refuelling and climbed back up for his final high-speed run across the western Atlantic toward New York. By that time Gary's eyes were tearful from the lack of crew rest. Thinking back on Jim's good night of sleep compared to his own experience, Gary was now pleased to see how well his pilot could refuel after six tracks, involving eleven tankers and more than five hours of flight above Mach 3.0. The other five hours had been filled with air refuellings, and climbs and descents but he was still going strong. Jim and Gary landed back at Griffiss after ten hours and eighteen minutes. Their reconnaissance 'take' was of 'high quality' and provided intelligence and defence analysts with the information they had been expecting.

The Syrian military situation was swinging in favour of the Israelis by 14 October. The Soviets had stepped up an airlift of military equipment and were aware that the Syrian front was collapsing. Washington had also begun supporting Israel with a huge airlift of US war materials. President Nixon had requested $2.2 billion in emergency aid for the Israelis, a request that incensed Abu Dhabi, Libya and Qatar, who had been meeting with oil companies in Vienna since 12 October. They immediately imposed a complete oil embargo on the US, a move quickly followed by the other OPEC oil producers.

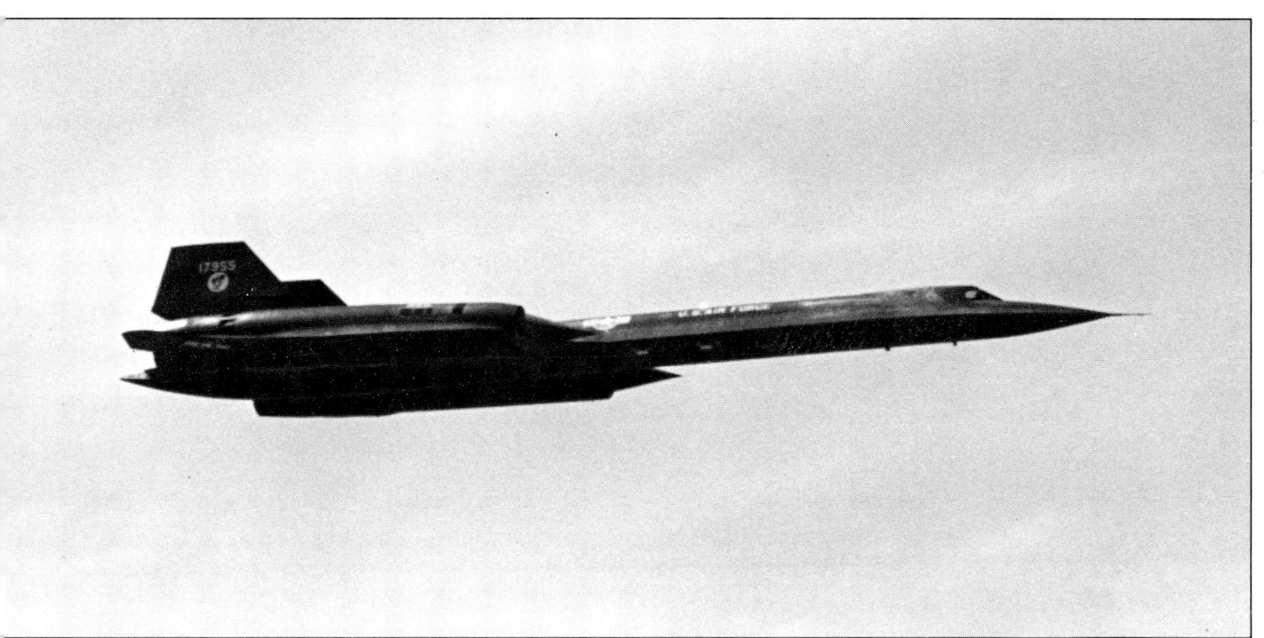

To further warn other western nations against supporting Israel, they unilaterally announced a 70 per cent rise in oil prices and a five per cent per month cut in petroleum production. The decision caused panic in western Europe, which depended on the Arab States for 80 per cent of their oil supply.

Meanwhile, in the Sinai desert the Egyptians launched a 100,000-strong offensive toward the east on 14 October, this attack resulting in one of the biggest tank battles in history. As Israeli forces gained ground, they also established a bridgehead west of the Suez Canal which threatened to cut off the Egyptian army. With the Egyptian military situation becoming more and more acute, President Nixon announced that US forces across the globe had been placed on military alert following the receipt of information which indicated that the Soviet Union was planning 'to send a very substantial force to the Middle East to relieve the beleaguered Egyptian Third Army, now completely encircled in the Sinai'.

This tense period in superpower relations was

The first SR-71A lost was aircraft 952, which broke up in a high speed pitch-up accident on 25 January 1966 (*Lockheed ADP*)

somewhat defused when Soviet Secretary Brezhnev supported a United Nations motion of 24 October which would end the Yom Kippur War. Meanwhile SR-71 surveillance missions continued. At 0200 hours on 25 October, Majs Al Joersz and John Fuller got airborne from Griffiss in 979 and chalked up another highly successful transatlantic sortie to the Middle East to provide US decision-makers with a much-needed update on the ground situation in the Sinai and around Galilee. Ever-reliable 979 was airborne yet again on another long mission on 2 November with Majs Bob Helt and Larry Elliott covering the same area of interest. One week later, Majs Jim Wilson and Bruce Douglass flew an even longer sortie which started at Griffiss and ended at Seymour Johnson AFB in North Carolina.

When it began to snow in New York, Pat Halloran decided to move SR-71 operations to the warmer climate at Seymour Johnson AFB for winter operations. Col Don Walbrecht headed up the new detachment, which had been pre-arranged with HQ TAC by Col Harlan Hain from the SAC Reconnaissance Center. Since the shooting war was over, reconnaissance would show compliance with the cease-fire agreement and provide irrefutable evidence for Secretary of State Kissinger's team, who were leading the delicately balanced withdrawal negotiations between the deeply distrusting Israelis and Arabs.

Fierce fighting broke out along the cease-fire line on 30 November which threatened to destroy the fragile agreement brokered by the US. Jim Sullivan and Noel Widdifield flew 964 across the Atlantic on 2 December to look at the situation. It proved to be a well-timed move since fighting had also begun that same day in the Golan Heights. Further diplomatic pressures put an end to the new skirmishes before Pat Bledsoe and Reg Blackwell went out in 979 on 10 December for another look at the belligerents. They flew their 'clock-work' 10-hour mission, arriving back at Seymour Johnson 'on the minute' of their

Tom Tilden and 'J T' Vida flew 955 on 17 March 1983 in KC-10 aerial refuelling tests (*Lockheed*)

Above The callsign 'Aspen' was used on all stateside training sorties. Here 'Aspen 31' approaches a KC-135Q for air refuelling practice (*P Crickmore*)

Right Fuelled to the point of pressure-disconnect, 'Aspen 31' prepares to disconnect and accelerate high over the Rocky Mountains (*P Crickmore*)

Below After refuelling, 'Aspen 31' prepares to accelerate and climb to altitude (*P Crickmore*)

flight plan. Thereafter, things were quiet for the next five weeks so the Beale Troops' went home for Christmas. In January they returned to base to carry on with Sinai surveillance.

On 25 January, Majs Buck Adams and Bill Machorek flew another perfect ten hour sortie, but they returned to Seymour to face a very low ceiling and visibility condition which 'mandated' a diversion to Griffiss which would put the 'take' out of position for processing. Don Walbrecht said: 'We had Buck grab some fuel from the standby tanker and jacked the ceiling up a bit (against the complaints of Harlan Hain at SAC headquarters) and Buck snuck in to a perfect landing at Seymour' under the lowest ceiling an SR-71 has ever landed'.

The detachment's spirited 'high-jinks' (after each outstanding mission of recognized national importance) annoyed the 4th Fighter Wing commander, Col Len Russell, whose fuel stocks had been quickly depleted by the five KC-135Q tankers which supported the SR-71 movements. With a serious shortage of fuel during the war, Seymour Johnson had not been resupplied for fighter training sorties. To further complicate matters, Beale's new 14th Air Divison commander, Brig Gen Don Pittman really messed things up by demeaning Col Russell, who was embittered by what had appeared to be SAC 'heavy-handedness'. The fuel embargo imposed by the OPEC nations caused the Air Force to husband its fuel supply and drastically reduce other flying to currency rides only. Because of Russell's complaints to his TAC boss Gen Dixon headquarters arbitration was necessary to put things back in perspective. In response, SAC's Deputy Chief of Staff for Logistics came to Seymour Johnson to thank Russell for supporting the Sinai effort and to solve his fuel problem. Within a few days the pipeline flowed with JP5 for the TAC F-4s and a trainload of JP7 arrived for the two SR-71s.

The success of international peace efforts soon began to show. On 18 January 1974 a military separation agreement was signed between Egyptian and Israeli defence officials which led to troop withdrawals. By mid-February, the Middle East peace process was beginning to go into 'overdrive' and on the 18th four Arab nations proposed a truce in the Golan Heights. To verify the pull-back, '971 was dispatched to the Suez on 25 January. There had been a great deal of suspicion on both sides that the opposing forces would not pull back; consequently, the 'Habu's' photography became the instrument of verification and was shown at the peace negotiations as proof. With that evidence in hand, full diplomatic ties were finally restored between Egypt and the US after a break lasting seven years.

Reg Blackwell was awarded the DFC for his part in the reconnaissance mission flown over the Golan Heights on 10 December 1973

As troop withdrawals continued Majs Ty Judkins and G T Morgan flew 979 on the next to last long sortie. Appropriately, this ever-green aircraft also flew the final sortie on 6 April 1974. It had flown two-thirds of the nine 'ten-hour' sorties, chalking up a remarkable rate of success. Despite the very demanding nature of these special-effort missions, all nine were flown in their entirety without ground or air aborts or diversions.

Those nine long-flights represented a pinnacle of operational professionalism. They were a tribute not only to the dedication of the aircrews, but also to that of the staff planners and of the small group of top ground technicians who maintained the SR-71s away from home. These sorties stood as a testament to the long reach of the aircraft, and its ability to operate with impunity in a high threat environment[1].

Simulator Tests

Capt Maury Rosenberg and another Air Force pilot were instructed to report to the General Dynamics plant at Carswell AFB near Fort Worth, Texas, in May 1976 to help in some research. The two officers were directed to an obscure room in the plant containing two very crude cockpits equipped with a stick, throttles and basic flight instruments. The room was a web of electrical wiring connected to racks of monitoring apparatus and a computer. The aircraft's 'capability' was Mach 3.0 at 100,000 ft with no simulated armament. The other cockpit was similar, but it also had radar, a fire control panel and carried missiles.

Two basic intercept profiles were flown. The first began with the missile-equipped interceptor scrambled from an alert pad when the unarmed 'aircraft' was detected 350 NM away and a repeat was flown when the 'target' was 450 NM away. In the second profile, the missile-equipped aircraft was in an airborne race-track pattern. As the unarmed aircraft entered the area, the interceptor was vectored

THE UNITED STATES OF AMERICA

TO ALL WHO SHALL SEE THESE PRESENTS, GREETING:

THIS IS TO CERTIFY THAT
THE PRESIDENT OF THE UNITED STATES OF AMERICA
AUTHORIZED BY ACT OF CONGRESS JULY 2, 1926
HAS AWARDED

THE DISTINGUISHED FLYING CROSS
(THIRD OAK LEAF CLUSTER)

TO

CAPTAIN REGINALD T. BLACKWELL

FOR
EXTRAORDINARY ACHIEVEMENT
WHILE PARTICIPATING IN AERIAL FLIGHT

10 DECEMBER 1973

GIVEN UNDER MY HAND IN THE CITY OF WASHINGTON
THIS 5th DAY OF NOVEMBER 19 74

David C Jones
CHIEF OF STAFF

John L. McLucas
SECRETARY OF THE AIR FORCE

CITATION TO ACCOMPANY THE AWARD OF

THE DISTINGUISHED FLYING CROSS
(THIRD OAK LEAF CLUSTER)

TO

REGINALD T. BLACKWELL

Captain Reginald T. Blackwell distinguished himself by extraordinary achievement while participating in aerial flight as an SR-71 Reconnaissance Systems Officer on 10 December 1973. On that date, his courageous accomplishments and superior professional skill resulted in the successful collection of significant intelligence vital to the highest national interests. While operating in a hazardous environment and despite conditions which threatened the effectiveness of this flight, Captain Blackwell applied his exceptional airmanship and successfully concluded this unique and important mission. The professional competence, aerial skill and devotion to duty displayed by Captain Blackwell reflect great credit upon himself and the United States Air Force.

From 80,000 ft above the mid-west, a contrail belonging to a commercial airliner some 45,000 ft below can be clearly seen (*Bill Flannigan*)

inbound on various intercept angles – head-on, abeam and tail-chase.

Four engineers monitored readouts as the scenarios were played out and would stop the proceedings to reset their instrumentation when they changed from one vector to another. It was dull, time-consuming work in which only 12 intercepts were to be completed in a full day. The engineers asked the pilots lots of performance questions to help verify some relevant flight data that they already gleaned from another source. It did not take long to abandon the scramble profile and to concentrate on an orbit-vector profile. Pat Bledsoe repeated those 'simulator flights' two weeks later. One of the other pilots involved in those tests was Maj Bob McConnell, who became an air attaché in Moscow.

Viktor Belenko defected from Siberia to Japan four months later in a MiG-25P. During his CIA debriefing, he talked about how he was trained to shoot down an SR-71 near Vladivostok, and how the Soviet contollers and pilots had reached the conclusion that their best chance to make an intercept would be achieved by being airborne in a holding pattern which faced the track of the high flyer. He admitted that experience against other *Foxbats* showed that the prospect of getting an SR-71 was quite remote at that time unless one carried a 'nuke' intercept missile.

Records

In 1976 SAC and HQ USAF agreed to show some of the SR-71's capabilities as part of the nation's bicentennial celebrations. The original plan was to set an 'around the world at the equator' speed record. Pat Bledsoe and John Fuller were the senior crew at that time and were chosen to make the flight. Initial planning showed that it could be done in 16 hours and 20 minutes with seven refuellings. The only modification required for the SR-71 would have been an additional liquid nitrogen dewar.

The crew was sceptical of their own physical limitations for a flight of that duration but believed that adrenilin would probably keep them going. Pat recalled 'Preparations proceeded well until the full plan reached HQ USAF. When the generals saw the cost of deploying the fuel and tankers to forward bases they were aghast. It would take nearly 100 KC-135 flights to carry out the operation safely. The word came back to Beale to ''do something more reasonable''.' Consequently, the 9th set a new series of world speed and altitude records on 27 and 28 July 1976.

The Falklands

Argentina invaded and captured the Falkland Islands on 2 April 1982. Three days later a Royal Navy task force set sail from Portsmouth with the objective of driving the invaders out and returning the islands to British rule. Twenty days later Royal Marine commandos recaptured South Georgia Island, and soon after President Reagan pledged American support for Britain in the crisis. He branded the Argentinians as 'aggressors' and ordered economic sanction against them. He also offered to supply Britain with 'unspecified' war materials to assist in the recapture.

Seventy-three days after the invasion, British troops completed their objective and the Union Jack flew over the Falklands again. Did the SR-71 fly over the islands during the conflict? An analysis of the problem took place at the Pentagon. The study showed that SR-71s could have covered the area easily if SAC could operate KC-135s from South American bases – this, however, was politically unacceptable. It was too difficult to operate the KC-135s exclusively from the US because they could not take on fuel in flight. KC-10s were not available to buddy refuel the tankers far enough forward so the idea was dropped and the task was left to 'other' sensors.

Giant Plate and *Clipper* Sorties

Early in the *Senior Crown* programme, Cuban reconnaissance became a task for the 9th SRW. Sorties flown from Beale were code-named *Giant Plate*; that designation was later changed to *Clipper*. Most sorties were 'stand-off' runs, flown alongside the island in international waters. The SR-71's sensors could record the entire array of targets on Cuba as the aircraft passed south of the island, before looping around for a northside pass on its way to a second refuelling before heading back to Beale. The whole trip would take three and a half hours and was considered a very routine sortie.

Occasionally the track was modified to take the

SR-71B 956 returns to its barn after completing a training sortie in November 1986 (*P Crickmore*)

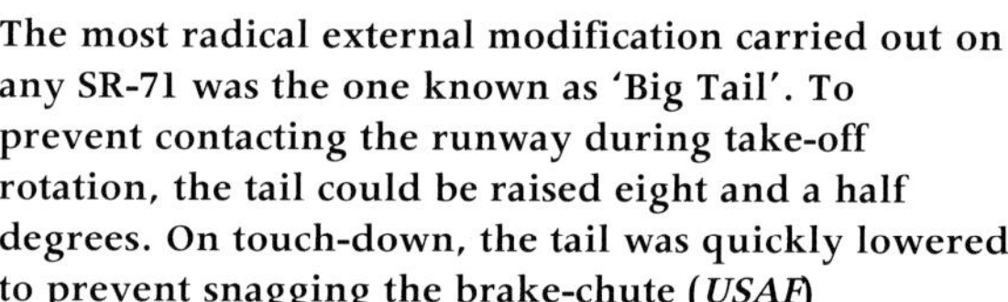

The most radical external modification carried out on any SR-71 was the one known as 'Big Tail'. To prevent contacting the runway during take-off rotation, the tail could be raised eight and a half degrees. On touch-down, the tail was quickly lowered to prevent snagging the brake-chute (*USAF*)

aircraft directly over Cuba. In an act of 'goodwill' towards the Caribbean nation, the incoming Carter administration suspended manned reconnaissance flights against the islands. In 1978, however, a reconnaissance satellite photographed a Soviet freighter in Havana harbour surrounded by large crates that were being moved to a nearby airbase where aircraft were being reassembled. It appeared that 15 MiG-23s had been supplied to Castro's Air Force. Such an upgrading of Cuban air strength was 'worrying'. The MiG-23BN *Flogger H* model was known to be capable of carrying nuclear weapons, and if it was indeed this variant of the MiG that had been exported, then the shipment violated the 1962 Soviet pledge of not deploying 'offensive' weapons to Cuba.

A decision was made in November 1978 to fly SR-71s over Cuba to identify the variant. Two sorties were carried out in conjunction with political announcements. On 20 November, President Carter said that the Soviet Union had assured him both publicly and privately that the MiG-23 jets were in Cuba for defensive purposes only. A Pravda commentary, citing the American press said 'The presence of such aircraft would run counter to the 1962 agreement'. It went on to say that the MiG reports 'were groundless and provocatory from beginning to end'. Photographs taken by SR-71s confirmed the Soviet claims – the aircraft were indeed MiG-23MS *Flogger Es* optimised for the air defence role.

Ten months later, a satellite revealed the presence of a large Soviet troop encampment southwest of Havana. An SR-71 flew over the island on 29 September 1979 to determine the strength of the unit, which turned out to be about 3000 men equipped with 40 tanks and other equipment. This new information concerned government authorities and threatened the Senate's ratification of the Strategic Arms Limitation Treaty. President Carter made a television address to the nation saying that there was no immediate threat to the US and that the Soviets claimed that the troop positions were only a training centre which would not be enlarged. The President went on to state that he would take steps to monitor activities in the area. SR-71 flights were a vital part of those continuing surveillance plans.

Seven years later Cuba was still being watched. Majs Stormy Boudreaux and Ted Ross departed Beale at 0400 hours on 19 June 1985 in 980 on a *Clipper* sortie. After their first air refuelling north of Salt Lake City, they turned southeast toward the target area. Castro had always held a belligerent attitude toward the US and his missile crews often spoofed SA-2 firings to annoy the overflyers. Many crews believed it was only a question of time before a SAM was fired their way, so advanced DEF systems were carried to counter such action. Part of the pre-penetration procedure saw the DEFs fully checked out, and to fly up to maximum speed before backing off to cruise speed to ensure that the inlets were performing at their best for SAM-dodging.

As 980 reached Mach 3.2 to test full-speed operations, Stormy began backing off to Mach 3.0 cruise while Ted checked out the new DEF system. At that point, the nose pitched up more than ten degrees before Stormy could reach the stick to stop the rise[2]. Since he was flying with his right hand on the autopilot's pitch wheel (where the right index finger moves a very small control wheel to adjust fine increments of nose-up or nose-down deflections), his hand was out of position for immediate reaction. He quickly moved his hand to the stick and exerted enough force to stop the dangerous pitching action.

Stormy had been flying fast and was beginning to slow down, and as a consequence the aircraft was in a nose-up trim condition when all three DAFICS computers shut down. The SR-71 was well out of

Between 30 October 1980 and 21 January 1981, 974 participated in ten sorties to evaluate NASA's new Tacan and S band radio. These items were designed for the Space Shuttle (*NASA*)

trim and the SAS was not there to help when it was most needed. Without SAS to dampen Stormy's sharp nose-down input, 980 responded with an equally sharp nose-down sweep of more than 15 degrees. He jerked the stick back, which caused a sudden up-sweep as Stormy recalled:

'I had litte time to analyse what was going on because things were happening so rapidly. Unfortunately, each oscillation was getting larger. It seemed that I was trying to learn the flight characteristics of a completely new airplane in a few seconds. Certainly, I'd never experienced anything like this before. In training we were only allowed to fly the aircraft with either pitch or roll or yaw SAS off, and that was at a benign 25,000 ft at 0.90 Mach. The loss of one channel of SAS was an abort item.

'I tried hard not to overcontrol the aircraft and to get the nose back on the horizon. As the nose reared up again to an ungodly 20 degrees, I knew that this would probably be the last chance I'd get before the aircraft exceeded the restoring capability of the controls. The aircraft would surely depart the flight envelope and disintegrate. Fortunately, I was still flying straight ahead, though we were still well above Mach 3. We hadn't deviated from our flight path and these oscillations were exposing the aircraft's underside forebody to awesome airstream loads. As the nose came up again, I hit the forward stop on the stick and still the nose kept rising. When it stopped I cranked in just a little forward trim and, by the grace of God, the nose started coming back down! I eased off some stick pressure, just enough to stop it deviating by much more than five degrees, from which I could progressively make smaller pitch movements. When I got that bucking bronco back to some proximity of level flight with the pitot tube near the horizon, I tried to maintain that position while I groped around the base of the stick for three red-cover 'guarded' re-set switches for the DAFICS computers. They were low and to the right and I was holding the stick with my right hand and trying with my left to reach around behind the back of the stick to reach these switches. Unfortunately, the metal cuff ring that secured my gloves to the rest of my pressure suit kept hitting the stick causing the aircraft to pitch or roll. I soon realised that I'd have to change hands. I managed to do that without overcontrolling and was finally able to engage the SAS channel. After that success, the rest was easy.

'When we analysed the MRS printout back at Beale, I learned that the inlet restart switch had activated

Bob Powell (in chocolate-brown pressure suit) receives his 1000-hour award from 9th SRW Wing Commander Col Pat Halloran on 10 January 1974 (*USAF*)

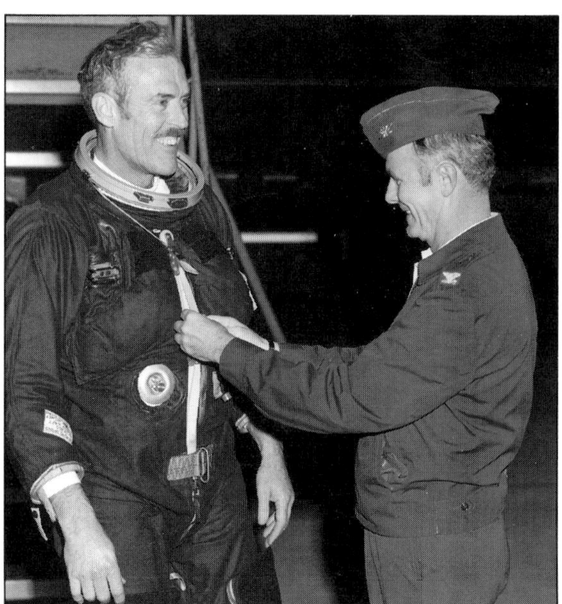

This group shot was taken after Lt Col Roger Jacks' last SR-71 flight. From left to right crewmembers (top row); John Murphy, Joe Vida, Don Emmons, Al Cirino, Tom Alison, John Fuller, Rich Graham (on own), Buzz Carpenter, Bill Groninger, Bruce Leibman. Standing at the left are Bill Keller, Chuck Sober, Joe Kinego (pressure suit left), Roger Jacks (bottom row) Jim Sullivan, Jay Reid and Tom Keck. Standing to the right of the shot are BC Thomas and Pat Bledsoe, who were almost obscured by John Storrie (*P Crickmore*)

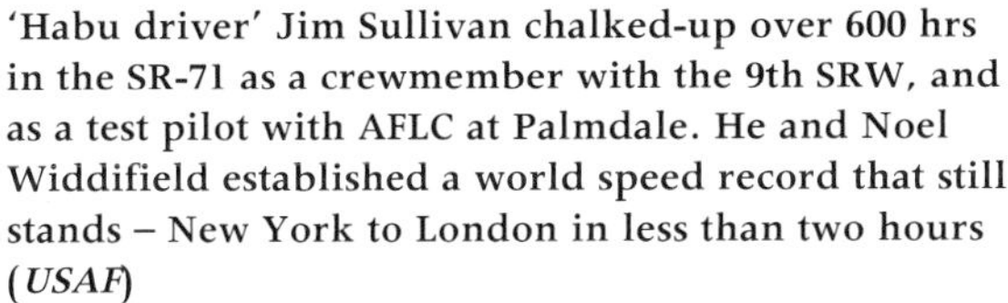
'Habu driver' Jim Sullivan chalked-up over 600 hrs in the SR-71 as a crewmember with the 9th SRW, and as a test pilot with AFLC at Palmdale. He and Noel Widdifield established a world speed record that still stands – New York to London in less than two hours (*USAF*)

Jim Eastham (left) was the second person to fly an SR-71. He and Ray Scalise are standing besides a YF-12 – an aircraft for which Jim was Lockheed's chief test pilot (*Lockheed*)

automatically following the DAFICS shutdown. This action caused the spikes to travel forward and had opened the forward bypass doors which prevented unstarts which would have added to our woes. Through all of this excitement, Ted remained remarkably calm despite the six-pound checklist ripping free from the two six-by-six inch velcro pads that had held it on his lap. It's during such frightening emergencies that I'm in awe of RSOs who have to read checklists and 'sit it out'. At least the pilots have plenty to keep themselves busy with, and less time to consider their fate.'

Stormy aborted the mission and recovered to Beale, where it was discovered that the triple DAFICS computer shutdown was caused by a voltage drop triggered when Ted activated the new DEF system (something the engineers said 'could never happen'). The 'fault circuitry' in the computer had detected this power loss and shut itself down.

Nicaragua

Some months earlier, SR-71s had overflown Nicarague for the first time. After the downfall of the dictator Samosa, a Marxist government was established who immediately requested Soviet military aid. In the autumn of 1984, a team of US 'crateologists' became interested in a cargo onboard a Soviet freighter that had docked in Nicaragua. The photographas taken by a US reconnaissance satellite showed what was believed to be MiG-21 interceptors. Nicaragua denied that the crates contained MiGs and maintained that the cargo consisted of Mi-8 *Hip* helicopters. After presidential clearance, six reconnaissance sorties were flown over Nicaragua from Beale. The first was flown on 7 November 1984 by Maj Bob Behler and Capt Ron Tabor (this crew flew three of the six sorties over Central America). As a result of their work and correlative intelligence, the MiG-21/Mi-8 wrangle slowly faded from the headlines, along with rumors of a possible US invasion of Nicaragua. Some months later, the world press confirmed that no MiG-21s had been shipped to Nicaragua – on this occasion the photo interpreters were 'off the mark'.

AFLC Command

The Palmdale facility was used as an acceptance test centre. An Advanced Systems Project Office (ASPO) was established and each new aircraft was subjected to extensive Functional Check Flights (FCF) before delivery to the Air Force. Each new and pristine SR-71 would then be picked up by a Beale

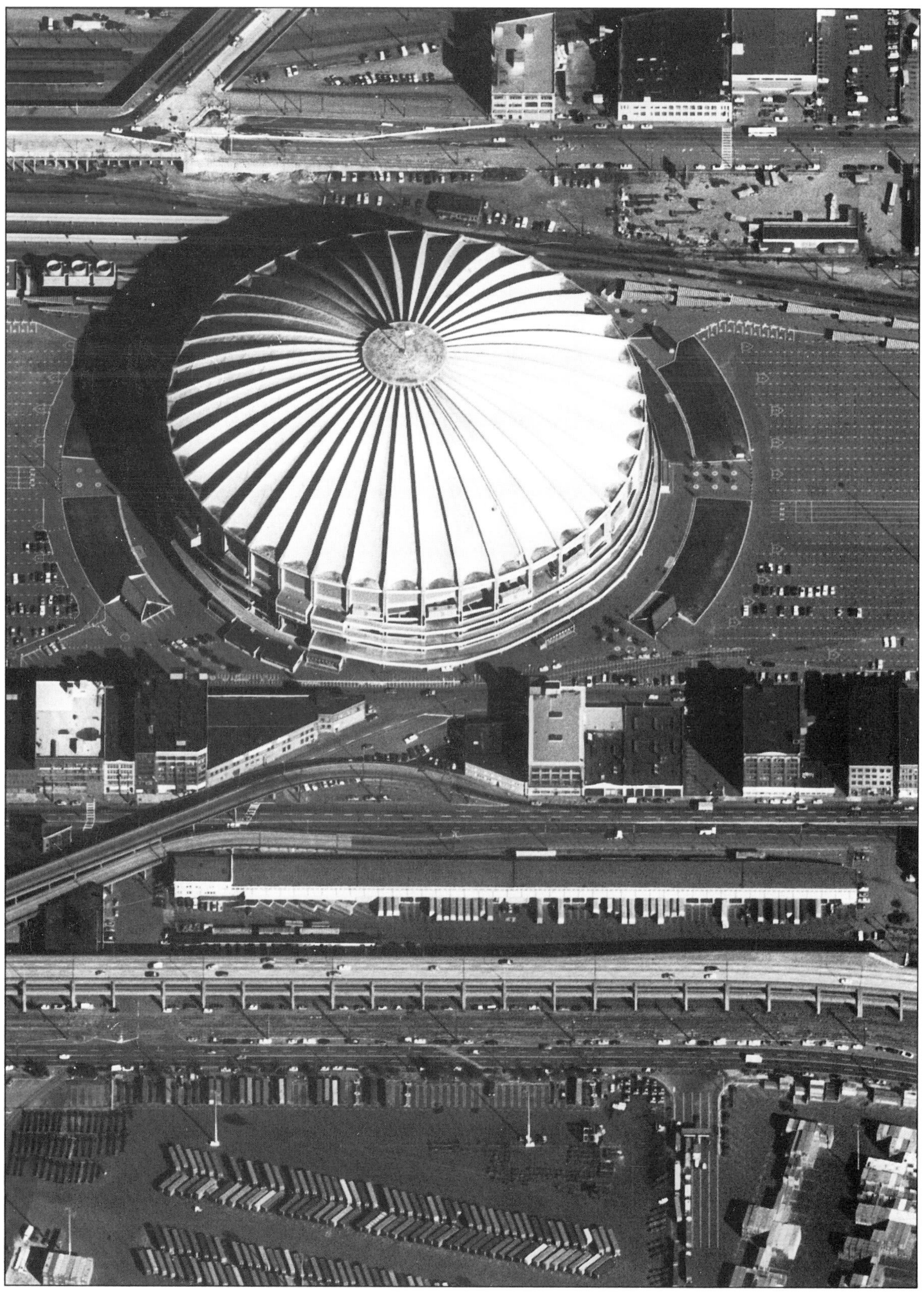

crew and delivered to the 9th SRW. On 31 December 1970 the functions of this unit were transferred from Air Force Systems Command (AFSC) to Air Force Logistics Command (AFLC), and Det 51 of AFLC was created. The unit reported to the Sacramento Air Logistics Center and had sub-division offices at Norton AFB at San Bernadino, California, near to the contractors and sub-contractors.

The function of the ASPO was to provide total logistics support to the SR-71 programme, including maintenance support (spares, major overhauls and testing and evaluation of new or upgraded systems). A September 1977 reorganisation placed the duties of Det 51 at Plant 42 in the hands of Det 6. Command of this new detachment was located at Norton, with further lines of command to Wright Patterson AFB in Ohio.

The two flight test crews of the Det 51/6 Flight Test Division flew missions on dedicated flight-test aircraft, and in addition conducted FCF's on recently overhauled fleet aircraft. All fleet modifications were first extensively flight tested at Palmdale. Such comprehensive testing encompassed all airframe, engine, subsystems and sensor/defensive systems that would ultimately be incorporated in improved fleet aircraft. Virtually all aspects of the SR-71's mechanical and sensor systems were modified and updated during the course of the programme. At any one time, contemporary and advanced technology systems and capabilities were fielded.

Significant programmes tested at Palmdale included High Mach/High Bank angle envelope clearance, a High Alpha (angle of attack) warning and protection system, DAFICS, electrical system replacement, stability system improvements and advanced sensor and defensive system qualification. Literally everything from nuts, bolts, fasteners and paint, to newly manufactured and uprated engines, were all extensively tested. The dedicated flight test crew (one crew selected from the USAF Test Pilot School, the other coming from the operational fleet) flew between 150 to 200 hours a year, and were supported by Lockheed ADP maintenance and engineering personnel from 1970 to 1990.

The high quality images obtained by the SR-71's cameras are perfectly illustrated by this impressive photograph of the Seattle Dome in Washington state while cruising at 82,000 ft and Mach 3 (*USAF*)

To remain ahead of Soviet missile development, the Air Force asked Lockheed engineers to develop an aft-directed ECM system to be used against advanced missiles. Additional fuselage space was necessary to accommodate the requirement and to allow sufficient space for real-time data transmitters. Design consideration was given to equipment pods and conformally-mounted packages, but an extended tail became the favoured option. Such a modification added considerably more volume, and involved minimum airframe and systems modifications, produced low aerodynamic drag and was relatively cheap. After the Air Force accepted the new design, 959 was transformed into the 'Big Tail' SR-71 configuration.

Proof of the concept began on 20 November 1975 when Lockheed test crew Darrell Greenamyer and Steve Belgeau conducted high speed taxy tests. The new tail unit was nearly nine feet long, weighed 1273 lbs, had an added volume of 49 cubic feet, and could carry a maximum payload of 864 lbs. To prevent the appendage from contacting the ground during take-off rotation, or the drag 'chute from fouling the unit during the landing roll, the tail was hydraulically repositioned eight and a half degrees up or down.

A second test was conducted by the same crew on 11 December. During that first airborne test, Greenamyer accelerated to Mach 1.27 so engineers could evaluate the stresses on the added fuselage section. Eleven flights later, Lockheed handed 'Big Tail' over to Det 51 at Palmdale. On 5 May 1976, Lt Col Tom Pugh and Maj John Carnochan chalked up the first Air Force test flight in the aircraft. On that sortie 959 was equipped with DEF 'J' and an Optical Bar nose camera. The test series included a Mach 3.0 flight on 4 August, after which the Air Force test crew certified the modification as 'having no detrimental effects on the aeroplane's handling characteristics, or its maximum Mach, while considerably enhancing the SR-71's overall mission capabilities'. To further demonstrate its enhanced mission capabilities, 'Big Tail' was flown with two Optical Bar Cameras, one in the nose and one in the tail. Later the chine bays were deepened to accommodate two further OBCs in each. It was later found that the intercept capabilities of the SA-5 was less of a threat to SR-71s than had been anticipated, and it was determined that the fleet would not require the Big Tail mod for an aft-facing ECM suite. After that test series was finished, Lt Col Pugh and

Maj Bill Frazier flew that unique aircraft on its final Det 51 flight on 24 October 1976.

The prime test airframe for many years had been 955, however, by 1985 this SR-71 had become so highly modified that it no longer represented the fleet configuration. Lt Cols Tom Tilden and Bill Flanagan flew 'ever-reliable' 955 on its 722nd and last sortie on 24 January 1985. Four days later, the same two crewmembers conducted a runway roughness evaluation in the jet, and then returned it to the Palmdale storage barn, where it remained for six years. In 1991 955 re-emerged once again, and was placed on permanent display at the Air Force Flight Test Center Museum at Edwards AFB.

The test role was passed on to 972, which was fresh out of Programmed Depot Maintenance, and flown by BC Thomas and JT Vida (the aircraft completed its FCF on 22 January 1985). Its final flight was on 6 March 1990 when Ed Yielding and JT Vida delivered the jet to the Smithsonian National Air and Space Museum following a record breaking flight across the US. During its time with the division, 972 flew 417.9 hours during 163 test sorties.

CHAPTER 6

'OL-8'

When President Johnson endorsed the CIA Director's 31 December 1966 decision to terminate the *Oxcart* programme, a schedule for the phase-out of the A-12 fleet was formulated to meet a 1 January 1968 deadline. On 10 January 1967 the head of the project advised Deputy Secretary of Defense Cyrus Vance that four A-12s would be placed in storage in July, two more in December, and the last four in January 1968.

In May 1967, Vance directed that the SR-71 assume contingency responsibility to conduct Cuban overflights in July and that the *Senior Crown* programme also be ready to cover Vietnam by 1 December 1967. His directive provided for a short overlap between the out-going 'covert' A-12 programme and the in-coming 'overt' SR-71 programme. The date of the change-over slipped five months, giving a brief stay of execution for *Oxcart*.

As the 1st SRS neared operational readiness, decisions were made by Colonel Bill Hayes (the 9th SRW Commander) and Colonel Hal Confer (the Director of Operations) as to which crews would be the first to be deployed to Kadena Air Base on the island of Okinawa. The eight crewmembers they selected began training for the deployment, flying simulator sorties depicting the oceanic route they would fly[1].

It was also decided that the crew who ferried the first aircraft to Kadena would fly the first operational sortie over Vietnam. The predetermined sequence would also include a fourth crew in the operational line-up who rode a tanker to Kadena. Each SR-71 departure would be backed-up by a spare (with the fourth crew) in the event of the primary aeroplane having to abort due to No-GO discrepancies, such as inlet malfunctions[2]. KC-135s were deployed to Hawaii and Kadena to support the three transpacific SR-71 deployment flights, code-named *Glowing Heat*.

The crews agreed to draw straws, leaving the choice of who would go first in the hands of Fate. Dave Dempster held the four straws of varying length and the RSOs from each of the other three crews drew one. With 'the luck of the draw', Dave Jensen's straw decided that he and Buddy Brown would fly the first aircraft across 'the Pond', and would hopefully fly the first 9th SRW ops sortie from Kadena. Jerry O'Malley and Ed Payne would fly the second deployment and Bob Spencer and Ruel (Keith) Branham the third. Dempster was left holding the short straw, so he and Watkins would ride the tanker unless one of the other crews came up with a 'sick' jet.

Command of the Operating Location would be alternated between the 9th SRW's wing commander and vice commander (and later the Deputy Chief of Operations). The first detachment commander would be the vice commander, Col Charles Minter, and Col Carl Estes would be the director of maintenance. Two days before the first *Glowing Heat* mission, six KC-135Q tankers were pre-positioned at Hickam AFB, Hawaii, from where Maj Harlon Hain (the 1st SRS operations officer) set up a down-range radio station on Wake Island to provide emergency radio coverage. All was ready for Brown and Jensen to make their record-breaking five-hour flight across the Pacific, the sortie being flown at a speed that was twice as fast as the existing world record.

Deployment

At 1000 hours on the morning prior to their departure, Brown and Jensen (along with their back-up crew, Watkins and Dempster) received their pre-mission briefing. Since this was the 9th's initial operational deployment, the briefing was attended by the wing commander and many others.

On 8 March 1968 Majs Buddy Brown and Dave Jensen left Beale in 978 as the first *Senior Crown* crew to deploy to Kadena. Above, Mort Jarvis (left) is pictured with Buddy Brown after they teamed up later in the programme (*USAF*)

Mission planners briefed the entire flight profile for the sortie which would begin at 1100 hours on 8 March. After take-off they would head west from Beale to a point 50 miles north of San Francisco, where they would 'light the burners' for a dash to 75,000 ft to check that all systems were functioning normally, before descending to the first air refuelling. With a clean bill of health on the 'Habu' and a top-up of fuel from the tankers, Buddy and Dave would race to another refuelling northwest of the Hawaiian Islands, where they would 'buddy cruise' with the tankers for an extra half an hour to take them to a point where they would be 'single-engine-capable' to the island of Iwo Jima as an emergency landing base.

After the mid-Pacific refuelling, a third Mach 3.0 dash would take them to their third and final top up west of Wake Island, where a maximum off-load would give them enough fuel to reach Kadena and to go to an alternate base on Taiwan should the weather deteriorate over Okinawa. During the briefing they were informed that the weather was expected to be good in the refuelling tracks, at Kadena, and at their emergency landing bases, and that they could expect a comfortable crossing. After a maintenance briefing and some good humour, the two crews began 'official crew rest'.

At 0730 the next morning the four crewmembers reported to the PSD for a final weather briefing and a maintenance report on their aircraft. This was followed by the standard preflight physical examination and high protein/low residue breakfast (steak and eggs, and orange juice[3]). After one last trip to the urinal, suit-up began. Two PSD suit technicians aided each crewmember as he donned his full pressure suit. A communications check and pressure suit integrity test confirmed that each garment was functioning properly, and after a ten-minute nap the crews were transported to their respective aircraft – Brown and Jensen to 978 and Watkins and Dempster to 980. After 'strapping in and connecting up' they began the normal 'challenge and response' cockpit checklists which would take them through engine start, taxy and pre-take-off procedures. With engines revved to full military power and all instruments 'in the green', Buddy

Above Lined-up sequentially, seven single-seat A-12s, plus 927 ('Titanium Goose') and two YF-12As, sit at Groom Dry Lake. In the foreground is 926, which became the first A-12 lost in an accident on 24 May 1963. The third aeroplane in the line-up was lost on 7 January 1967, while 929 was written-off on 28 December 1967 *(CIA)*

Below The engine exhaust plugs identify this M-12 as 134. A black A-12, sporting natural metal fins, is just visible behind the gantry *(Lockheed)*

Above The prototype M-12 and D-21 are pictured flying high above the Nevada desert. Aeroplane 940 survived the *Tagboard* flight test programme and can today be seen as the sole surviving example of its type at the Museum of Flight in Seattle, Washington *(Lockheed)*

Below left SR-71A 973, displays a 'star and bar' on the upper left wing – the national insignia was not incorporated on the fleet. Also shown are the longitudinal corrugations on the wing and the brake-chute storage compartment *(Lockheed)*

Below Agency pilot Jack Layton is pictured wearing a David Clark S-901 pressure suit in front of a single-seat A-12. The yellow 'box' to his left, is a portable oxygen and environmental control unit *(CIA)*

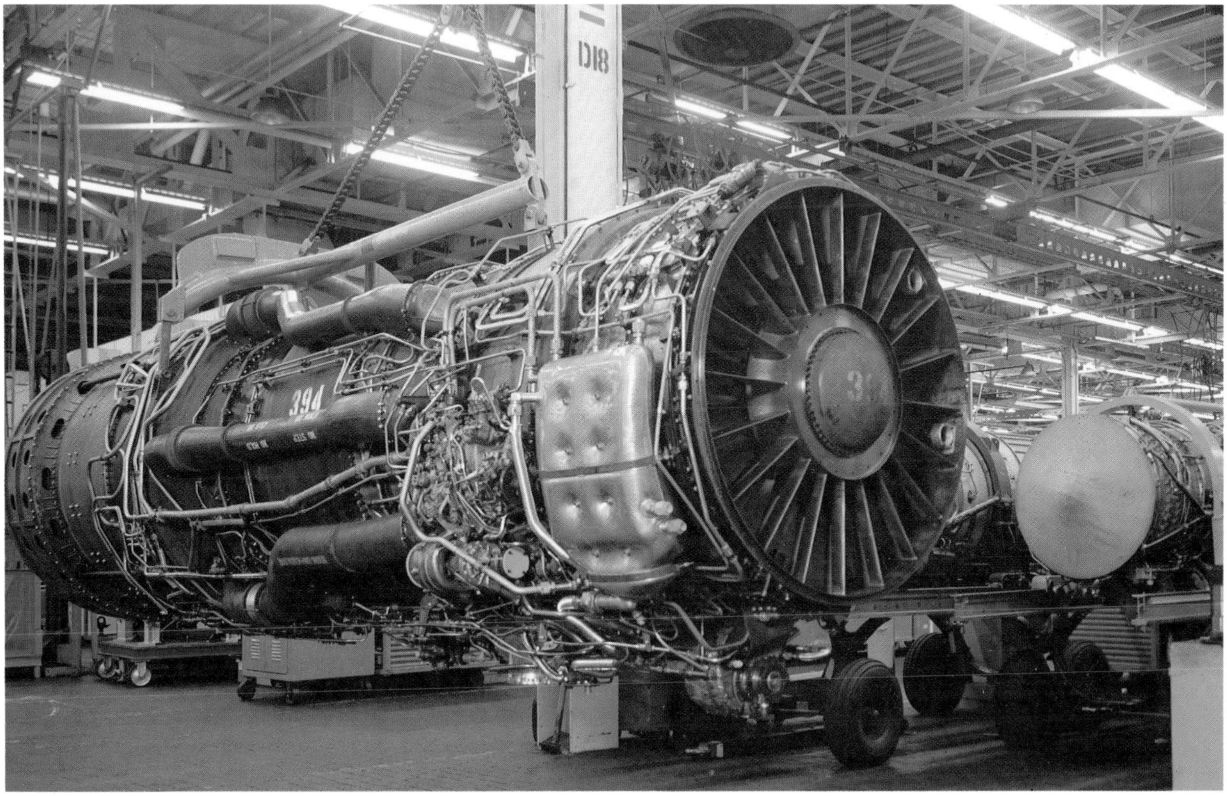

Above The engine that finally made the *Oxcart* and *Senior Crown* programmes possible was the Pratt & Whitney J58, masterfully designed by William H Brown *(Pratt & Whitney)*

Below One of the later flight-test teams at Palmdale consisted of Tom Tilden, BC Thomas, JT Vida and Phil Soucy. BC is wearing a non-standard S-1030 pressure suit; he and JT Vida acquired more flight hours in the SR-71 than any other crewmembers *(USAF)*

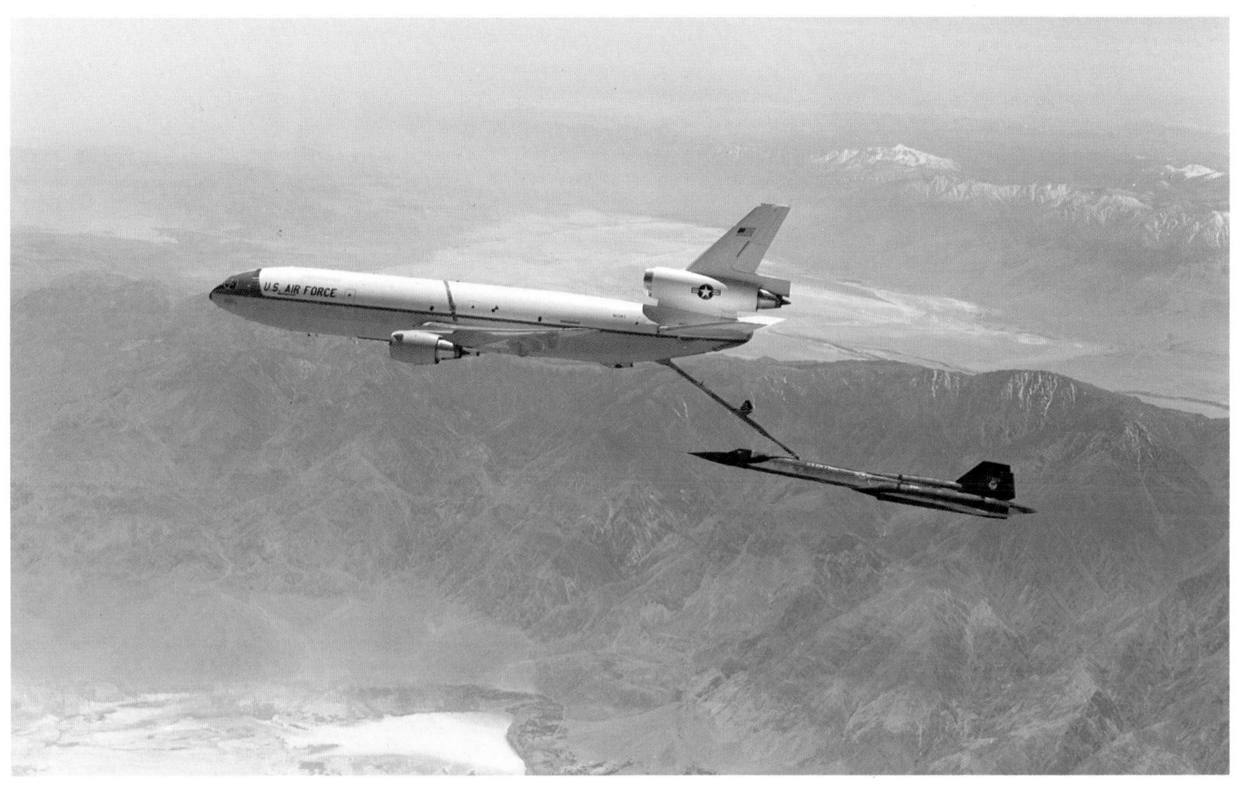

Above Flight number 559 in 955's long test career was conducted on 6 May 1981 when Palmdale flight test crew Cal Jewett and Bill Flanagan carried-out compatibility checks with McDonnell Douglas's KC-10, tail number N110KC *(USAF)*

Below Palmdale's 'evergreen' 955 completes yet another 'test-hop'. By the time the jet was retired it had accumulated 1993.5 flight hours during 712 sorties. It was last flown on 24 January 1985 by Tom Tilden and Bill Flanagan *(USAF)*

Above Lockheed test crew Darrell Greenamyer and Steve Belgau first flew the 'Big Tail' conversion of 959 on 11 December 1975. The feature was the most prominent external modification ever carried out on an SR-71A. Note the windows in the elongated tail for an OBC unit *(USAF)*

Below On 22 November 1989 the USAF terminated all SR-71 operations. In February 1990 Eric Schulzinger and Michael O'Leary were granted permission to group together the remaining SR-71s at Beale for this historic photograph *(Lockheed)*

Above Despite the prolonged and courageous efforts of Dan House and Blair Bozek to save 974, this aircraft has the dubious destinction of being the last SR-71 to be lost *(USAF)*

Above Ed Yeilding and JT Vida established a coast-to-coast speed record of 1 hour and 08 minutes on 6 March 1990 in SR-71A 64-17972. They are pictured at Palmdale before setting-off on their historic flight *(USAF)*

Below SR-71A 980 arrives at Edwards AFB sporting Det 4's Dartboard and Blackbird insignia, which were lovingly chalked upon its tail by Sgt Higley. The aeroplane is operated by NASA under the new tail number of 844, and was first flown by Steve Ishmael and Marta Bohn-Meyer on 24 September 1992 *(NASA)*

Right SR-71B 956 is currently being operated by the Dryden Research Center at Edwards AFB. The long-serving B-model was redesignated as 831 by NASA *(NASA)*

DET 1 - OKINAWA
1968 - 1990
CYGNUS
PSD
U-2
SR-71
1st STRAT RECON SQ
ROAD RUNNERS
"BEEP BEEP"
3+ FLIGHT TEST
SR-71
DET-6 (AFLC)
WSLO
SR-71
AERIAL RECONNAISSANCE
PROGRAMS
U-2
TR-1
DET 6,2762nd LOG SQ(SP)
SR-71
LOGISTICS SUPPORT
IN THRUST WE TRUST
PRATT& WHITNEY
PALMDALE ENGINE SHOP
A-1
OPERATIONAL DEMONSTRATION 1983

WEST COAST
1984
3+

released 978's brakes and lit both burners, the SR-71 rapidly rolling down the Beale runway and lifting off into the vivid blue morning sky. He recalls:

'After crossing the coast of California, I started our transonic acceleration climb profile to altitude. This portion of the flight was considered 'mission critical' because the spikes, forward and aft inlet doors, inlet guide vanes, and nozzles all had to check out prior to committing the bird to the Pacific high-flight. Everything was 'up tight' so we were on our way. Shortly after level-off at FL750 we picked up the tanker's ARC-50 radio signals and started getting ranging information to the aircraft, which was about 400 miles away. We had a solid 'lock on' so we made the radio-silent rendezvous. We pulled up into the pre-contact position, were waved in, got a contact and started our max off-load to a pressure disconnect. We took on about 60,000 lbs of fuel, said thanks and goodbye over the boom interphone and started on our way to AR #2. The second leg was uneventful, although the ARCP was changed slightly due to a line of thunderstorms in the AR track. We again accelerated on our next leg to the third and final refuelling. Approximately 20 minutes after level off at 79,000 ft, I encountered a problem which could have forced me to land at Johnson Island. My right spike (for no apparent reason) went full forward which caused a very large yaw moment (lots of drag). I checked my cockpit over and found a popped circuit breaker which (when reset) brought the spike back to its normal 'bottomed' position for high Mach flight.

'The third decel, AR and climb were also normal, but when we were back at altitude I encountered another potentially serious problem. My left generator went 'off-line' and I couldn't reset it. This was a No-GO situation which meant I should land as soon as practical. My decision was to continue on because we were less than a thousand miles (about 30 minutes) from Kadena. I used my coded call sign and contacted 'Mamma' and informed them that "I was lost, but making good time". We landed at Kadena with the failed generator, but the first SR-71 had arrived and was soon ready to start reconnaissance operations in Southeast Asia, and wherever else the National Authorities might require. We had taken off from Beale at 1100 and had arrived at Kadena at 0905 – nearly two hours earlier than take-off time (but in the next day because we had crossed the international date line). We beat the sun by a good margin.'

Bob Spencer and Keith Branham delivered 974 to Okinawa on Wednesday 13 March 1968 (*USAF*)

Jovial group shot snapped at Beale just prior to the first OL-8 transpac to Okinawa (*USAF*)

Two days later O'Malley and Payne delivered 976 to OL-8. They had departed Beale much earlier in the morning and landed at Kadena at 0330 hours Japan time. Spencer and Branham delivered 974 on 13 March. Three days later the KC-135 carrying Watkins and Dempster arrived at Kadena. It was late in the evening and raining hard when the tanker unloaded its weary passengers. As the last two SR-71 crewmembers (who had made the long Pacific trip 'the hard way') stepped from the tanker to what should have been a 'rapturous welcome' from the others, they were met by a junior NCO who was there to drive them to their Visiting Officers Quarters in a blue Air Force maintenance van. The newcomers felt deflated as the NCO murmured a weak apology for the sparse turnout, dismissing it as 'high work load due to operational requirements'. As they opened the door to their VOQ room they were greeted by the entire gang of crewmembers and senior staff who cried out the raucous wartime welcome, 'Hello Assholes. What took you so long getting here?' OL-8 was now fully manned and it was time for a 'little celebration'.

The Kadena detachment was known as Operating Location 8 (OL-8), which followed the numerical designation pattern of SAC's overseas reconnaissance locations. It was redesignated OLRK (Ryukyus – the name of the island chain which includes Okinawa) on 30 October 1970, and then changed to OLKA on 26 October 1971, changing yet again to Detachment 1 of the 9th SRW in August 1974, a title which it retained until 1990 when the SR-71 fleet was retired. The operational deployment of the SR-71s to Okinawa also gave the aeroplane the nickname of 'Habu' after a dark poisonous pit viper indigenous to the Ryukyu Island chain. Although the nickname 'Blackbird' has long been publicly associated with the SR-71, that title has been shunned by the crewmembers and others closely connected with the *Senior Crown* programme, who favoured the serpentine moniker. The name 'Habu' stuck permanently and Dave Jensen designed a colourful flight jacket patch with the snake interlaced around the figure eight.

Col Charlie Minter was the chief architect of most of the operating procedures for OL-8's crews. Those rules proved so sound and well-structured that most of them remained unchanged throughout the entire 22-year life of the Kadena operation. Maintenance teams from the 9th SRW that manned OL-8 were the best at their jobs and were considered the cream of Air Force maintainers. Col Carl Estes' hand-picked 'Habu'-technicians had done high-priority work on the three jets as they arrived and had all of them ready for operations by 0900 hours

on 15 March 1968, when the unit was declared 'fully OR' (Operationally Ready).

On Monday 18 March, OL-8 was ordered to fly its first operational sortie. As previously agreed, Buddy Brown and Dave Jensen began preparing themselves for the mission. As a hedge against crew illness or aircraft system failures, every operational sortie was backed up by a spare aircraft and a suited-up aircrew who were equally prepared for take-off orders. The standby crew on this occasion was Jerry O'Malley and Ed Payne. Although everyone was 'all set' for the mission, it was cancelled by higher authorities and Buddy and Dave flew a 'Cathy' training sortie[4]. As previously agreed back at Beale, the next crew to fly was Jerry and Ed. Lady Luck was on their side and on 21 March 1968 they flew the SR-71 on its first-ever operational sortie over 'enemy territory'.

Eyes and Ears

Shortly after their arrival on Okinawa, the crews were summoned to a briefing in a secure room where they heard of local efforts to observe their activities. Since the primary building material of Japanese houses was wood, tall watch towers had been built in numerous locations on Okinawa to detect fires in their earliest stages so the local fire departments could quickly contain them. One such tower existed just outside the perimeter fence on

Weary after their long tanker ride, Lt Col Jim Watkins and Maj Dave Dempster arrive on the wet island of Okinawa. Col Charles Minter (the first OL-8 commander) presents the crew with 'Senior Taxi Wings'; Watkins and Dempster had taxied out to Beale's hammerhead three times as back-up in 980 to cover the launch of the other three 'Habus' (*Dave Dempster*)

the north side of Kadena Air Base, near Kosser Circle. The so-called fire guards had unrivalled views of the entire base from its commanding platform.

During the year of A-12 operations, intelligence officers had correlated positively that whenever an A-12 emerged from its hangar, a red flag was run up the watch tower's flagpole. In addition, it had been ascertained that within five minutes of the flag's lofting, a Soviet 'trawler' (on radar picket duty just beyond the 12-mile limit off the coast of Okinawa) switched on its radar which remained on as long as the flag remained flying from the tower. All along the China coast to the Gulf of Tonkin the Soviets had positioned a string of such 'trawlers' to relay tracking information on the Vietnam-bound 'Habus'. An RSO later commented that it was almost like radar coverage back in America, but instead of FAA air traffic centres handing you off from one ATC centre to another, the Soviets were monitoring our every move. The co-ordinated tracking was also supported by Chinese *Tall King* surviellance radars along their coast and on Hainan Island. As an A-12 or SR-71 penetrated North Vietnamese airspace, the first SA-2 target acquisition radars would lock on at a slant range of approximately 80 miles. Such monitoring activities caused one crewmember to contemplate a radio transmission on the emergency frequency, saying 'с Лоброе УТРО ТАВ ТОВАРИШ' (Good Morning, Comrade).

What these crews were not told was that US Intelligence services had broken the Communists' communications codes. Lacking land-lines for point-to-point telephone contacts, the Vietnamese had to transmit 'Habu' tracking data to their command centres via broadcasted radio frequencies, which were immediately intercepted by US listeners on Okinawa, Taiwan, South Vietnam and Thailand, as well as by EC-130 airborne listening posts flying over the Gulf of Tonkin. Fluent Russian and Chinese linguists working at these stations would translate the broadcasts into English for secure retransmissions to various allied agencies. Back at Kadena, a handful of senior officers were privy to that information and could indirectly monitor their 'Habu's' progress via the enemy's conversations. As an A-12 or SR-71 departed Kadena on an operational sortie, the commander and a few of his key staff members would meet in the Special Activities Office, where a secure teleprinter known as a 'Dingy Whopper' would 'tell them about the sortie'. As one officer described this 'mail reading' exercise, 'We were able to listen to them, while they watched us'.

Fate was to frustrate the other 'Habu' crews who prepared to fly their own first operational sorties – each being cancelled and replaced with a training sortie instead. On 10 April 1968, Brown and Jensen were once again set as 'primary crew'. O'Malley and Payne were suited up as back-up. Buddy cranked 974's engines precisely on time and taxied out of the 'Little Creek' area to 'run-up' near the end of the runway. Jerry and Ed were sitting in 976 waiting to hear that Buddy and Dave were 'off and running'. Instead, Crew Chief Tech Sergeant Bill Campbell told them that 974 was taxying back to the hangar. While Jerry and Ed were getting ready to roll, Buddy and Dave parked 974 nearby, the stricken jet being duly 'swarmed' over by most of the OL-8 maintenance force. Even Col Estes clambered on top of the jet with his ANS specialists and 'was working like a GI mechanic' to help replace the astroinertial navigation set. Meanwhile Ed and Jerry were ready

As North Vietnam sortie rates increased, the three Kadena-based SR-71s began to notch up an impressive number of 'Habu' mission marks (*Lockheed ADP*)

to make Buddy's scheduled take-off time and relegate Buddy and Dave as their back-up. Ed recalled:

'We got out there and were running a fast checklist and I happened to look up and here comes Buddy taxying like a bat out of hell. It must have been a world record ANS change, but I was certain that Dave hadn't had time to get a 'star light' because the system hadn't had time to go through all of its BIT checks yet. Charlie Minter who was in the mobile control car, obviously was thinking the same thing. Since it was his duty as OL Commander to put the best aircraft over the target, he leapt from the car and wrote "YOU GO" on an 8 × 10 inch pad which he held up to Jerry and I, and "YOU STAY" on the other side which he showed to Buddy and Dave.'

As they climbed away, Jerry and Ed elected to adopt the primary aircraft's callsign since they had made that aircraft's take-off slot. They reasoned that the tankers would be expecting that call sign and that they would minimise confusion by keeping 974's identity. Unfortunately, the call sign change did not help Bill Boltersiders in the Command Post, who had to dispatch a coded report to HQ SAC immediately after take-off. In his uncertainty as to which aircraft actually departed, he had to wait for Col Minter's return from the flightline before having the necessary details to set HQ SAC straight. The mission got off to a good start and Jerry and Ed were again on their way toward Vietnam on the 'second' SR-71 combat sortie.

They coasted-in near Saigon, made a shallow turn to the right to fly northbound across the DMZ towards Vinh and then on to Hanoi. There was no shortage of high priority targets – Phuken and Ying-By airfields, the steel works, and dozens more. Unknown to the crew, President Johnson had stated that day in a broadcast that no US strike aircraft would fly further north than the 19th parallel. His decision had caused confusion within military circles to the meaning of 'strike aircraft'. The 'ground pounders' at higher headquarters decided to play it safe and sent out an HF Radio message intended to withhold the sortie from overflight. Ed received a coded message from *Sky King* on the *Giant Talk* network, but was too busy flying at 33 miles a minute over the prime target area to take time to decode the message, which instructed them to turn left and abort the mission. Some moments later the autopilot initiated a programmed turn which started them back toward the south. With a few moments between high workload events, Ed told Jerry of the abort order. After completing the turn, they exited North Vietnam near Dien Bien Phu and prepared for descent toward their air refuelling over Thailand.

The two fliers' spirits had been high throughout the sortie, particularly since their good luck had enabled them to fly both operational missions performed so far. The mission had been 'a piece of cake so far', or so they thought until Jerry eased back the throttles to the pre-assigned descent RPM. At that moment both engines rumbled slightly in a compression stall and immediately flamed-out.

An air-start required 450 knots KEAS and 7 PSI on the compressor face to get things 'turning and burning' again. That meant getting down to denser air where those higher aerodynamic values could be achieved. Jerry pushed the nose down hard and Ed recalled seeing the artificial horizon instrument showing all black[5]. As they rode the aircraft down to lower altitudes they decided that if Jerry could not get an airstart, Ed would call 'MAYDAY' at 23,000 ft and they would 'punch out' at 14,000. At 40,000 ft Jerry gave the throttles a nudge, which in turn gave the engines positive fuel flow and a shot of TEB for ignition. There was no response. He tried again as they were passing through 30,000 ft. Still nothing. Ed recalled further:

'By now we were both getting a little anxious. I saw the altimeter go through 26,000 ft and I was getting set to say "MAYDAY! MAYDAY! MAYDAY!" I got the word "MAY" out when I felt the aircraft shake a little. Realizing that Jerry had finally got something going, I didn't finish the rest of the message. A glance at the altimeter showed us just below 23,000 ft and still descending quite rapidly. Just then Jerry said "I've got one of them started." Shortly afterwards he got the second engine fired up and when we hit 20,000 ft we had both engines running fine.'

Having received the 'MAY' of Ed's message, the tanker crews knew that all was not well with the 'Habu' crew. This realization was confirmed as they monitored the air-to-air TACAN's Distance Measuring Equipment (DME) ranging. Ordinarily the SR-71 would make a 'hot' rate of supersonic closure on the tankers, slowing notably only in the final 30 miles. The DME meter would normally be clicking over between 20 to 30 miles per minute during the early part of the deceleration. Instead it quickly slowed to a closure rate of about eight miles per minute. That speed meant the 'Habu' was low and slow well before intended, and way up in 'bad guys' territory. Ed remembered:

'We got our act cleaned up and the first transmission we received from the tankers was, "Are you guys okay?" I answered, "No". They asked "What can we do?" I answered, "Turn North". The double-engine flame-out and rapid descent profile left 976 down at a 'gas-gobbling' 20,000 ft over northern Laos, some 300 miles short of our planned ARCP. We climbed back to 26,000 ft and headed south. I recall that the lead tanker navigator was a woman. I'm sure they must have violated operating procedures coming that far north without some form of fighter cover, but we were damn glad to see them. By the time we reached the tanker, 976 was below 8000 lbs of fuel. The tanker turned in front of us and the boomer plugged into our AR receptacle in a 'heartbeat'. We drained 80,000 lbs of JP7 out of two tankers and even used a little from the spare – perhaps a record off-load. We used the extra gas because we had to lengthen the air refuelling track from Laos to mid-Thailand. Had we just filled up and climbed for home we wouldn't have been able to fly the profile properly, so we just stayed behind those beautiful tankers until we reached the originally planned disengagement point.'

While Jerry and Ed were refuelling, they discussed what might have caused the double-engine flame-out and what would be the preferred action to get home safely. Ed was in favour of staying with the third KC-135 and flying all the way back at 0.90

Mach to meet some Kadena-launched spare tankers. Jerry, on the other hand, believed they should fly a normal profile to help determine the cause of the problem. Jerry discussed at length what data he wanted Ed to record and just prior to the final decel back into Kadena, he began reading out RPM, EGT and fuel flow information. He eased back the throttles and the engines spooled down normally. They recovered into Kadena without further incident, thus ending the second operational sortie of the SR-71's reconnaissance career. That double flame-out foreshadowed a spate of similar problems which would follow over Laos, and would earn the 'Habu' the nickname of 'Lead Sled' back at the SAC Reconnaissance Center.

With the first two ops missions under their belts, Jerry and Ed were relegated to flying test hops for the duration of their tour to ensure that the other crews had an opportunity of accumulating some combat time. The following week Buddy Brown and Dave Jensen were scheduled to fly a 'double looper' over North Vietnam. All went well with their first sortie until it was time to decelerate for their first Thailand refuelling. The tanker notified them that the ARCP had been moved due to thunderstorms in the AR area. As they began to decelerate the left generator went off-line and could not be reset. This failure was followed by a double-engine flame-out. Dave transmitted the necessary codes stating that they were going to make a precautionary landing at Takhli RTAFB, since generator failure was a 'land as soon as practicable' abort item. Without power they lost cabin pressurization and their 'moon suits' inflated, which made cockpit movements awkward. As they decended toward an altitude where the engines could be restarted, Buddy requested that the tankers come north to give them additional fuel after the early and rapid descent. At 35,000 feet he was able to restart the engines. He then adjusted the aircraft's centre of gravity for subsonic flight and called Takhli Approach Control, informing them of their impending arrival. The tower controller told them that the tankers had already alerted the Command Post and that they were ready to receive them. On approach, the nose gear's downlock light failed to illuminate. Buddy made a low pass by the tower to have the gear visually checked 'down' and then circled to an uneventful landing.

Since the CIA had a 'secure compound' on the airfield from where they conducted U-2 operations, Buddy was able to use one of their hangars. A recovery team arrived from Kadena and readied the SR-71 for a return to Kadena. As they were preparing to depart, the head of the Agency's detachment told Buddy, 'If you don't tell anyone

Another 'up North' sortie gets under way as a 'Habu' taxies out of its barn at Kadena (*USAF*)

you were here, I won't either'. Buddy laughed at the 'typical cloak and dagger' remark and thanked him for the first-rate support on their interrupted 'Habu' mission.

About a week later, Buddy and Dave flew their second ops sortie. As they started their descent into Thailand, they experienced another double-engine flame-out and another failed generator[6]. As they taxied back into the Agency's hangar at Takhli yet again, Buddy insisted he had not come to join the CIA but to enjoy their hospitality. On leaving the Thai base two days later, Buddy saluted them with a 'max burner' climb out that 'left them all smiling' as the lightly-fuelled 'Habu' climbed steeply away from its newfound second home in Southeast Asia.

Following cancellations and disappointments, Jim Watkins and Dave Dempster finally got airborne on 19 April in 974 . They topped-off their fuel tanks near Kadena and headed out for North Vietnam. Arcing around Hainan Island on their right, they entered the Gulf of Tonkin and reversed left onto their penetration track. This 'front door' entry took them over Haiphong and Hanoi, exiting via Dien Bien Phu. Like earlier flights, everything went well until it was time to come down for aerial refuelling. As soon as Jim slid the throttles out of burner, there was an enormous bang, followed by another double-engine flame-out. He got both engines started up again after wiping 50,000 ft of altitude off the altimeter's reading. The tanker crews responded immediately to the emergency call, heading north without fighter escort back into the 'bad lands' of Northern Laos.

Whilst the 'Habu' was 'on the boom' and taking on three tons of fuel a minute, Jim had time to reflect on the incident that could have ended in disaster. At that point he said to his RSO, 'Davey, I think I might know what happened and if I hold a couple hundred more RPMs above what it says in the check-list the next time I come out of burner, I might be able to keep the engines alive and we can complete the mission. What to you think?' Dave replied, 'Let's give it a try and do the next run.'

It seems that 'cowboy' Jim Watkins had the first glimmer of an idea which would later be proven when Don Walbrecht and Phil Loignon flew Vietnam to Thailand descents without a problem[7].

In 1968, OL-8's operational mission rate was approximately a mission a week. Jerry O'Malley and Ed Payne rotated home earlier than originally planned and were replaced by Maj Larry DeVall and Captain Clyde Shoemaker. Majs Bob Spencer and Keith Branham flew their first operational sortie on 22 April – a 'double-looper' over North Vietnam lasting five-and-a-half hours. They were airborne again on 8 May flying another 'double-looper' lasting another five-and-a-half hours. Their third and final operational flight of their first tour took place three days later. It was the first operational ELINT-gathering sortie flown by OL-8 and lasted four-and-a-half hours.

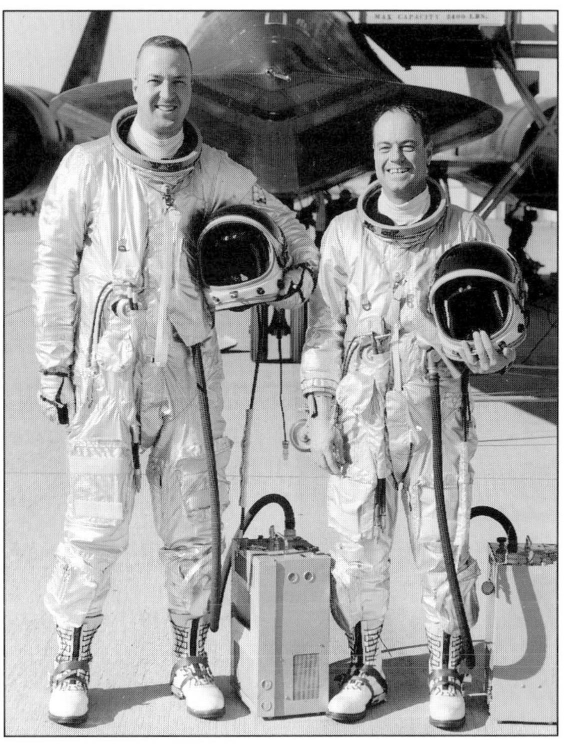

Dave Dempster (left) and Jim Watkins (right) came close to being the first casualties of OL-8 when Jim became hypoxic (*USAF*)

On 13 May 1968 Jim Watkins and Dave Dempster flew 974 on a two-loop route over North Vietnam using Side-Looking Radar. While on the KC-135's boom during the final air refuelling before the flight back to Kadena, Jim set the cabin pressure altitude switch to 10,000 ft. He told Dave he was raising his face plate for a drink of water – this was certainly an unusual procedure, momentarily breaking the old flying rule 'oxygen over 10,000ft'. After a refreshing libation, Jim closed his visor and informed Dempster that he was ready for the flight back home.

Dropping off the boom, he lit the burners and

headed up into the darkening tropical night sky. When he was established in an accelerating supersonic climb, Jim engaged the autopilot's 'Auto-Nav' function as the 'Habu' headed North East over the South China Sea. It was during this stage of the climb that Dave first percieved that 'all was not well with his pilot'. Jim's words were beginning to become slurred, but as far as Dave could tell, his actions were still okay. However, having trained together as a crew for well over 100 hours, the RSO was becoming increasingly concerned.

As the climb continued, Jim's speech deteriorated even further. Then the gut-twisting reality of the situation hit Dave with full force – his pilot was hypoxic and the RSO had no flight controls to overcome impending disaster. In a matter of minutes Jim would lose consciousness and shortly thereafter (unless Dave could get oxygen into his pilot's lungs), Jim would die and Dave would have to bail out in the vast South China Sea. The latter was not a realistic option for the RSO, and he wondered how he could get Jim's attention; he certainly could not get into the front cockpit where the flight controls were. Luckily the Autopilot and Auto-Nav functions were engaged which allowed Dempster to exercise the only control inputs that an RSO has in the back seat of an SR-71 – lateral steering using Nav steering commands, but absolutely no pitch controls. Dave dialled up 7700 on his IFF panel and squawked 'emergency' to alert the radar watchers in South Vietnam who were monitoring the flight and would know that 'all was not well'.

One option Dave considered was to turn the aircraft towards Cam Ranh Bay (the large PACAF base on the coast of South Vietnam). Dave dismissed this idea almost immediately for in a turn there was a greater chance of an inlet unstart and it was very doubtful if Jim could control the aeroplane in his current state of consciousness, which had become further degraded during the last minute of flight. Turning towards Vietnam would have taken the aircraft closer to the 'bad guys' and Dave was determined that he would not leave his pilot or allow any part of 'his' SR-71 to fall into enemy hands[8]. By now Jim was on the edge of unconsciousness. There was perhaps one possible remedy to this unbelievable situation. Dave summoned up every ounce of command authority in his voice and yelled over the intercom in a clear deliberate manner that 'We are now at the Start Descent check list'. Inlet Guide Vane switches to Lockout.' Surprisingly, Jim flicked the switches. 'Inlet Controls – Auto and Close.' Jim complied. 'Throttles, 720 degrees.' Again Jim carried out the RSO's instructions. Slowly 974's altimeter began to unwind. Dave recalled:

'Jim was one hell of a pilot. All of those thousands of hours of flying and training (and here he was about to pass out) and yet he was doing exactly what he was instucted to do. He came out of afterburner; he set the correct RPM and then threw the right switches for the bypass doors. Luckily, we didn't flame out or unstart, and Thank God, he didn't disconnect the Auto-Nav system so it was still steering us very accurately. On the way down, I monitored my Triple Display Indicator (Mach, KEAS and Altitude) readings and by using the profile card that we used to rendezvous with the tanker, I was able to give Jim additional commands like, "Okay, Jim, you're doing great; just ease it down a little bit; ease it down. Adjust your RPM slightly! Okay, you're right on profile." He was a disciplined flier and seemed to respond to those commands, and by the help of God, we raggedly descended and decelerated all the way down to subsonic speed, and he didn't pass out.

'We levelled off at about 25,000 ft and cruised at that altitude for awhile where Jim regained a bit of his normal consciousness. Slowly, Jim's voice began to return to normal and he suddenly said, "What the hell are we doing at this altitude!" I said, "Okay, Jim, the first thing I want you to do is to open your face plate and to close it again and to check that your bailer arm is down and firmly locked." He did exactly what I instructed and then started swearing at himself because the picture was beginning to return to him what had happened in the last ten minutes. We stayed 'low and slow' until he appeared 'clear and sharp' again.

'I calculated that we had enough fuel to fly subsonic all the way back to Taiwan, but Jim convinced me that everything was fine and that he clearly understood what had happened to him, although he had no real recollection of what had transpired during the ten-minute descent. Feeling comfortable that Jim now knew what was going on, I took the IFF out of emergency and he lit the burners and we flew supersonic to Kadena. One thing is for sure, you don't fly anywhere at Mach 3.0 and arrive at your destination fifteen minutes late.'

Col Minter and a few of the other SAO-watchers knew that something had happened, but no one knew what it was until the debrief (behind closed doors) when the problem was discussed in detail.

The initial rebuffs aimed at Jim soon gave way to more constructive dialogue when those who had not flown began to realise just how fortunate the crew of 974 had been. If Jim had not responded exactly as he had to Dave's instructions, the aircraft and crew would have vanished into the sea and the 'Habu' loss may have remained a mystery. It was therefore agreed that no disciplinary action would be taken and the story would be suppressed (which it duly was for 25 years).

As the experience of triple-sonic reconnaissance continued, crew changeovers brought other pioneers into the combat line-up at Kadena. In early May 1968, Maj Don Walbrecht and Capt Phil Loignon arrived to make their mark in operational flying. Their eight sorties from Kadena were typical of those flown at the time, and, in contrast to most of the initial missions flown in March and April, went quite smoothly. Like all crews, they started off with a two-hour training flight south of Okinawa in 976 on 19 May 1968 to get the feel of the vast oceanic area of the western Pacific.

Six days later they were airborne in 978 on their first North Vietnamese sortie which lasted five and a quarter hours. Completing the standard post-take-off refuelling, they were determined not to abort their mission unless 'a wing fell off'. Back in the US Don and Phil had experienced few inlet unstarts, but on their first important ops sortie while approaching Mach 2.4 and 55,000 ft one of the inlets let its shock wave go with an almighty bang. Phil asked, 'Isn't that a mandatory abort item?' 'Isn't what an abort item?' replied Don. Pressing on to 75,000 ft, the inlets kicked and bucked a few more times but all was as smooth as glass when they arrived at Mach 3.0. After entering the Gulf of Tonkin, Don pressed on to Mach 3.2, which gave the 'Habu' another 4000 ft above the enemy SAM-shooters.

Coasting in over Haiphong at 79,000 ft, they cruise-climbed to 81,000, where Phil noted a SAM target-acquisiton radar locking on. Immediately his ECM equipment nullified the threat and no missiles were fired. After crossing Hanoi and flying close to China, they exited North Vietnam over Laos, where Don eased the throttles out of burner for his descent (well aware of O'Malley, Brown, Watkins and DeVall's double flame-outs). Immediately there was a low rumble (the onset of an inlet-airflow mismatch which had probably caused the spate of flameouts). Instinctively, Don eased the throttles slightly forward, adding an additional two-hundred RPM to the engine speed. The rumble instantly disappeared and the engines remained alight for a notably smooth descent[9].

Don accelerated and climbed the *Playboy Rabbit*-adorned 978 on a southerly heading, rounding South Vietnam for another northbound run. They charged back up the Gulf of Tonkin offset from their first pass to make another uneventful run and a smooth deceleration at the slightly higher power settings, the mission terminating (after refuelling) in an uneventful recovery back to Kadena. They were airborne again the next day, taking 978 on a functional check flight to verify inlet performance

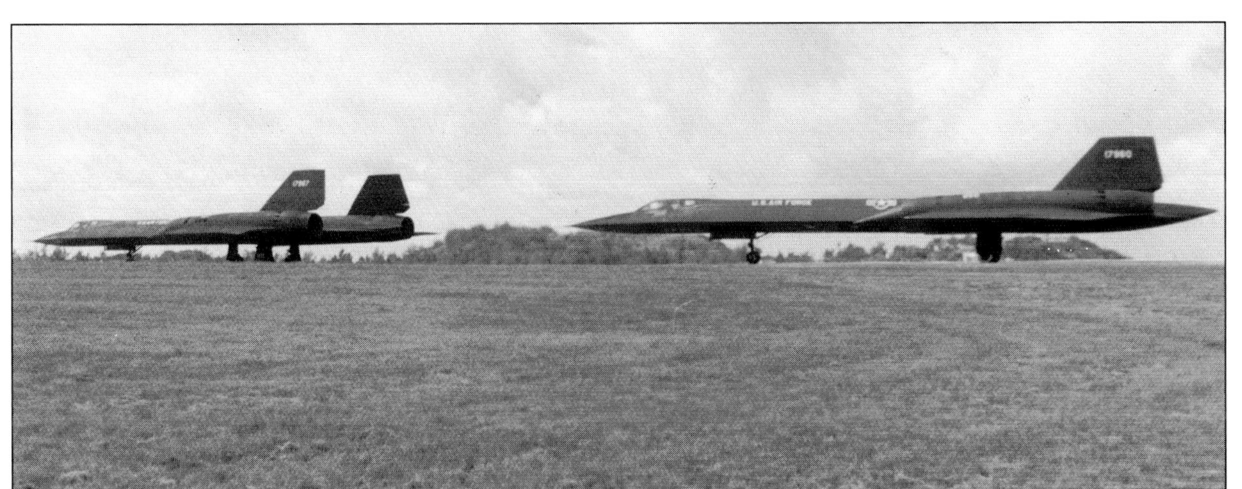

All top priority operational missions were 'spared' as a hedge against an air-abort. Here the primary and back-up aircraft wait at the hammerhead at Kadena (*USAF*)

and again on 8 June in the same jet to maintain aircrew currency. They completed their second operational sortie in 974 a few days later – a four and a half hour 'single looper' over North Vietnam.

Their third mission was again flown in 978 on 30 June (a 'two-looper' lasting five-and-a-half hours), for which they were each awarded the Distinguished Flying Cross. Don explained, 'Phil and I flew this important sortie in the face of a great typhoon, which was positioned off the southeast coast of Vietnam. It was extremely impressive to see from high altitude, easily visible from more than 500 miles away. Phil and I completed our two passes over denied territory and were heading back towards Kadena. By this time the typhoon had moved closer to the land mass of Vietnam and had pulled a great deal of moisture into its system. It was a remarkable sight, this enormous boiling maelstrom of great clouds stretching out before us, with vast columns of thunderstorms forced upwards on convective currents of air rising along its forward spiralling arms.

'The exceptionally tall storms looked like giant turrets which were guarding this mass of moving energy. Unable to see the storms which were lined up ahead of us, Phil was concerned that we might have to fly through the tops if they reached above 70,000 ft. When we got closer we could see that we had the better of them by at least 5000 ft. Flying at Mach 3.0, 15 miles up, one rarely approaches any other object closely enough to feel the spectacular sensation of 'great speed'. The typhoon had acted like a giant vacuum cleaner, drawing moist air away from the land mass and into the strom. The result was high-quality, clean air over all of the target areas, allowing us to obtain outstanding resolution of the 400 important targets Phil's cameras photographed.'

Don and Phil were especially proud of having been able to provide such a high qualilty 'take', but they modestly maintained that it was just good fortune that they happend to be airborne on such a good day, and that any crew back at the OL could have brought home the 'goods'. Thanks to the typhoon, Vietnam, China and Laos were all unusually clear and they got the 'good-goods', which saturated the attention of photo interpreters at all national and theatre intelligence centres.

On their final ops sortie in their 'always-in-the-green' 978 on 23 July 1968, Don and Phil flew another important 'double-looper' lasting five hours which yielded yet another superb-quality 'take' due to the proximity of the granddaddy of all thunderstorms which squatted over Haiphong. Don explained:

'Phil and I came zipping back up the Gulf clearly seeing all of Hainan and a great piece of China on our right. To our dismay, it appeared that too many clouds loomed ahead for a good run. I could see a great mass of high clouds standing over our target with a storm-pillar billowing up out of its middle – it was the 'superdome' of a single massive semi-tropical thunderstrom. I said to Phil, "it looks as if our sortie is going to be ruined by all of the undercast." We pressed on hoping for the best, accelerating and climbing to Mach 3.2 and 80,000 ft to make the run. By the time we topped out, we were beginning to cross over the storm, just barely above it.

'My attention was rivetted on the billowing top, which must have extended up to 79,000 ft – surely one of the highest cloud formations ever reported. We made a slight turn to the left to stay on track and went right over the top of the grand storm at an absolutely incredible rate of passage. Momentarily, I could feel the disturbing effects of the rising atmosphere's convective instability which made the 'Habu' wallow around more than I'd ever experienced at that high an altitude. As we shot over the top of it, the land mass ahead was sparklingly clear with perfect visibility all the way to mid-China. Phil photographed all of North Vietnam and much of southern China, and we turned south over Laos descending on our usual tanker track near Korat, Thailand. Again there were lots of medium-sized thunderstorms over Thailand but we found the tankers right where they were supposed to be.

'The tanker's boomer plugged into 978's receptacle immediately and the pilot started dodging all over the sky to avoid thunderstorms. It seemed we were heading west much longer than normal because of the sun's position and I recall looking out during a turn and asking Phil, "What's all that water down there?" He replied that it was the Andaman Sea, near Rangoon in Burma. We finally headed back to the southeast and after filling our tanks I asked the tanker's navigator for a heading that would take us clear of the thunderstorms, to which he replied, "There isn't one. You'll just have to take your chances." We climbed and accelerated, luckily missing all of the very turbulent thundercells. After we got above 50,000 ft and over the tops of most of the storms, we were in a continuous shroud of high thick cirrus which extended to the mid-sixties.

'We were moving at Mach 2.6 when we blasted from the cloud tops. It was like being shot from a rocket as we

This shot was taken at 82,000 ft by an SR-71 crewmember while flying near Vladivostok. Soviet fighters were particularly active during some of these 'Habu' PARPRO missions (*P Crickmore collection*)

bolted from the high tropopause into the clear stratosphere. We did another fast circuit of North Vietnam to see that the great single storm had already entered the post-mature phase with its anvil-top flattened out farther below. We then descended back into Thailand where the other storms had been. We were pleased that they had softened and moved further west. Having completed our third refuelling, we raced back to Kadena for an uneventful landing[10]. We flew our final Kadena training sortie, again in 978, shortly afterwards and redeployed back to California in the weekly Beale tanker.'

Majs Tony Bevacqua and Jerry Crew replaced Buddy and Dave and were flying 976 on 26 July 1968 on a 'double-looper' sortie over the 'North'. On their first pass, Jerry warned Tony that a SAM fire-control radar had locked-on them. Almost immediately he said, 'We've been fired upon'. The defensive systems performed as advertised, but Tony was unable to see the missiles, which ended up well behind them. During refuelling Jerry asked Tony if he intended to complete the sortie since their next track would again take them right back over the position from which they were fired upon. Tony replied, 'Why Not? They missed us.' On the next pass there was no reaction from any SAM battery. Back on the ground at Kadena, Tony recalled, 'As we got out of the aircraft we knew that the commander already knew about the incident. The first thing he asked was, "Did you see anything?" We said we hadn't, but we knew that it was for real. We were later told that the nearest of the two missiles was about one mile away.' It was the first occasion that an SR-71 had definitely been fired upon, and by chance, the terrain tracking camera took a picture of the SA-2s, recording Tony's 'first' for the record books.

Traditions and Antics

'All work and no play makes John a dull boy.' 'Habu' crew members certainly knew how to work and to get their job done, and they most definitely could not be accused of being dull, especially John Storrie, Buddy Brown, Larry DeVall and some of the more notorious pranksters. There was usually a genteel Sunday afternoon daiquiri party in the commander's quarters, which were only about 100 yards from the 'O' club, where many evening activities began. The favourite brew that one party group adopted was titled 'Velvet Punch', so-called because it could knock you out gently. Craven Givens (a tanker pilot of 'Habu' renown) was the undisputed master brewer of this 'smoothly lethal concoction', whose main constituents were three parts concentrated frozen lime juice, two parts beer and one part 'Everclear'. Light yellow-green in colour, 'Velvet Punch' was mixed in a stainless steel

Maj Dan House rests in the PSD van prior to an operational sortie. The bulkiness of his helmet is clearly evident (*P Crickmore collection*)

Maj Blair Bozek relaxes in the PSD van on the flightline. Once the crew were suited up, their movements were kept to a minimum (*P Crickmore collection*)

bowl that had been liberated from the kitchen. For the benefit of visitors, a clean jock and a pair of athletic socks were added. The stainless steel 'tanker bowl' was refuelled throughout the night until there was no one left capable of restocking the bowl.

At the south end of BOQ 310 (the 'Habu' home away from home) was a kitchen where the crews had their preflight (high-protein, low-residue) meal. Next to the kitchen was Doc Malley's room, where the crews received their preflight physical exam. The 'Habus' (under Buddy's leadership) convinced the Doc to give up his office for a crew lounge. They quickly set to work blanking out the entrance door and cutting an entry door into the now-isolated room through the kitchen's broom closet. A proper bar, fancy light fixtures, a music system and a refrigerator were added, and the walls were padded. The bright red decor of the 'Secret Bar' would have been more appropriate in a bath house. After the party room's reputation spread it became the envy of non-members, one of whom told the base commander who would not tolerate 'Habu' 'high jinks'.

Tony Bevacqua and Jerry Crew were the first OL-8 crewmembers to be positively fired upon by SA-2s, an event which occured over Hanoi on 26 July 1968 in SR-71A serial 976 (*USAF*)

Intelligence gathering was of course OL-8's livelihood, so it was not surprising that they learned of the impending visit before the actual inspection. The Secret Bar was quickly and quietly dismantled one night – the old entrance was reopened and the room returned to its former state. When the base commander conducted his 'surprise' visit the next day, he was surprised he could not find what had been reported. Soon after the inspection, the room was again transformed into the Secret Bar and it was 'business as usual'.

CMSgt Bill Gornik performs his famous neck tie cutting ceremony on Lt Col Pat Halloran in June 1968 (*USAF*)

Like an Indian chief displaying a prize collection of scalps, CMSgt Bill Gornik shows off 'his tie collection' (*P Crickmore*)

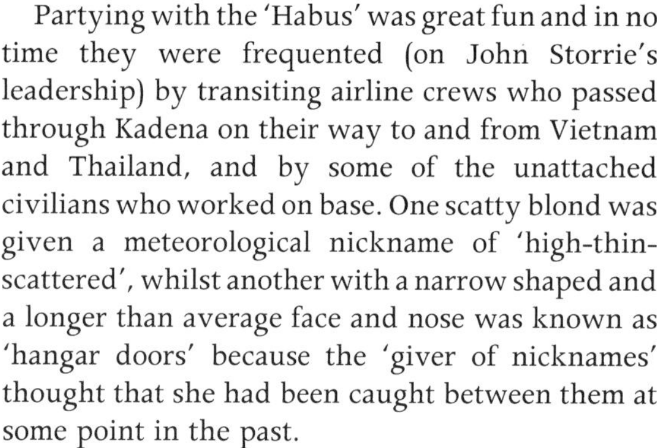

Partying with the 'Habus' was great fun and in no time they were frequented (on John Storrie's leadership) by transiting airline crews who passed through Kadena on their way to and from Vietnam and Thailand, and by some of the unattached civilians who worked on base. One scatty blond was given a meteorological nickname of 'high-thin-scattered', whilst another with a narrow shaped and a longer than average face and nose was known as 'hangar doors' because the 'giver of nicknames' thought that she had been caught between them at some point in the past.

On the night of 29 May 1968, the 'Habus' held a dinner at the Kadena Officers Club honouring Col Bill Hayes (the White Tornado), who had just completed his 30-day tour as OL commander and would return to Beale on the transpacific tanker in a few days. After dinner the party moved into the less formal Stag Bar, where Chief Master Sergeant Bill Gornik and two other senior NCOs crashed the party to say farewell to the colonel. Amid much hilarity, Bill Gornik produced a pen knife and severed the neckties of Bill Hayes and all the 'Habu' crew members. The next day he mounted the ties on a guide-on flag pole, just like the battle streamers on a command standard, or the feathers on an Indian ceremonial pole. At that moment a new tradition had been born.

In response, Don Walbrecht and Phil Loignon purchased a miniature Samurai sword and took it on a Mach 3.2 Hanoi flight before presenting it to Bill Gornik, the 'Chief-Master Necktie Cutter'. Thereafter, all crews flying their first operational mission from Kadena would wear a necktie inside their pressure suit. On completion of their sortie, they would emerge from the cockpit and have their tie ceremoniously cut off by Chief Gornik. Approximately 300 aircrew neckties all properly embroidered with names and dates, and hanging from Bill Gornick's 'Command Standard', which dates from 30 May 1968, are now displayed at Beale's 'Habu' museum.

Glowing Heat

By the fall of 1968, airframes 974, 976 and 978 had each amassed close to 300 flying hours at Okinawa. In so doing, they had easily validated the concept of long-range, triple-sonic, high-altitude strategic reconnaissance within hostile airspace. Their sensor systems had acquired intelligence data of national significance that had directly influenced the conduct of many air and ground operations. The dedicated professionalism of the maintenance teams working for Col Estes, and the high quality systems maintenance done by specialist company technical representatives, kept these deployed aircraft in top condition, but there were nevertheless certain 'heavy' depot-level maintenance tasks which lay beyond the capability of OL-8[11]. To carry out deep maintenance tech-order modification work, the original three aircraft had to be returned to Lockheed's Palmdale Plant 42. A complex every-other-day swap-out exercise code-named *Glowing Heat* was effected in late September, 974, 976 and 978 being replaced by 962, 970 and 980 – these aircraft were similarly replaced in the spring of 1969 by 971, 975 and 979.

Newly promoted Lt Col Tony Bevacqua and his new RSO were particpants in a *Glowing Heat* deployment from Beale to Kadena in 974 on 21 September 1969. They had just completed refuelling in the vicinity of Midway Island when one of the 'generator-out' lights illuminated on the telelight annunciator panel. It was a 'mandatory abort' item, so they dumped much of the fuel load that had just been taken on and diverted into the tiny island.

Midway is a renowned breeding ground for the Albatross. Luckily these large birds had all left the island a few days prior to Tony's arrival and he landed without incident (many of these creatures rest on the runway and are often hit by landing aircraft). Since Tony led off on the deployment, he was stuck on the island until all the other 'Habus' had been exchanged. A recovery team then came over from Kadena to solve their problem after all the other aircraft had been moved. Tony explained:

'The place was all Navy. Our BOQ was a cement block building with no air-conditioning and equipped with the world's most uncomfortable bed. To make matters less tolerable on this tiny island in the middle of nowhere, the 'O' Club didn't open until 1600 hours and we had to sit it out there on 'the rock' for ten days while our friends were laying sonic booms on us as they shuttled their 'Habus' back and forth across the Pacific. While there, I had the pleasure of meeting Judy Sides, a nationally-recognised and respected artist of the Gooney Bird.

'By the time 974 was ready to complete its trip to Kadena, she had painted a Gooney Bird symbol on each wheel-well door, applied another to each of the tails and another on the left side of the fuselage, near the cockpit where the white 'Habu'-snake mission symbols were normally painted. This shortlived artwork won the approval of the 'Habus' at Kadena, and constituted a new kind of 'first' in aviation art[12]',

Escalation of the Vietnam War generated an increase in the demand for timely, high-quality reconnaissance imagery. OL-8's SR-71 establishment was therefore increased in the spring of 1970 from three to four aircraft (969, 972, 973 and 974). The next three years would prove in many ways to be the detachment's 'Golden Era'.

(Left to right) Majs Charles 'Red' McNeer and George Bull (*USAF*)

Missiles

The first airborne recall of an SR-71 occurred on 4 October 1968. Majs Dale Shelton and Larry Boggess were just approaching the KC-135 to top off 970 after take-off when a coded message came through on HF Radio from *Sky King*, SAC's *Giant Talk* network, telling them to abort their mission and return to Kadena. Larry checked the authenticity of the message but could not retransmit on HF since Dale had already started refuelling. Larry recalled, 'When we didn't answer immediately, we got a curt UHF Radio call from the Kadena Command Post asking us if we'd received an earlier HF message transmission. We disconnected from the boom, dumped some fuel and recovered back to Kadena'. It seems that intelligence sources had discovered that the enemy knew of the 'Habu's' intended route, which would take the jet directly over the top of an active SAM site. Although SR-71s had been fired upon on an earlier sortie, it was deemed that offered the Vietnamese too much of an advantage on this occasion.

With a full-scale war raging in Southeast Asia, more and more crews got their chance to get their first TDY tour of duty at Okinawa, which was a great place to fly the 'Habu' from because it was a much more secure location. Majs Bobby Campbell and Jon Kraus flew their first sortie over Vietnam on 21 November 1968 – a 'double-looper' flown in 970 which lasted five-and-a-half hours. Majs Bob Powell and Bill Kendrick flew their first ops sortie on 29 December 1968 (again a 'double-looper' flight lasting nearly six hours) in which they were fired upon by two SA-2s. They brought back an especially high-quality 'take' by flying straight through their target run despite the rising missiles. They each earned a Distinguished Flying Cross for

A cell of three B-52s caught by an SR-71's Terrain Objective Camera as they coast into North Vietnam some 50,000 ft below the 'Habu' (*USAF*)

this mission. One 'Habu' driver later remarked to the author:

'Flying an SR-71 over the war at eighty-odd thousand feet was almost unreal. The Thud drivers were right down there in the middle of things while we were passing high overhead safely out of reach of the Soviet's best weapons. On a clear day, you'd see (and hear) the war going on 15 miles below. We could sometimes see flashes of fighter aircraft charging about and could often hear the excited radio conversations on guard channel, especially if an aircraft was down. We were only at risk for 15 minutes on both passes because we could cross North Vietnam in less than eight minutes flat. We always knew, however, that we'd really be in for it if we ever had to bail out over enemy territory for we would certainly have been a propaganda prize in our silver moon suits. We also had the advantage that in just a few hours we could be several thousand miles away back at the Secret Bar sipping a glass of *Chivas Regal*.'

Some of the crews who were fired upon by SA-2s spoke of seeing the SAMs through the RSO's view sight and the pilot's rear-view periscope. The missiles had to be fired 30 miles ahead of the jet to achieve the SR-71's altitude by the time it had arrived. Two white trails would appear well ahead of the 'Habu', but were normally not seen by the pilot since the aircraft's nose blocked his ground-view ahead. As the missiles approached the RSO could see them rising by looking through his down- and forward-looking view scope. When the missile exploded (usually above and behind) the pilot could get a quick glimpse of the explosion, which would first appear to billow out and then to collapse in on itself. That visual effect came about because of the rate of speed at which the jet could race away from the point of detonation. It was very strange to see, but the crews reported that it was also very comforting to know that the SAMs were ineffective because of the very long firing lead the missile-shooters needed to boost the SA-2 to altitude to 'point-intercept' the 3000 ft-per-second target.

Aircraft Loss

Throughout the early 1970s, OL-8's Vietnam sortie rate averaged two flights per week. The nature of high speed flight insured that those combat sorties would never become 'routine to the point of indifference'. OL-8 lost its first 'Habu' after more that two years of Kadena operations, which included over 200 operational and training sorties. On 10 May 1970 Majs Willie Lawson and Gil Martinez had completed one pass over North Vietnam and had refuelled 969 near Korat RTAFB. Willie had initiated an afterburner climb to prepare for a transonic 'dipsy-doddle'. Unfortunately, thunderstorms had built up rapidly across Thailand and no matter where they looked, a solid bank of clouds enshrouded the heavy thundercells which towered up to 50,000 ft.

Even an SR-71 needed climb distance to get above the clouds, and the dip-manoeuvre gave the aircraft a head-start on achieving the airspeed and Mach needed for a higher rate of climb. The 0.90 Mach preliminary climb was sluggish with a full fuel load, and Willie eased 969 into a slightly steeper climb to zoom up over the notch of a 30,000 ft-saddleback of connecting clouds between vertical storms, in order to stay clear of the cells ahead. At that moment, the aircraft entered turbulent clouds and both engines flamed out.

In heavy turbulence, without engine thrust, the aircraft's angle of attack increased. Suddenly the nose rose up into the dreaded pitch-up from which there was no recovery. Both crewmembers ejected safely and landed in the vicinity of U Tapao. Resplendent in their silver moon suits, they recruited the aid of a Thai who was driving a Saamlor (a three-wheeled vehicle common to Thailand) and were driven back to U Tapao and then flown back to Kadena in a KC-135. On their arrival, Col Hal Confer (the Det commander) and the entire unit had gathered to welcome them back. It was sad to lose a trusty 'Habu', but it was great to get the crew back. Overall, the pitch-up problem cost four aircraft in the 26 years of the SR-71 programme.

Kingpin

Son Tay prison camp was located 23 miles west of Hanoi, and it had gained notoriety for housing dozens of US POWs. It was the subject of numerous SR-71 'takes' which endeavoured over two years to establish the number of prisoners held within its stockade. On 10 June 1970, a Feasibility Study Group was convened by the Special Assistant for Counterinsurgency and Special Activities (SACSA) to look into the possibility of 'springing' Son Tay's inmates. A further planning group was established in early August to review reconnaissance imagery provided by Teledyne-Ryan's *Buffalo Hunter* reconnaissance drones and SR-71s. The low-flying drones were used sparingly over the target area for fear of alerting the North Vietnamese to the possibility of a future raid. The SR-71 with its long-axis camera capability was an ideal vehicle for obtaining spot photos of the camp.

In the last ten days before the planned raid, intense reconnaissance efforts were conducted, but every attempt was thwarted by poor weather. Continuous cloud cover had concealed Son Tay's targets from the 'Habu's high-altitude cameras, and two low altitude drones never returned. Nevertheless, a bold raid was mounted in the morning darkness of 21 November 1970 employing Florida-trained US Special Forces troops who used five HH-53 Jolly Green Giant helicopters in an attempt to rescue the 65 inmates thought to be at Son Tay. Unfortunately, the camp was completely empty. It was first thought that there may have been an intelligence leak at Hurlburt AFB, Florida, where a mock prison had been constructed for rehearsing the raid's swift action. However, it later transpired that the camp had been empty for some time due to the threat of flooding from a nearby river. The lack of timely photo-intelligence was a great embarrassment to Brig Gen LeRoy Manor's Son Tay raiders[13].

An OL-8 SR-71 was sent north following the unsuccessful Son Tay raid to obtain photographs of the damaged camp (*USAF*)

More Important Sorties

Flying time in the SR-71 (especially combat flying) was always considered a premium commodity

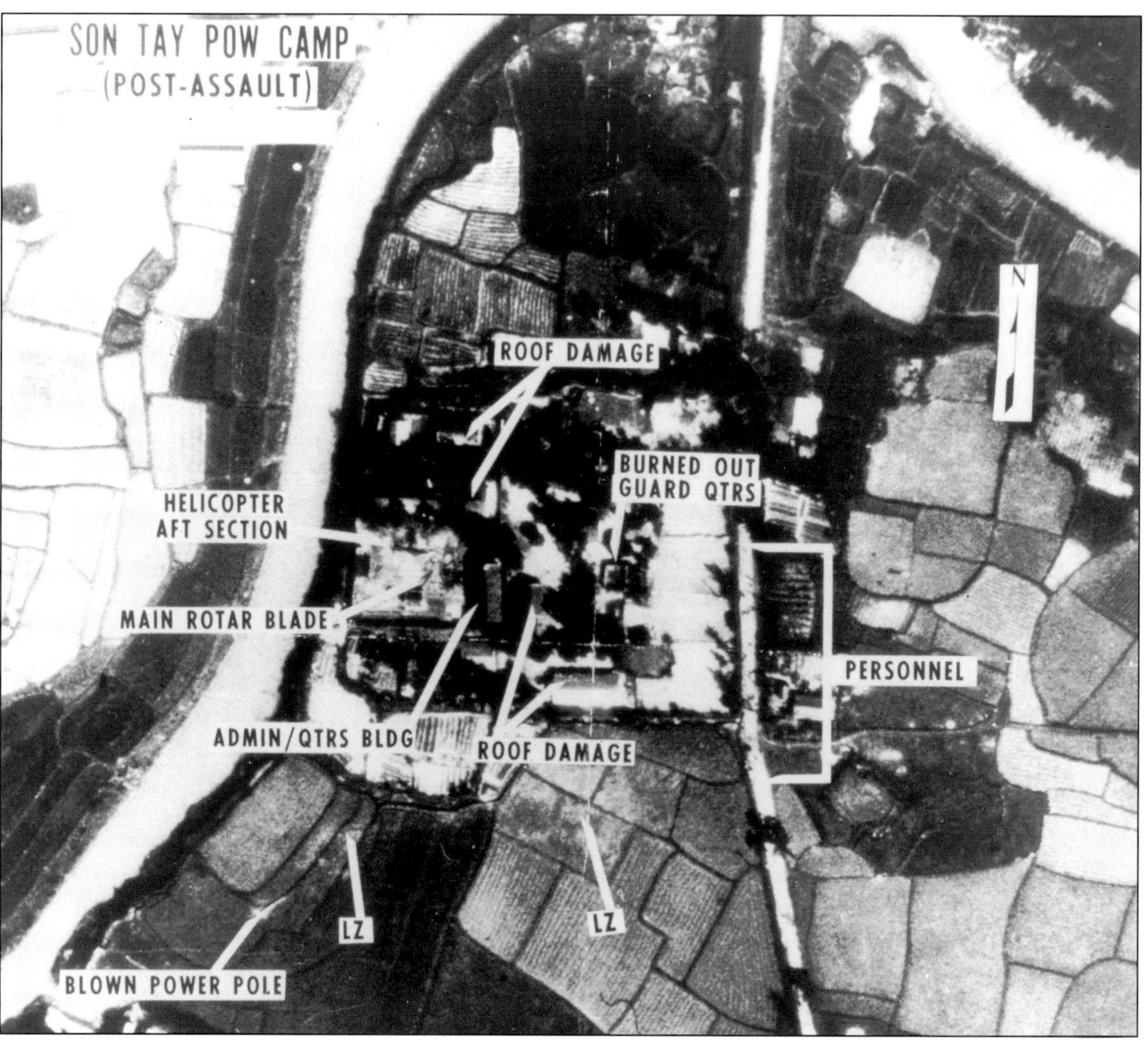

Butch Sheffield (left) and Bob Spencer (right) stirred up a hornet's nest on the night of 27 September 1971. In doing so they acquired the first detailed signal characteristics of the Soviet SA-5 *Gammon* SAM (*USAF*)

among the 20 crews, who would 'wheel-and-deal' with the staff schedulers for additional sorties. Although Southeast Asian sorties accounted for the majority of OL-8's flight hours, that area was not the exclusive domain of the 'Habu'. Majors Bob Spencer and Butch Sheffield were particularly pleased to be selected for one such prize sortie on the night of 27 September 1971. After completing the ritual post-take-off air refuelling in 980, they climbed away from the tankers on a northerly track opposite to the standard route down south into Vietnam. US intelligence had obtained details of the largest ever Soviet naval exercise to be held near Vladivostok, in the Sea of Japan. Undoubtedly, such an event could provide a rich source of intelligence data, and an SR-71 was the ideal vehicle through which to stir the Soviet fleet's defence systems into action.

National security officials were especially interested in obtaining fresh data on the signal characteristics of the Soviet's new SA-5 SAM system, codenamed *Gammon*[14]. If technical details of the signal characteristics like its radar's frequency, modulation, pulse-repetition frequency (PRF), pulse-repetition interval (PRI) and other factors could be measured, it might be possible to develop an effective ECM device to reduce or even negate the SA-5's highly-touted capabilities. The main problem was that the various ELINT recorders carried on the SR-71 filtered the vast range of electromagnetic emissions transmitted from all sources and actuated special recorders when receiving only certain signal types. Major Jack Clemence (an inventive Electronic Warfare Officer) who worked in the 9th SRW's Electronic Data Processing (EDP) Center, jury-rigged one of the ELINT sensors by electronically cutting and splicing the pulse-receiver's filtering system, which allowed it to receive a continuous-wave signal.

The possibility of night disorientation (caused by inlet unstarts and other hazards) over the dark northern Pacific, led the mission planners to restrict most turns to a 25-degree bank limit while night flying at Mach 3.2. The two crewmembers of 980 concentrated their attention on the naval target area just off Vladivostok while slicing through the night in full afterburner. If they maintained their current inbound track toward the Soviet port and turned at a 25-degree bank, they would overfly the USSR crossing high over the Khrebet Sikhote Alin and exit the area into the Sea of Japan, before returning to Kadena. As they bore down on the target area, dozens of Soviet radars were switched on to record what appeared to be shaping up as a certain violation of sovereign Soviet airspace. The deception worked well as 980 turned at the precise moment and failed to violate Siberian airspace due to it being programmed to roll into a full 35-degree bank, instead of the previously recorded 25-degree banks, so as to remain in international airspace.

On their approach to the target area, Bob noted to his great dismay that the right engine's oil pressure was dropping. Nevertheless, he pressed on. When they completed their target run, and were heading south toward home plate, he rechecked that critical oil pressure gauge. By then, its reading had fallen to 'zero', which was bad news indeed. After a brief consultation with Butch, he shut the engine down. Having already stirred up a hornet's nest of defence activity with their feinting pass over the Soviet's Pacific Fleet, they were now forced to descend and continue the rest of their flight at subsonic speeds, where they would soon be 'sitting ducks' for any fast jets that might be scrambled to intercept the oil-starved 'Habu'. To make matters worse, they encountered extreme headwinds which rapidly depleted their fuel supply. Butch calculated that a recovery back to Kadena was completely out of the question – instead, they would have to divert into South Korea.

The OL commander had been monitoring 980's suddenly-slowed progress and as the 'Habu' neared Korea, US listening posts reported the launch of several MiGs from Pyongyang, North Korea, on what appeared to be an intercept attempt. USAF F-102 Delta Daggers were immediately launched from a base near Hon Chew, South Korea, and vectored into a position which put them between the MiGs and the SR-71. It was later established that the MiG launch had been unconnected with the 'Habu's' descent. Bob recovered 980 into Taegu, South Korea, where the base commander had already received a call concerning his special visitor and was ready to receive the SR-71 and its crew. Their EMR 'take' turned out to be 'monumental'. In all, Bob and Butch had 'sniffed-out' emissions from 290 different radars. Of even greater significance to Western intelligence analysts was the 'beautiful' SA-5 signals that they had successfully captured – the first ever detected by Western 'observers'.

MPC's Blue Boxes

On 12 April 1972, Lt Col Ed Payne (by then, OL-8's chief of intelligence) received a phone call from a friend at Norton AFB, California, who spoke in indirect references about 'some blue boxes that would soon make Ed's job easier'. The call was so obscure that he did not know what his Norton contact was trying to tell him until a week later when he received a top secret message. The President had just signed the Defense Appropriation Bill, which allowed the OL to be equipped with a Mobile Processing Center that could perform post-mission processing at Okinawa, rather than having to send it to Japan or the US.

SR-71 operational tasking was driven by the intelligence requirements generated by; (1) the Commander-in-Chief Southeast Asia (CINCSEA); (2) the Defense Intelligence Agency (DIA); (3) the Central Intelligence Agency (CIA); (4) the Office of the Secretary of Defense (OSD); and (5) the National Security Agency (NSA). These requirements were correlated and prioritised by the Joint Chiefs of Staffs' Joint Reconnaissance Center (JCS-JRC), which organised the overall desires of those users into a monthly 'package of objectives'. Final planning was reviewed in a 'Monthly Reconnaissance Schedule' called the Peacetime Aerial Reconnaissance Program (PARPRO), which, once approved by the customer-agencies, would be fielded to the operating agency (SAC Headquarters at Omaha) and transmitted to the 'doers' (OL-8 at Kadena and other collector units in the USAF and Navy).

One OL commander recalled, 'There was a tendency to just by-pass the wing at Beale and consider our home unit as a training asset rather than a link in the operational chain of command[15]. Depending on the sensitivity of the proposed mission, clearance might also have had to be obtained from high State Department officials, members of the National Security Council's very secret '303 Committee', and sometimes the President himself.' On receipt of the SAC Reconnaissance Center's tasking order, the OL's own specialists carried out detailed planning for the mission which included the exact route, speeds, altitudes, turning and penetration points, as well as the many other mission details; sensor turn-on points, look-angles and turn-off points. Also logistical and safety details were fine-tuned, including aerial refuelling tracks and onloads, diversionary airfields and so forth. This planning information was then computer programmed and 'cut' onto a wide Milar tape-strip and 'loaded' into the 'Habu's' Astro-Inertial Navigation System computers. Finally, a 35 mm film-strip was prepared and loaded into the pilot's and RSO's Moving Map Projector.

After the mission had been flown, the palletised sensors were immediately down-loaded and sent to the processing centres. In the 1960s the photographic imagery was flown by special courier to the 67th RTS at Yokota Air Base near Tokyo. This recce-tech unit was closed shortly after the deactivation of the *Oxcart* programme; thereafter, the film was sent to Hickam Air Base at Honolulu for processing. Radar imagery was processed by the 9th's own RTS at Beale, while the ELINT data was handled by National-level agencies in and around Washington, DC, and in Omaha.

Just before the arrival of Ed's 'Blue Boxes', an area of Kadena was rapidly prepared for the MPC's many vans which were flown in by C-5 Galaxy . The blue trailers were quickly unloaded and towed to the newly-prepared area where they were interconnected to function as an in-theatre recce-tech unit. In a very short time, Ed was on the phone to the National Photographic Interpretation Center (NPIC) informing them that he was ready for quick-response intelligence processing. The OL could now process ELINT, COMINT, and black-and-white imagery, but the electronic reduction facility at Beale would still have to be used to process the radar imagery. With the MPC 'up and running', imagery was fast processed as soon as the 'Habu' landed, and was 'wet-read' by the photo interpreters who supplied an Initial Photo Interpretation Report (IPIR) on the highest priority targets.

This intelligence would be communicated in plain English on a secure telephone to 'appropriately cleared' persons on Henry Kissinger's staff who could provide a report to the President within four hours of an SR-71 overflying key targets. Such direct reporting of hot intelligence was called 'a remarkable achievement' for the time. Duplicate sets of photo negatives were immediately produced, with a set then being flown to Eielson AFB, Alaska, where it was transferred to another courier aircraft and flown to Washington, DC to be sped onward to the NPIC. Another courier would deliver a set of negatives to the 12th RTS at Saigon for the next day's air strike planning. Other high-priority recipients were; (1) Fleet Intelligence, Pacific (FINCPAC); (2) the 532nd RTS at Udorn RTAFB; (3) the 544th RTS at Offutt AFB, Nebraska; (4) SAC's B-52 force in Southeast Asia; (6) the DIA; (7) the JCS; and (8) the President and the National Security Council.

Enjoying 'sun-downers' are from left to right; unknown, Bruce Leibman, Bill Orcutt, Jack Madison, Russ Szczepanik, Don Emmons, Tom Alison, Joe Vida, Duane Noll, Tim Tilden and Jim Jiggens. Joe Vida and Tom Tilden joined their Det 1 hosts on a TDY deployment to conduct flight checks of a DAFICS-equipped SR-71 in tropical conditions (*P Crickmore collection*)

Booming the 'Hilton'

During the late spring of 1972, two intriguing and highly-classified sorties were flown from Kadena to North Vietnam on 2 and 4 May. Each mission was comprised of two primary aircraft and an airborne spare. The mission's objective was to 'lay down' two sonic booms within 15 seconds of one another for a signal to key prisoners of the notorious 'Hanoi Hilton' POW camp.

During one such sortie, Majs Tom Pugh and Ronnie Rice approached the target area at 75,000 ft from the south while Majs Bob Spencer and Butch Sheffield maintained 80,000 ft across the target from the southeast. Meanwhile Lt Col Darrel Cobb and Reg Blackwell were the airborne spare, and they were to cross the 'Hilton' at 70,000 ft from the west should either of the primary aircraft have to abort. The mission and the timing of the two booms were so critical that Darrel and Reggie flew all the way to the target area. A pre-arranged code-word had been established which would indicate that their services would not be needed. When that word was transmitted, Darrel broke off his run short of the target area.

Both missions were termed 'entirely successful' and accomplished their objective within the very tight time constraints – reconnaissance gathering was of secondary importance to the signal. Twenty years after the event, it is still unclear as to why these sorties were flown, or what the double booms were meant to signify to the POWs.

On 15 May 1972, Majs Tom Pugh and Ronnie Rice were airborne in 978 on Tom's 236th SR-71 sortie. They were flying a routine *Giant Scale* sortie, scheduled to be a 'double looper' up through the Gulf of Tonkin for a 'front door entry'. Just short of Haiphong Tom's concern over a strange cyclical hum in the interphone system was relieved when the generator bus-tie circuit split, allowing independent operation of each of the 60 KVA AC generators, one of which had been responsible for the varying frequency, hence the hum. Freed of the AC bus load sharing, the system seemingly returned to normal. The GO No-GO Checklist allowed the mission to proceed. While Tom was maintaining Mach 3.18 at 79,500 ft, a generator failed. That failure was a mandatory abort item so the crew began making provisions to divert into Thailand.

Majs Ronnie Rice (left) and Tom Pugh (right) overflew Hanoi in an SR-71 at just 41,000 ft on 15 May 1972, and amazingly got away with it. They are pictured wearing S-901J pressure suits (*USAF*)

Just over a minute later the other generator failed and they were in real trouble. Emergency AC and DC power did not come on-line and the fuel boost-pumps all stopped pumping JP7 to the engines. Without electrical power, the SAS cut out, and lacking boost pump pressure the fuel-flow to both engines stopped, causing them to flame out. To add to their grief, the inlet spikes went full forward and, as 978 began pitching and rolling rapidly, Tom knew the aircraft was approaching the limits of its supersonic flight envelope. Tom instructed Ron to 'get ready to bail. . .' but the intercom system failed before he could finish the statement. He held the stick gently while struggling to control the jet (without causing further pilot-induced oscillations), and while also trying to reach the all-important 'Standby-Electrical Switch' located on his right-hand panel. To reach that critical switch he had to move his left hand off the throttles and on to the control stick in order to free his right hand so he could restore some electrical power to the aeroplane. This accomplished, Tom initiated a

gentle 'needle ball and airspeed' turn towards a 'friendly piece of concrete'. Having descended to 41,000 ft and slowed to just Mach 1.1, he managed to get one generator back on-line and both engines re-lit. He then reaccelerated 978 to Mach 1.7 to exit the area as quickly as possible. Tom crossed Laos to recover 978 into Udorn RTAFB without further problems.

The serious nature of the malfunction necessitated that they return to Kadena subsonically. As they set off with two tankers (one carrying the recovery team), they heard another SR-71 diverting into U-Tapao RTAFB. The tanker with the maintenance team peeled away from 978 and headed back to Thailand to recover the other aircraft. At their post-flight analysis, Tom and Ron learned that they had overflown Hanoi at 41,000 ft. They had been extremely lucky considering the number of SAMs that encircled the city. It appeared that the Vietnamese radar operators and their Soviet advisers had been 'asleep at the switch' during 978's mid-altitude pass over one of the best defended cities in the world. The 'Bunny' had pulled off a lucky escape from what appeared to be an easy shoot down situation. After being repaired, 978 returned to operational status. Tom and Ben were each awarded Air Medals for Meritorious Achievement in 'the successful landing of their disabled aircraft'.

On the 9 June, 978 was involved in yet another scary episode. Majs Bob Powell[16] and Gary Coleman were approaching Hanoi on a front door entry when the SAS failed. They had just entered a 30-degree bank at Mach 3.2 and 81,000 ft when the aircraft started porpoising. As Bob struggled to master the destabilised flight characteristics, he found that he had to decelerate and descend to where the aircraft would be more manageable. Gary radioed the tanker with a delayed rendezvous time because they would be approaching at subsonic speeds. Bob completed a somewhat ragged aerial refuelling and trailed a spare tanker to the east coast of Vietnam, where they filled the tanks and slogged their way back to Kadena at 0.9 Mach (logging six and a half flying hours).

Farewell to the 'Bunny'

On 20 July 1972 OL-8 suffered the loss of 978. While returning from an operational mission, Majs Denny Bush and Jimmy Fagg approached Kadena to learn of excessive cross-wind landing conditions. On touch-down, Denny deployed the aeroplane's large braking parachute in a rapid deploy-jettison technique to prevent the 'Rapid Rabbit' from weather-cocking sharply into the wind and running off the side of the runway. Unhappy with the first touchdown he jettisoned the 'chute, pushed up the power, and 'took it around' for another landing approach. Although he successfully touched down on the second attempt, the crosswind was so strong that he was unable to keep the wind-cocked aircraft on the runway. During this 'off-runway' landing roll-out, one set of main wheels struck a low concrete structure, severely damaging the landing gear and causing substantial additional damage to the aeroplane. Both crewmembers clambered out unscathed, but 978 was written-off. The bits that were 'salvageable' were transported back to Norton AFB in a C-5 Galaxy, and were later used rather ignobly for spare parts for the other SR-71s. The remaining sections of the air frame were scrapped in Okinawa.

'Habu' Support of B-52s

The 'flexible response' strategy adopted by the Kennedy Administration to fight the Vietnam War caused SAC to examine the tactical potential of its strategic bombers in that war. By mounting two multiple-ejector racks on certain B-52s (in place of wing missile pylons), a further 24 bombs could supplement the 27 bombs that could already be hauled internally, thus nearly doubling a B-52F's bombload. As the situation in South Vietnam worsened, the JCS decided to deploy the modified B-52Fs to Andersen AFB, Guam, in February 1965. Code-named *Arc Light*, the aircraft could be used to strike targets in North Vietnam in reprisal for terrorist action against US personnel in the south. An ineffectual bombing raid was mounted by a large number of fighter-bombers against Viet Cong base camps near Black Virgin Mountain on 15 April 1965. Soon after, General Westmoreland obtained permission from Secretary of Defense McNamara to use B-52s in support of tactical operations in South Vietnam.

The first big strike took place on 18 June 1965 when 30 B-52s flew a 12-hour/5500-mile round trip from Guam to the Ben Cat Special Zone in Binh Duong Province northeast of Saigon. As these *Arc Light* sorties continued, a modification programme

THE UNITED STATES OF AMERICA

TO ALL WHO SHALL SEE THESE PRESENTS, GREETING:

THIS IS TO CERTIFY THAT
THE PRESIDENT OF THE UNITED STATES OF AMERICA
AUTHORIZED BY EXECUTIVE ORDER, MAY 11, 1942
HAS AWARDED

THE AIR MEDAL

(EIGHTH OAK LEAF CLUSTER)

TO

CAPTAIN REGINALD T. BLACKWELL
UNITED STATES AIR FORCE

FOR

MERITORIOUS ACHIEVEMENT
WHILE PARTICIPATING IN AERIAL FLIGHT

27 DECEMBER 1972

GIVEN UNDER MY HAND IN THE CITY OF WASHINGTON
THIS 17TH DAY OF DECEMBER 19 73

JOHN C. MEYER, General, USAF
Commander in Chief
Strategic Air Command

SECRETARY OF THE AIR FORCE

CITATION TO ACCOMPANY THE AWARD OF

THE AIR MEDAL
(EIGHTH OAK LEAF CLUSTER)

TO

REGINALD T. BLACKWELL

Captain Reginald T. Blackwell distinguished himself by meritorious achievement while participating in aerial flight as Reconnaissance Systems Officer on 27 December 1972. On that date, while operating from a forward location, his courageous accomplishments resulted in the acquisition of significant intelligence vitally important to the United States and the security of the free world. Despite the hazardous environment and the demanding conditions which threatened this mission, Captain Balckwell demonstrated his exceptional airmanship and brought this flight to a successful conclusion. The professional ability and outstanding aerial accomplishments of Captain Blackwell reflect great credit upon himself and the United States Air Force.

known as *Big Belly* got underway back in the US. Between December 1965 and September 1967, 82 B-52Ds received new radar transponders for ground-directed bombing and further bomb-rack mods which increased their carrying capacity from 15 bombs weighing 27,000 lbs to a staggering 108 bombs weighing 60,000 lbs.

On 1 April 1966, the 28th and 454th Bombardment Wings deployed to Guam and began flying regular *Arc Light* sorties. In addition to the great increase in firepower that these *Big Belly* bombers represented, the sortie rate was increased from 450 to 600 flights per month. Seven ground radar-directed bombing sites called *Combat Skyspot* were established, the first one coming on line at Bien Hoa in March 1966. These sites, working in conjunction with the B-52s' new radar transponders, helped to improve bombing accuracy. On 11 and 27 April 1966, B-52s struck North Vietnam for the first time, hitting targets in the Mu Gia Pass, which was the keystone of the notorious Ho Chi Minh Trail's supply network. The B-52 sortie rate increased as the ground war continued to deteriorate and by February it had reached 800 flights per month. Meanwhile, Guam had reached its saturation point in regards to the number of B-52s that it could support. Thereafter, additional aircraft were deployed to U-Tapao RTAFB at Sattahip, Thailand.

A year later McNamara approved yet another increase to 1200 and then finally 1800 B-52 sorties per month. On 1 November 1968, President Johnson called a halt to *Rolling Thunder* operations against North Vietnam. Target emphasis for the B-52s changed to *Commando Hunt* operations in an effort to stem the tide of men, equipment and fuel being infiltrated into South Vietnam via a supply network in Laos. Eight months after the election of President Nixon, Secretary of Defense Melvin Laird cut the B-52 sortie rate to 1400 per month. Two years later the monthly rate was further reduced to 1000 sorties and many aircraft and crews were returned to the US.

In early 1972, however, an enemy build-up along the Laotian trail network indicated the prospects of an imminent offensive. Gen Creighton Abrams and Adm John McCain (CINCPAC) requested additional *Arc Light* sorties to forestall this rising threat. On 8 February the JCS authorised 1200 monthly sorties and ordered 29 more B-52s to Guam. In a major invasion effort on 30 March 1972, the enemy hit South Vietnamese positions in Quang To, Kontum-Pleiku and Binh Long Provinces. As the situation worsened on all three fronts, B-52Gs were deployed for the first time. This increase brought the bomber force to 133 aircraft, which could fly as many as 2250 sorties per month. This new invasion prompted the President to lift the bombing halt of the North and on 21 and 23 April 1972, B-52s hit Vinh, the Bai Thuong airfield, the Haiphong petroleum products storage area, the Hamn Rong trans-shipment points and Thanh Hoa. It was the first time B-52s had ventured into the heavily-defended Hanoi-Haiphong area and they came away unscathed.

By late June there were 200 B-52s in theatre chalking up more than 3100 sorties per month. It was apparent to military planners that the aircraft had played a major role in blunting the Communists' spring offensive. In late October 1972, President Nixon called a halt to the bombing north of the 20th parallel in anticipation of a truce. As a hedge against the talks becoming deadlocked or breaking up, he also ordered the JCS to plan new strikes against the North which would concentrate on the Hanoi-Haiphong areas. On 13 December 1972, the North Vietnamese Delegation walked out of the Paris Peace Talks (throughout the long period of negotiations, North Vietnam had used the time to rebuild and strengthen their badly damaged positions). Two days later, Nixon ordered the execution of *Linebacker II*. Initially planned as a three-day, maximum night effort for B-52s, this big operation extended through 11 days of heavy bombing. The primary aim was to cut off the supply of equipment and supplies at their source to strangle the North's war effort.

On Day One (18 December), 121 B-52 sorties were flown. Two chaff corridors were sown by F-4s, but 100-knot winds blew the protective curtain away before the B-52s arrived. *Charcoal 1*, a B-52G leading nine other Guam-based aircraft against the Yen Vien/Ai Mo warehouse area, was hit by two SA-2s and became the first B-52 lost to hostile actions in the war. Two other bombers were also shot down by some of the 200 SAMs launched that night.

Day Two of the campaign saw B-52s hitting

Lt Col Darrell Cobb and Capt Reg Blackwell were awarded Air Medals for providing ECM support to B-52s taking part in operation *Linebacker* on the night of the 27/28 December 1972 (*USAF*)

targets at Hanoi, Kinh No, Yen Vien, Bac Giang and Thai Nguyen. Another 200 SA-2s were fired but no aircraft were lost. On the night of 20 December six B-52s fell to SAMs. By Christmas Eve (Day Seven of the campaign) 11 B-52s had been shot down. After a 36-hour pause over Christmas, operations resumed. Using revised tactics, 113 aircraft battered ten different targets in seven 15–minute waves. Two more B-52s were knocked down by SA-2s despite the fact that they had been supported by more than 100 fighter-bombers, which were used to suppress SAM batteries in the Haiphong area.

SR-71s were used to cover the most famous period of heavy bombing in the Vietnam War. Lt Col Darrell Cobb and Capt Reg Blackwell lifted off from Kadena in 975 an hour befor midnight on 27 December 1972. After topping off their fuel, they climbed and accelerated toward North Vietnam. There was no moonlight nor a visible horizon and they had to make timing points to arrive over the Haiphong and Hanoi areas at the precise moment the B-52s would be dropping their bombs. The intelligence planners knew that all the North Vietnamese defensive radar systems would be working 'flat out' to cope with 60 B-52s, and that such an electronic environment would be an especially rich ELINT collection opportunity. In addition, the SR-71's unmatched defensive electronics could provide additional ECM support for the B-52s.

As they arrived over the collection area on schedule, Cobb and Blackwell observed numerous SA-2 firings. During the fleeting moments when they were passing in the immediate target area, they were able to radiate a blinding ECM blanket using their advanced defensive systems. During the course of the raid, only one Guam-based B-52 was lost[17]. Darrell and Reg landed back at Kadena at 0239 hours in the morning. The next day they learned that their mission produced a wealth of intelligence data, which included the discovery of two unique emitters that had been responsible for heavy B-52 losses. Subsequent *Linebacker* raids were carried out without the loss of a single bomber.

Once again at midnight on 29 December 1972, the bombing north of the 20th parallel ceased. B-52s had flown a total of 729 sorties during the 11 days of *Linebacker II* operations (340 from U-Tapao and 389 from Guam). Thirty-four separate target areas had been hit by the B-52s which dropped 13,395 tons of bombs. The North Vietnamese had fired hundreds of SA-2s, distroying 15 of the bombers (nine B-52Ds and six B-52Gs), and damaging nine others. The stunning onslaught that the North had received from *Linebacker II* drove the North Vietnamese negotiators to the Paris Peace Talks to carry out deceptive negotiations in order to recover from what had been 'war-ending' destruction of their supplies and munitions.

A record of *Linebacker*'s enormous level of destruction had been faithfully recorded by the 'Habus'. The B-52s had clearly won the war at that point, but their victory was given away at the Paris Peace Conference. The conflict in Vietnam ended for the United States when the Paris Agreement was signed on 27 January 1973, which committed the withdrawal of US forces from South Vietnam. The agreement included; (1) the release of US prisoners of war within 60 days; (2) the formation of a Four-Party Joint Military Mission; (3) the establishment of an International Commission of Control and Supervision; (4) the clearance of mines from North Vietnamese waters; and (5) free elections for all Vietnamese. For the SR-71, it signalled a large reduction in target tasking, which was followed by a reduction in the number of Kadena-based aircraft from four to three. Another jet returned to Beale soon after, the remaining pair being tasked with performing stand-off reconnaissance flights to respect the newly-united, north-dominated Vietnam.

SS *Mayaguez* Incident

On Monday 12 May 1975, the US-registered freighter SS *Mayaguez* was stopped by a number of Khmer Rouge gunboats as it steamed in international waters some 60 NM southwest of Cambodia, near the Paulo Wai Islands in the Gulf of Thailand. The merchant ship was boarded, and the next day, under the control of its captors, the *Mayaguez* was moved to a point about two miles off the northeastern tip of Koh Tang Island.

The ship was initially located by two F-111s diverted from a routine training mission the day after the vessel's seizure. Thereafter, a round-the-clock surveillance plan was put into operation to monitor the *Mayaguez*'s movements. Just before dawn on 15 May an assault was launched on two beaches at the northern tip of Koh Tang and a search was made of the vessel in a bid to release the ship's crewmembers. However, a small Thai fishing boat had been used to move the crew to the Cambodian mainland the day before, and the Marine boarding party found the freighter to be empty. The assault force put ashore, but encountered stiffer resistance than had been anticipated from a much larger and well fortified group of Khmer troops. To make matters worse, during the assault on Koh Tang, which lasted 14 hours and resulted in 15 US Marines being killed, 3 Missing In Action (MIA), 50 wounded and four H-53 helicopters shot down, the same Thai fishing boat returned the ship's crew unharmed to the destroyer USS *Holt* in a gesture which seems to have been unconnected with the battle for their release.

The importance of this assault resulted in an SR-71 mission being scheduled to monitor the strike on Koh Tang. It was flown during the 15 May raid by Capts Al Cirino and Bruce Liebman, and their 'take' was to prove extremely useful during subsequent debriefings.

Despite the war in Southeast Asia having ended in August 1973, SR-71's from OLKA continued to conduct occasional overflights of Cambodia. Although never officially admitted, the large numbers of US troops listed as MIA continued to be a source of concern for the US government. This reason, together with occasional 'sightings' of MIAs and rumours of isolated prison compounds in inaccessible jungle areas, proved strong enough for various US intelligence agencies to request that such flights be sanctioned.

One such mission was flown by BC Thomas and Jay Reid in 976. The 5-hour 48-minute flight was conducted on 24 November 1980 – seven years after the cessation of hostilities. Unfortunately, no substantive evidence was produced by the aeroplane's sensors to back up such speculation.

China and the Soviet Union

The aftershocks of the Gary Powers incident insured that overflights of the Soviet Union in an A-12 or SR-71 remained politically unacceptable. Some extremely useful intelligence had, however, been obtained of Communist China by Chinese Nationalist pilots flying U-2s loaned from the CIA. The costs in pilots and machines had been high in that programme, with a number of aircraft being shot down by SA-2s. The only Peacetime Aerial Reconnaissance Programme options open to the United States when it came to gathering intelligence data over these enormous countries were satellites and stand-off viewing – OLKA performed the latter mission successfully over both countries.

When Viktor Belenko defected from his Siberian bases in a MiG-25P to Hakodate Air Base, Japan, in September 1976, he confided during his subsequent debriefings that Soviet fast-jet interceptor pilots had decided that the only way to get near a high-flying 'Habu' was to execute a snap-up manoeuvre well ahead of the target by four or more aircraft flying in trail formation. A salvo of missiles would then be fired by all aircraft in the hope of a lucky hit. Despite the fact that these stand-off flights were being conducted in international airspace, the 'Habu' crews remained convinced that the Soviet fighters would attempt a shoot-down and would argue about the aircraft's position afterwards. There can be no doubting the acute irritation that such flights caused the Soviet leadership since the USSR was eager to export its latest weapons systems to its Communist Allies but were failing in spectacular fashion to shoot down an aeroplane that was over 20 years old.

On 29 October 1979, Majs Rich Graham and Don Emmons were airborne from Kadena in 962 on just such a stand-off flight. Nearing Petropavlovsk (on the east coast of the Kamchatka peninsula) they observed two medium-altitude circular contrails ahead of them. As they continued, the two MiGs attempted a snap-up manoeuvre, but were unable to get anywhere near the 'Habu'. Rich and Don later observed four more contrails belonging to MiGs whose pilots were waiting to attempt a similar intercept. Rich said to Don, 'Let's show them that we know they're there and that we don't care'. Rich then dumped a small burst of fuel which created a high, fast vapour trail. No attempt was made by the MiGs to intercept the 3000 ft per second target which passed high above them. Such potential intercept actions were typical of the activity that greeted many stand-off flights during the Cold War.

There were not many possible track variations for a stand-off sortie. One can fly up or down a coastline or fly toward it and break away to the left or right! To keep the Soviet defence controllers guessing, Lt Col Tom Alison (the Det commander) thought up an innovative sortie with a difference. On the morning of 27 March 1984, Majors Stormy Boudreaux and Ted Ross got airborne from Kadena in 964. As they headed north-east near Vladivos-

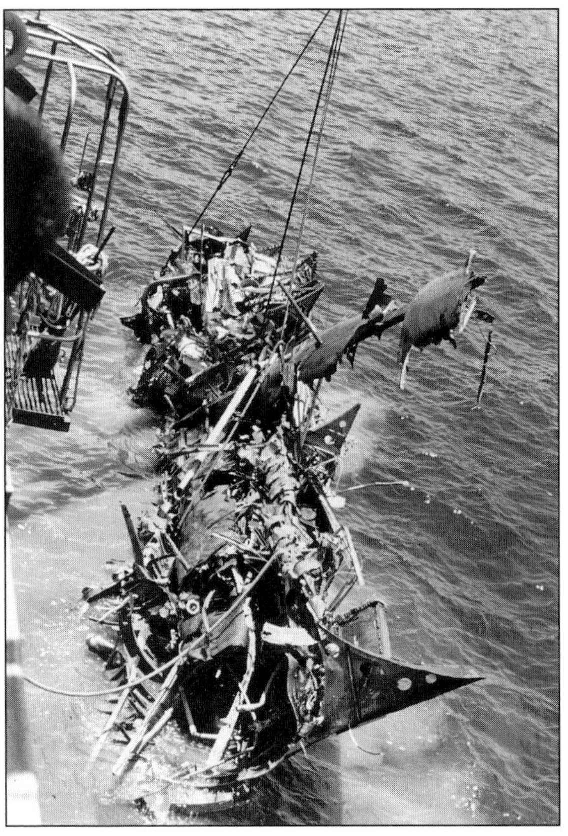

The forebody of 974 breaks the surface near Luzon Island. Furthest from the camera, the triangular front windshield framework and the air refuelling receptacle are barely distinguishable (*USAF*)

tock, SR-71 973 flown by Lt Col Les Dyer and Maj Dan Greenwood, which had taken off from Beale, streaked toward them from the opposite direction. At a closure speed of Mach 6, they flashed by each other only three miles apart. Stormy and Ted then turned right to trace Les and Dan who proceeded them south and then west across Korea just south of the Demilitarised Zone. Both aircraft were back on the ground at Kadena before noon with a very interesting collection of ELINT and photo intelligence.

Another Lost 'Habu'

After more than 21 years of operating from Kadena, and 17 years without the loss of a single 'Habu' at all locations, 974 crashed near the Philippines on 21 April 1989. Lt Col Dan House and Maj Blair Bozek had departed Kadena and headed 'straight out' to speed and altitude without a top-off air refuelling, ready to perform a routine stand-off sortie off the coast of Southeast Asia. After Dan levelled off at 75,000 ft and Mach 3, the aircraft began yawing to the left. Blair asked Dan, 'Is that an unstart?' Dan replied, 'I don't know'. It did not appear to be a typical unstart and the inlet had not re-cycled. Dan continued to monitor his instruments and saw that the left engine's gauges were winding down. He told Blair that the left engine had quit. By then there was no RPM, no EGT or oil pressure and the pressure gauges for the A and L hydraulic systems indicated 'zero'. The left engine had seized!

It had been a surprisingly gentle process but it was nonetheless an immediate abort item. Consequently, the crew began to plan for a diversionary landing base while following-up on their 'engine out' procedures. At that point, the right engine went through four unstarts during which another of the flight control's SAS channels failed, leaving them with only one out of six. As the aircraft lost speed and altitude, it entered a series of lateral gyrations which threatened to take the aeroplane beyond the limits of its flight envelope. Dan described the whole incident as follows:

'It felt like we were experiencing a series of falling-leaf manoeuvres. We were 'wrapping up' from one side to the other. I was ramming the stick through full-throw, back and forth, as quickly as I could but the aeroplane was doing pretty much what it wanted. That got me quite excited because from Mach 3 to Mach 2.5 I felt that I had no control whatsoever over the aircraft. I was most concerned because I didn't understand its cause. Well, somehow or other we flew out of that wild series of gyrations and I decided to divert into Clark AFB in the Philippines. We continued to descend and slow to subsonic speed on one engine and completed all our obligatory radio calls. Just when things appeared to be getting better, they suddenly got worse. I told Blair, "We've now got a B Hydro Light", which meant that our remaining hydraulic system was getting low on fluid. By then we were at 400 knots and 15,000 ft and the B system's pressure gauge started to fluctuate. Our situation was now really deteriorating. I quickly updated Blair on the potential failure of my flight controls and told him to 'hang on'.

'We were just off the north coast of the main Philippine island of Luzon and we agreed to remain over water as we proceeded toward Clark because if we had to leave the aircraft, we didn't want it dropping on peoples' heads,

The sad remains of 974's front cockpit (*USAF*)

and we didn't want classified material falling into the wrong hands. So we turned left into the dead engine, as that was the easiest way to turn, and flew along the coast looking for anywhere suitable to land. Blair thought he saw a field and asked me if I could still control where I was going. At that point, I was holding full left rudder and saw that the B hydro had 'zeroed'. As I replied to Blair, "No, I can't any longer", poor old 974 began wrapping up to the right very rapidly. I shouted, "Bail Out!, Bail Out!, Bail Out!" and pulled my ejection-seat's D-ring. I remember hitting the stop and the sensation of light coming into the cockpit as the canopy blew off. The next thing I recalled was the reassuring tug as my 'chute opened. We'd gone out at about 400 knots and 10,000 ft. The elapsed time from the initial yaw to ejection was about 16 minutes. I checked the 'chute which was fine and then started looking for Blair, whom I could not immediately spot. It seems he'd gone out after me because he wasn't in the correct sitting position for a safe bailout. Therefore, he was ahead and above me. When I finally located him, I started looking for 974 which was under me, falling straight down in planform. It happened to be upside-down and was not pitching or tumbling. As she hit the water, there was a splash and a brief fireball. Then all was gone.

'I readied myself for a feet-wet landing. My descent rate under that 35-ft-wide canopy was very slow, so I had plenty of time to look around. It was a sunny morning, there was no wind, the vegetation on the island was lush and green and the calm blue ocean which I was about to enter was flat with no waves. I could see fishing boats turn toward me and by the time I'd cleared my 'chute, a Bonka boat had arrived next to my position in the water. A Bonka boat is a 20-ft dug-out canoe with outriggers on either side and is powered by the noisiest internally-mounted two-stroke engine I have ever heard in my life. Two Philippino fishermen offered to lift me into their boat, and since one of my life rules was to never give up a free ride when you're shark bait, I gladly accepted. They retrieved all my life-support gear and lifted the parachute aboard their little boat and then we went over to where Blair was waiting. He'd gotten into his life-raft and was just climbing into another Bonka boat that had raced toward him as he descended. He tried the survival radio but couldn't hear anything because the search and rescue forces were still too far away. We went to the scene of the

968 taxies out to the hold at Kadena AB (*L Peacock*)

aeroplane's impact where there were only a few pieces of debris and some fuel floating nearby.

'We then asked the Philippino fishermen to take us ashore. They told us that the area opposite was controlled by the New People's Army (Communist insurgents who occupied the island), so they took us instead to a nearby town which was a two hour ride to the east. After handing us over to an officious policeman who was a member of the local militia, we tried to call Clark Air Base, but no one knew the phone number. Next, we asked to talk to the US Consulate in Manila but we had to wait our turn behind about 30 other people waiting to use the one phone. They eventually decided to take us to some local officials who could certainly help us. We'd taken our pressure suits off and were wearing the dark green nylon lining over our long underwear.

'We entered a large building carrying our survival gear and parachutes and were introduced to the Mayor and Town Council. They were very concerned for our well-being and asked if we needed to see a doctor. When we told them that it wasn't necessary, they invited us to have lunch with them. We had a wonderful meal of rice, pork, vegetables, pickled squid, plus the best ice-cold bottles of Coca-Cola we'd had in our lives. The Mayor then insisted that we take coffee with him at his home. While our survival radios were sending out their radiant signals,- "come save us, come save us", we were enjoying coffee on the mayor's lawn. We had asked if there was a radio-transmitter anywhere. Eventually they agreed to take us to one. As we were en-route, a Lockheed P-3 Orion flew overhead. We stopped the truck and made contact but our radio reception was not very good. On reaching the short-wave radio, we identified ourselves to the Orion crew and were told that a helicopter was on its way to pick us up. We drove back to the Mayor's house and Blair positioned himself in a dried-up rice field to greet the helicopter's crew. Meanwhile, I went back to the Mayor's house for a final cup of coffee and to thank him and his countrymen for their wonderful hospitality. I also picked up our mission gear which we'd left on the patio.

'The HH-53 Super Jolly Green Giant took us back to Clark Air Force Base. The crew was superb and wanted to take us to the O'club for a few 'coolers', but post-accident rules dictated that they had to hand us over to the medics for a physical examination. After this rather wild five-hour adventure, we were strapped to a stretcher by four medical corpsmen who put us in an ambulance. I had not been so helpless since 974 underwent the falling-leaf gyrations. Once we were in the ambulance, the doors were closed and the driver backed up no more than a hundred feet before the doors were flung open once again and they carried us into the hospital. Other than our bad attitudes for their seemingly stupid procedures, they found nothing wrong with us and after 24 hours of "observation" they released us.'

Side-scanning sonar operations of the crash site took place on 29 and 30 April and it was not long before the debris field of 974 was located. The 280ft-long salvage vessel USS *Beaufort* was dispatched to the site to lift the wreckage with its 10- and 15-ton cranes, fitted on the bow and stern of the ship respectively, and to find the sensors and defensive systems. Due to the proximity of the Communist New Peoples' Army, a number of Navy Seals (Special Forces) were onboard the *Beaufort* to provide protection to the divers and crew. An order for 'General Quarters' was sounded at 0400 hours one morning during the search. Crewmen rushed to their action stations in readiness for an immediate confrontation. They saw a large number of small vessels (which had been detected on the *Beaufort*'s radar) making for the ship. Tension mounted until it was discovered that the would-be attackers were really fishing boats which had come toward the bright lights of the naval vessel because a very large school of fish had congregated around it! The local fishermen were expecting to take full advantage of the unique situation.

When the inverted 974 had impacted the water, both engines smashed the sensors and other onboard equipment through the aeroplane's upper surfaces. Those objects were scattered on the ocean floor at varying distances away from the main wreckage. On the evening of 1 May, wire hausers were attached to one of the J58 engines. The late evening movements dislodged the TEB tank and caused a small leak which released tiny amounts of the chemical throughout the night. As a result, tiny amounts of the volatile chemical were released and bubbled to the surface, where it mixed with ambient air and exploded in small green puffs. The 'magic' of the 'Yankee' engineers caused quite a stir among the native fishermen who saw the eerie 'TEB-bubble show'.

The next day both engines were lifted and brought aboard the *Beaufort*'s fan-tail and two days later many of the sensors were also recovered. When the ship's crew attempted to lift the main section of the aircraft, the crane operator found that the large delta-shaped wing planform greatly exceeded the lifting capacity of his crane, and the wreckage refused to budge an inch. A yard-derrick was sent from Subic Bay and the forward fuselage section was recovered on 7 May, while the main structure was lifted aboard the *Beaufort*'s fan-tail the following day. The black wreckage was a sad end for a once-proud aeroplane, despite Dan's skilful and valiant efforts to save it.

Confrontation North Korea

The collapse of communism and the establishment of a so-called 'New World Order' has appeared to have produced an era of stability and co-operation among many formerly aggressive nations. Only a few outsider-countries of the communist 'old-guard' (China, Cuba and North Korea) still seem intent on clinging to political and economic systems that have clearly failed. In recent years, the US and China have become more tolerant of each other but Cuba and North Korea have chosen to remain as hostile outsiders. The continually belligerent attitude of North Korea has earned the country a reputation of being something of a 'wild card' in international politics, capable of igniting a war against South Korea and its western allies. As a consequence, North Korea has long been surveilled so US intelligence agencies might be able to constantly assess its military capabilities and learn something of its intentions.

North Korean reconnaissance sorties were first flown by A-12 pilots in 1967, but their short-lived efforts passed to SAC as a long-term role in early 1968 when the 9th SRW's OL-8 (OLRK) inherited the CIA's facilities at Kadena. OL-8's 'Habus' flew their first operational sortie over North Korea later that year, which in turn were followed by many similar missions over the next two decades. Only a few of the very first missions were flown directly over North Korean airspace, for it was found that all operational objectives could be achieved by flying south over the DMZ, or off the coast and looking in at an angle with the SR-71's long-range Technical Objective cameras or SLAR.

In April 1981, SR-71 flights began collecting ELINT cuts and other raw data on a suspected SA-2 site which was under construction on the island of *Chokta-ri* in an estuary near the western end of Korea's DMZ. In July and August of that year, Maj Maury Rosenberg and Capt ED McKim flew several passes over Korea to check on the progress of *Chokta-ri* SAM site. Before each flight, OL-8's Intelligence Officer briefed the crews about most recent developments since it was increasingly apparent that the North Koreans were about to embark upon another 'adventure in belligerence'.

On 25 August, Maj Nevin Cunningham and Geno

Wonsan harbour, North Korea, as seen from the cockpit of an SR-71 during an operational mission (*P Crickmore collection*)

Quist climbed into 967 for a similar two-loop sortie of the 'Z' area. Although it was a clear day over the target area, the primary sensor for this four-hour sortie was the Side-Looking-Radar (SLAR). During their fourth and final pass over the DMZ, the crew were still carrying excess fuel so Nevin flicked his fuel dump switch in quick Morse-Code bursts, which spelled out a four-letter expletive for the benefit of the ground trackers who were attempting to follow the SR-71 visually. Their humour was lost on the enemy, but it brought lots of laughs back at the 'Habu' bar at Kadena.

The next morning, Maury and ED were briefed for their mission, which entailed three passes along the DMZ. Once again they were briefed about the 'suspected' SA-2 site to which Maury asked the intelligence officer 'Who determines when a suspected site becomes a confirmed site?' He was told that the Defense Intelligence Agency made the final call on such issues and added, 'So what do we have to do before we can confirm it? See a missile?' The intelligence officer replied, 'Well, that would surely help'.

Maury and ED launched in 976 on their 'Z' sortie and headed for their first air refuelling. After tanking they flew through the Straits of Formosa and made their first high pass from west to east along Korea's DMZ. They then turned south and flew down the east coast of South Korea toward their second refuelling. Thereafter they reversed course and after reaching operational altitude off the west coast of South Korea, they repeated their west to east run across the DMZ. Coasting out to the east, Maury made a right and left 90–270 degree turn which put 976 on an east to west pass. While approaching the western side of Korea at Mach 3 and 77,000 ft, ED remarked that he was getting some DEF System activity, and that everything was turned on'. In the next breath, ED exclaimed, 'Wow! It looks like we've had a launch'. Maury accelerated to Mach 3.2 and told ED, 'I see a contrail! I'll be damned, it's coming right at us'. Maury made a slight turn to the left to turn away from the rising contrail which took them further into South Korean airspace and watched as the SA-2 missed by a good two miles, exploding behind and to the right of them at about 80,000 ft.

Always mindful of the sensitivity of such sorties, US authorities monitored these SR-71 flights very closely. Almost as soon as 976 came off track, ED received an encoded HF message from *Sky King* concerning the track deviation. There was no mention of the hostile missile firing. The RSO responded with the appropriate messages but found there was not a specific coded message that could be sent alluding to the missile incident. As a result of this mission, a coded message format was later added should a crew find themselves in similar circumstances. It was not until the 'Habu' crew arrived back on 'the Rock' that they could inform the staff that they had been shot at.

The incident was of such importance that a coded message was despatched to all interested agencies including the National Security Council. Secretary of Defense Casper Weinberger informed the President of the firing, after which a series of high-level briefings followed. Deputy Secretary of Defense Charles Carlucci recalled that President Reagan was 'furious' over the incident. Meanwhile, Dean Fischer, a spokesman for the State Department said, 'The Reagan Administration roundly denounces this act of lawlessness', adding that the attack violated 'accepted norms of international behaviour'. Despite faultless photographic evidence of the North Korean missile firing at an aircraft over South Korea, the North Korean government denied the missile charge. While the diplomatic rhetoric continued, Det 1 was told to move the reconnaissance track flown by the SR-71 even further to the south. Six days later, Nev Cunningham and Geno Quist flew a typical four-hour, two-loop sortie along the 'Z' in 976 with little reaction.

Majs BC Thomas and Jay Reid arrived at Kadena during the period of high-level interest in the Det Korean activity. On 26 September, Deputy SECDEF Frank Carlucci visited the island and was briefed on their operations and shown an SR-71 for the first time. Carlucci met with the 'Habu' crewmembers and explained that the DMZ route package had been moved further to the south for the moment but that

Tensions were strained to almost breaking point on 26 August 1981 when North Korea fired two SA-2s at an SR-71 conducting a PARPRO mission in international airspace. The RSO and pilot of that flight were ED McKim and Maury Rosenberg; the latter is pictured second from the left (*P Crickmore collection*)

Overleaf The SR-71's exploits, both planned and unplanned, often made headline news. These clippings cover the overflights of North Korea, and the unscheduled recovery into Norway – both events occuring in 1981 (*via Paul F Crickmore*)

Nordlands **FRAMTID**

Nr. 186 — Bodø, fredag 14. august 1981
73. årgang — Løssalg kr 2,50

US-spionfly nødlandet i Bodø i går

SIDE 27

På rekognoseringstur over Norskehavet og Barentshavet

Tekniske årsaker til amerikansk nødlanding i Bodø

Et fly av denne typen. Lockheed SR-71, et langtrekkende fly med maksimumshastighet på tre ganger lydens hastighet, står nå på Bodø flyplass etter en vellykket nødlanding i går. Dette er U-2-flyets etterfølger.

NF — Sverre Larsen:

Et meget avansert amerikansk rekognoseringsfly av typen Lockheed SR-71 måtte nødlande på Bodø Flyplass i går formiddag. Årsaken oppgis å være av teknisk art, idet flyet meldte om problemer med et av oljesystemene. Da dette skjedde var US-flyet på tokt over internasjonalt farvann i Norskehavet og Barentshavet. - Flyet landet i Bodø fordi flyplassen her var nærmest, og landingen ble gjennomført uten vansker. Ingen av de to ombord ble skadet, sier generalmajor Tønne Huitfeldt, sjefen for landstridskreftene i Nord-Norge i en kommentar til Nordlands Framtid.

— Er det ofte slike fly lander på flyplassen i Bodø?

— Meget sjelden er det at vi får inn slike fly, og denne gangen skjedde det jo fordi flyet hadde tekniske vansker, og derfor ba om å få lande her.

— Var noen ombord i det amerikanske flyet skadet?

— Nei, og som det står i pressemeldingen som vi har sendt ut, landet flyet uten vansker her i Bodø etter en normal radarinnflyging.

— Men hvorfor har da den amerikanske ambassade i Norge sendt ut en melding der en ber om at saken ikke blir offentliggjort før etter et nærmere angitt klokkeslett, idet alle pårørende til flyets besetning ennå ikke er varslet? Dette er jo en praksis som bare ellers brukes når det er skader eller dødsfall.

— Jeg har ikke kjennskap til meldingen ambassaden har sendt ut, sa Huitfeldt, som opplyste at flyet fortsatt står i Bodø i påvente av reparasjon.

Ikke ny U-2-historie

Lockheed SR 71 er kjent som U-2-flyets etterfølger, det amerikanske spionflyet som ble skutt ned over Sovjet først på 60-tallet, og som skapte en del diplomatiske problemer for Norge da russerne ble kjent med at Bodø hadde vært brukt som mellomlandingssted for U-2.

Pressetalsmann Geir Grung i Utenriksdepartementet uttaler til Nordlands Framtid at det på forhånd er umulig å si om gårdagens landing i Bodø kan skape en ny «U-2-historie». - Men på bakgrunn av at dette er en nødlanding, kan jeg vanskelig tro at en vil få diplomatisk noteveksling denne gangen, sier Grung, som ellers viser til Forsvaret for øvrige kommentarer.

Uforsiktig med sprengstoff

En mann fra Vestvågøy er ilagt en bot på 300 kroner for å ha opptrådt uforsiktig med sprengstoff. En ladning på 200 gram dynamitt ble dekket kun med trålposer. Dette førte til at en stein gikk gjennom taket og endte på kaldloftet i et nabohus.

Dagbladet

Løssalgspris 3,00 Nr. 187 - 113. årg. Fredag 14. august 1981

Sannheten om Johan Borgen

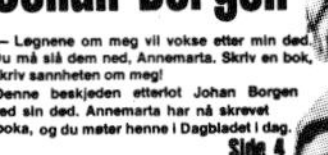

— Løgnene om meg vil vokse etter min død. Du må slå dem ned, Annemarta. Skriv en bok, skriv sannheten om meg!
Denne beskjeden etterlot Johan Borgen ved sin død. Annemarta har nå skrevet boka, og du møter henne i Dagbladet i dag.

Side 4

Super-spio[n] nødlandet i

USAs skarpeste øye mot Sovjet

■■ Det amerikanske superspionflyet SR 71 som måtte nødlande på Bodø flystasjon i går, er USAs skarpe øye mot Sovjet. Flyet driver skråfotofrafering fra ekstrem høyde over fremmede territorier.

■■ CIA utviklet flyet til spionasjeformål, men det disponeres nå av USAs flyvåpen.

Norske forsvarsmyndigheter hevder at det topphemmelige flyet tidligere ikke har vært observert på norsk jord.

Side 20

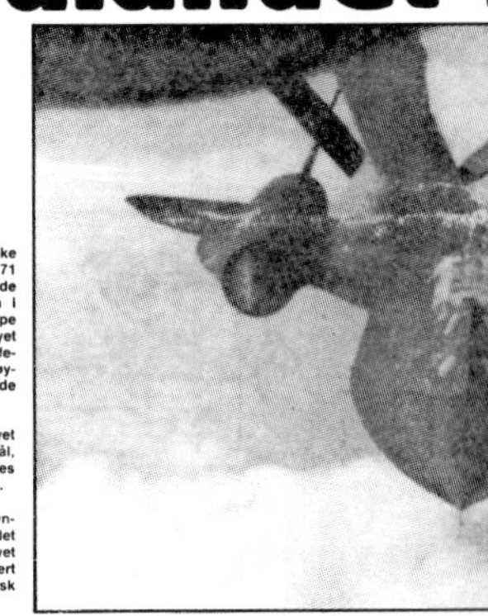

USAs superspion-fly SR 71 nødlandet i Bodø i går. Flyet kan fylle bensin i lufta (bildet) og er dermed ... lig over hele verden. CIA og Pentagon nekter overfor Dagbladet å kommentere saken.

VARSEL: Nordøst bris, tildels pent vær.

Løssalg kr. 2.50.

Nordlandsposten

(Nordlands Amtstidende)

Nr. 186, 119. årgang. Bodø, fredag 14. august 1981.

Topphemmelig rekognoseringsfly på Bodø flyplass:

Måtte nødlande etter tokt i Barentshavet

Det vakte nok berettiget oppsikt på Bodø flystasjon da et amerikansk rekognoseringsfly av den meget avanserte typen Lockheed SR-71 i går formiddag «nødlandet» i Bodø. Flyet var ikke i direkte vanskeligheter, men det var registrert feil med maskinens oljesystemer, og flyveren ba derfor om å få nødlande i Norge.

Lockheed SR-71 er et meget avansert rekognoseringsfly, og det er kjent for å kunne operere meget langt fra sine baser. Flyet som nå befinner seg på Bodø flyplass var på tokt i internasjonalt farvann i Norskehavet og i Barentshavet, og norske radarstasjoner fulgte flyet på den tid flyveren ba om å få lande i Norge.

Etter det vi har grunn til å tro, skal dette være første gang et slikt fly har landet i Skandinavia, men flytypen er

OVERGANG SISTE SIDE 2

TELEGRAPH

Vol. 101, No. 206 2 Sections, 16 Pages

North Platte Telegraph, 1981

Friday, August 28, 1981

25¢

Loverly day
Fair today and tonight with high in the upper 70s to low 80s. Low tonight in the mid to upper 50s. Mostly sunny and warmer on Saturday with high in the mid to upper 80s.
Weather on Page 6

Today

U.S. vows to protect planes

WASHINGTON (UPI) — The State Department said Thursday North Korea violated international law when it fired an anti-aircraft missile at a U.S. spy plane and vowed the United States will "take whatever steps necessary" to protect its pilots and planes.

A spokesman said both Moscow and Peking are being asked to reinforce the U.S. warning to North Korea that it will not tolerate a repetition of Wednesday's incident.

The missile exploded several miles from the high-flying, supersonic jet and posed no threat to the aircraft. Except for a stern warning, there was no immediate U.S. move to retaliate.

When the incident was announced Wednesday night, Pentagon officials refused to say when the event occured. But deputy White House press secretary Larry Speakes said Thursday the missile was fired about 3:30 a.m. EDT Wednesday.

Speakes, who is in California where President Reagan is vacationing, said Reagan was not told of the incident until his national security briefing at noon EDT, about 8 ½ hours later.

State Department spokesman Dean Fischer said flatly the missile was fired at the U.S. plane, which officials said never strayed over North Korean territory.

Fischer said, "We intend to continue to fly these routine flights and will take whatever steps are necessary to assure the future safety of our pilots and planes."

Fischer accused the North Koreans of violating the 1953 truce that ended hostilities on the Korean penninsula, and added, "Clearly, we are going to be watching North Korea's behavior very carefully." He said further U.S. action in response to the attack, "military or diplomatic, remains to be seen."

He said the incident "constitutes a violation of international law, the Korean Armistice Agreement, and accepted norms of international behavior.

The missile firing occurred just a week after two U.S. Navy fighters shot down a pair of Soviet-built Libyan jets that had fired at them over disputed Mediterranean waters. That prompted Reagan to declare, "If our men are fired on, our men are going to shoot back."

Reagan was not awakened to be told of the Libyan dogfight until 6 hours later. On Wednesday, White House counselor Edwin Meese told reporters in Sanata Barbara the even longer delay involving the Korean incident was because "there weren't really enough details from the Defense Department to evaluate the situation."

Reagan was briefed in more detail late Wednesday afternoon by Defense Secretary Caspar Weinberger, who went to the president's mountaintop ranch for a previously scheduled meeting.

In Seoul, South Korea's defense ministry issued a warning "that if North Korea continues provocative acts like this, it will be held responsible for any consequences that would arise therefrom."

Both State Department and Pentagon spokesmen declined to detail the mission of the U.S. plane — a SR-71 Blackbird capable of traveling three times the speed of sound at altitudes above 80,000 feet — but maintained the operation was "routine."

Fischer read a prepared statement that said, "We now have confirmation that early yesterday the North Koreans fired a missile at a U.S. Air Force plane flying in South Korean and international air space."

Fischer said the United Nations Command in Seoul — led by Americans — has called for a meeting Saturday of the commission that oversees enforcement of the 1953 armistice, but the North Korea had not yet responded to the request.

The United States does not have diplomatic relations with North Korea and thus no formal diplomatic protest could be lodged except through the Military Armistice Commission.

"In addition, we are contacting the governments of China and the Soviet Union to request that they convey our deep concern over this incident to North Korean authorities and that North Korea avoid any repetition of such dangerous activity," the State Department statement said.

China signed the 1953 truce agreement and the Soviets supply a large share of the North Korea arsenal, including SA-2 anti-aircraft missiles.

Chief Defense Department spokesman Henry Catto said Thursday the two-man crew of the sleek reconnaisance jet sighted the missile's contrail and its subsequent explosion several miles distant.

He said said the missile posed no threat to the Blackbird, and the plane returned unharmed to an undisclosed base — probably in Japan or Okinawa.

Catto refused to say exactly how far the SR-71 was from the demilitarized zone separating North and South Korea or from the North Korean coast during its mission, but said that at no time was the aircraft over North Korean territory.

An Air Force SR71 high-speed, high-altitude spy jet is shown at rest at the Kadena Air Base in Okinawa. An SR71 was fired upon over North Korea. (AP Laserphoto)

Airlines ... uced flight schedules

INTERNATIONAL Herald Tribune

Published with The New York Times and The Washington Post

LONDON, FRIDAY, AUGUST 28, 1981

Established 1887

...ME — Former U.S. President Jimmy Carter, greeted Thursday in Peking by the Communist ...ty chairman, Deng Xiaoping. Details, Page 2.

United Press International

N. Korea Fires Missile At U.S. Photo Aircraft

The Associated Press

WASHINGTON — The U.S. government said Thursday that it had confirmed that North Korea fired a missile at a U.S. reconnaissance plane flying in South Korean and international airspace Wednesday. The United States denounced the incident as an "act of lawlessness."

State Department spokesman Dean E. Fischer said: "We intend to continue to fly these routine flights and will take whatever steps are necessary to ensure the future safety of our pilots and our planes."

Pentagon spokesman Henry Catto said at a separate midday briefing that, during the mission, the U.S. jet, an SR-71 Blackbird, was "always in international airspace and South Korean airspace."

Mr. Catto said that the missile "undoubtedly" was fired from "one of several missile sites in North Korea."

He declined to discuss any details of the SR-71's mission, such as its route or how close it came to North Korean territory or airspace. Nor would he say what type of missile the North Koreans were believed to have fired at the plane.

It is policy not to discuss such sensitive, high-altitude reconnaissance operations, Mr. Catto said.

'Posed No Threat'

In announcing the episode, the Pentagon said only that the crew of the SR-71 "reported sighting a contrail and subsequent air burst several miles distant." The Pentagon said the incident "posed no threat to the aircraft, which landed safely."

Mr. Catto refused to say where the SR-71, which carried a crew of two, was based, but it is understood that these highly sophisticated strategic reconnaissance planes operate out of Okinawa.

The United States has never acknowledged any SR-71 flights over North Korea, but there have been repeated reports of such operations.

Mr. Catto said, "We intend to continue to fly these missions and I know of no limitation as a result of this incident." He said there had been no alert of U.S. forces in South Korea.

Asked whether the United States in any way provoked the incident, Mr. Catto replied: "No, sir."

At the time of the initial announcement Wednesday night, the wording of the Pentagon statement indicated that the missile had been fired from North Korea, but did not say so specifically.

However, the State Department spokesman, Mr. Fischer, said Thursday that there had been confirmation that "North Koreans fired a missile at a U.S. Air Force plane flying in South Korean and international airspace."

He said the United States views this incident with "serious concern." He called it an "act of lawlessness ... in violation of international law, the Korean Armistice Agreement and accepted norms of international behavior."

Mr. Fischer said the U.S. Command in Seoul had called for an Armistice Commission meeting Saturday "to protest directly to the North Koreans this violation of the 1953 armistice agreement." North Korea had not yet responded to the request for a meeting.

South Korea, meanwhile, accused North Korea on Thursday of "serious military provocation" and warned against any further "reckless" actions. Defense Ministry spokesman Park Chong Shik claimed that the missile attack, as well as the reported intrusion of North Korean MiG jets over Paengnyong-do Island on Aug. 21, "proved that the Communist North is always committing military adventures."

Mr. Fischer said the United States was contacting the Chinese and Soviet governments "to request that they convey our deep concern over this incident to North Korean authorities and that North Korea avoid any repetition of such dangerous activity."

High Speed

The twin-engine SR-71, which can fly at more than 2,000 miles (3,200 kilometers) an hour, is capable of photographing wide areas from altitudes of more than 80,000 feet (24,266 meters).

Mr. Fischer said there was no evidence of any connection between the Korean incident and the Libyan attack on U.S. aircraft off the coast of Libya last week.

President Reagan was not told about the Korean incident for 8½ hours, a spokesman said Thursday, but officials stressed that early reports lacked enough information to enable the president to evaluate the situation.

Presidential counselor Edwin Meese 3d said that Mr. Reagan, who is vacationing in California, was briefed about the incident Wednesday by Defense Secretary Caspar W. Weinberger during a previously scheduled meeting at Mr. Reagan's ranch.

"The president was concerned about it, obviously," said Mr. Meese, who attended the meeting with Mr. Weinberger. "But there weren't really enough details from the Defense Departmen...

...ns to Bar State Television

...thorities have ...ng the union ...r the tension ...ey will not al... silence newspa... ...es continued to ...ons, Solidarity ...usz Onyszkiewicz ...e government spokes... ...rzy Urban, but there were ...antive talks, the govern... office said.

...f Starvation'

...onal executive ...ent from its ...ansk, which ... inability to ...had placed ...onal obli...

going on is to save the country from the specter of starvation," the union's presidium said.

The statement echoed the words of Poland's new Roman Catholic primate, Archbishop Jozef Glemp, who said Wednesday that a power game was being played at the expense of the nation.

"Tensions and emotions are rising while poverty is lurking," the primate said.

The Warsaw daily Zycie Warszawy examined the situation from a different angle Thursday suggesting that far too often the words crisis and confrontation had been misplaced and abused.

Paper Accuses Media

The paper accused the official media — thereby apparently including itself — of panicking and said the government and Solidarity were closer to understanding than confrontation.

It said re-reading the press since ... ernment-society dialogue ... Today we know that the press was wrong," Zycie Warszawy said.

Solidarity also reported a strike in a sulphur mine near the southern city of Tarnobrzeg and said its branch in the city of Radom would go ahead with a one-hour regional strike Friday if talks with the government on local grievances did not begin.

Izvestia Charges Propaganda

MOSCOW (Reuters) — The Soviet government newspaper Izvestia charged Thursday that a massive propaganda campaign was being conducted by the West German news media to encourage counterrevolution in Poland.

Izvestia, in a report from Bonn, said the campaign amounted to open interference in Poland's internal affairs. The report said the campaign was linked to a strengthening of rightist forces in West Germany that were dissatified with Bonn's policy of good neighborly relations with Socialist countries.

...n Photo...

Han hjel...
Alma på N...

Frode Balseth heter ... gammel har han en so... vanlige. Han steller hus... Larsen på Mesøy i Mel... humør, men helsen er ikk... har fått besøk av Nordlan...

they would return to their former DMZ routes after 'certain preparations' were made. He did not explain what those preparations were but seemed angry about the attempted shoot-down. He added that the US government viewed such hostile actions with serious concern, and emphasized that the President would not stand for a repeat.

On Friday 2 October, BC and Jay flew 967 on a sortie off the eastern coast of China, North Korea and the USSR. They reported an unusual massing of ships off the coast of North Korea. The next day, Lt Gen Mathis (Assistant Vice Chief of Staff) held a special briefing for the Det's crewmembers in which he told of four special category missions which were to be flown on routes which would follow the same triple-pass track that Maury had flown when he was shot at on 26 August. He emphasized that the timing would be extremely important and that the 'Habu' was to be over the earlier mission's firing point within 30 seconds of their mission's prep-lanned timing. Timing control triangles would be built into the flight track after the second air refuelling to ensure that the precise timing constraints were met. One of the pilots asked why timing was so important. General Mathis explained that 'Wild Weasel' anti-radar strike aircraft would be poised to hit any North Korean SAM site within 60 seconds of a launch against the SR-71. The time constraint would ensure that the strike aircraft were headed in the right direction at the moment a missile was launched. President Reagan had personally approved the plan.

Operational sorties to the 'Z' continued to be flown along the ammended route until Monday 26 October 1981. Following extensive mission planning and detailed briefings, BC Thomas and Jay Reid took-off from Kadena exactly on time in 975. All four of these high-priority missions were ground-spared as insurance against an abort of the primary aircraft. BC recalled:

'We had to employ the timing triangles to lose a few minutes of 'pad'; we also delayed with the tanker all the way to the end of the second air refuelling for the same reason. We flew over the critical point within ten seconds of the designated time feeling very proud of ourselves.

'We all felt that it was this mission, which had such importance attached to it, and all of the preparation that had gone into it, to be the pinnacle of our professional efforts. Even though there was no firing, I experienced the greatest sense of well-being, knowing we did the whole operation 'exactly as planned'. I must admit that I'd hoped that the North Koreans would fire at us. Their missile capability never bothered us, and I believe that it is fair for me to say that by immediately smashing their launch facility, our national resolve would have been most graphically demonstrated.'

For whatever reason, the North Koreans chose not to launch a missile at this or any other trawling mission, and BC, and all who followed him, recovered safely after each four-hour flight.

Diego Garcia

The tiny island of Diego Garcia, located nearly half-way between the Maldives and Mauritius in the Indian Ocean, became an important operating location for B-52s participating in the Gulf War. Its strategic importance in relation to the western Middle East had been appreciated in US military circles over a decade earlier. As early as 1978, various engineering works began on the British-controlled base and the *Senior Crown* Programme Element Monitor (PEM) in the Pentagon obtained approval via a 'Chief of Staff Memo to the JCS' to acquire some JP7 fuel storage tanks for emplacement on the island. In addition, an SR-71 'barn' was moved from Beale for reconstruction in this unlikely sub-Asian location.

On Tuesday 1 July 1980 Bob Crowder and Don Emmons left Kadena in aircraft 962 on a four and a half hour flight down to the island to 'exercise the facility'. It was the first time that an SR-71 had ever visited the island, and after light maintenance the 'Habu' returned to Kadena. Despite having validated the good facilities, no SR-71 ever returned during subsequent operational sorties to 'points east' of the island.

The Gulf

On 24 September 1980 a simmering border war between Iraq and Iran flared into full-scale hostilities when Iraqi troops and tanks crashed across the border. Their dawn attack set the world's largest oil refinery, and many of Abadan's oil storage tanks, ablaze. The Iraqis quickly seized the port of Khorramshahr, and they advanced ten miles into Iranian territory. Despite initial successes by the Iraqi Army, the war turned into a stalemate with both sides digging in and fighting a long and bloody

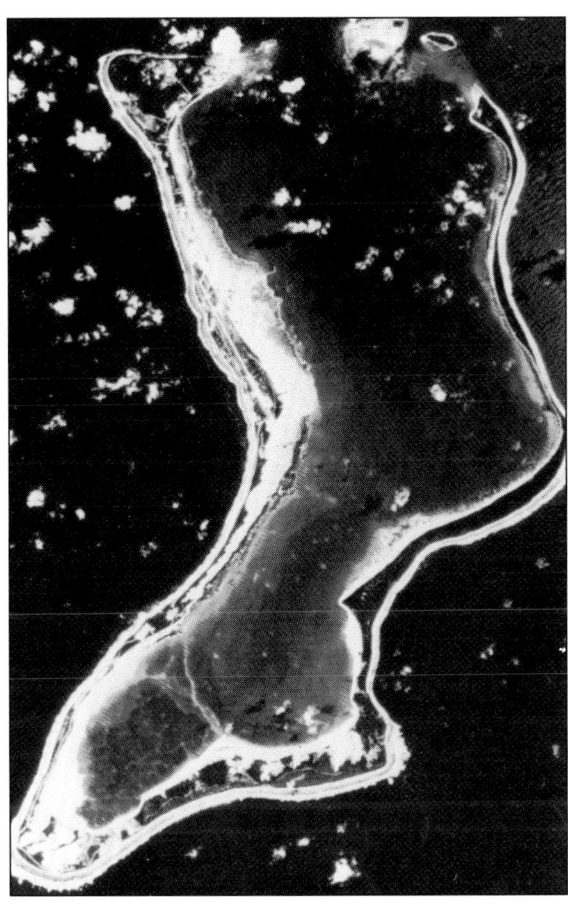

The island of Diego Garcia as photographed by the camera of 962 (*USAF*)

trench war, not too dissimilar to the battles fought in Flanders and Verdun some 65 years earlier.

Both the USSR and the US made it clear that neither side would get involved and that they would remain 'strictly neutral'. As the war dragged on, Iran began to exploit the 'oil pressure point' to take advantage of the 'hated West'. On 24 May 1984, two Iranian aircraft attacked an oil tanker off the Saudi Arabian coast. Reconnaissance of the area was provided by satellites and Det 1 SR-71s. As East-West countercharges continued over the next few years, Iraq's jets attacked the key Iranian oil terminals on Kharg Island and the Iranians attacked oil-laden supertankers bound for the West from Kuwait, Saudi Arabia and Bahrain. To offer greater protection to these unarmed vessels, the US government planned to 'reflag' such vessels as American ships and to escort them through the Straits of Hormuz. On 18 May 1987, two Iraqi Mirages F.1s, each carrying an AM.39 Exocet anti-ship missile, locked onto a surface target in the waters north of Bahrain. They both fired their sea-skimming missiles 12 miles from the target, but the warhead on one of the weapons failed to explode. The other missile, however, worked with devastating effect, hitting the frigate USS *Stark*, killing 28 sailors and leaving the sleek warship disabled and burning. President Reagan immediately demanded an Iraqi explanation for the attack, which a Baghdad spokesman said was due to the pilots identifying the frigate as Iranian.

Later in the summer of 1987, US intelligence believed that the Iranians had obtained a consignment of land-based *Silk Worm* anti-ship missiles from China, and were preparing to deploy them to threatening positions overlooking the Straits of Hormuz. Such actions could threaten the merchant tankers of many nations which transited the straits.

The first of four very long Kadena-based sorties to cover the Gulf region was flown by Majs Mike Smith and Doug Soifer on 22 July 1987. Majs Ed Yeilding and Curt Osterheld backed them up as spare crew in 967. As the primary crew stepped from the PSD van toward 975, Col Tom Alison and Lt Col Tom Henichek (the Det commander and ops officer) informed Mike and Doug that 975's ANS had not checked out properly and that they would have to take 967 instead, and that Ed and Curt would follow in 975 after its ANS problem was resolved.

The 11-hour sortie would involve two refuellings on the outbound leg and three on the return. As Mike and Doug approached their second aerial rendezvous, Doug called Ed and Curt, who were two hours behind in 967 and told them that everything was progressing well and that their services would not be required that day. The most distant second and third tankings were to be carried out by three KC-10s before and after 967 had flown over the 'cuckoo's nest'. The KC-10s were able to extend their range by 'buddy' refuelling each other. As a result of this, Mike was able to take on distant pre- and post-target split onloads from the two tankers during each AR.

The cloud cover had been almost continually undercast since they left Kadena, and as 967 was equipped with Technical Objective Cameras and an Optical Bar Panoramic Camera, it looked as if the mission could prove to be a very expensive failure. After much 'gas guzzling', they headed out 'hot and

Maj Mike Smith and Doug Soifer were the first to fly a Persian Gulf sortie on 22 July 1987 in 967 (*USAF*)

high' to boom the Gulf region; suddenly the undercast disappeared and conditions were perfect for their high-resolution cameras to do some of their finest work. Their fifth and final AR was completed ten hours after take-off. That night refuelling was complicated by the failure of one of the KC-10's boom lights, which made proper formation flying (in the close-in, contact position) very difficult. Despite that added strain to an already tiring flight (at the near limit of an SR-71's and an aircrew's flight duration), Mike landed an almost 'zero write-up' 'Habu' back at Kadena after a flight lasting 11 hours and 12 minutes.

On 9 August, Majs Terry Pappas and John Manzi left Kadena in 975 and headed out for the first of many aerial refuellings. After clearing the first tanker, they climbed and accelerated toward South-east Asia and then on south of India toward a second refuelling and their distant target area. Five hours after take-off they neared the collection area in the Persian Gulf. Everything had worked exactly as planned, and soon they were heading eastbound on their long trip back to Kadena. It had not been a simple, straightforward mission by any stretch of the imagination, however. Bad weather during two of the refuellings and a boom malfunction dictated that Terry had to maintain his contact position with the tankers for three-and-a-half hours during the mission. To make matters worse, nine hours into the sortie he became temporarily blinded by the combined effects of pure oxygen and an overheat condition which had affected his 'moon suit's' faceplate. The simple task of reading his instruments appeared almost impossible without opening his helmet visor, but such action was out of the question due to the greater dangers of decompression and hypoxia. Terry recalls that by squinting hard he could produce tears. That small bit of moisture revived his vison enough to continue the long mission. He finally completed the sortie with a smooth night landing back at Kadena after flying for more than 11 hours.

Warren McKendree and Randy Shelhorse completed a similar Gulf sortie, as did Dan House and Blair Bozek. These long-duration, high-priority missions revealed the presence of *Silk Worms* on Iranian soil and gathered extensive intelligence about the masses of military equipment in the Gulf. Thus, intelligence services were able to forewarn the US Navy of the *Silk Worm* threat, and diplomats were able to bring pressure to bear on Iran. The SR-71 had again performed its intelligence gathering service in a distant part of the world.

In earlier times, the crews would surely have received Distinguished Flying Crosses for these unique and important missions, but these sorties were being flown at the very time when the Chief of Staff, and other key SR-71 detractors, were under-mining the *Senior Crown* programme because of costs. The last thing they wanted were 'Habu Heroes' – therefore, the crews were only awarded Air Medals[8].

CHAPTER 7

DET 4

SR-71s would have staged through RAF Mildenhall during the Yom Kippur War in 1973 had it not been for the political posturing of the Heath Government. As a consequence, it was not until 9 September 1974 that the first 'Habu' visited England. On that historic day, Majs Jim Sullivan and Noel Widdifield established a world speed record across the Atlantic. Flying SR-71 number 972, they flew from New York to London in less than two hours[1], then 'stole the show' at Farnborough upon their arrival. Four days later, Capt 'Buck' Adams and Maj Bill Machorek set a return trip record in 972 of less than four hours back to Los Angeles[2].

Eighteen months later 972 again returned to the United Kingdom. Using the call-sign 'Burns 31', Majs 'Pat' Bledsoe and John Fuller flew 'old reliable' from Beale to Mildenhall in 4 hours and 42 minutes. This first operational deployment to Europe was made without the media attention that had accompanied the earlier visit – this was 'strictly business'.

The first operational sortie from Mildenhall was flown a few days later by Capts Maury Rosenberg and Don Bulloch. Their aircraft, equipped with Side Looking Radar for a through-the-clouds, stand-off look at north Russia, was to be flown over a route that would take Rosenberg and Bulloch high over the Barents Sea outside of Soviet airspace. As they were heading northbound west of Norway at 72,000 ft, Bulloch discovered that the outside air temperature was 30 degrees warmer than normal. After computing expected performance values in this abnormal subarctic flight condition by cross-correlating exhaust gas temperature against inlet door position, and interpolating the aircraft's true airspeed as read from the astro-inertial navigation system, the crew were alarmed to learn that their rate of fuel burn was considerably higher than calculated by the ground flight planners.

Realising that 972's fuel load would be 8000 lbs short by the time they arrived at their next air refuelling control point, and that they would barely be able to reach their tankers, the crew prudently decided to abort the mission and return to Milden-

Resplendent with its 9th SRW insignia emblazoned upon its tail, aircraft 976 arrives at RAF Mildenhall on 9 April 1980 for 30 days of European reconnaissance service (*P Crickmore*)

SR-71 974 first visited England on 30 April 1982 for eight months of European service (*L Peacock*)

hall. Following their safe recovery back in England, some staff members scoffed at the 'new guys'' decision to abort under such circumstances. Five days later, Bledsoe and Fuller flew 972 along the same route. They too aborted, confirming the outside air temperature was also more than 30 degrees above standard and that their preplanned fuel log was 'just out to lunch'. On 30 April 972 was flown back to Beale. The ten-day deployment, which was an intelligence 'bust', had nevertheless provided extremely useful operational information, highlighting the need to amend certain arctic airmass procedures before the next UK-based missions were attempted.

The purpose of 'Habu' deployments to Europe was 'to gather simultaneous, synoptic coverage (photographic, radar and electronic intelligence) of Soviet and Warsaw Pact facilities along the edge of the Eastern Bloc. They were initially staged during the winter months when cloud cover hindered satellite operations. The sensitive nature of such flights dictated that each deployment needed prior authorisation from Her Majesty's Government, which had to cover the full 20-day period of the det's activities.

Aircraft 962 arrived during *Exercise Teamwork* on 6 September 1976, and flew the very next day on a 'Barents Sea Mission' codenamed *Coldfire 001*. Majs Rich Graham and Don Emmons flew that and another round-robin sortie before returning 962 to Beale on 18 September. On 7 January 1977, aircraft number 958 arrived at Mildenhall as 'Ring 21'. It left at the end of a ten-day deployment as 'Power 86'. The same aircraft returned on 16 May as 'Indy 69' and returned to Beale 15 days later as 'Resay 35'. A third deployment took place on 24 October when 976 stayed for 23 days before returning to Beale on 16 November. Aircraft 964 deployed on two occasions during 1978 – it arrived the first time on 24 April for an 18-day stay and returned on 16 October for another 17 days.

After nearly two years of these short TDY deployments, Detachment 4 of the 9th SRW was activated at RAF Mildenhall to support U-2R and SR-71 operations[3].

Yemen

By 1979, Pat Halloran (the ex-9th SRW commander) had been promoted to Brigadier General. In March of that year, as SAC's Inspector General, he was conducting an Operational Readiness Inspection (ORI) at Beale. On the other side of the globe, tensions between Saudi Arabia and the Peoples' Republic of Yemen, were fast reaching breaking point. The US intelligence community believed that there was a very real risk that the Republic was on the brink of invading its northern neighbour. As a result, the 9th SRW had been restricted to base. Unaware of the real reasons behind such restrictions, most of the guys dismissed it as just an irritating part of the ORI.

On the night of Friday 9 March a party was in full

swing at the O' Club after a crew had 'bought the bar' following their first Mach 3 sortie earlier that day. At about 2200 hours Col Willie Lawaon (the Deputy Commander for Operations) asked Majs Buzz Carpenter and John Murphy to meet him in one of the planning rooms at 1000 hours the next morning. At 0700 hours the crewmembers received a phone call instructing them to report to headquarters immediately.

On arrival, they were briefed about the situation prevailing in the Yemen and began planning a 'Habu' mission into the region that would be conducted from RAF Mildenhall. As the crew's 'Saturday off' became dominated by mission planning, Buzz and John phoned their wives and asked them to pack their bags 'for an indeterminate period at an undisclosed destination' – it was the type of call that 'Habu' wives were used to. Arriving back at their homes at 0200 hours on Sunday, they grabbed a few hours sleep and were on a KC-135 the same day bound for Mildenhall. They touched down at the Suffolk base on the morning of Monday 12 March, and were escorted to a radio car from which they provided mobile recovery supervision for Majs Rich Graham and Don Emmons, who were due to land in 972 from their ferry flight from Beale.

Tanker support for the Yemen sorties had nearly cleared the Beale ramp of its KC-135s, and there was very little left for Inspector General Pat Halloran to inspect! At that point, Pat remarked to an SR-71 crewmember, 'Well, this is what it's really all about'. The three planned sorties into the region called for the aeroplane to be configured with an OBC in the nose and TEOC 'close-look' cameras in chine bays P and Q. Cloud cover over the collection area caused the first missions to be continually postponed. On three occasions an execution message was received, whereupon the crews would eat and go to bed at 1800 hours for crew rest before being awakened at 0200 hours to start their long day. On two snowy mornings the crew was strapped into their aeroplane with adrenaline pumping (ready for an 0430 hours engine start) only to have the mission put on a 24-hour hold and the crew returned to Det 4's accommodation block.

Finally, Buzz and John were able to get airborne in 972 and head for their first air refuelling off Land's End. Unfortunately, Buzz suffered a violent attack of diarrhoea while on the tanker boom, but despite his discomfort, he elected to continue the mission. Having convinced John that he now felt much better, they completed the full fuel off-load and accelerated due south.

Since they were unable to overfly France, it became necessary to skirt the Iberian penninsula. They therefore entered the Mediterranean Sea through the Straits of Gibraltar and completed a second refuelling before returning to high Mach flight. After overflying the Suez Canal, they descended for their third tanker rendezvous over the Red Sea. The planned double-loop coverage of the collection area was interrupted by the ANS, which tried to initiate a pre-programmed turn prior to reaching the correct destination point (DP). Upon recognizing the error, the pilot flew the aeroplane manually while trying to work out what had cause the AUTONAV 'glitch'. As a result of this miscue, they overshot the turn point but completed the rest of the route and made their way back to the tankers for another 'Red Sea' top-up. A fifth air refuelling was completed east of Gibraltar and an hour-and-a-half later they recovered 972 back at Mildenhall after a full ten-hour mission.

The mission had generated considerable interest within the 9th SRW as well as at SAC Headquarters and in Washington. As a result, Buzz and John were greeted by a large number of their colleagues as they stepped off of the gantry (including Col Dave Young, the 9th SRW vice commander), who presented Buzz with a brown SR-71 tie tack to commemorate the inflight incident when, to misquote a well-known phrase, 'the world fell out of Buzz's bottom'.

When the 'take' was processed, it was of exceptional quality and the incident which had delayed their turn had yielded the most important information. That unexpected success made additional flights to the area unnecessary. Consequently, Rich Graham and Don Emmons returned 972 to Beale on 28 March. Two other deployments to Mildenhall were carried out in 1979 – 979 spent 15 days in the UK between 17 April and 2 May, and 976 arrived on 18 October and left on 13 November.

By early 1980, the SR-71 operations at Mildenhall had become much more routine and the rate of 'deployment clearances' increased. The three deployments for 1980 used aircraft numbers 976, 972 and 964. The first two stayed for one month each and the third remained at Mildenhall for four months. In 1981 aircraft 972 arrived on 6 March and departed on 5 May. Not all transits were flown as planned – the mission of 12 August 1981 was

Aircraft 964 is seen taking the first half of a 'split-load' from a KC-135Q (*P Crickmore*)

scheduled to fly from Beale to the Barents, and back to Beale. On that flight Majs BC Thomas and Jay Reid took off from Beale at 2200 hours to fly a ten-and-a-half-hour sortie with refuellings over Idaho, Goose Bay, twice over the North Sea and again over Goose Bay, before returning to Beale. Between the two North Sea refuellings they would make their important, high-fast run over the Barents Sea, where their side-looking radar would pick up targets on the Kolskiy Poluostrov and in Murmansk harbour.

The mission went like clock-work until they were in the 'take' area when BC noted that his left-engine low 'oil-quantity' warning light was flashing on and off. After completing the important radar run, he hooked 964 up with one of the KC-135Qs and began taking on the much-needed fuel load. It was during refuelling that he noted the oil warning light was shining continuously. That situation was a 'mandatory abort' item on his emergency procedures checklist because prolonged flight under such degraded conditions could easily result in engine seizure. There were two preferred bases in northwest Europe for diversionary aborts – Mildenhall, a two-and-a-half hour subsonic flight away, or Bödo in Norway, which was just 20 minutes away. BC decided that prudence was the better part of valour on this occasion and diverted into Bödo. There he was greeted by the base commander, Gen Ohmount, whom, as BC recalled, was very polite but very nervous. It later transpired that Ohmount had been a young lieutenant at the base in 1960 when Gary Powers had been shot down, and when it had become widely known that the intention was for the CIA pilot to have landed at Bödo, the Norwegian government disclamed any knowledge of the plan and fired Ohmount's 1960 boss – this event was still strongly etched on his memory.

Having notified the SAC Reconnaissance Center of his intentions to divert, BC was anxious to provide 'Home-Plate' with other details. The Norwegian general directed the 'Habu' pilot towards his underground command post, a very impressive place built into the side of a mountain, from where

(Left to right) BC Thomas and Jay Reid were the first 'Habu' crew to land an SR-71 on a Continental European base. On 12 August 1981 they diverted 964 into Bödo, Norway (*via BC Thomas*)

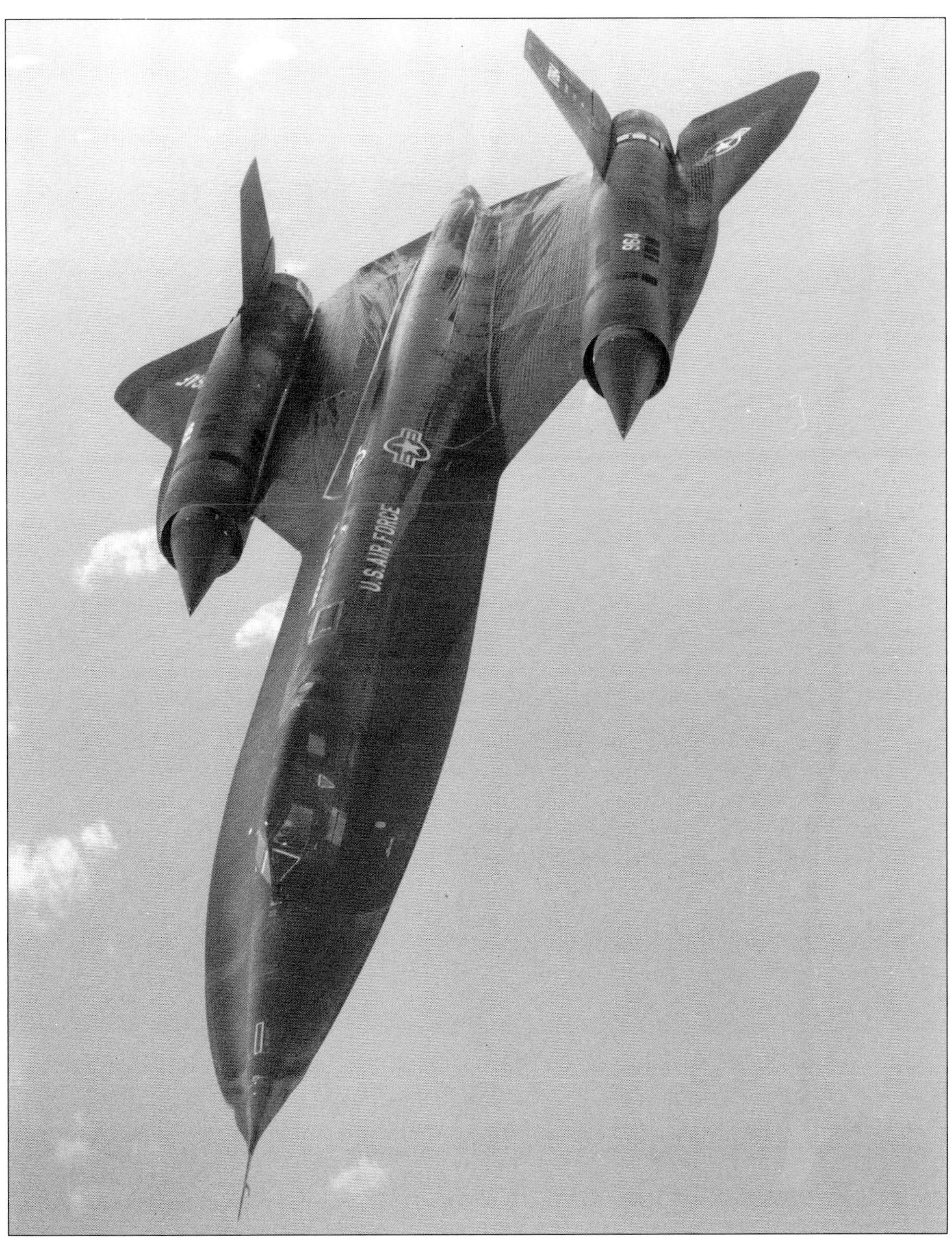

On 6 October 1981 964 was flown on a Barents/Baltic sortie by Maj Rich Judson and Frank Kelly. Note the JP7 fuel streaming from dozens of tiny cracks following a max fuel load disconnect

BC could tell Col Dave Young (the 9th SRW commander) of the nature of 964's mechanical problem. Young asked at what stage the decision had been made to abort, to which BC gave the total mission time and the third air refuelling plus-time. From that answer, Col Young was able to ascertain that the aircraft had the reconnaissance 'take' on board, and that certain specialists would have to accompany the recovery crew to down-load the data.

Two officers were then assigned to each of the US fliers – BC recalled that his 'minder' was Lt Roar Strand, a 331st Fighter Squadron F-104 pilot. The two Norwegian pilots did not let their charges out of their sight, and even slept in the same room. The recovery team, headed-up by Lt Col Randy Hertzog, arrived in a KC-135Q on 15 August. Gen Ohmount had requested that the recovery team wear military uniforms and not civilian clothes to ensure that all was kept 'above board'. Unfortunately this message did not reach the new arrivals, who were quickly ushered back into the tanker and instructed to don their fatigues.

With a million members of the Polish Solidarity movement going on strike on 7 August, and mounting tension between communist state officials and the rest of the Polish population, it was decided that 964 should remain in Europe to monitor any possible Soviet response. Consequently at 1342 hours on 16 August, BC and Jay departed Bödo in the company of their trusty tanker for a return flight to Mildenhall, which was performed without fuss at subsonic speed. Now christened 'The Bödonian Express', 964 touched down at 1452. The crew were met at the bottom of the gantry-platform by two other 'Habu' crew-members, Majs Jerry Glasser and Mac Hornbaker, who would fly the next sortie.

BC and Jay Reid returned 964 to Mildenhall on 16 August after a subsonic flight from Norway (*L Peacock*)

On 22 August, Jerry and Mac flew 'The Bödonian Express' on a sortie into the Baltic near Poland. One week later, BC and Jay flew another sortie in the vicinity of Poland. A third sortie to the area was conducted by Capts Rich Young and Ed Bethart on 31 August, and on 2 September BC and Jay were finally returned to Beale by tanker after their scheduled ten-hour sortie had lasted 21 days. Aircraft 964 continued flying operational sorties until 6 November when it was returned to Beale. The political situation in Poland continued to deteriorate as the clamour for reforms and democracy gathered momentum. By early December the situation had reached breaking point. Late during the night of 12 December 1981, the communist leader, Gen Jaruzelski, cut all communication links with the West and deployed troops and armour to set up road blocks and occupy strategic installations. He then declared a state of martial law and appeared on television to announce the formation of a Military Council of National Salvation. He claimed that strikes, protest demonstrations and crime had brought the country 'to the border of mental endurance, . . . the verge of an abyss'. Two days later it became apparent that at least 14,000 trade union activists had been arrested and seven people had been shot in the Selesian coalfields while resisting martial law. Would Jaruzelski turn to the Soviet Union for help in his struggle to retain control of Poland? Or would President Leonid Brezhnev commit Soviet troops to crush the uprising as he had done in Czechoslovakia on 21 August 1968? Clearly, the Reagan Administration needed some answers, and fast, and the Det 4 crews were tasked with providing them.

Maj Jack Madison and Steve Lee stand in-front of Det 4's very 'Anglophied' emblem (*P Crickmore*)

Majs Gil Bertelson and Frank Stampf were on the roster for this important sortie. The significance of their mission dictated that it be backed-up with a spare aircraft; consequently, Majs Nevin Cunningham and Geno Quist (known within the crew force as 'Neno' and 'Geno') were also suited-up as 'spares'. As Gil and Frank disappeared with their SR-71 into the cold, wet, night, Nevin and Geno waited at the end of the runway in 958 for the code-words which would either send them 'back to the barn', or on their way on a long mission over much of the north Atlantic and northern Europe. Soon after, Frank called back to Geno on their discrete HF radio frequency saying simply, 'Your guys have got it'. To which both spare crewmen simultaneously said, 'Oh Shit!' and off they went. The weather in the first air refuelling area over Nevada and Utah was so bad that it was all the 'Habu' crew could do to find the tanker in the thick clouds. When they finally located it, and were 'on the boom', it proved extremely difficult for Nevin to maintain the connection due to the heavy turbulence. The updrafts bounced the KC-135 all over the sky to the degree that its autopilot was unable to react fast enough to the unstable conditions. This refuelling was therefore one of the most difficult experienced by both the tanker and SR-71 crews. Nevin asked the tanker pilot to forget the autopilot and 'go manual' to achieve a better 'offload platform'. Meanwhile, the transfer operation was enshrouded in Saint Elmo's Fire, which lit-up both aircraft like glowing Christmas trees.

After finally completing the ragged refuelling operation, Nevin lit both burners and pressed-on to the second ARCP over Maritime Canada. Again the weather did its utmost to make the operation as uncomfortable as possible. After quickly crossing the black Atlantic, they headed towards their third refuelling track off the west coast of Norway. Here they were sandwiched between layers of cloud, but the air was smooth in the arctic twilight and the top off went smoothly. The long Atlantic crossing required a fill-up from two tankers. After taking the first half of his load from one KC-135, Nevin looked for the other tanker. As he closed in on the second aircraft, he discovered he was joining up with what turned out to be a Soviet Ilyushin Il-20 *Coot* ELINT aircraft! Nevin flew 958 up to the 'would-be' tanker, who was no doubt equally startled by the presence of a mysterious 'Habu'. Nevin and Geno quickly dropped back to find the second tanker, and after they 'topped-off', the pilot lit the burners for the next high-hot run. At 72,000 ft they headed into the 'take' area, where it was especially dark at altitude (it seemed that the only source of light was from the two J58 afterburners 100 ft behind them). Having completed an inner 'loop' around the Baltic Sea, they were on their way back down to the fourth refuelling when the sun popped back up over the horizon.

To further complicate matters on this long and difficult mission, Geno was unable to make radio contact with the tankers. Fortunately, Nevin spotted their contrails well below and ahead of them, and simply followed the aerial 'railroad tracks' for a join-up. While on the boom, Geno broke further bad news to Nevin about their Astro-Inertial Navigation System, which had failed. Clearly it would not be possible to return to Beale since 'ANS Failure' was a mandatory abort item. They therefore settled into formation with the tankers, who led them to Mildenhall, where snow and ice covered the runway and taxyways. Finally, after what had turned out to be 'a very entertaining' mission, 958 slithered to a halt outside the dedicated SR-71 barn, and Nevin and Geno climbed out after their eight-and-a-half hour 'fun-filled' mission – their 27th operational sortie together.

Back at Beale AFB the Californian weather was much less severe. As BC Thomas and Jay Reid climbed from the tandem cockpits of a T-38 on completion of a routine training flight on Wednesday 16 December, they were met by Col Randy

Nevin Cunningham, who was no stranger to Mildenhall, became the detachment's commander, and he is seen here talking to Lt Col Joe Kinego, commander of the 1st SRs at that time (*P Crickmore*)

All sensor data collected by the Det was processed in these Mobile Processing Center Units (MPC), located within a secure compound inside hanger 538 at Mildenhall

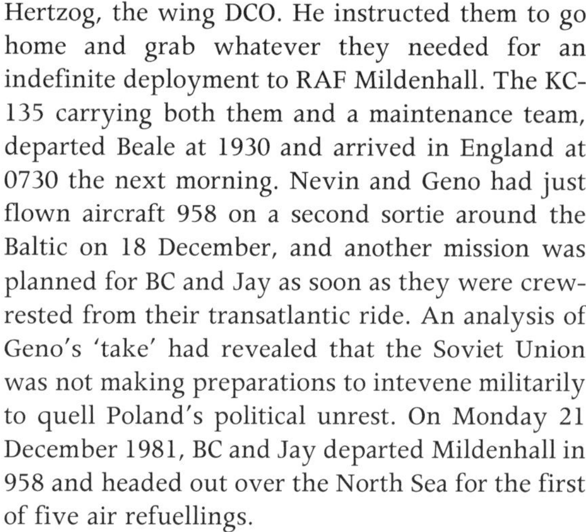

Hertzog, the wing DCO. He instructed them to go home and grab whatever they needed for an indefinite deployment to RAF Mildenhall. The KC-135 carrying both them and a maintenance team, departed Beale at 1930 and arrived in England at 0730 the next morning. Nevin and Geno had just flown aircraft 958 on a second sortie around the Baltic on 18 December, and another mission was planned for BC and Jay as soon as they were crew-rested from their transatlantic ride. An analysis of Geno's 'take' had revealed that the Soviet Union was not making preparations to intevene militarily to quell Poland's political unrest. On Monday 21 December 1981, BC and Jay departed Mildenhall in 958 and headed out over the North Sea for the first of five air refuellings.

Their flight was also tasked to monitor the Soviet-Polish border situation from a stand-off position in international airspace over the Baltic Sea, and to include a long northern run around the coast of Norway along Russia's north coast. Jay activated the sensors as they cruised at Mach 3 on their northern loop, which exited the 'take' area near Murmansk on a westerly heading toward the fourth refuelling. Out over the North Atlantic, the right generator cut off but BC managed to get it reset. After the fifth tank near Goose Bay, Labrador, another problem arose that would limit their cruise speed inbound to Beale. During acceleration BC noted that 958's supply of liquid nitrogen had been depleted, and that the fuel tanks could not be pressurised to inert fuel fumes at high Mach. He limited the cruise Mach to 2.6 in accordance with emergency operating procedures and made his final descent into Beale somewhat low on fuel after a flight of almost ten hours. The series of Baltic sorties not only obtained invaluable intelligence at a time of high international tension, but also vividly demonstrated US resolve to stay actively engaged in the situation by using its key surveillance assets in the NATO-Warsaw Pact theatre of operations.

Det 4's capability was doubled during the closing stages of 1982 when two SR-71s were based 'permanently' at Mildenhall for the first time, the aircraft being manned by a number of crews on 30-day deployments who flew a succession of 'routine but highly productive missions' across the North Sea and eastern Europe. After 972 had been deployed for seven months, it was ready to be returned to Beale for periodic 'heavy maintenance', which included replacing fuel tank sealant that tended to burn away after repeated high-Mach flights. Nevin and Geno got the big redeployment sortie and left Mildenall at 1000 hours on Tuesday 5 July 1983 via the Barents/Baltic Seas, and returned across the North Atlantic to California. After completing their first 'take' run on a 'northern loop' over the Barents Sea, they decelerated into the

'Viking North' air refuelling track in international airspace west of Bödo, Norway. Topped off, they climbed back to altitude and entered their second 'collection area' within the narrow Baltic corridor to complete the reconnaissance portion of the mission. Preparing to head home, they again decelerated and descended into the Viking North area over the North Sea. Back at high altitude, Geno calculated that Nevin would have to accelerate to maximum Mach to improve the aircraft's range to ensure that they would have enough fuel to reach the next set of tankers near Labrador.

During this high-hot phase of the flight, the left engine's exhaust gas temperature indicator showed that the EGT had become uncontrollable and that 972 should not be flown faster than 3.05 Mach to ensure that engine damage would not occur. By flying at this 'less than optimum speed', the SR-71 would not be able to reach the KC-135s. Manual control of the inlet spikes and doors made matters worse and they were only able to maintain Mach 3 in that configuration. Slowing to subsonic speeds would further exacerbate their low fuel predicament and they found that they could not go back to Bödo. Therefore, they had to press on toward their tankers in the hope that they might be able to improve their fuel flow rate or to divert into Iceland. For the next 45 minutes Nevin flew at 3.09 Mach before slowing to 3.05 to allow the EGT to drop back into the 'green'.

As they approached the 'point-of-no-return' off Iceland, Geno recalculated the fuel situation, which had improved slightly. Nevin decided to 'press on' and told Geno to get the tankers to fly toward them to further shorten their distance to hook-up. After completing a hook-up in record-breaking time (much to their great relief), the fuel streamed into 972 at more than 6000 lbs per minute. Back at Beale after another seven hours of SR-71 excitement, neither crewmember would admit to how much (or how little) fuel they had remaining before they made contact with their everlasting friends in the tanker.

Aircraft Number 955

In May 1983 it was decided by HQ SAC and Air Force Systems Command officials to demonstrate the Loral Company's Advanced Synthetic Aperature Radar System (ASARS-1) on an SR-71 before upgrading the rest of the 'Habu' fleet with this new high-definition, ground-mapping radar system. After aircraft number 955[4] was equipped with the new system, BC Thomas and John Morgan were

On the 9 July 1983, Maury Rosenberg and ED McKim touched down at RAF Mildenhall in aircraft 955. The serial number had been changed to 962 to prevent unwanted attention. Here BC Thomas carries out post-flight checks in the aircraft at Palmdale. Note the bulbous 'duck-bill'-like nose, characteristic of an ASARS 1-equipped sensor package (*USAF*)

assigned the task of conducting the first operational test flight. On 1 July 1983, they made SAC's first ASARS familiarisation flight, which lasted just over five hours, and during which John learned ASARS 'switchology' and operating techniques. Five days later, Maury Rosenberg and ED McKim also flew the modified SR-71 on a five-hour sortie, recovering into Beale AFB rather than Palmdale. On 9 July, Maury and ED deployed 955 on a seven-hour flight to Mildenhall, via the Barents/Baltic collection area.

Local British plane spotters peering through binoculars and telescopes from various off-base vantage points, excitedly recorded the 'Habu's' arrival, some noting the slightly bumpy ASARS nose, but an 'already familiar' tail number which many people lovingly kept in their log books. On that occasion, all of them logged a false serial as a cover-number was being used to conceal the fact that the test-bird was overseas. As 955 was already known by military aviation enthusiasts as 'the Palmdale test-ship', it had been decided by the maintenance folks back at Beale to temporarily rechristen 955 as 962 for this deployment. The latter jet had visited Mildenhall earlier, and would not therefore draw unwelcome attention and speculation to the unique test deployment.

Nine days later on 18 July 1983 BC and John took the aircraft on a 2.6 hours ASARS operational test sortie to monitor military installations in East Germany. On 21 July, Maury and ED took their turn on a four hour mission. The next day BC and John flew 980 to Greenham Common to participate in the International Air Tattoo to help raise money for the RAF's Benevolent Fund. Among the many thousands of people who came to see the aircraft were some of the 'Greenham Women', who had long been demonstrating against many political issues, and who had been camping outside the base to gain public recognition[5]. The day before the SR-71 was due to return to Mildenhall, some of the demonstrators managed to daub white paint on the 'Habu'. They were quickly arrested for causing a disturbance, and for possible damage to the aircraft's titanium, which a later laboratory analysis proved was unharmed.

Several days later Maj Jim Jiggens and Capt Joe McCue performed an unforgettable departure from the base. After a morning take-off on 26 July for the short flight back to Mildenhall, Jim (an ex-*Thunderbirds* airshow demonstration pilot, who had obtained prior permission from the base commander to do a farewell flyby) flew a wide circular pattern at 250 knots towards the Greenham Peace Camp. As 980 reached a strategic point, Jim pushed both trottles to full afterburner, whereupon the SR-71 thundered over the encampment at a very low altitude. Applying sharp back pressure to the control stick and lofting the 'Habu' into a spectacular climb, Jim allowed his sleek aircraft to trumpet the 'sound of freedom' as only an SR-71 could.

Aircraft 964 prepares to leave its 'barn' on 17 December 1987 for a 0745 launch. Ground technicians would have begun their activities four-and-a-half hours earlier. Their first task was to warm the tar-like engine oil prior to start-up, which in UK winter temperatures was a solid mass (*P Crickmore*)

The final ASARS demonstration flight was conducted on 30 July when BC and John flew 955 on a 7.3 hour flight back to Beale, via the Baltic and Barents Seas. The series of tests were extremely successful, proving that ASARS 1 represented a quantum leap in radar resolution and capability for reconnaissance purposes. Capts Gary Luloff and Bob Coats ferried the aircraft back to Palmdale on 2 August, where further tests were conducted prior to completing two production radar sets for the operational fleet.

Permanent Deployment

Although the 1983 deployment to Mildhenall was still called a 'temporary' operation, two SR-71s remained at the base throughout the entire year (apart from a period lasting 33 days in early 1983, and three days in the autumn). As early as 1980, SAC had begun planning changes in the SR-71's European operations to cut the cost of deployments and to increase the frequency of surveillance flights. Such changes required actions of 'air diplomacy' on the part of HQ 3rd Air Force negotiators, and USAF and SAC staff specialists. On instructions from the JCS, HQ USAF and HQ SAC, Col Don Walbrecht of the Third Air Force (accompanied by Lt Col John Fuller and Lt Col Dwight Kealoa of HQ USAF/XOXX and Lt Col Kenneth Hagemann of HQ SAC/XP[6]) proposed to Assistant Secretary Martin Scicluna, and to Gp Capt Frank Appleyard, Deputy Director of Operations in the RAF's Directorate of Organisation (DGO/RAF), that SR-71 operations at Mildenhall should be 'bedded down' on a more permanent basis.

Scicluna (Head of MoD's 5-9 (Air)) led the British contingent who reviewed the proposal. Although he thought that the SR-71's high-visibility image might cause 'political difficulties' at senior levels, he took the issue forward to Secretary of State for Defence, Sir Francis Pym, who agreed to consider it. After specialised briefings to a few MoD 'insiders', which included certain intelligence officers who had 'special access' to US reconnaissance information, their recommendations were taken to Pym who agreed to the initiative. Another meeting held three days later worked out the politics of the proposal. The following week, each member of the US team briefed his respective CINC or Deputy Chief of Staff in Ramstein, Omaha or Washington that the programme was 'on track' in Whitehall[7]. Soon after, Prime Minister Thatcher's approval was noted as a simple 'change of mode of operations' from temporary deployments to a permanent presence at RAF Mildenhall. U-2 operations were to be moved from Mildenhall to Alconbury as both bases were 'beefed-up' for their expanded intelligence roles.

During the next two months, Walbrecht made regular trips to London to answer questions from MoD officials who prepared authority documents for ministerial signature. Scicluna later confided that the SR-71 initiative went down very well because of long-standing intelligence sharing connections, and because one of his junior staff officers had suggested calling the proposal a simple 'change of mode' of current operations from intermittent to permanent basing. The permissive loop was then closed, and the SR-71s could come to England, where they would remain the 'plane spotters' favourite attraction for many years.

On 5 April 1984, Prime Minister Thatcher announced that a detatchment of SR-71 aircraft had been formed at the Suffolk base. A blanket clearance to operate two 'Habus' from the United Kingdom had been granted by the government, but certain sorties would still require prior high-level approval from the MoD. Moreover, those especially sensitive operations would require 'a clearance' from the PM herself.

Anglo-American co-operation extended into SR-71 missions themselves, 'Habu' sorties venturing into the Barents and the Baltic areas being coordinated with the RAF's small fleet of Nimrod R.1 ELINT aircraft, operated from RAF Wyton in

Maj Jim Jiggens and Ted Ross begin accelerating 960 down Mildenhall's runway. The slight flash from the right engine was from TEB ignition. The left engine is already delivering max thrust. On 'light-up' a sharp rudder deflection is often necessary to correct for the asymmetrical thrust (*P Crickmore*)

Maj Brian Shul and Walt Watkins work through the 'challenge and response' checklist prior to launching 973 on an operational sortie. Note rudder deflection during controllability checks (*P Crickmore*)

Leicestershire by No 51 Sqn. Such co-operation also extended to the Luftwaffe, which used Atlantiques in a similar role to the Nimrods. During such sorties, the SR-71 took on the role of a 'provocateur'. Tracks would be changed, and the SR-71 flown on a profile which, if continued straight ahead, would penetrate Soviet or Warsaw Pact airspace. On such occasions, the 'Habu' would always break off at the last possible second and remain in international airspace.

Soviet Fighters

At 1010 hours on 3 June 1986, Majs Stormy Boudreaux and Ted Ross left Mildenhall in 980, heading out across the North Sea toward their first refuelling west of Norway on another Barents/Baltic sortie. At 26,000 ft in the refuelling track, they found the sun directly ahead of them and clouds all around as they closed for contact with the KC-135s in diffuse and strangely-angled sunlight, which reflected brightly off the bottoms of the tankers.

As soon as the boomer made contact, Stormy found himself flying formation in almost blinding conditions, with the SR-71's cockpit instruments obscured (in the dark shadow of the dashboard below the windscreen), forcing him to arrange his tiltable car-like sunvisor to shield against the high-contrast conditions. That effort proved of little value, for while in the contact position 'on the boom', the tanker's reference points for formation flying were flashing in such extreme contrast that they appeared to be surrounded by 'sea or sky or whatever'. A stong sensation of vertigo overtook Stormy, leaving him with a false sense of diving and climbing (and with the even more powerful sensation of flying inverted while refuelling. An interphone call to Ted assured Stormy that he was not upside-down; he was then able to continue filling 980's tanks while fighting his sense of flying 'straight up or straight down'.

After clearing the tanker, and his senses, Stormy climbed through 60,000 ft, where he noted through his periscope that 980 was still pulling contrails which should have stopped above FL600. Another check at 70,000 revealed that he was 'still conning', which he hoped would surely stop before they approached their target area. Upon entering the Barent Sea zone, the aircraft began a programmed left turn to the north east and then reversed in a large sweeping right turn to roll out on a westerly heading, which would take them on the 'collection run' and back across the entry point. When established on the westerly heading north of Archangel, they noted that they were still 'conning', which was most abnormal at high altitudes. To add to their dismay, Stormy spotted three other contrails ahead of them and to the left, but turning to converge in what might be an intercept. Another southerly glance revealed three more 'cons' closing from the left but at a lower altitude.

MiG-25s often put in an appearance during missions up to the Barents Sea

These six Soviet fighters, each separated by approximately 15 miles, were executing what appeared to be a well-rehearsed turning intercept manoeuvre to pop up somewhere in the vicinity of the fast-moving 'Habu' and fire off some sophisticated new air-to-air missiles. The Soviet fighter pilots had executed an in-place turn which would have placed them in a perfect position for a head-on attack had 980's track penetrated Soviet air space. As Ted monitored the fighters' electronic activities, Stormy increased speed and altitude.

Suddenly a contrail shot by just beneath the nose of 980, leaving both crewmembers waiting for a missile or another aircraft to appear which might have 'spoiled their whole day'. It was with great relief that Stormy realised they were now paralleling their inbound contrail, and the contrail they had just crossed was their own that they had laid while turning northeast before heading west. For a few moments their hearts missed several beats in the thought of having unwanted high-Mach company 15 miles above the cold Arctic seas.

Stormy eased off some power and settled back into their routine of high-Mach cruise, the autopilot completed a long 'lazy turn' around the north shore of Norway, before Stormy started his descent toward another refuelling. To complete the mission, the crew made an easy high altitude dash into the Baltic corridor and down through the former West Germany, before heading home to Mildenhall.

Lebanon

By the mid-1970s, the Middle East's complicated politics that had bonded Christian and Moslem factions together in relative peace in the Lebanon since that country had declared its independence in November 1943 had broken down. Soon after, a long and tragic civil war erupted which was further complicated by the wider implications of the region's power politics. In an effort to restore peace, President Assad of Syria dissipated more than 40,000 of his best troops in a series of fruitless battles. Assad's forces were backed by a number of Palestine Liberation Organisation (PLO) fanatics who stiffened the resolve of the various Moslem militia groups in the area. By August 1982, the grim catalogue of human carnage had reached many thousand dead on both sides of the rising conflict.

Some 15 terrorist organisations sympathetic to the Palestinian cause operated from numerous bases in southern Lebanon, and periodically launched attacks against neighbouring Israel. These acts of terrorism became progressively more numerous and violent. After several retalitory strikes, Israel responded on 6 June 1982 with a major land, sea and air invasion aimed at destroying the PLO leadership, and its armed forces. Twenty-three days later Israeli troops were at the gates of Beirut, and were in a position to fulfil their stated objective. Prime Minister Mehachem Begin was forced to modify his fierce demands when faced with threats of Soviet intervention to aid Syria, and American disapproval of the invasion. An Israeli seige of Beirut culminated in some 7000 PLO fighters abandoning the city and fleeing the Lebanon into sympathetic Arab sanctuaries in Syria, Jordan, the Sudan, North and South Yemen, Algeria, Iraq and Tunisia, where their leader, Yasser Arafat, set up his headquarters.

On 28 September President Reagan announced that the US Marines were to resume their peacekeeping role in Beirut, which had been interrupted by the Israeli invasion of the Lebanon. Reagan said that he believed it was important that the US maintain a military presence in the area until the Lebanese government was in full control. France, Italy and the United Kingdom also dispatched contingents of troops to the region in attempts to add world pressure to the policing of the area, for the departure of the PLO heralded the beginning of a new era of terrorism in the Lebanon.

On 18 April 1983, a suicidal member of *Islamic Jihad*, a pro-Iranian network of fanatical Shi'ites, drove a truck loaded with 300 lbs of explosives up to the entrance of the US Embassy in Beruit, which he then detonated, killing 40 people, including eight Americans. Two more of these *Kamikaze*-type raids followed on 23 October, resulting in 241 US Marines and 58 French paratroopers being killed. Another such raid on 4 November claimed the lives of 39 Israeli troops within their guarded camp. By early 1984, the peacekeeping positions had become untenable and the troops were withdrawn, leaving behind only the Syrians and the Israelis. By February, the Lebanon was once again embroiled in its ever-worsening civil war.

The resurgence of Islamic Fundamentalism had been sparked off by the Ayatollah Khomeini on 1 April 1979 when he declared Iran to be an Islamic Republic. Khomeini was a zealot whose unquestioned devotion to Islam was only equalled by his all-consuming hatred for the West and, in particular, the United States. According to most Western intelligence sources, Islamic Fundamentalism would represent the most destabilising influence in the Middle East throughout the 1980s.

Once again, the capabilities of the SR-71 would be called upon in this 'hot-spot' to serve the needs of the transatlantic intelligence community, and of those friendly nations who also shared in the revelations of the 'Habu's' high quality photographic and electronic surveillance. Missions over the Lebanon were flown by Mildenhall's Det 4 crews to keep tabs on the Syrian and Israeli armies, as well as on various contraband movements which supplied Islamic Jihad warriors and other supporting groups. The 'Habu' flights also monitored the movements of key terrorist leaders as their small executive support aircraft slipped from one tiny airstrip to another in the desert.

One such Middle Eastern SR-71 sortie took place on 27 July 1984 when at 0730 hours Stormy Boudreaux and Ted Ross again departed Mildenhall in 979 using the call sign 'Boyce 64'. This important flight (the crew's 30th together) was complicated by several factors; (1) refusal of overflight transit across France, which necessitated entering the Mediterranean area via the Straits of Gibraltar; (2) inlet control problems during acceleration to high Mach, which forced Stormy to 'go manual' on bypass door operations; and (3) spike control problems at 2.2 Mach which caused an inlet disturbance (unstart), which further aggravated control.

By this time 979 was eastbound and nearing Mach 2.5, and the flight path was committed to entering the 'Med' on the preplanned heading, or overflying West Africa or Spain during an abort. Consequently, Stormy elected to 'go manual' on both inlet spike and door operations. Emergency operating procedures dictated that an aircraft in a 'double-manual' configuration should not be flown above Mach 3 and 70,000 ft. Therefore, Stormy held 979 at that degraded limit and pressed on through the Straits of Gibraltar high over the Mediterranean. Off the southern coast of Italy they decelerated and descended for a second refuelling. Standard procedures (once returning to subsonic flight) included resetting all inlet switches back to 'automatic', and to continue the next leg of the flight in 'auto' since such inlet 'glitches' often tended to clear themselves on another acceleration cycle.

Stormy and Ted followed this logical procedure, but 979 repeated the previous disturbances. At that point 'according to the book', they should have aborted the flight. The mission had been planned around a single high-speed, high-altitude pass over the target area. The well-seasoned crew reasoned that they had already come so far that they could make that one pass easily and collect the needed reconnaissance data within imposed operating constraints, especially since they could easily 'break off' over the waters of the Eastern Mediterranean should they have any serious difficulties over land.

Consequently, they completed the 'manual' recce run but found that 979 (operated in the less fuel-efficient 'manual' inlet configuration) ended the run in a notably depleted fuel state. Ted urgently contacted the tankers which were orbiting near the island of Crete and asked that they head east to meet the thirsty 'Habu'. As the SR-71 descended, Stormy caught sight of the tankers some 30,000 ft below, and executed what he described loosely as 'an extremely large variation of a barrel-roll' and slid in behind the tankers 'in no time flat'. The boomer plugged in immediately and 979 began taking on the much needed JP7. Hooking up well east of the normal ARCP, 'Boyce 64' had to stay with the tankers much longer than the normal 12 to 15

This map shows the targets attacked during *Eldorado Canyon* on 15 April 1986 (*DoD*)

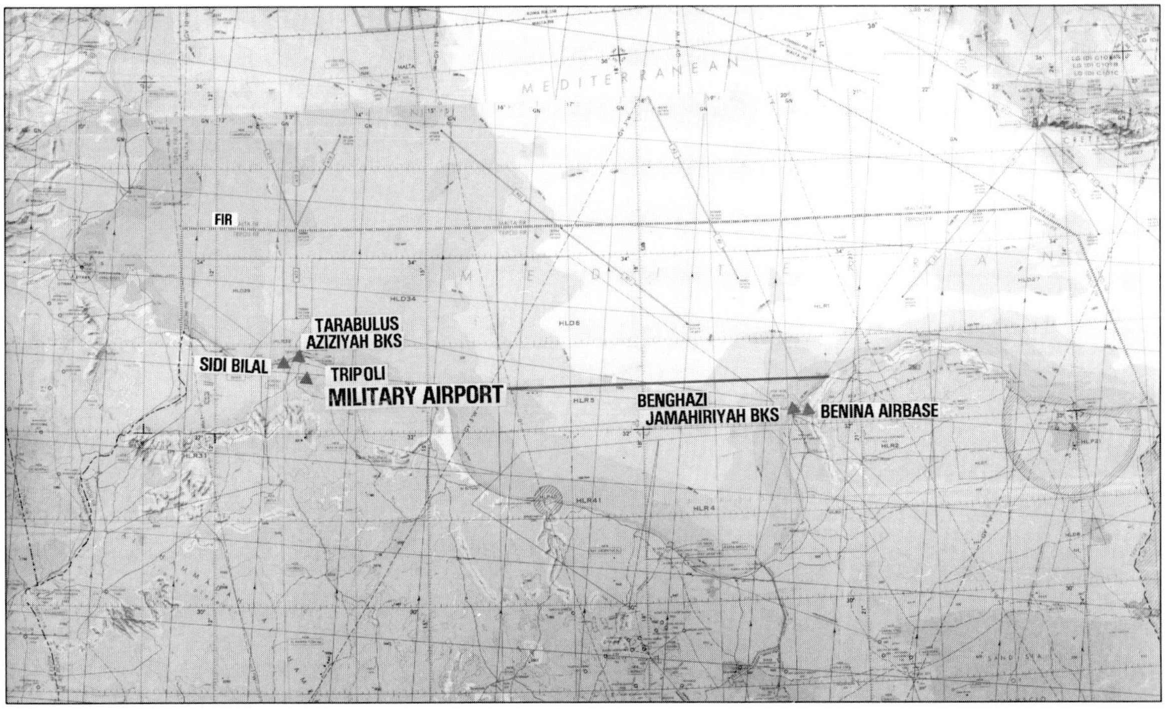

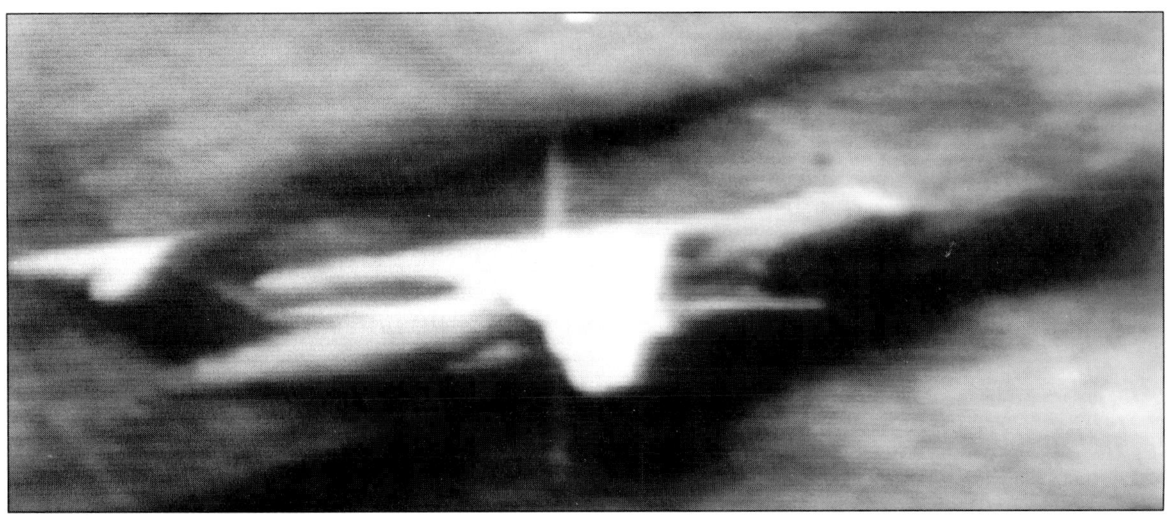

A Libyan Air Force Il-76 *Candid* at Tripoli Airport, as seen through a F-111F's Pave Tack/ laser-guided delivery system. The notation at the top right indicated the Time To Impact (TTI) of the 500 lb general purpose bombs (*USAF*)

minutes of 'on the boom time' to drop off at the scheduled 'end-AR' point, before proceeding back to England.

With 979's tanks filled to a pressure disconnect, Stormy and Ted climbed to high altitude on the final leg back through the Straits of Gibraltar and home to Mildenhall, where they landed after nearly seven hours, four of which had been spent at supersonic speed while carefully controlling both inlet spikes and doors manually. The good news was that their 'take' was of exceptional quality as a result of a cold front which covered the eastern Mediterranean and produced very clear air for 'razor sharp' photographic imagery. Det 4's commander, Col Jay Murphy, was especially proud of his crew's very notable mission accomplishments, but the bad news was that they had flown a 'degraded' aircraft over a known Soviet SA-5 SAM site. Overweighing that concern, however, was word from Washington that the 'take' was 'most valuable' for the analysts back at the National Photographic Interpretation Center (NPIC).

Three dark camels were printed on the left nose-gear door of 980 after its participation in the April raid. The white colouration of the middle camel is due to photo-flash bounce back (*P Crickmore Collection*)

Libya

A group of revolutionary army officers seized power on 1 September 1969 while King Idris of Libya was on holiday in Turkey. In that revolt, led by a subaltern named Moamar Ghadaffi, the officers proclaimed Libya to be a republic in the name of 'freedom, socialism and unity'. Washington recognised the new regime just five days later, allowing Ghadaffi to consolidate his position of power over the next two-and-a-half years, during which time he nationalised foreign banking and petroleum interests within Libya and was called a 'strongman' by Western news editors.

Ghadaffi made his interpretation of 'freedom, socialism and unity' clear to the world on 11 June 1972 when he announced he was giving aid to the Irish Republican Army. That support was also extended to similar terrorist organisations within Europe and the Middle East. When Ghadaffi decided to lay claim to territorial rights over much of the Gulf of Sidra on Libya's northern shore, the United States refused to recognise any extension beyond the traditional three-mile limit. To back up the 'international waters' claim to the Gulf, the USS *Nimitz* (CVN-68), attached to the 6th Fleet, began an exercise within the disputed area on 18 August. Interference by Libyan Mirages, Su-22s, MiG-23s and -25s culminated in the shooting down of two Su-22 *Fitter Js* by F-14 Tomcats from VF-41 'Black Aces'. Libyan-American relations plunged to an all-time low as Ghadaffi's aggression continued. Northern Chad was annexed by Libyan forces, an English police woman was shot dead by a Libyan 'diplomat' in London, arms were sent to the Nicaraguan Sandinistas and continued support was given to countless terrorist organisations throughout the world.

US patience was running out. In an address to the American Bar Association on 8 July 1985, President Reagan branded Libya, Iran, North Korea, Cuba and Nicaragua as members of a 'confederation of terrorist states'. Libya's political ruse finally reached its end after further actions in the Gulf of Sidra, the hijacking of a TWA Boeing 727 airliner on a flight from Rome to Athens and the bombing of the *La Belle* discotheque in Berlin.

In Operation *Eldorado Canyon* (a co-ordinated strike on military targets at Benia and Tripoli), air elements of the US Navy and Air Force attacked Libya on 15 April 1986. The main part of the strike was carried out by 18 F-111Fs from RAF Lakenheath, split into six flights of three aircraft each using call signs 'Puffy', 'Lujan', 'Remit', 'Elton', 'Karma' and 'Jewel'[8]. More than 20 KC-10s and KC-135s were used to provide air refuelling support for the strike force. In addition, three EF-111s from RAF Upper Heyford used high-powered jamming equipment to 'blind' Libyan radars.

Det 4 was tasked with providing post-strike reconnaissance, which called for an SR-71 mission to be launched from Mildenhall at 0500 hours the following morning. Hours before the 'Habu'

The Det 4 SR-71s provided analysts in the Pentagon with concrete proof of the damage inflicted on Benina Airfield by the US Navy strikes, the quality of the images taken clearly showing destroyed MiG-23s on the tarmac and burnt-out hangars (*USAF*)

launch, the following four KC-135s and KC-10s left the base for their refuelling orbits;

'Finey 50' and 'Finey 51' launched at 0230 and 0240 hours (KC-135 #91520 and KC-10 #30079)
'Finey 52' and 'Finey 53' launched at 0402 and 0405 hours (KC-135 #80125 and KC-10 #30082)
'Finey 54' and 'Finey 55' launched at 0412 and 0415 hours (KC-135s #00342 and #80094)
'Finey 56' launched at 0740 hours (KC-10 #30075)

Lt Cols Jerry Glasser and Ron Tabor took-off as scheduled at 0500 in SR-71 number 980 (callsign 'Tromp 30') to meet up with with 'Finey 54' and 'Finey 55' which had entered a holding pattern off the southwest coast of England to top-off the thirsty 'Habu'. The importance of the mission dictated that 'Tromp 30' would be backed-up by another SR-71 in case of an abort or sensor failure of the primary aircraft. Accordingly, Majs Brian Shul and Walt Watson launched at 0615 hours in aircraft 960 (callsign 'Tromp 31') and duplicated the route flown by Glasser and Tabor. Approaching their first ARCP with 'Finey 54' and '55' off Cornwall, Shul spotted the returning F-111s approaching head-on, several thousand feet below. 'Lujac 21's' pilot (the F-111 flight leader) rocked his wings in recognition; Shul rocked 'Tromp 31's' wings in a return salute.

The final tanker (KC-10 #30075) joined *Eldorado Canyon* to support the return of the two 'Habus'. The SR-71s had been equipped with two chine-mounted Technical Objective Cameras (TEOCs) for spot coverage, and a nose-mounted Optical Bar Camera (OBC) for horizon-to-horizon coverage. Since the F-111s and the Navy A-6s had struck six hours earlier, the two 'Habu' crews could expect Libya's entire air defence network to be on full alert, and eager to retaliate for the bombing. Missiles were indeed launched at both aircraft, but the SR-71 again proved that it could fly with impunity against such SAM threats.

At 0910 a KC-135Q (callsign 'Java 90') landed at Mildenhall carrying senior members of 9th SRW staff from Beale to witness the mission debriefing. Twenty minutes later tankers 'Finey 54' and '55' touched down followed at 0935 by 'Tromp 30', which had flown a mission lasting four-and-a-half hours. One hour and 13 minutes later Shul landed the back-up 'Habu', 'Tromp 31'. The five remaining tankers returned over the next four-and-a-half hours. 'Finey 51' flew a twelve-and-a-half hour sortie. When 'Finey 56' landed at 1526 hours, *Eldorado Canyon* was completed, with the exception of search efforts for Ribas-Dominicci and Lorance, whose F-111 had been lost the previous night just off the coast of Libya.

The mission's 'take' was processed in the Mobile Processing Center located in one of Mildenhall's disused hangars. It was then transported by a KC-135 ('Trout 99') to Andrews AFB, Maryland (only 25 miles from the Pentagon and the White House), where national-level officials were eagerly awaiting post-strike briefings which showed both the good and bad effects of the strike. The world news media

Tom McCleary and Stan Gudmundson arrive at the 'barn' and say their farewells to the team of ground technicians (*P Crickmore*)

Tom and Stan depart in 964. Soon after they performed the final UK flyby for the press before heading to California for the last time (*P Crickmore*)

had been quick to show the bad side of the story, BBC reporter Kate Adie being used as a propaganda dupe to show not only where one F-111's bomb load went astray near the French Embassy, but also where Libyan SAMs had fallen back on the city to be blamed as US bombs. Fortunately, she also proved useful in post-strike reconnaissance by showing the accurately bombed terrorist camp, referred to by her as a 'cadet' school.

The 'Habu's' reconnaissance mission was repeated on both 16 and 17 April with minor time and route changes. To preserve security, call signs were changed. The names 'Fatty' and 'Lute' were given to the tankers and SR-71s on 16 April, and 'Minor' and 'Phony' were used the next day. Shul and Watson were the primary crew on the 16th and Smith and Whalen took the primary slot the following day. This intense period of reconnaissance activity was the first time that both of Det 4's SR-71s had been airborne simultaneously, and represented a great accomplishment by the Det's support personnel under the command of Lt Col Barry MacKean. In addition, it was the first time that KC-10s had been used to refuel SR-71s in the European theatre. Also for the first time, photos taken by the SR-71s were released to the press, although the source was never officially admitted. The first sorties yielded no photos of Tripoli since

The last Det 4 SR-71 was returned to Beale by Maj Don Watkins and Bob Fowlkes soon after 964's departure (*P Crickmore*)

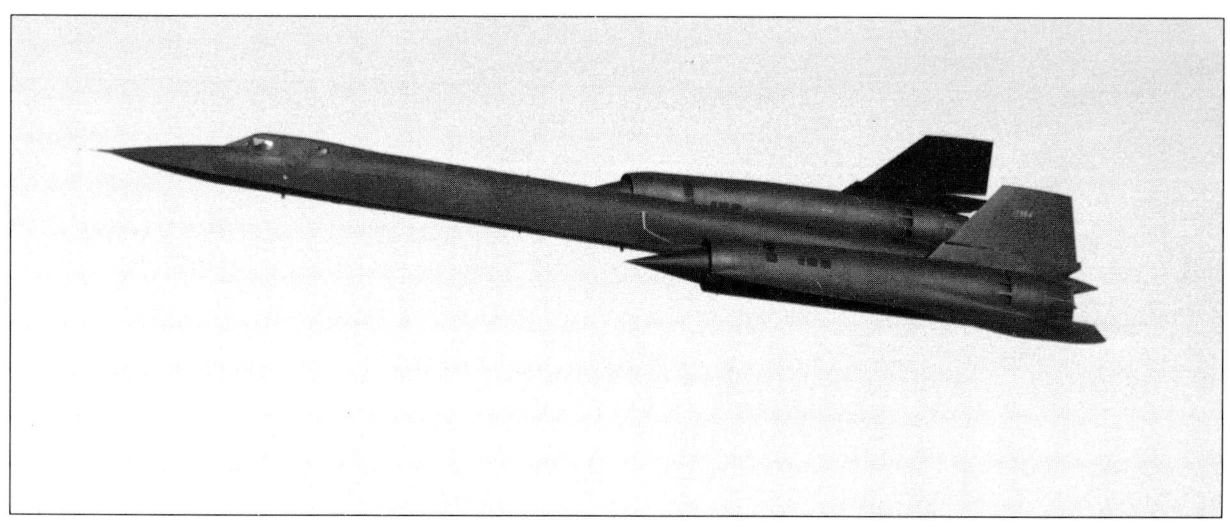

The grey overcast sky reflected the UK 'birdwatchers'' gloom as Don and Bob headed west (*P Crickmore*)

impenetrable clouds had blinded the cameras to the damage wrought by Lakenheath's F-111s. Later sorties accounted for all the weapons dropped.

Bellicose rumblings[9] from Ghadaffi continued after the raid, and 14 months later, the West's intelligence services believed that Libya had received a number of MiG-29 *Fulcrums*. This outstanding fighter, with a ground attack capability, would considerably enhance Libya's air defence network. It was therefore decided that Det 4 should fly another series of sorties over the Libyan region to try and confirm these intelligence reports. On 27, 28 and 30 August 1987 both SR-71s were launched from Mildenhall to photograph all the Libyan bases. Tanker support for each operation consisted of three KC-135s and two KC-10s. The tankers and the 'Habus' used the call signs of 'Mug', 'Sokey' and 'Baffy'. Two other KC-135s ('Gamit 99' and 'Myer 99') flew courier missions to Andrews AFB, Maryland, on 29 August and 9 September to transport the 'take' to the Pentagon, where intelligence analysts failed to find the MiGs they had suspected.

From that time on, it appears as if the Libyan leader may have learned a lesson from *Eldorado Canyon*, with his political profile on an the international stage being much reduced. Nevertheless, the 'desert thorn' remained an annoyance, despite operating with a diminished level of personal confidence and public support within an increasingly isolated nation[10].

An ex-B-52 'driver', Don Watkins illustrates a manoeuvre he could perform easily in the SR-71 that was unattainable in the BUFF. Bob Fowlkes looks on unimpressed!

It fell to Lt Col Tom Henichek to officiate reluctantly over the deactivation of Det 4. His obvious fatigue 'says it all' (*P Crickmore*)

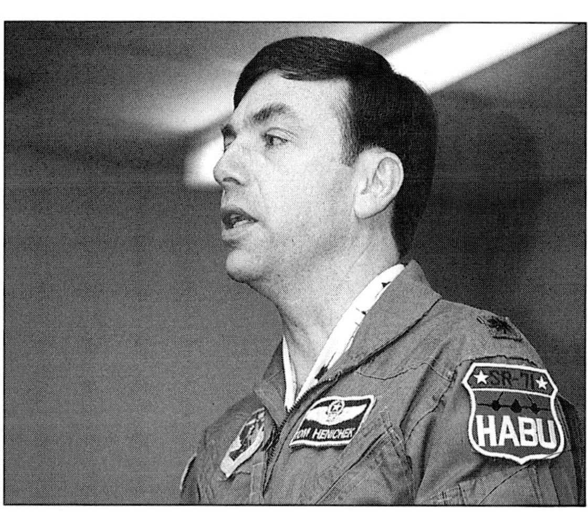

CHAPTER 8

Politics

Air Force Manual (AFM) 1-1 states that surveillance and reconnaissance constitute one of the nine basic operational missions of the US Air Force. Those two intelligence tasks are defined in JCS Publication 1 as follows: 'Reconnaissance is a mission undertaken to obtain, by visual observation or other detection methods, information about the activities and resources of an enemy or potential enemy; or to secure data concerning the meteorological, hydrographic or geographic characteristics of a particular area. Surveillance is 'the systematic observation of aerospace, surface, or subsurface areas, places, persons, or things by visual, aural, electronic, photographic, or other means'.

The main difference between reconnaissance and surveillance is one of duration and specification. The former is directed toward localized or specific targets, while the latter uses systems that collect information continuously. Such information is analysed, evaluated and processed into intelligence reports which form the informed basis of political and military decision-making. The function being supported determines whether the collection operation is 'strategic or tactical – surveillance or reconnaissance'.

AFM 1-1 further defines the nature of strategic and tactical surveillance as follows:

'Strategic surveillance and reconnaissance operations support the needs for national strategic intelligence. They also help fill the information requirements of tactical commanders. Through

When small-minded officials at HQ SAC refused to allow Lockheed access to an SR-71 for a film they were making about the aeroplane, Air Force Logistics Command came to the rescue. The Skunk, featured so prominently on the tail of Palmdale aircraft, was sprayed over, hence the colour variation under the serial number. Such pettiness blossomed into full-scale vindictiveness when the Senior Crown **programme ended: some crew members were passed over for promotion, something previously unheard of for ex-'Habus'** (USAF)

When 962 returned to Kadena to Beale, its tail was embellished with this masterpiece. The quip was not well received in some quarters, and an order soon arrived for its removal *(via Don Emmons)*

strategic operations, we can assess the total capacity of a foreign nation to wage war and can monitor the progress of war. Strategic operations provide information essential to:

Identifying targets for strategic and tactical attack.
Providing indications and warning of hostile intent and actions.
Assessing damage to enemy and friendly targets.
Determining force structure.
Determining requirements for research and development of warfighting systems.
Helping to verify compliance with treaties and agreements.

'Target surveillance and reconnaissance operations support theater and tactical field commanders. When tactical systems are assigned targets, the resulting information may fill both national and strategic intelligence requirements. Tactical systems provide indications of hostile intent and information from which intelligence is derived. Tactical operations provide information for:

Assessing the disposition, composition, and movement of enemy forces.
Locating enemy lines of communication, installations, and electronic emissions.
Verifying post-strike damage.
Observing conditions in surface battle areas.
Providing weather and terrain information'.

JCS Publication 1 clearly clarifies the distinction between strategic and tactical intelligence with these definitions:

'Strategic intelligence is information required for the formation of policy and military plans at national and international levels.

Tactical intelligence is information required for planning and conducting tactical operations.

Strategic and tactical intelligence differ only in scope, point-of-view, and level of employment'.

The SR-71 has been an ideal 'atmospheric' vehicle for conducting strategic and tactical reconnaissance operations. The aeroplane's size and power have provided a secure platform for optical, radar and ELINT systems which view wide areas of the earth. Although the requirement for aerial reconnaissance has not ended, the SR-71 was prematurely retired from the USAF's active aircraft inventory before a suitable replacement system was found. Just how and why this situation was allowed to develop is certainly intriguing.

Streamlined Operations

After the Yom Kippur War, an intelligence official asked Bob Murphy of the 'Skunk Works' what it would take to operate SR-71s out of a Middle East location. Bob's response was 'everything could be worked around if the runway was long enough'. Murphy was asked to draw up a contract maintenance plan to support U-2s and SR-71s. Such operations were not new to Lockheed, since they had already provided contract support for the CIA's U-2s and A-12s. After studying all aspects of the maintenance concept, Murphy discovered that the Air Force's 2400 people at four locations could be replaced by 450 civilian contract personnel. Lockheed's financial staff advised Bob not to submit such a low figure – 'it would make the Air Force look bad'. He therefore proposed 650 civilian contractors for the entire task.

Once the initial opposition was overcome, a colonel asked Murphy if he could also take over the maintenance of the KC-135Qs and T-38s as well as all of the SR-71s sensors. Gen Rogers (Commander

A-12 number 925 was dismantled at Palmdale and trucked to New York City, where it was lifted aboard the *USS Intrepid*, a de-commissioned aircraft carrier which had become a military museum in New York Harbour (*via Don Emmons*)

of AFLC) and Gen Daugherty (CINCSAC) later approved the plan and Bob Murphy began looking for a house near Beale. Unfortunately, the plan was scuttled by the Air Council when one of its three-star members warned against a contractor 'buying his way in, and once established, [who] would raise manning levels and costs and have the Air Force over a barrel'. Such remarks were unfounded, as the CIA could have vouched, but the argument was strong enough to overturn a plan that would surely have significantly lowered *Senior Crown* costs.

Scaledown

Early in the programme, the total number of PAA SR-71s was scaled down. The two flying squadrons became one in April 1971. As the US disengaged itself from Vietnam and with the 1973 Middle East crisis over, the number of unit-authorised aircraft also declined. By 1977, the SR-71A Primary Authorised Aircraft (PAA) stood at six aircraft, and funding was reduced proportionately. Since the SR-71 was primarily an imagery platform, it had lost support from the National Intelligence Committee, which had become enamoured with overhead products. Having lost much of the 'clout' of that powerful constituency, the SR-71 had to be funded by the Air Force, although it was still tasked by national agencies to support a variety of their theatre intelligence requirements.

Even HQ SAC was hostile towards *Senior Crown* because SR-71 costs detracted from the parent command's bomber and tanker mission. Although SAC's SIOP needed SIGINT to keep it up to date, the SR-71 could not gather long on-station samples of SIGINT, unlike the RC-135s and U-2Rs. The loss of its SAC patronage left *Senior Crown* increasingly isolated; to survive continued budget raids, it was apparent that the SR-71's utility had to be improved by flying longer missions over many parts of the world. It had to become more flexible and more competitive with overhead systems. Consequently, the aircraft had to undergo a series of sensor updates and, most importantly, it had to be equipped with an air-to-ground data–link system which would give it a 'near real–time capability'.

A new 'marketing package' was assembled which included details of the SR-71's performance and imagery capabilities. In the mid-seventies, *Senior Crown* advocates embarked on a public relations campaign within the Washington intelligence community to garner support for what appeared to be a mortally wounded programme.

Following an SR–71 briefing to intelligence officers of the Navy's Atlantic fleet, Bill Flexenhar (an analyst at the Naval Intelligence Support Centre at Suitland, Maryland), expressed an interest in the SR-71's sea-scanning radar capabilities to detect submarines in their home ports in the Baltic and Arctic areas. Flexenhar requested those areas to be 'SLAR–imaged' for his analysis.

A new requirement might thus have arisen which would give the SR-71 a new lease of life. A call was made to the SAC Reconnaissance Centre for SR-71 missions over those oceanic areas, but the response was not encouraging. It was agreed instead that sorties flown from Kadena over the Soviet's Pacific fleet near Vladivostok could be used to test the concept. After two missions, Flexenhar was impressed with the results and a presentation was made to high-level naval and national intelligence officials. At Mildenhall, a short term operation (unconnected with oceanic surveillance) gave the 9th SRW the opportunity to collect the specific type of imagery that Flexenhar had requested. This new material whetted the Navy's appetite for more of what they considered 'very valuable intelligence'.

To fulfil the requirement, it would be necessary permanently to base two SR-71's at Mildenhall. Such a move would reduce mission response times and be much more cost effective. A permanent operating location in Europe would require permission from Britain's Ministry of Defence and the Prime Minister, and would need close co-ordination with the US State Department and the Congressional Intelligence Oversight Committee. More funding would be needed for new support facilities at Mildenhall (a maintenance complex, two single-aircraft hangers, added fuel storage and an engine run-up 'hush-house').

The cost was estimated to be about $14 million for these and other needs. A funding programme was steered through various Washington agencies by the Pentagon-based Senior Crown Program Element Monitor (PEM), who by that time was on Lt Gen Jerry O'Malley's Plans and Operations staff.

Not surprisingly, parts of the Air Staff resisted an expensive initiative for the Navy. Many officers (including Lt Gen Larry Welch[1], then in charge of Air Force Programming and Budgeting) believed that the national and naval users should 'pick up the whole tab' for intelligence services provided by the Air Force. The same kind of resistance came from the HQ SAC because an expanded *Senior Crown* program would take operations and maintenance money away from SAC's bomber and missile programs.

Cost cutting elements were incorporated into the proposal, including recycled Beale hangers, a renovated mobile processing centre and other cost-conscious innovations. Maintenance would be 'civilian contract' carried out by 52 Lockheed and subsystem specialists. The result was a $4 million saving, bringing costs down to about $10 million.

Missions were planned at a rate of ten per month – the actual requirement was much higher, but this information was suppressed from SAC HQ, who would then have insisted upon a three-aeroplane complement, which in turn would have increased costs to a point that would have jeopardised the entire proposal.

Under the title 'SR-71 Permanent Basing Initiative', the 100-page report was forwarded for final budgetary considerations. The budgetary cut-off line for Air Force programs usually reached through the first 200 prioritised 'line items' of the Program Objective Memorandum (POM), which had to be forwarded through the Chief to the Secretary

SR-71A number 959 was similarly dismantled and is now displayed at the Air Force Armament Museum at Eglin AFB, Florida (*via Don Emmons*)

Col Rod Dyckman (left) checked out NASA pilot Steve Ishmael (right) in the SR-71B during July 1991 (NASA)

SR-71B number 956 was re-numbered 831 by NASA. Rod Dyckman and Steve Ishmael delivered the aeroplane to the Dryden Flight Research Facility, Edwards AFB, California on 25 July 1991 *(NASA)*

of the Air Force, and onward to the Secretary of Defence (SECDEF), where the OSD staff would tear great holes in all of the services finely tuned POMs. As the Air Force POM was being finalised for forwarding to the secretaries, the President and Congress, *Senior Crown* supporters at the Pentagon were aghast to see that the Air Staff board and the Air Force Council (a three-star panel, chaired by the Vice Chief) had ranked the European ops proposal 250 lines below the 'cut–off line'. It was so far below the line that it was abundantly clear where the Navy's initiative ranked within the Air Force's own list of priorities.

The initiative was about to 'fall through the budgetary crack' when a totally unrelated event was used to the advantage of the Senior Crown program. CINCSAC, Gen Dick Ellis, sent a message to the Air Force Chief of Staff, Gen Allen, complaining that SAC's recce force was over-tasked. The message was really focused on U-2 and RC-135 assets, not the unwanted SR-71. This message required a personal response back to CINCSAC. A draft response addressed a broad range of issues and included the line 'I have an initiative working to bring two SR-71s out of storage and permanently base them at RAF Mildenhall'.

Needless to say, as the draft message worked its way up through the Air Staff co-ordination process, the line was initially deleted. It seems, however, that when the response document appeared in Ellis' office for final signature, it had been reinstated. When the Air Force council saw what the chief had signed, the Permanent Basing Initiative leaped from 450th position to 7th in the budgetary line-up. Concurrences came in from all parties; the POM 'went to bed' and *Senior Crown* was alive and well, to fulfil its new role from Mildenhall.

Tragic Loss

Jerry O'Malley helped keep the SR-71 program alive for years, and would have probably kept it going for at least another five had he completed his rise to the top job in the Air Force – a promotion that seemed certain in 1985. Ed Payne remembered one day back in 1966 when Jerry asked him what his career plans were. Ed thought briefly and answered, 'Well, I want to be the best RSO in the 9th.' 'That's a given' replied Jerry, 'but what about the future?' Ed admitted that he had never thought that far ahead. 'Well I have,' answered Jerry. 'I want to be Chief of Staff of the Air Force.' Ed added, 'Jerry was not egotistical or unrealistic, but had planned a long way ahead. He knew his qualifications and capabilities' and had told Ed that he had served as aide to a three-star general who had a drinking problem. As a consequence, Jerry had made decisions for his boss and had developed a sense of responsibility and assurance way beyond his rank and years. After SR-71 crew duty, O'Malley progressed much more rapidly than all of his fellow officers and was back to command the 9th SRW by 1973.

After a second tour of duty in South-east Asia, Jerry earned his first star by 1974 (only 21 years after graduating from West Point). Every two years thereafter he rose in rank to become Vice Chief of the Air Force in 1980, CINCPACAF in 1982 and commander of TAC in 1984. He had made all the

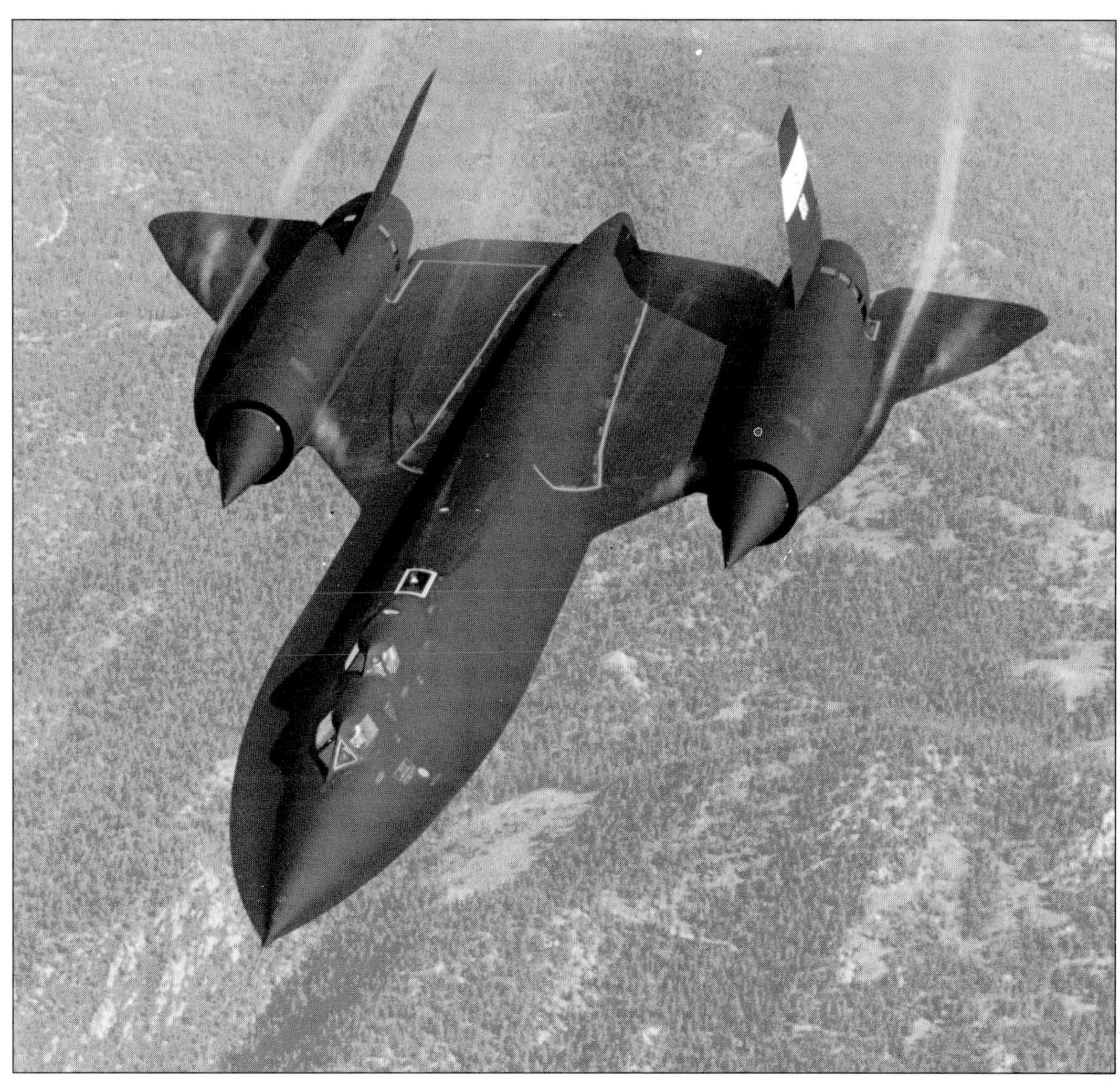

right moves to become Chief of Staff in 1986 and perhaps Chairman of the Joint Chiefs of Staff in 1987; and everyone in the Air Force knew it was likely to happen because Gen Charlie Gabriel had carefully steered his friend and fellow officer over all the hurdles to the top. Then on 20 April 1985 an appalling tragedy struck the O'Malley family, the Air Force and the SR-71 programme.

As a four-star general commander, Jerry was in great demand as a guest speaker and ceremonial figure. Top generals have the congressionally authorised privilege of taking their wives along on ceremonial and official activities which fill many of their days and evenings. After a full day at his office at TAC Headquarters, Jerry departed Langley AFB, Virginia, with his wife Dianne (along with his bright young captain aide, another mission pilot and a crew-chief) for a quick flight to Western Pennsylvannia where they were to be guests of honour at a boy scout convention.

The T-39 Sabreliner executive jet was the least likely aircraft for such a terrible accident. However, the runway was short, their approach speed was fast, and a sharp drop-off lay at the far end of the runway. When their aircraft could not be stopped in time, it skidded over the small cliff and jammed the escape hatch. No one aboard was able to exit the aircraft, which burst into flames. Jerry and Dianne were mourned by their thousands of friends and admirers all over the world, and were buried near President Taft in the Arlington National Cemetery in Washington DC.

The Air Force lost a top officer who could have been one of their finest Chiefs of Staff. The SR-71 programme also began dying without his guiding hand. The only senior staff officer who had filled the right Pentagon positions was Gen Larry Welch. One of the vagaries of change in any large organization, especially at the top, is that the incumbent has his own agenda – *Senior Crown* did not feature in the non-O'Malley Air Force.

Heroes and Villains

The programme was 'living on borrowed time' without an electro-optical system and without the ASARS-1 connected to a data link system. Eventually funds were appropriated for the development of Senior King, the much needed data link which, like ASARS-1, was built by the Loral Company, and would have featured a fuselage spine-mounted antenna to provide secure 'near real–time' data via satellite, 'right down to the commanders in the field'. While the prototype was undergoing development, a Congressman from Wyoming, serving on the House Permanent Select Committee on Intelligence, commissioned a study to evaluate the cost and effectiveness of such a system. Taking the title from his name, 'The Cheney Study', proceeded at the pace of a snail on Valium. Also serving on the HPSCI study were Dewain Andrews and Bob Fitch, both of whom trumpeted overheads and articulated an anti SR-71 position to the point of making programme shut-down a personal crusade. Andrews became Assistant Secretary of Defense for Command, Control and Communication (ASD/C 3), Fitch became a leading figure in the National Reconnaissance Office (NRO) and to complete the irony, Dick Cheney became SECDEF, playing an executive role in terminating *Senior Crown*. By the time the Cheney Study recommended the go ahead with Senior King, two years later, Gen Welch was winding down the programme.

Unequivocally the programme's main detractor was Chief of Staff, General Larry Welch. Other prominent staff officers included General Dougan, AF/XO, General John Chain, CINSAC, General Ron Fogleman, AF/Program Requirements, General Doyle, Chief of SAC Intelligence (SAC/IN), Colonel Tanner also in SAC/IN and General Leo Smith of the Budget Review Board. Their assault got underway from mid-1986. Cost and marginal benefits over satellites were cited as the main reasons for retiring the SR-71; in addition an air-breathing replacement was under development and during a meeting on Capitol Hill, Welch testified that the SR-71 had become vulnerable to SA-5s and SA-10s.

By 1988 it looked as though the efforts of the above mentioned would be successful. But all was not quite lost: Admiral Lee Baggot, Commander in Chief Atlantic (CINCLANT) needed SR-71 coverage of the Kola peninsula as there were no other means of obtaining the quality of coverage required. He took the battle to retain the SR-71 right to the Joint Chiefs of Staff (JCS) and obtained funding for Det 4 for a further year. Meanwhile the SR-71 PEM and his action officer took a late evening trip to visit a staffer on the Senate Appropriations Committee. They were asked what they needed to keep Palmdale and Kadena open for fiscal year (FY) '89. Their answer was $20 million for Palmdale and $26

SR-71B, 831 is readied for an early morning flight with NASA *(P Crickmore)*

million for Kadena. The staffer replied simply; 'You got it; enjoy your evening gentlemen.' And so *Senior Crown* survived another year. Unfortunately, FY90 would see a different outcome. Despite several ex Habu crewmembers placing the importance of the *Senior Crown* programme before their personal career and promotion prospects, outstanding officers like Rich Graham, Curt Osterheld, Tom Veltri and especially 'Geno' Quist, the axe finally fell on 30 September 1989 (end of FY '89). During an interview with Barbara Amouyal (published in the 12 June 1989 issue of the *Air Force Times*) General Welch was asked 'Has the Air Force developed a program to compensate for capabilities about to be lost with the deactivation of the SR-71? If not, should we be relying on satellites for our strategic reconnaissance requirements?' Gen Welch answered, pointing to a mounted control stick on a coffee table:

"That stick is from an SR-71. I'm an SR-71 pilot. No one has more sympathy for the capabilities of the SR-71 than I do, yet I am recommending we discontinue operations of that airplane and the reason is purely cost and benefits. Today to operate six SR-71s it costs $208 million per year. We operate 72 F-16s for $160 million per year. So if you're going to pay that much money, you have to have a fairly decent return on your investment. The overhead systems have improved greatly, both in radar and imaging. That is not to say that you can do with an overhead system all those things you can do with the SR-71. But the combination of what you can do with overhead systems today, and what you can do with the TR-1 (U-2R) which also had new sensors on it, gives you a sense that the marginal contributions of the SR-71 are in my view, simply not cost–effective.'

To users of SR-71 collected intelligence materials, such comments from the Chief of Staff were alarming to say the least. Welch was no SR-71 pilot. He did 'ride' in an SR-71B with a highly qualified instructor pilot. After his ride at Mach 3.2 and 82,000ft, he commented, 'Is that all it can do?' He had demonstrated his 'fighter–pilot intolerance' for all of SAC's weapons systems which he had commanded. To claim that F-16s were cheaper to operate really missed the point. It was not a like-for-like comparison because their respective roles were completely different.

The SR–71 operating cost figure that Gen Welch flagged up was based on an inventory of nine SR-71s. Later figures revealed that six SR-71s could actually be operated for $150 million a year on a 'no frills' basis.

Gen Welch's third reason for scrapping the Senior Crown programme was its vulnerability to enemy defences. Again this was erroneous. Before the axe fell on 'Habu' operations, a brand new DEF system known as DEF A2C had been developed which could be programmed against all forecast air- and ground-launched threats – unfortunately it could not be programmed against the 'ground threat' in Washington.

What was to be the final Air Force SR-71 flight took place on 6 March 1990, when Ed Yeilding and JT Vida flew 972 on a West to East coast record-breaking flight before landing at the Smithsonian National Aerospace Museum, Washington DC. The next day, Apollo astronaut Senator John Glenn delivered an eloquent speech from the floor of the senate, reflecting upon the SR-71's achievements:

'Mr President, I rise to note a sad landmark in aviation history. Yesterday, the SR-71 reconnaissance plane, the fastest and highest-flying US aircraft was retired after making a record-setting 68-minute flight from California to Dulles Airport here in Washington, where it was turned over to the Smithsonian's Air and Space Museum.

'As a member of both the Senate Select Committee on Intelligence as well as the Senate Armed Services Committee, I am deeply concerned about last year's decision to terminate this proven, outstanding reconnaissance asset.

'Last year's DoD Authorization Conference Report stated that 'while the conferees believe there is substantial inherent military value in the SR-71 fleet, it is clear that the Department (of Defence) has no intention of operating the aircraft to achieve or exploit that potential.

Ed Yeilding and J T Vida established a coast-to-coast speed record in 972 on 6 March 1990, when they 'ferried' it from Palmdale to the National Aerospace Museum at Dulles Airport, Washington DC, the last USAF SR-71 flight *(Lockheed)*

The high cost of continued operation of an asset so ill used by the Department cannot be justified.'

'While it is undoubtedly true that the SR-71 fleet was not being utilized to its fullest potential, I believe that this shortcoming could have easily been redressed by the Department of Defense, and by no means warranted termination. In view of the high cost of other Air Force programs, the costs of this program and its benefits were both affordable and reasonable.

'Mr President, the SR-71 is a proven reconnaissance asset that brought a truly unique capability to America's intelligence community. The SR-71 is a high altitude, high speed, long range airborne reconnaissance platform that has served our nation well since it first flew in the mid-1960s. The SR-71 is able to penetrate hostile territory with comparatively little vulnerability to attack unlike other reconnaissance platforms. This makes it particularly useful in crisis situations like the Persian Gulf. While opponents of the SR-71 have argued that National Technical Means are capable of performing the same mission, these systems are far less flexible and survivable than the SR-71.

'It is interesting to note that for some years now, the DoD has been making the case that the US needs an anti-satellite capability, in large part due to the threat posed to our satellites by the Soviets. Should the US go forward with the deployment of an ASAT system, it would seem likely that the Soviets would end their moratorium on testing an advance ASAT program. Given the increased threat such a super power ASAT race would pose to our already vulnerable satellites it would seem the height of folly to cancel the only truly survivable air-breathing reconnaissance platform in our inventory – the SR-71.

'In retiring the SR-71, the United States has essentially removed itself from the strategic aerial reconnaissance business. Intelligence systems such as the SR-71 are the eyes and ears for our nation's defense and are therefore true force-multipliers. I am convinced that the US will be placed at a serious disadvantage in future crisis situations by the termination of the SR–71.

'I think that few members of the Congress and certainly few in the public truly realise the magnitude of the decision to terminate the SR-71. In part, this is due to the fact that the vast majority of our nation's intelligence capabilities such as the SR-71 cannot be fully discussed in public, if at all. Because these programs are classified, few members of Congress are even aware of many of these systems unless the member serves on one of the committees that conducts oversight of these programs.

'Also, because they are classified, intelligence systems have virtually no public constituency. In increasingly constrained budget environments, it is simply a fact of life that systems and programs that bring highly visible benefits to constituents are far more likely to survive the budget cutters axe than valuable intelligence programs such as the SR-71.

'The retirement of the SR-71 highlights another problem our nation will confront in the years to come. With the revolutionary changes taking place in the Communist bloc, the prospect for reaching sweeping and truly meaningful arms control agreements with the Soviet Union are better than they have ever been since World War II.

'Indeed, it seems likely that this year, we will reach a sweeping array of arms control agreements with the Soviets – verification protocols of the RRBT and FNET nuclear testing treaties, START, CPE, a bilateral agreement on chemical weapons, and an 'open skies' agreement.

'While I am second to no one in my enthusiasm at this prospect, we must be aware that these agreements will necessarily be very complex and therefore very difficult to adequately monitor. Enormously expensive intelligence systems that enable us to adequately monitor Soviet compliance with these complex agreements constitute the hidden costs of arms control. If these essential intelligence systems are sacrificed like the SR-71 to narrow budgetary considerations, our ability to adequately monitor these agreements will be placed at risk – endangering our nation's security as well as the public's consensus behind the arms control process.

'Mr President, the termination of the SR-71 was a grave mistake and could place our nation at a serious disadvantage in the event of a future crisis. Yesterday's historic transcontinental flight was a sad memorial to our short-sighted policy in strategic aerial reconnaissance.'

More than forty other members of Congress, including the chairman of the Senate Committee on Armed Services, Senator Sam Nunn, were equally concerned and perturbed about the decision to retire the SR-71. Misgivings were also voiced outside Congress. A former director of the National Security Agency confided in Ben Rich, President of Lockheed ADP, 'Satellites will never fully compensate for the loss of the Blackbird. They have nothing in the wings to replace it and we may be in for some nasty surprises and a whole new set of intelligence problems because of this.'

On the 2nd August 1990, three Iraqi Republican Guard Divisions invaded Kuwait. Within days of the invasion Ben Rich was on the phone to General Michael Loh, the Air Force Vice Chief of Staff and informed him that he could have three SR-71s ready for operations over the Gulf within ninety days. General Loh said that he'd float the idea and get back. About a week later Ben received a call saying that Secretary of Defence Dick Cheney had vetoed the idea, and commented along the lines 'I retired that aeroplane once I'm not going to do it again. If I bring it back now I'll never get rid of it.'

Senator Bryd, Chairman of the Senate Appropriation Committee, sent a classified letter to Senator Boran, Chairman of the Senate Select Committee on Intelligence requesting that the SR-71 program be reactivated to cover Desert Shield (the build up of allied coalition forces in the Gulf). Senator Boran declined the request, stating that other aircraft, including the U-2, together with national satellite systems could fulfill the mission requirements. As it became increasingly apparent that force would almost certainly be required to dislodge Saddam Hussein's troops from occupied Kuwait, General Norman Schwarzkopf asked the Chairman of the Joint Chiefs of Staff, General Colin Powell, to request the reactivation of the SR-71. Initially, Powell refused, but a second request was passed up the line to Secretary of Defence Cheney, who yet again refused to reactivate the program he had deactivated ten months earlier. At 03:00hrs (local), on 17 January 1991, the coalition air campaign against Iraq began. That Desert Storm was an overwhelming success for coalition forces is beyond dispute; however, there were lessons to be learned from the 41-day campaign and one deficiency was certainly the lack of timely reconnaissance material available to General Schwarzkopf's field commanders.

Discontent rumbled on until March/April 1994, when events in the international arena once more took a turn. Relations between North Korea and the

SR-71A 844 (ex-980) was flown for the first time by its NASA crew on 24 September 1996; the pilot was Steve Ishmael and the Research Systems Operator was Marta Bohn-Meyer *(NASA)*

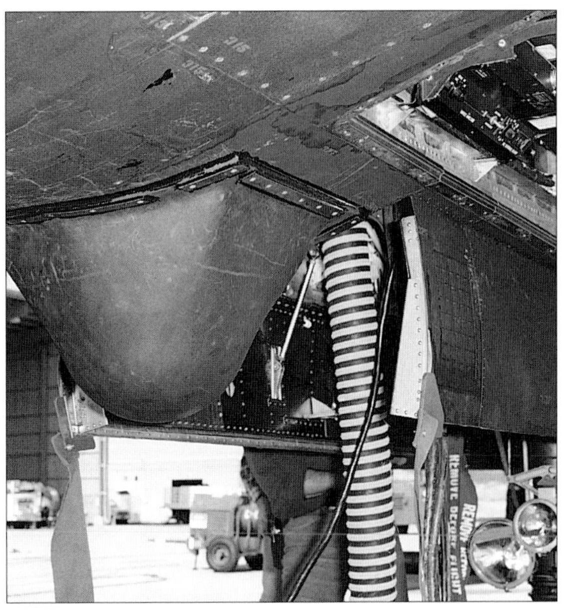

The radome housing the data-link antenna is located below bay C, just forward of the front undercarriage well. A digital cassette recorder system (DCRsi) provides recording and playback of both ASARS and ELINT data. Real-time data can be provided if the aircraft is within 300nm line–of–sight range of a receiving station; if not, the entire recorded collection can be downloaded in ten minutes once within station range *(USAF)*

United States, at best always strained, reached a new low over the north's refusal to allow inspection of their nuclear sites. At this point Senator Robert Byrd took centre stage. Together with several members of the Armed Services, and various members of Congress he contended that back in 1990 the Pentagon had consistently lied about the supposed readiness of a replacement for the SR-71. The motivation behind such comments was not the usual politicking, but one of genuine concern for the maintenance of a platform capable of broad area synoptic coverage.

The campaigning and lobbying paid off as noted in 'Department of Defence Appropriation Bill 1995' report 103–321 dated July 20.

'The committee agrees to make available $100,000,000 for reactivation of a modest (three-plane) SR-71 Blackbird reconnaissance aircraft contingent for intelligence operations as recommended by the Senate Armed Services Committee. The committee believes reactivation is justified because of the unique operational capability that, at present and for the next few years, only this aircraft can provide. Cost estimates for the first year of operation, including one–time costs to reactivate such a contingency group, and the out-years operation and maintenance costs, are based on estimates from the Defense Airborne Reconnaissance Office, and on the recent experience of NASA, which is currently flying the aircraft for scientific experimentation. To control cost growth, the committee recommends a cap on funding for fiscal year 1995. Further, the Committee believes that an appropriate operation and maintenance estimate for the out-years is less than $50,000,000 per year, depending on the extent of emergency usage, based on at least one month of operational activity, with 10 to 15 sorties.

The SR-71 Program was terminated in 1990 as a full-fledged operational activity involving 12 aircraft on the grounds of costs, lack of need as a result of the end of the cold war, and the promise of follow–on systems which would be able to accomplish the missions for which the SR-71 was designed: oncall strategic and tactical reconnaissance through surprise, assured and invulnerable penetration of the target nation's airspace to defeat deceptive practices aimed at our other reconnaissance techniques. All three grounds for termination no longer pertain. First, the end of the cold war did not remove the need for a capability to overfly nations for intelligence considered in the vital interests of our nation and our allies. During the Persian Gulf War, our commanders on the scene badly needed the capabilities of the SR-71. The final report to Congress on the "Conduct of the Persian Gulf War", April 1992, stated that:

> Imagery was vital to coalition operations, especially to support targeting development for precision-guided munitions and Tomahawk land attack missile attacks, and for BDA. Operations Desert Shield and Desert Storm placed great demands on national, theater, and tactical imagery reconnaissance systems. The insatiable appetite for imagery and imagery-derived products could not be met.
>
> The SR-71 could have been useful during Operation Desert Shield if overflight of Iraq had been permitted. In that case, the system would have provided broad area coverage of a large number of Iraqi units. During Operation Desert Storm air operations, the SR-71 would have been of value for BDA and determining Iraqi force dispositions.

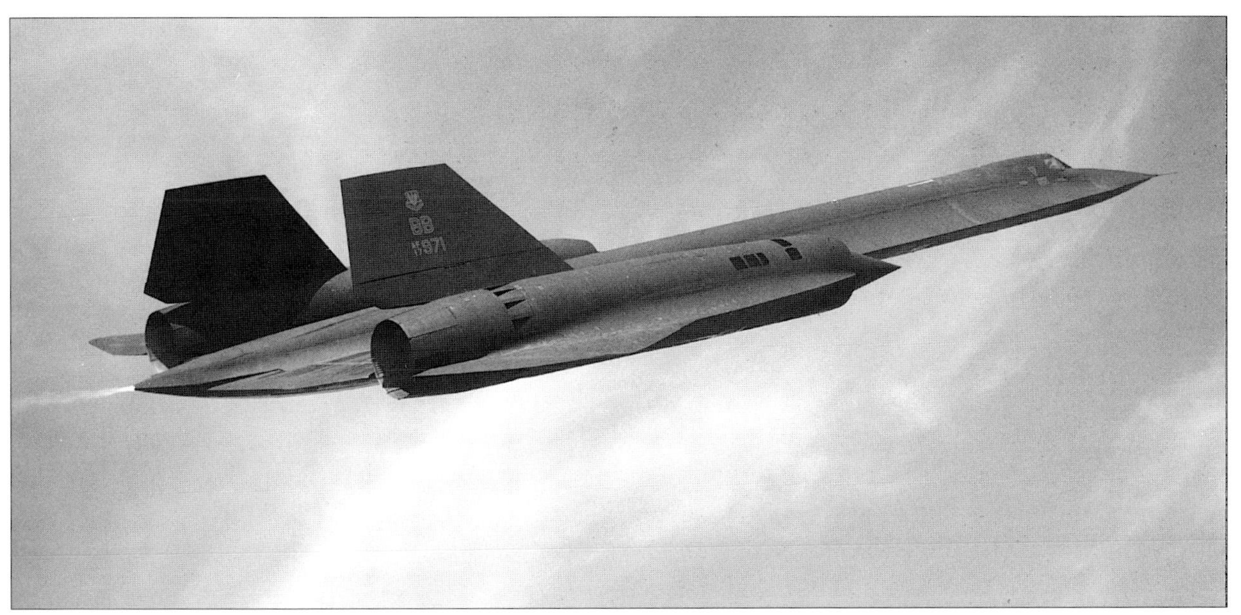

Call Sign 'NASA 832' vents JP-7 from its rear fuselage vent several minutes after take off during its functional test flight from Runway 25 at Air Force Plant 42, Palmdale, CA. The test pilot is Ed Schneider and flight test engineer Bob Meyer. (Photo Jim Ross/NASA)

The fact is that the SR–71 could have mapped Iraq in three hours and provided intelligence that was not available to the United States planners for the duration of the conflict. Furthermore, the tremendous extent of Iraqi nuclear weapons development activity that became increasingly clear only many months after the war could have been detected through the use of the SR-71.

Second, the systems which some hoped would be developed and procured as a follow-on to the SR-71 have not materialised, leaving the SR-71 the only asset in our inventory which has the capability to provide wide-area synoptic coverage in all weather, day and night; can cover any target on short notice; has the sensor flexibility to fly photographic, radar, signals intercept, or other missions responding to the needs of the on-scene commander; can defeat deceptive practices that are currently being engaged in by a variety of nations who may have precise knowledge of the overhead times and orbits of our reconnaissance satellites; that is, according to a new DARO study, still invulnerable to interdiction; that is a mechanism that the President can use selectively to demonstrate national will as a political instrument.

Further, the aircraft allows for surges in collection capability; and provides high–quality synoptic coverage of large areas without drawing national collection systems from other areas of interest.

None of these qualities can be attributed to other air–breathing systems in our inventory, such as the U-2, nor to satellite coverage.

Regarding cost, the Committee has allocated $100,000,000 for the first year reactivation and operation and maintenance costs of the aircraft. The Committee believes that it would take about $60,000,000 to prepare three aircraft now in storage at Edwards Air Force Base and Palmdale, for operational service. The Committee, therefore, directs that no more than $60,000,000 be available for this purpose. Estimates for operations support amount to some $40,000,000, roughly equally divided between Air Force and contractor support. These cost estimates have been validated in a July 15, 1994, report by the Defense Airborne Reconnaissance Office on "The Reactivation of an SR-71 Contingency Capability." The Committee notes that NASA currently operates three SR-71 aircraft on loan from USAF at a cost of $6,210,000 per year in direct and indirect costs, flying 10 missions. The assumptions upon which those estimates are based include 12 months of operations and training and one 30-day deployment during which 10 operational sorties would be conducted.

Further savings may be available by establishing an organizational concept of a combined Air Force/NASA, contractor team based at the Air Force Flight Test Center (AFFTC) at Edwards AFB, CA, where the NASA operations are currently conducted. This basing provides synergism from combined operations, collocation of operations and training, and a combined maintenance/logistics concept extending from current SR-71 logistic support for NASA. Under this concept, according to the Commander of the AFFTC, the "SR–71's unique capabilities could additionally be used to support national advanced technology demonstration and testing. AFFTC is prepared to fully support this combined ACC/AFMC/NASA SR–71 unit." The Air Force is directed to work with NASA and the contractor to collocate all possible logistics and operational support facilities for the SR-71 Program, under the combined concept developed by the Flight Test Center.

Given the utility of the system to both national and tactical intelligence and commanders, the Committee believes costs should be evenly shared by the intelligence community and the TIARA (Tactical Intelligence And Related Activities) budget and has included funds in the bill divided along these lines.

Last, a robust sensor suite should be incorporated in this contingency group proposal. First, the advanced synthetic aperture radar system (ASAR-1) should be included.

This provides a demonstrated air-to-ground system with high data rate, providing all weather, day-night capability. Second, regarding optical imagery, both a broad area optical bar camera and a targetable tactical resolution camera will be included, allowing selection from a range of sensors, depending on the mission profile that is determined.As a result of the recommended adjustments, the committee approves $544,980,000, increasing the budget request by $16,690,000. The House allowance is $64,310,000 above the Senate allocation.'

NASA 832 is on a two-mile, ILS final approach for landing Runway 25 at Air Force Plant 42, Palmdale, CA to complete its NASA Dryden-crewed functional check flight on 26 June 95. SR- 71A #971 will next fly as 'Aspen 30' with an Air Force crew. Palmdale, Canyon Country, and the San Gabriel Mountains lie in the background. *(Photo Jim Ross/NASA)*

Lt Cols Gil Luloff and Jim Greenwood cruise by Lake Isabella (in California's Sierra Nevada Mountains) at .9 Mach and 24,000 feet in SR–71A #967, some 50 nautical miles and six minutes from takeoff at Edwards AFB Runway 22, en route to air refuelling with KC-135T Callsign 'Sled 71'. Lt Col Lulloff exercises the engine inlet controls and autopilot functions en route to the tanker while Lt Col Greenwood fine tunes the tanker rendezvous and massages the sensors and navigation systems. *(Lt Col Blair Bozek/USAF)*

The conferees went on to reaffirm their support for the goals and objectives of the department's endurance unmanned aerial vehicle program, while an Authorization Conference Report tasked the Secretary of Defence to provide to the congressional defence committees classified and unclassified reports by January 1 1995 detailing:–

1. How the SR-71 will be integrated into the department's reconnaissance modernisation plan.

2. How the SR-71 will provide additional capabilities to contribute to the departments' reconnaissance and intelligence collection capability.

3. The time it will take to fully reactivate the SR-71, and

4. The impact on Future Years' Defence Program (FYDP) costs to provide this additional reconnaissance capability until new endurance UAVs are fielded.

The conferees further directed that the SR-71 program be wholly designated as a TIARA program and that the Air Force assume total responsibility for sustaining out-year budget requirements.

In a memo to the Deputy Chief of Staff, Plans and Operations USAF, from the Director, DARO, Major General Kenneth R Israel, dated 24 Oct 1994, the latter recognised the AF as the executive Agent for the modest (three-plane) SR-71 aircraft contingency reconnaissance capability, and continued, 'The SR-71 program is limited to $100.0 million for FY1995. Congress appropriated $65.0 million in Air Force Procurement funds in the Defense Airborne Reconnaissance Program (DARP). The additional $35.0 million for O & M is embedded in the Air Force O & M budget. Currently, no funding has been identified for FY1996 and out.'

The last sentence rings ominously. Notwithstanding, minds were aligned, if not focused, as the reactivation got underway. To ensure costs were kept to a minimum it was decided that the USAF operation would indeed be based at Edwards AFB. Of the three SR-71As placed in deep storage by the Air Force at site 2, Palmdale (aircraft #962, #967 and #968) only 967 was called to arms. The other A model to be recommissioned was #971, which had been loaned to NASA, re-numbered 832 and regularly ground tested but never flown by its civilian caretakers. Pilot trainer SR-71B, together with the flight simulator, would be shared. On January 29 1994, three crews were selected to fly the aircraft, pilots Gil Luloff, Tom McCleary and Don Watkins together with RSO's Blair Bozak, Mike Finan and Jim Greenwood, the plan being that two crews would always be Mission Ready, and a third

Mid–morning sun reflects off JP-7 fuel streaks as 'Aspen 30' proceeds from its air refuelling with 'Sled 71' *(Lt Col Blair Bozek/USAF)*

crew Mission Capable. Designated Det 2 of the 9th Reconnaissance Wing, and currently under the command of ex-HABU RSO Col Stan Gudmundson, command and control of the unit is exercised at Beale AFB. Lockheed Program Manager is ex SR-71 pilot Col Jay Murphy (Ret) while former RSO's, Cols Don Emmons (Ret) and Barry MacKean (Ret) are rebuilding the necessary logistics and support structure. Capt Mike Zimmerman is the sole active duty officer co-ordinating the reactivation.

Aircraft reactivation began on January 5 1995 with fuel leak evaluation of aircraft 967. Seven days later, at 11:26 hrs Steve Ishmael and Marta Bohn–Meyer got airborne from Edwards in 971 on a 26-minute ferry–flight which terminated at Lockheed Martins Skunk Works, Plant 10, Building 602, Palmdale, California. Over the next three months ASARS sensors previously in storage at Luke AFB, Arizona were installed, as were other sensors, DEF and ELINT systems. At 10:18 hrs on April 26 Ed Schneider and Marta took 971 on a one hour 34-minute Functional Check Flight for the Air Force. A month later on May 23, Ed and Marta's husband Bob Meyer conducted 971's second and final FCF which lasted 2.5 hours, during which the aircraft was air refuelled and achieved a maximum speed and altitude of Mach 3.23 and 81,400 ft. Both flights were completed with just minor write-ups. NASA crews undertook five further flights in 971 (see appendices) the last on October 17th 1995, after which the aircraft completed five sorties with Air Force crews.

Aircraft 967's path back to operational status wasn't as trouble-free. She undertook her first flight after a break of 216 days, on August 28 1995. It proved to be the first of nine FCF attempts, one of which ended with a diversion into Nellis AFB due to a miswired fuel system. The aircraft was finally handed over to the Air Force following a successful FCF conducted by Rogers Smith and Marta on January 12 1996. Eighteen days later, after a flight lasting 2.6 hrs, 967 joined its stable mate at Edwards AFB.

On 27 June 1995, following an intense period in the flight simulator, Lt Col Gill Luloff with IP Rogers Smith got airborne from Edwards AFB in SR–71B 956 (NASA 831). The flight lasted 3.1 hrs, was supported by tankers from Fairchild AFB and achieved a maximum speed and altitude of Mach 3.23 and 78,245 ft. By early February 1996, Air Force and NASA crews had completed fifteen crew re-qualification and proficiency flights in the 'B' model. Back in Washington however, opponents of the program were beginning to prepare their case for a complete shut-down.

Elements of DARO's five-page 'Report to Congress on Reactivation of the SR–71,' released on 1 January 1995, were seized upon by antagonists of the reactivation plan and in a letter dated 18 January, addressed to the Hon John Kasich, Chairman of the Committee on the Budget and the Hon Robert Livingston, Chairman of the Committee on Appropriations, twenty members of Congress belonging to the Conservative Opportunity Society voiced their objections. The most influential opponent of the program on Capitol Hill was House Intelligence Committee Chairman, Larry Combest, who also formally requested that John Kasich cancel FY1995 spending authority for the SR-71. Several key officers in the Air Force were also strongly resentful of the Congressionally Directed Action (CDA) to reactivate the SR-71, including none other than the now USAF Chief of Staff, General Ronald R Fogleman, as evidenced from his hand-written memo to two other senior Air Force Officers (see overleaf, page 192). Caught up in the middle of all this was Lt Col Sam Torrey, the Air Force Program Manager who worked in the Manned Reconnaissance Division of DARA. In a paper to the Air Staff dated 15 March he recommended, 'Continue with reactivation at slowest rate possible to achieve capability by 1 Sept '95 and expedite reprogramming request to determine if program will be executable.' Basically, the Air Force were planning for a twelve-month womb to tomb scenario and figuring that Congress would be unable to push through additional funding for a second year. They therefore wanted to ensure that compliance with budget appropriation was met but not exceeded as they would then have to 'eat' excess spending.

However, further funds for the SR-71 were appropriated as detailed in Conference Report 104-101 of April 5, 1995 which notes, 'Of the

Gathering of Blackbirds large and small. Det 2's 29 Mar 1996 ribbon cutting ceremony saw all its aircraft on display. Ironically the programme was terminated 17 days after this photo was taken.
(Lt Col Blair Bozek/USAF)

$100,000,000 appropriated for the SR-71 activation in fiscal year 1995, the conferees agree to rescind $27,500,000 and transfer $23,500,000 from Aircraft Procurement, Air Force (APAF) 95/97 to Operation and Maintenance, Air Force (OMAF) 95 as follows:–

FY 95

Appropriation		Rescission	Transfer	Net
APAF	65	-27.5	-23.5	14
OMAF	35	0	+23,5	58.5
TOTAL	100	-27.5	0	72.5

On 16 June, Senator John Glenn and Robert Byrd wrote to Senator Strom Thurmond, Chairman of the Committee on Armed Services, urging him to 'include in his report language that would authorise the continuation of the contingency force of the SR-71 reconnaissance aircraft that was initiated in last year's bill.' Noting the program had 'revived an unmatched reconnaissance asset' and that 'The SR-71 is a cost-effective hedge until unmanned aerial vehicles become widely available.' The National Defense Authorization Act for Fiscal year 1996, dated July 12 1995 notes:

'The committee is pleased with the timely and cost-effective reconstitution of a contingency force manned, high speed, penetrating reconnaissance aircraft as a hedge until penetrating unmanned aerial vehicles are widely fielded. The contingency capability of two SR-71 aircraft was accomplished by the Air Force under the direction of the Defense Airborne Reconnaissance Office for substantially less than the $100.0 million appropriated for this purpose last year. The committee therefore encourages the Air Force and the Defense Airborne Reconnaissance Office to retain this capability in fiscal year 1996 from such funds as are made available."

Unfortunately despite monies being appropriated there is no mention of it in the Senate Authorisation Bill.

A member of Staff on the House Select Committee on Intelligence, recently retired RC-135 Chief Master Sergeant Mike Meermans, pointed out to his Committee's Chairman that section 504 of the 1947 National Security Act prohibits the obligation of funds for intelligence activities not specifically authorised.

This was taken up during a meeting of Congress on 15 December 1995, when Combest asked, 'Mr Speaker, I understand that the conference report currently before the House does not authorize any operations and maintenance funds for the SR-71 reconnaissance program; is that correct?'

'Mr Spence. Mr Speaker, if the gentleman will yield, the gentleman is correct. Neither the House nor the Senate Defense authorisation bill contained any specific O & M in the authorisation for the SR-71. Therefore the conference report, similarly does not authorize any funds for this purpose.'

'Mr Combest. Mr Speaker, I thank the gentleman for that response.

Mr Speaker, it remains my view that this system is no longer a cost-effective platform for conducting strategic reconnaissance and should be retired to storage in the coming year. I would also note that

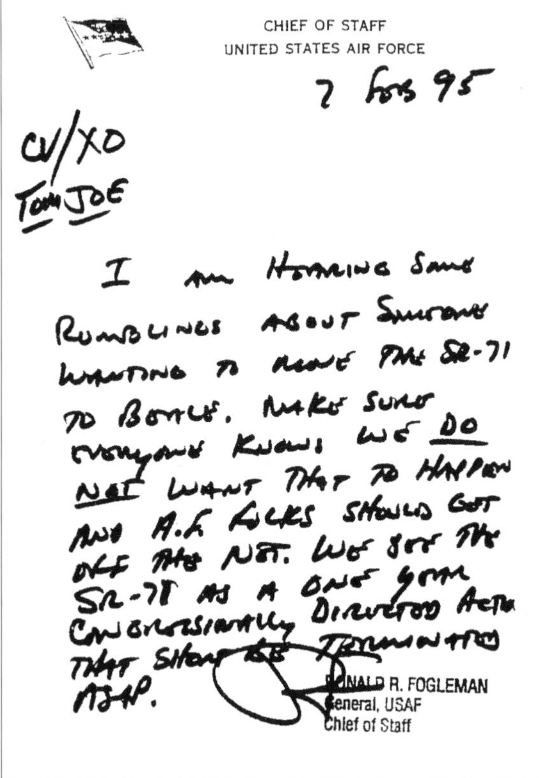
CHIEF OF STAFF
UNITED STATES AIR FORCE

7 FEB 95

CV/XO
Tom/Joe

I am hearing some rumblings about someone wanting to move the SR-71 to Beale. Make sure everyone knows we do not want that to happen and A.F. folks should get off the net. We see the SR-71 as a one year congressionally directed action that should be terminated ASAP.

NALD R. FOGLEMAN
eneral, USAF
hief of Staff

'I am hearing some rumbling about someone wanting to move the SR-71 to Beale. Make sure everyone knows we do not want that to happen and A.F. folks should get off the net. We see the SR-71 as a one year congressionally directed action that should be terminated ASAP.'
USAF Chief of Staff General Ronald R. Fogleman makes his position clear.

section 504 of the National Security Act specifically denies the ability for the purpose without a specific corresponding authorization.'

'Mr Spence. Mr Speaker, I concur with the gentleman's assessment and agree that the denial on O&M authorisation for the SR-71 should lead to the termination of this program during fiscal year 1996.'

Not surprisingly this prompted a debate within the Air Staff as to where this left the SR-71 reactivation program, with conflicting guidance being given depending upon whether the individual was a proponent or opponent of the SR-71. Appropriators contended that 504 didn't apply, therefore the aircraft should continue to fly; while authorizers took the opposing view, that it does apply, therefore the plane should be retired.

In a letter dated 1 March 1996, Don Fox, a lawyer serving in the office of the General Counsel, wrote

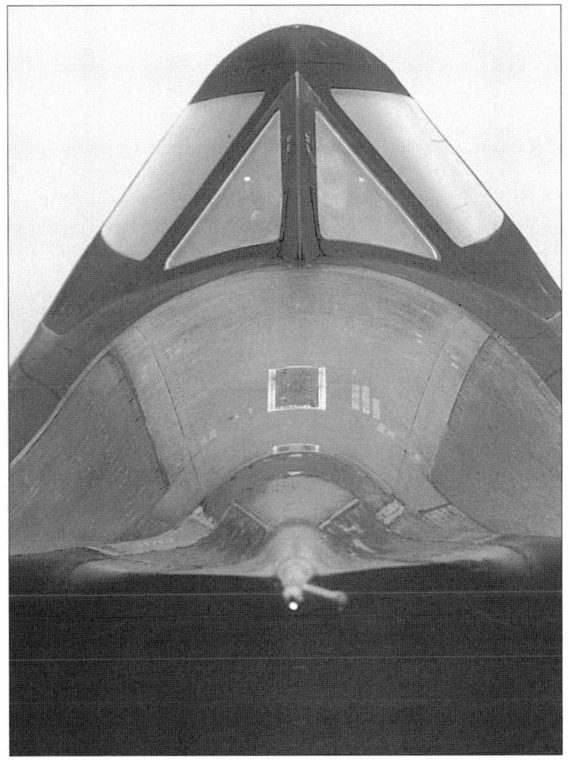

The materials used and the curvaceous lines of the SR-71 confirmed that stealth was an inherent aim of the SR-71 from its conception. *(Paul Crickmore)*

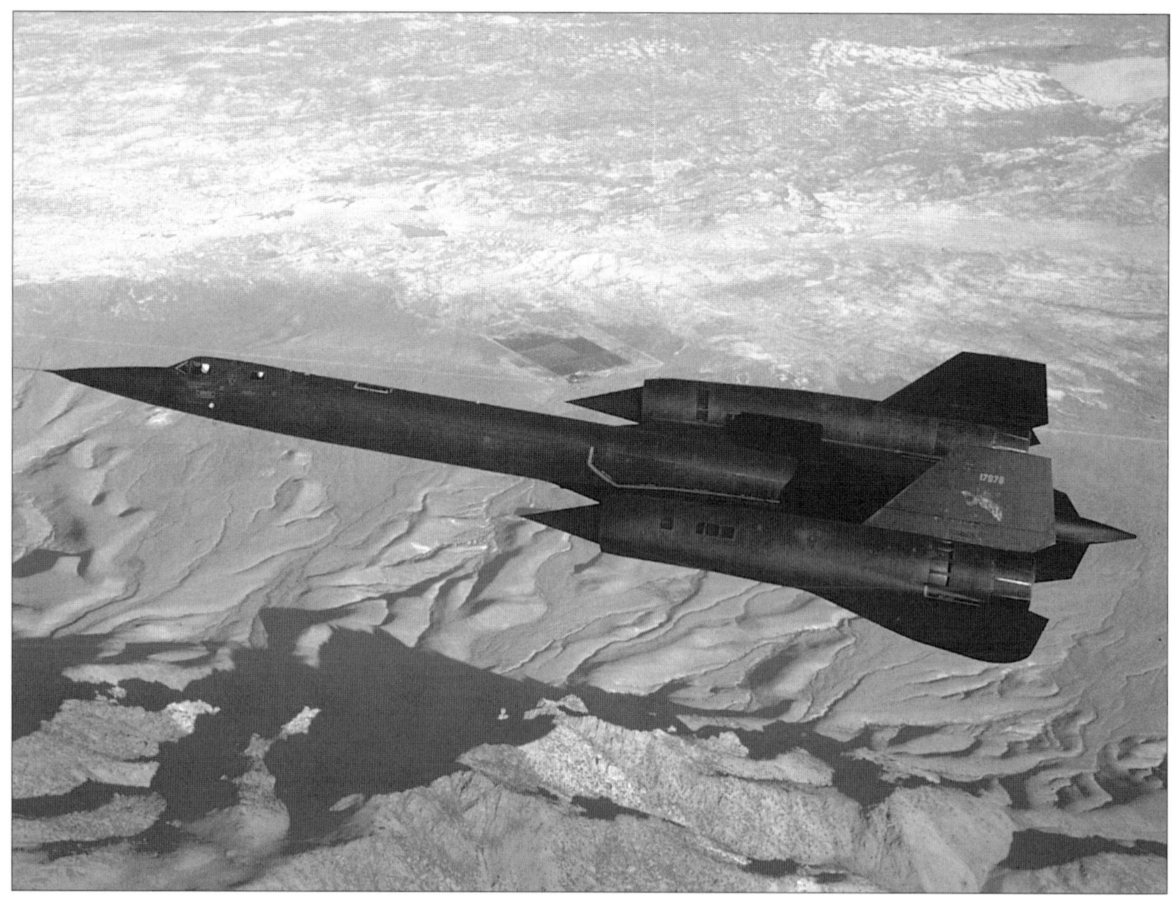

Photographed in the twilight of its career, 976 flew the first ever Habu mission. Now retired, it can be seen at the Air Force Museum, Wright Patterson AFB, Ohio *(Eric Schulzinger)*

to Sam Torrey giving some guidance and interpretation of the National Security Act and newly structured Intelligence Authorisation Act in relation to SR-71 funding; the last paragraph noted 'Resolution of the authorization question is key to the issue of the SR-71 funding in FY96. If funding is not authorized in the classified schedule of authorizations then obligation and expenditure of funds is prohibited. If the funds were authorised, then depending on the wording of the authorisation the Air Force may still retain some discretion as to whether the 3010 (Aircraft Procurement, Air Force) and 3400 (Operation and Maintenance) funds must be obligated and expended.' It is significant that in the Intelligence Authorisation Committee's classified annex relating to Operations and Maintenance accounts, the line item for the SR-71 had been zeroed. Programme manager Sam Torrey believed he was caught between a rock and a hard place and requested an unequivocal mandate to either operate or not operate the SR–71. On Friday 12 April John White (Deputy Secretary of Defence) received a letter from John Hamre, Under Secretary of Defence (Comptroller) which outlined the 'significant disagreement within Congress' concerning the SR-71, pointing out that 'Last year the appropriations act provided $30 million to operate the SR-71, but the Intelligence Authorisation Act provided no funds and explicitly denied authorisation. The letter continued: 'For whatever reason, we didn't focus on this until about a month ago when someone from the House Intelligence Committee asked us if we were complying with the law. We researched it and have concluded that we have no option but to suspend operations of the SR-71.'

Following an informal meeting that night between Steve Cortese, Staff Director on the Senate Subcommittee on Defense, Committee on Appropriations and John White, a letter was sent

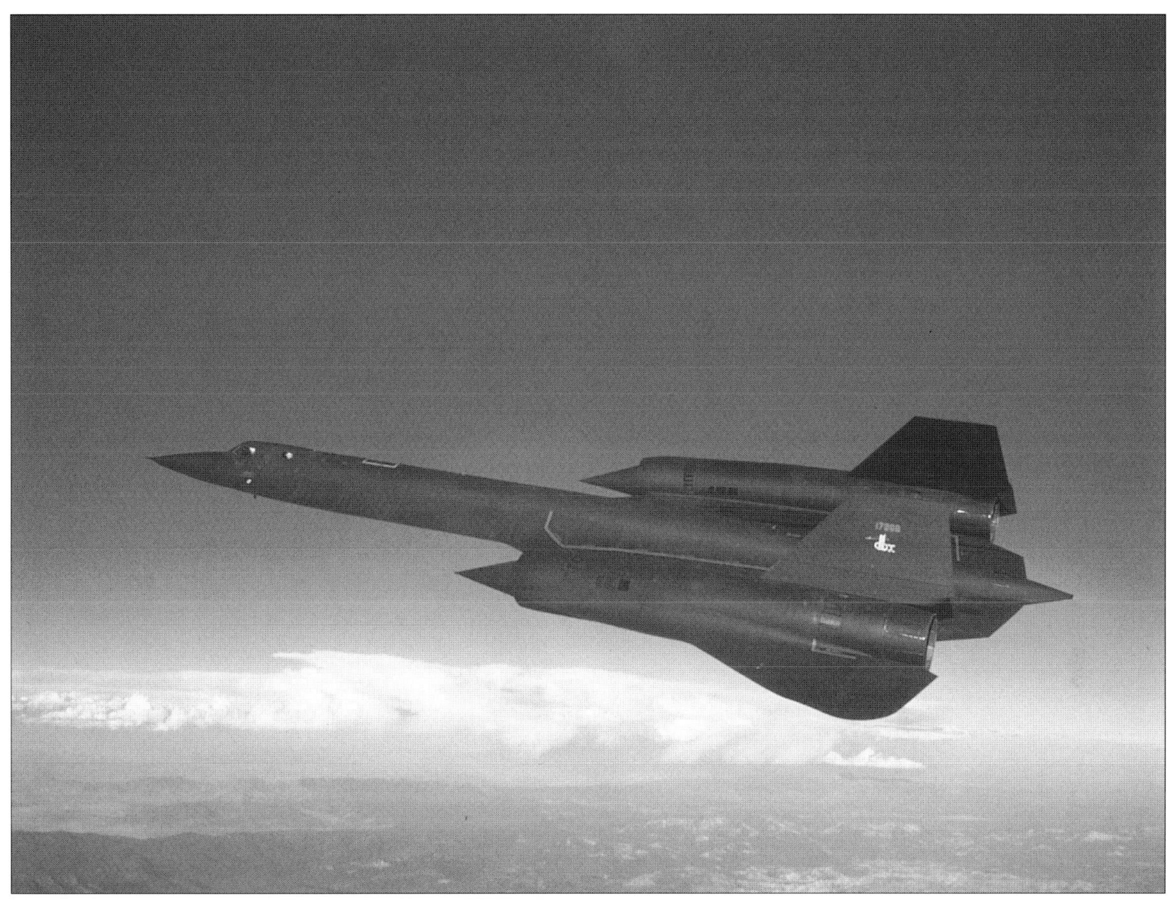

Wearing the tail art 'dbx' (Dolby X), aircraft 968 is seen trumpeting the sound of freedom in happier days. Today, she remains in storage at Palmdale, while younger sister 967 is back. *(Eric Schulzinger)*

direct to Senator Ted Stevens, chairman of the above committee and reads:

'I am writing about an unfortunate development which has forced the Department to take action which I know will not please you concerning the SR-71.

'The SR-71, like other intelligence programs, is governed by somewhat different legislation arrangements. Section 504 of the National Security Act of 1947 stipulates that the Department may not obligate or expend funds for any intelligence program, even though it has been appropriated, unless there is an independent authorization for the intelligence or intelligence-related activity. This is further complicated by the legislation Congress passed in the Intelligence Authorization Act which gives statutory force of law to the conference report accompanying the act. In this very critical way, the intelligence authorization process differs markedly from the normal defense authorization process.

'Section 102 of the Intelligence Authorization Act for FY96 provides that "the amounts authorized to be appropriated for Intelligence and intelligence-related activities are those specified in the classified Schedule of Authorizations prepared to accompany the conference report on bill H.R.1655 of the One Hundred Fourth Congress."

'The FY96 Schedule of Authorizations denied authorization of funds to operate the SR-71, although the Schedule authorized funds to modify the aircraft. We have confirmed with the intelligence committees that they did intend to modify but not operate the SR–71. The DoD General Counsel and Air Force General Counsel have determined that the combination of section 504 and section 102 have the consequence of making it illegal for the Department to continue to operate the SR-71. Consequently, I have directed the Air Force to suspend operation of the SR-71 immediately. The

Department will proceed with the modification program as provided by the legislation.

'We regret having to take this action, for it rekindles an unfortunate periodic struggle among our oversight committees, to avoid this action, but there appears to be no legal basis for us to continue operating the SR-71. Should Congress act subsequently to remove the legal impediment to operate the SR-71, the Department is prepared to comply with congressional direction. I would be pleased to review this with you at your convenience.'

At 23:00 (Z) on 16 April 1996 a signal was dispatched suspending SR-71 operations with immediate effect. By coincidence,Gil Luloff and Mike Finan flew 967 that very day. Gil and Jim Greenwood were airborne for 2.3 hrs in 967 on 9 May, testing the aircraft's Data Link. It would not fly again until FY97.

Ed Scheider and Blair Bozek flew aircraft 971 on 14 June, again using 3010 funds to check the ASARS data link, but it too would not fly again until the new fiscal.

At least two classified, official messages requesting SR-71 operations were made subsequent to the aircraft being grounded. One, made on 28 May 1996, came from the NSA and was directed to Air Force Combat Command and Air Forces Directorate for plans and operations. The second request in June, was from the DIA and originated by the CINC US Pacific Command. Both requests were denied, based upon, the interpretation of the aforementioned intelligence laws.

A letter to John White from Arlen Specter and J. Robert Kerrey, Chairman and Vice Chairman respectively of the Senate Select Committee on intelligence (SSCI) dated 24 April noted:

'For the record, we wish to clarify that the SSCI played no role in the initial authorization of the SR-71 by the Senate, or in the subsequent conference negotiations on the SR-71. The Senate Armed

A reminder from the Lockheed literature of the hot spots involving SR-71 throughout its long history. *(Lockheed)*

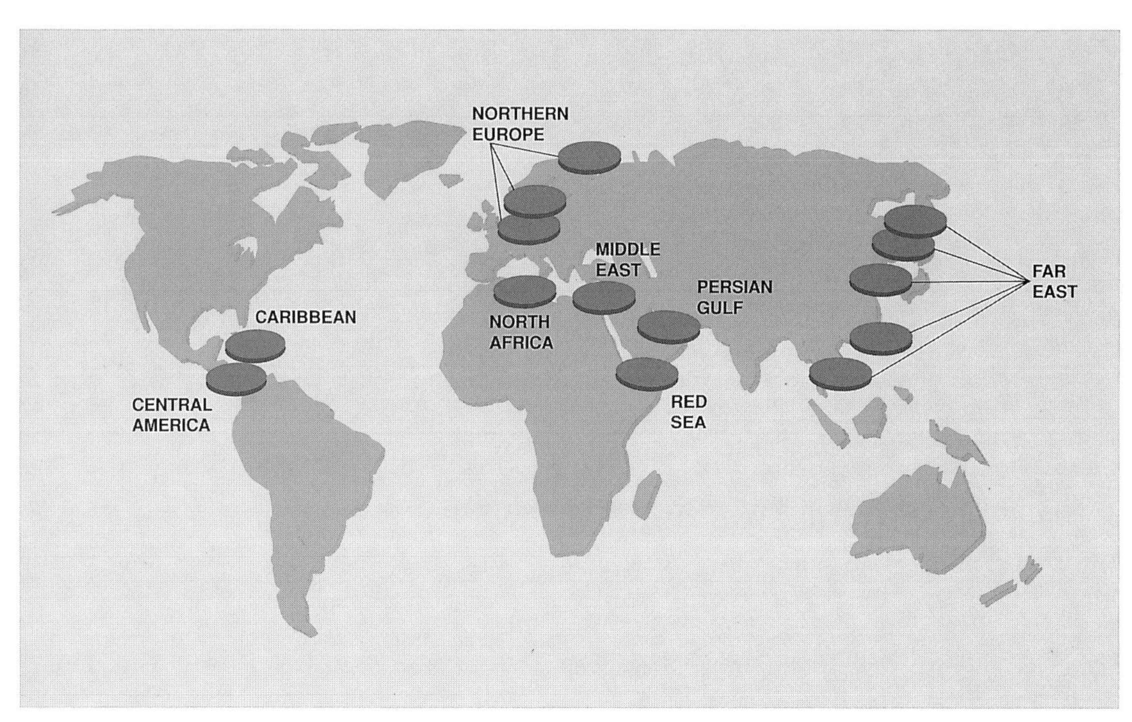

Mission Profile

Mission profiles vary greatly, depending on distance between operating base and target areas as well as other factors. From a forward operating location (FOL), it may be possible to access a target area using a single-legged, 1-hour mission. Where range to target is greater, mission is multi-legged. Where extra range is required for a mission, top-off refueling is performed after takeoff, before ascent to first supersonic leg. During supersonic leg, airplane altitude increases as fuel is consumed. Reconnaissance legs are flown at higher altitude and speed to optimize survivability. The following is a simplified diagram of both single and multi-legged missions. The diagram shows airplane returning to original base; however, depending on mission plan, it may land at an alternate base.

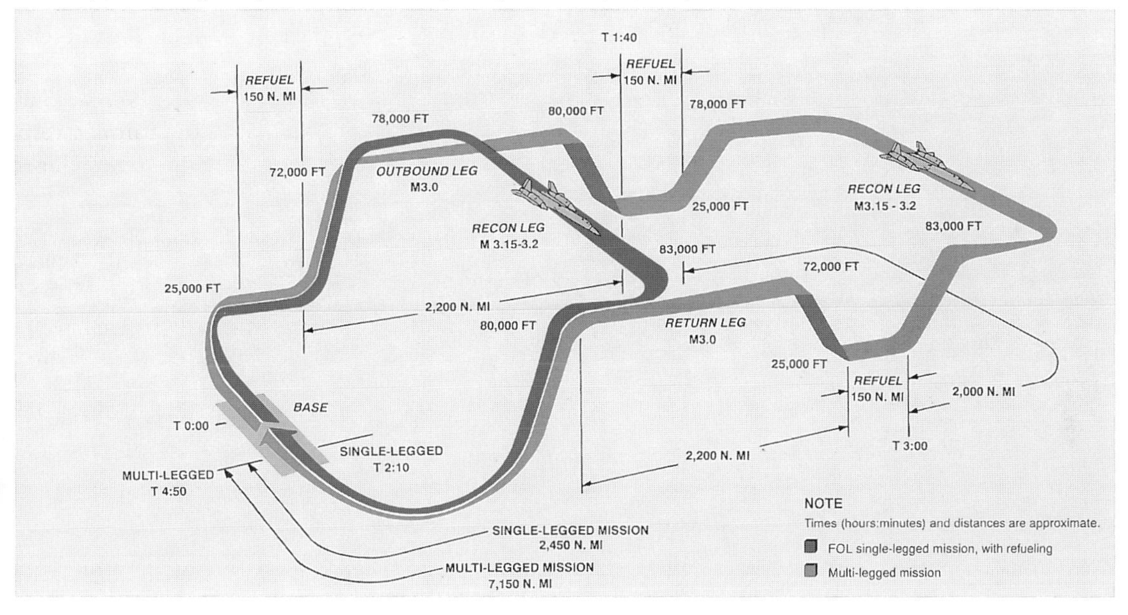

This simplified schematic shows two mission profiles. Note that both rely upon tanker support to top up tanks shortly after take-off. *(Lockheed)*

Services Committee performed both functions. The JMIP and TIARA sections of the annual intelligence authorization bill and report, including the classified annex, are the product of a three-way negotiation between the HPSCI and HASC for the House and the SASC for the Senate, in the context of the defense authorization conference. Finally, at no point did anyone seek or receive "confirmation" related to the SSCI's views on the intended funding restrictions pertaining to the SR-71."

Members of the Senate Appropriations Committee were enraged at the way they had been completely circumvented over the decision to suspend SR-71 operations and were quick to make known their possible course of action if they encountered similar obstructions during the appropriation of funds for FY97. The clear threat was that the SAC would move to have section 8080 of the Appropriations Act eliminated.

This section authorises intelligence activities for which funds are appropriated, until the Intelligence Authorisation Bill is enacted. The SAC's next tactic would be to defeat the Intelligence Authorisation Act for FY97 in the House and Senate floors.

With no section 8080 from the Appropriations Act and no Intelligence Authorisation Act, virtually all intelligence activities would grind to a halt. One can imagine the alarm in AF, DIA, CIA and NSA circles!

Of the $253 billion total Department of Defense Appropriation Bill for 1997, $30 million has been allocated for SR-71 O & M,and a further $9 million for procurement. This spend has now been ratified and signed off by the President and it looks as though the Habu programme is once more up and running – well, at least for 1997!

What of Aurora?

Throughout 1988-1990, speculation was rife concerning the existence of a high altitude,

Seen here in NASA markings, the sole surviving SR-71B has proved to be a real workhorse, as evidenced by the flight record on page 251. *(NASA)*

hypersonic replacement for the SR-71, which informed commentators asserted was powered by an exotic, high-tech ramjet. The aviation press ran numerous articles about this amazing machine which some enthusiasts claim to have seen operating from Area 51 and on this side of the Atlantic, from the ubiquitous 'underground hanger' at Macrahanish. This warp-speed platform we were all reliably informed was named Aurora. In fact, we now know that Aurora was the name used to hide funds for the B-2 competition. The intended SR-71 replacement was far less glitzy than all the glamorous hype and fiction had led us to believe: it was intended to have been a highly stealthy, subsonic, Unmanned Aerial Vehicle or UAV.

Built by Lockheed-Martin/Boeing, the highly classified Tier 3 project became a victim of the peace dividend and escalating costs. In its place, a two platform UAV competition has been established. The parent companies behind Tier 3 fielded their entry, the Tier 3 minus (Darkstar), which is expected to cost around $10-12 million per article.

This Very Low Observable (VLO) flying wing is reported to have an 'on-target' loiter time of more than 8 hours. Its competitor, the Tier 2 plus UAV (Global Hawk) is believed to have a target loiter capability of 24 hours and possess a range of 3,000 miles at 65,000 feet. Both UAV's are said to carry the same SAR and electro-optical camera system. However, in Rich Graham's excellent book *SR-71 Revealed: The Inside Story,* he states that the Tier 3 minus can only be equipped with one sensor at a time. If this is the case, it must be seen as a retrograde step, as field commanders require a comprehensive picture of the enemy's Order of Battle, which in turn requires simultaneous synoptic area coverage.

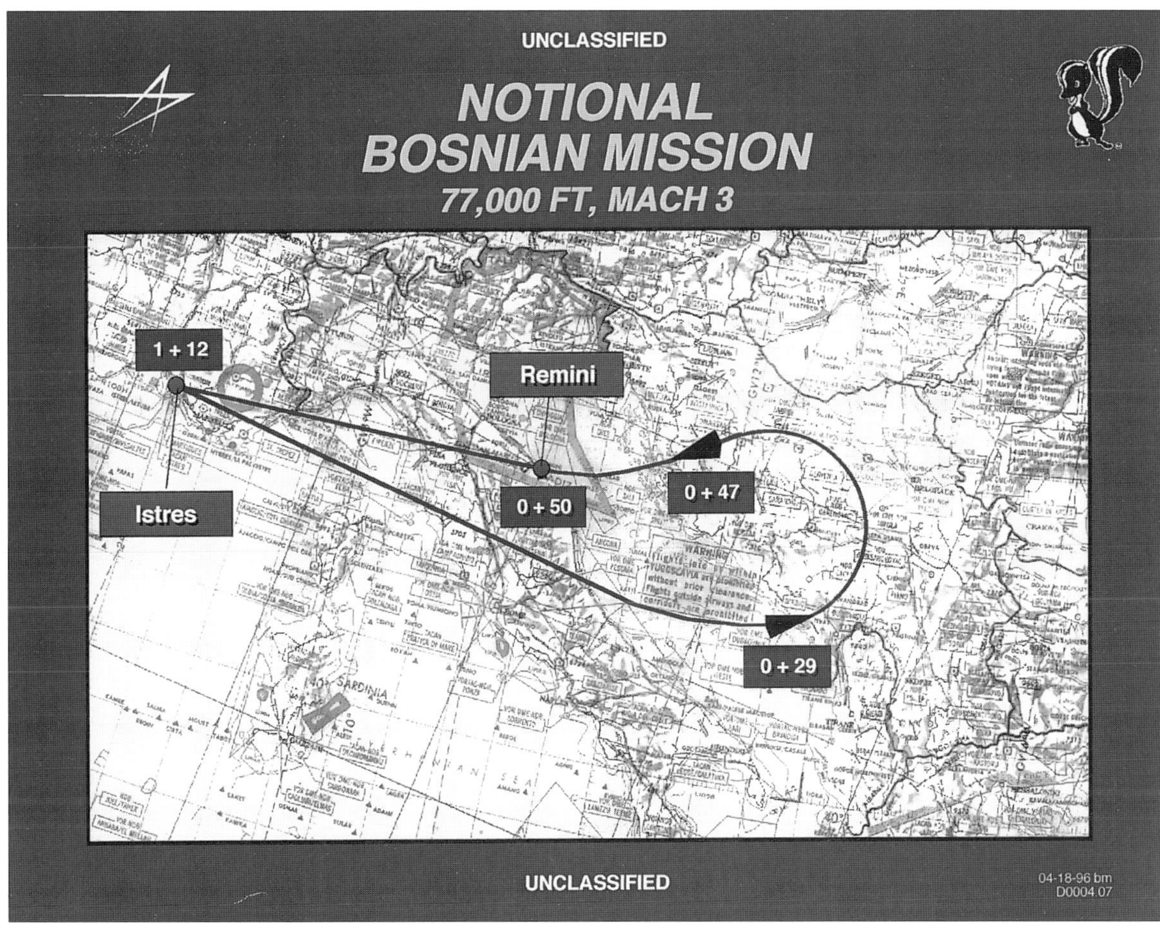

On 28 May, 1996 the NSA requested an SR-71 mission over Bosnia, for which this schematic was produced by Lockheed. *(Lockheed)*

The development of long range, highly sensitive Infra Red tracking systems could conceivably prove to be stealth technology's Achilles' heel. While the need to develop and exploit UAV/stealth technology is self evident, there would appear to be valid questions regarding the platform's ability to be mission survivable.

Interception depends upon the resolution of two basic criteria – an ability to detect and track and the ability to bring to bear a weapon system capable of defeating the platform. The use of stealth technology and ECM can certainly frustrate detection, and it can also play a role in helping to defeat a weapon system. But speed, altitude and manoeuvrability are the most obvious necessary attributes if engagement is to be successfully avoided. The number of weapon systems capable of defeating an extremely high altitude aircraft is tiny. Add high speed to the equation and interceptability, together with exposure time to a weapon system, is further reduced. We have seen how satellite doctrine within certain influential circles of the intelligence community has evolved into entrenched satellite dogma; we have also seen the shortsightedness of such policies. Could UAV's be going the same way? Surely what is needed is a mutually inclusive approach to the development of the airborne reconnaissance-gathering triad – satellites, UAV's and aircraft – as each brings its own unique capabilities.

The world in which the SR-71 was conceived has thankfully changed dramatically; the degree of intellectual authority that was attached to such policies as Mutually Assured Destruction (MAD) and General Curtis LeMay's vehicle for getting us all there, 'Project Control', is hopefully assigned forever to the history books. But there will always be enemies of freedom and democracy. Deterrence

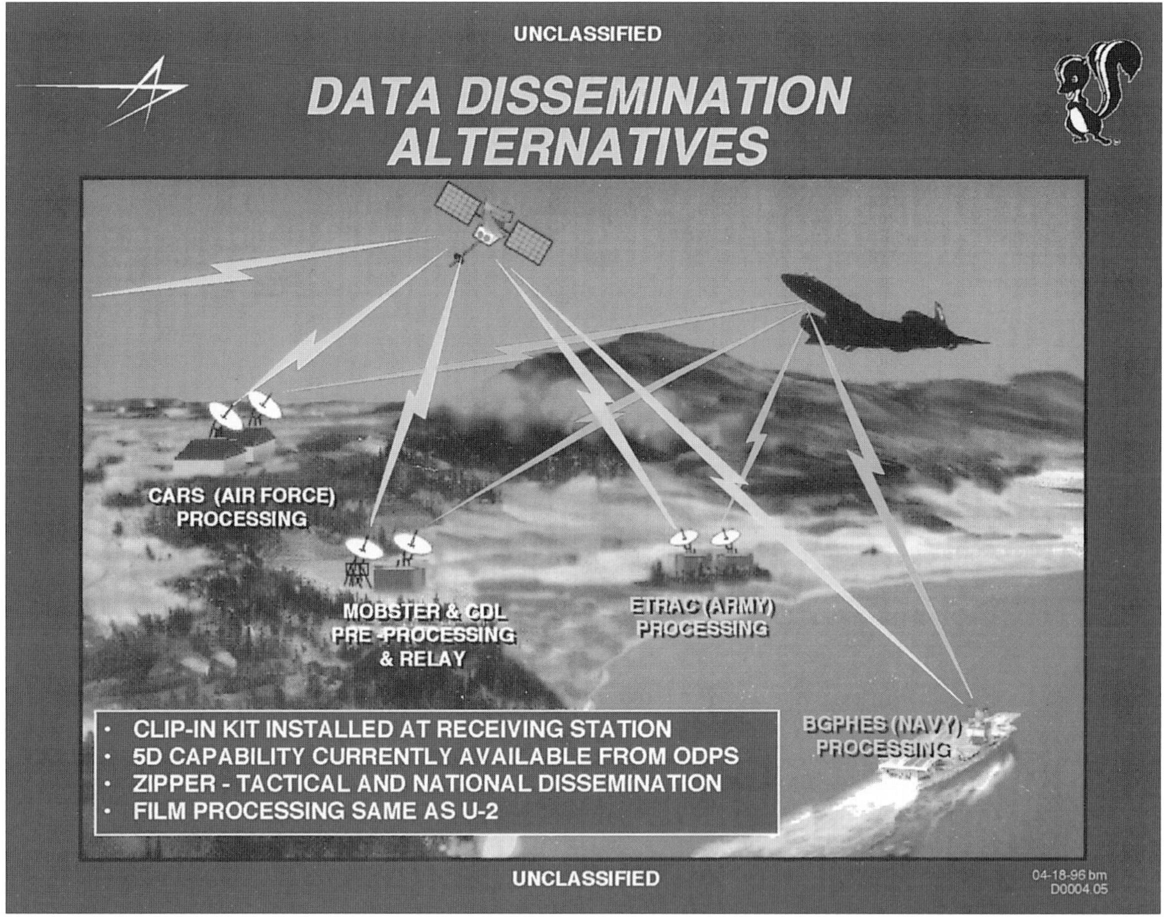

As emphasised by this schematic, the data link is compatible with US Army, Navy and Air Force processing systems. *(Lockheed)*

is unquestionably the best form of defence, even though its success can only be located in the abstract, shadow world of potential destruction that never was. A keystone to maintaining deterrence is the pursuit of truth; and to this end the SR-71 can still make an invaluable contribution, particularly to theatre commanders.

The SR-71's utility has increased immeasurably with the introduction of the Loral Unisys (now Lockheed–Martin, Tactical Communications Division), data link. Apart from the two flights mentioned earlier, flight testing ground to a halt until October 1996.

It is anticipated that the system will be operational by December/January 1996/97. The next major sensor enhancement will take place with the deployment of an electro-optical backplane for the Technical Objective Cameras (TEOC), these units are being developed by Recon Optical, located in Barrington, Illinois. This will facilitate the transmission of 'close-look', high quality images, via the data link in 'real-time' (radar imagery is transmitted in 'near-real-time', due to the slight time delay needed to convert the picture into a digitised format for transmission).

The two key individuals responsible for re-establishing logistical support, Barry MacKean and Don Emmons, have done a masterful job. They have 31 spare J-58 engines, and Ashland Petroleum Company in Kentucky is once again manufacturing JP-7 fuel. Tanker support is provided by the 92nd Air Refueling Wing, flying KC-135Ts from Fairchild AFB (fuel has been pre-postioned to RAF Fairford for possible support of EUCOM and CENTCOM). They also have several hundred spare tyres, all beyond their shelf life; in practical terms this means that BF Goodrich have to periodically re-certify them, which results in fewer landings per tyre.

One for the archives, taken at the 1993 Blackbird Reunion at Reno, Nevada. From left to right: Ed Yeilding, who established a coast-to-coast record in what was intended to have been the USAF's final SR-71 flight, on 6 March 1990; Lou Schalk, Chief Test Pilot of the A-12 progamme; and Bob Gilliland, Chief Test Pilot of the SR-71 programme *(Paul Crickmore)*

This increased capability brought about by the deployment of upgraded sensors should lead to greater tactical utilisation of the platform – all things being equal, the SR-71 might just make 2001, the article number conferred on the SR-71 prototype, by its brilliant designer, the great Clarence L 'Kelly' Johnson.

Abbreviations

AAA	Anti-Aircraft Artillery
ADP	Advanced Development Projects
ADS	Accessory Drive System
AFCS	Automatic Flight Control System
AICS	Air Inlet Control System
ANS	Astro-inertial Navigation System
ARCP	Air Refueling Control Point
ASARS	Advanced Synthetic Aperature Radar System
BIT	Built-In Test
CCT	Computer Compatible Tape
CG	Centre of Gravity
CIA	Central Intelligence Agency
CIS	Chemical Ignition System
COMINT	Communications Intelligence
CP	Control Point
DAFICS	Digital Automatic Flight Inlet Control System
Det	Detachment
DFC	Distinguished Flying Cross
DIA	Defense Intelligence Agency
DME	Distance Measuring Equipment
DoD	Department of Defense
DP	Destination Point
ECCM	Electronic Counter-Counter Measures
ECM	Electronic Counter Measures
ECS	Environmental Control System
EDP	Electronic Data Processing
ELINT	Electronic Intelligence
EOB	Electronic Order of Battle
FCF	Functional Check Flight
FCO	Fire Control Officer
FMC	Forward Motion Compensation
FRDC	Florida Research and Development Centre
IFF	Identification Friend/Foe
IGV	Inlet Guide Vanes
INS	Inertial Navigation System
IPIR	Initial Photo Interpretation Report
MGFU	Mobile Ground Formatter Unit
MPC	Mobile Processing Center
MRS	Mission Recorder System
NASA	National Aeronautics and Space Administation
NPIC	National Photographic Interpretation Center
NSA	National Security Agency
OBC	Optical Bar Camera
OL	Operating Location
OSD	Office of the Secretary of Defense
PACAF	Pacific Air Force
PARPRO	Peacetime Aerial Reconnaissance Programme
PEM	Programme Element Manager
PEN	Programme Element Number
POM	Programme Objective Memorandum
PRF	Pulse Repetition Frequency
PRI	Pulse Repetition Interval
PSD	Physiological Support Division
PVD	Peripheral Vision Display
RAM	Radar Absorbing Materials
RCD	Radar Corrolated Display
RCS	Radar Cross-Section
RHWR	Radar Homing and Warning Receiver
RSO	Reconnaissance Systems Officer
SAC	Strategic Air Command
SACSA	Special Assistant for Counterinsurgency and Special Activities
SAM	Surface-to-Air-Missile
SAO	Special Activities Office
SAS	Stability Augmentation System
SIGINT	Signals Intelligence
SLAR	Side-ways Looking Airborne Radar
SRS	Strategic Reconnaissance Squadron
SRW	Strategic Reconnaissance Wing
TACAN	Tactical Air Navigation
TCU	Tape-Copy-Unit
TEB	Triethylborane

Footnotes

Chapter 1

1. 'Cocked' – Readied the aircraft for engine start by pre-checking its exterior, pre-positioning cockpit switches and reviewing nearly 100 checklist items for the mission crew.
2. TEB – Triethylborane is a volatile chemical starter fluid that produces flash ignition when exposed to air. Each engine had a less than litre-sized, gold-plated tank which held the chemical to be injected into the engine's burner cans, or afterburner, by simply moving the throttle from the 'Off' to the 'Idle' position, or from the 'Mil-power' to 'Minimum-AB' position. TEB counters reeled down from 16 to 0, although the TEB supply could give more than the indicated number. On a typical flight, each engine used four to six TEB shots: engine starts, take-off AB light-up (maybe an AB light-up during aerial refuelling), post refuelling AB light-up for climb to altitude and a second post refuelling AB light-up on longer missions. The remaining TEB was in reserve for airstarts in the rare event of an engine flame-out, or for additional AB light-ups.
3. Checked for full deflection and freedom of travel in both directions, with all movements called out and positively confirmed by the crew chief, and acknowledged by the pilot.
4. For example: Mach 2.6/450 KEAS – Mach 2.7/440 KEAS – Mach 2.8/430 KEAS – Mach 2.9/420 KEAS – Mach 3.0/ 410 KEAS – Mach 3.1/400 KEAS – Mach 3.2/390 KEAS – whereupon the KEAS could be traded off for altitude down to a minimum of 310 KEAS.

Chapter 2

1. The bank angle was restricted to 40 degrees at high speed, and a 180-degree turn had a diameter of 130 miles.
2. 'Murphy's Law' – If its humanly possible to misconnect wiring or to get things backward, it will surely be done. Conversely, in order to prevent such errors, it is necessary for engineers to make connections 'Murphy-proof' with deliberate connection differences.
3. All A-12/YF-12 and SR-71 aircraft were identified by two separate numbering systems in which Lockheed and the CIA gave them article numbers between 121 and 135. The Air Force however, used conventional number coding which indicated year of manufacture and tail number. To clarify the two sets of numbers given in this book, the A-12s and YF-12s have been double indentified as follows;

Article 121 – 60-6924
Article 122 – 60-6925
Article 123 – 60-6926
Article 124 – 60-6927
Article 125 – 60-6928
Article 126 – 60-6929
Article 127 – 60-6930
Article 130 – 60-6933
Article 1001 – 60-6934
Article 1002 – 60-6935
Article 1003 – 60-6936
Article 131 – 60-6937
Article 132 – 60-6938
Article 133 – 60-6939
Article 128 – 60-6931
Article 129 – 60-6932
Article 134 – 60-6940
Article 135 – 60-6941

Although the *Oxcart* pilots and the Agency tended to use the article numbers, the Air Force crews used the last three numbers in its serial for individual aircraft indentity. 'Dutch' was used for A-12 and early SR-71 test flights. Stateside SR-71 training flights always used the call-sign 'Aspen', followed by a two-digit sub-identifier to highlight SR-71s to air traffic controllers for priority handling. Over the years most air- and groundcrew members called each aircraft by its final three tail numbers, and this is how they are referred to in this volume.
4. 'Butt-Snappers' were designed to forcibly boost a crewmember from his rocket-fired escape seat after bail-out. The cradled Snapper-Straps were contoured behind the parachute and ran from the seat's shoulder position under the knees to a position at the front edge of the seat. After bail-out and seat stabilisation, the shoulder and lap belts were guillotined and the snappers automatically tightened to thrust the crewman clear of the seat, prior to automatic or manual parachute deployment.
5. By summer's end the processing time was greatly reduced by equipping the 67th RTS with A-12 related processing equipment. This speed-up allowed the photo-intelligence 'product' to be in the hands of US commanders in Vietnam within 24 hours of the A-12 landing.
6. A 'double looper' mission entailed overflying North Vietnam, followed by an air refuelling over Thailand, and then another pass over North Vietnam (the second route displaced further north or south of the first pass), followed by another refuelling over Thailand before flying back to Kadena. The duration of such flights was approximately five-and-a-half hours, and during this time the aircraft would cover over 6000 nautical miles.
7. Many years later, Denny Sullivan still has in his possession a most notable souvenir of that 1967 flight – a very small piece of brass from the fuse of the Soviet-made SA-2. This was the only hit ever made on any A-12/SR-71 during more than 1000 flights over 'denied territory'. It is also worth mentioning that Denny's A-12 was the only American aircraft over Hanoi at that time, which gave the North Vietnamese, and their Soviet advisers, ideal conditions for tracking and attempting to bag a 'Cygnus'.
8. That 20 April meeting included Assistant Secretary of Defense and Deputy Director of Defense for Research and Engineering, Dr Eugene G Fubins; Chief of Naval Operations, Adm David L McDonald; Director of Naval Intelligence, Vice Adm Rufus L Taylor; and Assistant Director for Collection for the Defence Intelligence Agency, Rear Adm Frederic J Harlfinger.
9. That group included the Budget's CW Fisher, DoD's

Herbert Bennington and the CIA's John Paragosky.
10. A-12 numbers 127, 129 and 131 stayed on Okinawa throughout *Black Shield*, and flew all of the operational missions during the *Oxcart* deployment.

Chapter 3
1. The J58 engine's design team was headed by William H Brown and included Don Pascal, Norm Cotter, Dick Coar and Ed Esmeier. William Gorton, Pratt & Whitney's Florida General Manager, provided the interface between the engine manufacturer and Lockheed, while W Stanley Dees was the J58 programme manager.
2. USAF Regulation 60-16 requires that pressure suits be worn on all flights above 50,000 ft.
3. The A-12 and SR-71 design engineers used certain descriptive nicknames for identifying various parts of the aircrafts' sometimes unique assemblies. The free-floating trailing-edge nacelle flaps that were used to help shape the exhaust plume were referred to as 'tail-feathers'. The forward bypass door mechanisms were called 'onion-slicers', and the aft bypass doors were known as 'cabbage-slicers'. Although the use of proper engineering terminology was encouraged, those and other light-hearted nicknames stuck throughout the SR-71's life.
4. A left generator bus, a right generator bus, an essential AC bus, an emergency AC bus and a hot AC bus. In addition there were 26-volt essential and emergency AC buses.
5. Abe Kardong once noted a large island under his track whilst streaking over the western Pacific between Okinawa and Vietnam. When he asked his RSO what that unexpected land mass might be, Art Kogler said 'Its Luzon Abe. You'd better check your autopilot to see if it's in the Auto Nav mode'. Since it was not, the aircraft had failed to turn at the previous DP turn-point, and was departing rapidly from its programmed course. Naturally, a big corrective turn was made and another quick lesson was learnt about checking and rechecking heading, track and position.
6. 'Slow' film (low ASA rating) was used to obtain the highest possible image-resolving clarity for maximum enlargement.
7. Resolution is not the ability to distinguish a single football on a grassy pitch, but rather to count the number of individual footballs when placed closely together (in the case of the Type H camera, only two inches apart).
8. With the exception of additional sensors carried in the extended tail modification of SR-71 17959.

Chapter 4
1. Optical correlation is now carried out digitally, but back in the early 1960s a small double-ended vacuum tube was used. At one end was stored a pre-programmed reconnaissance photo; the other end scanned the ground. Look-rate filters were used to ensure accurate photo correlation. During the terminal guidance phase of its flight, the missile would pitch down and check its position relative to the target, make a dog-leg turn if necessary, and repeat this procedure up to three times before impact.
2. Prior to their departure to Burbank, Nelson thoroughly briefed the ten on how they were to conduct themselves while away from Beale. To preserve security they were told to leave their uniforms behind and to wear only civilian clothes. They were each given a cover story and told that they had been booked into the Burbank Travel Lodge. They then set off in unmarked cars down Highway 99, each one feeling very excited at their new-found *James Bond* lifestyle. As they arrived at their hotel, they noticed a large billboard upon which the word 'Topless' appeared in very bold print. It advertised the 'Brewmistresses' Beer Bar' which was the first topless bar any of them had ever seen. Clearly, it warranted further investigation. They walked into the bar in blue-jeans and casual shirts and with their cover stories, each felt as if he was the perfect undercover agent. While adjusting to the topless bar phenomenon, they were taken aback by the observation of one of the waitresses, who asked Tom Schmittou how long he had been in the Air Force. Tom stammered that he was not in the Air Force, whereupon the waitress countered that he and the others were most certainly in the Air Force because 'you're all wearing those funny black-faced Air Force watches'. Having fallen at the first encounter, the crews just laughed as their *James Bond* egos were shot to pieces. The incident cleared the air however, and although no reference was made to the reason for their presence in Burbank, they took themselves a little less seriously.
3. The SR-71/YF-12 test force, functioning as an autonomous self-contained unit complete with its own maintenance and support facilities, reported to Maj Gen Alton Slay, commander of the Air Force Flight Test Center at Edwards, which was under the overall command of the AFSC. This unique unit was redesignated the 4786th Test Squadron (TS) on 16 January 1970. The test force were charged with performing Category II, or 'Developmental', testing, and USAF acceptance of new aircraft from the factory. The test crews validated aircraft safety and provided detailed performance characteristics which were incorporated into the flight manual, and tested progressive improvements made as aircraft systems evolved. After Phase I and II of the SR-71/YF-12 test programme were satisfactorily completed, the 4786th TS was deactivated on 12 May 1972. For their pioneering contributions Lou Schalk, Bill Park, Jim Eastham and Bob Gilliland each received the Ivan Kinchloe Award for 1964 from the Society of Experimental Test Pilots.
4. The first system used in the 1960s lacked the three-axis movement of today's flight simulators, however, the rear cockpit utilised overhead satellite imagery projected through the RSO's optical viewsight, and had a rating of top secret because of the satellite photography.
5. More than a year later, and after two shocking night accidents, the night portion of the training syllabus was ammended for safety considerations. Thereafter, a pilot did not complete his first night sortie until he had logged 50 hours of SR-71 flying (about 16 daytime flights).

6. By this time an SR-71 pilot had accumulated 35 hours in the SR-71A and B, and nearly 100 hours in the flight simulator; his RSO had flown fewer aircraft hours but had amassed more hours in the simulator.
7. Lockheed developed an interim fix that detuned the inlet system allowing the aeroplane to be flown in the automatic mode. This softer programme reduced the margin of unstarts. The ultimate panacea for unstarts proved to be DAFICS, a system developed much later in the programme, which was more accurate, faster responding, and less apt to drift out of calibration, thus smoothing out inlet pressures and preventing inlet disturbances.
8. Earle's silver 'moon-suit' was 'toasty brown' following his 'punch out' through the 1800-degree hot fireball, and the blisters on his fingers were the result of him having his gloved hands (which had grasped the between-the-knees ejection 'D'-ring) pointing downward as he streaked through the the explosive burst. Earle miraculously survived the fireball primarily because his 'moon-suit' provided a thick extra skin and a self-contained environment, which shielded him from the searing heat. The thickness of the suit also saved both the pilot and the RSO from suffering extensive abrasions during their 'trip' across the desert floor.
9. Jim Watkins, who was ten years older than the other crewmembers, was a real 'Texas cowboy' and an outstanding horseman (during an on-base rodeo, arranged during the 1969 Labour Day holiday, he roped a cow from a horse whilst wearing his full pressure suit and helmet). He had joined the US Army Air Force in 1944 and had flown B-24 Liberators. After a postwar break in service, he flew fighters during the Korean War, then C-46 transports before moving to KC-97 tankers. That experience led him into KC-135s, and his connection with the A-12 programme, which put him into close touch with Col Nelson, who accepted Jim into the SR-71 flying force firstly as a staff officer and then as a crewmember.
10. The primary power source for the pilot's Flight Director Instruments was changed to the Astro-inertial Navigation gyroscope, whilst the RSO's attitude indicator and the pilot's standby attitude instrument were powered by the Flight Reference System. This set of instruments consisted of a gyro unit similar to that used on the T-38 and other aircraft, and they were eventually replaced with a new INS gyro unit based on that fitted in the latest fighters like the F-16.

Chapter 5

1. The SR-71 was designed to be statically stable, should flight be interrupted by a perturbation, because an aeroplane is supposed to have a natural tendency toward a restoring moment. The SR-71 was dynamically unstable without SAS, and its stability was exacerbated by high speeds and high bank angles. The faster and higher the aircraft flew, the less damping there was available. With an aft movement of the 'centre of pressure', and a corresponding movement in the centre of gravity to reduce trim drag, it can be seen that flight without SAS was barely possible at high Mach and high altitude. Therefore, a pilot had to make a correct restoring control movement quickly and decisively, without overcontrolling. At the time of this incident, 980 had been modified with DAFICS – a system architecturally suited to the SR-71.
2. Summary of the Long-Duration Reconnaissance Flights flown from Griffiss and Seymour Johnson:

Date	A/C	Crew	Duration	Mileage	Time at Mach
13 Oct 73	979	Shelton/Coleman	11:13	11979	6:08
25 Oct 73	979	Joersz/Fuller	11:13	11859	5:56
2 Nov 73	979	Helt/Elliott	11:22	11973	6:00
11 Nov 73	964	Wilson/Douglass	10:49	12181	6:41
2 Dec 73	964	Sullivan/ Widdifield	9:56	12320	6:46
10 Dec 73	979	Bledsoe/Blackwell	10:00	12320	6:45
25 Jan 74	971	Adams/Machorek	10:04	12147	6:40
7 Mar 74	979	Judkins/Morgan	9:45	11865	7:02
6 Apr 74	979	Ransom/Gersten	9:46	11905	7:03

Chapter 6

1. It was a 9th SRW standard operating procedure for a new mission to be first flown in the simulator to familiarise the crews with communications and air refuelling requirements, missed air-refuelling procedures, 'points-of-no-return' abort decision points, recall procedures, locations of emergency landing airfields and other general procedures to be employed in the event of emergencies far from home bases. The transpacific deployment was to be made 'in the black' (without radio transmissions, except in codewords) and a rendezvous with the tankers was also to be 'radio silent'.
2. To assure that the deployer's inlets functioned properly, the *Glowing Heat* mission profile included an immediate climb to high altitude and Mach 3, and then a descent to the first pair of tankers which were waiting 1000 miles off the California coast.
3. They were also given some inflight foods which could be dispensed from a tooth paste-like tube, via a straw that was inserted through a re-sealable feeding port in the lower part of the helmet.
4. The Okinawa training flights, which were flown southeast of Kadena, were dubbed 'Cathy' sorties after mission planner Chuck Ferris' girlfriend back in the US.
5. The Attitude Director Instrument, sometimes called the artificial horizon, is a bi-coloured sphere in which the top half is white for sky and the bottom half black for ground. As an aircraft is banked, climbed or dived, its attitude is accurately represented on the instrument in relation to a horizon shown by the black-white separation line. In the case of a sharp dive, the white synthetic 'sky' disappears.
6. Early generator failures were frequent and difficult to rectify because the offending equipment often worked properly during ground tests after the aborted aircraft

had landed and cooled. Col Carl Estes recalled that one day a bright young NCO came to him with the answer. At sustained high Mach and prolonged heat-soaks, lead solder used in connecting wires to the generator was melting, which in turn caused the wires to loosen and the generator to fail. On the ground the solder resolidified and the generator worked again. The fix was simple once the problem had been isolated – alloyed solder was used, as it possessed a much higher melting point.
7. The standard descent procedure that had been written into the Dash-1 hand checklist had been arrived at after numerous training sorties flown in the United States. Atmosphereic conditions prevailing in those temperate latitudes were considerably different from those in the tropics. The standard atmospheric temperature lapse rate is a drop of two degrees centigrade for every 1000 ft increase in altitude, which places the tropopause (the line delineating the troposphere from the stratosphere) at about 55,000 ft. Generally speaking, at this altitude the temperature of the ambient air would reach -55 degrees Centigrade. However, the *Oxcart* and *Senior Crown* programmes were breaking new ground in the field of sustained high-speed, high-altitude flight. They soon discovered that the tropical tropopause could rise considerably higher. In Southeast Asia the atmosphere could expand into a dome 10 to 12,000 ft higher, allowing the tropospheric air temperature to drop to -70 degrees centigrade (15 degrees below the standard temperature, while the stratospheric air above it was stable at -55). As the aircraft descended on reduced power settings it would penetrate the 'domed' tropopause into the troposphere, where it was suddenly immersed into sharply colder air. Subjected to these lower T_2 (air temperature at the engines' compressor face) values, engine RPM also decreased to levels lower than those experienced in the United States. This reduced airflow to a point where the inlets could not bypass enough air from the engine, even with the forward bypass doors fully open. The increased inlet pressure then expelled the shockwave forward in an unstart. Now operating in a low pressure condition, the engines flamed out. Descending with the engines set some 1500 to 2000 RPM higher provided the additional margin to cope with the new atmospheric environment.
8. There was no command eject system fitted to the aircraft that would enable one crew member to eject the other before following suit.
9. As the air refuelling operation was completed near Korat Air Base, Thailand, one of the KC-135s recovered into U-Tapao to replenish its fuel tanks. This procedure was regularly carried out by all the KC-135Qs, which recovered into Korat prior to returning to Kadena five or six hours after the SR-71.
10. On 1 August 1968 Don and Phil flew their final Kadena 'Cathy' sortie (again in 978), and redeployed back to California on the weekly Beale transpacific tanker.
11. The tech reps were headed up by Paul Mellinger. Others worked for Pratt & Whitney, Northrop, Itek, Goodyear and Honeywell. Their combined expertise was responsible for the low levels of air aborts due to maintenance problems, and was therefore central to the overall success of *Senior Crown*.
12. Early in OL-8's operations, the snake-symbol on the side of an SR-71 accounted for a completed recon mission. After a dozen or so miniature Habu-symbols appeared on each aircraft, a senior 'staff toad' (reportedly at HQ SAC) decried these symbols as 'too revealing' of US intelligence activities. Also, by that time 978 was sporting a large white *Playboy Bunny* symbol on each vertical stabilizer, 974 had gained similar super-sized 'Habu'-symbols, and another jet wore an Irish four-leafed clover. It was not long before SAC instructed the wing to remove the mission symbols and the tail art from the SR-71s. Thereafter, even the standard USAF insignia and tail numbers were 'muted'.
13. It appears as if the *Kingpin* planners had not been told about a parallel CIA programme codenamed *Operation Popeye*, which involved the air-dropping of silver-iodide cloud-seeding pellets for rain-making over Laos. This rather bizarre activity had been going on for more than three and a half years prior to the launch of *Kingpin*. The purpose of *Popeye* had been to cause landslides along the north-south roadways, and to wash away river crossings which were being used by the North Vietnamese to supply their army in South Vietnam. Such was the compartmentalised nature of covert operations, that one most-secret programme may have stymied another.
14. Reported in the late 1960s as the SA-5 *Griffon*, this much-improved variant was over 50 ft long, weighed nearly 12 tons and possessed a range of 180 miles. It could be fired upward at a speed of Mach 3.5 to an altitude of 100,000 ft, where its 135-lb high-explosive warhead had the theoretical capability of intercepting an SR-71. In addition to obtaining target-guidance instructions from its ground-based target-acquisiton radars (called *Square Pair*), the SA-5 was believed to also carry a 60-cm wave-length radar receiver in its nose to carry out active radar homing, through the use of a rocket motor in its third stage, to terminally guide the warhead to its target.
15. Nevertheless, the home unit and their intermediate command headquarters, HQ 15th Air Force, were kept very well informed of all activity by top secret message traffic. It was vital that they were kept in the loop as they were responsible for providing trained crews and maintenance personnel, ensuring aircraft reliability for effective combat sorties and for the movement of all assets other than the planning and execution of the operational missions themselves. There was a strong tendency of higher headquarters to abuse chain-of-command principles in the so-called 'interest of security', and when 'old-boy' connections were established among key personalities. It was often characteristic of 'hot' activites in very secret operations to leave someone out of the loop who was cleared to know, but was bypassed in the name of 'expediency'.
16. Bob Powell was the first pilot to log 1000 flight hours in the SR-71.

17. A U-Tapao-based B-52 flown by Capt John Mize was badly crippled. He nursed his damaged aircraft toward Nakhon Phanom RTAFB, Thailand, where the crew bailed out. Mize was the first SAC pilot to be awarded the Air Force Cross for valorous action during the Vietnam conflict.
18. These long SR-71 sorties were flown over the Persian Gulf area in 1987 and 1988 on the following dates;

22 July 1987 – 967, crewed by Majs Mike Smith and Doug Soifer
9 Aug 1987 – 975, crewed by Majs Terry Pappas and John Manzi
26 Oct 1987 – 967, crewed by Majs Warren McKendree and Randy Shelhorse
30 Apr 1988 – 974, crewed by Majs Dan House and Blair Bozek

Chapter 7

1. SR-71 eastbound transatlantic record flight time, 1 hour and 55 minutes – 3490 nautical miles covered.
2. SR-71 westbound transatlantic record flight time, 3 hours and 48 minutes – 5645 nautical miles covered.
3. Det 4 was a U-2R detachment at first, manned by crews of the 99th SRS, who were tasked with obtaining ELINT and COMINT from northern European operational areas under the SAC mission code-name of *Senior Ruby*.
4. SR-71 number 64-17955 was an early-build airframe that was assigned to the AFLC (Plant 42) at Palmdale. It had long been used as a test aircraft for thoroughly evaluating new systems being developed for SR-71s prior to their fitment on operational jets.
5. The Greenham Women were described as a group of 'travellers' who thought they had a better understanding of world power politics than elected officials, and they had set-up a permanent camp-site outside the cruise-missile base. Over the preceding months they had done their utmost to disrupt the movement of vehicles that entered and left the base.
6. USAF/XOXX – HQ USAF Directorate of Plans and Policy; SAC/XP – HQ SAC Deputy Chief of Staff Plans.
7. The 'air diplomacy' effort was part of other on-going agreement-making efforts being undertaken at that time by the Third Air Force Commander, Maj Gen Robert W Bazley, and his planner-negotiator, Col Walbrecht, who served as the US Air Staff's EUCOM and USAFE sub-theatre representative on military matters and basing issues in the UK. As part of the larger 'package' of initiatives under discussion at that time, the SR-71 effort fitted into a set of arrangements being made with British government officials which included the first deployments of cruise missiles to Greenham Common, the future bed-down of TR-1s at Alconbury, an expansion of tanker deployments at Fairford and the preparation of an underground EUCOM command bunker at Daw Hill (High Wycombe Air Station).
8. Once again, the French government refused to allow American aircraft to overfly its territory. It was therefore necessary for the 18 Lakenheath aircraft to fly around Spain to enter the Mediterranean area via the Straits of Gibraltar. The obstructive action of the French added considerable distance to the mission, resulting in additional night air refuellings. It is believed that fatigue and disorientation caused F-111F number 02389 ('Karma 52'), crewed by pilot Capt Fernando Ribas-Dominicci and Weapons Systems Officer Capt Paul Lorence, to crash into the sea, killing both crew members.
9. At a time when several Middle Eastern governments were providing shelter and tacit approval to various terrorist organizations that 'exported' their murderous trade throughout the Western World, *Eldorado Canyon*'s direct and decisive action helped to shatter the image of the so-called 'Lion of Libya', who had dogged US foreign policy.
10. *Eldorado Canyon* post-strike sorties were flown over Libya from RAF Mildenhall on the following dates;

15 April 1986 980
16 April 1986 960
17 April 1986 980

Chapter 8

1. Gen Larry D Welch was a flying training instructor and a fighter pilot for most of his career. He spent his first nine years in Air Training Command and the next sixteen in TAC. In the early 1970s Welch climbed the TAC command ladder as DCO and vice commander of the F-4 Phantom II-equipped 35th TFW at George AFB, California, and earned his first star as commander of the F-15 Eagle-equipped 1st TFW at Langley AFB, Virginia. Thereafter, he rose further as a quiet and perceptive staff officer, although he had little chance of becoming chief with O'Malley clearly in line for the top position. The Air Force had become increasingly TAC-dominated after nuclear scientist Gen Lew Allen turned executive leadership over to Gen Charles Gabriel. For years the air chiefs had come from SAC. TAC's generals took the lead in 1982, and the USAF became a 'fighter-minded' service; hence, no more SAC. The following is a complete list of all 15 air chiefs from 1940 to 1993:

Gen Henry H Arnold 1940–1946
Gen Carl Spaatz 1947–1948
Gen Hoyt S Vandenberg 1948–1953
Gen Nathan F Twining 1953–1957
Gen Thomas D White 1957–1961
Gen Curtis E LeMay 1961–1965
Gen John P McConnell 1965–1969
Gen John D Ryan 1969–1973
Gen George S Brown 1973–1974
Gen David C Jones 1974–1978
Gen Lew Allen 1978–1982
Gen Charles A Gabriel 1982–1986
Gen Larry D Welch 1986–1990
Gen Michael Dugan 1990
Gen Merrill A McPeak 1990–present

Flight Log

During more than twenty years of its existence, the SR-71 detachment at Kadena AB, Okinawa was scheduled to fly in excess of 2,700 operational or Habu missions. Deducting ground and air aborts from this total reveals that the unit completed a staggering 2,410 Habu missions.

Intelligence requirements of the Vietnam war dominated the det's early activities. Flight duration times varied from 2.5 to 5.5 hours, depending upon the number of targets scheduled into the mission; this in turn dictated the aircraft's air refuelling requirements, etc.

It wasn't until 25 July 1970 that the det. broadend its area of interest to include North Korea. Again, flight duration times varied from between two to four hours, the determining of course being the intelligence community's requirements.

PARPRO sorties were also flown from Okinawa off China and the Soviet Union. Round-robin missions from the island lasted about four hours, often though, these collection areas were targeted during aircraft change-arounds, as an SR-71 returned to Beale or conversely was positioned to complete a stint of TDY on the island.

Later still came the eleven-hour return flights to the Gulf.

An analysis of Det 4's flight log clearly demonstrates the reach capability of this remarkable aircraft, together with the willingness of successive US administrations to deploy this high value asset to all hot-spots of the world, in the pursuit of truth. It also depicts in bold relief the ability of both flight and ground support staff to successfully execute the most demanding of missions.

Footnotes to Kadena flight log.

1. First confirmed firing of an SA-2 against an SR-71.
2.3.4 &5. First aircraft changeovers.
6. First and only aircraft recall due to enemy preparedness along the aircraft's intended route.
7. Aircraft stalled post air – refuelling and crashed in Thailand, the crew ejected safely.
8. First SR-71 mission over North Korea (all prior ops sorties from Kadena were flown in support of the Vietnam war)
9. First night operational sortie flown from Kadena, the collection area was Vladivostok.
10. Co-ordinated sorties to lay – down sonic booms over the Hanoi Hilton POW camp. Take off times were:– #979, 14:16 hrs(L), #980, 14:18 hrs (L) and #968, 15:22 hrs (L).
11. Second series of missions to boom the Hanoi Hilton. Take-off times were :– #980, 14:16hrs (L), #978, 14:18 (L) and #968 15:22hrs (L).
12. Close call over Hanoi following generator failure and double flame-out.
13. Aircraft was written-off during recovery back at Kadena. Crew escaped injury.
14. Missions for the remainder of the year flown in support of Linebacker II.
15. First operational mission flown over North Vietnam at night.
16. Mission flown in support of the SS Mayaguez incident.
17. Successful mission flown off the coast of Okinawa to locate a Soviet Intelligence gathering 'Trawler'.
18. On ...September 1976, Viktor Belenko successfully defected to Habodate Air Base, Japan in a Mig – 25P. SR-71 missions from Kadena to points off the coast of Petropavlovsk were typically of about 4 hour duration.
19. Special flight co-ordinated with the US Navy.
20. Special mission.
21. Special flight co-ordinated with the US Navy.
22. 'Brave Shield' mission flown in the region of Kawajelin Island and co-ordinated with missile tests from Vandenberg AFB in order to validate elements of SIOP.
23. Fight off the coast of Petropavlovsk.
24. Aircraft flown to Diego Garcia to 'exercise' facilities should they be required to support future SR-71 operations.
25. Aircraft returned from Diego Garcia.
26. Special flight conducted over North Vietnam, Cambodia and Laos in search of substantive evidence claims of MIA POW camps.
27. Nearing completion of a third pass along the DMZ between North & South Korea, the crew were fired upon by a SA-2.
28. Flight conducted off the eastern coast of China and North Korea; The crew report an unusual massing of shipping.
29. Flight path of the 26 August '81 mission repeated with full support of strike and wild weasel aircraft incase North Korea again elected to launch an SA-2 – wisely, they refrained.
30. The aircraft was airborne at 14:15hrs (L), the collection area being the vicinity of the Kamchatka peninsula. upon return to Kadena the RSO reported increased tracking and ECM activity in the collection area. Later that night an RC-135 ELINT/COMINT gathering aircraft of the 55th SRW also undertook a mission to the same area. Shortly thereafter, Korean Airlines flight KE007, a Boeing 747 – 200B, on a commercial flight from Anchorage, Alaska to Seoul was shot-down having strayed well into Soviet airspace and the highly sensitive area of Kamchatka. The aircraft failed to respond to various warnings and was eventually shot-down by force consisting of three SU-15's and a Mig – 23. All 269 passengers and crew on board the airliner lost their lives.
31. Co-ordinated mission off the coast of Vladivostok between # '964 flying a round – robin and # '973 inbound from Beale.
32. First mission flown from Kadena into the Gulf and back, during the war between Iran and Iraq.
33. Second mission to the Gulf.
34. Third mission to the Gulf.
35. Fourth mission to the Gulf.
36. Aircraft crashed into the sea off Luzon, the Philippines, the crew ejected safely.

Complete SR-71 Missions Record, Det 1

Date	Instal. No.	T.O. Time	Pilot Name	RSO Name	Mission Type	Duration	Remarks
09/03/68	978	10:00	BROWN Buddy	JENSEN Dave	Ferry to OL-8	6.6	
11/03/68	976	10:00	O'MALLEY Jerome/Jerry	PAYNE Edward/Ed.	Ferry to OL-8	6.5	
13/03/68	974	10:00	SPENCER Bob	BRANHAM Keith	Ferry to OL-8	6.3	
18/03/68	978	10:00	BROWN Buddy	JENSEN Dave	CCTM	1.5	
21/03/68	976	12:30	O'MALLEY Jerry	PAYNE Ed.	HABU	5.1	
24/03/68	976	11:00	O'MALLEY Jerry	PAYNE Ed.	RTB FERRY	1.5	
26/03/68	974	11:51	WATKINS Jim	DEMPSTER Dave	CCTM	1.7	
28/03/68	976	11:00	SPENCER Bob	BRANHAM Keith	CCTM	1.7	
01/04/68	978	12:00	BROWN Buddy	JENSEN Dave	CCTM	1.7	
04/04/68	976	12:00	O'MALLEY Jerry	PAYNE Ed.	FCF/E	1.7	
05/04/68	974	14:00	WATKINS Jim	DEMPSTER Dave	CCTM	1.7	
08/04/68	978	12:00	SPENCER Bob	BRANHAM Keith	CCTM	1.6	
10/04/68	978		BROWN Buddy	JENSEN Dave	CCTM		A
10/04/68	976	14:00	O'MALLEY Jerry	PAYNE Ed.	HABU	3.9	
12/04/68	974	12:00	BROWN Buddy	JENSEN Dave	CCTM	1.7	
15/04/68	976	13:22	WATKINS Jim	DEMPSTER Dave	CCTM	2.4	
16/04/68	976	16:00	SPENCER Bob	BRANHAM Keith	FCF/E	1.1	
18/04/68	978	11:00	BROWN Buddy	JENSEN Dave	HABU	2.4	A
19/04/68	974	12:00	WATKINS Jim	DEMPSTER Dave	HABU	5.4	
20/04/68	978	13:00	BROWN Buddy	JENSEN Dave	RTB FERRY	2.3	
22/04/68	974	11:00	SPENCER Bob	BRANHAM Keith	HABU	5.6	
24/04/68	978	10:00	O'MALLEY Jerry	PAYNE Ed.	FCF/E	1.9	A
27/04/68	976	12:20	BROWN Buddy	JENSEN Dave	HABU	3	A
28/04/68	974	14:00	WATKINS Jim	DEMPSTER Dave	HABU	3.8	
28/04/68	978	15:00	O'MALLEY Jerry	PAYNE Ed.	FCF/ELECT	1.6	
29/04/68	976	10:58	BROWN Buddy	JENSEN Dave	RTB FERRY TO OL-8	2.3	
02/05/68	976	12:00	SPENCER Bob	BRANHAM Keith	CCTM	2.6	
04/05/68	974		WATKINS Jim	DEMPSTER Dave	FCF/E	1.6	
05/05/68	978		SPENCER Bob	BRANHAM Keith	HABU	5.4	
08/05/68	976		WATKINS Jim	DEMPSTER Dave	HABU	5.7	
09/05/68	978		DEVALL Larry	SHOEMAKER Clyde	FCF/E	2.3	
11/05/68	976		STORRIE John	MALLOZZIE Cos	FCF/E	1.7	
11/05/68	974		SPENCER Bob	BRANHAM Keith	HABU	4.5	
13/05/68	974		WATKINS Jim	DEMPSTER Dave	HABU	5.6	
16/05/68	976		STORRIE John	MALLOZZIE Cos	HABU	5.2	
17/05/68	978		DEVALL Larry	SHOEMAKER Clyde	HABU	4.3	
19/05/68	976		WALBRECHT Don	LOIGNON Phil	FCF/E	1.7	
19/05/68	978		WATKINS Jim	DEMPSTER Dave	FCF/E	1.9	
22/05/68	974		STORRIE John	MALLOZZIE Cos	HABU	3.1	
24/05/68	976		DEVALL Larry	SHOEMAKER Clyde	HABU	5.5	
25/05/68	978		WALBRECHT Don	LOIGNON Phil	HABU	5.3	
27/05/68	978		WALBRECHT Don	LOIGNON Phil	FCF/E	1.8	
29/05/68	974		WATKINS Jim	DEMPSTER Dave	CCTM	2.5	
03/06/68	976		STORRIE John	MALLOZZIE Cos	HABU	1.3	A
03/06/68	978		DEVALL Larry	SHOEMAKER Clyde	HABU	4.3	
05/06/68	974		BEVACQUA Tony	CREWS Mac	CCTM	2.3	
07/06/68	978		WALBRECHT Don	LOIGNON Phil	CCTM	2.3	
11/06/68	976		STORRIE John	MALLOZZIE Cos	CCTM	2.7	
14/06/68	974		DEVALL Larry	SHOEMAKER Clyde	CCTM	1.7	
15/06/68	978		BEVACQUA Tony	MALLOZZIE Cos	CCTM	1.8	
17/06/68	976		WALBRECHT Don	LOIGNON Phil	CCTM		A
18/06/68	974		WALBRECHT Don	LOIGNON Phil	HABU	4.1	
19/06/68	976		STORRIE John	MALLOZZIE Cos	CCTM	1.9	
23/06/68	978		BEVACQUA Tony	CREWS Mac	HABU	5.4	
25/06/68	974		STORRIE John	MALLOZZIE Cos	HABU	4.3	
26/06/68	976		DEVALL Larry	SHOEMAKER Clyde	CCTM	0.8	A
29/06/68	974		COLLINS Pete	SHOEMAKER Clyde	CCTM	2.3	A
30/06/68	978		WALBRECHT Don	LOIGNON Phil	HABU	5.2	
03/07/68	974		COLLINS Pete	SEAGROVES Connie	CCTM		A
04/07/68	976		BEVACQUA Tony	CREWS Mac	HABU	6	
05/07/68	974		COLLINS Pete	SEAGROVES Connie	CCTM	1.6	A
07/07/68	978		STORRIE John	MALLOZZIE Cos	CCTM	2.7	
08/07/68	976	11:00	WALBRECHT Don	LOIGNON Phil	CCTM	1.5	
10/07/68	978	11:00	BEVACQUA Tony	CREWS Mac	CCTM	1.7	A
12/07/68	976	14:00	STORRIE John	MALLOZZIE Cos	HABU	3.9	
14/07/68	978	10:00	COLLINS Pete	SEAGROVES Connie	CCTM	2.3	
15/07/68	974	10:00	WALBRECHT Don	LOIGNON Phil	CCTM	1.6	
17/07/68	976	10:15	STORRIE John	MALLOZZIE Cos	CCTM	2.6	
18/07/68	976	14:00	COLLINS Pete	SEAGROVES Connie	HABU	5.3	
19/07/68	974	12:00	BEVACQUA Tony	CREWS Mac	CCTM	1.8	
20/07/68	978	15:00	HALLORAN Pat	JARVIS Mort	CCTM	2.1	
23/07/68	978	13:45	WALBRECHT Don	LOIGNON Phil	HABU	5.1	
24/07/68	976	14:00	COLLINS Pete	SEAGROVES Connie	FCF/PHASE	2.3	
26/07/68	974	09:01	HALLORAN Pat	JARVIS Mort	HABU	2.1	A
26/07/68	976	10:08	BEVACQUA Tony	CREWS Mac	HABU	6	1
28/07/68	974	09:10	HALLORAN Pat	JARVIS Mort	HABU	5.3	
01/08/68	978	10:15	WALBRECHT Don	LOIGNON Phil	CCTM	2.5	
02/08/68	974	10:30	COLLINS Pete	SEAGROVES Connie	CCTM	1.6	
04/08/68	974	10:00	ST MARTIN Roy	BREADEN Cecil	FCF	1.7	
05/08/68	976	13:25	BEVACQUA Tony	CREWS Mac	CCTM	2.3	
07/08/68	978	10:45	HALLORAN Pat	JARVIS Mort	CCTM	2.3	
09/08/68	974	10:45	COLLINS Pete	SEAGROVES Connie	CCTM	2.3	
11/08/68	978	10:05	ST MARTIN Roy	BREADEN Cecil	CCTM	0.5	
12/08/68	974	08:50	BEVACQUA Tony	CREWS Mac	HABU	5.5	
14/08/68	976	10:50	HALLORAN Pat	JARVIS Mort	CCTM	2.4	
16/08/68	976	10:25	COLLINS Pete	SEAGROVES Connie	FCF	2.1	
17/08/68	974	14:58	HALLORAN Pat	JARVIS Mort	HABU	0.6	A
17/08/68	978	14:00	COLLINS Pete	SEAGROVES Connie	HABU	1.9	A
18/08/68	978	13:35	COLLINS Pete	SEAGROVES Connie	HABU	4	
18/08/68	974	14:35	HALLORAN Pat	JARVIS Mort	HABU	4.1	
19/08/68	976	11:05	BULL George	Mc NEER Red	CCTM	2.4	
21/08/68	978	08:50	ST MARTIN Roy	BREADEN Cecil	HABU	5.4	
23/08/68	978	11:55	COLLINS Pete	SEAGROVES Connie	CCTM	2.3	
29/08/68	974	10:06	COLLINS Pete	SEAGROVES Connie	HABU	1.7	A
01/09/68	976	12:55	HALLORAN Pat	JARVIS Mort	CCTM	1.3	
02/09/68	974	11:35	BULL George	Mc NEER Red	CCTM	1.3	
06/09/68	978	12:00	ST MARTIN Roy	BREADEN Cecil	CCTM	1.1	
06/09/68	974	13:00	HALLORAN Pat	JARVIS Mort	CCTM	1	
08/09/68	974	09:05	BULL George	Mc NEER Red	HABU	4.3	
09/09/68	978	12:05	COLLINS Pete	SEAGROVES Connie	CCTM	0.9	
10/09/68	976	09:50	HALLORAN Pat	JARVIS Mort	CCTM	2.3	
12/09/68	980	08:00	SHELTON Dale	BOGGESS Larry	FERRY TO OL-8	6.3	2
13/09/68	976	06:00	COLLINS Pete	SEAGROVES Connie	FERRY TO SC-5		2
14/09/68	980	11:55	SHELTON Dale	BOGGESS Larry	CCTM K3	2.5	
15/09/68	970	02:00	HICHEW Al	SCHMITTOU Tom	FERRY TO OL-8	6.3	3
16/09/68	974	06:00	HALLORAN Pat	JARVIS Mort	FERRY TO SC-5		3
17/09/68	980	10:00	ST MARTIN Roy	BREADEN Cecil	HABU	3.9	
17/09/68	970	11:16	BULL George	Mc NEER Red	CCTM K3	2.4	
18/09/68	962	02:00	CAMPBELL Bill	PENNINGTON Al	FERRY TO OL-8	5.9	4
18/09/68	980	13:00	BULL George	Mc NEER Red	HABU	4	
19/09/68	978	06:00	HICHEW Al	SCHMITTOU Tom	FERRY TO SC-5		5
19/09/68	962	13:05	CAMPBELL Bill	PENNINGTON Al	CCTM K3	2.3	
20/09/68	980	09:05	SHELTON Dale	BOGGESS Larry	CCTM K3	2.2	
25/09/68	970	09:25	SHELTON Dale	BOGGESS Larry	HABU	5.7	
26/09/68	980		ST MARTIN Roy	BREADEN Cecil	CCTM		A
30/09/68	962	12:00	CAMPBELL Bill	PENNINGTON Al	HABU	5.8	
01/10/68	970	10:55	ST MARTIN Roy	BREADEN Cecil	HABU	6.1	
02/10/68	980	10:55	BULL George	Mc NEER Red	CCTM K3	0.4	A
03/10/68	962	11:20	BULL George	Mc NEER Red	HABU	5.7	
04/10/68	970	09:15	SHELTON Dale	BOGGESS Larry	HABU	1	R,6
05/10/68	980	10:15	Mc CALLUM Brian	LOCKE Bobby	CCTM K3	0.6	A
07/10/68	980	10:40	CAMPBELL Bill	PENNINGTON Al	CCTM K3	2.4	
10/10/68	970	09:30	BULL George	Mc NEER Red	CCTM K3	2.2	
12/10/68	980	11:55	SHELTON Dale	BOGGESS Larry	CCTM K3	2.4	
13/10/68	970	11:40	SHELTON Dale	BOGGESS Larry	HABU	4.1	
16/10/68	980	10:55	CAMPBELL Bill	PENNINGTON Al	HABU	4.6	A
17/10/68	962	12:00	Mc CALLUM Brian	LOCKE Bobby	HABU	4.6	A
18/10/68	980	14:32	CAMPBELL Bill	PENNINGTON Al	RTB FERRY	2.3	
20/10/68	970	12:00	BULL George	Mc NEER Red	HABU	5.7	
23/10/68	980	11:31	SHELTON Dale	BOGGESS Larry	CCTM K3	1.1	A
25/10/68	980	09:30	CAMPBELL Bill	PENNINGTON Al	CCTM K3	2.3	A
26/10/68	962	10:30	DAUBS Larry	ROETCISOENDER Bob	CCTM K3	2.4	
26/10/68	980	11:40	Mc CALLUM Brian	LOCKE Bobby	CCTM K3	2.4	
27/10/68	970		SHELTON Dale	BOGGESS Larry	CCTM K3		A
29/10/68	980	10:30	SHELTON Dale	BOGGESS Larry	CCTM K3	2.4	
30/10/68	970	11:30	CAMPBALL Bill	PENNINGTON Al	CCTM K3	2.4	
03/11/68	970	11:45	CAMPBALL Bill	PENNINGTON Al	HABU	5.7	
04/11/68	962	10:00	CAMPBELL Bobby	KRAUS Jon	CCTM K3	2.6	
04/11/68	980	12:00	Mc CALLUM Brian	LOCKE Bobby	CCTM K4	1	
05/11/68	962	10:00	DAUBS Larry	ROETCISOENDER Bob	CCTM K3	2.7	
10/11/68	970	11:30	DAUBS Larry	ROETCISOENDER Bob	CCTM K4	1.1	
10/11/68	980	10:10	Mc CALLUM Brian	LOCKE Bobby	HABU	5.9	
11/11/68	962	10:00	CAMPBELL Bill	PENNINGTON Al	CCTM K3	2.2	
12/11/68	962	10:00	CAMPBELL Bobby	KRAUS Jon	CCTM K3	2.5	
13/11/68	980	10:00	Mc CALLUM Brian	LOCKE Bobby	CCTM K3	2.4	
15/11/68	962	10:30	DAUBS Larry	ROETCISOENDER Bob	CCTM K3	2.5	
16/11/68	970	10:30	CAMPBELL Bobby	KRAUS Jon	CCTM K3	2.5	
18/11/68	962	09:50	BOWLES Ben	FAGG Jimmy	CCTM K3	2.3	
21/11/68	980		DAUBS Larry	ROETCISOENDER Bob	HABU		A
21/11/68	970	11:10	CAMPBELL Bobby	KRAUS Jon	HABU	5.9	
22/11/68	962	09:30	DAUBS Larry	ROETCISOENDER Bob	HABU	5.9	
23/11/68	980	10:35	BOWELS Ben	FAGG Jimmy	HABU	5.8	
24/11/68	962	11:45	Mc CALLUM Brian	LOCKE Bobby	CCTM K4	1.1	
26/11/68	962	14:15	CAMPBELL Bobby	KRAUS Jon	CCTM K3	2.5	
27/11/68	970	11:55	Mc CALLUM Brian	LOCKE Bobby	CCTM K3	2.4	
29/11/68	962	09:30	DAUBS Larry	ROETCISOENDER Bob	CCTM K3	0.9	A
30/11/68	962	09:30	BOWELS Ben	FAGG Jimmy	CCTM K3	2.5	
02/12/68	980	12:45	DAUBS Larry	ROETCISOENDER Bob	HABU	4.1	
03/12/68	962	10:00	CAMPBELL Bobby	KRAUS Jon	HABU	1.5	A
03/12/68	970	11:00	BOWELS Ben	FAGG Jimmy	HABU	5.7	
04/12/68	980	10:45	SPENCER Bob	BRANHAM Keith	CCTM K4	0.9	
04/12/68	962	09:30	CAMPBELL Bobby	KRAUS Jon	HABU	5.4	
05/12/68	980	12:00	SPENCER Bob	BRANHAM Keith	HABU	1.7	A
07/12/68	980	10:00	DAUBS Larry	ROETCISOENDER Bob	CCTM K3	2.5	
08/12/68	970	09:30	BOWELS Ben	FAGG Jimmy	CCTM K3	2.5	
09/12/68	962	11:00	SPENCER Bob	BRANHAM Keith	HABU	5.3	
10/12/68	970	11:50	DAUBS Larry	ROETCISOENDER Bob	HABU	5.4	
10/12/68	980	13:06	CAMPBELL Bobby	KRAUS Jon	CCTM K3	1	
11/12/68	962	10:55	CAMPBELL Bobby	KRAUS Jon	HABU	5.5	
13/12/68	970	11:45	BOWELS Ben	FAGG Jimmy	HABU	5.7	
13/12/68	980	13:00	SPENCER Bob	BRANHAM Keith	CCTM K4	1	
17/12/68	970	10:00	LAWSON Willie	MARTINEZ Gil	CCTM K3	2.7	
19/12/68	980	12:15	CAMPBELL Bobby	KRAUS Jon	CCTM K4	1.2	
20/12/68	962	10:30	SPENCER Bob	BRANHAM Keith	HABU	5.7	
21/12/68	980	10:00	BOWELS Ben	FAGG Jimmy	CCTM K3	2.3	
24/12/68	970	10:00	LAWSON Willie	MARTINEZ Gil	HABU	6.2	
27/12/68	970	10:00	POWELL Robert (Bob)	KENDRICK Bill	CCTM K3	2.5	
29/12/68	980	11:50	POWELL Bob	KENDRICK Bill	HABU	5.8	
30/12/68	962	11:35	BOWELS Ben	FAGG Jimmy	HABU	6.1	
30/12/68	970	12:50	SPENCER Bob	BRANHAM Keith	CCTM K4	1	

Date	Instal. No.	T.O. Time	Pilot Name	RSO Name	Mission Type	Duration	Remarks
03/01/69	980	10:00	LAWSON Willie	MARTINEZ Gil	CCTM K3	2.5	
06/01/69	962	10:00	POWELL Bob	KENDRICK Bill	CCTM K3	2.3	
10/01/69	970	12:25	SPENCER Bob	BRANHAM Keith	HABU	4.2	
10/01/69	980	13:41	LAWSON Willie	MARTINEZ Gil	CCTM K4	1.3	
13/01/69	980	10:00	O'MALLEY Jerry	PAYNE Ed	CCTM K3	2.3	
14/01/69	962	10:15	POWELL Bob	KENDRICK Bill	CCTM K3	2.2	
16/01/69	980	10:30	SPENCER Bob	BRANHAM Keith	CCTM K3	2.4	
18/01/69	970		LAWSON Willie	MARTINEZ Gil	CCTM		A
20/01/69	980	12:00	POWELL Bob	KENDRICK Bill	CCTM K4	1.1	
20/01/69	962	11:55	LAWSON Willie	MARTINEZ Gil	CCTM K3	2.3	
21/01/69	970	09:55	O'MALLEY Jerry	PAYNE Ed	CCTM K3	2.3	
23/01/69	962	12:30	LAWSON Willie	MARTINEZ Gil	CCTM K3	2.5	
25/01/69	980	13:56	POWELL Bob	KENDRICK Bill	CCTM K4	1.2	
26/01/69	970	09:30	KARDONG Abe	KOGLER Jim	CCTM K3	2.5	
27/01/69	980	12:00	LAWSON Willie	MARTINEZ Gil	HABU	5.9	
28/01/69	970	12:00	POWELL Bob	KENDRICK Bill	HABU	6	
29/01/69	962	12:00	O'MALLEY Jerry	PAYNE Ed	HABU	5.3	
31/01/69	980	10:00	KARDONG Abe	KOGLER Jim	FCF/S/K3	0.7	A
02/02/69	980	10:00	KARDONG Abe	KOGLER Jim	CCTM K3	2.4	
03/02/69	980	10:15	LAWSON Willie	MARTINEZ Gil	CCTM K3	2.5	
06/02/69	962	12:10	POWELL Bob	KENDRICK Bill	CCTM K3	2.3	
07/02/69	980	10:15	O'MALLEY Jerry	PAYNE Ed	FCF/E/K3	2.6	
08/02/69	970		FRUEHAUF Dave	PAYNE Al	CCTM K3		A
11/02/69	980	10:55	FRUEHAUF Dave	PAYNE Al	FCF/E/K3	2.1	
12/02/69	970	10:15	KARDONG Abe	KENDRICK Bill	CCTM K5	2	
13/02/69	980	11:45	POWELL Bob	KOGLER Jim	FCF/E/K3	2.3	
14/02/69	962	13:00	KARDONG Abe	KOGLER Jim	HABU	4.1	
15/02/69	970	12:55	POWELL Bob	KENDRICK Bill	HABU	4.2	
17/02/69	980	09:50	O'MALLEY Jerry	PAYNE Ed	FCF/E/K3	2.5	
19/02/69	970		FRUEHAUF Dave	PAYNE Al	CCTM		
20/02/69	980	13:06	KARDONG Abe	PAYNE Al	CCTM K3	1.7	A
21/02/69	962	10:30	KARDONG Abe	KOGLER Jim	FCF/PHASE/K3	2.4	
23/02/69	980	09:50	DEVALL Larry	SHOEMAKER Clyde	CCTM K5	2.4	
25/02/69	970	10:30	O'MALLEY Jerry	PAYNE Ed	CCTM K3	0.4	A
26/02/69	962	10:30	FRUEHAUF Dave	PAYNE Al	CCTM K5	2.6	
28/02/69	970	09:30	KARDONG Abe	KOGLER Jim	CCTM K3	2.5	
03/03/69	962	09:30	DEVALL Larry	SHOEMAKER Clyde	CCTM K5	2.3	
04/03/69	980	09:30	O'MALLEY Jerry	PAYNE Ed	FCF/PHASE/K3	2.5	
06/03/69	980		FRUEHAUF Dave	PAYNE Al	CCTM K3		A
07/03/69	980	10:15	FRUEHAUF Dave	PAYNE Al	CCTM K3	2.5	
09/03/69	962	11:30	FRUEHAUF Dave	PAYNE Al	HABU	6.1	
10/03/69	980	11:55	DEVALL Larry	SHOEMAKER Clyde	HABU	5.3	
11/03/69	970	11:00	BROWN Buddy	JARVIS Mort	FCS/PHASE/K4	1.2	
12/03/69	962	11:00	KARDONG Abe	KOGLER Jim	HABU	5.2	
13/03/69	962	11:35	KARDONG Abe	KOGLER Jim	RTB FERRY	0.7	
14/03/69	980	13:00	BROWN Buddy	JARVIS Mort	CCTM K3	2.5	
18/03/69	962	13:00	DEVALL Larry	SHOEMAKER Clyde	CCTM K4	1.2	
18/03/69	970	12:20	FRUEHAUF Dave	PAYNE Al	CCTM K3	2.4	
19/03/69	980	13:10	BROWN Buddy	JARVIS Mort	HABU	4.2	
20/03/69	962	12:30	FRUEHAUF Dave	PAYNE Al	HABU	6	
21/03/69	970		DEVALL Larry	SHOEMAKER Clyde	HABU		A
21/03/69	980	13:50	KARDONG Abe	KOGLER Jim	HABU	4	
25/03/69	962	11:40	HUDSON Jim	BUDZINSKI Norb	CCTM K3	2.4	
26/03/69	970	13:00	DEVALL Larry	SHOEMAKER Clyde	HABU	5.3	
27/03/69	980	13:05	BROWN Buddy	JARVIS Mort	HABU	4.2	
27/03/69	962	14:40	HUDSON Jim	BUDZINSKI Norb	CCTM K3	2.3	
01/04/69	980	11:00	FRUEHAUF Dave	PAYNE Al	CCTM K3	2.4	
05/04/69	970	12:30	DEVALL Larry	SHOEMAKER Clyde	CCTM K3	1.3	A
06/04/69	962	11:30	HUDSON Jim	BUDZINSKI Norb	HABU	5.5	
07/04/69	980	10:00	DEVALL Larry	SHOEMAKER Clyde	HABU	4.1	
08/04/69	962	13:20	BROWN Buddy	JARVIS Mort	HABU	4.2	
08/04/69	980	14:35	ESTES Tom	VICK Dewain	CCTM K3	2.4	
09/04/69	970	11:40	ESTES Tom	VICK Dewain	HABU	0.9	A
09/04/69	962	12:40	HUDSON Jim	BUDZINSKI Norb	HABU	5.6	
11/04/69	970	11:00	DEVALL Larry	SHOEMAKER Clyde	CCTM K3	1.6	A
13/04/69	962	10:00	BROWN Buddy	JARVIS Mort	CCTM K3	2.3	
15/04/69	962	13:30	ESTES Tom	VICK Dewain	HABU	4.2	
16/04/69	970		HUDSON Jim	BUDZINSKI Norb	CCTM		A
17/04/69	970	11:00	HUDSON Jim	BUDZINSKI Norb	CCTM K4	1	
18/04/69	971	03:00	BULL George	Mc NEER Red	FERRY TO OL-8	5.6	
19/04/69	980	06:00	DEVALL Larry	SHOEMAKER Clyde	FERRY TO SC-5		
21/04/69	979	03:27	STORRIE John	MALLOZZIE Cos	FERRY TO OL-8	5.3	
22/04/69	970	06:00	BULL George	Mc NEER Red	FERRY TO SC-5		
23/04/69	971	14:00	BROWN Buddy	JARVIS Mort	HABU	4.1	
24/04/69	975	03:53	WATKINS Jim	LOIGNON Phil	FERRY TO OL-8	5.5	
25/04/69	962	06:00	BROWN Buddy	JARVIS Mort	FERRY TO SC-5		
26/04/69	979	10:00	ESTES Tom	VICK Dewain	CCTM K3	1.8	
29/04/69	975	10:30	HUDSON Jim	BUDZINSKI Norb	CCTM K3	2.3	
01/05/69	979	12:30	HUDSON Jim	BUDZINSKI Norb	HABU	0.7	A
01/05/69	971	13:30	ESTES Tom	VICK Dewain	HABU	5.2	
02/05/69	975	10:15	STORRIE John	MALLOZZIE Cos	CCTM K3	2.4	
04/05/69	979	10:30	WATKINS Jim	LOIGNON Phil	CCTM K3	2.4	
09/05/69	975	11:06	HUDSON Jim	BUDZINSKI Norb	CCTM K5	2.3	
10/05/69	979	13:35	HUDSON Jim	BUDZINSKI Norb	HABU	0.4	A
10/05/69	971	14:35	STORRIE John	MALLOZZIE Cos	HABU	0.7	A
11/05/69	975	13:00	HUDSON Jim	BUDZINSKI Norb	HABU	5.4	
12/05/69	971	13:35	STORRIE John	MALLOZZIE Cos	HABU	4.2	
14/05/69	971	13:35	WATKINS Jim	LOIGNON Phil	HABU	3.4	A
14/05/69	975	14:50	ESTES Tom	VICK Dewain	CCTM K3	2.4	
16/05/69	971	14:00	WATKINS Jim	LOIGNON Phil	RTB FERRY	2.5	
16/05/69	979	13:50	ESTES Tom	VICK Dewain	HABU	1.2	A
16/05/69	975	14:50	STORRIE John	MALLOZZIE Cos	HABU	2.2	A
18/05/69	971	13:50	ESTES Tom	VICK Dewain	HABU	4	
18/05/69	975	15:05	STORRIE John	MALLOZZIE Cos	CCTM K3	2.3	
20/05/69	979	11:15	WATKINS Jim	LOIGNON Phil	CCTM K5	0.7	A
20/05/69	975	10:00	SHELTON Jim	SCHMITTOU Tom	CCTM K3	2.5	
21/05/69	979	13:50	WATKINS Jim	LOIGNON Phil	CCTM K5	2.4	
22/05/69	975	12:40	STORRIE John	MALLOZZIE Cos	HABU	5.1	
23/05/69	971	10:15	ESTES Tom	VICK Dewain	CCTM K3	2.4	
24/05/69	979	10:00	WATKINS Jim	LOIGNON Phil	HABU	3.5	
25/05/69	975	13:00	SHELTON Jim	SCHMITTOU Tom	HABU	5.4	
26/05/69	979	10:00	STORRIE John	MALLOZZIE Cos	CCTM K3	2.3	
28/05/69	979	09:05	ESTES Tom	VICK Dewain	HABU	5.9	
29/05/69	971	09:30	STORRIE John	MALLOZZIE Cos	HABU	4.1	
31/05/69	975	10:00	ST MARTIN Roy	BREADEN Cecil	CCTM K3	2.5	
03/06/69	975	11:00	WATKINS Jim	LOIGNON Phil	CCTM K3	2.4	
04/06/69	979	10:15	SHELTON Jim	SCHMITTOU Tom	CCTM K5	2.3	
05/06/69	971		SHELTON Jim	SCHMITTOU Tom	HABU		A
05/06/69	975	13:55	WATKINS Jim	LOIGNON Phil	HABU	5.6	A
07/06/69	975	09:05	WATKINS Jim	LOIGNON Phil	RTB FERRY	1.2	
10/06/69	975	10:15	STORRIE John	MALLOZZIE Cos	CCTM K3	2.3	
11/06/69	971	10:48	ST MARTIN Roy	BREADEN Cecil	CCTM K3	2.3	
13/06/69	979	12:50	SHELTON Jim	SCHMITTOU Tom	HABU	1.3	A
13/06/69	975	13:50	ST MARTIN Roy	BREADEN Cecil	HABU	5.4	
17/06/69	975	10:01	BULL George	Mc NEER Red	CCTM K3	1.3	A
18/06/69	975	14:15	STORRIE John	MALLOZZIE Cos	CCTM K3	2.3	
22/06/69	979	09:46	ST MARTIN Roy	BREADEN Cecil	CCTM K3	2.3	
23/06/69	971	10:15	SHELTON Jim	SCHMITTOU Tom	CCTM K3	2.3	
25/06/69	975		BULL George	Mc NEER Red	CCTM K3		A
29/06/69	975		STORRIE John	MALLOZZIE Cos	HABU		A
29/06/69	971	09:45	BULL George	Mc NEER Red	CCTM K3	1.6	A
30/06/69	979	09:15	ST MARTIN Roy	BREADEN Cecil	HABU	3.5	
01/07/69	975	10:00	STORRIE John	MALLOZZIE Cos	CCTM K4	0.4	A
02/07/69	979	12:30	STORRIE John	MALLOZZIE Cos	HABU	3.8	
04/07/69	975		Mc CALLUM Brian	LOCKE Bobby	CCTM		A
04/07/69	971	10:00	SHELTON Jim	SCHMITTOU Tom	CCTM K3	2.5	
05/07/69	971	14:00	SHELTON Jim	SCHMITTOU Tom	HABU	4.1	
06/07/69	975	10:50	Mc CALLUM Brian	LOCKE Bobby	CCTM K3	2.6	
08/07/69	979	10:10	ST MARTIN Roy	BREADEN Cecil	HABU	3.5	
08/07/69	975	09:10	BULL George	Mc NEER Red	HABU	1.5	A
10/07/69	971		Mc CALLUM Brian	LOCKE Bobby	CCTM		A
11/07/69	971	10:40	Mc CALLUM Brian	LOCKE Bobby	CCTM K3	2.4	
12/07/69	975	10:15	CAMPBELL Bobby	KRAUS Jon	CCTM K3	2.5	
15/07/69	971	10:10	BULL George	Mc NEER Red	CCTM K3	2.4	
16/07/69	979	10:20	ST MARTIN Roy	BREADEN Cecil	CCTM K3	2.3	
18/07/69	975	09:30	Mc CALLUM Brian	LOCKE Bobby	CCTM K3	2.5	
21/07/69	971	10:47	CAMPBELL Bobby	KRAUS Jon	CCTM K4	1.1	
22/07/69	979	10:30	ST MARTIN Roy	BREADEN Cecil	CCTM K3	1.6	A
23/07/69	975	13:30	BULL George	Mc NEER Red	HABU	5.8	
25/07/69	979	09:45	Mc CALLUM Brian	LOCKE Bobby	CCTM K3	2.4	
26/07/69	971	09:45	DAUBS Larry	ROETCISOENDER Bob	FCF K3	2.4	A
28/07/69	979	12:45	Mc CALLUM Brian	LOCKE Bobby	HABU	5.7	
30/07/69	971	10:17	CAMPBELL Bobby	KRAUS Jon	FCF K3	2.3	A
01/08/69	975	10:00	BULL George	Mc NEER Red	FCF K4	1.2	A
03/08/69	971		CAMPBELL Bobby	KRAUS Jon	FCF K4		A
03/08/69	975	14:50	DAUBS Larry	ROETCISOENDER Bob	HABU	4.2	
04/08/69	979	09:45	CAMPBELL Bobby	KRAUS Jon	HABU	4.8	
09/08/69	971	10:00	Mc CALLUM Brian	LOCKE Bobby	FCF K3	1.9	A
11/08/69	979	10:00	DAUBS Larry	ROETCISOENDER Bob	FCF K3	2.4	
13/08/69	979		BOWLES Ben	FAGG Jimmy	FCF K3		A
14/08/69	975	10:00	BOWLES Ben	FAGG Jimmy	CCTM K3	2.6	
15/08/69	979	12:05	CAMPBELL Bobby	KRAUS Jon	FCF K4	1.2	A
16/08/69	971	12:00	Mc CALLUM Brian	LOCKE Bobby	HABU	3.6	
18/08/69	979		DAUBS Larry	ROETCISOENDER Bob	FCF		A
22/08/69	979	12:00	DAUBS Larry	ROETCISOENDER Bob	FCF K3	2.3	A
23/08/69	975	12:35	DAUBS Larry	ROETCISOENDER Bob	HABU	5.4	
24/08/69	971	13:35	BOWLES Ben	FAGG Jimmy	HABU	4	
25/08/69	975	11:00	CAMPBELL Bobby	KRAUS Jon	FCF K3	2.4	A
27/08/69	971	10:00	POWELL Bob	COLEMAN Gary	FCF K3	2.4	A
31/08/69	979		CAMPBELL Bobby	KRAUS Jon	HABU		A
31/08/69	975	14:30	POWELL Bob	COLEMAN Gary	HABU	4	
03/09/69	979		DAUBS Larry	ROETCISOENDER Bob	FCF		A
04/09/69	979	10:00	DAUBS Larry	ROETCISOENDER Bob	FCF K3	2.3	
06/09/69	975	14:35	BOWLES Ben	FAGG Jimmy	CCTM K4	1.1	
08/09/69	971	13:20	DAUBS Larry	ROETCISOENDER Bob	HABU	4.1	
09/09/69	979	13:20	BOWLES Ben	FAGG Jimmy	HABU	4.3	
10/09/69	975	13:15	LAWSON Willie	MARTINEZ Gil	HABU	2.1	A
10/09/69	971	14:20	POWELL Bob	COLEMAN Gary	HABU	4.1	
12/09/69	971		BOWLES Ben	FAGG Jimmy	FCF		A
15/09/69	979	12:30	LAWSON Willie	MARTINEZ Gil	HABU	5.4	
15/09/69	971	13:30	BOWLES Ben	FAGG Jimmy	K7	2.5	
16/09/69	975	11:20	DAUBS Larry	ROETCISOENDER Bob	HABU	5.7	
18/09/69	975	10:00	POWELL Bob	COLEMAN Gary	FCF K3	2.2	A
19/09/69	971	10:00	BOWLES Ben	FAGG Jimmy	HABU	1.4	A
19/09/69	979	11:00	POWELL Bob	COLEMAN Gary	HABU	3.7	
21/09/69	974	03:00	BEVACQUA Tony	KOGLER Jim	FERRY TO OL-8	2.9	A
24/09/69	969	09:00	SHELTON Jim	SCHMITTOU Tom	FERRY TO OL-8	5.4	
25/09/69	979	06:00	BOWELS Ben	FAGG Jimmy	FERRY OUT		
27/09/69	973	02:00	FRUEHAUF Dave	PAYNE Al	FERRY TO OL-8	5.2	
28/09/69	971	06:00	SHELTON Jim	SCHMITTOU Tom	FERRY TO SC-5	2.7	A
29/09/69	971	13:00	SHELTON Jim	SCHMITTOU Tom	FCF K3	2.2	A
29/09/69	969	11:40	LAWSON Willie	MARTINEZ Gil	HABU	5.3	
30/09/69	972	09:00	SPENCER Bob	SHEFFIELD Butch	FERRY TO OL-8	5.3	
01/10/69	971	06:00	SHELTON Jim	SCHMITTOU Tom	FERRY OUT		
03/10/69	974	02:17	BEVACQUA Tony	KOGLER Jim	FERRY TO OL-8	2.9	
03/10/69	973	12:30	POWELL Bob	COLEMAN Gary	HABU	4.5	
04/10/69	973	09:45	FRUEHAUF Dave	PAYNE Al	HABU	1.6	A
04/10/69	972	10:45	SPENCER Bob	SHEFFIELD Butch	HABU	6	
08/10/69	969	10:00	LAWSON Willie	MARTINEZ Gil	K3	2.5	
08/10/69	973	11:01	POWELL Bob	COLEMAN Gary	K7	2.4	
09/10/69	973	10:00	FRUEHAUF Dave	PAYNE Al	HABU	3.8	
10/10/69	969	10:00	SPENCER Bob	SHEFFIELD Butch	K3	1.6	A
12/10/69	972		LAWSON Willie	MARTINEZ Gil	HABU		A
12/10/69	973	11:50	POWELL Bob	COLEMAN Gary	HABU	5.6	
13/10/69	969	10:15	LAWSON Willie	MARTINEZ Gil	K7	2.4	
17/10/69	972	10:20	LAWSON Willie	MARTINEZ Gil	HABU	3.7	

Date	Instal. No.	T.O. Time	Pilot Name	RSO Name	Mission Type	Duration	Remarks
20/10/69	972		FRUEHAUF Dave	PAYNE Al	K3		A
20/10/69	969	11:00	FRUEHAUF Dave	PAYNE Al	K7	2.5	
22/10/69	975	06:00	DAUBS Larry	ROETCISOENDER Bob	FERRY OUT		
22/10/69	972	10:00	DEVALL Larry	SHOEMAKER Clyde	K3	2.5	
22/10/69	973	11:00	SPENCER Bob	SHEFFIELD Butch	K7	2.5	
24/10/69	969	10:15	LAWSON Willie	MARTINEZ Gil	K7	2.5	
27/10/69	972	10:00	FRUEHAUF Dave	PAYNE Al	K3	2.4	
29/10/69	969	09:50	LAWSON Willie	MARTINEZ Gil	K3	2.4	
31/10/69	973	09:30	DEVALL Larry	SHOEMAKER Clyde	K3	2.3	
31/10/69	972	10:30	SPENCER Bob	SHEFFIELD Butch	K3	2.3	
03/11/69	972	10:00	HUDSON Jim	BUDZINSKI Norb	K3	2.2	
06/11/69	973	12:20	SPENCER Bob	SHEFFIELD Butch	HABU	4.1	
07/11/69	974	10:05	FRUEHAUF Dave	PAYNE Al	K7	2.4	
09/11/69	973	12:00	DEVALL Larry	SHOEMAKER Clyde	HABU	4.2	
10/11/69	974	09:55	HUDSON Jim	BUDZINSKI Norb	K3	2.4	
11/11/69	969	12:00	FRUEHAUF Dave	PAYNE Al	HABU	4.2	
13/11/69	973	09:45	SPENCER Bob	SHEFFIELD Butch	K3	2.4	
16/11/69	972	10:00	ESTES Tom	VICK Dewain	K3	2.3	
22/11/69	974	11:00	SPENCER Bob	SHEFFIELD Butch	HABU	3.4	A
22/11/69	972	13:30	DEVALL Larry	SHOEMAKER Clyde	K3	2.3	
23/11/69	974	16:03	SPENCER Bob	SHEFFIELD Butch	RTB FERRY	1.5	
24/11/69	969		HUDSON Jim	BUDZINSKI Norb	K3		A
26/11/69	973	11:00	HUDSON Jim	BUDZINSKI Norb	HABU	4	A
27/11/69	969	11:15	ESTES Tom	VICK Dewain	K3	2.3	
27/11/69	972	10:00	DEVALL Larry	SHOEMAKER Clyde	HABU	5.2	
28/11/69	969	11:00	ESTES Tom	VICK Dewain	HABU	6	
01/12/69	974	10:50	BROWN Buddy	JARVIS Mort	K7	2.4	
03/12/69	972	10:00	HUDSON Jim	BUDZINSKI Norb	K3	2.3	
03/12/69	974	11:00	DEVALL Larry	SHOEMAKER Clyde	K3	2.5	
05/12/69	969	10:30	HUDSON Jim	BUDZINSKI Norb	HABU	5.6	
06/12/69	974	10:19	ESTES Tom	VICK Dewain	K7	2.4	
08/12/69	974	10:15	BROWN Buddy	JARVIS Mort	K3	2.2	
09/12/69	972	10:15	DEVALL Larry	SHOEMAKER Clyde	K3	2.1	
11/12/69	973	10:10	HUDSON Jim	BUDZINSKI Norb	K3	2.3	
12/12/69	974	10:20	BROWN Buddy	JARVIS Mort	HABU	5.2	
15/12/69	969	10:15	ESTES Tom	VICK Dewain	K3	2.4	
16/12/69	973	10:00	SHELTON Jim	SCHMITTOU Tom	K3	1.4	A
17/12/69	974	10:15	HUDSON Jim	BUDZINSKI Norb	K3	2.3	
19/12/69	973	10:00	SHELTON Jim	SCHMITTOU Tom	K3	2.4	
20/12/69	972	10:15	BROWN Buddy	JARVIS Mort	K3	2.3	
22/12/69	972	10:15	HUDSON Jim	BUDZINSKI Norb	K7	2.3	
23/12/69	974	12:10	ESTES Tom	VICK Dewain	HABU	2.1	A
23/12/69	973	13:16	SHELTON Jim	SCHMITTOU Tom	HABU	4.1	
26/12/69	972	10:43	ST MARTIN Roy	BREADEN Cecil	K7	2.3	
29/12/69	972	10:30	ESTES Tom	VICK Dewain	HABU	5.8	
30/12/69	969	09:55	BROWN Buddy	JARVIS Mort	K8	2	
01/01/70	972	12:20	BROWN Buddy	JARVIS Mort	HABU	4	
02/01/70	973	12:05	SHELTON Jim	SCHMITTOU Tom	K3	2.2	
06/01/70	972	10:15	ESTES Tom	VICK Dewain	K3	2.4	
06/01/70	969	11:15	ST MARTIN Roy	BREADEN Cecil	K3	2.3	
07/01/70	972	10:15	BROWN Buddy	JARVIS Mort	K3	2.3	
09/01/70	972	11:10	SHELTON Jim	SCHMITTOU Tom*	HABU	5.3	
12/01/70	974	10:15	BULL George	KRAUS Jon	K3	2.3	
13/01/70	969	10:15	ST MARTIN Roy	BREADEN Cecil	K7	2.3	
15/01/70	972	11:53	ST MARTIN Roy	BREADEN Cecil	HABU	3.9	
16/01/70	974	14:20	SHELTON Jim	SCHMITTOU Tom	K3	2.3	
19/01/70	972	10:15	BROWN Buddy	JARVIS Mort	K11	2.1	
20/01/70	969	10:15	BULL George	KRAUS Jon	K11	2.2	
21/01/70	974	10:15	ST MARTIN Roy	BREADEN Cecil	K3	2.3	
24/01/70	974	12:58	STORRIE John	MALLOZZIE Cos	K3	2.3	
28/01/70	972	10:15	SHELTON Jim	SCHMITTOU Tom	K3	2.4	
28/01/70	969	11:15	BULL George	KRAUS Jon	K7	2.3	
29/01/70	973	12:55	ST MARTIN Roy	BREADEN Cecil	K3	1.3	A
29/01/70	974	11:35	BULL George	KRAUS Jon	HABU	5.5	
01/02/70	973	12:45	STORRIE John	MALLOZZIE Cos	K3	2.3	
03/02/70	969	11:30	SHELTON Jim	SCHMITTOU Tom	HABU	1.4	A
03/02/70	974	12:30	ST MARTIN Roy	BREADEN Cecil	HABU	5.5	
04/02/70	973	10:15	BULL George	KRAUS Jon	K7	2.4	
07/02/70	969	10:15	POWELL Bob	COLEMAN Gary	K3	2.4	
08/02/70	969	11:50	STORRIE John	MALLOZZIE Cos	HABU	5.6	
09/02/70	974	10:15	ST MARTIN Roy	BREADEN Cecil	K10	2.2	
11/02/70	972	10:15	BULL George	KRAUS Jon	K11	2.4	
13/02/70	972	10:15	POWELL Bob	COLEMAN Gary	K11	2.3	
14/02/70	973	11:02	STORRIE John	MALLOZZIE Cos	K11	2.3	
16/02/70	973	10:00	ST MARTIN Roy	BREADEN Cecil	HABU	2.6	A
18/02/70	974	11:55	BULL George	KRAUS Jon	K3	2.3	
19/02/70	972	10:14	POWELL Bob	COLEMAN Gary	K7	2.4	
20/02/70	973	12:00	STORRIE John	MALLOZZIE Cos	K3	2.2	
21/02/70	972	12:00	BEVACQUA Tony	KOGLER Jim	K3	2.3	
23/02/70	974	09:45	BULL George	KRAUS Jon	K7	2.4	
25/02/70	974	12:00	BULL George	KRAUS Jon	HABU	5.6	
28/02/70	972	10:10	POWELL Bob	COLEMAN Gary	K11	2.2	
02/03/70	973	10:15	STORRIE John	MALLOZZIE Cos	K11	2.5	
04/03/70	973	11:50	BEVACQUA Tony	KOGLER Jim	K7	2.4	
06/03/70	973	10:24	POWELL Bob	COLEMAN Gary	K7	2.3	
08/03/70	974	10:15	Mc CALLUM Brian	LOCKE Bobby	K11	2.4	
09/03/70	969	10:15	STORRIE John	MALLOZZIE Cos	K11	2.4	
11/03/70	973	11:00	BEVACQUA Tony	KOGLER Jim	K3	1.4	A
12/03/70	969	10:14	POWELL Bob	COLEMAN Gary	K7	2.5	
14/03/70	972	11:00	BEVACQUA Tony	KOGLER Jim	K11	2.4	
14/03/70	973	10:00	Mc CALLUM Brian	LOCKE Bobby	K3	2.3	
19/03/70	969	09:26	POWELL Bob	COLEMAN Gary	HABU	5.3	
20/03/70	972	13:25	BEVACQUA Tony	KOGLER Jim	K11	2.6	
22/03/70	972	10:15	BOWELS Ben	FAGG Jimmy	K3	2.5	
22/03/70	969	11:15	Mc CALLUM Brian	LOCKE Bobby	K11	2.5	
24/03/70	972	10:15	POWELL Bob	COLEMAN Gary	K11	2.3	
25/03/70	973	10:15	BEVACQUA Tony	KOGLER Jim	K11	1.5	A
30/03/70	973	11:50	Mc CALLUM Brian	LOCKE Bobby	K7	2.5	

Date	Instal. No.	T.O. Time	Pilot Name	RSO Name	Mission Type	Duration	Remarks
31/03/70	972	10:15	BOWELS Ben	FAGG Jimmy	K3	2.4	
03/04/70	972	11:20	BEVACQUA Tony	KOGLER Jim	HABU	5.7	
04/04/70	969	10:15	LAWSON Willie	MARTINEZ Gil	K11	2.4	
06/04/70	972	10:15	Mc CALLUM Brian	LOCKE Bobby	K11	2.4	
09/04/70	969	12:00	Mc CALLUM Brian	LOCKE Bobby	HABU	5.5	
10/04/70	973	12:00	BOWELS Ben	FAGG Jimmy	HABU	5.3	
12/04/70	972		BEVACQUA Tony	KOGLER Jim	K7		A
12/04/70	973	11:30	LAWSON Willie	MARTINEZ Gil	K11	2.2	
13/04/70	972	10:15	BEVACQUA Tony	KOGLER Jim	K7	2.4	
17/04/70	972	10:00	Mc CALLUM Brian	LOCKE Bobby	K7	2.4	
19/04/70	972	10:15	FRUEHAUF Dave	PAYNE Al	K3	2.2	
19/04/70	973	11:15	BOWLES Ben	FAGG Jimmy	K11	2.4	
21/04/70	974	12:15	LAWSON Willie	MARTINEZ Gil	K11	2.5	
22/04/70	969		Mc CALLUM Brian	LOCKE Bobby	K7		A
23/04/70	974	12:45	BOWLES Ben	FAGG Jimmy	K3	2.4	
23/04/70	969	11:15	FRUEHAUF Dave	PAYNE Al	K7	2.3	
25/04/70	969	10:15	DEVALL Larry	SHOEMAKER Clyde	K11	2.4	
26/04/70	974	10:22	BOWLES Ben	FAGG Jimmy	HABU	1.8	A
26/04/70	973	11:43	LAWSON Willie	MARTINEZ Gil	HABU	5.4	A
28/04/70	974		FRUEHAUF Dave	PAYNE Al	K3		A
29/04/70	974	10:15	FRUEHAUF Dave	PAYNE Al	K3	2.5	
30/04/70	973	13:10	DEVALL Larry	SHOEMAKER Clyde	K7	2.4	
01/05/70	969	12:10	LAWSON Willie	MARTINEZ Gil	HABU	5.5	
02/05/70	973	12:05	BOWLES Ben	FAGG Jimmy	HABU	5.5	
04/05/70	969	10:15	FRUEHAUF Dave	PAYNE Al	K3	2.4	
05/05/70	973	10:15	DEVALL Larry	SHOEMAKER Clyde	K3	2.3	
06/05/70	974	08:30	FRUEHAUF Dave	PAYNE Al	HABU	4.2	
07/05/70	969	10:56	BOWLES Ben	FAGG Jimmy	HABU	3.6	
08/05/70	972	10:15	LAWSON Willie	MARTINEZ Gil	K3	2.3	
09/05/70	973	12:10	DEVALL Larry	SHOEMAKER Clyde	HABU	5.4	
10/05/70	969	10:30	LAWSON Willie	MARTINEZ Gil	HABU		
CRASH,7							
17/05/70	974	10:15	SPENCER Bob	SHEFFIELD Butch	K7	2.5	
18/05/70	973	10:45	FRUEHAUF Dave	PAYNE Al	K3	2.3	
19/05/70	972	10:15	BOWLES Ben	FAGG Jimmy	K3	2.3	
21/05/70	973	10:15	DEVALL Larry	SHOEMAKER Clyde	K3	2.3	
23/05/70	974	10:15	HUDSON Jim	BUDZINSKI Norb	K3	2.3	
25/05/70	972		SPENCER Bob	SHEFFIELD Butch	K7		A
29/05/70	972	10:15	SPENCER Bob	SHEFFIELD Butch	K7	2.2	
02/06/70	972	12:11	HUDSON Jim	BUDZINSKI Norb	K7	1.1	A
02/06/70	974	13:30	FRUEHAUF Dave	PAYNE Al	HABU	4.1	
03/06/70	972	12:10	DEVALL Larry	SHOEMAKER Clyde	K3	2.3	
05/06/70	974	10:50	FRUEHAUF Dave	PAYNE Al	HABU	3.6	
06/06/70	973	14:50	SPENCER Bob	SHEFFIELD Butch	K3	2.3	
06/06/70	972	13:30	DEVALL Larry	SHOEMAKER Clyde	HABU	4	
09/06/70	974	10:35	HUDSON Jim	BUDZINSKI Norb	K7	2.4	
10/06/70	972		FRUEHAUF Dave	PAYNE Al	K7		A
11/06/70	972	10:00	FRUEHAUF Dave	PAYNE Al	K4	1.1	
15/06/70	973	12:00	SPENCER Bob	SHEFFIELD Butch	HABU	4.1	
17/06/70	973	12:15	HUDSON Jim	BUDZINSKI Norb	HABU	5.8	
17/06/70	972	13:35	ESTES Tom	VICK Dewain	K7	2.4	
26/06/70	974	11:00	SPENCER Bob	SHEFFIELD Butch	HABU	5	
12/07/70	972	11:04	ESTES Tom	VICK Dewain	K4	0.9	A
12/07/70	973	11:15	HUDSON Jim	BUDZINSKI Norb	K4	1.3	
14/07/70	973		SPENCER Bob	SHEFFIELD Butch	K4		A
14/07/70	974	10:10	STORRIE John	MALLOZZIE Cos	K4	1.2	
14/07/70	973	13:30	SPENCER Bob	SHEFFIELD Butch	K4	1.2	
15/07/70	972	11:24	ESTES Tom	VICK Dewain	K4	1.3	
15/07/70	973	12:21	HUDSON Jim	BUDZINSKI Norb	K4	1.3	
17/07/70	973	10:30	STORRIE John	MALLOZZIE Cos	K4	1.2	
18/07/70	972	10:05	SHELTON Jim	SCHMITTOU Tom	K4	1.3	
20/07/70	972	16:01	HUDSON Jim	BUDZINSKI Norb	K4	1.1	
21/07/70	974	10:00	STORRIE John	MALLOZZIE Cos	K4	1	
22/07/70	973	10:00	ESTES Tom	VICK Dewain	HABU	2	A
22/07/70	972	11:39	SHELTON Jim	SCHMITTOU Tom	K4	1.1	
22/07/70	974	11:00	HUDSON Jim	BUDZINSKI Norb	HABU	1.6	A
25/07/70	974		STORRIE John	MALLOZZIE Cos	HABU		A
25/07/70	972	10:00	STORRIE John	MALLOZZIE Cos	HABU	2.1	8
26/07/70	973	10:04	COBB Darryl	GANTT Myron	K4	1.2	
27/07/70	972	10:15	SHELTON Jim	SCHMITTOU Tom	K7	2.4	
28/07/70	974	09:10	ESTES Tom	VICK Dewain	HABU	0.7	A
28/07/70	972	10:10	STORRIE John	MALLOZZIE Cos	HABU	1.8	A
31/07/70	973	13:15	COBB Darryl	GANTT Myron	K3	2.3	
31/07/70	974	11:50	ESTES Tom	VICK Dewain	HABU	5.8	
05/08/70	972	09:45	STORRIE John	MALLOZZIE Cos	K4	0.9	
05/08/70	974	10:00	SHELTON Jim	SCHMITTOU Tom	K4	1.1	
06/08/70	973	09:50	COBB Darryl	GANTT Myron	K4	1.1	
08/08/70	974	10:15	BULL George	KRAUS Jon	K3	2.3	
10/08/70	972	10:30	STORRIE John	MALLOZZIE Cos	K7	1.5	A
11/08/70	974		SHELTON Jim	SCHMITTOU Tom	K3		A
15/08/70	972	11:15	SHELTON Jim	SCHMITTOU Tom	K3	2.3	
16/08/70	974	09:45	COBB Darryl	GANTT Myron	K3	2.3	
17/08/70	973	12:00	BULL George	KRAUS Jon	K7	2.3	
19/08/70	972	09:45	STORRIE John	MALLOZZIE Cos	K3	2.4	
21/08/70	973	09:45	COBB Darryl	GANTT Myron	K9	2.4	
21/08/70	974	11:15	BULL George	KRAUS Jon	K7	2.3	
22/08/70	972	10:00	ST MARTIN Roy	BREADEN CECIL	K7	2.6	
24/08/70	974	09:45	COBB Darryl	GANTT Myron	K9	2.4	
25/08/70	974		BULL George	KRAUS Jon	K3		A
25/08/70	973	10:00	STORRIE John	MALLOZZIE Cos	K3	2.2	
26/08/70	974	09:45	BULL George	KRAUS Jon	K3	2.1	
30/08/70	973	13:10	STORRIE John	MALLOZZIE Cos	HABU	4.1	
01/09/70	974	09:45	ST MARTIN Roy	BREADEN Cecil	K9	2.3	
01/09/70	972	11:42	COBB Darryl	GANTT Myron	K9	2.3	
02/09/70	973	12:50	COBB Darryl	GANTT Myron	HABU	4.1	
08/09/70	972	11:00	BROWN Buddy	JARVIS Mort	HABU	3.7	
09/09/70	972	11:45	BULL George	KRAUS Jon	HABU	2.9	A
11/09/70	974	10:00	ST MARTIN Roy	BREADEN Cecil	K9	2.2	A

Date	Instal. No.	T.O. Time	Pilot Name	RSO Name	Mission	Duration	Remarks
11/09/70	972	10:32	BULL George	KRAUS Jon	RTB FERRY	0.3	A
13/09/70	972	15:35	BULL George	KRAUS Jon	RTB FERRY	2.6	
14/09/70	974	13:05	COBB Darryl	GANTT Myron	K9	2.4	
17/09/70	973	11:30	ST MARTIN Roy	BREADEN Cecil	HABU	5.5	
18/09/70	974	10:00	BULL George	KRAUS Jon	HABU	3.5	
19/09/70	973	09:10	BULL George	KRAUS Jon	HABU	5	
20/09/70	972	10:00	BROWN Buddy	JARVIS Mort	K7	2.3	
21/09/70	972	09:30	POWELL Bob	COLEMAN Gary	HABU	3.5	
23/09/70	973	11:30	BROWN Buddy	JARVIS Mort	HABU	4.2	
24/09/70	974	10:15	ST MARTIN Roy	BREADEN Cecil	K9	2.4	
26/09/70	972	12:00	ST MARTIN Roy	BREADEN Cecil	HABU	3.5	
28/09/70	972	10:23	BULL George	KRAUS Jon	K7	2.4	
30/09/70	974	10:15	POWELL Bob	COLEMAN Gary	K9	2.2	
01/10/70	972	10:00	BROWN Buddy	JARVIS Mort	K9	2.3	
03/10/70	974	10:00	ST MARTIN Roy	BREADEN Cecil	HABU	5.5	
06/10/70	974	13:00	BEVACQUA Tony	KOGLER Jim	HABU	3.6	
07/10/70	973	11:00	BROWN Buddy	JARVIS Mort	HABU	5.4	
08/10/70	972	09:45	POWELL Bob	COLEMAN Gary	K9	2.2	
10/10/70	972	10:00	ST MARTIN Roy	BREADEN Cecil	K9	2.4	
12/10/70	972		BEVACQUA Tony	KOGLER Jim	K9		A
13/10/70	972	09:45	BEVACQUA Tony	KOGLER Jim	K9	2.4	
13/10/70	974	11:00	BROWN Buddy	JARVIS Mort	K9	2.3	
15/10/70	974	07:00	POWELL Bob	COLEMAN Gary	HABU	3.7	
19/10/70	973	10:15	FRUEHAUF Dave	PAYNE Al	K3	2.5	
22/10/70	972		BEVACQUA Tony	KOGLER Jim	K9		A
23/10/70	973	12:15	POWELL Bob	COLEMAN Gary	HABU	4.1	
24/10/70	972		FRUEHAUF Dave	PAYNE Al	HABU B/U		A
24/10/70	974	11:15	BEVACQUA Tony	KOGLER Jim	HABU	5.5	
26/10/70	972	10:00	BROWN Buddy	JARVIS Mort	K7	2.4	
27/10/70	973	10:45	FRUEHAUF Dave	PAYNE Al	HABU	3.6	
28/10/70	974	10:15	POWELL Bob	COLEMAN Gary	K7	2.3	
31/10/70	974	11:30	BOWLES Ben	FAGG Jimmy	HABU	2	A
31/10/70	973	12:30	BEVACQUA Tony	KOGLER Jim	HABU	3.6	
02/11/70	972	11:15	POWELL Bob	COLEMAN Gary	HABU	5.1	
02/11/70	974	12:30	BEVACQUA Tony	KOGLER Jim	K9	2.3	
04/11/70	974	10:50	BEVACQUA Tony	KOGLER Jim	HABU	5.6	
05/11/70	974	11:00	FRUEHAUF Dave	PAYNE Al	HABU	3.7	
06/11/70	973	12:10	BOWLES Ben	FAGG Jimmy	K9	2.3	
06/11/70	974	10:50	FRUEHAUF Dave	PAYNE Al	HABU	5.6	
09/11/70	972	10:00	POWELL Bob	COLEMAN Gary	K7	2.4	
11/11/70	973	09:45	BEVACQUA Tony	KOGLER Jim	HABU	3.5	
11/11/70	974	12:30	FRUEHAUF Dave	PAYNE Al	K7	2.5	
13/11/70	972	10:50	BOWLES Ben	FAGG Jimmy	HABU	5.4	
16/11/70	973	10:15	PUGH Tom	RICE Ron	K3	2.5	
18/11/70	974	11:30	PUGH Tom	RICE Ron	HABU	4.2	A
20/11/70	972	08:25	BEVACQUA Tony	KOGLER Jim	HABU	5.5	
20/11/70	974	13:35	PUGH Tom	RICE Ron	RTB FERRY	2.4	
21/11/70	973	09:20	FRUEHAUF Dave	PAYNE Al	HABU	5.5	
24/11/70	974	10:15	BOWLES Ben	FAGG Jimmy	K7	2.4	
25/11/70	972	08:17	BOWLES Ben	FAGG Jimmy	HABU	3.6	
27/11/70	972	11:45	PUGH Tom	RICE Ron	K3	2.5	
28/11/70	973	10:00	FRUEHAUF Dave	PAYNE Al	K7	2.4	
29/11/70	974	12:29	PUGH Tom	RICE Ron	HABU	3.5	A
30/11/70	972	10:15	BUSH Denny	LOIGNON Phil	K7	2.4	
03/12/70	974	10:00	BOWLES Ben	FAGG Jimmy	K3	0.7	A
04/12/70	974	13:15	BUSH Denny	FAGG Jimmy	K4	0.9	
04/12/70	972	12:59	PUGH Tom	RICE Ron	HABU	1.7	A
04/12/70	973	11:53	FRUEHAUF Dave	PAYNE Al	HABU	1.8	A
07/12/70	973	10:30	BOWLES Ben	FAGG Jimmy	HABU	3.5	
11/12/70	972	10:00	PUGH Tom	RICE Ron	K7	2.4	
13/12/70	974	10:10	HUDSON Jim	BUDZINSKI Norb	K3	2.4	
14/12/70	972	10:00	BUSH Denny	LOIGNON Phil	K3	2.3	
16/12/70	973	10:00	BOWLES Ben	FAGG Jimmy	K3	2.5	
18/12/70	975	10:00	SPENCER Bob	SHEFFIELD Butch	FERRY TO OL-8	5.7	
18/12/70	972	12:00	PUGH Tom	RICE Ron	HABU	6.1	
19/12/70	974	12:05	BUSH Denny	LOIGNON Phil	HABU	6	A
21/12/70	973	11:00	HUDSON Jim	BUDZINSKI Norb	HABU	3.6	
23/12/70	974	10:00	SPENCER Bob	SHEFFIELD Butch	K3	2.3	
24/12/70	973	10:00	PUGH Tom	RICE Ron	HABU	3.6	
25/12/70	972	08:35	PUGH Tom	RICE Ron	HABU	1.5	A
25/12/70	974	10:18	PUGH Tom	RICE Ron	HABU	2.2	A
29/12/70	973	11:00	HUDSON Jim	BUDZINSKI Norb	HABU	1.8	A
29/12/70	972	12:00	SPENCER Bob	SHEFFIELD Butch	HABU	2.1	A
02/01/71	974	10:00	SPENCER Bob	SHEFFIELD Butch	K3	2.2	
02/01/71	972	11:15	BUSH Denny	LOIGNON Phil	K9	2.3	
03/01/71	973	12:20	HUDSON Jim	BUDZINSKI Norb	K3	2.3	
03/01/71	972	11:00	PUGH Tom	RICE Ron	HABU	5.8	
04/01/71	975	09:00	BUSH Denny	LOIGNON Phil	K7	2.4	
04/01/71	974	08:09	SPENCER Bob	SHEFFIELD Butch	HABU	3.9	
07/01/71	974	17:30	HUDSON Jim	BUDZINSKI Norb	K12	0.7	
08/01/71	975	12:15	BUSH Denny	LOIGNON Phil	HABU	5.3	
09/01/71	973	08:55	HUDSON Jim	BUDZINSKI Norb	HABU	3.9	A
09/01/71	975	14:14	SPENCER Bob	SHEFFIELD Butch	HABU	1.5	A
10/01/71	972	13:30	ESTES Tom	VICK Dewain	K3	2.6	
11/01/71	975	13:00	BUSH Denny	LOIGNON Phil	K3	1.8	A
13/01/71	975	10:30	HUDSON Jim	BUDZINSKI Norb	HABU	3.7	
13/01/71	973	13:40	ESTES Tom	VICK Dewain	K9	1	A
15/01/71	975	11:30	SPENCER Bob	SHEFFIELD Butch	HABU	3.7	
15/01/71	973	14:30	ESTES Tom	VICK Dewain	K9	2.2	
16/01/71	972	11:00	HUDSON Jim	BUDZINSKI Norb	HABU	3	A
18/01/71	972	12:00	HUDSON Jim	BUDZINSKI Norb	RTB FERRY	2.5	
19/01/71	973	16:30	SPENCER Bob	SHEFFIELD Butch	K3	2.3	
22/01/71	975	11:40	ESTES Tom	VICK Dewain	HABU	3.8	
24/01/71	972	11:00	SHELTON Jim	SCHMITTOU Tom	K3	2.4	
25/01/71	973	10:00	HUDSON Jim	BUDZINSKI Norb	K3	2.4	
28/01/71	973	11:50	SPENCER Bob	SHEFFIELD Butch	HABU	3.8	
31/01/71	975	16:15	ESTES Tom	VICK Dewain	NK3	2.3	
01/02/71	974	10:00	SHELTON Jim	SCHMITTOU Tom	K9	2.3	
02/02/71	975	10:00	HUDSON Jim	BUDZINSKI Norb	HABU	3.7	
06/02/71	973	12:30	SPENCER Bob	SHEFFIELD Butch	HABU	1.5	A
06/02/71	972	13:30	ESTES Tom	VICK Dewain	HABU	1.8	A
07/02/71	973	11:15	SHELTON Jim	SCHMITTOU Tom	K7	0.8	A
07/02/71	974	10:00	COBB Darryl	GANTT Myron	K3	2.3	
08/02/71	972	13:00	ESTES Tom	VICK Dewain	RTB FERRY OL-RK	1.5	
10/02/71	974	11:00	SPENCER Bob	SHEFFIELD Butch	HABU	1.6	A
10/02/71	973	12:15	COBB Darryl	GANTT Myron	HABU	3.7	
10/02/71	972	14:30	SHELTON Jim	SCHMITTOU Tom	K7	2.4	
12/02/71	973	11:01	COBB Darryl	GANTT Myron	K7	2.3	
13/02/71	972	10:00	ESTES Tom	VICK Dewain	K9	2.5	
13/02/71	974	11:04	SPENCER Bob	SHEFFIELD Butch	RTB FERRY (OL-RK)	1.6	
15/02/71	973	12:50	SHELTON Jim	SCHMITTOU Tom	HABU	4	
15/02/71	974	14:30	COBB Darryl	GANTT Myron	K9	2.4	
18/02/71	973	17:45	SHELTON Jim	SCHMITTOU Tom	NK4	1.2	
19/02/71	974	10:00	ESTES Tom	VICK Dewain	K7	2.4	
20/02/71	973	12:20	ESTES Tom	VICK Dewain	HABU	5.4	
21/02/71	975	10:15	STORRIE John	MALLOZZIE Cos	FCF K9	2.4	
23/02/71	974	12:30	SHELTON Jim	SCHMITTOU Tom	HABU	5.3	
23/02/71	972	14:35	COBB Darryl	GANTT Myron	K7	1.4	A
25/02/71	973	10:45	COBB Darryl	GANTT Myron	HABU	3.8	
25/02/71	972	12:45	ESTES Tom	VICK Dewain	K7	2.4	
26/02/71	974	13:37	STORRIE John	MALLOZZIE Cos	HABU	1.8	A
26/02/71	973	14:40	SHELTON Jim	SCHMITTOU Tom	HABU	3.7	
27/02/71	975	11:00	COBB Darryl	GANTT Myron	K9	2.3	
01/03/71	974	12:00	ESTES Tom	VICK Dewain	HABU	5.2	
01/03/71	972	18:00	STORRIE John	MALLOZZIE Cos	NK12	0.8	
02/03/71	975	10:00	SHELTON Jim	SCHMITTOU Tom	K7	2.4	
04/03/71	972	11:51	STORRIE John	MALLOZZIE Cos	HABU	3.7	
05/03/71	975	12:15	COBB Darryl	GANTT Myron	K9	2.5	
07/03/71	974	11:30	SHELTON Jim	SCHMITTOU Tom	HABU	3.9	
07/03/71	975	14:00	BULL George	KRAUS Jon	K3	2.4	
09/03/71	972		COBB Darryl	GANTT Myron	K9		A
10/03/71	972	12:00	COBB Darryl	GANTT Myron	K9	1.7	A
12/03/71	974	11:35	BULL George	KRAUS Jon	HABU	4	
12/03/71	973	13:30	STORRIE John	GANTT Myron	K9	2.3	
14/03/71	975	09:30	SHELTON Jim	SCHMITTOU Tom	HABU	5.1	
15/03/71	973	10:00	COBB Darryl	GANTT Myron	K7	2.4	
16/03/71	974	10:15	BULL George	KRAUS Jon	K9	2.4	
16/03/71	975	11:15	STORRIE John	SCHMITTOU Tom	K9	2.3	
17/03/71	972	11:50	COBB Darryl	GANTT Myron	HABU	7.6	
20/03/71	973	10:00	ST MARTIN Roy	BREADEN Cecil	K9	0.7	A
21/03/71	973	13:20	ST MARTIN Roy	BREADEN Cecil	K9	2.1	
21/03/71	974	12:00	STORRIE John	MALLOZZIE Cos	HABU	3.9	
24/03/71	975	12:30	BULL George	KRAUS Jon	HABU	4.2	
25/03/71	974	10:00	COBB Darryl	GANTT Myron	HABU	3.5	
27/03/71	975	12:00	ST MARTIN Roy	BREADEN Cecil	HABU	1.7	A
27/03/71	974	13:00	COBB Darryl	GANTT Myron	HABU	3.9	A
28/03/71	975	12:20	ST MARTIN Roy	BREADEN Cecil	HABU	5.1	
29/03/71	973	12:10	STORRIE John	MALLOZZIE Cos	HABU	5.4	
30/03/71	974	10:00	BULL George	KRAUS Jon	HABU	3.5	
04/04/71	975	11:30	ST MARTIN Roy	BREADEN Cecil	HABU	1.7	A
04/04/71	974	12:30	STORRIE John	MALLOZZIE Cos	HABU	2.1	A
05/04/71	973	10:00	HERTZOG Randy	CARNOCHAN John	K7	1.6	A
06/04/71	975	13:30	STORRIE John	MALLOZZIE Cos	HABU	3.9	
07/04/71	973	10:15	HERTZOG Randy	CARNOCHAN John	K7	2.1	
09/04/71	972		STORRIE John	MALLOZZIE Cos	K9		A
10/04/71	972	14:40	STORRIE John	MALLOZZIE Cos	K9	2.4	
12/04/71	975	12:00	BULL George	KRAUS Jon	HABU	1.8	A
12/04/71	974	13:03	ST MARTIN Roy	BREADEN Cecil	HABU	2.5	
12/04/71	972	13:49	HERTZOG Randy	CARNOCHAN John	K9	1.8	
13/04/71	975	09:45	STORRIE John	MALLOZZIE Cos	K7	2.4	
15/04/71	975	12:50	BULL George	KRAUS Jon	HABU	3.8	
19/04/71	974	10:15	BROWN Buddy	JARVIS Mort	K9	2.4	
20/04/71	972	10:15	HERTZOG Randy	CARNOCHAN John	K9	2.2	
21/04/71	974	12:00	HERTZOG Randy	CARNOCHAN John	HABU	5.5	
23/04/71	975	11:45	BULL George	KRAUS Jon	HABU	3.5	
24/04/71	974		BROWN Buddy	JARVIS Mort	K3		A
25/04/71	974	10:00	BROWN Buddy	JARVIS Mort	K3	2.2	
28/04/71	972	11:30	ST MARTIN Roy	BREADEN Cecil	K3	2.2	
29/04/71	974	11:30	HERTZOG Randy	CARNOCHAN John	HABU	3.4	
30/04/71	975	09:30	BROWN Buddy	JARVIS Mort	HABU	1.7	A
30/04/71	972	11:36	ST MARTIN Roy	BREADEN Cecil	HABU	3.7	
02/05/71	975	09:30	FRUEHAUF Dave	PAYNE Al	K7	2.5	
03/05/71	973	10:00	BROWN Buddy	JARVIS Mort	K9	2.1	
07/05/71	975	10:00	HERTZOG Randy	CARNOCHAN John	K9	2.4	
08/05/71	972	12:00	ST MARTIN Roy	BREADEN Cecil	HABU	1.6	A
08/05/71	973	13:00	FRUEHAUF Dave	PAYNE Al	HABU	3.5	
09/05/71	973	10:00	ST MARTIN Roy	BREADEN Cecil	HABU	5.8	A
09/05/71	972	11:15	HERTZOG Randy	CARNOCHAN John	K9	2.2	
10/05/71	975	10:00	BROWN Buddy	JARVIS Mort	K9	2.2	
11/05/71	972	13:45	HERTZOG Randy	CARNOCHAN John	HABU	3.9	
12/05/71	975	09:45	ST MARTIN Roy	BREADEN Cecil	K9	1.5	A
14/05/71	973	11:00	FRUEHAUF Dave	PAYNE Al	HABU	2.3	
15/05/71	974	10:00	POWELL Bob	COLEMAN Gary	K9	2.3	
16/05/71	975	10:00	BROWN Buddy	JARVIS Mort	K9	2.1	
17/05/71	972	11:30	HERTZOG Randy	CARNOCHAN John	HABU	3.3	
18/05/71	974	10:00	FRUEHAUF Dave	PAYNE Al	K9	2.4	
20/05/71	973	10:10	POWELL Bob	COLEMAN Gary	HABU	3.5	
23/05/71	974	10:00	BROWN Buddy	JARVIS Mort	K9	2.2	
24/05/71	973	10:00	HERTZOG Randy	CARNOCHAN John	K9	2.3	
25/05/71	974	10:00	FRUEHAUF Dave	PAYNE Al	K9	2.3	
25/05/71	973	10:00	POWELL Bob	COLEMAN Gary	K9	2.2	
27/05/71	972	12:50	BROWN Buddy	JARVIS Mort	HABU	1.6	A
27/05/71	973	13:50	FRUEHAUF Dave	PAYNE Al	HABU	5.6	
28/05/71	975	13:45	POWELL Bob	COLEMAN Gary	K9	2.3	
28/05/71	974	12:30	BROWN Buddy	JARVIS Mort	HABU	5.5	
29/05/71	972	13:00	HERTZOG Randy	CARNOCHAN John	HABU	3.4	

Date	Instal. No.	T.O. Time	Pilot Name	RSO Name	Mission	Duration	Remarks
01/06/71	973	09:45	FRUEHAUF Dave	PAYNE Al	K9	1	A
03/06/71	973	09:45	POWELL Bob	COLEMAN Gary	K9	2.4	
04/06/71	972	09:45	BROWN Buddy	JARVIS Mort	K9	2.3	
06/06/71	975	09:30	FRUEHAUF Dave	PAYNE Al	HABU	3.2	
08/06/71	973	06:00	BROWN Buddy	JARVIS Mort	FERRY OUT		
10/06/71	968	03:00	BEVACQUA Tony	KOGLER Jim	FERRY TO OL-RK	5.3	
11/06/71	972	06:00	HERTZOG Randy	CARNOCHAN John	FERRY OUT		
13/06/71	979	03:00	ESTES Tom	VICK Dewain	FERRY TO OL-RK	5.4	
14/06/71	974	06:00	FRUEHAUF Dave	PAYNE Al	FERRY OUT		
14/06/71	968	07:30	POWELL Bob	COLEMAN Gary	K7	2.4	
16/06/71	978	03:00	BOWLES Ben	FAGG Jimmy	FERRY TO OL-RK	5.3	
16/06/71	968	10:30	POWELL Bob	COLEMAN Gary	HABU	3.9	
17/06/71	975	06:00	ESTES Tom	VICK Dewain	FERRY OUT		
17/06/71	979	10:20	BEVACQUA Tony	KOGLER Jim	HABU	2.3	
18/06/71	978	10:30	BEVACQUA Tony	KOGLER Jim	HABU	4	
19/06/71	980	03:09	PUGH Tom	RICE Ron	FERRY TO OL-RK	5.2	
19/06/71	979	11:00	POWELL Bob	COLEMAN Gary	K9	2.3	
21/06/71	978	10:00	BOWLES Ben	RICE Ron	K2	2.4	
22/06/71	980		PUGH Tom	RICE Ron	K2		A
23/06/71	978		BEVACQUA Tony	KOGLER Jim	HABU-BACKUP		
23/06/71	979	13:51	PUGH Tom	RICE Ron	HABU	3.5	
24/06/71	980	10:00	BEVACQUA Tony	KOGLER Jim	K2	2.2	
26/06/71	979	13:30	BOWLES Ben	FAGG Jimmy	HABU	5.7	
27/06/71	978	13:00	PUGH Tom	RICE Ron	HABU	3.9	
30/06/71	980	13:00	POWELL Bob	COLEMAN Gary	HABU	3.4	
01/07/71	968	10:15	PUGH Tom	RICE Ron	K9	2.3	
03/07/71	968	10:00	BEVACQUA Tony	KOGLER Jim	K9	2.3	
04/07/71	980	11:00	POWELL Bob	COLEMAN Gary	HABU	3.7	A
05/07/71	978	13:00	BEVACQUA Tony	KOGLER Jim	HABU	5.3	
08/07/71	968	10:00	BOWLES Ben	FAGG Jimmy	K9	2.4	
10/07/71	979	10:19	BUSH Denny	LOIGNON Phil	K9	2.3	
11/07/71	978	13:00	BOWLES Ben	FAGG Jimmy	HABU	5.5	
13/07/71	978	12:00	PUGH Tom	RICE Ron	HABU	3.5	
15/07/71	979	10:00	BEVACQUA Tony	KOGLER Jim	K7	2.3	
17/07/71	979	11:30	BUSH Denny	LOIGNON Phil	HABU	1.5	A
17/07/71	978	12:30	BOWLES Ben	FAGG Jimmy	HABU	3.5	
19/07/71	980	10:00	PUGH Tom	RICE Ron	K9	2.3	
21/07/71	968		PUGH Tom	RICE Ron	HABU		A
21/07/71	979	14:30	BUSH Denny	LOIGNON Phil	HABU	5.8	
23/07/71	968	12:00	BOWLES Ben	FAGG Jimmy	HABU	3.4	
24/07/71	979	10:00	SHELTON Jim	SCHMITTOU Tom	K9	1.8	A
27/07/71	979		PUGH Tom	RICE Ron	K9		A
28/07/71	980		BUSH Denny	MARTINEZ Gil	K9		A
28/07/71	979		PUGH Tom	RICE Ron	K9		A
28/07/71	979	13:00	PUGH Tom	RICE Ron	K9	2.3	
29/07/71	978	10:00	BUSH Denny	LOIGNON Phil	K9	1.5	A
30/07/71	979	11:30	BOWLES Ben	FAGG Jimmy	HABU	3.5	
31/07/71	968	13:30	SHELTON Jim	SCHMITTOU Tom	K9	2.3	
01/08/71	980	12:00	PUGH Tom	RICE Ron	K9	2.2	
06/08/71	978		BUSH Denny	LOIGNON Phil	K7		A
07/08/71	979	13:30	BUSH Denny	LOIGNON Phil	HABU	1.5	A
07/08/71	968	14:35	SHELTON Jim	SCHMITTOU Tom	HABU	3.6	
08/08/71	978	10:10	SPENCER Bob	SHEFFIELD Butch	K9	2.2	
08/08/71	979	13:55	BUSH Denny	LOIGNON Phil	RTB FERRY TO OL-KA	1.4	
11/08/71	978	11:16	PUGH Tom	RICE Ron	K9	2.3	
12/08/71	979	10:00	SHELTON Jim	SCHMITTOU Tom	K9	1.5	A
13/08/71	968	13:00	SPENCER Bob	SHEFFIELD Butch	HABU	1.4	A
13/08/71	978	14:00	BUSH Denny	LOIGNON Phil	HABU	3.5	
14/08/71	979	10:00	SPENCER Bob	SHEFFIELD Butch	K9	2.3	
15/08/71	968	12:15	SHELTON Jim	SCHMITTOU Tom	K9	2.2	
18/08/71	978	09:07	PUGH Tom	RICE Ron	K9	1.4	A
19/08/71	968	09:00	BUSH Denny	LOIGNON Phil	K7	2.4	
20/08/71	980	13:15	SPENCER Bob	SHEFFIELD Butch	K7	2.4	
21/08/71	979	09:30	SHELTON Jim	SCHMITTOU Tom	HABU	3.5	
23/08/71	980	10:15	CUNNINGHAM Bob	MORGAN George	K9	2.4	
24/08/71	968	09:00	BUSH Denny	LOIGNON Phil	K7	1.6	A
26/08/71	978	09:45	SPENCER Bob	SHEFFIELD Butch	K9	1.6	A
27/08/71	978	10:00	SHELTON Jim	SCHMITTOU Tom	K7	2.3	
30/08/71	978	12:30	SHELTON Jim	SCHMITTOU Tom	HABU	3.3	A
31/08/71	980	08:50	CUNNINGHAM Bob	MORGAN George	HABU	3.7	
31/08/71	978	14:18	SHELTON Jim	SCHMITTOU Tom	RTB FERRY TO OL-RK	3.9	
01/09/71	979	09:00	SPENCER Bob	SHEFFIELD Butch	K4	1.1	
01/09/71	980	08:30	BUSH Denny	LOIGNON Phil	HABU	1.9	
02/09/71	968	09:45	CUNNINGHAM Bob	MORGAN George	K9	2.5	
03/09/71	979	11:30	SHELTON Jim	SCHMITTOU Tom	HABU	4.1	
04/09/71	978	10:00	HERTZOG Randy	CARNOCHAN John	K7	1.5	A
09/09/71	968	08:24	SPENCER Bob	SHEFFIELD Butch	HABU	2.3	
10/09/71	978	10:15	CUNNINGHAM Bob	MORGAN George	K7	0.5	A
11/09/71	968	11:30	SPENCER Bob	SHEFFIELD Butch	HABU	5.3	
12/09/71	968	11:00	HERTZOG Randy	CARNOCHAN John	HABU	3.5	
13/09/71	978	10:30	HERTZOG Randy	CARNOCHAN John	K9	2.3	
15/09/71	979	10:00	CUNNINGHAM Bob	MORGAN George	HABU	4	
16/09/71	978	10:00	SHELTON Jim	SCHMITTOU Tom	K9	2.1	
17/09/71	968	11:30	HERTZOG Randy	CARNOCHAN John	HABU	5.8	
18/09/71	980	10:38	COBB Darryl	BLACKWELL Reggie	K4	1.1	A
19/09/71	968	13:00	CUNNINGHAM Bob	MORGAN George	HABU	1.7	
20/09/71	980	12:55	COBB Darryl	BLACKWELL Reggie	K9	2.3	
20/09/71	979	11:30	SPENCER Bob	SHEFFIELD Butch	HABU	4.9	
25/09/71	979	12:30	COBB Darryl	BLACKWELL Reggie	HABU	1.5	A
25/09/71	980	13:30	CUNNINGHAM Bob	MORGAN George	HABU	0.8	A
26/09/71	978	13:30	HERTZOG Randy	CARNOCHAN John	K9	1.6	A
27/09/71	979	11:32	COBB Darryl	BLACKWELL Reggie	K9	2.2	
27/09/71	980	18:15	SPENCER Bob	SHEFFIELD Butch	N/HABU	2.6	A,9
28/09/71	978		CUNNINGHAM Bob	MORGAN George	K9		A
28/09/71	980	19:43	SPENCER Bob	SHEFFIELD Butch	N/RTB FERRY	1.4	
28/09/71	979	12:30	HERTZOG Randy	CARNOCHAN John	HABU	1.9	
29/09/71	979	13:30	COBB Darryl	BLACKWELL Reggie	HABU	1.9	A
29/09/71	980	14:35	CUNNINGHAM Bob	MORGAN George	HABU	5.2	
30/09/71	980		COBB Darryl	BLACKWELL Reggie	HABU		A
30/09/71	978	10:05	HERTZOG Randy	CARNOCHAN John	K9	2.5	
03/10/71	978	09:00	ESTES Tom	MORGAN George	K2	3.5	
03/10/71	968	10:00	COBB Darryl	BLACKWELL Reggie	K9	2.3	
04/10/71	980	11:00	HERTZOG Randy	CARNOCHAN John	K7	2.3	
05/10/71	978	12:00	CUNNINGHAM Bob	MORGAN George	HABU	3.4	
07/10/71	980	12:30	CUNNINGHAM Bob	MORGAN George	HABU	5.4	
07/10/71	968	13:55	ESTES Tom	VICK Dewain	K9	2.3	
10/10/71	978	10:00	COBB Darryl	BLACKWELL Reggie	K9	2.4	
12/10/71	968	10:40	CUNNINGHAM Bob	MORGAN George	HABU	3.6	
14/10/71	980	09:55	ESTES Tom	VICK Dewain	HABU	2.2	
14/10/71	978	14:00	HERTZOG Randy	CARNOCHAN John	HABU	3.8	
16/10/71	978	10:00	FRUEHAUF Dave	MARTINEZ Gil	K9	2.3	
16/10/71	979	11:00	COBB Darryl	BLACKWELL Reggie	K9	2.2	
17/10/71	968	11:15	ESTES Tom	VICK Dewain	HABU	1.5	A
17/10/71	980	12:15	HERTZOG Randy	CARNOCHAN John	HABU	1.6	A
18/10/71	979	11:30	COBB Darryl	BLACKWELL Reggie	HABU	1.6	A
18/10/71	980	12:30	ESTES Tom	VICK Dewain	HABU	5.1	
19/10/71	968	12:15	FRUEHAUF Dave	MARTINEZ Gil	HABU	3.6	
20/10/71	979	09:00	HERTZOG Randy	CARNOCHAN John	K9	2.3	
22/10/71	979	12:00	COBB Darryl	BLACKWELL Reggie	HABU	5.1	
24/10/71	978	10:00	ESTES Tom	VICK Dewain	K9	1.8	A
25/10/71	978	12:00	FRUEHAUF Dave	MARTINEZ Gil	K9	1.7	A
27/10/71	980	08:50	HERTZOG Randy	CARNOCHAN John	HABU	2.3	
31/10/71	979	12:00	POWELL Bob	COLEMAN Gary	HABU	1.8	
01/11/71	980	10:00	ESTES Tom	VICK Dewain	K5	0.8	A
01/11/71	978	09:45	COBB Darryl	BLACKWELL Reggie	K9	2.3	
02/11/71	978	11:00	COBB Darryl	BLACKWELL Reggie	HABU	7.2	A
03/11/71	979	11:00	FRUEHAUF Dave	MARTINEZ Gil	HABU	2.2	A
04/11/71	980	09:00	POWELL Bob	COLEMAN Gary	K5	1.6	A
06/11/71	980	10:00	ESTES Tom	VICK Dewain	K5	2.3	
07/11/71	978	13:30	ESTES Tom	VICK Dewain	HABU	3.8	
09/11/71	980	10:10	COBB Darryl	BLACKWELL Reggie	K5	2.4	
10/11/71	979	12:00	FRUEHAUF Dave	MARTINEZ Gil	HABU	1.8	
11/11/71	980	08:10	POWELL Bob	COLEMAN Gary	HABU	2.3	
16/11/71	980	12:31	PUGH Tom	RICE Ron	K7	2.5	
17/11/71	978	11:15	FRUEHAUF Dave	MARTINEZ Gil	HABU	5.6	
18/11/71	980	11:30	ESTES Tom	VICK Dewain	HABU	3.4	
18/11/71	968	12:45	POWELL Bob	COLEMAN Gary	K5	2.4	
21/11/71	979	09:30	PUGH Tom	RICE Ron	K7	2.3	
23/11/71	979	06:24	ESTES Tom	VICK Dewain	HABU	2.3	
27/11/71	980	12:30	FRUEHAUF Dave	MARTINEZ Gil	HABU	1.9	
27/11/71	968	13:45	POWELL Bob	COLEMAN Gary	K5	2.2	
30/11/71	968	10:30	PUGH Tom	RICE Ron	K9	2.3	
02/12/71	968	10:57	BULL George	KRAUS Jon	K5	2.3	
05/12/71	979	11:15	FRUEHAUF Dave	MARTINEZ Gil	HABU	1.9	
05/12/71	980	13:00	PUGH Tom	RICE Ron	K7	2.4	
07/12/71	979	11:15	FRUEHAUF Dave	MARTINEZ Gil	HABU	3.3	
09/12/71	980	11:30	POWELL Bob	COLEMAN Gary	K7	2.4	
10/12/71	979	12:30	PUGH Tom	RICE Ron	HABU	3.8	
10/12/71	968	13:45	BUSH Denny	KOGLER Jim	K5	2.4	
12/12/71	979	11:45	POWELL Bob	COLEMAN Gary	HABU	5.4	
13/12/71	978	10:00	PUGH Tom	RICE Ron	K7	2	
13/12/71	968	13:52	BULL George	KRAUS Jon	HABU	2.4	
15/12/71	968		BUSH Denny	KOGLER Jim	K7		A
16/12/71	968	09:45	BUSH Denny	KOGLER Jim	K7	2.4	
17/12/71	978	11:30	POWELL Bob	COLEMAN Gary	HABU	3.3	A
19/12/71	980	11:00	PUGH Tom	RICE Ron	HABU	5.5	
20/12/71	978	10:00	BUSH Denny	KOGLER Jim	K9	2.3	
20/12/71	968	13:15	BULL George	KRAUS Jon	HABU	2.4	
21/12/71	968	12:15	BULL George	KRAUS Jon	HABU	5.3	
21/12/71	980	13:30	BUSH Denny	KOGLER Jim	K9	2.3	
23/12/71	980	09:45	PUGH Tom	RICE Ron	K9	1.8	A
28/12/71	978		BUSH Denny	KOGLER Jim	HABU		A
28/12/71	980	13:00	BULL George	KRAUS Jon	HABU	1.9	
28/12/71	979	09:00	SHELTON JIm	SCHMITTOU Tom	K3	2.5	
31/12/71	979	10:00	BUSH Denny	KOGLER Jim	K3	2.3	
02/01/72	978	11:00	BUSH Denny	KOGLER Jim	HABU	3.5	
04/01/72	978	10:00	PUGH Tom	RICE Ron	K9	2.3	
06/01/72	980	10:15	SHELTON Jim	SCHMITTOU Tom	K9	2.4	
07/01/72	979	09:45	JUDKINS Ty	SHOEMAKER Clyde	K9	2.6	
08/01/72	980	10:15	BULL George	KRAUS Jon	K3	2.3	
12/01/72	980		JUDKINS Ty	SHOEMAKER Clyde	K5		A
13/01/72	980	12:00	BUSH Denny	KOGLER Jim	HABU	4.2	
14/01/72	978	10:00	SHELTON Jim	SCHMITTOU Tom	K9	2.4	
16/01/72	980	12:30	SHELTON Jim	SCHMITTOU Tom	HABU	1.9	
16/01/72	979	13:45	JUDKINS Ty	SHOEMAKER Clyde	K5	2.3	
17/01/72	968	10:17	BULL George	KRAUS Jon	K9	2.3	
18/01/72	978	10:15	BUSH Denny	KOGLER Jim	K7	2.5	
20/01/72	978	12:47	BUSH Denny	KOGLER Jim	HABU	5.5	
21/01/72	979	12:00	SHELTON Jim	SCHMITTOU Tom	HABU	5.1	
22/01/72	968	12:30	JUDKINS Ty	SHOEMAKER Clyde	HABU	3.6	
22/01/72	978	13:45	BOWLES Ben	FAGG Jimmy	K7	2.6	
24/01/72	968	12:45	SHELTON Jim	SCHMITTOU Tom	K9	2.4	
24/01/72	979	11:40	JUDKINS Ty	SHOEMAKER Clyde	HABU	5.4	
27/01/72	968		SHELTON Jim	SCHMITTOU Tom	K9		A
27/01/72	979	13:45	BOWLES Ben	FAGG Jimmy	HABU	2.3	
28/01/72	968		BUSH Denny	KOGLER Jim	K5		A
28/01/72	978	11:30	SHELTON Jim	SCHMITTOU Tom	HABU	1.9	
30/01/72	968	10:00	BUSH Denny	KOGLER Jim	K9	2.3	
01/02/72	978	13:00	BUSH Denny	KOGLER Jim	HABU	5.5	
02/02/72	968	11:15	SHELTON Jim	SCHMITTOU Tom	K7	2.3	
02/02/72	979	10:00	JUDKINS Ty	SHOEMAKER Clyde	HABU	3.6	
04/02/72	968	12:00	SHELTON Jim	SCHMITTOU Tom	K5	2.4	
05/02/72	979	12:15	BOWLES Ben	FAGG Jimmy	HABU	3.6	
08/02/72	978	10:15	CUNNINGHAM Bob	MORGAN George	K4	1	
10/02/72	979	10:35	JUDKINS Ty	SHOEMAKER Clyde	HABU	3.4	A
11/02/72	968	13:15	CUNNINGHAM Bob	MORGAN George	HABU	1.5	A

Date	Instal. No.	T.O. Time	Pilot Name	RSO Name	Mission	Duration	Remarks
11/02/72	978	14:15	SHELTON Jim	SCHMITTOU Tom	HABU	3.8	
14/02/72	979	11:15	BOWLES Ben	FAGG Jimmy	HABU	1.8	
15/02/72	980	10:15	CUNNINGHAM Bob	MORGAN George	K9	1.7	A
16/02/72	968	11:15	JUDKINS Ty	SHOEMAKER Clyde	K9	2.3	
17/02/72	980	10:00	BOWLES Ben	FAGG Jimmy	K9	2.2	
18/02/72	968	09:45	HERTZOG Randy	FAGG Jimmy	K9	2.2	
19/02/72	979	13:00	BOWLES Ben	FAGG Jimmy	HABU	5.5	
24/02/72	979	10:30	JUDKINS Ty	SHOEMAKER Clyde	K9	2.3	
25/02/72	980	13:00	JUDKINS Ty	SHOEMAKER Clyde	HABU	5.4	
29/02/72	968	13:00	CUNNINGHAM Bob	MORGAN George	K9	2.3	
02/03/72	979	10:15	HERTZOG Randy	CARNOCHAN John	K9	2.3	
03/03/72	980	10:00	SULLIVAN Jim	WIDDIFIELD Noel	K9	2.3	
03/03/72	968	11:15	BOWLES Ben	FAGG Jimmy	K9	2.3	
04/03/72	979	13:00	BOWLES Ben	FAGG Jimmy	HABU	4.1	A
05/03/72	968	10:30	CUNNINGHAM Bob	MORGAN George	HABU	3.5	
05/03/72	979	17:10	BOWLES Ben	FAGG Jimmy	RTB FERRY	3.7	
06/03/72	980	13:15	CUNNINGHAM Bob	MORGAN George	HABU	5.3	
08/03/72	979	10:30	HERTZOG Randy	CARNOCHAN John	K9	2.3	
09/03/72	980	08:00	SULLIVAN Jim	WIDDIFIELD Noel	HABU	2.3	
11/03/72	968	10:00	BOWLES Ben	FAGG Jimmy	K9	2.3	
12/03/72	980	10:30	HERTZOG Randy	CARNOCHAN John	K9	2.2	
15/03/72	979	13:45	HERTZOG Randy	CARNOCHAN John	HABU	4	
16/03/72	980	10:15	CUNNINGHAM Bob	MORGAN George	K9	2.3	
17/03/72	978	11:15	SPENCER Bob	SHEFFIELD Butch	K9	2.4	
17/03/72	968	12:30	SULLIVAN Jim	WIDDIFIELD Noel	HABU	1.5	A
18/03/72	968	09:45	SULLIVAN Jim	WIDDIFIELD Noel	RTB FERRY	1.3	
20/03/72	980	12:30	SULLIVAN Jim	WIDDIFIELD Noel	HABU	4.1	
22/03/72	968	09:15	HERTZOG Randy	CARNOCHAN John	K9	2.2	
22/03/72	979	10:30	CUNNINGHAM Bob	MORGAN George	K9	1.5	A
23/03/72	978	14:00	SPENCER Bob	SHEFFIELD Butch	HABU	4.1	
26/03/72	980	10:00	HERTZOG Randy	CARNOCHAN John	K9	2.3	
26/03/72	978	14:00	CUNNINGHAM Bob	MORGAN George	HABU	1.8	
28/03/72	979	10:25	SULLIVAN Jim	WIDDIFIELD Noel	K9	2.3	
29/03/72	978	07:14	SPENCER Bob	SHEFFIELD Butch	HABU	2.3	
30/03/72	980	10:00	SULLIVAN Jim	WIDDIFIELD Noel	K9	1.5	A
31/03/72	980	15:16	COBB Darryl	BLACKWELL Reggie	K4	1.2	
01/04/72	979	08:30	HERTZOG Randy	CARNOCHAN John	HABU	1.9	
02/04/72	968	10:15	SPENCER Bob	SHEFFIELD Butch	K9	2.4	
03/04/72	979		SULLIVAN Jim	WIDDIFIELD Noel	HABU		A
04/04/72	980	09:15	COBB Darryl	BLACKWELL Reggie	K7	2.4	
04/04/72	968	13:30	SULLIVAN Jim	WIDDIFIELD Noel	HABU	3.6	
05/04/72	980	14:00	HERTZOG Randy	CARNOCHAN John	HABU	3.8	
07/04/72	979	11:05	SULLIVAN Jim	WIDDIFIELD Noel	HABU	4	
08/04/72	980	10:00	COBB Darryl	BLACKWELL Reggie	K4	1.1	
09/04/72	968	11:30	HERTZOG Randy	CARNOCHAN John	HABU	1.9	
11/04/72	968	13:30	SPENCER Bob	SHEFFIELD Butch	HABU	3.7	A
12/04/72	968	12:15	COBB Darryl	BLACKWELL Reggie	HABU	3.9	
13/04/72	978	14:00	SULLIVAN Jim	WIDDIFIELD Noel	HABU	3.9	
14/04/72	978	14:00	FRUEHAUF Dave	MARTINEZ Gil	HABU	4.1	
16/04/72	980	14:55	SPENCER Bob	SHEFFIELD Butch	HABU	3.8	A
17/04/72	978	13:00	COBB Darryl	BLACKWELL Reggie	HABU	4.1	
17/04/72	968	14:00	SULLIVAN Jim	WIDDIFIELD Noel	HABU	4.1	A
18/04/72	980	09:00	SPENCER Bob	SHEFFIELD Butch	K9	2.3	
18/04/72	979	10:00	SULLIVAN Jim	WIDDIFIELD Noel	K9	2	A
19/04/72	968	09:00	FRUEHAUF Dave	MARTINEZ Gil	K9	2.3	
19/04/72	980	10:00	COBB Darryl	BLACKWELL Reggie	K9	2.3	
20/04/72	978		FRUEHAUF Dave	MARTINEZ Gil	HABU		A
20/04/72	980	13:00	SPENCER Bob	SHEFFIELD Butch	HABU	4.2	
23/04/72	979	14:30	FRUEHAUF Dave	MARTINEZ Gil	HABU	4.1	
25/04/72	979	10:00	SULLIVAN Jim	WIDDIFIELD Noel	K9	2.3	
26/04/72	978	10:00	COBB Darryl	BLACKWELL Reggie	HABU	3.9	
27/04/72	980	14:30	SPENCER Bob	SHEFFIELD Butch	HABU	4.1	
29/04/72	979	12:09	PUGH Tom	RICE Ron	HABU	2.4	A
30/04/72	980	11:00	COBB Darryl	BLACKWELL Reggie	K9	2.3	
30/04/72	968	14:54	FRUEHAUF Dave	MARTINEZ Gil	K9	2.3	
01/05/72	979	10:30	PUGH Tom	RICE Ron	RTB FERRY	2.1	
02/05/72	980	14:18	COBB Darryl	BLACKWELL Reggie	HABU	3.8	10
02/05/72	979	14:16	SPENCER Bob	SHEFFIELD Butch	HABU	4.8	A,10
02/05/72	968	15:22	FRUEHAUF Dave	MARTINEZ Gil	HABU	4.1	10
03/05/72	978	13:00	PUGH Tom	RICE Ron	K9	2.3	
04/05/72	980	14:16	SPENCER Bob	SHEFFIELD Butch	HABU	3.9	11
04/05/72	978	14:18	COBB Darryl	BLACKWELL Reggie	HABU	4.1	11
04/05/72	968	15:22	PUGH Tom	RICE Ron	HABU	4.2	11
08/05/72	979		FRUEHAUF Dave	MARTINEZ Gil	HABU		A
08/05/72	978	15:05	COBB Darryl	BLACKWELL Reggie	HABU	4.1	
09/05/72	980	12:00	SPENCER Bob	SHEFFIELD Butch	HABU	4.2	
10/05/72	980	14:03	FRUEHAUF Dave	MARTINEZ Gil	HABU	4.2	
10/05/72	979	15:50	PUGH Tom	RICE Ron	K9	1.8	
11/05/72	978	12:00	PUGH Tom	RICE Ron	HABU	4.4	
12/05/72	979	13:00	ESTES Tom	VICK Dewain	HABU	4.2	
13/05/72	968		ESTES Tom	VICK Dewain	K9		A
13/05/72	978	13:00	COBB Darryl	BLACKWELL Reggie	HABU	4.2	
14/05/72	968	09:30	ESTES Tom	VICK Dewain	K9	1.7	
14/05/72	979	12:50	FRUEHAUF Dave	MARTINEZ Gil	HABU	4	A
15/05/72	978	11:45	PUGH Tom	RICE Ron	HABU	1.6	A,12
16/05/72	979	14:15	COBB Darryl	BLACKWELL Reggie	K9	1.6	
16/05/72	968	13:00	ESTES Tom	VICK Dewain	HABU	4.1	
17/05/72	979	13:00	COBB Darryl	BLACKWELL Reggie	HABU	2.3	A
17/05/72	978	14:00	PUGH Tom	RICE Ron	RTB FERRY	3.6	
17/05/72	968	14:14	FRUEHAUF Dave	MARTINEZ Gil	HABU	2.5	A
18/05/72	968	11:52	FRUEHAUF Dave	MARTINEZ Gil	RTB FERRY	2.6	
18/05/72	978	12:42	PUGH Tom	RICE Ron	K9	2.3	
18/05/72	979	11:40	COBB Darryl	BLACKWELL Reggie	HABU	4	
19/05/72	978	11:50	PUGH Tom	RICE Ron	HABU	4.1	
20/05/72	979	12:15	ESTES Tom	VICK Dewain	HABU	4.1	
21/05/72	978	12:00	FRUEHAUF Dave	MARTINEZ Gil	HABU	4.1	
22/05/72	968	11:50	COBB Darryl	BLACKWELL Reggie	HABU	4.2	
23/05/72	980		COBB Darryl	BLACKWELL Reggie	K9		A
23/05/72	979	12:20	PUGH Tom	RICE Ron	HABU	4.1	
24/05/72	980	09:30	COBB Darryl	BLACKWELL Reggie	K9	2.3	
24/05/72	978	12:50	ESTES Tom	VICK Dewain	HABU	3.8	A
25/05/72	968	14:30	FRUEFAUF Dave	MARTINEZ Gil	HABU	4	
26/05/72	980	16:05	PUGH Tom	RICE Ron	K9	2.3	
26/05/72	979	14:50	POWELL Bob	COLEMAN Gary	HABU	4.1	
27/05/72	968	12:30	PUGH Tom	RICE Ron	HABU	4.1	
28/05/72	980	14:45	FRUEHAUF Dave	MARTINEZ Gil	HABU	1.9	
28/05/72	978	13:00	ESTES Tom	VICK Dewain	HABU	4.2	
29/05/72	968	14:00	FRUEHAUF Dave	MARTINEZ Gil	HABU	4.1	
30/05/72	978	13:30	POWELL Bob	COLEMAN Gary	HABU	4.2	
31/05/72	980	14:15	PUGH Tom	RICE Ron	HABU	4.2	
01/06/72	968	12:00	FRUEHAUF Dave	MARTINEZ Gil	HABU	4.2	A
02/06/72	978	13:00	ESTES Tom	VICK Dewain	HABU	3.8	A
03/06/72	979	12:00	POWELL Bob	COLEMAN Gary	HABU	4.3	A
04/06/72	968	11:30	PUGH Tom	RICE Ron	HABU	2.3	A
05/06/72	979	13:30	FRUEHAUF Dave	MARTINEZ Gil	HABU	4.3	A
06/06/72	980	13:05	ESTES Tom	VICK Dewain	HABU	4.2	
07/06/72	978	13:30	POWELL Bob	COLEMAN Gary	HABU	4.4	
08/06/72	979	13:40	PUGH Tom	RICE Ron	HABU	2	A
08/06/72	980	15:20	ESTES Tom	VICK Dewain	HABU	4	A
09/06/72	968	09:00	GUNTHER Bud	ALLOCCA Tom	K7	2.4	
09/06/72	978	10:45	POWELL Bob	COLEMAN Gary	HABU	6.3	A
10/06/72	979	12:00	PUGH Tom	RICE Ron	HABU	4.2	A
11/06/72	980	14:00	GUNTHER Bud	ALLOCCA Tom	HABU	4.2	
12/06/72	979	13:00	ESTES Tom	VICK Dewain	HABU	4.1	
13/06/72	978	13:30	POWELL Bob	COLEMAN Gary	HABU	4.5	
14/06/72	980	12:00	PUGH Tom	RICE Ron	HABU	4.2	
15/06/72	968	10:30	GUNTHER Bud	ALLOCCA Tom	HABU	4.1	
16/06/72	978	10:00	ESTES Tom	VICK Dewain	HABU	4.2	
17/06/72	980	11:00	POWELL Bob	COLEMAN Gary	HABU	4.1	
18/06/72	978		PUGH Tom	RICE Ron	HABU		A
19/06/72	968	13:30	PUGH Tom	RICE Ron	HABU	4.1	A
20/06/72	978		GUNTHER Bud	ALLOCCA Tom	HABU		A
20/06/72	980	13:30	ESTES Tom	VICK Dewain	HABU	3.9	A
21/06/72	978	14:15	GUNTHER Bud	ALLOCCA Tom	HABU	4.1	
22/06/72	979	13:00	POWELL Bob	COLEMAN Gary	HABU	4	
23/06/72	979	13:30	ESTES Tom	VICK Dewain	HABU	4.1	A
24/06/72	980	13:00	BUSH Denny	FAGG Jimmy	HABU	4	
25/06/72	968	12:30	GUNTHER Bud	ALLOCCA Tom	HABU	4.2	
26/06/72	978	13:30	POWELL Bob	COLEMAN Gary	HABU	4	
27/06/72	979	13:00	ESTES Tom	VICK Dewain	HABU	3.8	A
29/06/72	968	12:00	BUSH Denny	FAGG Jimmy	HABU	4.1	
30/06/72	980	11:00	GUNTHER Bud	ALLOCCA Tom	HABU	4.3	A
01/07/72	978	12:30	POWELL Bob	COLEMAN Gary	HABU	1.9	A
01/07/72	979	14:10	ESTES Tom	VICK Dewain	HABU	3.8	A
02/07/72	978	12:25	POWELL Bob	COLEMAN Gary	RTB FERRY	2.2	A
02/07/72	968	13:30	BUSH Denny	FAGG Jimmy	HABU	4.2	A
03/07/72	980	12:15	GUNTHER Bud	ALLOCCA Tom	HABU	6.3	A
04/07/72	978	13:40	ESTES Tom	VICK Dewain	HABU	4	A
05/07/72	979	13:00	POWELL Bob	COLEMAN Gary	HABU	2.1	A
05/07/72	968	14:30	BUSH Denny	FAGG Jimmy	HABU	4	A
06/07/72	968	12:30	GUNTHER Bud	ALLOCCA Tom	HABU	4.1	
07/07/72	979	13:00	POWELL Bob	COLEMAN Gary	HABU	1.9	A
07/07/72	980	14:30	BUSH Denny	FAGG Jimmy	HABU	4.1	A
08/07/72	968	13:00	JUDKINS Ty	KRAUS Jon	HABU	4.3	A
09/07/72	980	09:15	GUNTHER Bud	ALLOCCA Tom	HABU	4.1	
10/07/72	968	11:30	POWELL Bob	COLEMAN Gary	HABU	4.3	
11/07/72	979		GUNTHER Bud	ALLOCCA Tom	K9		A
11/07/72	968	11:00	BUSH Denny	FAGG Jimmy	HABU	4	A
13/07/72	979		GUNTHER Bud	ALLOCCA Tom	K9		A
13/07/72	978	09:30	JUDKINS Ty	KRAUS Jon	K7	2.4	A
13/07/72	979	12:38	GUNTHER Bud	ALLOCCA Tom	K9	1.9	
14/07/72	968	12:00	JUDKINS Ty	KRAUS Jon	HABU	4.2	A
14/07/72	979	14:00	POWELL Bob	COLEMAN Gary	K9	2.1	
15/07/72	978	11:30	GUNTHER Bud	ALLOCCA Tom	HABU	4.2	A
16/07/72	978	08:34	GUNTHER Bud	ALLOCCA Tom	RTB FERRY TO OL-KA	1.2	A
16/07/72	980	09:10	POWELL Bob	COLEMAN Gary	HABU	1.9	A
16/07/72	979	10:40	JUDKINS Ty	KRAUS Jon	HABU	1.5	A
17/07/72	979	10:00	POWELL Bob	COLEMAN Gary	HABU	4.1	A
18/07/72	978	11:00	GUNTHER Bud	ALLOCCA Tom	HABU	4.1	A
18/07/72	980	13:00	POWELL Bob	COLEMAN Gary	K9	2.2	
19/07/72	979	13:00	JUDKINS Ty	KRAUS Jon	HABU	4.1	A
20/07/72	978	12:20	BUSH Denny	FAGG Jimmy	HABU	4	,13 CRASH
27/07/72	980	11:15	CUNNINGHAM Bob	MORGAN George	HABU	1.7	A
27/07/72	979	12:45	GUNTHER Bud	ALLOCCA Tom	HABU	1.2	A
28/07/72	968		JUDKINS Ty	KRAUS Jon	K9		A
28/07/72	979	10:30	CUNNINGHAM Bob	MORGAN George	HABU	4	A
29/07/72	968		CUNNINGHAM Bob	MORGAN George	K9		A
29/07/72	979	13:00	GUNTHER Bud	ALLOCCA Tom	HABU	4	A
30/07/72	979	13:15	CUNNINGHAM Bob	MORGAN George	HABU	3.9	
30/07/72	968	16:00	GUNTHER Bud	ALLOCCA Tom	K9	2.2	A
31/07/72	968		JUDKINS Ty	KRAUS Jon	HABU		A
31/07/72	979	13:45	GUNTHER Bud	ALLOCCA Tom	HABU	4.5	A
01/08/72	979		CUNNINGHAM Bob	MORGAN George	HABU		A
01/08/72	968	12:30	JUDKINS Ty	KRAUS Jon	HABU	0.6	A
02/08/72	968	13:20	CUNNINGHAM Bob	MORGAN George	K9	2.2	A
02/08/72	979	11:30	JUDKINS Ty	KRAUS Jon	HABU	4.2	
03/08/72	968	11:00	CUNNINGHAM Bob	MORGAN George	HABU	4.2	
03/08/72	980	12:50	GUNTHER Bud	ALLOCCA Tom	K9	2.4	
04/08/72	968	12:34	GUNTHER Bud	ALLOCCA Tom	HABU	4.5	
05/08/72	980	11:30	JUDKINS Ty	KRAUS Jon	HABU	4	A
06/08/72	968	12:30	CUNNINGHAM Bob	MORGAN George	HABU	4.1	
06/08/72	979	14:20	GUNTHER Bud	ALLOCCA Tom	K7	2.3	
07/08/72	979	12:00	GUNTHER Bud	ALLOCCA Tom	HABU	4.4	
08/08/72	968		JUDKINS Ty	KRAUS Jon	HABU		A
08/08/72	979	14:00	JUDKINS Ty	KRAUS Jon	HABU	4	A

Date	Instal. No.	T.O. Time	Pilot Name	RSO Name	Mission	Duration	Remarks
09/08/72	979	11:00	CUNNINGHAM Bob	MORGAN George	HABU	4.1	
10/08/72	968	?	JUDKINS Ty	KRAUS Jon	HABU	4	
11/08/72	975	11:00	POWELL Bob	COLEMAN Gary	FERRY TO OL-KA	5.4	
11/08/72	979	?	CUNNINGHAM Bob	MORGAN George	HABU	3.3	
12/08/72	980		GUNTHER Bud	ALLOCCA Tom	FERRY OUT BACKUP		
12/08/72	979	06:30	JUDKINS Ty	KRAUS Jon	FERRY OUT		
12/08/72	968	15:30	POWELL Bob	COLEMAN Gary	HABU	0.7	A
12/08/72	975	15:45	CUNNINGHAM Bob	MORGAN George	HABU	4.1	A
13/08/72	975	12:30	GUNTHER Bud	ALLOCCA Tom	HABU	4.1	
14/08/72	968	11:30	POWELL Bob	COLEMAN Gary	HABU	4.1	A
14/08/72	971	03:00	SULLIVAN Jim	WIDDIFIELD Noel	FERRY TO OL-KA	5.3	
15/08/72	980	06:00	GUNTHER Bud	ALLOCCA Tom	FERRY OUT		
15/08/72	971	13:00	SULLIVAN Jim	WIDDIFIELD Noel	HABU	3.1	A
18/08/72	961	03:00	SHELTON Jim	SCHMITTOU Tom	FERRY TO OL-KA	5.3	A
18/08/72	975	12:00	SULLIVAN Jim	WIDDIFIELD Noel	HABU	4.2	
19/08/72	968	06:00	POWELL Bob	COLEMAN Gary	FERRY OUT		
19/08/72	961	12:30	CUNNINGHAM Bob	MORGAN George	HABU	4.2	A
20/08/72	975	12:15	SHELTON Jim	SCHMITTOU Tom	HABU	4.3	
21/08/72	963	03:00	COBB Darryl	BLACKWELL Reggie	FERRY TO OL-KA	5.1	A
21/08/72	961	11:00	SULLIVAN Jim	WIDDIFIELD Noel	HABU	4	
22/08/72	971	13:00	COBB Darryl	BLACKWELL Reggie	HABU	4.1	
23/08/72	963	12:00	CUNNINGHAM Bob	MORGAN George	HABU	4.3	
23/08/72	961	14:45	SHELTON Jim	SCHMITTOU Tom	K5	2.3	
24/08/72	975	10:30	SULLIVAN Jim	WIDDIFIELD Noel	HABU	1.6	A
24/08/72	971	12:00	SHELTON Jim	SCHMITTOU Tom	HABU	4.3	A
25/08/72	961		SHELTON Jim	SCHMITTOU Tom	K5		A
25/08/72	963	12:15	SULLIVAN Jim	WIDDIFIELD Noel	HABU	4.3	A
26/08/72	975	11:00	COBB Darryl	BLACKWELL Reggie	HABU	3.5	A
27/08/72	975	13:15	COBB Darryl	BLACKWELL Reggie	RTB FERRY	2.4	A
27/08/72	971	12:00	CUNNINGHAM Bob	MORGAN George	HABU	4.1	
28/08/72	963	11:30	SHELTON Jim	SCHMITTOU Tom	HABU	4.3	
29/08/72	961	11:20	CUNNINGHAM Bob	MORGAN George	K4	0.7	A
29/08/72	971	09:30	SULLIVAN Jim	WIDDIFIELD Noel	HABU	3.9	
29/08/72	963	12:30	COBB Darryl	BLACKWELL Reggie	HABU	2.3	
31/08/72	971		CUNNINGHAM Bob	MORGAN George	HABU		A
31/08/72	963	12:44	CUNNINGHAM Bob	MORGAN George	HABU	3.9	A
01/09/72	971	14:15	SHELTON Jim	SCHMITTOU Tom	HABU	4	
02/09/72	975		SHELTON Jim	SCHMITTOU Tom	K4		A
02/09/72	961		SULLIVAN Jim	WIDDIFIELD Noel	HABU		A
02/09/72	963	11:30	COBB Darryl	BLACKWELL Reggie	HABU	4.1	A
03/09/72	961	08:30	SULLIVAN Jim	WIDDIFIELD Noel	HABU	2.5	A
04/09/72	961	16:15	SULLIVAN Jim	WIDDIFIELD Noel	RTB FERRY	2	A
04/09/72	971	09:30	CUNNINGHAM Bob	MORGAN George	HABU	4.1	A
05/09/72	971	11:30	SHELTON Jim	SCHMITTOU Tom	HABU	4.1	
06/09/72	961	13:00	COBB Darryl	BLACKWELL Reggie	HABU	1.6	A
06/09/72	975	14:30	SULLIVAN Jim	WIDDIFIELD Noel	HABU	4.2	A
07/09/72	961	12:00	COBB Darryl	BLACKWELL Reggie	HABU	4.3	
08/09/72	975	13:45	SHELTON Jim	SCHMITTOU Tom	HABU	4.3	A
09/09/72	975		SULLIVAN Jim	WIDDIFIELD Noel	HABU		A
09/09/72	971	15:15	COBB Darryl	BLACKWELL Reggie	HABU	4.1	A
10/09/72	975	11:45	SULLIVAN Jim	WIDDIFIELD Noel	HABU	4	
11/09/72	975	13:30	SHELTON Jim	SCHMITTOU Tom	HABU	4.1	
12/09/72	961	12:00	COBB Darryl	BLACKWELL Reggie	HABU	4.1	
12/09/72	963	14:37	HALLER Carl	FULLER John	K9	2.2	
13/09/72	961	08:30	SULLIVAN Jim	WIDDIFIELD Noel	HABU	1.7	A
13/09/72	971	10:00	HALLER Carl	FULLER John	HABU	4.4	A
14/09/72	963	09:30	SULLIVAN Jim	WIDDIFIELD Noel	HABU	4	A
15/09/72	961	08:30	COBB Darryl	BLACKWELL Reggie	HABU	1.7	A
15/09/72	963	10:00	SHELTON Jim	SCHMITTOU Tom	HABU	4	A
15/09/72	971	11:00	HALLER Carl	FULLER John	HABU	3.6	A
17/09/72	963	11:30	COBB Darryl	BLACKWELL Reggie	HABU	4.1	
18/09/72	963	12:00	SULLIVAN Jim	WIDDIFIELD Noel	HABU	4.2	
18/09/72	975	14:03	COBB Darryl	BLACKWELL Reggie	HABU	3.4	
19/09/72	975	13:00	HALLER Carl	FULLER John	HABU	4	
20/09/72	975	08:00	SHELTON Jim	SCHMITTOU Tom	HABU	4.2	A
21/09/72	971	09:30	COBB Darryl	BLACKWELL Reggie	HABU	3.8	
22/09/72	975	11:00	SULLIVAN Jim	WIDDIFIELD Noel	HABU	4.1	
22/09/72	961	12:50	COBB Darryl	BLACKWELL Reggie	K9	2.3	A
23/09/72	963	12:00	HALLER Carl	FULLER John	HABU	4.3	A
23/09/72	971	12:45	SULLIVAN Jim	WIDDIFIELD Noel	HABU	3.6	
24/09/72	961	13:00	SHELTON Jim	SCHMITTOU Tom	HABU	4.1	
25/09/72	963	13:15	COBB Darryl	BLACKWELL Reggie	HABU	1.8	A
25/09/72	971	14:45	SULLIVAN Jim	WIDDIFIELD Noel	HABU	2.3	A
26/09/72	961	10:30	COBB Darryl	BLACKWELL Reggie	HABU	4.1	A
27/09/72	961	12:00	HALLER Carl	FULLER John	HABU	2.2	A
27/09/72	963	13:30	SHELTON Jim	SCHMITTOU Tom	HABU	4	A
28/09/72	963	10:00	HALLER Carl	FULLER John	HABU	4.3	
28/09/72	971	11:50	COBB Darryl	BLACKWELL Reggie	K4	1.1	A
29/09/72	971	12:00	POWELL Bob	COLEMAN Gary	HABU	3.9	A
30/09/72	971	11:30	COBB Darryl	BLACKWELL Reggie	HABU	4.1	
30/09/72	961	14:00	POWELL Bob	COLEMAN Gary	HABU	3.4	A
01/10/72	961	12:10	SHELTON Jim	SCHMITTOU Tom	HABU	4.1	
02/10/72	961	09:45	HALLER Carl	FULLER John	HABU	4	A
03/10/72	963	09:15	POWELL Bob	COLEMAN Gary	HABU	3.9	
04/10/72	975		POWELL Bob	COLEMAN Gary	K9		A
04/10/72	961	10:00	COBB Darryl	BLACKWELL Reggie	HABU	4	A
05/10/72	975	10:00	COBB Darryl	BLACKWELL Reggie	K9	1.8	
05/10/72	971	13:00	SHELTON Jim	SCHMITTOU Tom	HABU	4.1	A
06/10/72	963	12:15	HALLER Carl	FULLER John	HABU	4.1	A
07/10/72	971	09:30	POWELL Bob	COLEMAN Gary	HABU	4.1	
07/10/72	975	11:20	HALLER Carl	FULLER John	K9	2.2	
08/10/72	975	12:00	COBB Darryl	BLACKWELL Reggie	HABU	4.1	
09/10/72	971	12:30	SHELTON Jim	SCHMITTOU Tom	HABU	4.2	
10/10/72	963	12:15	HALLER Carl	FULLER John	HABU	6.9	
10/10/72	975	13:50	POWELL Bob	COLEMAN Gary	K4	0.9	
11/10/72	971	10:00	POWELL Bob	COLEMAN Gary	HABU	3.4	A
12/10/72	963	11:30	COBB Darryl	BLACKWELL Reggie	HABU	1	A
12/10/72	971	13:00	HALLER Carl	FULLER John	HABU	4	A
13/10/72	963	12:30	COBB Darryl	BLACKWELL Reggie	HABU	2.2	A
13/10/72	975	14:20	HERTZOG Randy	RICE Ron	K4	1	A
14/10/72	971	13:00	COBB Darryl	BLACKWELL Reggie	HABU	4.1	
14/10/72	961	14:58	POWELL Bob	COLEMAN Gary	K9	2.2	
15/10/72	975	08:45	HERTZOG Randy	RICE Ron	HABU	3.9	
16/10/72	975	11:00	POWELL Bob	COLEMAN Gary	HABU	3.9	A
16/10/72	961	14:15	HERTZOG Randy	RICE Ron	HABU	1.7	A
17/10/72	963	12:30	HALLER Carl	FULLER John	HABU	4.2	A
18/10/72	961	12:04	COBB Darryl	BLACKWELL Reggie	HABU	4.2	
20/10/72	975	12:20	HERTZOG Randy	RICE Ron	HABU	4	
21/10/72	961	10:00	POWELL Bob	COLEMAN Gary	HABU	3.5	
24/10/72	963	11:45	HALLER Carl	FULLER John	HABU	4.2	
25/10/72	975	12:00	COBB Darryl	BLACKWELL Reggie	K5	2.3	
26/10/72	961	14:13	HERTZOG Randy	RICE Ron	HABU	1.7	
28/10/72	975	12:00	POWELL Bob	COLEMAN Gary	HABU	3.8	
29/10/72	971	10:00	BLEDSOE Pat	CARNOCHAN John	K9	2.3	A
30/10/72	961	12:45	BLEDSOE Pat	CARNOCHAN John	HABU	4	
31/10/72	963	12:15	HALLER Carl	FULLER John	HABU	3.5	
02/11/72	975		HALLER Carl	FULLER John	HABU		A
02/11/72	963	11:33	HERTZOG Randy	RICE Ron	HABU	4.1	A
02/11/72	975	13:18	POWELL Bob	COLEMAN Gary	HABU	0.3	A
03/11/72	971	12:44	HALLER Carl	FULLER John	HABU	4.3	A
04/11/72	971	13:30	POWELL Bob	COLEMAN Gary	HABU	4.9	
07/11/72	975	10:00	BLEDSOE Pat	CARNOCHAN John	HABU	3.4	A
09/11/72	961	10:00	HERTZOG Randy	RICE Ron	K9	2.3	
10/11/72	971	11:00	BLEDSOE Pat	CARNOCHAN John	HABU	4.1	
11/11/72	971	13:45	POWELL Bob	COLEMAN Gary	HABU	1.8	
12/11/72	975	12:00	JUDKINS Ty	MORGAN George	HABU	4.1	A
14/11/72	963	13:00	HERTZOG Randy	RICE Ron	HABU	4.2	
15/11/72	963	11:00	BLEDSOE Pat	CARNOCHAN John	HABU	4	A
18/11/72	961		JUDKINS Ty	MORGAN George	HABU		A
18/11/72	961	13:15	JUDKINS Ty	MORGAN George	HABU	3.5	A
19/11/72	975	12:30	HERTZOG Randy	RICE Ron	HABU	1.6	A
19/11/72	961	14:00	JUDKINS Ty	MORGAN George	HABU	4.2	A
21/11/72	975	10:00	BLEDSOE Pat	CARNOCHAN John	K9	2.4	
21/11/72	961	11:00	GUNTHER Bud	ALLOCCA Tom	HABU	3.6	A
25/11/72	971	13:30	SULLIVAN Jim	WIDDDIFIELD Noel	HABU	1.9	
28/11/72	961	10:20	BLEDSOE Pat	CARNOCHAN John	K9	2.4	A
01/12/72	975	08:30	BLEDSOE Pat	CARNOCHAN John	HABU	2.2	A
02/12/72	971	12:00	GUNTHER Bud	ALLOCCA Tom	HABU	4.1	A
02/12/72	975	12:50	BLEDSOE Pat	CARNOCHAN John	RTB FERRY	3.8	
04/12/72	963		RANSOM Lee	GERSTEN Mark	K9		A
04/12/72	961	11:00	SULLIVAN Jim	WIDDIFIELD Noel	HABU	4.1	A
05/12/72	971	10:30	JUDKINS Ty	MORGAN George	HABU	4	A
05/12/72	963	12:12	RANSOM Lee	GERSTEN Mark	K9	2.4	A
06/12/72	971	12:00	RANSOM Lee	GERSTEN Mark	HABU	4	
08/12/72	963	12:30	GUNTHER Bud	ALLOCCA Tom	HABU	4	
11/12/72	975	10:00	RANSOM Lee	GERSTEN Mark	K9	2.2	
11/12/72	961	11:30	SULLIVAN Jim	WIDDIFIELD Noel	HABU	4	
12/12/72	975	13:30	RANSOM Lee	GERSTEN Mark	HABU	3.7	
15/12/72	975	10:00	COBB Darryl	BLACKWELL Reggie	HABU	4.2	
15/12/72	963	13:00	RANSOM Lee	GERSTEN Mark	HABU	3.5	
19/12/72	975		SULLIVAN Jim	WIDDIFIELD Noel	HABU		A
19/12/72	961	14:00	SULLIVAN Jim	WIDDIFIELD Noel	HABU	4.1	A,14
20/12/72	961	12:00	COBB Darryl	BLACKWELL Reggie	HABU	4.2	
21/12/72	975	11:45	RANSOM Lee	GERSTEN Mark	HABU	4.1	
22/12/72	963	12:10	COBB Darryl	BLACKWELL Reggie	HABU	4	
23/12/72	975	12:30	CUNNINGHAM Bob	FAGG Jimmy	HABU	4.9	A
23/12/72	961	14:12	RANSOM Lee	GERSTEN Mark	HABU	4.3	A
24/12/72	971	13:00	COBB Darryl	BLACKWELL Reggie	HABU	4.1	A
25/12/72	975	13:00	CUNNINGHAM Bob	FAGG Jimmy	HABU	4	
27/12/72	963		RANSOM Lee	GERSTEN Mark	HABU		A
27/12/72	963	14:20	RANSOM Lee	GERSTEN Mark	HABU	3.8	A
28/12/72	975	22:43	COBB Darryl	BLACKWELL Reggie	N-HABU	3.9	A,15
29/12/72	971	13:00	CUNNINGHAM Bob	FAGG Jimmy	HABU	4.1	
01/01/73	975		RANSOM Lee	GERSTEN Mark	HABU		A
01/01/73	963		COBB Darryl	BLACKWELL Reggie	HABU		A
02/01/73	975	10:00	RANSOM Lee	GERSTEN Mark	HABU	5.9	A
03/01/73	963	12:39	COBB Darryl	BLACKWELL Reggie	HABU	4.3	A
04/01/73	961	12:40	CUNNINGHAM Bob	FAGG Jimmy	HABU	3.4	
07/01/73	971	11:46	BLEDSOE Pat	CARNOCHAN John	HABU	4.4	A
08/01/73	963	10:00	COBB Darryl	BLACKWELL Reggie	HABU	4.3	A
10/01/73	961	12:30	BLEDSOE Pat	CARNOCHAN John	HABU	3.5	A
13/01/73	963	12:00	CUNNINGHAM Bob	FAGG Jimmy	HABU	4	A
14/01/73	971	14:00	SHELTON Jim	SCHMITTOU Tom	HABU	4.2	
15/01/73	961	12:00	BLEDSOE Pat	CARNOCHAN John	HABU	3.9	
16/01/73	963	12:05	SHELTON Jim	SCHMITTOU Tom	HABU	2.3	
19/01/73	963	12:00	CUNNINGHAM Bob	FAGG Jimmy	K9	2.3	A
20/01/73	961	12:45	CUNNINGHAM Bob	FAGG Jimmy	HABU	4	
20/01/73	975	15:15	SHELTON Jim	SCHMITTOU Tom	K9	2	
21/01/73	961	12:00	SHELTON Jim	SCHMITTOU Tom	HABU	4.1	A
22/01/73	971	12:00	BLEDSOE Pat	CARNOCHAN John	HABU	4.1	
23/01/73	975	12:00	CUNNINGHAM Bob	FAGG Jimmy	HABU	4.3	
24/01/73	971	12:50	SHELTON Jim	SCHMITTOU Tom	HABU	4.3	
25/01/73	963	12:30	BLEDSOE Pat	CARNOCHAN John	HABU	3.9	
26/01/73	975	11:45	SHELTON Jim	SCHMITTOU Tom	K9	2.2	A
30/01/73	971	10:00	JUDKINS Ty	MORGAN George	K10	2.2	
31/01/73	963	12:45	JUDKINS Ty	MORGAN George	HABU	3.5	
01/02/73	971	11:00	SHELTON Jim	SCHMITTOU Tom	HABU	4	
06/02/73	975	12:00	JUDKINS Ty	MORGAN George	HABU	3.9	
07/02/73	961	09:35	SHELTON Jim	SCHMITTOU Tom	K10	2.2	A
07/02/73	963	11:00	GUNTHER Bud	ALLOCCA Tom	HABU	3.5	
10/02/73	971	12:00	GUNTHER Bud	ALLOCCA Tom	HABU	4.1	
11/02/73	963	13:00	POWELL Bob	COLEMAN Gary	HABU	3.9	
13/02/73	971	12:30	JUDKINS Ty	MORGAN George	HABU	4	A
14/02/73	975	12:00	GUNTHER Bud	ALLOCCA Tom	HABU	4.2	A
15/02/73	961	10:00	POWELL Bob	COLEMAN Gary	HABU	5.2	
16/02/73	971	12:00	JUDKINS Ty	MORGAN George	HABU	4.1	

Date	Instal. No.	T.O. Time	Pilot Name	RSO Name	Mission	Duration	Remarks
17/02/73	975	13:00	GUNTHER Bud	ALLOCCA Tom	HABU	4	
18/02/73	963	10:00	POWELL Bob	COLEMAN Gary	HABU	3.7	
19/02/73	975	11:00	JUDKINS Ty	MORGAN George	HABU	4	
20/02/73	961	10:00	GUNTHER Bud	ALLOCCA Tom	HABU	4	A
22/02/73	975	10:40	POWELL Bob	COLEMAN Gary	HABU	3.8	
23/02/73	975	12:30	JUDKINS Ty	MORGAN George	HABU	3.5	A
24/02/73	961	11:00	GUNTHER Bud	ALLOCCA Tom	HABU	4	A
25/02/73	963	10:40	POWELL Bob	COLEMAN Gary	HABU	2.2	
27/02/73	975		JUDKINS Ty	MORGAN George	HABU		A
27/02/73	961		JUDKINS Ty	MORGAN George	HABU		A
27/02/73	975	11:14	GUNTHER Bud	ALLOCCA Tom	HABU	4.1	A
28/02/73	963	09:45	POWELL Bob	COLEMAN Gary	HABU	3.5	
01/03/73	975	10:00	JUDKINS Ty	MORGAN George	HABU	2	A
01/03/73	963	11:30	GUNTHER Bud	ALLOCCA Tom	HABU	3.7	A
03/03/73	975	11:00	JUDKINS Ty	MORGAN George	HABU	4	
06/03/73	961	12:30	POWELL Bob	COLEMAN Gary	HABU	3.9	
07/03/73	971	10:00	JUDKINS Ty	MORGAN George	K3	2.4	
08/03/73	963	12:30	GUNTHER Bud	ALLOCCA Tom	HABU	3.6	
10/03/73	961	10:00	SULLIVAN Jim	WIDDIFIELD Noel	HABU	3.6	A
11/03/73	971	12:00	POWELL Bob	COLEMAN Gary	HABU	2.6	A
13/03/73	975	09:15	GUNTHER Bud	ALLOCCA Tom	HABU	4.3	A
14/03/73	971	10:00	SULLIVAN Jim	WIDDIFIELD Noel	HABU	3.6	A
18/03/73	961	14:00	RANSOM Lee	GERSTEN Mark	HABU	3.6	
19/03/73	975	11:50	RANSOM Lee	GERSTEN Mark	HABU	4.2	
23/03/73	971	10:00	SULLIVAN Jim	WIDDIFIELD Noel	HABU	3.9	
26/03/73	961	08:20	RANSOM Lee	GERSTEN Mark	HABU	2.3	
26/03/73	971	10:00	ADAMS Buck	MACHOREK Bill	K9	2.4	A
27/03/73	961	11:00	ADAMS Buck	MACHOREK Bill	HABU	4	
30/03/73	971	12:00	SULLIVAN Jim	WIDDIFIELD Noel	HABU	3	
31/03/73	975	09:45	RANSOM Lee	GERSTEN Mark	HABU	3.7	
03/04/73	971	10:30	SULLIVAN Jim	WIDDIFIELD Noel	HABU	3.9	
04/04/73	963	12:00	SULLIVAN Jim	WIDDIFIELD Noel	K4	0.8	A
04/04/73	961	10:00	ADAMS Buck	MACHOREK Bill	HABU	3.7	A
06/04/73	961	09:10	ADAMS Buck	MACHOREK Bill	HABU	4.5	A
08/04/73	961	12:30	BLEDSOE Pat	BLACKWELL Reggie	HABU	3.2	
09/04/73	975	10:30	SULLIVAN Jim	WIDDIFIELD Noel	HABU	0.6	A
09/04/73	971	10:35	ADAMS Buck	MACHOREK Bill	HABU	4.4	A
11/04/73	963	12:50	BLEDSOE Pat	BLACKWELL Reggie	HABU	3.5	
12/04/73	975	08:30	SULLIVAN Jim	WIDDIFIELD Noel	HABU	3.8	A
14/04/73	963	10:45	ADAMS Buck	MACHOREK Bill	HABU	2.2	A
14/04/73	961	12:15	BLEDSOE Pat	BLACKWELL Reggie	HABU	0.4	A
16/04/73	971	12:15	SULLIVAN Jim	WIDDIFIELD Noel	HABU	3.9	A
18/04/73	961	07:05	BLEDSOE Pat	BLACKWELL Reggie	HABU	2.3	A
19/04/73	971	12:00	ADAMS Buck	MACHOREK Bill	HABU	4.1	
22/04/73	963	11:44	CUNNINGHAM Bob	FAGG Jimmy	HABU	5.3	
24/04/73	963	11:45	BLEDSOE Pat	BLACKWELL Reggie	HABU	5.5	A
26/04/73	961	14:00	ADAMS Buck	MACHOREK Bill	HABU	3.5	A
28/04/73	971	09:15	CUNNINGHAM Bob	FAGG Jimmy	HABU	3.5	A
30/04/73	963	10:00	BLEDSOE Pat	BLACKWELL Reggie	HABU	3.5	
01/05/73	975	10:00	ADAMS Buck	MACHOREK Bill	K5	2.2	
05/05/73	975	12:25	CUNNINGHAM Bob	FAGG Jimmy	K5	2	
06/05/73	961	09:46	RANSOM Lee	GERSTEN Mark	K4	1	A
07/05/73	975	12:00	ADAMS Buck	MACHOREK Bill	HABU	3	A
08/05/73	975	18:30	ADAMS Buck	MACHOREK Bill	N-RTB FERRY	2.3	A
11/05/73	971	10:00	CUNNINGHAM Bob	FAGG Jimmy	K4	1.1	
12/05/73	971	10:00	CUNNINGHAM Bob	FAGG Jimmy	HABU	4.3	
13/05/73	963	10:25	RANSOM Lee	GERSTEN Mark	HABU	4	
16/05/73	963	09:40	CUNNINGHAM Bob	FAGG Jimmy	HABU	3.8	A
17/05/73	975	13:30	RANSOM Lee	GERSTEN Mark	HABU	2.6	A
19/05/73	971	10:30	HERTZOG Randy	CARNOCHAN John	HABU	4.3	A
19/05/73	963	13:30	CUNNINGHAM Bob	FAGG Jimmy	HABU	1.8	
20/05/73	961	11:30	RANSOM Lee	GERSTEN Mark	HABU	3.1	A
21/05/73	975	11:00	HERTZOG Randy	CARNOCHAN John	K3	2.2	A
24/05/73	961	10:00	RANSOM Lee	GERSTEN Mark	HABU	2	A
27/05/73	963	12:15	CUNNINGHAM Bob	FAGG Jimmy	HABU	4.3	A
28/05/73	971	10:00	HERTZOG Randy	CARNOCHAN John	K4	1	
30/05/73	961	10:45	HERTZOG Randy	CARNOCHAN John	HABU	2.3	
30/05/73	975	11:45	RANSOM Lee	GERSTEN Mark	K5	2.2	A
31/05/73	971	12:30	JUDKINS Ty	MORGAN George	K4	1	
01/06/73	961		CUNNINGHAM Bob	FAGG Jimmy	HABU		A
01/06/73	975	13:58	RANSOM Lee	GERSTEN Mark	HABU	3.1	A
03/06/73	971	10:00	HERTZOG Randy	CARNOCHAN John	HABU	3.9	
04/06/73	975	06:00	CUNNINGHAM Bob	FAGG Jimmy	FERRY OUT		A
06/06/73	962	03:00	BLEDSOE Pat	BLACKWELL Reggie	FERRY IN (OL-KA)	5.3	
07/06/73	961	06:00	BLEDSOE Pat	BLACKWELL Reggie	FERRY OUT		
08/06/73	963	09:30	BLEDSOE Pat	BLACKWELL Reggie	HABU	4	
08/06/73	962	10:00	JUDKINS Ty	MORGAN George	K5	2.1	
09/06/73	972	03:00	ADAMS Buck	MACHOREK Bill	FERRY TO OL-KA	5.3	
10/06/73	971	06:00	RANSOM Lee	GERSTEN Mark	FERRY OUT		
11/06/73	972	11:00	HERTZOG Randy	CARNOCHAN John	HABU	3.6	
12/06/73	968	03:08	HELT Bob	ELLIOTT Larry	FERRY TO OL-KA	5.5	
13/06/73	963	06:00	ADAMS Buck	MACHOREK Bill	FERRY OUT		
14/06/73	972	10:00	JUDKINS Ty	MORGAN George	HABU	0.6	A
14/06/73	968	10:19	HELT Bob	ELLIOTT Larry	K9	2.3	A
15/06/73	968	07:00	JUDKINS Ty	MORGAN George	HABU	3.5	A
16/06/73	972	10:00	HERTZOG Randy	CARNOCHAN John	K9	2.5	
19/06/73	962	10:00	HELT Bob	ELLIOTT Larry	K9	3.9	
20/06/73	968	11:15	JUDKINS Ty	MORGAN George	HABU	4.3	A
21/06/73	972	10:00	HERTZOG Randy	CARNOCHAN John	K5	1.8	
22/06/73	968	16:00	HERTZOG Randy	CARNOCHAN John	HABU	2.2	
23/06/73	962	12:20	HELT Bob	ELLIOTT Larry	HABU	3.3	
24/06/73	968		JUDKINS Ty	MORGAN George	K4		A
24/06/73	972	11:30	HERTZOG Randy	CARNOCHAN John	HABU	3.9	A
26/06/73	972	10:00	JUDKINS Ty	MORGAN George	K9	2.1	
28/06/73	962	10:10	JUDKINS Ty	MORGAN George	HABU	3.9	
29/06/73	968	13:25	HELT Bob	ELLIOTT Larry	HABU	3.5	
02/07/73	972	10:00	GUNTHER Bud	ALLOCCA Tom	K9	2.1	
05/07/73	962	11:30	JUNKINS Ty	MORGAN George	HABU	2.2	A
05/07/73	968	13:08	HELT Bob	ELLIOTT Larry	HABU	3.6	A
06/07/73	962		JUDKINS Ty	MORGAN George	RTB FERRY		A
07/07/73	972	12:00	GUNTHER Bud	ALLOCCA Tom	HABU	2	A
07/07/73	962	18:06	JUDKINS Ty	MORGAN George	N-RTB FERRY	2.4	A
10/07/73	972	10:10	HELT Bob	ELLIOTT Larry	K9/5	2.1	A
11/07/73	962	12:00	GUNTHER Bud	ALLOCCA Tom	HABU	3.6	A
13/07/73	972	09:30	JOERSZ Al	FULLER John	K3	2.3	
13/07/73	962	14:15	HELT Bob	ELLIOTT Larry	HABU	3.6	
21/07/73	968	13:30	JOERSZ Al	FULLER John	HABU	3.3	
22/07/73	962	11:10	HELT Bob	ELLIOTT Larry	HABU	3.6	
24/07/73	972	11:00	GUNTHER Bud	ALLOCCA Tom	K4	1	
25/07/73	962	14:30	JOERSZ Al	FULLER John	HABU	3.5	
27/07/73	972	09:30	SHELTON Jim	COLEMAN Gary	HABU	3.8	
29/07/73	968	11:00	GUNTHER Bud	ALLOCCA Tom	HABU	3.5	A
31/07/73	962	09:30	JOERSZ Al	FULLER John	HABU	3.9	
02/08/73	968	14:30	SHELTON Jim	COLEMAN Gary	HABU	3.6	
03/08/73	962	10:30	GUNTHER Bud	ALLOCCA Tom	HABU	3.1	
04/08/73	972		WILSON Jim	DOUGLASS Bruce	K10		A
05/08/73	968	10:08	WILSON Jim	DOUGLASS Bruce	K10	2.4	A
07/08/73	972	11:00	JOERSZ Al	FULLER John	HABU	1.9	A
07/08/73	968	12:41	SHELTON Jim	COLEMAN Gary	HABU	3.9	A
10/08/73	962	13:30	JOERSZ Al	FULLER John	HABU	3.5	A
17/08/73	968	13:00	JOERSZ Al	FULLER John	HABU	3.9	
17/08/73	962	14:50	WILSON Jim	DOUGLASS Bruce	K9	2.3	
19/08/73	972		ADAMS Buck	MACHOREK Bill	K11		A
19/08/73	972	14:40	ADAMS Buck	MACHOREK Bill	K4	1.1	A
20/08/73	962	14:00	SHELTON Jim	COLEMAN Gary	HABU	3.6	A
24/08/73	972	13:00	WILSON Jim	DOUGLASS Bruce	HABU	4.2	A
26/08/73	968		ADAMS Buck	MACHOREK Bill	K11B		A
28/08/73	962	10:00	ADAMS Buck	MACHOREK Bill	K11B	2.3	A
28/08/73	968	11:00	SHELTON Jim	COLEMAN Gary	K11A	2.1	
30/08/73	962		WILSON Jim	DOUGLASS Bruce	HABU		A
30/08/73	972	14:07	WILSON Jim	DOUGLASS Bruce	HABU	3.5	A
31/08/73	968	10:00	ADAMS Buck	MACHOREK Bill	K6	2.7	
03/09/73	962	10:00	WILSON Jim	DOUGLASS Bruce	K11B	2.2	
04/09/73	972	10:00	ADAMS Buck	MACHOREK Bill	K11C	2.2	
06/09/73	962	11:00	WILSON Jim	DOUGLASS Bruce	HABU	4.5	A
07/09/73	972	12:00	ADAMS Buck	MACHOREK Bill	HABU	3.5	
09/09/73	972	09:30	ADAMS Buck	MACHOREK Bill	HABU	3.7	A
10/09/73	968	10:00	SULLIVAN Jim	WIDDIFIELD Noel	K11	2.3	A
11/09/73	968	12:30	SULLIVAN Jim	WIDDIFIELD Noel	HABU	3.5	
13/09/73	972	10:00	SULLIVAN Jim	WIDDIFIELD Noel	HABU	3.9	A
15/09/73	962	10:00	WILSON Jim	DOUGLASS Bruce	K11A	2.4	A
18/09/73	972	07:00	WILSON Jim	DOUGLASS Bruce	K13	2.1	
20/09/73	962	13:15	ADAMS Buck	MACHOREK Bill	HABU	3.4	
23/09/73	962	11:55	SULLIVAN Jim	WIDDIFIELD Noel	K4	0.9	
23/09/73	972	10:10	BLEDSOE Pat	BLACKWELL Reggie	HABU	4.4	
26/09/73	968	10:00	ADAMS Buck	MACHOREK Bill	K12	3.8	A
27/09/73	962	13:30	BLEDSOE Pat	BLACKWELL Reggie	HABU	3.5	
30/09/73	968	10:00	SULLIVAN Jim	WIDDIFIELD Noel	K12	3.4	A
02/10/73	968		SULLIVAN Jim	WIDDIFIELD Noel	HABU		A
02/10/73	962	11:00	ADAMS Buck	MACHOREK Bill	HABU	0.8	A
04/10/73	972	09:30	SULLIVAN Jim	WIDDIFIELD Noel	HABU	3.9	A
05/10/73	962	13:30	BLEDSOE Pat	BLACKWELL Reggie	HABU	3.6	A
07/10/73	972	13:03	RANSOM Lee	ALLOCCA Tom	K12	2	A
08/10/73	968	13:12	SULLIVAN Jim	WIDDIFIELD Noel	HABU	1.9	A
10/10/73	968	10:00	BLEDSOE Pat	BLACKWELL Reggie	K11B	3.3	A
12/10/73	972		RANSOM Lee	ALLOCCA Tom	K12		A
13/10/73	962		SULLIVAN Jim	WIDDIFIELD Noel	K4		A
13/10/73	972	13:07	RANSOM Lee	ALLOCCA Tom	K11B	1	A
13/10/73	962	13:28	SULLIVAN Jim	WIDDIFIELD Noel	K4	1	A
15/10/73	968	13:17	RANSOM Lee	ALLOCCA Tom	HABU	2.5	A
17/10/73	972	10:06	BLEDSOE Pat	BLACKWELL Reggie	K9	2.2	A
18/10/73	968	13:30	BLEDSOE Pat	BLACKWELL Reggie	HABU	3.6	
19/10/73	962	10:00	HERTZOG Randy	CARNOCHAN John	K9	2.4	
21/10/73	968	09:30	BLEDSOE Pat	BLACKWELL Reggie	HABU	4.1	
23/10/73	972	10:09	RANSOM Lee	ALLOCCA Tom	K9	2.2	A
25/10/73	962	10:00	HERTZOG Randy	CARNOCHAN John	K9	1.8	A
28/10/73	972	10:00	BLEDSOE Pat	BLACKWELL Reggie	K9	2.3	A
29/10/73	962		RANSOM Lee	ALLOCCA Tom	K9		A
30/10/73	968	11:00	RANSOM Lee	ALLOCCA Tom	HABU	4	A
31/10/73	972	14:00	RANSOM Lee	ALLOCCA Tom	K9	2.2	
01/11/73	962	10:00	HERTZOG Randy	ALLOCCA Tom	K9	1.8	A
03/11/73	972	12:30	JUDKINS Ty	MORGAN George	HABU	3.5	A
06/11/73	962	10:00	HERTZOG Randy	CARNOCHAN John	K9	2.3	
08/11/73	968	12:00	RANSOM Lee	ALLOCCA Tom	HABU	4.1	A
08/11/73	972	15:45	JUDKINS Ty	MORGAN George	K4	0.9	A
12/11/73	962	10:00	HERTZOG Randy	CARNOCHAN John	K9	2.2	
14/11/73	972	10:00	RANSOM Lee	ALLOCCA Tom	K9	2.1	
14/11/73	968	11:00	JUDKINS Ty	MORGAN George	K9	2.1	A
17/11/73	962	10:00	HELT Bob	ELLIOTT Larry	K12	3.4	
18/11/73	968	12:30	HELT Bob	ELLIOTT Larry	HABU	3.6	
19/11/73	972	11:30	HERTZOG Randy	CARNOCHAN John	HABU	4.2	
21/11/73	968	10:00	JUDKINS Ty	MORGAN George	HABU	4.4	
22/11/73	962	12:30	HERTZOG Randy	CARNOCHAN John	HABU	3.6	
26/11/73	968	10:00	HELT Bob	ELLIOTT Larry	K4	1.4	
28/11/73	962	11:15	HELT Bob	ELLIOTT Larry	HABU	3.9	
29/11/73	968	12:20	JUDKINS Ty	MORGAN George	HABU	3.6	
02/12/73	972	10:10	HELT Bob	ELLIOTT Larry	K9	2.5	
03/12/73	962	11:00	JUDKINS Ty	MORGAN George	HABU	4.1	
04/12/73	962	11:15	SHELTON Jim	COLEMAN Gary	HABU	4.8	
05/12/73	968	09:30	HELT Bob	ELLIOTT Larry	K9	2.3	
07/12/73	968	10:15	HELT Bob	ELLIOTT Larry	K10	2.5	
08/12/73	962	09:30	HELT Bob	ELLIOTT Larry	HABU	4.1	
10/12/73	962	11:30	JUDKINS Ty	MORGAN George	HABU	4.8	A
11/12/73	972	10:00	SHELTON Jim	COLEMAN Gary	K4	1	
16/12/73	972	13:23	SHELTON Jim	COLEMAN Gary	HABU	0.5	A
17/12/73	972	12:15	SHELTON Jim	COLEMAN Gary	HABU	4.2	A

Date	Instal. No.	T.O. Time	Pilot Name	RSO Name	Mission	Duration	Remarks
18/12/73	968	10:00	JOERSZ Al	FULLER John	K9	0.8	
19/12/73	972	12:15	JOERSZ Al	FULLER John	HABU	4.9	
21/12/73	968	10:00	HELT Bob	ELLIOTT Larry	K9	1.5	
26/12/73	962	10:00	JOERSZ Al	FULLER John	K9	2.1	A
27/12/73	962	10:06	SHELTON Jim	COLEMAN Gary	K9	2.6	A
28/12/73	972	12:15	JOERSZ Al	FULLER John	HABU	3.5	
29/12/73	968	10:00	WILSON Jim	DOUGLASS Bruce	K9	2.5	A
31/12/73	972	11:15	JOERSZ Al	FULLER John	HABU	4.2	
03/01/74	962	10:00	WILSOM Jim	DOUGLASS Bruce	K9	1.8	A
04/01/74	972	11:45	SHELTON Jim	COLEMAN Gary	HABU	4.9	A
06/01/74	968	10:00	JOERSZ Al	FULLER John	K9	2.6	
08/01/74	972	10:30	WILSON Jim	DOUGLASS Bruce	HABU	4.1	
09/01/74	962	10:00	JOERSZ Al	FULLER John	K9	2.6	
12/01/74	968	11:00	WILSON Jim	DOUGLASS Bruce	HABU	3.6	
14/01/74	972	11:20	SULLIVAN Jim	WIDDIFIELD Noel	K9	2.5	
15/01/74	962	11:00	ROSENBERG Maury	BULLUCH Don	K9	2.5	
17/01/74	968	10:11	ROSENBERG Maury	BULLUCH Don	K1	3.7	
18/01/74	972	10:00	WILSON Jim	DOUGLASS Bruce	K9	2.6	
19/01/74	972	12:00	SULLIVAN Jim	WIDDIFIELD Noel	HABU	4.8	
22/01/74	972	12:00	WILSON Jim	DOUGLASS Bruce	K9	2.4	
23/01/74	968	10:31	ROSENBERG Maury	BULLUCH Don	K9	2.6	A
24/01/74	962	11:30	WILSON Jim	DOUGLASS Bruce	HABU	4.1	A
25/01/74	968	10:00	ROSENBERG Maury	BULLUCH Don	K9	1.4	A
28/01/74	968	13:10	ROSENBERG Maury	BULLUCH Don	K9	2.4	A
30/01/74	972	12:00	SULLIVAN Jim	WIDDIFIELD Noel	HABU	3.5	A
31/01/74	968	10:00	WILSON Jim	DOUGLASS Bruce	K9	2.3	
02/02/74	962	11:30	WILSON Jim	DOUGLASS Bruce	HABU	4.1	
04/02/74	968	09:45	ROSENBERG Maury	BULLUCH Don	K9	2.5	
05/02/74	968	10:00	ROSENBERG Maury	BULLUCH Don	K1	1.4	A
06/02/74	962	10:00	SULLIVAN Jim	WIDDIFIELD Noel	HABU	3.8	A
07/02/74	968	10:00	ROSENBERG Maury	BULLUCH Don	K1	3.7	
10/02/74	962	12:15	ADAMS Buck	MACHOREK Bill	HABU	3.6	
11/02/74	972	10:05	ROSENBERG Maury	BULLUCH Don	K1	4.1	
13/02/74	962	12:30	SULLIVAN Jim	WIDDIFIELD Noel	HABU	1.9	A
15/02/74	962	11:55	SULLIVAN Jim	WIDDIFIELD Noel	HABU	3.9	A
18/02/74	968	12:30	ADAMS Buck	MACHOREK Bill	HABU	3.5	
19/02/74	972	10:00	RANSOM Lee	ALLOCCA Tom	K9	2.3	
22/02/74	968		RANSOM Lee	ALLOCCA Tom	HABU		A
23/02/74	962		RANSOM Lee	ALLOCCA Tom	HABU		A
25/02/74	968	11:30	RANSOM Lee	ALLOCCA Tom	HABU	3.7	A
26/02/74	972	10:15	BLEDSOE Pat	BLACKWELL Reggie	K9	2.4	
27/02/74	968	09:05	ADAMS Buck	MACHOREK Bill	HABU	3.6	A
02/03/74	962	12:00	BLEDSOE Pat	BLACKWELL Reggie	HABU	4.4	
04/03/74	962		RANSOM Lee	ALLOCCA Tom	K9		A
05/03/74	962	10:17	RANSOM Lee	ALLOCCA Tom	K9	2.2	A
06/03/74	972	10:20	ADAMS Buck	MACHOREK Bill	K9	1.1	A
07/03/74	962	12:00	RANSOM Lee	ALLOCCA Tom	HABU	1.1	A
08/03/74	968	09:30	RANSOM Lee	ALLOCCA Tom	HABU	3.7	A
11/03/74	972	11:00	ADAMS Buck	MACHOREK Bill	HABU	4.4	
12/03/74	962	13:15	RANSOM Lee	ALLOCCA Tom	K4	0.9	
12/03/74	972	12:15	BLEDSOE Pat	BLACKWELL Reggie	HABU	4.3	A
16/03/74	968	10:00	JUDKINS Ty	MORGAN George	K9	2.4	A
18/03/74	962	12:00	RANSOM Lee	ALLOCCA Tom	HABU	3.5	
19/03/74	972		BLEDSOE Pat	BLACKWELL Reggie	K9		A
20/03/74	972	09:45	BLEDSOE Pat	BLACKWELL Reggie	K9	2.3	A
25/03/74	962	10:00	HELT Bob	ELLIOTT Larry	K9	2.4	A
26/03/74	968	13:00	JUDKINS Ty	MORGAN George	K9	2.1	
27/03/74	972	10:00	JUDKINS Ty	MORGAN George	HABU	3.7	
28/03/74	972	13:00	BLEDSOE Pat	BLACKWELL Reggie	HABU	4.3	
31/03/74	972	12:15	HELT Bob	ELLIOTT Larry	HABU	3.8	
04/04/74	962	13:00	BLEDSOE Pat	BLACKWELL Reggie	K4	1.1	
05/04/74	972	11:30	JUDKINS Ty	MORGAN George	HABU	4.8	
07/04/74	962	10:30	BLEDSOE Pat	BLACKWELL Reggie	HABU	4.1	
10/04/74	972	09:45	HELT Bob	ELLIOTT Larry	K9	2.8	
11/04/74	962	11:00	HELT Bob	ELLIOTT Larry	HABU	5	
13/04/74	972	10:00	HERTZOG Randy	CARNOCHAN John	K9	2.4	
16/04/74	962	09:46	JUDKINS Ty	MORGAN George	K9	2.4	A
20/04/74	972	11:30	HERTZOG Randy	CARNOCHAN John	HABU	3.7	A
22/04/74	968	10:00	JOERSZ Al	FULLER John	D1	1.3	
23/04/74	962	10:00	HELT Bob	ELLIOTT Larry	D1	1.2	A
27/04/74	968	12:20	JOERSZ Al	FULLER John	D3	2	
29/04/74	972	14:30	HELT Bob	ELLIOTT Larry	HABU	3.9	
30/04/74	968	10:00	HERTZOG Randy	CARNOCHAN John	D3	2.5	
01/05/74	962	12:35	JOERSZ Al	FULLER John	HABU	5	
06/05/74	962	11:10	HERTZOG Randy	CARNOCHAN John	HABU	5.1	
07/05/74	972	10:00	WILSON Jim	DOUGLASS Bruce	D4	2.7	
10/05/74	972	10:00	JOERSZ Al	FULLER John	HABU	3.9	
13/05/74	962	10:00	HERTZOG Randy	CARNOCHAN John	D6	2.4	
14/05/74	962	13:35	WILSON Jim	DOUGLASS Bruce	D4	2.8	
17/05/74	968	11:03	WILSON Jim	DOUGLASS Bruce	HABU	3.7	
18/05/74	962	10:05	JOERSZ Al	FULLER John	D4	2.4	
19/05/74	968	09:30	JOERSZ Al	FULLER John	HABU	3.7	
20/05/74	962	18:50	WILSON Jim	DOUGLASS Bruce	D1	1	
22/05/74	968	10:00	ROSENBERG Maury	BULLUCH Don	D4	2.4	
27/05/74	968	10:45	ROSENBERG Maury	BULLUCH Don	HABU	5.1	
28/05/74	962	10:00	JOERSZ Al	FULLER John	D3	2.5	
03/06/74	972	10:15	WILSON Jim	DOUGLASS Bruce	D5	2.1	
04/06/74	962	09:45	SULLIVAN Jim	WIDDIFIELD Noel	D4	2.5	
05/06/74	968	10:05	WILSON Jim	DOUGLASS Bruce	HABU	2.3	A
06/06/74	972	10:20	ROSENBERG Maury	BULLUCH Don	D8	4.2	
07/06/74	972	10:15	SULLIVAN Jim	WIDDIFIELD Noel	D8	4	
10/06/74	968	10:03	WILSON Jim	DOUGLASS Bruce	D8	4.3	
11/06/74	968	10:45	ROSENBERG MAURY	BULLUCH Don	D8	4.2	
12/06/74	962	10:45	WILSON Jim	DOUGLASS Bruce	D8	4.2	
14/06/74	972	13:00	ROSENBERG Maury	BULLUCH Don	HABU	2	A
15/06/74	972	14:00	ROSENBERG Maury	BULLUCH Don	HABU	4.7	
17/06/74	962	09:00	ADAMS Buck	MACHOREK BIll	D8	3.9	
18/06/74	972	09:02	SULLIVAN Jim	WIDDIFIELD Noel	D7	2	

Date	Instal. No.	T.O. Time	Pilot Name	RSO Name	Mission	Duration	Remarks
21/06/74	962		ROSENBERG Maury	BULLUCH Don	D8		A
22/06/74	972	11:00	SULLIVAN Jim	WIDDIFIELD Noel	HABU	3.6	
24/06/74	962	10:00	ROSENBERG Maury	BULLUCH Don	D8	2.3	A
25/06/74	972	10:04	ADAMS Buck	MACHOREK Bill	D8	4	
26/06/74	972		SULLIVAN Jim	WIDDIFIELD Noel	D8		A
27/06/74	962	13:44	ADAMS Buck	MACHOREK Bill	HABU	1.8	A
28/06/74	972	13:30	ADAMS Buck	MACHOREK Bill	HABU	1.3	A
29/06/74	972	11:30	SULLIVAN Jim	WIDDIFIELD Noel	HABU	3.6	
02/07/74	968	10:06	HELT Bob	ELLIOTT Larry	D8	2	A
03/07/74	962	10:20	ADAMS Buck	MACHOREK Bill	D8	2.1	
08/07/74	972	11:00	HELT Bob	ELLIOTT Larry	HABU	3	A
09/07/74	962	10:00	SULLIVAN Jim	WIDDIFIELD Noel	D3	2.2	
10/07/74	962	11:30	SULLIVAN Jim	WIDDIFIELD Noel	HABU	4.1	
11/07/74	968	10:05	ADAMS Buck	MACHOREK Bill	D8	3.9	
12/07/74	972		HELT Bob	ELLIOTT Larry	D8		A
15/07/74	968	12:30	ADAMS Buck	MACHOREK Bill	HABU	3.6	
16/07/74	972	10:30	HELT Bob	ELLIOTT Larry	D8	4.1	
18/07/74	968		BLEDSOE Pat	BLACKWELL Reggie	D7		A
19/07/74	968	10:30	BLEDSOE Pat	BLACKWELL Reggie	D1	1.1	
23/07/74	968	11:03	HELT Bob	ELLIOTT Larry	HABU	4	
24/07/74	972	10:30	ADAMS Buck	MACHOREK Bill	D4	2.3	
26/07/74	968	09:10	BLEDSOE Pat	BLACKWELL Reggie	HABU	4.2	
29/07/74	972	10:00	HELT Bob	ELLIOTT Larry	HABU	2.1	A
30/07/74	962	11:23	RANSOM Lee	PAYNE Al	D8	4.1	
31/07/74	968	11:00	BLEDSOE Pat	BLACKWELL Reggie	D7	2.3	
02/08/74	968	10:15	HELT Bob	ELLIOTT Larry	D8	4.1	
06/08/74	972	12:30	RANSOM Lee	PAYNE Al	HABU	1.5	A
07/08/74	962	10:15	BLEDSOE Pat	BLACKWELL Reggie	D8	4	
08/08/74	968	10:30	RANSOM Lee	PAYNE Al	HABU	4	
09/08/74	962	12:00	HELT Bob	ELLIOTT Larry	HABU	2.3	A
09/08/74	968	13:23	BLEDSOE Pat	BLACKWELL Reggie	HABU	4.2	
11/08/74	968		RANSOM Lee	PAYNE Al	D4		A
12/08/74	968	10:00	HELT Bob	ELLIOTT Larry	D1	1.1	
13/08/74	963	03:00	JOERSZ Al	FULLER John	FERRY IN	5.3	
13/08/74	972	10:00	RANSOM Lee	PAYNE Al	D3	2.4	
14/08/74	968	06:00	HELT Bob	ELLIOTT Larry	FERRY OUT		
15/08/74	962	11:00	BLEDSOE Pat	BLACKWELL Reggie	HABU	3.7	
15/08/74	963	10:00	JOERSZ Al	FULLER John	D3	2.4	
16/08/74	961	03:00	WILSON Jim	DOUGLASS Bruce	FERRY IN	5.3	
17/08/74	972	06:00	BLEDSOE Pat	BLACKWELL Reggie	FERRY OUT		
18/08/74	963	12:34	RANSOM Lee	PAYNE Al	HABU	3.4	A
19/08/74	976	03:00	HERTZOG Randy	MORGAN George	FERRY IN	5.3	
20/08/74	962	06:00	WILSON Jim	DOUGLASS Bruce	FERRY OUT		
20/08/74	961	09:30	JOERSZ Al	FULLER John	D3	0.8	A
22/08/74	963	09:45	RANSOM Lee	PAYNE Al	HABU	1.5	A
22/08/74	976	11:00	JOERSZ Al	FULLER John	HABU	1.7	A
23/08/74	963	09:45	RANSOM Lee	PAYNE Al	HABU	4.3	
26/08/74	976	10:00	HERTZOG Randy	MORGAN George	D4	2.3	
26/08/74	961	10:35	JOERSZ Al	FULLER John	HABU	4.8	
27/08/74	963	10:00	RANSOM Lee	PAYNE Al	D1	1.1	
28/08/74	976	10:15	HERTZOG Randy	MORGAN George	D4	1.5	A
03/09/74	976	10:15	JOERSZ Al	FULLER John	D8	4.1	
04/09/74	961	10:17	RANSOM Lee	PAYNE AL	D1	1	
04/09/74	963	10:30	HERTZOG Randy	MORGAN George	D3	2.4	
05/09/74	963	10:30	HERTZOG Randy	MORGAN George	HABU	4.9	
09/09/74	976	10:52	ROSENBERG Maury	BULLUCH Don	D8	4	
10/09/74	963	10:30	JOERSZ Al	FULLER John	HABU	4.9	
11/09/74	961	11:55	JOERSZ Al	FULLER John	HABU	4	
13/09/74	963	10:45	HERTZOG Randy	MORGAN George	D3	2.4	
17/09/74	961	10:32	JOERSZ Al	FULLER John	D3	2.5	
19/09/74	976	10:00	ROSENBERG Maury	BULLUCH Don	HABU	4.9	
20/09/74	963	10:15	HERTZOG Randy	MORGAN George	D3	2.3	
23/09/74	961	10:40	WILSON Jim	DOUGLASS Bruce	D8	4.1	
24/09/74	976	10:15	ROSENBERG Maury	BULLUCH Don	D4	1.8	A
25/09/74	963	10:45	HERTZOG Randy	MORGAN George	HABU	5	
27/09/74	961	12:00	HERTZOG Randy	MORGAN George	HABU	2.1	A
27/09/74	963	13:24	ROSENBERG Maury	BOLLUCH Don	HABU	4.3	
02/10/74	963	10:14	WILSON Jim	DOUGLASS Bruce	D2	2.5	
04/10/74	961	10:13	ROSENBERG Maury	BULLUCH Don	D1	1.2	
09/10/74	961	11:45	ROSENBERG Maury	BULLUCH Don	HABU	3.7	
10/10/74	963	10:34	WILSON Jim	DOUGLASS Bruce	D8	3.6	
12/10/74	963	12:30	WILSON Jim	DOUGLASS Bruce	HABU	4.2	
15/10/74	963		ADAMS Buck	MACHOREK Bill	D4		A
16/10/74	961	11:44	WILSON Jim	DOUGLASS Bruce	HABU	5.1	
17/10/74	963		ADAMS Buck	MACHOREK Bill	D4		A
18/10/74	961	12:27	ROSENBERG Maury	BULLUCH Don	D7	1.8	
18/10/74	963	10:34	ADAMS Buck	MACHOREK Bill	HABU	4.1	
22/10/74	961	10:15	WILSON Jim	DOUGLASS Bruce	D3	2.5	
26/10/74	963	12:50	ADAMS Buck	MACHOREK Bill	HABU	3.7	
28/10/74	963	12:50	WILSON Jim	DOUGLASS Bruce	HABU	3.8	
29/10/74	961	10:15	SULLIVAN Jim	WIDDIFIELD Noel	D3	2.4	
01/11/74	963		SULLIVAN Jim	WIDDIFIELD Noel	HABU		A
02/11/74	963	10:30	SULLIVAN Jim	WIDDIFIELD Noel	HABU	3.6	
11/11/74	961	13:15	HELT Bob	ELLIOTT Larry	D3	2.5	
12/11/74	963	10:35	SULLIVAN Jim	WIDDIFIELD Noel	D3	2.3	
13/11/74	961	11:00	HELT Bob	ELLIOTT Larry	HABU	5.1	
15/11/74	963	13:30	SULLIVAN Jim	WIDDIFIELD Noel	D3	2.4	
17/11/74	961	10:00	RANSOM Lee	PAYNE Al	D8	2.6	A
23/11/74	963	11:30	HELT Bob	ELLIOTT Larry	HABU	4.2	
25/11/74	963	13:00	RANSOM Lee	PAYNE Al	D8	3.9	
26/11/74	971	03:31	BLEDSOE Pat	BLACKWELL Reggie	FERRY IN (DET-1)	5.5	
28/11/74	963	11:30	HELT Bob	ELLIOTT Larry	HABU	4.2	
29/11/74	961	10:50	RANSOM Lee	PAYNE Al	D3	2.5	
02/12/74	971	10:31	BLEDSOE Pat	BLACKWELL Reggie	D8	1.5	A
03/12/74	961	11:30	BLEDSOE Pat	BLACKWELL Reggie	HABU	4.4	
04/12/74	971	10:15	HELT Bob	ELLIOTT Larry	D8	1.4	A
06/12/74	961	10:45	RANSOM Lee	PAYNE Al	HABU	5	
09/12/74	971	12:00	HELT Bob	ELLIOTT Larry	D8	2	A

Date	Instal. No.	T.O. Time	Pilot Name	RSO Name	Mission	Duration	Remarks
10/12/74	971		BLEDSOE Pat	BLACKWELL Reggie	D9		A
11/12/74	971	11:15	BLEDSOE Pat	BLACKWELL Reggie	D1	1.1	
11/12/74	963	10:15	HELT Bob	ELLIOTT Larry	HABU	3.7	
13/12/74	971	10:15	RANSOM Lee	PAYNE Al	D9	2.7	
17/12/74	971	12:00	KINEGO Joe	JACKS Roger	D3	2.5	
19/12/74	963		BLEDSOE Pat	BLACKWELL Reggie	HABU		A
20/12/74	961	10:30	BLEDSOE Pat	BLACKWELL Reggie	D8	3.8	
21/12/74	963		BLEDSOE Pat	BLACKWELL Reggie	HABU		A
23/12/74	961	10:50	RANSOM Lee	PAYNE Al	D1	1	
23/12/74	963	09:30	BLEDSOE Pat	BLACKWELL Reggie	HABU	3.7	
27/12/74	971	11:30	KINEGO Joe	JACKS Roger	D5	3.9	
28/12/74	963	11:15	KINEGO Joe	JACKS Roger	HABU	3.7	
30/12/74	961	11:30	BLEDSOE Pat	BLACKWELL Reggie	HABU	2.1	A
30/12/74	971	12:45	KINEGO Joe	JACKS Roger	HABU	1.4	A
31/12/74	961	11:30	BLEDSOE Pat	BLACKWELL Reggie	HABU	6.2	A
02/01/75	963	10:30	ROSENBERG Maury	BULLUCH Don	HABU	4.3	
03/01/75	961	09:30	ROSENBERG Maury	BULLUCH Don	D4	2.4	
04/01/75	961		KINEGO Joe	JACKS Roger	HABU		A
04/01/75	963	12:15	ROSENBERG Maury	BULLUCH Don	HABU	4.1	
06/01/75	971	10:00	BLEDSOE Pat	BLACKWELL Reggie	D8	4.2	
07/01/75	961	10:30	KINEGO Joe	JACKS Roger	HABU	3.3	
09/01/75	961	10:30	ROSENBERG Maury	BULLUCH Don	HABU	4.3	
10/01/75	976	10:00	SMITH Tom	CARNOCHAN John	FCF	0.7	A
10/01/75	971	11:30	KINEGO Joe	JACKS Roger	HABU	5	
11/01/75	961	11:31	KINEGO Joe	JACKS Roger	HABU	4.3	
13/01/75	976		PUGH Tom	CARNOCHAN John	FCF		A
13/01/75	976	13:15	PUGH Tom	CARNOCHAN John	FCF	1.4	A
14/01/75	976	13:30	SMITH Tom	CARNOCHAN John	FCF	2.4	
15/01/75	963	11:00	JOERSZ Al	MACHOREK Bill	D9	2.5	
16/01/75	971	10:50	ROSENBERG Maury	BULLUCH Don	HABU	5.2	
17/01/75	976	13:00	PUGH Tom	CARNOCHAN John	D1	1	
17/01/75	961	11:00	JOERSZ Al	MACHOREK Bill	HABU	3.9	
23/01/75	963	10:00	KINEGO Joe	MACHOREK Bill	D1	1	
24/01/75	961	11:30	JOERSZ Al	MACHOREK Bill	HABU	4.1	
25/01/75	963	10:45	ROSENBERG Maury	BULLUCH Don	HABU	4	
27/01/75	961	11:00	ROSENBERG Maury	BULLUCH Don	HABU	1.7	A
28/01/75	961	11:00	HERTZOG Randy	MORGAN George	HABU	3.6	A
29/01/75	976	13:00	PUGH Tom	CARNOCHAN John	D1	1	
29/01/75	963	11:45	JOERSZ Al	MACHOREK Bill	HABU	3.1	A
30/01/75	976	06:50	PUGH Tom	CARNOCHAN John	FERRY OUT		
31/01/75	971		ROSENBERG Maury	BULLUCH Don	HABU		A
31/01/75	961	12:30	HERTZOG Randy	MORGAN George	HABU	4.2	
01/02/75	971	10:28	ROSENBERG Maury	BULLUCH Don	D8	4	
04/02/75	971	10:32	JOERSZ Al	MACHOREK Bill	D8	4	
07/02/75	961	10:15	HERTZOG Randy	MORGAN George	HABU	4.2	
08/02/75	963		JOERSZ Al	MACHOREK Bill	HABU		A
10/02/75	971		JOERSZ Al	MACHOREK Bill	HABU		A
10/02/75	971	12:33	JOERSZ Al	MACHOREK Bill	HABU	4.9	
11/02/75	963	10:15	WILSON Jim	DOUGLASS Bruce	D3	2.1	
13/02/75	971	10:45	HERTZOG Randy	MORGAN George	HABU	4.9	
18/02/75	971	11:20	WILSON Jim	DOUGLASS Bruce	HABU	4.3	
18/02/75	961	12:50	JOERSZ Al	MACHOREK Bill	D3	2.3	
19/02/75	963	10:15	HERTZOG Randy	MORGAN George	D1	1.1	
24/02/75	961	12:00	HERTZOG Randy	MORGAN George	HABU	4.3	
25/02/75	971	11:30	WILSON Jim	DOUGLASS Bruce	HABU	3.8	
28/02/75	971	11:05	ADAMS Buck	GERSTEN Mark	HABU	4.8	
04/03/75	961	12:15	HERTZOG Randy	MORGAN George	D3	2.4	
06/03/75	971	12:00	WILSON Jim	DOUGLASS Bruce	HABU	4.2	
07/03/75	961	12:00	WILSON Jim	DOUGLASS Bruce	HABU	5	
09/03/75	963	09:00	SULLIVAN Jim	WIDDIFIELD Noel	D1	1.1	
10/03/75	963	12:38	ADAMS Buck	GERSTEN Mark	D8 MODIFIED	2.5	
12/03/75	961	11:00	ADAMS Buck	GERSTEN Mark	HABU	0.6	A
13/03/75	971		ADAMS Buck	GERSTEN Mark	HABU		A
14/03/75	971		ADAMS Buck	GERSTEN Mark	HABU		A
14/03/75	971	13:10	ADAMS Buck	GERSTEN Mark	HABU	4.1	
15/03/75	971	12:00	SULLIVAN Jim	WIDDIFIELD Noel	HABU	4.9	
17/03/75	963	11:00	WILSON Jim	DOUGLASS Bruce	D8	4.1	
19/03/75	961	11:00	ADAMS Buck	GERSTEN Mark	D8	2.2	
20/03/75	963	11:00	SULLIVAN Jim	WIDDIFIELD Noel	D1	1.1	
21/03/75	971	11:15	ADAMS Buck	GERSTEN Mark	HABU	5	
22/03/75	963	10:16	SULLIVAN Jim	WIDDIFIELD Noel	D1	0.9	
24/03/75	961	10:15	RANSOM Lee	PAYNE Al	D3	1.3	A
25/03/75	963	10:45	SULLIVAN Jim	WIDDIFIELD Noel	HABU	4.8	
26/03/75	963	13:10	SULLIVAN Jim	WIDDIFIELD Noel	HABU	3.3	
27/03/75	963	12:00	RANSOM Lee	PAYNE Al	HABU	4	
28/03/75	963	11:30	ADAMS Buck	GERSTEN Mark	HABU	3.5	
28/03/75	971	13:00	SULLIVAN Jim	WIDDIFIELD Noel	D1	0.8	A
01/04/75	971	11:30	ADAMS Buck	GERSTEN Mark	HABU	4	
02/04/75	961	11:37	RANSOM Lee	PAYNE Al	D1	1	
03/04/75	963		RANSOM Lee	PAYNE Al	HABU		A
03/04/75	963	12:32	RANSOM Lee	PAYNE Al	HABU	4.9	
04/04/75	961	10:30	SULLIVAN Jim	WIDDIFIELD Noel	D3	2.2	
05/04/75	971	12:00	SULLIVAN Jim	WIDDIFIELD Noel	HABU	4.2	
07/04/75	961		HELT Bob	ELLIOTT Larry	D1		A
09/04/75	971	11:00	HELT Bob	ELLIOTT Larry	D8	3.9	
10/04/75	963	11:20	RANSOM Lee	PAYNE Al	HABU	4.9	A
11/04/75	961	10:15	SULLIVAN Jim	WIDDIFIELD Noel	D1	0.9	
12/04/75	961	10:00	HELT Bob	ELLIOTT Larry	HABU	0.9	A
13/04/75	961	11:01	HELT Bob	ELLIOTT Larry	HABU	3.6	
15/04/75	971	09:30	SULLIVAN Jim	WIDDIFIELD Noel	HABU	4.4	
16/04/75	963	11:30	SULLIVAN Jim	WIDDIFIELD Noel	HABU	3.5	
17/04/75	971	10:15	RANSOM Lee	PAYNE Al	HABU	1	A
17/04/75	963	11:35	HELT Bob	ELLIOTT Larry	HABU	3.5	
19/04/75	963		RANSOM Lee	PAYNE Al	HABU		A
19/04/75	971	11:20	RANSOM Lee	PAYNE Al	HABU	0.9	A
21/04/75	963	10:00	RANSOM Lee	PAYNE Al	HABU	4.4	
22/04/75	961	10:33	CIRINO AL	LIEBMAN Bruce	D3	2.5	
23/04/75	963	09:30	CIRINO AL	LIEBMAN Bruce	HABU	0.6	A
24/04/75	961		CIRINO AL	LIEBMAN Bruce	HABU		A
24/04/75	961	10:50	CIRINO AL	LIEBMAN Bruce	HABU	4.4	
25/04/75	963	10:00	HELT Bob	ELLIOTT Larry	HABU	3.3	A
26/04/75	971	09:05	RANSOM Lee	PAYNE Al	HABU	4.5	
27/04/75	971	10:30	CIRINO Al	LIEBMAN Bruce	HABU	3.5	
27/04/75	963	22:40	HELT Bob	ELLIOTT Larry	RTB FERRY NITE	2	
28/04/75	971	09:50	RANSOM Lee	PAYNE Al	HABU	3.4	
29/04/75	961	10:09	HELT Bob	ELLIOTT Larry	HABU	3.4	
30/04/75	971	09:30	CIRINO Al	LIEBMAN Bruce	HABU	3.5	
06/05/75	963	10:20	BLEDSOE Pat	BLACKWELL Reggie	D3	2.2	
07/05/75	961	11:40	HELT Bob	ELLIOTT Larry	D4	2.3	
09/05/75	963	11:30	HELT Bob	ELLIOTT Larry	HABU	1.6	A
10/05/75	961	11:30	CIRINO Al	LIEBAMN Bruce	HABU	3.8	
11/05/75	971	10:30	CIRINO Al	LIEBAMN Bruce	D1	0.9	
11/05/75	961	08:30	HELT Bob	ELLIOTT Larry	HABU	4.2	
15/05/75	963	11:20	BLEDSOE Pat	BLACKWELL Reggie	D1	1.1	
17/05/75	963	09:30	KINEGO Joe	JACKS Roger	D1	1	
19/05/75	961	08:30	CIRINO Al	LIEBMAN Bruce	HABU	7.4	A,16
20/05/75	963	12:20	BLEDSOE Pat	BLACKWELL Reggie	HABU	5.1	
22/05/75	961	09:50	BLEDSOE Pat	BLACKWELL Reggie	HABU	4.1	
24/05/75	961	12:00	CIRINO Al	LIEBMAN Bruce	HABU	0.5	A
26/05/75	963	10:30	CIRINO Al	LIEBMAN Bruce	HABU	2.2	A
27/05/75	971	10:35	KINEGO Joe	JACKS Roger	D9	1.2	
28/05/75	961	10:30	CIRINO Al	LIEBMAN Bruce	HABU	2.4	A
30/05/75	963	11:01	KINEGO Joe	JACKS Roger	HABU	3.9	
02/06/75	971		RANSOM Lee	PAYNE Al	D9		A
03/06/75	963	11:00	BLEDSOE Pat	BLACKWELL Reggie	HABU	3.7	
03/06/75	971	11:40	RANSOM Lee	PAYNE Al	D4	2.4	
06/06/75	971		KINEGO Joe	JACKS Roger	D8		A
06/06/75	971	15:02	KINEGO Joe	JACKS Roger	D4	1.9	A
10/06/75	971	11:32	BLEDSOE Pat	BLACKWELL Reggie	D4	1.9	A
13/06/75	961	09:16	RANSOM Lee	PAYNE Al	D4	1.9	A
13/06/75	963	10:10	KINEGO Joe	JACKS Roger	HABU	5	
16/06/75	971	10:15	WILSON Jim	DOUGLASS Bruce	D3	2.6	
17/06/75	963	10:15	JOERSZ AL	MORGAN George	D4	2.4	
18/06/75	961		KINEGO Joe	JACKS Roger	D4		A
19/06/75	963	10:15	WILSON Jim	DOUGLASS Bruce	D6	2.4	
20/06/75	971	11:15	KINEGO Joe	JACKS Roger	HABU	2.4	
23/06/75	961	09:30	JOERSZ Al	MORGAN George	D8	1.7	A
24/06/75	963	09:30	KINEGO Joe	JACKS Roger	HABU	3.2	
24/06/75	961	13:30	WILSON Jim	DOUGLASS Bruce	D9	2.5	
25/06/75	971	10:15	JOERSZ Al	MORGAN George	D9	1.3	
27/06/75	961	12:27	JOERSZ Al	MORGAN George	D9	2.2	
30/06/75	971		MURPHY Jay	BILLINGSLEY John	D4		A
01/07/75	963	10:15	MURPHY Jay	BILLINGSLEY John	D3	2.3	
02/07/75	961	09:00	WILSON Jim	DOUGLASS Bruce	D4	2.3	
02/07/75	971	13:03	JOERSZ Al	MORGAN George	HABU	3.6	
03/07/75	971	11:53	WILSON Jim	DOUGLASS Bruce	HABU	3.5	
07/07/75	963		MURPHY Jay	BILLINGSLEY John	D9		A
07/07/75	963	11:30	MURPHY Jay	BILLINGSLEY John	D9	1.3	
09/07/75	961	10:15	MURPHY Jay	BILLINGSLEY John	D9	2.9	
11/07/75	971	10:00	WILSON Jim	DOUGLASS Bruce	HABU	3.7	
11/07/75	963	12:33	JOERSZ Al	MORGAN George	K9	2.7	
14/07/75	961	12:49	MURPHY Jay	BILLINGSLEY John	D8	1.7	A
16/07/75	963	11:59	WILSON Jim	DOUGLASS Bruce	D9	2.7	
17/07/75	971	13:00	MURPHY Jay	BILLINGSLEY John	HABU	2.2	
18/07/75	961	13:37	JOERSZ Al	MORGAN George	D9	2.4	
19/07/75	971	09:15	JOERSZ Al	MORGAN George	HABU	3.5	
21/07/75	971	09:26	MURPHY Jay	BILLINGSLEY John	D8	3.8	
22/07/75	961	10:18	WILSON Jim	DOUGLASS Bruce	D8	2.5	A
23/07/75	961	10:00	JOERSZ Al	MORGAN George	D8	4.1	
24/07/75	963		MURPHY Jay	BILLINGSLEY John	HABU		A
25/07/75	963		MURPHY Jay	BILLINGSLEY John	D1		A
25/07/75	963	13:00	MURPHY Jay	BILLINGSLEY John	D3	1	
28/07/75	961	10:10	MURPHY Jay	BILLINGSLEY John	HABU	4.2	A
30/07/75	961	11:20	HELT Bob	ELLIOTT Larry	HABU	3.6	
31/07/75	963	08:35	HELT Bob	ELLIOTT Larry	HABU	4.3	
01/08/75	961	11:15	SULLIVAN Jim	GERSTEN Mark	D4	2.4	
04/08/75	963	09:30	SULLIVAN Jim	GERSTEN Mark	HABU	1.4	A
08/08/75	961	11:14	SULLIVAN Jim	GERSTEN Mark	HABU	3.5	
13/08/75	971	12:51	ROSENBERG Maury	BULLUCH Don	D10	2.2	
14/08/75	963	12:00	HELT Bob	ELLIOTT Larry	D10	2.4	
15/08/75	963	09:30	HELT Bob	ELLIOTT Larry	HABU	3.8	
15/08/75	971	12:09	SULLIVAN Jim	GERSTEN Mark	D10	2.3	
22/08/75	961		ROSENBERG Maury	BULLUCH Don	D10		A
22/08/75	963	14:20	SULLIVAN Jim	GERSTEN Mark	D4	2.4	
24/08/75	971		SULLIVAN Jim	GERSTEN Mark	HABU		A
25/08/75	963	10:30	SULLIVAN Jim	GERSTEN Mark	HABU	2.1	A
26/08/75	963	10:30	SULLIVAN Jim	GERSTEN Mark	HABU	3.6	
26/08/75	961	13:15	ROSENBERG Maury	BULLUCH Don	D10	2.2	
27/08/75	971	11:18	CIRINO Al	LIEBMAN Bruce	HABU	3.8	
28/08/75	961	10:30	SULLIVAN Jim	GERSTEN Mark	D10	2.2	
29/08/75	971		SULLIVAN Jim	GERSTEN Mark	HABU		A
29/08/75	961	14:13	CIRINO Al	LIEBMAN Bruce	HABU	3.6	
02/09/75	961	10:00	ROSENBERG Maury	BULLUCH Don	D8	2.6	
03/09/75	961	10:35	SULLIVAN Jim	GERSTEN Mark	D4	2.5	
04/09/75	971	09:45	CIRINO Al	LIEBMAN Bruce	D8	4.2	
05/09/75	963		ROSENBERG Maury	BULLUCH Don	D10		A
05/09/75	963	16:01	ROSENBERG Maury	BULLUCH Don	D10	2.3	
08/09/75	963		BLEDSOE Pat	BLACKWELL Reggie	D10		A
08/09/75	961	09:50	ROSENBERG Maury	BULLUCH Don	HABU	3.5	
09/09/75	963	10:00	BLEDSOE Pat	BLACKWELL Reggie	D8	4	
09/09/75	971	10:45	CIRINO Al	LIEBMAN Bruce	D3	2.6	A
10/09/75	963	10:28	ROSENBERG Maury	BULLUCH Don	D8	3.8	
11/09/75	971	10:00	BLEDSOE Pat	BLACKWELL Reggie	D8	1.4	A
15/09/75	961	10:15	ROSENBERG Maury	BULLUCH Don	D8	4.2	
16/09/75	971	14:42	CIRINO Al	LIEBMAN Bruce	HABU	3.5	
17/09/75	961	10:30	BLEDSOE Pat	BLACKWELL Reggie	D8	4.1	

Date	Instal. No.	T.O. Time	Pilot Name	RSO Name	Mission	Duration	Remarks
19/09/75	961		CIRINO Al	LIEBMAN Bruce	D8		A
22/09/75	971	10:15	BLEDSOE Pat	BLACKWELL Reggie	HABU	4.9	
22/09/75	961	12:30	GRAHAM Rich	EMMONS Don	D5	3.6	
24/09/75	961	11:15	CIRINO Al	LIEBMAN Bruce	D8	2.5	A
26/09/75	961		GRAHAM Rich	EMMONS Don	D8		A
29/09/75	961		CIRINO Al	LIEBMAN Bruce	D5		A
29/09/75	961	14:47	CIRINO Al	LIEBMAN Bruce	D8	2.6	
30/09/75	971	11:00	GRAHAM Rich	EMMONS Don	HABU	3.6	
03/10/75	961	11:00	BLEDSOE Pat	BLACKWELL Reggie	D8	2.8	
06/10/75	971		BLEDSOE Pat	BLACKWELL Reggie	HABU		A
07/10/75	971	09:00	KINIGO Joe	JACKS Roger	D11	5.6	
09/10/75	961	10:10	BLEDSOE Pat	BLACKWELL Reggie	HABU	4.9	
10/10/75	971	09:38	GRAHAM Rich	EMMONS Don	D11	5.7	
13/10/75	971	10:07	GRAHAM Rich	EMMONS Don	HABU	3.5	
17/10/75	961	11:15	KINEGO Joe	JACKS Roger	HABU	1.9	
22/10/75	963		RANSOM Lee	PAYNE Al	D8		A
23/10/75	963	10:15	RANSOM Lee	PAYNE Al	D8	4.1	
28/10/75	971	10:15	GRAHAM Rich	EMMONS Don	D11	2.1	
29/10/75	963	12:30	RANSOM Lee	PAYNE Al	HABU	3.6	
30/10/75	961	11:00	KINEGO Joe	JACKS Roger	HABU	2.6	A
31/10/75	963	11:00	KINEGO Joe	JACKS Roger	HABU	1	A
31/10/75	961	12:15	RANSOM Lee	PAYNE Al	HABU	3.5	
03/11/75	971	10:14	WILSON Jim	DOUGLASS Bruce	D8	4.1	
05/11/75	961	11:10	WILSON Jim	DOUGLASS Bruce	HABU	3.8	
06/11/75	963	10:15	KINEGO Joe	JACKS Roger	D8	4.2	
07/11/75	961		RANSOM Lee	PAYNE Al	D8		A
12/11/75	971	11:00	KINEGO Joe	JACKS Roger	HABU	3.7	
14/11/75	963	10:15	RANSOM Lee	PAYNE Al	D4	2.5	
17/11/75	971	12:55	WILSON Jim	DOUGLASS Bruce	HABU	3.7	
18/11/75	963	12:00	MURPHY Jay	BILLINGSLEY John	HABU	3.8	
19/11/75	971		RANSOM Lee	PAYNE Al	D8		A
21/11/75	971	10:17	RANSOM Lee	PAYNE Al	D8	3.8	
24/11/75	963	10:15	WILSON Jim	DOUGLASS Bruce	D4	2.6	
26/11/75	971	10:15	RANSOM Lee	PAYNE Al	D8	3.9	
27/11/75	963	12:15	MURPHY Jim	BILLINGSLEY John	HABU	1.9	
01/12/75	963	09:31	JOERSZ Al	MORGAN George	D4	2.5	
04/12/75	963	10:00	WILSON Jim	DOUGLASS Bruce	HABU	2.6	
05/12/75	963	10:15	MURPHY Jay	BILLINGSLEY John	D8	4.1	
08/12/75	971	10:16	JOERSZ Al	MORGAN George	D8	4.3	
09/12/75	963	11:00	JOERSZ Al	MORGAN George	HABU	3.6	
10/12/75	971	10:15	WILSON Jim	DOUGLASS Bruce	D4	2.7	
12/12/75	963	11:00	MURPHY Jay	BILLINGSLEY John	HABU	5	
15/12/75	971	09:10	JOERSZ Al	MORGAN George	HABU	0.7	A
16/12/75	963	10:30	JOERSZ Al	MORGAN George	HABU	3.6	
16/12/75	971	12:05	ALISON Tom	VIDA Joe (J.T.)	D4	2.7	
18/12/75	963	10:00	ALISON Tom	VIDA Joe	HABU	3.6	A
20/12/75	963	07:00	MURPHY Jay	BILLINGSLEY John	HABU	3.8	
22/12/75	971	10:50	ALISON Tom	VIDA Joe	HABU	4.9	
29/12/75	963	10:04	JOERSZ Al	MORGAN George	D4	2.6	
30/12/75	971	09:30	ROSENBERG Maury	BULLUCH Don	HABU	3.6	
31/12/75	963	10:05	ALISON Tom	VIDA Joe	D4	2.5	
05/01/76	963	10:50	JOERSZ Al	MORGAN George	HABU	4.9	
08/01/76	971	09:30	ALISON Tom	VIDA Joe	HABU	3.7	
10/01/76	963	10:14	ROSENBERG Maury	BULLUCH Don	D4	2.5	
12/01/76	963	10:15	ROSENBERG Maury	BULLUCH Don	HABU	3.6	
14/01/76	961	14:04	ALISON Tom	VIDA Joe	D4	2.6	
17/01/76	963	12:15	HELT Bob	ELLIOTT Larry	HABU	1.1	A
20/01/76	971	11:42	ALISON Tom	VIDA Joe	HABU	3.5	A
21/01/76	961	10:03	ROSENBERG Maury	BULLUCH Don	D8	4.1	
23/01/76	961	11:30	HELT Bob	ELLIOTT Larry	HABU	3.7	
23/01/76	963	13:05	ROSENBERG Maury	BULLUCH Don	D7	1.7	
24/01/76	971	10:30	ROSENBERG Maury	BULLUCH Don	HABU	3.7	
27/01/76	961	11:00	BLEDSOE Pat	FULLER John	HABU	3.6	
29/01/76	963	12:40	HELT Bob	ELLIOTT Larry	HABU	4.3	
02/02/76	961	10:15	ROSENBERG Maury	BULLUCH Don	D4	2.7	
06/02/76	963	10:02	BLEDSOE Pat	FULLER John	HABU	4.8	
07/02/76	961	10:31	HELT Bob	ELLIOTT Larry	HABU	3.8	
10/02/76	963	11:30	CIRINO Al	LIEBMAN Bruce	HABU	2.4	
11/02/76	961	10:15	HELT Bob	ELLIOTT Larry	D4	2.6	
12/02/76	963		BLEDSOE Pat	FULLER John	HABU		A
13/02/76	963	11:22	BLEDSOE Pat	FULLER John	HABU	3.9	
16/02/76	971	10:56	CIRINO Al	LIEBMAN Bruce	D8	4.5	
18/02/76	961	11:50	HELT Bob	ELLIOTT Larry	HABU	3.7	
19/02/76	963	10:20	BLEDSOE Pat	FULLER John	D4	2.4	
20/02/76	971	09:10	CIRINO Al	LIEBMAN Bruce	HABU	1.3	A
20/02/76	961	10:10	BLEDSOE Pat	FULLER John	HABU	2	
23/02/76	961	10:17	GRAHAM Rich	EMMONS Don	D8	4.1	
24/02/76	971		CIRINO Al	LIEBMAN Bruce	HABU		A
24/02/76	961	11:30	GRAHAM Rich	EMMONS Don	HABU	3.6	
26/02/76	971	10:18	CIRINO Al	LIEBMAN Bruce	D4	2.6	
27/02/76	963	11:05	BLEDSOE Pat	EMMONS Don	D4	2.7	
27/02/76	961	12:30	CIRINO Al	LIEBMAN Bruce	HABU	3.7	
01/03/76	971		GRAHAM Rich	EMMONS Don	D4		A
02/03/76	961	10:30	BLEDSOE Pat	FULLER John	HABU	2.7	A
03/03/76	971	10:15	GRAHAM Rich	EMMONS Don	D4	2.6	
04/03/76	971	10:30	GRAHAM Rich	EMMONS Don	HABU	3.5	
08/03/76	971	10:15	CIRINO Al	LIEBMAN Bruce	D8	4	
09/03/76	971	10:00	CIRINO Al	LIEBMAN Bruce	HABU	2.4	
10/03/76	961	10:15	RANSOM Lee	PAYNE Al	D4	2.6	
12/03/76	961	11:00	GRAHAM Rich	EMMONS Don	SPECIAL-CAPSTAN DRAGON SNAPPER	1.9	17
15/03/76	971	10:18	CIRINO Al	LIEBMAN Bruce	D4	2.6	
17/03/76	961	10:50	GRAHAM Rich	EMMONS Don	HABU	3.6	
19/03/76	971		RANSOM Lee	PAYNE Al	D4		A
20/03/76	961	09:30	RANSOM Lee	PAYNE Al	HABU	4.8	
22/03/76	971	10:30	MURPHY Jay	BILLINGSLEY John	D4	2	A
23/03/76	963		GRAHAM Rich	EMMONS Don	D8		A
24/03/76	961	09:45	GRAHAM Rich	EMMONS Don	HABU	3.7	
25/03/76	963		RANSOM Lee	PAYNE Al	D8		A
25/03/76	963		RANSOM Lee	PAYNE Al	D8		A
26/03/76	963	11:47	RANSOM Lee	PAYNE Al	D4	2.4	
26/03/76	971	10:17	MURPHY Jay	BILLINGSLEY John	D4	2.3	
29/03/76	961	10:58	MURPHY Jay	BILLINGSLEY John	HABU	3.6	
30/03/76	963	10:19	GRAHAM Rich	EMMONS Don	D4	2.5	
02/04/76	971	14:05	RANSOM Lee	PAYNE Al	D4	1.7	A
05/04/76	961	10:22	KINEGO Joe	JACKS Roger	D4	2.4	
06/04/76	961	12:08	RANSOM Lee	PAYNE Al	HABU	2.1	A
07/04/76	963	10:15	WILSON Jim	DOUGLASS Bruce	D8	4.3	
08/04/76	971	13:05	WILSON Jim	DOUGLASS Bruce	HABU	2	A
10/04/76	971	11:30	KINEGO Joe	JACKS Roger	HABU	2.3	
12/04/76	961	11:46	RANSOM Lee	PAYNE Al	D8	2.3	A
13/04/76	963	10:16	WILSON Jim	DOUGLASS Bruce	D4	2.6	
14/04/76	971	10:48	KINEGO Joe	JACKS Roger	D8	4.2	
19/04/76	963	10:20	JOERSZ Al	MORGAN George	D4	2.5	
20/04/76	971	10:22	WILSON Jim	DOUGLASS Bruce	HABU	3.7	
22/04/76	963	10:25	KINEGO Joe	JACKS Roger	D4	2.5	
23/04/76	971	09:30	KINEGO Joe	JACKS Roger	HABU	3.5	
26/04/76	971	10:00	JOERSZ Al	MORGAN George	HABU	3.5	
27/04/76	961	10:42	WILSON Jim	DOUGLASS Bruce	D8	4.2	
28/04/76	963		KINEGO Joe	JACKS Roger	D4		A
28/04/76	963	11:20	KINEGO Joe	JACKS Roger	D4	2.5	
30/04/76	961	11:15	JOERSZ Al	MORGAN George	D4	2.5	
03/05/76	971	10:31	WILSON Jim	DOUGLASS Bruce	D4	2.5	
04/05/76	961	12:30	WILSON Jim	DOUGLASS Bruce	HABU	4	A
06/05/76	963	09:30	KINEGO Joe	JACKS Roger	HABU	0.8	A
06/05/76	971	10:37	JOERSZ Al	MORGAN George	HABU	4.6	
08/05/76	961	09:40	KINEGO Joe	JACKS Roger	HABU	4.9	
10/05/76	971	10:30	WILSON Jim	DOUGLASS Bruce	D4	2.6	
11/05/76	961	10:00	JOERSZ Al	MORGAN George	D4	2.3	
12/05/76	963	10:15	KINEGO Joe	JACKS Roger	D4	2.4	
17/05/76	971	10:15	MURPHY Jay	BILLINGSLEY John	D4	1.5	A
18/05/76	963	13:47	WILSON Jim	DOUGLASS Bruce	HABU	3.6	
21/05/76	963	10:15	JOERSZ Al	MORGAN George	HABU	1	A
24/05/76	963	10:15	JOERSZ Al	MORGAN George	HABU	3.1	A
25/05/76	961	10:01	WILSON Jim	DOUGLASS Bruce	D2	2.4	
26/05/76	971	09:45	MURPHY Jay	BILLINGSLEY John	HABU	3.9	
28/05/76	971		MURPHY Jay	BILLINGSLEY John	HABU		A
28/05/76	971	14:55	MURPHY Jay	BILLINGSLEY John	HABU	2.2	
01/06/76	963	10:17	ALISON Tom	VIDA Joe	D4	2.3	
02/06/76	961	11:15	ROSENBERG Maury	BULLUCH Don	D4	2.2	
03/06/76	971	10:15	ALISON Tom	VIDA Joe	HABU	3.8	
07/06/76	963	10:27	MURPHY Jay	BILLINGSLEY John	D4	2.3	
08/06/76	961	11:05	ROSENBERG Maury	BULLUCH Don	HABU	2.1	
09/06/76	971	10:17	ALISON Tom	VIDA Joe	D2	2.3	
10/06/76	961	13:00	ALISON Tom	VIDA Joe	HABU	2.2	
14/06/76	963	10:15	BLEDSOE Pat	FULLER John	D2	2.2	
15/06/76	971	11:30	ROSENBERG Maury	BULLUCH Don	HABU	3.7	
18/06/76	963	10:39	ALISON Tom	VIDA Joe	D4	2.3	
21/06/76	963	12:00	BLEDSOE Pat	FULLER John	D4	2.5	
22/06/76	971	09:30	ALISON Tom	VIDA Joe	HABU	3.6	
23/06/76	963	10:15	ROSENBERG Maury	BULLUCH Don	D4	2.6	
26/06/76	971		BLEDSOE Pat	FULLER John	HABU		A
26/06/76	963	12:57	ROSENBERG Maury	BULLUCH Don	HABU	3.6	
27/06/76	971	13:00	BLEDSOE Pat	FULLER John	HABU	2.4	
28/06/76	963		ALISON Tom	VIDA Joe	D11		A
29/06/76	963	12:15	ALISON Tom	VIDA Joe	HABU	3.9	
03/07/76	961	11:17	ROSENBERG Maury	BULLUCH Don	D4	2.4	
06/07/76	963	11:48	BLEDSOE Pat	FULLER John	D4	2.4	
07/07/76	971	10:15	ROSENBERG Maury	BULLUCH Don	HABU	3.6	
07/07/76	961	15:43	ALISON Tom	VIDA Joe	D4	2.2	
08/07/76	963	12:00	BLEDSOE Pat	FULLER John	HABU	2.2	
12/07/76	961	13:10	ALISON Tom	VIDA Joe	HABU	2.7	A
13/07/76	979	04:00	GRAHAM Rich	EMMONS Don	FERRY IN	5.3	
13/07/76	963	10:23	BLEDSOE Pat	FULLER John	D4	2.2	
14/07/76	971	06:00	ROSENBERG Maury	BULLUCH Don	FERRY OUT		
14/07/76	979	13:38	BLEDSOE Pat	FULLER John	HABU	2.3	
15/07/76	972	04:00	MURPHY Jay	BILLINGSLEY John	FERRY IN	5.1	
16/07/76	963	06:00	ALISON Tom	VIDA Joe	FERRY OUT		
16/07/76	961	06:42	MURPHY Jay	BILLINGSLEY John	D1	1.2	
20/07/76	976	04:00	CIRINO Al	LIEBMAN Bruce	FERRY IN	5.2	
20/07/76	979	13:30	GRAHAM Rich	EMMONS Don	HABU	3.7	
21/07/76	961	06:42	MURPHY Jay	BILLINGSLEY John	FERRY OUT		
21/07/76	972	10:15	BLEDSOE Pat	FULLER John	D4	2.3	
23/07/76	976	14:05	CIRINO Al	LIEBMAN Bruce	HABU	3.6	
26/07/76	976	13:15	GRAHAM Rich	EMMONS Don	HABU	3.8	
27/07/76	979	10:17	KINEGO Joe	JACKS Roger	D4	2.5	
29/07/76	972	10:45	CIRINO Al	LIEBMAN Bruce	D4	2.5	
30/07/76	976		KINEGO Joe	JACKS Roger	HABU	3	A
02/08/76	976	10:21	GRAHAM Rich	EMMONS Don	D4	2.5	
03/08/76	972	10:15	CIRINO Al	LIEBMAN Bruce	D4	1.9	A
05/08/76	976	11:50	KINEGO Joe	JACKS Roger	D4	2.4	
06/08/76	979	13:45	CIRINO Al	LIEBMAN Bruce	HABU	3.9	
11/08/76	979	11:03	GRAHAM Rich	EMMONS Don	HABU	3.6	
12/08/76	972	10:19	KINEGO Joe	JACKS Roger	D4	2.5	
13/08/76	976	10:15	CIRINO Al	LIEBMAN Bruce	D8	3.4	A
14/08/76	972	09:50	KINEGO Joe	JACKS Roger	HABU	3.7	
16/08/76	979	10:18	CIRINO Al	LIEBMAN Bruce	D4	2.3	
18/08/76	976	11:00	GRAHAM Rich	EMMONS Don	D1	0.9	
19/08/76	972	14:15	KINEGO Joe	JACKS Roger	HABU	2.4	
21/08/76	976	09:01	MURPHY Jay	BILLINGSLEY John	HABU	3.9	
23/08/76	979	08:00	GILMORE Bill	PAYNE Al	HABU	4	
26/08/76	976	13:00	KINEGO Joe	JACKS Roger	HABU	2.1	
28/08/76	979	10:00	MURPHY Jay	BILLINGSLEY John	HABU	3.3	
31/08/76	976	10:00	MURPHY Jay	BILLINGSLEY John	HABU	2.2	
03/09/76	976	10:30	GILMORE Bill	PAYNE Al	HABU	3.9	
04/09/76	979	09:30	JOERSZ AL	MORGAN George	HABU	3.5	

Date	Instal. No.	T.O. Time	Pilot Name	RSO Name	Mission	Duration	Remarks
07/09/76	972		GILMORE Bill	PAYNE Al	D8		A
07/09/76	976	10:00	MURPHY Jay	BILLINGSLEY John	HABU	4.2	18
11/09/76	979	10:31	GILMORE Bill	PAYNE Al	D4	2.3	
13/09/76	976	10:30	GILMORE Bill	PAYNE Al	HABU	2.4	
15/09/76	979	10:46	JOERSZ Al	MORGAN George	D3	2.3	
16/09/76	972	11:01	GILMORE Bill	PAYNE Al	D8	4.1	
17/09/76	979	13:30	JOERSZ Al	MORGAN George	HABU	3.5	
20/09/76	976	10:30	ALISON Tom	VIDA Joe	D8	4	
21/09/76	976	11:02	GILMORE Bill	PAYNE Al	D4	2.4	
22/09/76	972	11:00	GILMORE Bill	PAYNE Al	HABU	5.3	
23/09/76	976	09:30	ALISON Tom	VIDA Joe	HABU	2.2	
24/09/76	972	10:13	JORESZ Al	MORGAN George	D8	4.1	
27/09/76	979	10:25	GILMORE Bill	PAYNE Al	D5	3.7	
28/09/76	972	11:16	ALISON Tom	VIDA Joe	D5	3.6	
29/09/76	979	11:15	JOERSZ Al	MORGAN George	HABU	2.4	A
01/10/76	972	11:01	ALISON Tom	VIDA Joe	D8	4	
04/10/76	972	10:14	ROSENBERG Maury	BULLUCH Don	D8	4	
06/10/76	976	09:30	ALISON Tom	VIDA Joe	HABU	3.6	
07/10/76	972	11:10	JOERSZ Al	MORGAN George	D8	3.7	
12/10/76	976	10:00	JOERSZ Al	MORGAN George	HABU	3.5	
13/10/76	972	10:01	ROSENBERG Maury	BULLUCH Don	D8	4.1	
14/10/76	976	10:30	ROSENBERG Maury	BULLUCH Don	HABU	5.2	
15/10/76	972	11:00	ALISON Tom	VIDA Joe	HABU	3.7	
18/10/76	972	14:25	BLEDSOE Pat	FULLER John	D12	2.4	
19/10/76	976	10:00	ALISON Tom	VIDA Joe	D3	2.2	
21/10/76	972	10:30	ROSENBERG Maury	BULLUCH Don	D8	1.6	A
22/10/76	976	11:31	BLEDSOE Pat	FULLER John	HABU	2.5	A
25/10/76	979	10:00	ALISON Tom	VIDA Joe	D8	4.1	
26/10/76	972	14:00	ROSENBERG Maury	BULLUCH Don	HABU	4	A
27/10/76	979		BLEDSOE Pat	FULLER John	D8		A
28/10/76	979	10:34	BLEDSOE Pat	FULLER John	D3	1.6	A
29/10/76	972	14:30	ALISON Tom	VIDA Joe	HABU	3.8	
30/10/76	976	12:00	ROSENBERG Maury	BULLUCH Don	SAROO1	4.1	
02/11/76	972	11:10	BLEDSOE Pat	FULLER John	D3	2.6	
04/11/76	972	08:20	BLEDSOE Pat	FULLER John	HABU	4	
05/11/76	976	10:55	ALISON Tom	VIDA Joe	D12	1.8	A
08/11/76	979		ROSENBERG Maury	BULLUCH Don	D8		A
12/11/76	979	11:15	BLEDSOE Pat	FULLER John	D7	2.3	
13/11/76	972	09:45	GRAHAM Rich	EMMONS Don	D3	2.3	
15/11/76	972	11:00	BLEDSOE Pat	FULLER John	HABU	5.3	
16/11/76	979	09:25	CIRINO Al	LIEBMAN Bruce	D7	2.5	
18/11/76	979	10:46	CIRINO Al	LIEBMAN Bruce	HABU	3.9	
19/11/76	976	10:07	GRAHAM Rich	EMMONS Don	D12	2.4	
20/11/76	979		GRAHAM Rich	EMMONS Don	HABU		A
22/11/76	976	13:00	GRAHAM Rich	EMMONS Don	HABU	3.6	
23/11/76	979	11:30	BLEDSOE Pat	FULLER John	HABU	5.5	
27/11/76	976	09:30	CIRINO Al	LIEBMAN Bruce	HABU	3.6	
29/11/76	979	10:50	GRAHAM Rich	EMMONS Don	HABU	3.9	
30/11/76	972	11:10	KINEGO Joe	JACKS Roger	HABU	2.1	
03/12/76	972	12:00	CIRINO Al	LIEBMAN Bruce	HABU	3.6	
07/12/76	979	13:15	GRAHAM Rich	EMMONS Don	HABU	3.7	
11/12/76	972	10:30	KINEGO Joe	JACKS Roger	HABU	2.3	
13/12/76	979	10:20	CROWDER Bob	MORGAN John	D3	2.5	
15/12/76	972	11:15	GRAHAM Rich	EMMONS Don	HABU	3.5	
17/12/76	976		KINEGO Joe	JACKS Roger	D8		A
20/12/76	979	13:45	GRAHAM Rich	EMMONS Don	HABU	3.6	
21/12/76	976		CROWDER Bob	MORGAN John	D8		A
23/12/76	976	10:08	KINEGO Joe	JACKS Roger	D8	4.2	
24/12/76	972	10:12	CROWDER Bob	MORGAN John	HABU	3.9	
28/12/76	976	10:34	CROWDER Bob	MORGAN John	D8	4.3	
29/12/76	979	12:08	KINEGO Joe	JACKS Roger	HABU	2.8	A
30/12/76	972	10:10	CROWDER Bob	MORGAN John	D5	3.7	
03/01/77	976	11:00	KINEGO Joe	JACKS Roger	D4	2.7	
05/01/77	979	06:55	CROWDER Bob	MORGAN John	HABU	3.5	
07/01/77	972	11:08	MURPHY Jay	BILLINGSLEY John	D12	2.6	
10/01/77	979	09:58	JOERSZ Al	PAYNE Al	D8	2.2	A
11/01/77	976	11:00	CROWDER Bob	MORGAN John	HABU	3.6	
12/01/77	972	10:41	MURPHY Jay	BILLINGSLEY John	D3	2.4	
13/01/77	976	10:40	JOERSZ Al	PAYNE Al	HABU	3.5	
14/01/77	979	10:00	CROWDER Bob	MORGAN John	D11	6.1	
15/01/77	972	09:55	MURPHY Jay	BILLINGSLEY John	HABU	3.7	
17/01/77	972	12:30	CROWDER Bob	MORGAN John	HABU	4	
20/01/77	976	11:00	MURPHY Jay	BILLINGSLEY John	D8	2.3	A
21/01/77	979	13:15	JOERSZ Al	PAYNE Al	HABU	4	
24/01/77	972	10:59	ROSENBERG Maury	BULLUCH Don	D3	2.3	
26/01/77	979	09:30	ROSENBERG Maury	BULLUCH Don	HABU	3.1	A
27/01/77	976	13:50	JOERSZ Al	PAYNE Al	HABU	3.8	
31/01/77	979	10:03	MURPHY Jay	BILLINGSLEY John	D8	4.2	
04/02/77	972	09:30	ROSENBERG Maury	BULLUCH Don	D2	2.4	
05/02/77	976	10:00	MURPHY Jay	BILLINGSLEY John	HABU	1.5	A
07/02/77	979	09:30	JOERSZ Al	PAYNE Al	D4	2.6	
08/02/77	976	11:02	MURPHY Jay	BILLINGSLEY John	HABU	4.1	
10/02/77	972		ROSENBERG Maury	BULLUCH Don	HABU		A
14/02/77	976	14:17	ROSENBERG Maury	BULLUCH Don	HABU	1.5	A
16/02/77	976	11:00	JOERSZ Al	PAYNE Al	HABU	2.3	
17/02/77	976	09:30	ROSENBERG Maury	BULLUCH Don	HABU	2.4	
18/02/77	979	10:00	CIRINO Al	LIEBMAN Bruce	P2	2.5	
19/02/77	976	09:10	ROSENBERG Maury	BULLUCH Don	HABU	4.2	
21/02/77	979	10:15	ALISON Tom	VIDA Joe	HABU	4	
22/02/77	976	13:15	CIRINO Al	LIEBMAN Bruce	HABU	2.3	A
24/02/77	979	10:00	ROSENBERG Maury	BULLUCH Don	HABU	3.7	
26/02/77	976	10:30	ALISON Tom	VIDA Joe	HABU	4	
28/02/77	979	10:00	ROSENBERG Maury	BULLUCH Don	P2	2.5	
01/03/77	976	09:10	ALISON Tom	VIDA Joe	P2	2.4	
03/03/77	979	12:00	ALISON Tom	VIDA Joe	HABU	3.6	
07/03/77	976	11:00	CIRINO Al	LIEBMAN Bruce	HABU	2.2	
08/03/77	972	10:37	BLEDSOE Pat	FULLER John	P8	3.6	A
09/03/77	979	09:52	BLEDSOE Pat	FULLER John	HABU	4.1	
10/03/77	972	09:45	CIRINO Al	LIEBMAN Bruce	P8	4.1	
11/03/77	976	11:03	ALISON Tom	VIDA Joe	P4	3.8	
15/03/77	979	12:22	CIRINO Al	LIEBMAN Bruce	HABU	2.7	A
17/03/77	976	10:30	BLEDSOE Pat	FULLER John	P2	2.3	
18/03/77	979	09:30	ALISON Tom	VIDA Joe	HABU	4.1	
21/03/77	972	10:20	CARPENTER Buzz	MURPHY John	P8	4.2	
22/03/77	976	10:15	BLEDSOE Pat	FULLER John	D8	1.8	A
23/03/77	979	11:30	BLEDSOE Pat	FULLER John	HABU	4.1	
24/03/77	972	13:02	ALISON Tom	VIDA Joe	P8	4.2	
25/03/77	976	10:30	CARPENTER Buzz	MURPHY John	D8	4.1	
28/03/77	979	11:36	CARPENTER Buzz	MURPHY John	HABU	4	
01/04/77	976	10:30	BLEDSOE Pat	FULLER John	P8	3.8	
04/04/77	972	11:00	GRAHAM Rich	EMMONS Don	P8	4.1	
05/04/77	979	09:30	BLEDSOE Pat	FULLER John	HABU	4.2	
06/04/77	972	10:30	CARPENTER Buzz	MURPHY John	P8	3.8	
08/04/77	979	13:00	CARPENTER Buzz	MURPHY John	HABU	4.2	
11/04/77	976	10:33	BLEDSOE Pat	FULLER John	P8	4.3	
12/04/77	972	11:00	GRAHAM Rich	EMMONS Don	P8	3.6	
14/04/77	976	10:16	CARPENTER Buzz	MURPHY John	D8	3.8	
16/04/77	972	09:05	GRAHAM Rich	EMMONS Don	HABU	4	
19/04/77	972	13:00	CARPENTER Buzz	MURPHY John	HABU	2.4	
19/04/77	976	09:30	KINEGO Joe	JACKS Roger	HABU	1.4	A
22/04/77	972	10:06	GRAHAM Rich	EMMONS Don	HABU	2.6	
22/04/77	976		KINEGO Joe	JACKS Roger	HABU		A
22/04/77	972		GRAHAM Rich	EMMONS Don	HABU		A
25/04/77	976	11:00	KINEGO Joe	JACKS Roger	HABU	2.5	A
26/04/77	972	12:00	GRAHAM Rich	EMMONS Don	HABU	2.5	A
29/04/77	976	09:20	KINEGO Joe	JACKS Roger	HABU	3.8	
02/05/77	979	10:12	CROWDER Bob	MORGAN John	D8	4	
03/05/77	972	10:13	GRAHAM Rich	EMMONS Don	P8	3.9	
04/05/77	979		GRAHAM Rich	EMMONS Don	HABU		A
06/05/77	979	09:20	GRAHAM Rich	EMMONS Don	HABU	4.1	
07/05/77	972	11:00	CROWDER Bob	MORGAN John	HABU	3.5	
10/05/77	976	09:45	KINEGO Joe	JACKS Roger	HABU	3.6	
12/05/77	976	14:15	CROWDER Bob	MORGAN John	HABU	4.3	
13/05/77	972	10:09	KINEGO Joe	JACKS Roger	FERRY TO GUAM	2.5	
					STATIC DISPLAY		
15/05/77	972	11:00	CROWDER Bob	MORGAN John	RTB FERRY	3	
17/05/77	979	10:30	MURPHY Jay	BILLINGSLEY John	P8	1.2	A
18/05/77	976	10:15	CROWDER Bob	MORGAN John	D8	4.1	
19/05/77	972	13:07	KINEGO Joe	JACKS Roger	P2	2.5	
21/05/77	976	14:00	KINEGO Joe	JACKS Roger	HABU	3.9	
23/05/77	972		MURPHY Jay	BILLINGSLEY John	D8		A
23/05/77	972	11:45	MURPHY Jay	BILLINGSLEY John	P8	4.1	
24/05/77	979	10:15	CROWDER Bob	MORGAN John	P8	4	
26/05/77	976	12:11	MURPHY Jay	BILLINGSLEY John	P2	2.3	
27/05/77	979	15:00	MURPHY Jay	BILLINGSLEY John	HABU	2.2	A
31/05/77	979	14:00	JOERSZ Al	BULLUCH Don	HABU	3.5	
01/06/77	976	10:45	CROWDER Bob	MORGAN John	D8	3.9	
03/06/77	972	10:30	MURPHY Jay	BILLINGSLEY John	D8	3.7	
04/06/77	979		CROWDER Bob	MORGAN John	HABU		A
04/06/77	979	11:05	CROWDER Bob	MORGAN John	HABU	1.8	A
06/06/77	972	11:00	MURPHY Jay	BILLINGSLEY John	HABU	2.4	
07/06/77	979		CROWDER Bob	MORGAN John	HABU		A
07/06/77	979	12:49	CROWDER Bob	MORGAN John	HABU	4	A
10/06/77	972	11:04	JOERSZ Al	BULLUCH Don	P7	2.1	
14/06/77	979	09:20	JOERSZ Al	BULLUCH Don	HABU	3.8	
15/06/77	972	10:15	ROSENBERG Maury	PAYNE Al	P7	2.3	
17/06/77	979	10:05	MURPHY Jay	BILLINGSLEY John	HABU	2.6	A
23/06/77	972	11:00	ROSENBERG Maury	PAYNE Al	P13	2.5	
24/06/77	979	13:33	ROSENBERG Maury	PAYNE Al	HABU	4.1	
25/06/77	972	09:30	CIRINO Al	LIEBMAN Bruce	HABU	4.1	
27/06/77	979	13:39	ALISON Tom	VIDA Joe	HABU	2.5	A
27/06/77	976	12:44	CIRINO Al	LIEBMAN Bruce	P7	2.5	
27/06/77	979		ALISON Tom	VIDA Joe	HABU		A
30/06/77	976		ROSENBERG Maury	PAYNE Al	HABU		A
30/06/77	976	12:18	ROSENBERG Maury	PAYNE Al	HABU	3.9	
01/07/77	976	10:51	ALISON Tom	VIDA Joe	D13	2.5	
05/07/77	976	10:00	CIRINO Al	LIEBMAN Bruce	P8	4	
07/07/77	979	11:44	ROSENBERG Maury	PAYNE Al	D8	3.8	
07/07/77	979		ROSENBERG Maury	PAYNE Al	D8		A
08/07/77	976	07:00	CIRINO Al	LIEBMAN Bruce	HABU	2.3	A
11/07/77	976	14:00	ALISON Tom	VIDA Joe	HABU	3.8	
12/07/77	979	09:53	ROSENBERG Maury	PAYNE Al	D8	3.3	A
14/07/77	976	08:00	ALISON Tom	VIDA Joe	HABU	4.1	
15/07/77	979	10:00	CIRINO Al	LIEBMAN Bruce	P5	3.7	
18/07/77	972		ALISON Tom	VIDA Joe	D7		A
19/07/77	979	09:29	ROSENBERG Maury	PAYNE Al	HABU	4.1	
19/07/77	972	09:00	ALISON Tom	VIDA Joe	P1	1.1	
19/07/77	979		ROSENBERG Maury	PAYNE Al	HABU		A
21/07/77	976	10:07	CIRINO Al	LIEBMAN Bruce	P5	2.5	
23/07/77	976	09:15	CIRINO Al	LIEBMAN Bruce	HABU	4.3	
25/07/77	972	21:20	BLEDSOE Pat	FULLER John	N-D7	2.4	
27/07/77	972	13:00	CARPENTER Buzz	MURPHY John	HABU	4.2	A
28/07/77	976	10:09	CIRINO Al	LIEBMAN Bruce	D7	3.1	A
31/07/77	976	14:00	BLEDSOE Pat	FULLER John	HABU	2.3	
01/08/77	979	10:00	CARPENTER Buzz	MURPHY John	D4	2.5	A
02/08/77	976	09:33	CIRINO Al	LIEBMAN Bruce	HABU	1	A
04/08/77	976	14:58	BLEDSOE Pat	FULLER John	HABU	4.2	
05/08/77	972	13:07	CARPENTER Buzz	MURPHY John	HABU	2.5	
08/08/77	979	08:50	CIRINO Al	FULLER John	P4	3.5	
09/08/77	976	06:00	CIRINO Al	LIEBMAN Bruce	H/FERRY OUT		
10/08/77	960	04:00	ROSENBERG Maury	PAYNE Al	FERRY IN / HABU	5.5	
11/08/77	972	06:00	BLEDSOE Pat	FULLER John	FERRY OUT		
12/08/77	960	08:45	ROSENBERG Maury	PAYNE Al	D4	2.6	
12/08/77	975	04:00	GRAHAM Rich	EMMONS Don	FERRY IN	5	
13/08/77	979	06:20	ROSENBERG Maury	PAYNE Al	FERRY OUT		
14/08/77	967	04:00	KINEGO Joe	ELLIOTT Larry	FERRY IN	5.3	

Date	Instal. No.	T.O. Time	Pilot Name	RSO Name	Mission	Duration	Remarks
15/08/77	967	09:52	CARPENTER Buzz	MURPHY John	HABU	5.4	
18/08/77	967	10:18	GRAHAM Rich	EMMONS Don	HABU	4	
19/08/77	960	10:09	CARPENTER Buzz	MURPHY John	D4	4.1	
23/08/77	960	15:12	CARPENTER Buzz	MURPHY John	HABU	2.1	A
23/08/77	967		GRAHAM Rich	EMMONS Don	D4		A
24/08/77	975	10:00	GRAHAM Rich	EMMONS Don	D4	2.4	
25/08/77	975	09:26	KINEGO Joe	ELLIOTT Larry	HABU	2.2	A
27/08/77	975	12:32	CARPENTER Buzz	MURPHY John	HABU	4.2	
29/08/77	967	12:00	KINEGO Joe	ELLIOTT Larry	D4	4.4	
30/08/77	975	09:15	GRAHAM Rich	EMMONS Don	HABU	3.8	
02/09/77	967	10:48	KINEGO Joe	ELLIOTT Larry	HABU	3.8	
02/09/77	960	10:48	VETH Jack	KELLER Bill	D7	2.5	
07/09/77	960	09:30	GRAHAM Rich	EMMONS Don	HABU	2.4	
07/09/77	975	10:31	VETH Jack	KELLER Bill	D7	2.4	
12/09/77	967	10:23	KINEGO Joe	ELLIOTT Larry	D4	3.4	A
13/09/77	975	09:10	VETH Jack	KELLER Bill	HABU	3.8	
15/09/77	967	11:55	VETH Jack	KELLER Bill	D7	4.1	A
16/09/77	960	13:00	KINEGO Joe	ELLIOTT Larry	HABU	3.9	
19/09/77	960	21:05	VETH Jack	KELLER Bill	N-HABU	4.1	
21/09/77	960		CROWDER Bob	MORGAN John	D11		A
22/09/77	975	10:20	CROWDER Bob	MORGAN John	HABU	4.1	
23/09/77	960	10:03	KINEGO Joe	ELLIOTT Larry	D4	2.5	
23/09/77	967	09:53	VETH Jack	KELLER Bill	P13	2.1	
26/09/77	960	09:36	CROWDER Bob	MORGAN John	P11	6.3	
27/09/77	967	21:30	KINEGO Joe	ELLIOTT Larry	N-HABU	4.3	
29/09/77	960	12:18	VETH Jack	KELLER Bill	P11	5.9	
03/10/77	975	10:45	VETH Jack	KELLER Bill	HABU	4.3	
04/10/77	960	09:30	MURPHY Jay	BILLINGSLEY John	D4	2.5	
07/10/77	975	09:12	CROWDER Bob	MORGAN John	HABU	3.9	
11/10/77	967	09:15	VETH Jack	KELLER Bill	HABU	3.8	
12/10/77	960	06:50	MURPHY Jay	BILLINGSLEY John	D4	2.4	
14/10/77	967	09:05	MURPHY Jay	BILLINGSLEY John	HABU	4.2	
19/10/77	975	11:15	CROWDER Bob	MORGAN John	HABU	2.3	A
20/10/77	967	10:00	ROSENBERG Maury	PAYNE Al	D8	4.4	
21/10/77	975	10:15	MURPHY Jay	BILLINGSLEY John	D8	4.1	
22/10/77	967	10:40	ROSENBERG Maury	PAYNE Al	HABU	4.3	
25/10/77	975	18:30	CROWDER Bob	MORGAN John	N-D4	2.5	
27/10/77	967	14:00	ROSENBERG Maury	PAYNE Al	HABU	4.2	A
28/10/77	975	10:00	ALISON Tom	VIDA Joe	D8	3.3	A
01/11/77	967	10:15	MURPHY Jay	BILLINGSLEY John	HABU	2	A
03/11/77	967	14:00	MURPHY Jay	BILLINGSLEY John	RTB FERRY	1.8	
05/11/77	975	14:33	ALISON Tom	VIDA Joe	HABU	4.3	
07/11/77	967	09:58	ROSENBERG Maury	PAYNE Al	D4	2.3	
08/11/77	975	10:00	MURPHY Jay	BILLINGSLEY John	D8	2.4	A
10/11/77	975	09:53	ROSENBERG Maury	PAYNE Al	D4	2.5	
11/11/77	967	09:30	ROSENBERG Maury	PAYNE Al	HABU	3.4	
14/11/77	960	10:18	CARPENTER Buzz	MURPHY John	D8	3.4	
15/11/77	975	11:00	ALISON Tom	VIDA Joe	D8	4.6	
16/11/77	967	20:15	ALISON Tom	VIDA Joe	N-HABU	2.5	A
18/11/77	960		CARPENTER Buzz	MURPHY John	HABU		A
21/11/77	967	10:02	ROSENBERG Maury	PAYNE Al	D8	3.9	
22/11/77	960		CARPENTER Buzz	MURPHY John	P4		A
23/11/77	967	09:15	CARPENTER Buzz	MURPHY John	HABU	3.6	
23/11/77	960	14:45	ALISON Tom	VIDA Joe	P2	2.4	
25/11/77	960	20:00	ALISON Tom	VIDA Joe	N-HABU	2.3	
28/11/77	967	12:48	CARPENTER Buzz	MURPHY John	HABU	4.4	
29/11/77	960	10:00	GRAHAM Rich	EMMONS Don	P13	3.2	A
02/12/77	960	10:40	GRAHAM Rich	EMMONS Don	HABU	3.8	
05/12/77	967	12:19	ALISON Tom	VIDA Joe	D8	2.5	A
06/12/77	960	10:00	ALISON Tom	VIDA Joe	HABU	5.3	
08/12/77	967	10:24	CARPENTER Buzz	MURPHY John	D8	3.8	
10/12/77	960	11:02	GRAHAM Rich	EMMONS Don	GIANT BARNACLE	3.9	19
12/12/77	967	11:00	GRONINGER Bill	SOBER Chuck	GIANT BARNACLE	4.1	19
13/12/77	960	21:00	CARPENTER Buzz	MURPHY John	N-HABU	2.4	
15/12/77	975	10:06	GRONINGER Bill	SOBER Chuck	D8	3.2	
16/12/77	960	13:15	GRAHAM Rich	EMMONS Don	HABU	4	
19/12/77	960	11:15	GRONINGER Bill	SOBER Chuck	HABU	2.3	
20/12/77	975	10:14	CARPENTER Buzz	MURPHY John	P4	2.4	
22/12/77	960	19:00	GRAHAM Rich	EMMONS Don	N-HABU	2.4	
23/12/77	975	13:00	VETH Jack	KELLER Bill	P2	2.3	
28/12/77	975	14:45	GRAHAM Rich	EMMONS Don	D8	3.2	
28/12/77	960	12:03	GRONINGER Bill	SOBER Chuck	HABU	4	
03/01/78	975	13:16	VETH Jack	KELLER Bill	HABU	4.3	
06/01/78	967	08:56	VETH Jack	KELLER Bill	D4	1.4	
06/01/78	975	08:04	GRONINGER Bill	SOBER Chuck	SPECIAL MISSION	4.4	20
09/01/78	975	10:06	KINEGO Joe	ELLIOTT Larry	D8	4.3	
10/01/78	967	10:10	GRONINGER Bill	SOBER Chuck	HABU	2.5	
11/01/78	960	08:05	VETH Jack	KELLER Bill	D8	4.7	
13/01/78	960	10:00	KINEGO Joe	ELLIOTT Larry	D8	5.1	A
16/01/78	967	13:15	VETH Jack	KELLER Bill	D8	2	A
17/01/78	960	09:36	GRONINGER Bill	SOBER Chuck	D11	2.7	A
19/01/78	975	10:00	VETH Jack	KELLER Bill	P2	2.4	
20/01/78	967		KINEGO Joe	ELLIOTT Larry	HABU		A
20/01/78	967		KINEGO Joe	ELLIOTT Larry	HABU		A
20/01/78	960	14:30	CROWDER Bob	MORGAN John	P2	2.6	
23/01/78	960	09:40	KINEGO Joe	ELLIOTT Larry	HABU	4.1	
24/01/78	975	13:30	CROWDER Bob	MORGAN John	P2	2.6	
25/01/78	967	08:15	VETH Jack	KELLER Bill	HABU	4.1	
27/01/78	960		CROWDER Bob	MORGAN John	HABU		A
27/01/78	960		CROWDER Bob	MORGAN John	HABU		A
28/01/78	975	10:05	CROWDER Bob	MORGAN John	HABU	4.3	
30/01/78	967	09:15	KINEGO Joe	ELLIOTT Larry	HABU	3.7	
30/01/78	960		VETH Jack	KELLER Bill	D4		A
01/02/78	960	10:15	VETH Jack	ELLIOTT Larry	P2	2.8	A
03/02/78	967	10:15	CROWDER Bob	MORGAN John	HABU	2.4	
03/02/78	960	13:15	MURPHY Jay	BILLINGSLEY John	P2	2.8	A
04/02/78	975	10:30	KINEGO Joe	ELLIOTT Larry	D1	1.1	
06/02/78	975	20:33	KINEGO Joe	ELLIOTT Larry	N-HABU	2.3	
07/02/78	960	14:30	CROWDER Bob	MORGAN John	D4	2.6	
08/02/78	967		MURPHY Jay	BILLINGSLEY John	D3		A
09/02/78	967	10:15	MURPHY Jay	BILLINGSLEY John	D4	2.2	
10/02/78	960	09:30	KINEGO Joe	ELLIOTT Larry	HABU	4	
13/02/78	960	13:15	CROWDER Bob	MORGAN John	HABU	3.9	
14/02/78	975	10:33	KINEGO Joe	ELLIOTT Larry	D4	2.2	
18/02/78	975	18:00	CROWDER Bob	MORGAN John	N-HABU	2.4	
18/02/78	960		CROWDER Bob	MORGAN John	HABU		A
20/02/78	960	09:43	MURPHY Jay	BILLINGSLEY John	HABU	3.7	
23/02/78	975	16:15	ALISON Tom	VIDA Joe	HABU	2.3	
25/02/78	960	14:48	CROWDER Bob	MORGAN John	HABU	2.2	
02/03/78	960	16:30	MURPHY Jay	BILLINGSLEY John	N-HABU	2.3	
06/03/78	960	13:40	ALISON Tom	VIDA Joe	HABU	2.2	
11/03/78	975	19:00	MURPHY Jay	BILLINGSLEY John	N-HABU	0.9	A
12/03/78	975	19:00	ROSENBERG Maury	PAYNE Al	N-HABU	2.3	
14/03/78	960	21:30	ALISON Tom	VIDA Joe	N-HABU	2.4	
17/03/78	975	10:00	ROSENBERG Maury	PAYNE Al	HABU	3.8	
20/03/78	960	15:16	CARPENTER Buzz	MURPHY John	D4	0.9	A
22/03/78	975	11:25	ALISON Tom	VIDA Joe	HABU	4.1	
22/03/78	960	13:35	ROSENBERG Maury	PAYNE Al	D4	2.5	
24/03/78	975	11:30	CARPENTER Buzz	MURPHY John	D8	2.9	A
29/03/78	975	15:30	ROSENBERG Maury	PAYNE Al	HABU	4.1	
30/03/78	975	17:30	CARPENTER Buzz	MURPHY John	N-HABU	2.2	
03/04/78	975	18:30	CARPENTER Buzz	MURPHY John	N-HABU	1.9	A
05/04/78	967	12:15	THOMAS B.C.	REID Jay	D8	4.2	
06/04/78	975	13:15	ROSENBERG Maury	PAYNE Al	HABU	4.1	
07/04/78	967		CARPENTER Buzz	MURPHY John	D4		A
08/04/78	967	11:00	CARPENTER Buzz	MURPHY John	D4	1.2	A
11/04/78	975	10:10	CARPENTER Buzz	MURPHY John	HABU	3.7	
15/04/78	975	10:30	THOMAS B.C.	REID Jay	HABU	4.1	
18/04/78	967	10:35	GRAHAM Rich	EMMONS Don	P4	3.9	
20/04/78	975	13:16	CARPENTER Buzz	MURPHY John	HABU	2.4	A
21/04/78	967	11:00	GRAHAM Rich	EMMONS Don	HABU	3.9	
21/04/78	975	10:38	CARPENTER Buzz	MURPHY John	RTB FERRY	1.6	
24/04/78	967	12:55	THOMAS B.C.	REID Jay	D8	4.1	
24/04/78	960	15:30	CARPENTER Buzz	MURPHY John	D9	2.6	A
25/04/78	975	20:05	CARPENTER Buzz	MURPHY John	N-HABU	2.3	
27/04/78	967	13:35	GRAHAM Rich	EMMONS Don	D8	4.2	
28/04/78	960	07:30	THOMAS B.C.	REID Jay	HABU	3.9	
01/05/78	960	10:00	GRONINGER Bill	SOBER Chuck	D8	3.9	
02/05/78	967		GRAHAM Rich	EMMONS Don	HABU		A
03/05/78	960	10:27	THOMAS B.C.	REID Jay	D9	3.9	
04/05/78	967	09:05	GRAHAM Rich	EMMONS Don	HABU	4.1	A
08/05/78	960	14:00	GRONINGER Bill	SOBER Chuck	HABU	4.1	
09/05/78	967	14:00	THOMAS B.C.	REID Jay	D4	2.5	
11/05/78	960	10:00	GRAHAM Rich	SOBER Chuck	D8	3.9	
12/05/78	967		GRONINGER Bill	SOBER Chuck	HABU		A
13/05/78	967	08:30	GRONINGER Bill	SOBER Chuck	HABU	2.3	
15/05/78	975		VETH Jack	ELLIOTT Larry	D9		A
17/05/78	967	12:45	GRAHAM Rich	EMMONS Don	HABU	1.8	A
19/05/78	967	06:38	VETH Jack	KELLER Bill	HHQ GIANT BARNACLE	3.3	21
20/05/78	975	06:30	GRAHAM Rich	EMMONS Don	HABU	2.3	
21/05/78	967	11:08	VETH Jack	KELLER Bill	RTB FERRY	2.9	
22/05/78	967	11:20	GRONINGER Bill	SOBER Chuck	HABU	4.4	
25/05/78	967	21:13	VETH Jack	KELLER Bill	N-HABU	2.4	
30/05/78	967	11:25	GRONINGER Bill	SOBER Chuck	HABU	2	A
31/05/78	967	13:25	GRONINGER Bill	SOBER Chuck	HABU	3.6	
01/06/78	975	10:30	KINEGO Joe	KELLER Bill	D8	3.8	
02/06/78	967	09:30	KINEGO Joe	LIEBMAN Bruce	HABU	4.2	
06/06/78	967	13:45	VETH Jack	KELLER Bill	HABU	4.2	
08/06/78	975	13:05	KINEGO Joe	LIEBMAN Bruce	P4	2.6	
08/06/78	975		KINEGO Joe	LIEBMAN Bruce	P4		A
09/06/78	960	13:38	VETH Jack	ELLIOTT Larry	P4 / FCF COMPLETED	2.5	
12/06/78	975	10:00	CROWDER Bob	MORGAN John	D8	4	
13/06/78	967		KINEGO Joe	LIEBMAN Bruce	D5		A
15/06/78	960	10:30	KINEGO Joe	LIEBMAN Bruce	HABU	3.9	
16/06/78	975	10:30	VETH Jack	LIEBMAN Bruce	D8	4.3	
20/06/78	975	21:00	VETH Jack	KELLER Bill	N-HABU	2.4	
22/06/78	975	09:27	CROWDER Bob	MORGAN John	HABU	2.3	
23/06/78	975	11:40	KINEGO Joe	LIEBMAN Bruce	HABU	3.9	
26/06/78	960	11:54	KECK Tom	SHAW Tim	D8	3.9	
26/06/78	960		KECK Tom	SHAW Tim	D8		A
27/06/78	967	10:28	CROWDER Bob	MORGAN John	P4	5.7	
28/06/78	960	09:30	KECK Tom	SHAW Tim	HABU	0.7	A
29/06/78	960	09:51	KECK Tom	SHAW Tim	HABU	4.3	
30/06/78	975	10:00	KINEGO Joe	LIEBMAN Bruce	D3	2.5	
05/07/78	960	09:15	KECK Tom	SHAW Tim	D3	2.5	
06/07/78	967	21:25	CROWDER Bob	MORGAN John	N-HABU	2.3	
10/07/78	967	10:00	ALISON Tom	VIDA Joe	D8	3.8	
12/07/78	960	06:00	KECK Tom	SHAW Tim	HABU	4.3	
14/07/78	967	10:10	CROWDER Bob	MORGAN John	HABU	2.9	A
17/07/78	967	13:15	ALISON Tom	VIDA Joe	HABU	2.2	A
18/07/78	960	10:00	KECK Tom	SHAW Tim	D8	4	
21/07/78	967	14:44	KECK Tom	SHAW Tim	HABU	4.2	
24/07/78	960	18:31	ALISON Tom	VIDA Joe	HABU	1.1	A
26/07/78	967	07:15	ALISON Tom	VIDA Joe	HABU	3.9	
30/07/78	967	12:15	CARPENTER Buzz	MURPHY John	HABU	0.5	A
31/07/78	967	12:15	CARPENTER Buzz	MURPHY John	HABU	2.3	
01/08/78	960	09:27	KECK Tom	SHAW Tim	D8	3.2	A
03/08/78	960	14:55	ALISON Tom	VIDA Joe	HABU	3.7	
05/08/78	967	09:33	CARPENTER Buzz	MURPHY John	HABU	2.3	
07/08/78	960	09:15	THOMAS B.C.	REID Jay	HABU	3.8	
09/08/78	975		ALISON Tom	VIDA Joe	P4		A
10/08/78	975	14:20	ALISON Tom	VIDA Joe	D8	3.8	
11/08/78	967	13:16	CARPENTER Buzz	MURPHY John	D7	2.4	
14/08/78	975	10:35	THOMAS B.C.	REID Jay	FCF2	3.9	
18/08/78	975	04:02	CARPENTER Buzz	MURPHY John	HABU	4.1	

Date	Instal. No.	T.O. Time	Pilot Name	RSO Name	Mission	Duration	Remarks
21/08/78	975	09:16	THOMAS B.C.	REID Jay	HABU	2.8	A
23/08/78	975	11:24	GRAHAM Rich	EMMONS Don	HABU	3.6	
24/08/78	960	12:14	CARPENTER Buzz	MURPHY John	FCF2	2.7	A
24/08/78	960		CARPENTER Buzz	MURPHY John	FCF2		A
25/08/78	967	09:15	CARPENTER Buzz	MURPHY John	HABU	3.8	
28/08/78	967	10:34	GRAHAM Rich	EMMONS Don	D8	2.2	
28/08/78	960	12:35	THOMAS B.C.	REID Jay	D7	2.5	A
29/08/78	975	21:24	THOMAS B.C.	REID Jay	N-HABU	1.7	A
30/08/78	975	21:43	THOMAS B.C.	REID Jay	N-HABU	2.3	
01/09/78	967		GRAHAM Rich	EMMONS Don	HABU		A
05/09/78	975	21:04	GRAHAM Rich	EMMONS Don	N-HABU	2.2	
06/09/78	960	14:41	CROWDER Bob	MORGAN John	D8	2.5	A
08/09/78	960	11:30	CROWDER Bob	MORGAN John	HABU	4.2	
08/09/78	975	12:45	THOMAS B.C.	REID Jay	D1	1.2	
11/09/78	960	10:35	THOMAS B.C.	REID Jay	HABU	3.9	
12/09/78	975	10:35	GRAHAM Rich	EMMONS Don	HABU	2.3	
14/09/78	960	09:58	CROWDER Bob	MORGAN John	D4	2.5	
15/09/78	975	13:00	CROWDER Bob	MORGAN John	HABU	4.1	
18/09/78	960	12:53	GRONINGER Bill	SOBER Chuck	D8	4.2	
19/09/78	975	21:30	GRAHAM Rich	EMMONS Don	N-HABU	2.4	
20/09/78	960	13:00	CROWDER Bob	MORGAN John	FCF2	2.5	
22/09/78	975	04:30	GRONINGER Bill	SOBER Chuck	HABU	4.3	
25/09/78	960	09:40	CROWDER Bob	MORGAN John	HABU	3.7	
25/09/78	975	10:48	GRAHAM Rich	EMMONS Don	D1	1.2	
26/09/78	967	10:20	GRONINGER Bill	SOBER Chuck	FCF2	4.1	
28/09/78	975	14:45	GRONINGER Bill	SOBER Chuck	HABU	2.2	A
29/09/78	967	10:15	CROWDER Bob	MORGAN John	D8	4	
02/10/78	967	13:04	CROWDER Bob	MORGAN John	HABU	2.3	
04/10/78	967	09:01	VETH Jack	KELLER Bill	HABU	4.3	
05/10/78	975	10:15	VETH Jack	KELLER Bill	D8	4.2	
06/10/78	967	10:00	CROWDER Bob	MORGAN John	HABU	2.4	
10/10/78	975	13:48	VETH Jack	KELLER Bill	HABU	1.1	A
10/10/78	967	14:19	CROWDER Bob	MORGAN John	HABU	4.4	
12/10/78	960		VETH Jack	KELLER Bill	D7		A
16/10/78	960	13:29	KECK Tom	SHAW Tim	D1	1	
16/10/78	967	11:15	GRONINGER Bill	SOBER Chuck	HABU	2.4	
17/10/78	967	19:45	VETH Jack	KELLER Bill	N-HABU	2.3	
19/10/78	967	07:10	KECK Tom	SHAW Tim	HABU	1.4	A
20/10/78	967	15:00	KECK Tom	SHAW Tim	HABU	3.9	
22/10/78	960	12:10	GRONINGER Bill	SOBER Chuck	HABU	1.4	A
24/10/78	960	21:00	VETH Jack	KELLER Bill	N-HABU	2	A
25/10/78	967	21:15	VETH Jack	KELLER Bill	N-HABU	2.3	
26/10/78	960	12:00	GRONINGER Bill	SOBER Chuck	HABU	1.4	
28/10/78	960	10:15	KECK Tom	SHAW Tim	HABU	1.3	A
30/10/78	967	07:10	KECK Tom	SHAW Tim	HABU	4.3	
31/10/78	960	12:15	VETH Jack	KELLER Bill	HABU	0.9	A
01/11/78	967	21:45	VETH Jack	KELLER Bill	N-HABU	2.3	
03/11/78	967	10:10	KINEGO Joe	LIEBMAN Bruce	HABU	4.1	
03/11/78	975	13:19	KECK Tom	SHAW Tim	D4	2.6	
06/11/78	960	14:21	KECK Tom	SHAW Tim	HABU	4.4	
08/11/78	967	06:00	VETH Jack	KELLER Bill	HABU	2.5	
09/11/78	960	13:00	KINEGO Joe	LIEBMAN Bruce	FCF2	4.2	
11/11/78	960	07:00	KINEGO Joe	LIEBMAN Bruce	HABU	4.4	
13/11/78	960	09:31	KECK Tom	SHAW Tim	HABU	1.4	
14/11/78	975	10:04	PETERS Dave	BETHART Ed	D4	1.4	A
15/11/78	960	09:05	PETERS Dave	BETHART Ed	HABU	4.1	
16/11/78	960	20:20	KINEGO Joe	LIEBMAN Bruce	N-HABU	3.2	A
17/11/78	975	13:00	KECK Tom	SHAW Tim	D8	3.4	A
20/11/78	967	13:00	KECK Tom	SHAW Tim	HABU	4.2	
21/11/78	975	21:30	KINEGO Joe	LIEBMAN Bruce	N-HABU	2.3	
27/11/78	967	11:15	PETERS Dave	BETHART Ed	HABU	4.1	A
28/11/78	975	10:02	CARPENTER Buzz	MURPHY John	D2	2.2	
29/11/78	967	10:43	PETERS Dave	BETHART Ed	RTB FERRY	1.9	
30/11/78	967	10:30	KINEGO Joe	LIEBMAN Bruce	HABU	2.4	A
01/12/78	975	10:05	CARPENTER Buzz	MURPHY John	D8	4.1	
04/12/78	975	11:45	CARPENTER Buzz	MURPHY John	HABU	4.3	A
05/12/78	967		PETERS Dave	BETHART Ed	HABU		A
06/12/78	975		CARPENTER Buzz	MURPHY John	RTB FERRY		A
07/12/78	975	11:22	CARPENTER Buzz	MURPHY John	RTB FERRY	1.8	
09/12/78	975	11:10	CARPENTER Buzz	MURPHY John	HABU	2.2	A
11/12/78	967	12:40	ALISON Tom	VIDA Joe	HABU	2.9	A
11/12/78	960	14:44	CARPENTER Buzz	BETHART Ed	P2	2.2	A
13/12/78	960	09:58	CARPENTER Buzz	MURPHY John	FCF2	2.4	
13/12/78	967	14:47	ALISON Tom	VIDA Joe	RTB FERRY	1.6	
14/12/78	960	11:01	CARPENTER Buzz	MURPHY John	HABU	2.3	
15/12/78	967	12:00	ALISON Tom	VIDA Joe	HABU	1.2	A
16/12/78	967	11:15	ALISON Tom	VIDA Joe	HABU	4.2	
19/12/78	967	19:45	CARPENTER Buzz	MURPHY John	N-HABU	2.4	
20/12/78	960	15:08	PETERS Dave	BETHART Ed	FCF2	2.3	
20/12/78	960		PETERS Dave	BETHART Ed	FCF2		A
21/12/78	967	10:30	ALISON Tom	VIDA Joe	HABU	3.7	
27/12/78	960	13:19	CARPENTER Buzz	MURPHY John	HABU	1.4	A
28/12/78	960	10:04	CARPENTER Buzz	MURPHY John	HABU	4.3	
29/12/78	967	11:00	THOMAS B.C.	REID Jay	HABU	2.3	
02/01/79	975	10:31	CARPENTER Buzz	MURPHY John	FCF	2.6	
02/01/79	960	10:30	ALISON Tom	VIDA Joe	HABU	3.8	
04/01/79	960	14:10	THOMAS B.C.	REID Jay	HABU	2.4	
05/01/79	975	10:00	ALISON Tom	VIDA Joe	FCF	4	
06/01/79	960	09:11	ALISON Tom	VIDA Joe	HABU	1.4	
08/01/79	975	09:43	GRONINGER Bill	SOBER Chuck	FCF	4.1	
09/01/79	967	10:15	GRONINGER Bill	SOBER Chuck	HABU	2.3	A
11/01/79	960	19:10	THOMAS B.C.	REID Jay	N-HABU	2.4	
15/01/79	975	08:30	ALISON Tom	VIDA Joe	HABU	3.9	
17/01/79	967	13:45	THOMAS B.C.	REID Jay	HABU	3.1	A
17/01/79	960	12:55	GRONINGER Bill	SOBER Chuck	HABU	1.5	A
19/01/79	975	20:05	GRONINGER Bill	SOBER Chuck	N-HABU	2.3	
23/01/79	975	10:09	THOMAS B.C.	REID Jay	HABU	1.3	A
24/01/79	960	10:00	THOMAS B.C.	REID Jay	HABU	2.4	
26/01/79	960	18:30	GRAHAM Rich	EMMONS Don	N-HABU	1.3	
30/01/79	960	09:16	GRONINGER BIll	SOBER Chuck	HABU	2.4	
31/01/79	967	11:10	THOMAS B.C.	REID Jay	HABU	2.4	
03/02/79	960	10:30	GRAHAM Rich	EMMONS Don	HABU	1.5	
05/02/79	960	19:00	GRONINGER BIll	SOBER Chuck	N-HABU	2.3	
07/02/79	960	13:15	GRAHAM Rich	EMMONS Don	HABU	3.6	
08/02/79	967	09:30	SHELTON Lee	MACKEAN Barry	FCF2	2.5	
09/02/79	967	08:33	SHELTON Lee	MACKEAN Barry	HABU	2.5	
12/02/79	960	20:16	GRONINGER Bill	SOBER Chuck	N-HABU	2.3	
15/02/79	967	10:30	GRAHAM Rich	EMMONS Don	HABU	2.4	
16/02/79	960	11:50	SHELTON Lee	MACKEAN Barry	HABU	4.1	
19/02/79	960	08:00	GRAHAM Rich	EMMONS Don	HABU	4	
22/02/79	967	09:28	VETH Jack	KELLER Bill	HABU	2.3	
23/02/79	960	13:42	SHELTON Lee	MACKEAN Barry	HABU	3.9	
23/02/79	960		SHELTON Lee	MACKEAN Barry	HABU		A
26/02/79	967	21:30	GRAHAM Rich	EMMONS Don	N-HABU	2.3	
27/02/79	967		VETH Jack	KELLER Bill	HABU		A
27/02/79	975	11:47	VETH Jack	KELLER Bill	FCF2	4.2	
02/03/79	967	13:10	SHELTON Lee	MACKEAN Barry	HABU	4.5	
05/03/79	975	10:11	KINEGO Joe	LIEBMAN Bruce	FCF2	4.3	
06/03/79	967	10:35	VETH Jack	KELLER Bill	HABU	4.2	
08/03/79	975	22:00	KINEGO Joe	LIEBMAN Bruce	N-HABU	2.1	A
10/03/79	960	12:00	SHELTON Lee	MACKEAN Barry	HABU	2.1	A
12/03/79	975	10:00	VETH Jack	KELLER Bill	FCF2	2.2	
13/03/79	960	09:10	VETH Jack	KELLER Bill	HABU	4.1	
16/03/79	960	23:30	KINEGO Joe	LIEBMAN Bruce	N-HABU	2.4	
20/03/79	960	10:15	VETH Jack	KELLER Bill	HABU	2.4	
22/03/79	960	19:45	CROWDER Bob	MORGAN John	N-HABU	2.4	
24/03/79	975	11:30	KINEGO Joe	LIEBMAN Bruce	HABU	3.9	
25/03/79	960	10:00	VETH Jack	KELLER Bill	HABU	0.5	A
25/03/79	960	12:14	VETH Jack	KELLER Bill	HABU	1.6	A
27/03/79	975	10:15	CROWDER BOb	MORGAN John	HABU	2.3	
30/03/79	960	09:10	KINEGO Joe	LIEBMAN Bruce	HABU	4.2	
02/04/79	975	18:05	CROWDER Bob	MORGAN John	N-HABU	2.3	
04/04/79	967		KECK Tom	SHAW Tim	HABU		A
05/04/79	960	09:10	KECK Tom	SHAW Tim	HABU	1.4	
06/04/79	967	16:00	KINEGO Joe	LIEBMAN Bruce	HABU	2.2	A
10/04/79	975	12:45	CROWDER Bob	MORGAN John	HABU	4.1	
11/04/79	967		KECK Tom	SHAW Tim	FCF2		A
11/04/79	967	10:05	KECK Tom	SHAW Tim	FCF2	4	
12/04/79	960	19:30	KECK Tom	SHAW Tim	N-HABU	2.5	
14/04/79	967	09:30	CROWDER Bob	MORGAN John	HABU	4.4	
16/04/79	975	21:45	PETERS Dave	BETHART Ed	N-HABU	2.2	A
18/04/79	960	10:55	KECK Tom	SHAW Tim	HABU	4.1	
20/04/79	975	10:21	CROWDER Bob	MORGAN John	HABU	2.3	
20/04/79	975		CROWDER Bob	MORGAN John	HABU		A
23/04/79	975	23:30	PETERS Dave	BETHART Ed	N-HABU	2.2	
27/04/79	967	13:47	KECK Tom	SHAW Tim	HABU	4.1	
28/04/79	960	10:35	PETERS Dave	BETHART Ed	HABU	1.4	A
30/04/79	967	12:09	ALISON Tom	VIDA Joe	FCF2	3.8	
02/05/79	975	09:40	KECK Tom	SHAW Tim	HABU	2.4	A
03/05/79	960		PETERS Dave	BETHART Ed	D4		A
04/05/79	960	16:31	PETERS Dave	BETHART Ed	FCF1	2.3	A
04/05/79	967	16:30	ALISON Tom	VIDA Joe	HABU	2.3	A
07/05/79	967	09:05	KECK Tom	SHAW Tim	HABU	4.1	
10/05/79	975	10:30	ALISON Tom	VIDA Joe	D1	1.2	
11/05/79	967	08:00	PETERS Dave	BETHART Ed	HABU	1.2	A
12/05/79	960	10:00	ALISON Tom	VIDA Joe	HABU	2.3	
14/05/79	967		PETERS Dave	BETHART Ed	HABU		A
15/05/79	975	13:00	ALISON Tom	VIDA Joe	D8	4.1	
16/05/79	960	19:30	PETERS Dave	BETHART Ed	N-HABU	2.3	
18/05/79	975	11:43	CARPENTER Buzz	MURPHY John	HABU	3.8	
19/05/79	967	09:50	ALISON Tom	VIDA Joe	HABU	4.1	A
21/05/79	975	13:15	PETERS Dave	BETHART Ed	HABU	0.5	A
25/05/79	960	14:10	ALISON Tom	VIDA Joe	HABU	4.1	
29/05/79	967	20:10	CARPENTER Buzz	MURPHY John	N-HABU	2.3	
01/06/79	975	10:00	PETERS Dave	MURPHY John	FCF	2.3	
02/06/79	967	11:25	ALISON Tom	VIDA Joe	HABU	4.2	
04/06/79	960	17:15	CARPENTER Buzz	MURPHY John	N-HABU	4.1	
05/06/79	975		ALISON Tom	VIDA Joe	?		A
07/06/79	967	13:32	CARPENTER Buzz	MURPHY John	HABU	4	
09/06/79	975	09:05	CARPENTER Buzz	MURPHY John	HABU	4.1	
13/06/79	967	15:05	GRAHAM Rich	EMMONS Don	HABU	2.3	
15/06/79	975	09:05	GRONINGER Bill	SOBER Chuck	HABU	2.5	
18/06/79	967	14:11	CARPENTER Buzz	MURPHY John	HABU	4.4	
19/06/79	960	13:00	GRAHAM Rich	EMMONS Don	FCF	2.3	
20/06/79	975	11:10	GRONINGER Bill	SOBER Chuck	HABU	2.4	
22/06/79	962	02:00	SHELTON Lee	MacKEAN Barry	FERRY IN - H	6.7	
23/06/79	960	06:00	CARPENTER Buzz	MURPHY John	H-FERRY OUT		
25/06/79	975	09:30	GRAHAM Rich	EMMONS Don	HABU	4.1	
26/06/79	967	19:25	GRONINGER Bill	SOBER Chuck	N-HABU	2.3	
28/06/79	975	10:43	SHELTON Lee	MACKEAN Barry	HABU	4.1	
02/07/79	975	10:02	GRAHAM Rich	EMMONS Don	HABU	5.2	
05/07/79	962	20:20	SHELTON Lee	MacKEAN Barry	N-HABU	2.5	
09/07/79	967	14:09	GRAHAM Rich	EMMONS Don	HABU	4.2	
11/07/79	975		THOMAS B.C.	REID Jay	HABU		A
11/07/79	975	06:23	SHELTON Lee	MACKEAN Barry	HABU	1.4	
11/07/79	962	03:58	THOMAS B.C.	REID Jay	HHQ SPECIAL -	4.5	22
					NIGHT GLOBAL SHIELD		
13/07/79	975	10:45	GRAHAM Rich	EMMONS Don	HABU	4	
16/07/79	975	18:45	SHELTON Lee	MACKEAN Barry	N-HABU	2.3	
19/07/79	972	02:00	KINEGO Joe	KELLER Bill	FERRY IN / HABU	6.4	
20/07/79	967	08:15	SHELTON Lee	MACKEAN Barry	HABU	2.3	
20/07/79	975	06:00	GRAHAM Rich	EMMONS Don	H-FERRY OUT		
24/07/79	962	00:13	THOMAS B.C.	REID Jay	N-HABU	2.3	
25/07/79	962	09:35	KINEGO Joe	KELLER Bill	HABU	2.2	
27/07/79	962	09:45	SHELTON Lee	MacKEAN Barry	HABU	3.8	
30/07/79	972	09:45	THOMAS B.C.	REID Jay	HABU	4.1	

Date	Instal. No.	T.O. Time	Pilot Name	RSO Name	Mission	Duration	Remarks
31/07/79	967	10:00	KINEGO Joe	KELLER Bill	FCF	2.3	
02/08/79	979	02:03	VETH Jack	MACHOREK Bill	FERRY IN / HABU	6.1	A
03/08/79	967	06:00	SHELTON Lee	MACKEAN Barry	FERRY OUT		
06/08/79	962		THOMAS B.C.	REID Jay	HABU		A
06/08/79	962	13:26	THOMAS B.C.	REID Jay	HABU	4.2	
07/08/79	972	19:50	KINEGO Joe	KELLER Bill	N-HABU	2.3	
10/08/79	962	10:45	VETH Jack	MACHOREK Bill	HABU	3.8	
11/08/79	979	08:30	THOMAS B.C.	REID Jay	HABU	2.4	
20/08/79	979	13:43	VETH Jack	KELLER Bill	FCF	2.2	
25/08/79	972	11:30	YOUNG Rich	SZCZEPANIK Russ	FCF	2.5	A
27/08/79	962	15:22	VETH Jack	MACHOREK Bill	HABU	4.1	
30/08/79	979	08:05	YOUNG Rich	SZCZEPANIK Russ	HABU	3.9	
31/08/79	962	20:05	VETH Jack	MACHOREK Bill	N-HABU	2.3	
03/09/79	972	10:05	YOUNG Rich	SZCZEPANIK Russ	HABU	2.6	A
05/09/79	962	10:25	ALISON Tom	VIDA Joe	HABU	2.3	
07/09/79	962	18:00	VETH Jack	MACHOREK Bill	N-HABU	2.2	
10/09/79	979	21:20	ALISON Tom	VIDA Joe	N-HABU	2.3	
11/09/79	972	13:30	VETH Jack	MACHOREK Bill	FCF	2.4	
12/09/79	962	12:15	YOUNG Rick	SZCZEPANIK Russ	HABU	3.2	A
14/09/79	979	09:10	ALISON Tom	VIDA Joe	HABU	4.1	
17/09/79	979	10:35	YOUNG Rick	SZCZEPANIK Russ	HABU	4	
18/09/79	979	22:30	KECK Tom	SHAW Tim	N-HABU	2.4	
19/09/79	972		ALISON Tom	VIDA Joe	FCF		A
20/09/79	962	11:10	ALISON Tom	VIDA Joe	HABU	3.7	
21/09/79	972	14:47	KECK Tom	SHAW Tim	FCF	2.5	
21/09/79	962	14:46	YOUNG Rick	SZCZEPANIK Russ	HABU	4.1	
24/09/79	972	10:15	ALISON Tom	VIDA Joe	HABU	3.5	A
01/10/79	979	11:30	KECK Tom	SHAW Tim	HABU	4.2	
03/10/79	972	19:40	ALISON Tom	VIDA Joe	N-HABU	2.3	
05/10/79	979	12:30	KECK Tom	SHAW Tim	HABU	2.3	
10/10/79	972	09:05	PETERS Dave	BETHART Ed	HABU	2.3	
11/10/79	972	13:45	ALISON Tom	VIDA Joe	HABU	3.8	
13/10/79	979	10:40	KECK Tom	SHAW Tim	HABU	2.2	
20/10/79	972	15:05	PETERS Dave	BETHART Ed	HABU	2.3	
22/10/79	962	13:59	KECK Tom	SHAW Tim	FCF	4.3	
22/10/79	979	20:02	GRAHAM Rich	EMMONS Don	N-HABU	2.3	
24/10/79	972	11:15	PETERS Dave	BETHART Ed	HABU	2.4	A
25/10/79	979	22:35	KECK Tom	SHAW Tim	N-HABU	2.4	
29/10/79	962	09:17	GRAHAM Rich	EMMONS Don	HABU	3.9	23
30/10/79	979	20:20	CARPENTER Buzz	SOBER Chuck	N-HABU	2.3	
05/11/79	972	19:25	PETERS Dave	BETHART Ed	N-HABU	2.4	
07/11/79	962	11:45	GRAHAM Rich	EMMONS Don	HABU	3.7	
08/11/79	979	10:45	CARPENTER Buzz	SOBER Chuck	HABU	2.4	
09/11/79	972	18:40	GRAHAM Rich	EMMONS Don	N-HABU	2.3	
13/11/79	962	07:40	CARPENTER Buzz	SOBER Chuck	HABU	2.4	A
14/11/79	972	19:05	GRAHAM Rich	EMMONS Don	N-HABU	2.3	
16/11/79	962	12:15	THOMAS B.C.	REID Jay	HABU	4.2	
21/11/79	979	15:10	CARPENTER Buzz	SOBER Chuck	N-HABU	4.8	
24/11/79	972	10:30	SHELTON Lee	MacKEAN Barry	HABU	2.2	
26/11/79	962	11:45	CARPENTER Buzz	SOBER Chuck	HABU	3.9	
27/11/79	972	20:10	SHELTON Lee	MacKEAN Barry	N-HABU	2.3	
29/11/79	979	14:50	CARPENTER Buzz	SOBER Chuck	HABU	2.4	
03/12/79	962	18:55	SHELTON Lee	MacKEAN Barry	N-HABU	2.3	
05/12/79	972	09:05	CARPENTER Buzz	SOBER Chuck	HABU	4.2	
10/12/79	979	11:00	SHELTON Lee	MacKEAN Barry	HABU	2.3	
12/12/79	962	07:55	THOMAS B.C.	REID Jay	HABU	4	
13/12/79	979	17:45	SHELTON Lee	MacKEAN Barry	N-HABU	2.3	
14/12/79	962	12:30	THOMAS B.C.	REID Jay	HABU	4	A
17/12/79	962	09:25	SHELTON Lee	MacKEAN Barry	HABU	4.3	
18/12/79	979	21:45	THOMAS B.C.	REID Jay	N-HABU	2.3	
20/12/79	962	12:30	THOMAS B.C.	REID Jay	HABU	2.3	
21/12/79	979	11:15	SHELTON Lee	MacKEAN Barry	HABU	2.3	
27/12/79	962	13:15	YOUNG Rick	SZCZEPANIK Russ	HABU	4.3	
29/12/79	979	08:21	SHELTON Lee	MacKEAN Barry	HABU	3.9	
03/01/80	962		YOUNG Rick	SZCZEPANIK Russ	N-HABU		A
03/01/80	962	21:30	YOUNG Rick	SZCZEPANIK Russ	N-HABU	2.5	A
04/01/80	972	15:30	SHELTON Lee	MacKEAN Barry	FCF-2	2	A
05/01/80	979		YOUNG Rick	SZCZEPANIK Russ	HABU		A
07/01/80	962	09:05	YOUNG Rick	SZCZEPANIK Russ	HABU	4.2	
09/01/80	979	11:10	ALISON Tom	VIDA Joe	HABU	4.2	
10/01/80	962	10:55	SHELTON Lee	MacKEAN Barry	HABU	2.3	
15/01/80	972		YOUNG Rick	SZCZEPANIK Russ	HABU		A
16/01/80	972	10:00	YOUNG Rick	SZCZEPANIK Russ	HABU	2.3	A
17/01/80	979	20:20	ALISON Tom	VIDA Joe	N-HABU	2.3	
19/01/80	962	10:20	YOUNG Rick	SZCZEPANIK Russ	HABU	2.7	A
21/01/80	962	10:00	ALISON Tom	VIDA Joe	HABU	2.3	A
22/01/80	962	19:05	KECK Tom	SHAW Tim	HABU	2.4	
24/01/80	962	10:46	YOUNG Rick	SZCZEPANIK Russ	HABU	2.3	A
25/01/80	962	14:30	ALISON Tom	VIDA Joe	HABU	3.8	
28/01/80	979	07:30	KECK Tom	SHAW Tim	HABU	3.9	
29/01/80	972	09:20	YOUNG Rick	SZCZEPANIK Russ	HABU	2.4	A
30/01/80	979	20:15	ALISON Tom	VIDA Joe	N-HABU	2.4	
01/02/80	979	10:50	KECK Tom	SHAW Tim	HABU	2.3	
01/02/80	972	10:51	YOUNG Rick	SZCZEPANIK Russ	FCF	1.2	A
04/02/80	962	19:00	KECK Tom	SHAW Tim	HABU	2.6	
05/02/80	972	15:00	ALISON Tom	VIDA Joe	FCF	2.3	
07/02/80	979	07:15	ALISON Tom	VIDA Joe	HABU	4.1	
09/02/80	972	07:35	PETERS Dave	BETHART Ed	HABU	2.5	A
11/02/80	979	09:55	KECK Tom	SHAW Tim	HABU	4.3	
12/02/80	962	22:45	ALISON Tom	VIDA Joe	N-HABU	2.3	
15/02/80	972	10:30	PETERS Dave	BETHART Ed	HABU	1.8	A
17/02/80	979	09:15	KECK Tom	SHAW Tim	HABU	5.9	
20/02/80	962	18:45	CROWDER Bob	EMMONS Don	N-HABU	2.3	
22/02/80	972	13:12	KECK Tom	SHAW Tim	HABU	4.1	
25/02/80	979	09:05	PETERS Dave	BETHART Ed	HABU	2.3	
25/02/80	972	09:06	CROWDER Bob	EMMONS Don	FCF	4.1	
27/02/80	972	12:10	KECK Tom	SHAW Tim	HABU	3.9	
28/02/80	962	11:36	PETERS Dave	BETHART Ed	HABU	2.1	A
03/03/80	962	20:05	CROWDER Bob	EMMONS Don	N-HABU	2.3	
05/03/80	972	10:10	CARPENTER Buzz	SOBER Chuck	HABU	4.2	
06/03/80	962	15:50	CROWDER Bob	EMMONS Don	HABU	2.3	
10/03/80	972	07:50	CARPENTER Buzz	SOBER Chuck	HABU	4.2	
11/03/80	962	22:05	CROWDER Bob	EMMONS Don	N-HABU	2.4	
15/03/80	972	10:38	CARPENTER Buzz	SOBER Chuck	HABU	2.4	
17/03/80	962	18:50	CROWDER Bob	EMMONS Don	N-HABU	2.2	
18/03/80	979	13:00	THOMAS B.C.	REID Jay	FCF	4.3	
19/03/80	972	11:33	CARPENTER Buzz	SOBER Chuck	HABU	3.9	
21/03/80	979	08:40	CROWDER Bob	EMMONS Don	HABU	3.8	
24/03/80	972	11:30	THOMAS B.C.	REID Jay	HABU	4	
25/03/80	962	21:20	CARPENTER Buzz	SOBER Chuck	N-HABU	2.3	
27/03/80	979	11:00	CROWDER Bob	EMMONS Don	HABU	2.4	
28/03/80	962	22:00	THOMAS B.C.	REID Jay	N-HABU	2.4	
29/03/80	972	19:10	CARPENTER Buzz	SOBER Chuck	N-HABU	2.3	
31/03/80	979		KINEGO Joe	KELLER Bill	HABU		A
31/03/80	979	19:53	KINEGO Joe	KELLER Bill	N-HABU	2.3	
02/04/80	962	19:05	THOMAS B.C.	REID Jay	N-HABU	2.4	
04/04/80	972	10:35	CARPENTER Buzz	SOBER Chuck	HABU	1.4	A
07/04/80	979		CARPENTER Buzz	SOBER Chuck	HABU		A
07/04/80	979	13:44	CARPENTER Buzz	SOBER Chuck	HABU	0.5	A
08/04/80	979	19:49	CARPENTER Buzz	SOBER Chuck	N-HABU	2.4	
12/04/80	962	09:15	KINEGO Joe	KELLER Bill	HABU	4.1	A
14/04/80	972	10:46	THOMAS B.C.	REID Jay	HABU	4.4	
15/04/80	962	20:30	SHELTON Lee	MacKEAN Barry	N-HABU	2.4	
17/04/80	979	12:20	KINEGO Joe	KELLER Bill	HABU	1.9	A
19/04/80	972	09:51	THOMAS B.C.	REID Jay	HABU	2.5	
21/04/80	962	10:30	SHELTON Lee	MacKEAN Barry	HABU	2.4	
23/04/80	979	09:25	THOMAS B.C.	REID Jay	HABU	2.5	A
24/04/80	972	21:40	KINEGO Joe	KELLER Bill	N-HABU	2.2	
29/04/80	972	11:15	SHELTON Lee	MacKEAN Barry	HABU	4.4	
01/05/80	979	10:30	KINEGO Joe	KELLER Bill	HABU	2.3	
03/05/80	979	09:15	YOUNG Rick	SZCZEPANIK Russ	HABU	6	
05/05/80	962	10:00	SHELTON Lee	MacKEAN Barry	FCF	2.5	
06/05/80	972	18:30	KINEGO Joe	KELLER Bill	N-HABU	2.3	
07/05/80	979	19:15	YOUNG Rick	SZCZEPANIK Russ	N-HABU	2.3	
09/05/80	962	09:05	SHELTON Lee	MacKEAN Barry	HABU	2.6	
12/05/80	962	13:08	YOUNG Rick	SZCZEPANIK Russ	HABU	2.5	
13/05/80	972	21:05	ALISON Tom	VIDA Joe	N-HABU	2.3	
15/05/80	979	12:30	SHELTON Lee	MacKEAN Barry	HABU	2.4	A
19/05/80	962	11:15	YOUNG Rick	SZCZEPANIK Russ	HABU	4.4	
23/05/80	972	20:45	ALISON Tom	VIDA Joe	N-HABU	2.5	
28/05/80	979	09:30	YOUNG Rick	SZCZEPANIK Russ	HABU	2.4	
30/05/80	962	06:00	KECK Tom	SHAW Tim	HABU	4.3	
02/06/80	979	11:30	ALISON Tom	VIDA Joe	HABU	2.4	
04/06/80	962	11:09	YOUNG Rick	SZCZEPANIK Russ	HABU	2.3	
05/06/80	972	20:40	KECK Tom	SHAW Tim	N-HABU	2.4	
09/06/80	979	21:05	ALISON Tom	VIDA Joe	N-HABU	2.3	
11/06/80	962	19:55	PETERS Dave	BETHART Ed	N-HABU	2.3	
13/06/80	972	14:50	KECK Tom	SHAW Tim	HABU	4.1	
16/06/80	962	09:10	ALISON Tom	VIDA Joe	HABU	2.3	A
18/06/80	979	07:20	KECK Tom	SHAW Tim	HABU	3.8	A
19/06/80	962	20:50	ALISON Tom	VIDA Joe	N-HABU	2.3	
23/06/80	979	07:02	PETERS Dave	BETHART Ed	FCF	2.3	
24/06/80	972	09:23	ALISON Tom	VIDA Joe	H-FERRY OUT		
24/06/80	962	09:42	KECK Tom	SHAW Tim	H-FERRY OUT	1.3	
					AIR SPARE		
24/06/80	976	03:08	CROWDER Bob	EMMONS Don	FERRY IN-H	5.7	
26/06/80	979	12:10	PETERS Dave	BETHART Ed	HABU	1.1	A
28/06/80	976	12:00	KECK Tom	SHAW Tim	HABU	2.9	A
01/07/80	962	10:05	CROWDER Bob	EMMONS Don	SPECIAL	4.4	24
03/07/80	979		PETERS Dave	BETHART Ed	HABU		A
04/07/80	962	10:55	CROWDER Bob	EMMONS Don	SPECIAL RTB FERRY	4.9	25
05/07/80	979	12:00	PETERS Dave	BETHART Ed	HABU	2.3	
08/07/80	979	09:05	CROWDER Bob	EMMONS Don	HABU	4.1	
09/07/80	962	20:40	PETERS Dave	BETHART Ed	N-HABU	2.1	
10/07/80	976	12:00	BERTELSON Gil	STAMPF Frank	FCF	4.1	
11/07/80	979	11:10	BERTELSON Gil	STAMPF Frank	HABU	4	
14/07/80	976	08:10	CROWDER Bob	EMMONS Don	HABU	3.9	
15/07/80	962	21:50	PETERS Dave	BETHART Ed	N-HABU	2.2	
17/07/80	958	08:30	THOMAS B.C.	REID Jay	FERRY IN-H	6.5	
19/07/80	962	09:15	PETERS Dave	BETHART Ed	H-FERRY OUT		
21/07/80	979		BERTELSON Gil	STAMPF Frank	HABU		A
21/07/80	979	12:40	BERTELSON Gil	STAMPF Frank	HABU	2.3	A
23/07/80	958	10:10	CROWDER Bob	EMMONS Don	HABU	4.1	
24/07/80	976	20:00	THOMAS B.C.	REID Jay	N-HABU	2.2	
29/07/80	976	06:00	BERTELSON Gil	STAMPF Frank	HABU	4.2	
30/07/80	979	13:10	CROWDER Bob	EMMONS Don	HABU	2.4	
01/08/80	976	09:15	THOMAS B.C.	REID Jay	HABU	1.9	A
03/08/80	979	08:15	BERTELSON Gil	STAMPF Frank	HABU	6.2	
05/08/80	976	10:10	CARPENTER Buzz	KELLER Bill	HABU	3.8	
07/08/80	958	14:05	BERTELSON Gil	STAMPF Frank	HABU	4.1	
11/08/80	976	07:55	CARPENTER Buzz	KELLER Bill	HABU	3.9	
12/08/80	979	20:03	THOMAS B.C.	REID Jay	N-HABU	2.3	
14/08/80	976	10:42	BERTELSON Gil	STAMPF Frank	HABU	2.4	
19/08/80	958	11:19	CARPENTER Buzz	KELLER Bill	HABU	4.1	
20/08/80	979	21:10	THOMAS B.C.	REID Jay	N-HABU	2.2	
23/08/80	958	12:50	SHELTON Lee	MacKEAN Barry	HABU	2.3	
25/08/80	979	20:50	CARPENTER Buzz	KELLER Bill	N-HABU	2.1	
26/08/80	976	10:03	THOMAS B.C.	REID Jay	FCF	2.2	
29/08/80	979	12:13	SHELTON Lee	MacKEAN Barry	HABU	2.5	A
02/09/80	979	19:59	CARPENTER Buzz	KELLER Bill	N-HABU	2.3	
04/09/80	976	09:44	SHELTON Lee	MacKEAN Barry	HABU	2.4	
04/09/80	960	05:57	ALISON Tom	VIDA Joe	H-FERRY IN	6.2	
05/09/80	979	10:30	CARPENTER Buzz	KELLER Bill	H/FERRY OUT		
08/09/80	958	10:15	YOUNG Rick	SZCZEPANIK Russ	HABU	2.2	
12/09/80	976	14:00	SHELTON Lee	MacKEAN Barry	HABU	2.3	
16/09/80	960	08:00	ALISON Tom	VIDA Joe	HABU	4.2	

Date	Instal. No.	T.O. Time	Pilot Name	RSO Name	Mission	Duration	Remarks
17/09/80	958		YOUNG Rick	SZCZEPANIK Russ	HABU		A
18/09/80	958	21:10	YOUNG Rick	SZCZEPANIK Russ	N-HABU	2.4	
20/09/80	960	09:30	SHELTON Lee	MacKEAN Barry	HABU	2.3	
22/09/80	958	12:05	ALISON Tom	VIDA Joe	HABU	4.1	
24/09/80	976	08:20	YOUNG Rick	SZCZEPANIK Russ	HABU	0.4	A
25/09/80	960	19:10	YOUNG Rick	SZCZEPANIK Russ	N-HABU	2.3	
26/09/80	960	13:00	ALISON Tom	VIDA Joe	HABU	2.3	
29/09/80	958	10:10	YOUNG Rick	SZCZEPANIK Russ	HABU	2.3	
01/10/80	960	10:05	PETERS Dave	BETHART Ed	HABU	4	
02/10/80	976	22:35	ALISON Tom	VIDA Joe	N-HABU	2.4	
06/10/80	960	15:05	YOUNG Rick	SZCZEPANIK Russ	N-HABU	4.2	
10/10/80	976	12:05	PETERS Dave	BETHART Ed	HABU	2.3	
14/10/80	960	20:00	ALISON Tom	VIDA Joe	N-HABU	2.4	
16/10/80	976	14:02	PETERS Dave	BETHART Ed	HABU	2.3	
18/10/80	960	10:40	ALISON Tom	VIDA Joe	HABU	2.3	
20/10/80	960	10:15	PETERS Dave	BETHART Ed	HABU	2.4	
21/10/80	976	14:50	ALISON Tom	VIDA Joe	HABU	4.3	
23/10/80	976		PETERS Dave	BETHART Ed	N-HABU		A
25/10/80	976	11:00	PETERS Dave	BETHART Ed	HABU	2.3	
28/10/80	960	10:30	CROWDER Bob	MORGAN John	HABU	2.4	
29/10/80	976	12:43	JUDSON Rich	KELLY Frank	FCF	4.2	
30/10/80	960	20:15	CROWDER Bob	MORGAN John	N-HABU	2.3	
31/10/80	958	14:00	JUDSON Rich	KELLY Frank	FCF	3.9	
03/11/80	976	13:00	JUDSON Rich	KELLY Frank	HABU	4.2	
04/11/80	960	19:50	PETERS Dave	BETHART Ed	N-HABU	2.3	
06/11/80	976	11:05	CROWDER Bob	MORGAN John	HABU	4.1	
08/11/80	960	12:10	JUDSON Rich	KELLY Frank	HABU	2.3	
10/11/80	960	11:15	CROWDER Bob	MORGAN John	HABU	4.3	
13/11/80	960	11:15	THOMAS B.C.	REID Jay	HABU	2.5	
14/11/80	960	11:15	JUDSON Rich	KELLY Frank	HABU	2.4	
17/11/80	976	07:50	CROWDER Bob	MORGAN John	HABU	4.2	
18/11/80	960	21:05	THOMAS B.C.	REID Jay	N-HABU	2.3	
20/11/80	958	20:30	THOMAS B.C.	REID Jay	N-HABU	2.2	A
21/11/80	976	12:00	JUDSON Rich	KELLY Frank	FCF	2.5	
22/11/80	960	10:25	CROWDER Bob	MORGAN John	HABU	5.7	
24/11/80	976	10:30	THOMAS B.C.	REID Jay	HABU-S	5.8	26
25/11/80	976	21:20	BERTELSON Gil	STAMPF Frank	N-HABU	2.3	
26/11/80	958	12:00	CROWDER Bob	MORGAN John	FCF	1.7	A
28/11/80	958	13:10	THOMAS B.C.	REID Jay	HABU	4.2	
01/12/80	958	12:55	BERTELSON Gil	STAMPF Frank	HABU	1.2	A
02/12/80	958	11:43	CROWDER Bob	MORGAN John	HABU	4.2	
03/12/80	976	18:40	THOMAS B.C.	REID Jay	N-HABU	2.3	
05/12/80	960	10:35	BERTELSON Gil	STAMPF Frank	HABU	3.8	
09/12/80	958	07:51	THOMAS B.C.	REID Jay	HABU	2.3	A
10/12/80	976	15:10	PETERS Dave	BETHART Ed	HABU	1.9	A
11/12/80	976	15:10	BERTELSON Gil	STAMPF Frank	HABU	2.3	
12/12/80	958	12:08	THOMAS B.C.	REID Jay	HABU	2.3	
15/12/80	960	19:30	PETERS Dave	BETHART Ed	N-HABU	2.3	
17/12/80	958		BERTELSON Gil	STAMPF Frank	HABU		A
18/12/80	958	09:30	BERTELSON Gil	STAMPF Frank	HABU	4.2	
19/12/80	960	10:30	BERTELSON Gil	STAMPF Frank	HABU	4.1	
23/12/80	976	08:02	BERTELSON Gil	STAMPF Frank	HABU	3.8	
23/12/80	960	08:41	CUNNINGHAM Nevin	QUIST Gene	FCF	3.3	
27/12/80	976	12:00	CUNNINGHAM Nevin	QUIST Gene	HABU	4.2	
29/12/80	958	18:30	CARPENTER Buzz	SHAW Tim	N-HABU	2.4	
03/01/81	958	10:40	CUNNINGHAM Nevin	QUIST Gene	HABU	4.1	
05/01/81	976	15:17	CARPENTER Buzz	SHAW Tim	HABU	4.2	A
06/01/81	960	20:15	SHELTON Lee	MacKEAN Barry	N-HABU	2.4	
08/01/81	976	10:00	CUNNINGHAM Nevin	QUIST Gene	HABU	4.3	
10/01/81	958	12:00	SHELTON Lee	MacKEAN Barry	HABU	2.2	
14/01/81	960	10:00	CARPENTER Buzz	SHAW Tim	HABU	4.1	
15/01/81	960	08:05	CARPENTER Buzz	SHAW Tim	RTB FERRY	4.8	
15/01/81	976	14:05	CUNNINGHAM Nevin	QUIST Gene	HABU	2.3	
19/01/81	976	12:30	SHELTON Lee	MacKEAN Barry	HABU	4.2	
20/01/81	958	10:11	CUNNINGHAM Nevin	QUIST Gene	HABU	1.6	A
21/01/81	960	12:00	CUNNINGHAM Nevin	QUIST Gene	HABU	4.2	
22/01/81	960	21:00	ALISON Tom	REID Jay	N-HABU	2.5	
26/01/81	958	07:55	SHELTON Lee	MacKEAN Barry	HABU	2.3	A
28/01/81	960	10:40	CUNNINGHAM Nevin	QUIST Gene	HABU	3.9	
29/01/81	976	18:30	ALISON Tom	REID Jay	N-HABU	2.5	A
30/01/81	958	18:30	ALISON Tom	REID Jay	N-HABU	2.2	
02/02/81	958	12:30	SHELTON Lee	MacKEAN Barry	HABU	3.9	
04/02/81	976	14:00	YOUNG Rick	SZCZEPANIK Russ	HABU	2.4	
06/02/81	958	09:10	ALISON Tom	REID Jay	HABU	4.2	
09/02/81	976	10:35	SHELTON Lee	MacKEAN Barry	HABU	3.9	
11/02/81	958	14:55	YOUNG Rick	SZCZEPANIK Russ	HABU	2.3	
13/02/81	958	19:55	ALISON Tom	REID Jay	N-HABU	2.4	
17/02/81	976	20:15	YOUNG Rick	SZCZEPANIK Russ	N-HABU	2.3	
19/02/81	958	13:19	ALISON Tom	REID Jay	HABU	3.9	
21/02/81	976	10:25	YOUNG Rick	SZCZEPANIK Russ	HABU	4	
23/02/81	976	19:30	ALISON Tom	REID Jay	N-HABU	2.3	
25/02/81	958	13:45	ALISON Tom	REID Jay	HABU	2.4	
27/02/81	958	07:45	YOUNG Rick	SZCZEPANIK Russ	HABU	4.2	
02/03/81	976	20:05	PETERS Dave	BETHART Ed	N-HABU	2	A
04/03/81	958	12:05	YOUNG Rick	SZCZEPANIK Russ	HABU	4.3	
05/03/81	960	09:30	PETERS Dave	BETHART Ed	FCF	2.2	
06/03/81	958	10:30	YOUNG Rick	SZCZEPANIK Russ	HABU	3.9	
09/03/81	958	21:00	PETERS Dave	BETHART Ed	N-HABU	2.4	
11/03/81	960	09:30	YOUNG Rick	SZCZEPANIK Russ	FCF	2.5	
12/03/81	976	06:45	JUDSON Rich	KELLY Frank	HABU	4.3	
14/03/81	976	12:05	JUDSON Rich	KELLY Frank	HABU	4.3	
16/03/81	960	13:00	JUDSON Rich	KELLY Frank	HABU	2.4	
17/03/81	958	22:00	JUDSON Rich	KELLY Frank	N-HABU	2.3	
20/03/81	960	08:30	PETERS Dave	BETHART Ed	HABU	1.5	A
21/03/81	960	08:30	JUDSON Rich	KELLY Frank	HABU	3.2	A
24/03/81	958	10:00	PETERS Dave	BETHART Ed	HABU	4.1	
26/03/81	960	11:55	JUDSON Rich	KELLY Frank	HABU	4.2	
27/03/81	958	10:30	JUDSON Rich	KELLY Frank	HABU	3.7	

Date	Instal. No.	T.O. Time	Pilot Name	RSO Name	Mission	Duration	Remarks
01/04/81	958	09:05	CROWDER Bob	MORGAN John	HABU	4	
02/04/81	958	20:05	JUDSON Rich	KELLY Frank	N-HABU	2.3	
06/04/81	960	07:32	CROWDER Bob	MORGAN John	HABU	4.4	
07/04/81	958	10:10	JUDSON Rich	KELLY Frank	HABU	4.1	
09/04/81	960	13:45	CROWDER Bob	MORGAN John	HABU	3.7	
13/04/81	958	21:02	BERTELSON Gil	STAMPF Frank	N-HABU	2.3	
15/04/81	958	12:55	CARPENTER Buzz	SHAW Tim	HABU	4.2	
16/04/81	976	09:30	CROWDER Bob	MORGAN John	FCF	2.5	A
17/04/81	958	08:30	BERTELSON Gil	STAMPF Frank	HABU	4	
20/04/81	976	19:45	CARPENTER Buzz	SHAW Tim	N-HABU	2.3	
22/04/81	960	14:20	CROWDER Bob	MORGAN John	HABU	4.3	
25/04/81	976	09:55	BERTELSON Gil	STAMPF Frank	HABU	2.4	
28/04/81	960	12:50	CUNNINGHAM Nevin	QUIST Gene	HABU	2.2	A
29/04/81	960	12:50	CUNNINGHAM Nevin	QUIST Gene	HABU	4.1	
01/05/81	976	10:31	BERTELSON Gil	STAMPF Frank	HABU	2.4	
04/05/81	960	20:17	CUNNINGHAM Nevin	QUIST Gene	N-HABU	2.2	
06/05/81	976	09:05	CARPENTER Buzz	SHAW Tim	HABU	4	
07/05/81	960	13:40	BERTELSON Gil	STAMPF Frank	HABU	4.1	
11/05/81	960	19:45	CUNNINGHAM Nevin	QUIST Gene	N-HABU	2.3	
13/05/81	960	10:30	CARPENTER Buzz	SHAW Tim	HABU	4	
14/05/81	958	09:19	SHELTON Lee	MacKEAN Barry	FCF	3.8	
15/05/81	958	10:00	CUNNINGHAM Nevin	QUIST Gene	HABU	4.2	
18/05/81	976	11:45	CARPENTER Buzz	SHAW Tim	HABU	4.1	
19/05/81	958	20:15	SHELTON Lee	MacKEAN Barry	N-HABU	2.3	
22/05/81	960	09:55	CUNNINGHAM Nevin	QUIST Gene	HABU	3.9	
26/05/81	976	14:00	SHELTON Lee	MacKEAN Barry	HABU	1.1	A
27/05/81	976	14:30	SHELTON Lee	MacKEAN Barry	HABU	4.1	
29/05/81	958	09:30	ALISON Tom	REID Jay	HABU	5.8	
30/05/81	976	16:00	CUNNINGHAM Nevin	QUIST Gene	N-HABU	5.2	
02/06/81	958	10:30	SHELTON Lee	MacKEAN Barry	HABU	3.9	
04/06/81	960	09:15	ALISON Tom	REID Jay	HABU	2	
08/06/81	960	10:00	ALISON Tom	REID Jay	HABU	3.9	
09/06/81	976	14:00	SHELTON Lee	MacKEAN Barry	HABU	4.1	
11/06/81	958	20:15	YOUNG Rich	SZCZEPANIK Russ	N-HABU	2.3	
13/06/81	976	07:50	ALISON Tom	REID Jay	HABU	4.2	
15/06/81	958	19:45	SHELTON Lee	MacKEAN Barry	N-HABU	2.2	
17/06/81	960	09:15	YOUNG Rich	SZCZEPANIK Russ	HABU	4.1	
19/06/81	958	10:35	ALISON Tom	REID Jay	HABU	2.3	
22/06/81	958	21:10	ALISON Tom	REID Jay	N-HABU	2.3	
25/06/81	958	09:50	BERTELSON Gil	STAMPF Frank	HABU	4.1	
25/06/81	960	10:05	GLASSER Jerry	HORNBAKER Mac	FCF	4.2	
26/06/81	976	13:00	ALISON Tom	REID Jay	HABU	4.1	
29/06/81	976	14:00	GLASSER Jerry	HORNBAKER Mac	HABU	4.1	
02/07/81	960	08:00	BERTELSON Gil	STAMPF Frank	HABU	4.1	
06/07/81	958	12:05	GLASSER Jerry	HORNBAKER Mac	HABU	4	
07/07/81	960	20:30	BERTELSON Gil	STAMPF Frank	N-HABU	2.2	
09/07/81	958	10:00	PETERS Dave	BETHART Ed	HABU	4	
10/07/81	976	14:20	GLASSER Jerry	HORNBAKER Mac	HABU	4.1	
14/07/81	975	03:40	ROSENBERG Maury	McKIM E.D.	FERRY IN-H	6.3	
15/07/81	960	05:00	BERTELSON Gil	STAMPF Frank	H-FERRY OUT		
16/07/81	958	05:52	YOUNG Rich	SZCZEPANIK Russ	H-FERRY OUT		
16/07/81	976	05:58	GLASSER Jerry	HORNBAKER Mac	FERRY OUT AIR SPARE	1.2	
16/07/81	967	04:19	JUDSON Rich	KELLY Frank	FERRY IN-H	6.7	
20/07/81	975	21:00	PETERS Dave	BETHART Ed	N-HABU	2	A
23/07/81	976	10:00	GLASSER Jerry	HORNBAKER Mac	HABU	1.7	A
24/07/81	975	10:00	GLASSER Jerry	HORNBAKER Mac	HABU	3.6	A
24/07/81	976	12:00	ROSENBERG Maury	McKIM E.D.	FCF	3.9	
27/07/81	975	15:25	GLASSER Jerry	HORNBAKER Mac	RTB FERRY	1.5	
27/07/81	976	20:38	PETERS Dave	BETHART Ed	N-HABU	2.3	
29/07/81	976	10:15	ROSENBERG Maury	McKIM E.D.	HABU	3.9	
31/07/81	976	09:30	PETERS Dave	BETHART Ed	HABU	2.4	
03/08/81	975	20:45	JUDSON Rich	KELLY Frank	N-HABU	1	A
04/08/81	967	11:00	PETERS Dave	BETHART Ed	FCF	2.2	
05/08/81	975	09:18	ROSENBERG Maury	McKIM E.D.	HABU	2.1	A
06/08/81	975	17:00	JUDSON Rich	KELLY Frank	N-HABU	4.1	
11/08/81	967	07:40	PETERS Dave	BETHART Ed	HABU	4.2	
12/08/81	975	20:48	JUDSON Rich	KELLY Frank	N-HABU	2.3	
14/08/81	975	10:15	ROSENBERG Maury	McKIM E.D.	HABU	2.3	
15/08/81	967	20:00	JUDSON Rich	KELLY Frank	N-HABU	2.3	
17/08/81	975	09:30	CUNNINGHAM Nevin	QUIST Gene	HABU	4.2	
19/08/81	976	10:00	ROSENBERG Maury	McKIM E.D.	HABU	4	
20/08/81	967	14:00	JUDSON Rich	KELLY Frank	HABU	2.3	
24/08/81	975	12:00	CUNNINGHAM Nevin	QUIST Gene	HABU	1	A
25/08/81	967	10:00	CUNNINGHAM Nevin	QUIST Gene	HABU	4.2	
26/08/81	976	13:15	ROSENBERG Maury	McKIM E.D.	HABU	4.1	27
02/09/81	976		JUDSON Rich	KELLY Frank	HABU		A
02/09/81	967	11:00	CROWDER Bob	MORGAN John	HABU	2.4	
03/09/81	967	11:45	BERTELSON Gil	STAMPF Frank	HABU	0.9	
03/09/81	975	11:00	JUDSON Rich	KELLY Frank	HABU	4	
04/09/81	967	09:15	BERTELSON Gil	STAMPF Frank	HABU	3.5	A
08/09/81	967	12:00	CROWDER Bob	MORGAN John	HABU	2.9	
10/09/81	975	04:15	JUDSON Rich	KELLY Frank	N-HABU	2.3	
12/09/81	976	09:15	BERTELSON Gil	STAMPF Frank	HABU	2.3	
14/09/81	976	18:50	CROWDER Bob	MORGAN John	N-HABU	2.4	
16/09/81	976	11:10	CUNNINGHAM Nevin	QUIST Gene	HABU	3.9	
18/09/81	976		BERTELSON Gil	STAMPF Frank	HABU		A
18/09/81	967		CROWDER Bob	MORGAN John	HABU		A
21/09/81	976	19:25	BERTELSON Gil	STAMPF Frank	N-HABU	2.3	
24/09/81	967	08:55	CUNNINGHAM Nevin	QUIST Gene	HABU	1.4	
24/09/81	976	08:45	CROWDER Bob	MORGAN John	HABU	4.8	
28/09/81	975	10:00	BERTELSON Gil	STAMPF Frank	HABU	4.2	
29/09/81	976	16:05	CUNNINGHAM Nevin	QUIST Gene	HABU	2.4	
02/10/81	967	14:00	THOMAS B.C.	REID Jay	HABU	2.4	28
03/10/81	975	09:30	CUNNINGHAM Nevin	QUIST Gene	HABU	4	
05/10/81	967	13:00	BERTELSON Gil	STAMPF Frank	HABU	3.1	
08/10/81	975		THOMAS B.C.	REID Jay	HABU		A
09/10/81	967	10:15	THOMAS B.C.	REID Jay	HABU	2.2	
14/10/81	975	19:03	CUNNINGHAM Nevin	QUIST Gene	N-HABU	2.3	

Date	Instal. No.	T.O. Time	Pilot Name	RSO Name	Mission	Duration	Remarks
15/10/81	975	12:20	THOMAS B.C.	REID Jay	HABU	2.3	
19/10/81	975	13:05	CUNNINGHAM Nevin	QUIST Gene	HABU	2.3	
20/10/81	975	10:00	CUNNINGHAM Nevin	QUIST Gene	HABU	3.9	
23/10/81	975	11:00	THOMAS B.C.	REID Jay	HABU	2.5	
24/10/81	967	18:30	CUNNINGHAM Nevin	QUIST Gene	N-HABU	3.2	
26/10/81	975	08:12	THOMAS B.C.	REID Jay	HABU	4.2	29
27/10/81	975	08:30	YOUNG Rick	BETHART Ed	HABU	4.2	
02/11/81	975	08:00	THOMAS B.C.	REID Jay	HABU	3	
03/11/81	975		YOUNG Rick	BETHART Ed	HABU		A
03/11/81	967	08:00	THOMAS B.C.	REID Jay	HABU	4.3	
04/11/81	976	10:00	McCRARY Rick	LAWRENCE Dave	FCF	4.2	
05/11/81	967	08:30	YOUNG Rick	BETHART Ed	HABU	4	
09/11/81	976	18:45	YOUNG Rick	BETHART Ed	N-HABU	2.3	
12/11/81	967	09:30	McCRARY Rick	LAWRENCE Dave	HABU	4.2	
13/11/81	976	10:30	PETERS Dave	SZCZEPANIK Russ	HABU	1.7	A
15/11/81	976	10:25	PETERS Dave	SZCZEPANIK Russ	RTB FERRY	1.6	
16/11/81	967	07:12	YOUNG Rick	BETHART Ed	HABU	4.1	
17/11/81	976	07:05	McCRARY Rick	LAWRENCE Dave	HABU	1.8	A
17/11/81	967	08:01	PETERS Dave	SZCZEPANIK Russ	HABU	4.1	
20/11/81	976		McCRARY Rick	LAWRENCE Dave	HABU		A
20/11/81	967		PETERS Dave	SZCZEPANIK Russ	HABU		A
23/11/81	976	11:45	McCRARY Rick	LAWRENCE Dave	HABU	2.3	
24/11/81	967	09:56	PETERS Dave	SZCZEPANIK Russ	HABU	2.5	A
28/11/81	976	12:30	GLASSER Jerry	HORNBAKER Mac	HABU	2.4	
30/11/81	967	08:31	McCRARY Rick	LAWRENCE Dave	HABU	4.2	
01/12/81	976	18:15	PETERS Dave	SZCZEPANIK Russ	N-HABU	2.3	
03/12/81	967	23:00	GLASSER Jerry	HORNBAKER Mac	N-HABU	2.4	
07/12/81	976	10:30	PETERS Dave	SZCZEPANIK Russ	HABU	3.8	
08/12/81	967	13:00	ROSENBERG Maury	McKIM E.D.	HABU	4.1	
09/12/81	975	09:15	GLASSER Jerry	HORNBAKER Mac	FCF	3.8	
10/12/81	976	08:57	PETERS Dave	SZCZEPANIK Russ	HABU	4	
14/12/81	967	08:30	ROSENBERG Maury	McKIM E.D.	HABU	2.4	
15/12/81	976	12:00	GLASSER Jerry	HORNBAKER Mac	HABU	4.2	
17/12/81	975	09:01	ROSENBERG Maury	McKIM E.D.	HABU	3.9	
21/12/81	967	09:02	GLASSER Jerry	HORNBAKER Mac	HABU	3.9	
23/12/81	975	09:27	CROWDER Bob	MORGAN John	HABU	4	
29/12/81	967	10:02	GLASSER Jerry	HORNBAKER Mac	HABU	4	
30/12/81	975	18:30	ROSENBERG Maury	McKIM E.D.	N-HABU	2.3	
04/01/82	976	07:10	CROWDER Bob	MORGAN John	HABU	3.9	
06/01/82	967	10:47	SMITH Bernie	WHALEN Denny	FCF	4.2	
07/01/82	975	09:30	ROSENBERG Maury	McKIM E.D.	HABU	4.4	
08/01/82	976	12:05	SMITH Bernie	WHALEN Denny	HABU	4.4	
12/01/82	975	17:30	ROSENBERG Maury	McKIM E.D.	N-HABU	2.3	
14/01/82	967	07:20	CROWDER Bob	MORGAN John	HABU	4	
15/01/82	976	09:30	SMITH Bernie	WHALEN Denny	HABU	2.3	
16/01/82	967	10:30	CROWDER Bob	MORGAN John	HABU	3.8	
18/01/82	975	18:00	JUDSON Rich	KELLY Frank	N-HABU	2.3	
20/01/82	976	10:00	SMITH Bernie	WHALEN Denny	HABU	3.9	
25/01/82	975	08:15	CROWDER Bob	MORGAN John	HABU	2.4	
26/01/82	967	18:25	JUDSON Rich	KELLY Frank	N-HABU	2.3	
28/01/82	976	11:00	SMITH Bernie	WHALEN Denny	HABU	1.6	A
29/01/82	975	09:30	SMITH Bernie	WHALEN Denny	HABU	3.9	
01/02/82	967	10:02	JUDSON Rich	KELLY Frank	HABU	4	
02/02/82	975	18:45	THOMAS B.C.	REID Jay	N-HABU	2.3	
05/02/82	976	10:00	SMITH Bernie	WHALEN Denny	HABU	3.9	
08/02/82	975	20:00	JUDSON Rich	KELLY Frank	N-HABU	2.3	
10/02/82	967	07:45	THOMAS B.C.	REID Jay	HABU	2.3	
12/02/82	976	10:38	JUDSON Rich	KELLY Frank	HABU	3.7	
16/02/82	975	19:05	THOMAS B.C.	REID Jay	N-HABU	2.3	
19/02/82	975	10:18	JUDSON Rich	KELLY Frank	HABU	4.4	
20/02/82	967	10:10	BERTELSON Gil	STAMPF Frank	HABU	2.3	
22/02/82	976	08:30	THOMAS B.C.	REID Jay	HABU	4.2	
24/02/82	975	09:30	JUDSON Rich	KELLY Frank	HABU	4.3	
25/02/82	967	10:15	BERTELSON Gil	STAMPF Frank	HABU	2.4	
01/03/82	975	09:05	BERTELSON Gil	STAMPF Frank	HABU	1.7	A
02/03/82	976	10:01	CUNNINGHAM Nevin	QUIST Gene	HABU	4	
04/03/82	975	10:00	SHELTON Lee	KELLER Bill	HABU	4.1	
05/03/82	976	12:30	BERTELSON Gil	STAMPF Frank	HABU	4.3	
08/03/82	976	18:45	CUNNINGHAM Nevin	QUIST Gene	N-HABU	2.3	
10/03/82	976	15:00	SHELTON Lee	KELLER Bill	HABU	2.4	
12/03/82	976	11:45	BERTELSON Gil	STAMPF Frank	HABU	2.4	
16/03/82	976	14:40	CUNNINGHAM Nevin	QUIST Gene	HABU	4	
17/03/82	967	14:46	SHELTON Lee	KELLER Bill	FCF	3	A
18/03/82	976		BERTELSON Gil	STAMPF Frank	HABU		A
20/03/82	975		BERTELSON Gil	STAMPF Frank	HABU		A
20/03/82	975	13:15	BERTELSON Gil	STAMPF Frank	HABU	0.4	A
22/03/82	967	19:00	SHELTON Lee	KELLER Bill	HABU	2.3	
24/03/82	976	09:05	BERTELSON Gil	STAMPF Frank	HABU	4	
25/03/82	967	10:15	CUNNINGHAM Nevin	QUIST Gene	HABU	4.2	
29/03/82	976	06:50	CUNNINGHAM Nevin	QUIST Gene	HABU	2.3	
30/03/82	967	20:50	McCRARY Rick	LAWRENCE Dave	N-HABU	2.4	
01/04/82	976	09:15	YOUNG Rick	BETHART Ed	HABU	2.8	A
02/04/82	967	13:00	CUNNINGHAM Nevin	QUIST Gene	HABU	2.4	
05/04/82	967	09:20	McCRARY Rick	LAWRENCE Dave	HABU	4.1	
06/04/82	976	21:07	CUNNINGHAM Nevin	QUIST Gene	N-HABU	2.2	
09/04/82	976	12:40	McCRARY Rick	LAWRENCE Dave	HABU	2.2	A
12/04/82	967	19:05	YOUNG Rick	BETHART Ed	N-HABU	2.3	
14/04/82	976	12:30	McCRARY Rick	LAWRENCE Dave	HABU	4.1	
16/04/82	967	10:00	YOUNG Rick	BETHART Ed	HABU	4	
19/04/82	976	19:45	YOUNG Rick	BETHART Ed	N-HABU	2.3	
22/04/82	967	08:30	McCRARY Rick	LAWRENCE Dave	HABU	4.2	
27/04/82	967	11:00	McCRARY Rick	LAWRENCE Dave	HABU	4.3	
29/04/82	976	10:30	CROWDER Bob	MORGAN John	HABU	4.1	
03/05/82	976	11:15	CROWDER Bob	MORGAN John	HABU	4.2	
04/05/82	967	19:30	McCRARY Rick	LAWRENCE Dave	N-HABU	2.3	
05/05/82	975	?	CROWDER Bob	MORGAN John	FCF	4.2	
07/05/82	976	10:30	McCRARY Rick	LAWRENCE Dave	HABU	2.3	
08/05/82	967	10:00	CROWDER Bob	LAWRENCE Dave	FCF	2.7	
10/05/82	976	09:35	GLASSER Jerry	HORNBAKER Mac	HABU	4	
12/05/82	976	20:03	GLASSER Jerry	HORNBAKER Mac	N-HABU	2.4	
13/05/82	975	14:00	CROWDER Bob	HORNBAKER Mac	FCF	2.4	
17/05/82	976	20:05	CROWDER Bob	MORGAN John	N-HABU	2.2	
19/05/82	967	09:20	GLASSER Jerry	HORNBAKER Mac	HABU	4.3	
20/05/82	967	11:00	CROWDER Bob	MORGAN John	HABU	1.7	A
22/05/82	967		CROWDER Bob	MORGAN John	RTB FERRY		A
24/05/82	976	09:30	GLASSER Jerry	HORNBAKER Mac	HABU	3.6	
26/05/82	975	08:00	ROSENBERG Maury	McKIM E.D.	HABU	2.4	
27/05/82	976	10:15	GLASSER Jerry	HORNBAKER Mac	HABU	4.1	
28/05/82	975	12:10	ROSENBERG Maury	McKIM E.D.	HABU	1.6	A
29/05/82	975	14:00	ROSENBERG Maury	McKIM E.D.	HABU	2.2	
31/05/82	975	11:00	GLASSER Jerry	HORNBAKER Mac	HABU	2.3	
01/06/82	976	20:15	ROSENBERG Maury	McKIM E.D.	N-HABU	2.2	
03/06/82	975	15:00	GLASSER Jerry	HORNBAKER Mac	HABU	2.2	
06/06/82	980	04:25	SHELTON Lee	SZCZEPANIK Russ	FERRY IN	5.9	
07/06/82	976	6:00	CROWDER Bob	MORGAN John	FERRY OUT		
09/06/82	975	09:05	GLASSER Jerry	HORNBAKER Mac	HABU	3.8	
11/06/82	980	08:40	SHELTON Lee	SZCZEPANIK Russ	HABU	2.4	
15/06/82	980	08:22	GLASSER Jerry	HORNBAKER Mac	HABU	4	
16/06/82	967	09:50	SHELTON Lee	SZCZEPANIK Russ	RTB FERRY	1.9	
17/06/82	980	12:00	LULOFF Gil	COATS Bob	FCF	4.1	
17/06/82	975	16:45	SHELTON Lee	SZCZEPANIK Russ	FCF	2	A
18/06/82	975	12:51	LULOFF Gil	COATS Bob	HABU	2.3	A
19/06/82	975	10:00	LULOFF Gil	COATS Bob	HABU	2.4	
22/06/82	975	09:31	SHELTON Lee	SZCZEPANIK Russ	HABU	2.6	
23/06/82	980	21:00	SMITH Bernie	WHALEN Denny	N-HABU	2.2	
24/06/82	967		SHELTON Lee	SZCZEPANIK Russ	FCF		A
24/06/82	967	14:01	SHELTON Lee	SZCZEPANIK Russ	FCF	1.7	A
25/06/82	975		LULOFF Gil	COATS Bob	HABU		A
25/06/82	975	12:00	LULOFF Gil	COATS Bob	HABU	4	
26/06/82	980	11:00	SMITH Bernie	WHALEN Denny	HABU	2.3	
26/06/82	967	15:00	SHELTON Lee	SZCZEPANIK Russ	FCF	2.2	
28/06/82	980	19:30	SHELTON Lee	SZCZEPANIK Russ	N-HABU	2.3	
30/06/82	967	06:00	SMITH Bernie	WHALEN Denny	FERRY OUT		
02/07/82	980	11:00	LULOFF Gil	COATS Bob	HABU	2.3	
06/07/82	975	10:15	SHELTON Lee	SZCZEPANIK Russ	HABU	4.1	
07/07/82	980	19:45	SHELTON Lee	SZCZEPANIK Russ	N-HABU	2.4	
09/07/82	980	09:45	LULOFF Gil	COATS Bob	HABU	4.2	
13/07/82	975	10:35	SHELTON Lee	SZCZEPANIK Russ	HABU	2.6	
13/07/82	980	09:40	LULOFF Gil	COATS Bob	HABU	3.8	
15/07/82	975	10:00	JUDSON Rich	HORNBAKER Mac	HABU	4	
19/07/82	975	20:09	LULOFF Gil	COATS Bob	N-HABU	2.2	
21/07/82	980	13:15	JUDSON Rich	HORNBAKER Mac	HABU	4.1	
23/07/82	975	09:30	LULOFF Gil	COATS Bob	HABU	2.3	
27/07/82	980	20:45	LULOFF Gil	COATS Bob	N-HABU	2.3	
29/07/82	975	10:15	JUDSON Rich	HORNBAKER Mac	HABU	2.3	
02/08/82	980	10:06	JUDSON Rich	HORNBAKER Mac	HABU	4.2	
03/08/82	975	20:05	SMITH Bernie	WHALEN Denny	N-HABU	2.3	
05/08/82	980	10:22	JUDSON Rich	HORNBAKER Mac	HABU	4.1	
12/08/82	975	11:09	SMITH Bernie	WHALEN Denny	HABU	2.4	
13/08/82	980	11:00	JUSDON Rich	HORNBAKER Mac	HABU	4	
19/08/82	975	08:00	SMITH Bernie	WHALEN Denny	HABU	2.3	
21/08/82	975	10:00	JUDSON Rich	HORNBAKER Mac	HABU	1.8	A
23/08/82	975	12:00	SMITH Bernie	WHALEN Denny	HABU	3.7	
27/08/82	975	11:30	SMITH Bernie	WHALEN Denny	HABU	2.4	
28/08/82	975	13:00	SMITH Bernie	WHALEN Denny	HABU	2.3	
30/08/82	975		SMITH Bernie	WHALEN Denny	HABU		A
31/08/82	975	18:45	SMITH Bernie	WHALEN Denny	N-HABU	2.3	
01/09/82	975	12:00	BERTELSON Gil	STAMPF Frank	HABU	3.9	
02/09/82	980	19:15	SMITH Bernie	WHALEN Denny	N-HABU	2.3	
06/09/82	975	11:00	BERTELSON Gil	STAMPF Frank	HABU	3.8	
08/09/82	980	20:30	SMITH Bernie	WHALEN Denny	N-HABU	2.5	
10/09/82	980	09:45	BERTELSON Gil	STAMPF Frank	HABU	2.3	
14/09/82	980	08:30	BERTELSON Gil	STAMPF Frank	HABU	4	
15/09/82	980	11:30	DYER Les	GREENWOOD Dan	FCF	4.1	
17/09/82	980	10:00	DYER Les	GREENWOOD Dan	HABU	4.1	
20/09/82	980	10:30	BERTELSON Gil	STAMPF Frank	HABU	3.9	
22/09/82	980	10:45	DYER Les	GREENWOOD Dan	HABU	3.8	
23/09/82	975	07:57	BERTELSON Gil	STAMPF Frank	FCF	1.1	
24/09/82	980	14:02	DYER Les	GREENWOOD Dan	HABU	2.3	
27/09/82	975	20:07	BERTELSON Gil	STAMPF Frank	N-HABU	2.3	
29/09/82	980	11:30	DYER Les	GREENWOOD Dan	HABU	4	
02/10/82	975	10:30	BERTELSON Gil	STAMPF Frank	HABU	3.8	
04/10/82	975	12:25	BERTELSON Gil	STAMPF Frank	HABU	3.8	
08/10/82	980	08:00	CUNNINGHAM Nevin	QUIST Gene	HABU	4.6	
08/10/82	975	08:46	DYER Les	GREENWOOD Dan	HABU	5.5	
12/10/82	975	10:04	CUNNINGHAM Nevin	QUIST Gene	HABU	2.3	
13/10/82	980	19:30	DYER Les	GREENWOOD Dan	N-HABU	2.2	
15/10/82	975	09:30	CUNNINGHAM Nevin	QUIST Gene	HABU	0.5	A
15/10/82	975	14:00	CUNNINGHAM Nevin	QUIST Gene	HABU	2.3	
18/10/82	980	12:30	DYER Les	GREENWOOD Dan	HABU	4.1	
19/10/82	975	20:15	CUNNINGHAM Nevin	QUIST Gene	N-HABU	2.2	
22/10/82	980	11:00	DYER Les	GREENWOOD Dan	HABU	4	
26/10/82	980	10:45	DYER Les	GREENWOOD Dan	HABU	2.2	
28/10/82	975	10:00	CUNNINGHAM Nevin	QUIST Gene	HABU	2.6	
30/10/82	980	08:45	CUNNINGHAM Nevin	QUIST Gene	HABU	5.4	
02/11/82	980	21:30	McCRARY Rick	WHALEN Denny	N-HABU	2.3	
04/11/82	975	10:36	CUNNINGHAM Nevin	QUIST Gene	HABU	3.7	
06/11/82	980		McCRARY Rick	WHALEN Denny	HABU		A
06/11/82	980	11:04	McCRARY Rick	WHALEN Denny	HABU	2.2	
08/11/82	975	09:30	McCRARY Rick	WHALEN Denny	HABU	2.2	
12/11/82	960	04:15	ROSENBERG Maury	BETHART Ed	FERRY IN-H	6.2	
13/11/82	980	08:12	CUNNINGHAM Nevin	QUIST Gene	H-FERRY OUT		
15/11/82	975	14:58	McCRARY Rick	WHALEN Denny	HABU	2.2	
17/11/82	960	09:15	McCRARY Rick	WHALEN Denny	HABU	2.3	
18/11/82	960	09:45	ROSENBERG Maury	BETHART Ed	HABU	2.3	
24/11/82	975	10:30	ROSENBERG Maury	BETHART Ed	HABU	3.8	

Date	Instal. No.	T.O. Time	Pilot Name	RSO Name	Mission	Duration	Remarks
26/11/82	960	11:00	BURK Bill	HENICHEK Tom	FCF	2.5	
27/11/82	975	09:45	BURK Bill	HENICHEK Tom	HABU	2.8	A
30/11/82	960	12:15	ROSENBERG Maury	BETHART Ed	HABU	2.3	
01/12/82	960	10:00	BURK Bill	HENICHEK Tom	HABU	3.9	
03/12/82	960	10:00	ROSENBERG Maury	BETHART Ed	HABU	2.3	
06/12/82	975	10:03	BURK Bill	HENICHEK Tom	HABU	2.5	
08/12/82	960	10:00	BURK Bill	HENICHEK Tom	HABU	3.6	
09/12/82	975	09:05	BURK Bill	HENICHEK Tom	HABU	2.3	
14/12/82	975	13:00	ROSENBERG Maury	BETHART Ed	HABU	2.3	
16/12/82	960	10:30	BURK Bill	HENICHEK Tom	HABU	3.2	A
18/12/82	975	11:00	ROSENBERG Maury	BETHART Ed	HABU	3.6	
20/12/82	960	18:00	BURK Bill	HENICHEK Tom	N-HABU	2.3	
22/12/82	975	14:09	ROSENBERG Maury	BETHART Ed	HABU	2.3	
27/12/82	960	18:30	ROSENBERG Maury	BETHART Ed	N-HABU	2.3	
29/12/82	975	10:00	BURK Bill	HENICHEK Tom	HABU	2.3	
05/01/83	960		SHELTON Lee	MORGAN John	HABU		A
06/01/83	975	19:00	SHELTON Lee	MORGAN John	N-HABU	2.5	
08/01/83	960	10:43	GLASSER Jerry	LAWRENCE Dave	HABU	2.3	
10/01/83	975	10:30	SHELTON Lee	MORGAN John	HABU	3.7	
12/01/83	960	11:30	GLASSER Jerry	LAWRENCE Dave	HABU	2.4	
14/01/83	975	08:00	SHELTON Lee	MORGAN John	HABU	2.4	
17/01/83	960	11:00	GLASSER Jerry	LAWRENCE Dave	HABU	2.8	A
18/01/83	975	14:00	SHELTON Lee	MORGAN John	HABU	2.4	
20/01/83	975	09:30	GLASSER Jerry	MORGAN John	HABU	2.3	
21/01/83	960	10:30	SHELTON Lee	MORGAN John	HABU	2.4	A
25/01/83	960	09:05	GLASSER Jerry	LAWRENCE Dave	HABU	2.8	
26/01/83	975	18:45	GLASSER Jerry	LAWRENCE Dave	N-HABU	1.7	A
27/01/83	960	18:45	GLASSER Jerry	LAWRENCE Dave	N-HABU	2.3	
28/01/83	960	13:00	LULOFF Gil	COATS Bob	HABU	2.4	
01/02/83	975	09:45	GLASSER Jerry	LAWRENCE Dave	HABU	4.1	
02/02/83	975	21:00	LULOFF Gil	COATS Bob	N-HABU	2.3	
04/02/83	960	12:13	GLASSER Jerry	LAWRENCE Dave	HABU	2.3	
07/02/83	975	11:30	LULOFF Gil	COATS Bob	HABU	2.3	
12/02/83	960		LULOFF Gil	COATS Bob	HABU		A
13/02/83	975	11:00	GLASSER Jerry	LAWRENCE Dave	HABU	2.3	
14/02/83	975	10:00	LULOFF Gil	COATS Bob	HABU	2.4	
15/02/83	964	04:00	JUDSON Rich	HORNBAKER Mac	FERRY IN-H	6.2	A
17/02/83	975	08:00	GLASSER Jerry	LAWRENCE Dave	H-FERRY OUT		
18/02/83	960	10:00	JUDSON Rich	HORNBAKER Mac	HABU	4	
22/02/83	960	18:45	LULOFF Gil	COATS Bob	N-HABU	2.4	
24/02/83	964	09:30	JUDSON Rich	HORNBAKER Mac	HABU	2.3	
25/02/83	960	10:00	LULOFF Gil	COATS Bob	HABU	4.1	
01/03/83	964	20:30	LULOFF Gil	COATS Bob	N-HABU	2.3	
03/03/83	960	08:30	JUDSON Rich	HORNBAKER Mac	HABU	2.2	
07/03/83	960	09:30	JUDSON Rich	HORNBAKER Mac	HABU	3.5	
09/03/83	960	09:30	SMITH Bernie	McKIM E.D.	HABU	2.3	
11/03/83	964	11:30	JUDSON Rich	HORNBAKER Mac	HABU	3.8	
15/03/83	964	06:00	SMITH Bernie	McKIM E.D.	HABU	2.3	
16/03/83	960	13:00	JUDSON Rich	HORNBAKER Mac	HABU	2.5	
18/03/83	964	10:00	SMITH Bernie	McKIM E.D.	HABU	4	
21/03/83	960	20:00	JUDSON Rich	HORNBAKER Mac	N-HABU	2.3	
23/03/83	960	08:20	JUDSON Rich	HORNBAKER Mac	HABU	4.2	
24/03/83	960	09:05	SMITH Bernie	McKIM E.D.	HABU	2.8	
28/03/83	964	19:30	SMITH Bernie	McKIM E.D.	N-HABU	2.3	
30/03/83	960	10:30	JIGGENS Jim	McCUE Joe	FCF	4.2	
01/04/83	960	09:15	JIGGENS Jim	McCUE Joe	HABU	2.4	
04/04/83	964	18:45	SMITH Bernie	McKIM E.D.	N-HABU	2.3	
06/04/83	960	10:15	JIGGENS Jim	McCUE Joe	HABU	4.2	
08/04/83	964	09:30	SMITH Bernie	McKIM E.D.	HABU	2.7	
11/04/83	960	10:00	JIGGENS Jim	McCUE Joe	HABU	2.3	
12/04/83	960	13:15	SMITH Bernie	McKIM E.D.	HABU	4	
14/04/83	960	09:05	JIGGENS Jim	McCUE Joe	HABU	2.4	
18/04/83	964	19:15	PETERS Dave	KELLER Bill	N-HABU	1.3	A
19/04/83	964	19:15	PETERS Dave	KELLER Bill	N-HABU	2.5	
21/04/83	964	10:30	JIGGENS Jim	McCUE Joe	HABU	3	A
22/04/83	960	12:14	PETERS Dave	KELLER Bill	HABU	2.2	
26/04/83	964	21:00	JIGGENS Jim	McCUE Joe	N-HABU	2.3	
28/04/83	964	11:30	PETERS Dave	KELLER Bill	HABU	4	
02/05/83	964	10:17	PETERS Dave	KELLER Bill	HABU	4.1	
03/05/83	960	19:00	JIGGENS Jim	McCUE Joe	N-HABU	1.9	A
05/05/83	964	09:05	PETERS Dave	KELLER Bill	HABU	2.4	
09/05/83	960	08:15	PETERS Dave	KELLER Bill	HABU	2.2	
11/05/83	964	08:30	BEHLER Bob	TABOR Ron	FCF	4.1	
12/05/83	964	13:00	BEHLER Bob	TABOR Ron	HABU	4.1	
13/05/83	960	13:30	PETERS Dave	KELLER Bill	HABU	2.5	
16/05/83	964	11:30	BEHLER Bob	TABOR Ron	HABU	3.8	
18/05/83	960	20:58	PETERS Dave	KELLER Bill	N-HABU	2.3	
20/05/83	964	10:08	BEHLER Bob	TABOR Ron	HABU	3.9	
24/05/83	964	19:35	PETERS Dave	KELLER Bill	N-HABU	2.3	
25/05/83	960	12:30	BEHLER Bob	TABOR Ron	HABU	2.3	
27/05/83	964	10:00	BEHLER Bob	TABOR Ron	HABU	1.8	A
01/06/83	964	09:15	McCRARY Rick	LAWRENCE Dave	HABU	4.1	
02/06/83	960	20:55	BEHLER Bob	TABOR Ron	N-HABU	2.2	
06/06/83	964	08:30	McCRARY Rick	LAWRENCE Dave	HABU	3.8	
07/06/83	960	14:00	BEHLER Bob	TABOR Ron	HABU	2.2	
10/06/83	964	11:00	McCRARY Rick	LAWRENCE Dave	HABU	3.9	
13/06/83	960	12:30	BEHLER Bob	TABOR Ron	HABU	2.2	
14/06/83	964	19:30	BEHLER Bob	TABOR Ron	N-HABU	2.3	
16/06/83	964	09:05	McCRARY Rick	LAWRENCE Dave	HABU	2.4	
20/06/83	964	20:00	McCRARY Rick	LAWRENCE Dave	N-HABU	2.2	
22/06/83	960	10:00	BURK Bill	HENICHEK Tom	HABU	2.2	
27/06/83	964	05:00	BURK Bill	HENICHEK Tom	HABU	4.9	
27/06/83	960	05:30	McCRARY Rick	LAWRENCE Dave	HABU	3.9	
01/07/83	960	09:15	McCRARY Rick	LAWRENCE Dave	HABU	4.1	
05/07/83	964	19:50	BURK Bill	HENICHEK Tom	N-HABU	2.5	
07/07/83	964	09:30	McCRARY Rick	LAWRENCE Dave	HABU	2.3	
11/07/83	964	12:00	BURK Bill	HENICHEK Tom	HABU	3.9	
14/07/83	964	08:30	CUNNINGHAM Nevin	QUIST Gene	HABU	2.3	

Date	Instal. No.	T.O. Time	Pilot Name	RSO Name	Mission	Duration	Remarks
15/07/83	964	12:00	BURK Bill	HENICHEK Tom	HABU	3.7	
18/07/83	964	11:30	CUNNINGHAM Nevin	QUIST Gene	HABU	2.3	
20/07/83	964	10:04	BURK Bill	HENICHEK Tom	HABU	4.2	
21/07/83	964	20:00	CUNNINGHAM Nevin	QUIST Gene	N-HABU	2.3	
22/07/83	960	14:00	BURK Bill	HENICHEK Tom	FCF	4.1	
25/07/83	960	10:30	CUNNINGHAM Nevin	QUIST Gene	HABU	3.9	
26/07/83	960	19:45	BURK Bill	HENICHEK Tom	N-HABU	1.4	A
27/07/83	960	24:00	BURK Bill	HENICHEK Tom	N-HABU	2.2	
28/07/83	960	09:45	CUNNINGHAM Nevin	QUIST Gene	HABU	2.2	
01/08/83	964	12:15	CUNNINGHAM Nevin	QUIST Gene	HABU	4.1	
03/08/83	960	11:48	BOUDREAUX Stormy	NEWGREEN Terry	FCF	4.2	
04/08/83	960	19:15	CUNNINGHAM Nevin	QUIST Gene	N-HABU	2.3	
06/08/83	960	12:00	BOUDREAUX Stormy	NEWGREEN Terry	HABU	3.7	
10/08/83	964	08:30	CUNNINGHAM Nevin	QUIST Gene	HABU	2.2	
16/08/83	960	19:30	CUNNINGHAM Nevin	QUIST Gene	N-HABU	2.4	
18/08/83	964	09:15	BOUDREAUX Stormy	NEWGREEN Terry	HABU	2.3	
20/08/83	964	12:13	BOUDREAUX Stormy	NEWGREEN Terry	HABU	2.3	
23/08/83	964	10:30	BOUDREAUX Stormy	NEWGREEN Terry	HABU	2.3	
24/08/83	960	20:00	DYER Les	WHALEN Denny	N-HABU	2.4	
27/08/83	960	13:15	BOUDREAUX Stormy	NEWGREEN Terry	HABU	4.3	
29/08/83	960	09:45	DYER Les	WHALEN Denny	HABU	3.9	
30/08/83	964	10:15	BOUDREAUX Stormy	NEWGREEN Terry	HABU	2.4	
01/09/83	964	09:05	DYER Les	WHALEN Denny	HABU	2.2	A,30
02/09/83	960	12:00	BOUDREAUX Stormy	NEWGREEN Terry	HABU	2.3	
06/09/83	960	11:00	DYER Les	WHALEN Denny	HABU	0.9	
06/09/83	960	14:15	DYER Les	WHALEN Denny	HABU	3.9	
08/09/83	960	09:30	DYER Les	WHALEN Denny	HABU	2.2	
12/09/83	960	18:45	ROSENBERG Maury	McKIM E.D.	HABU	1.2	A
14/09/83	960	08:30	ROSENBERG Maury	McKIM E.D.	HABU	4	
16/09/83	960	10:15	DYER Les	GREENWOOD Dan	HABU	1.7	A
19/09/83	960	13:00	DYER Les	GREENWOOD Dan	HABU	3.8	
20/09/83	960	19:15	ROSENBERG Maury	McKIM E.D.	N-HABU	2.2	
22/09/83	960	13:00	DYER Les	GREENWOOD Dan	HABU	4.4	
23/09/83	964	13:00	ROSENBERG Maury	McKIM E.D.	FCF	2.3	
24/09/83	960	09:45	DYER Les	GREENWOOD Dan	HABU	4.1	
29/09/83	964	10:00	ROSENBERG Maury	McKIM E.D.	HABU	2.3	
01/10/83	964	10:04	ROSENBERG Maury	McKIM E.D.	HABU	2.2	
03/10/83	964	18:45	LULOFF Gil	COATS Bob	N-HABU	2.3	
05/10/83	964	12:00	ROSENBERG Maury	McKIM E.D.	HABU	4.1	
06/10/83	960		LULOFF Gil	COATS Bob	HABU		A
06/10/83	960	14:16	LULOFF Gil	COATS Bob	HABU	3.6	
11/10/83	964	18:30	ROSENBERG Maury	McKIM E.D.	N-HABU	2.3	
14/10/83	960	09:45	LULOFF Gil	COATS Bob	HABU	2.4	
17/10/83	960	10:04	ROSENBERG Maury	McKIM E.D.	HABU	4.1	
18/10/83	960	09:30	LULOFF Gil	COATS Bob	HABU	2.4	
20/10/83	964	09:05	LULOFF Gil	COATS Bob	HABU	2.3	
24/10/83	960	10:30	LULOFF Gil	COATS Bob	HABU	1.3	A
25/10/83	964	10:30	LULOFF Gil	COATS Bob	HABU	3.7	
26/10/83	960	20:00	THOMAS B.C.	MORGAN John	N-HABU	2.3	
28/10/83	960	11:03	LULOFF Gil	COATS Bob	HABU	3.8	
01/11/83	964	18:00	THOMAS B.C.	MORGAN John	N-HABU	2.5	
03/11/83	960	11:20	LULOFF Gil	COATS Bob	HABU	4.1	
04/11/83	960	09:45	THOMAS B.C.	MORGAN John	HABU	2.4	
07/11/83	964	10:30	LULOFF Gil	COATS Bob	HABU	3.9	
08/11/83	960	11:00	THOMAS B.C.	MORGAN John	HABU	4.1	
10/11/83	964	09:05	THOMAS B.C.	MORGAN John	HABU	2.4	
14/11/83	960	18:15	LULOFF Gil	COATS Bob	N-HABU	2.4	
16/11/83	964	09:30	THOMAS B.C.	MORGAN John	HABU	2.4	
19/11/83	976	05:00	GLASSER Jerry	ROSS Ted	FERRY IN-H	6.6	
20/11/83	960	08:00	LULOFF Gil	COATS Bob	FERRY OUT		
23/11/83	964	07:15	THOMAS B.C.	MORGAN John	HABU	4	
28/11/83	964	21:08	GLASSER Jerry	ROSS Ted	N-HABU	2.4	
01/12/83	976		GLASSER Jerry	ROSS Ted	HABU		A
01/12/83	976	11:20	GLASSER Jerry	ROSS Ted	HABU	2.4	
05/12/83	964	18:00	GLASSER Jerry	ROSS Ted	N-HABU	2.3	
07/12/83	976	14:00	BEHLER Bob	TABOR Ron	HABU	2.3	
09/12/83	964	09:45	GLASSER Jerry	ROSS Ted	HABU	3.8	
12/12/83	964	12:00	BEHLER Bob	TABOR Ron	HABU	3.8	
14/12/83	976	09:05	GLASSER Jerry	ROSS Ted	HABU	3.9	
15/12/83	976		BEHLER Bob	TABOR Ron	HABU		A
15/12/83	964	21:46	BEHLER Bob	TABOR Ron	N-HABU	2.2	
19/12/83	964	17:45	GLASSER Jerry	ROSS Ted	N-HABU	2.4	
20/12/83	976	13:00	BEHLER Bob	TABOR Ron	HABU	2.3	
22/12/83	976	09:15	BEHLER Bob	TABOR Ron	HABU	2.3	
27/12/83	964	10:00	SMITH Bernie	WHALEN Denny	HABU	4	
29/12/83	976	12:00	BEHLER Bob	TABOR Ron	HABU	3	A
03/01/84	964	11:15	SMITH Bernie	WHALEN Denny	HABU	1.5	A
03/01/84	964	16:15	SMITH Bernie	WHALEN Denny	HABU	2.3	
05/01/84	964	09:45	BEHLER Bob	TABOR Ron	HABU	2.3	
06/01/84	964	10:00	SMITH Bernie	WHALEN Dennis	HABU	3.8	
09/01/84	964	18:00	BEHLER Bob	TABOR Ron	N-HABU	2.3	
11/01/84	976	09:30	SMITH Bernie	WHALEN Dennis	HABU	2.3	
12/01/84	976	09:30	SMITH Bernie	WHALEN Dennis	HABU	2.3	
17/01/84	964	11:00	MATTHEWS Joe	OSTERHELD Curt	FCF	2.7	
17/01/84	976	18:30	SMITH Bernie	WHALEN Dennis	N-HABU	2.2	
19/01/84	964	11:00	MATTHEWS Joe	OSTERHELD Curt	HABU	0.8	A
20/01/84	964	10:00	MATTHEWS Joe	OSTERHELD Curt	HABU	4.3	
23/01/84	976	13:00	MATTHEWS Joe	OSTERHELD Curt	HABU	1.5	A
25/01/84	964	18:15	SMITH Bernie	WHALEN DENNIS	N-HABU	2.2	
25/01/84	976	12:14	MATTHEWS Joe	OSTERHELD Curt	RTB FERRY	1.5	
27/01/84	964	10:00	MATTHEWS Joe	OSTERHELD Curt	HABU	3.9	
30/01/84	976	10:15	SMITH Bernie	WHALEN Dennis	HABU	2.3	
01/02/84	964	10:00	MATTHEWS Joe	OSTERHALD Curt	HABU	2.3	A
02/02/84	976	10:55	MATTHEWS Joe	OSTERHALD Curt	HABU	2.3	
06/02/84	976	18:38	MATTHEWS Joe	OSTERHALD Curt	HABU	2.3	
08/02/84	976	10:30	PETERS Dave	BETHART Ed	HABU	2	A
10/02/84	964	12:02	MATTHEWS Joe	OSTERHELD Curt	HABU	2.5	
14/02/84	976	12:15	PETERS Dave	BETHART Ed	HABU	2.3	

Date	Instal. No.	T.O. Time	Pilot Name	RSO Name	Mission	Duration	Remarks
15/02/84	964	18:45	MATTHEWS Joe	OSTERHELD Curt	N-HABU	2.3	
17/02/84	976	10:02	PETERS Dave	BETHART Ed	HABU	3.7	
21/02/84	964	18:35	MATTHEWS Joe	OSTERHELD Curt	N-HABU	2.3	
23/02/84	976	09:30	PETERS Dave	BETHART Ed	HABU	2.3	
27/02/84	964	10:00	PETERS Dave	BETHART Ed	HABU	3.8	
28/02/84	964	13:00	JIGGENS Jim	McCUE Joe	HABU	2.9	A
03/03/84	976	10:00	PETERS Dave	BETHART Ed	HABU	3.8	
05/03/84	964	18:45	JIGGENS Jim	McCUE JOE	N-HABU	2.3	
07/03/84	964	11:00	PETERS Dave	BETHART Ed	HABU	2.3	A
09/03/84	964	10:00	JIGGENS Jim	McCUE Joe	HABU	2.2	
12/03/84	964	19:00	PETERS Dave	BETHART Ed	N-HABU	2.4	
13/03/84	976	14:00	JIGGENS Jim	McCUE Joe	HABU	2.4	
15/03/84	976	09:30	JIGGENS Jim	McCUE Joe	HABU	2.3	
20/03/84	964	19:15	BOUDREAUX Stormy	NEWGREEN Terry	N-HABU	2.3	
23/03/84	964	11:00	JIGGENS Jim	McCUE Joe	HABU	2.3	
27/03/84	964	09:02	BOUDREAUX Stormy	NEWGREEN Terry	HABU	2.3	31
27/03/84	973	04:45	DYER Les	GREENWOOD Dan	FERRY IN-H	6.7	31
29/03/84	964		JIGGENS Jim	McCUE Joe	HABU		A
30/03/84	964	08:10	JIGGENS Jim	McCUE Joe	H-FERRY OUT		
02/04/84	976	09:45	BOUDREAUX Stormy	NEWGREEN Terry	HABU	2.3	
03/04/84	976	14:00	DYER Les	GREENWOOD Dan	HABU	2.1	
05/04/84	973	09:15	BOUDREAUX Stormy	NEWGREEN Terry	HABU	2.4	
09/04/84	976	10:15	DYER Les	GREENWOOD Dan	HABU	2.2	
11/04/84	973	19:05	BOUDREAUX Stormy	NEWGREEN Terry	N-HABU	2.3	
13/04/84	973	09:05	DYER Les	GREENWOOD Dan	HABU	2.2	
16/04/84	973	19:00	BOUDREAUX Stormy	NEWGREEN Terry	N-HABU	2.3	
18/04/84	973	14:30	DYER Les	GREENWOOD Dan	HABU	2.2	
20/04/84	976	09:30	BOUDREAUX Stormy	NEWGREEN Terry	HABU	2.2	
23/04/84	973	13:00	DYER Les	GREENWOOD Dan	HABU	2.3	
24/04/84	976	19:15	BOUDREAUX Stormy	NEWGREEN Terry	N-HABU	2.3	
29/04/84	973	10:00	DYER Les	GREENWOOD Dan	HABU	2.3	
01/05/84	976	16:00	CUNNINGHAM Nevin	QUIST Gene	HABU	1.4	A
02/05/84	976	12:00	CUNNINGHAM Nevin	QUIST Gene	HABU	2.3	
03/05/84	976	09:30	DYER Les	GREENWOOD Dan	HABU	2.2	
08/05/84	976		CUNNINGHAM Nevin	QUIST Gene	HABU		A
08/05/84	976	10:35	CUNNINGHAM Nevin	QUIST Gene	HABU	3.7	
09/05/84	973	21:00	DYER Les	GREENWOOD Dan	N-HABU	2.2	
11/05/84	976	06:00	CUNNINGHAM Nenin	QUIST Gene	HABU	2.3	
14/05/84	976	21:21	DYER Les	GREENWOOD Dan	N-HABU	2.1	
16/05/84	973	09:47	DYER Les	GREENWOOD Dan	HABU	2.3	
17/05/84	976	09:30	CUNNINGHAM Nevin	QUIST Gene	HABU	2.4	
21/05/84	976	17:30	CUNNINGHAM Nevin	QUIST Gene	N-HABU	2.1	A
23/05/84	973	22:00	BURK Bill	HENICHEK Tom	N-HABU	2.3	
25/05/84	976		CUNNINGHAM Nevin	QUIST Gene	HABU		A
25/05/84	976	11:15	CUNNINGHAM Nevin	QUIST Gene	HABU	2.4	
29/05/84	976	18:00	BURK Bill	HENICHEK Tom	HABU	2.2	
30/05/84	976	12:30	CUNNINGHAM Nevin	QUIST Gene	HABU	2.2	
01/06/84	976	13:00	BURK Bill	HENICHEK Tom	HABU	2.4	
04/06/84	976	20:00	CUNNINGHAM Nevin	QUIST Gene	N-HABU	2.5	
06/06/84	973	07:30	BURK Bill	HENICHEK Tom	HABU	2.4	
07/06/84	976	09:15	BURK Bill	HENICHEK Tom	HABU	2.2	
11/06/84	973	16:30	PETERS Dave	BETHART Ed	HABU	2.2	
13/06/84	973	20:10	BURK Bill	HENICHEK Tom	N-HABU	2.2	
15/06/84	973	08:15	PETERS Dave	BETHART Ed	HABU	1.6	A
18/06/84	973	16:50	BURK Bill	HENICHEK Tom	HABU	2.1	
21/06/84	976	14:22	PETERS Dave	BETHART Ed	FCF	0.9	A
22/06/84	973	19:30	BURK Bill	HENICHEK Tom	N-HABU	2.3	
25/06/84	976	11:25	BURK Bill	HENICHEK Tom	FCF	2.6	
27/06/84	976	07:50	PETERS Dave	BETHART Ed	HABU	3.8	
28/06/84	973	09:30	BURK Bill	HENICHEK Tom	HABU	1.7	A
29/06/84	973	11:00	PETERS Dave	BETHART Ed	HABU	2.3	
02/07/84	973	19:45	PETERS Dave	BETHART Ed	N-HABU	2.2	
05/07/84	973	13:15	MADISON Jack	ORCUTT Bill	FCF	2.5	
06/07/84	973	09:15	MADISON Jack	ORCUTT Bill	HABU	2.4	
09/07/84	973		PETERS Dave	BETHART Ed	N-HABU		A
10/07/84	976	19:30	PETERS Dave	BETHART Ed	N-HABU	2.3	
12/07/84	976	09:58	MADISON Jack	ORCUTT Bill	HABU	2.2	
13/07/84	976	09:45	PETERS Dave	BETHART Ed	HABU	2.4	
16/07/84	976	16:41	MADISON Jack	ORCUTT Bill	HABU	2.2	
18/07/84	976	14:00	PETERS Dave	BETHART Ed	HABU	2.2	
20/07/84	976	12:32	MADISON Jack	ORCUTT Bill	HABU	3.8	
23/07/84	976		MADISON Jack	ORCUTT Bill	HABU		A
24/07/84	976	20:00	LULOFF Gil	COATS Bob	N-HABU	2.3	
26/07/84	976	09:30	MADISON Jack	ORCUTT Bill	HABU	2.4	
27/07/84	976	10:00	LULOFF Gil	COATS Bob	HABU	2.3	
31/07/84	973	11:00	MADISON Jack	ORCUTT Bill	HABU	2.3	
01/08/84	976	19:45	MADISON Jack	ORCUTT Bill	N-HABU	2.2	
03/08/84	976	13:00	LULOFF Gil	COATS Bob	HABU	0.6	A
06/08/84	973	13:00	LULOFF Gil	COATS Bob	HABU	2.3	
07/08/84	973	10:15	MADISON Jack	ORCUTT Bill	HABU	2.3	
09/08/84	973	09:15	LULOFF Gil	COATS Bob	HABU	1.5	A
10/08/84	976	10:30	LULOFF Gil	COATS Bob	HABU	2.2	
13/08/84	976	19:15	GLASSER Jerry	TABOR Ron	N-HABU	2.4	
15/08/84	973	11:00	LULOFF Gil	COATS Bob	HABU	2.4	
17/08/84	973	08:00	GLASSER Jerry	TABOR Ron	HABU	2.3	
22/08/84	976	19:10	LULOFF Gil	COATS Bob	N-HABU	2.2	
24/08/84	976	09:45	GLASSER Jerry	TABOR Ron	HABU	2.4	
27/08/84	976		LULOFF Gil	COATS Bob	HABU		
28/08/84	973	10:00	LULOFF Gil	COATS Bob	HABU	2.2	
29/08/84	973	09:45	GLASSER Jerry	TABOR Ron	HABU	2.2	
30/08/84	976	09:30	GLASSER Jerry	TABOR Ron	HABU	2.3	
04/09/84	976	19:00	GLASSER Jerry	TABOR Ron	N-HABU	2.3	
05/09/84	973	13:00	YEILDING Edward	LEE Steve	FCF	2.5	
07/09/84	976	10:05	GLASSER Jerry	TABOR Ron	HABU	2.4	
08/09/84	973	10:00	YEILDING Edward	LEE Steve	HABU	2.2	
10/09/84	973	18:55	GLASSER Jerry	TABOR Ron	N-HABU	2.4	
12/09/84	973	13:00	YEILDING Edward	LEE Steve	HABU	2.2	
14/09/84	973	10:00	YEILDING Edward	LEE Steve	HABU	3.6	

Date	Instal. No.	T.O. Time	Pilot Name	RSO Name	Mission	Duration	Remarks
17/09/84	976	11:30	GLASSER Jerry	TABOR Ron	HABU	2.6	
19/09/84	976	18:35	GLASSER Jerry	TABOR Ron	N-HABU	2.6	
21/09/84	973	10:00	YEILDING Edward	LEE Steve	HABU	1.4	A
23/09/84	973	11:26	YEILDING Edward	LEE Steve	RTB FERRY	1.5	
24/09/84	976	13:30	SMITH Bernie	WHALEN Denny	HABU	2.3	
26/09/84	976	10:00	YEILDING Edward	LEE Steve	HABU	3.8	
27/09/84	973	15:15	SMITH Bernie	WHALEN Denny	HABU	2.2	
01/10/84	976	14:00	YEILDING Edward	LEE Steve	HABU	2.2	
03/10/84	973	10:00	SMITH Bernie	WHALEN Denny	HABU	2.3	
05/10/84	973	10:30	YEILDING Edward	LEE Steve	HABU	3.7	
09/10/84	976	18:15	YEILDING Edward	LEE Steve	N-HABU	2.2	
11/10/84	973	09:15	SMITH Bernie	WHALEN Denny	HABU	2.3	
15/10/84	973	21:00	JIGGENS Jim	McCUE Joe	N-HABU	2.4	
17/10/84	976	10:30	SMITH Bernie	WHALEN Denny	HABU	3.7	
19/10/84	976	10:00	JIGGENS Jim	McCUE Joe	HABU	3.8	
23/10/84	973	12:00	SMITH Bernie	WHALEN Denny	HABU	2.2	
24/10/84	973	18:31	JIGGENS Jim	McCUE Joe	N-HABU	2.3	
26/10/84	973		SMITH Bernie	WHALEN Denny	HABU		
30/10/84	976	12:42	SMITH Bernie	WHALEN Denny	HABU	2.3	
31/10/84	976	11:30	JIGGENS Jim	McCUE Joe	HABU	3.8	
01/11/84	976	09:30	CUNNINGHAM Nevin	MORGAN John	HABU	2.3	
05/11/84	976	18:30	BOUDREAUX Stormy	ROSS Ted	N-HABU	2.5	
07/11/84	976	11:30	CUNNINGHAM Nevin	MORGAN John	HABU	2.4	
08/11/84	973	10:00	BOUDREAUX Stormy	ROSS Ted	FCF	2.4	
09/11/84	976	11:00	CUNNINGHAM Nevin	MORGAN John	HABU	2.3	
13/11/84	976	17:45	BOUDREAUX Stormy	ROSS Ted	N-HABU	2.3	
14/11/84	973	16:00	CUNNINGHAM Nevin	MORGAN John	N-HABU	0.4	A
14/11/84	973	18:25	CUNNINGHAM Nevin	MORGAN John	N-HABU	2.4	
16/11/84	976		BOUDREAUX Stormy	ROSS Ted	HABU		
17/11/84	976	11:00	BOUDREAUX Stormy	ROSS Ted	HABU	3.7	
19/11/84	973	18:15	CUNNINGHAM Nevin	MORGAN John	N-HABU	2.3	
21/11/84	976	09:15	BOUDREAUX Stormy	ROSS Ted	HABU	2.3	
23/11/84	973	09:45	BOUDREAUX Stormy	ROSS Ted	HABU	2.3	
27/11/84	973	15:00	BEHLER Bob	TABOR Ron	HABU	2.3	
29/11/84	976	10:30	BOUDREAUX Stormy	ROSS Ted	HABU	4.1	
03/12/84	973	11:15	BEHLER Bob	TABOR Ron	HABU	0.6	A
04/12/84	973	19:30	BEHLER Bob	TABOR Ron	N-HABU	2.3	
06/12/84	976	10:15	BOUDREAUX Stormy	ROSS Ted	HABU	3.9	
07/12/84	973	10:00	BEHLER Bob	TABOR Ron	HABU	2.3	
11/12/84	964	06:04	BURK Bill	HENICHEK Tom	FERRY IN-H	6.6	
13/12/84	976	08:00	BOUDREAUX Stormy	ROSS Ted	H-FERRY OUT		
15/12/84	973	09:15	BEHLER Bob	TABOR Ron	HABU	2.3	
17/12/84	973	09:30	BEHLER Bob	TABOR Ron	HABU	5.6	
19/12/84	964	17:45	BURK Bill	HENICHEK Tom	N-HABU	2.2	
21/12/84	973	07:00	BURK Bill	HENICHEK Tom	HABU	6.2	A
26/12/84	964	18:15	BEHLER Bob	TABOR Ron	N-HABU	2.3	
27/12/84	973	11:00	BURK Bill	HENICHEK Tom	HABU	2.5	
28/12/84	964	09:05	BEHLER Bob	TABOR Ron	HABU	2.4	
30/12/84	973	10:00	BURK Bill	HENICHEK Tom	HABU	3.6	
02/01/85	964	10:00	BEHLER Bob	TABOR Ron	HABU	2.4	
03/01/85	973	09:15	BURK Bill	HENICHEK Tom	HABU	1.9	
07/01/85	964	10:30	MATTHEWS Joe	OSTERHELD Curt	HABU	3.8	
09/01/85	973	23:30	BURK Bill	HENICHEK Tom	N-HABU	2.2	
11/01/85	964	10:45	MATTHEWS Joe	OSTERHELD Curt	HABU	2.3	
14/01/85	964	11:00	BURK Bill	HENICHEK Tom	HABU	3.7	
17/01/85	964	07:30	MATTHEWS Joe	OSTERHELD Curt	HABU	4	
21/01/85	964	09:30	BURK Bill	HENICHEK Tom	HABU	3.8	
22/01/85	973	18:58	BURK Bill	HENICHEK Tom	HABU	0.5	A
23/01/85	973	18:30	BURK Bill	HENICHEK Tom	HABU	0.5	A
24/01/85	964	18:30	MATTHEWS Joe	OSTERHELD Curt	N-HABU	2.2	
26/01/85	964	08:00	MATTHEWS Joe	OSTERHELD Curt	HABU	2.3	
28/01/85	964	21:00	MATTHEWS Joe	OSTERHELD Curt	N-HABU	2.3	
29/01/85	973	14:00	SHUL Brian	WATSON Walter	FCF	2.8	
31/01/85	964	14:00	SHUL Brian	WATSON Walter	HABU	2.4	
01/02/85	973	11:00	MATTHEWS Joe	OSTERHALD Curt	HABU	2.3	
05/02/85	964	13:51	SHUL Brian	WATSON Walter	HABU	2.3	
06/02/85	973	19:50	MATTHEWS Joe	OSTERHELD Curt	N-HABU	2.3	
08/02/85	964	09:30	SHUL Brian	WATSON Walter	HABU	2.6	
12/02/85	973	12:00	MATTHEWS Joe	OSTERHELD Curt	HABU	2.3	
14/02/85	964	11:30	SHUL Brian	WATSON Walter	HABU	4.2	
19/02/85	964	21:04	DYER Les	TABOR Ron	N-HABU	2.3	
22/02/85	973	11:00	SHUL Brian	WATSON Walter	HABU	2.5	A
25/02/85	964	10:15	DYER Les	TABOR Ron	HABU	2.3	
27/02/85	964	12:00	SHUL Brian	WATSON Walter	HABU	2.4	
01/03/85	964	10:00	DYER Les	TABOR Ron	HABU	2.2	
04/03/85	964	19:00	SHUL Brian	WATSON Walter	N-HABU	2.2	
07/03/85	964	09:30	DYER Les	TABOR Ron	HABU	2.2	
11/03/85	973	13:00	YEILDING Edward	LEE Steve	HABU	2.3	
13/03/85	964	08:45	DYER Les	TABOR Ron	HABU	2.2	
15/03/85	973	09:10	YEILDING Edward	LEE Steve	HABU	2.3	
19/03/85	973	19:30	DYER Les	TABOR Ron	HABU	2.2	
22/03/85	964	10:00	YEILDING Edward	LEE Steve	HABU	2.3	
26/03/85	973	12:00	DYER Les	TABOR Ron	HABU	2.3	
28/03/85	964		YEILDING Edward	LEE Steve	HABU		A
28/03/85	973	14:00	YEILDING Edward	LEE Steve	HABU	2.3	
01/04/85	973	11:00	SMITH Bernie	WHALEN Denny	HABU	2.3	
03/04/85	964	11:00	YEILDING Edward	LEE Steve	HABU	2.3	
05/04/85	973	11:30	SMITH Bernie	WHALEN Denny	HABU	3.9	
09/04/85	973	09:10	YEILDING Edward	LEE Steve	HABU	2.2	
10/04/85	964	19:30	SMITH Bernie	WHALEN Denny	N-HABU	1.9	A
12/04/85	964	11:38	YEILDING Edward	LEE Steve	HABU	2.3	
15/04/85	964	11:00	SMITH Bernie	WHALEN Denny	HABU	2.4	
16/04/85	973	12:00	YEILDING Edward	LEE Steve	HABU	2.6	
18/04/85	964	15:00	SMITH Bernie	WHALEN Denny	HABU	2.3	
22/04/85	964	10:45	SMITH Bernie	WHALEN Denny	HABU	2.3	
23/04/85	964	09:50	DEAL Duane	VELTRI Tom	FCF	2.4	
24/04/85	973	10:15	SMITH Bernie	WHALEN Denny	HABU	0.4	A
26/04/85	973	09:30	DEAL Duane	VELTRI Tom	HABU	2.4	

Date	*Instal. No.*	*T.O. Time*	*Pilot Name*	*RSO Name*	*Mission*	*Duration*	*Remarks*
29/04/85	964	12:01	DEAL Duane	VELTRI Tom	HABU	4	
01/05/85	973	18:55	SMITH Bernie	WHALEN Denny	N-HABU	2.3	
03/05/85	964	11:00	SMITH Bernie	WHALEN Denny	HABU	2.3	
06/05/85	964	12:00	DEAL Duane	VELTRI Tom	HABU	2.4	
07/05/85	973	10:15	SMITH Bernie	WHALEN Denny	HABU	2.3	
09/05/85	964	10:00	DEAL Duane	VELTRI Tom	HABU	3.7	
13/05/85	964	23:00	JIGGENS Jim	McCUE Joe	N-HABU	1.4	A
15/05/85	973	11:34	JIGGENS Jim	McCUE Joe	HABU	2.2	A
16/05/85	964	09:45	DEAL Duane	VELTRI Tom	HABU	2.2	
21/05/85	973	19:30	DEAL Duane	VELTRI Tom	N-HABU	2.3	
27/05/85	973	08:00	JIGGENS Jim	McCUE Joe	FCF	2.1	
29/05/85	973	13:40	JIGGENS Jim	McCUE Joe	HABU	2.4	
31/05/85	973	09:30	JIGGENS Jim	McCUE Joe	HABU	2.3	
03/06/85	973	15:00	JIGGENS Jim	McCUE Joe	HABU	2.2	
04/06/85	964	10:22	NOLL Duane	MORGAN Charlie	FCF	2.5	
05/06/85	973	20:15	JIGGENS Jim	McCUE Joe	N-HABU	2.3	
07/06/85	973	10:00	NOLL Duane	MORGAN Charlie	HABU	2.3	A
10/06/85	964	09:45	NOLL Duane	MORGAN Charlie	HABU	2.2	
11/06/85	958	04:01	MADISON Jack	ORCUTT Bill	FERRY IN-H	6.6	
12/06/85	964	19:20	JIGGENS Jim	McCUE Joe	N-HABU	2.3	
13/06/85	958	11:00	TILDEN Tom	VIDA Joe	FCF DAFICS	3.6	
14/06/85	973	10:00	MADISON Jack	ORCUTT Bill	HABU	4.5	
17/06/85	958	13:10	TILDEN Tom	VIDA Joe	FCF DAFICS	3.7	
18/06/85	964	20:18	JIGGENS Jim	McCUE Joe	N-HABU	2.5	
19/06/85	958	11:53	TILDEN Tom	VIDA Joe	FCF DAFICS	2.6	
21/06/85	973	11:20	NOLL Duane	MORGAN Charlie	HABU	2.2	
24/06/85	958	10:15	NOLL Duane	MORGAN Charlie	HABU	2.3	
25/06/85	973		JIGGENS Jim	McCUE Joe	H-FERRY OUT		A
26/06/85	973	08:00	JIGGENS Jim	McCUE Joe	H-FERRY OUT		
28/06/85	964	12:00	MADISON Jack	ORCUTT Bill	HABU	2.4	
01/07/85	964	19:30	NOLL Duane	MORGAN Charlie	N-HABU	2.2	
03/07/85	958	09:30	MADISON Jack	ORCUTT Bill	HABU	2.2	
09/07/85	958	12:00	NOLL Duane	MORGAN Charlie	HABU	2.3	
11/07/85	958	09:15	MADISON Jack	ORCUTT Bill	HABU	2.3	
16/07/85	964	09:45	BOUDREAUX Stormy	ROSS Ted	HABU	2.3	
17/07/85	958	13:00	MADISON Jack	ORCUTT Bill	HABU	2.3	
18/07/85	958	10:35	BOUDREAUX Stormy	ROSS Ted	HABU	2.4	
21/07/85	958	10:00	BOUDREAUX Stormy	ROSS Ted	HABU	4.5	
22/07/85	964	20:00	MADISON Jack	ORCUTT Bill	N-HABU	2.3	
25/07/85	964	13:45	BOUDREAUX Stormy	ROSS Ted	HABU	2.3	
31/07/85	968	04:30	SMITH Bernie	WHALEN Denny	FERRY IN-H	6	
01/08/85	964	08:00	MADISON Jack	ORCUTT Bill	H-FERRY OUT		
02/08/85	968	09:20	BOUDREAUX Stormy	ROSS Ted	HABU	2.3	
05/08/85	958	19:30	SMITH Bernie	WHALEN Denny	N-HABU	2.3	
07/08/85	968	11:15	BOUDREAUX Stormy	ROSS Ted	HABU	2.3	
09/08/85	968	10:15	SMITH Bernie	WHALEN Denny	HABU	2.2	
14/08/85	958		BOUDREAUX Stormy	ROSS Ted	HABU		A
19/08/85	968	11:03	SMITH Bernie	WHALEN Denny	HABU	3.9	
23/08/85	968	11:30	BOUDREAUX Stormy	ROSS Ted	HABU	2.3	
25/08/85	968	10:00	SMITH Bernie	WHALEN Denny	HABU	4.5	
26/08/85	958	09:30	DYCKMAN Rod	BERGAM Tom	FCF	2.4	
27/08/85	968	11:00	DYCKMAN Rod	BERGAM Tom	HABU	2.3	
28/08/85	968	19:15	SMITH Bernie	WHALEN Denny	N-HABU	2.3	
03/09/85	968	20:04	SMITH Bernie	WHALEN Denny	N-HABU	2.2	
05/09/85	968	12:00	DYCKMAN Rod	BERGAM Tom	HABU	2.3	
07/09/85	958	10:00	SMITH Bernie	WHALEN Denny	HABU	2.3	
10/09/85	968	10:00	DYCKMAN Rod	BERGAM Tom	HABU	2.4	
11/09/85	968	09:15	SMITH Bernie	WHALEN Denny	HABU	2.3	
12/09/85	958		DYCKMAN Rod	BERGAM Tom	HABU		A
13/09/85	968	10:00	DYCKMAN Rod	BERGAM Tom	HABU	0.5	A
14/09/85	968	10:00	DYCKMAN Rod	BERGAM Tom	HABU	1.5	A
17/09/85	958	11:00	MATTHEWS Joe	OSTERHELD Curt	HABU	2.2	
18/09/85	968	18:35	MATTHEWS Joe	OSTERHELD Curt	N-HABU	2.3	
21/09/85	958	09:34	DYCKMAN Rod	BERGAM Tom	HABU	2.1	
23/09/85	968	18:45	DYCKMAN Rod	BERGAM Tom	N-HABU	2.3	
26/09/85	958	08:15	MATTHEWS Joe	OSTERHELD Curt	HABU	2.3	
27/09/85	968	10:30	DYCKMAN Rod	BERGAM Tom	HABU	2.3	
01/10/85	958	11:09	DYCKMAN Rod	BERGAM Tom	HABU	2.2	
02/10/85	968	11:00	MATTHEWS Joe	OSTERHELD Curt	HABU	2.5	A
07/10/85	958	18:33	MATTHEWS Joe	OSTERHELD Curt	N-HABU	2.3	
09/10/85	968	12:10	MATTHEWS Joe	OSTERHELD Curt	HABU	2.3	
11/10/85	958	09:45	GLASSER Jerry	TABOR Ron	HABU	2.4	
15/10/85	968	18:15	MATTHEWS Joe	OSTERHELD Curt	HABU	0.3	A
17/10/85	958	12:02	MATTHEWS Joe	OSTERHELD Curt	HABU	2.3	
18/10/85	958	10:45	GLASSER Jerry	TABOR Ron	HABU	3.7	
21/10/85	968	10:30	MATTHEWS Joe	OSTERHELD Curt	FCF	2.1	
22/10/85	958	13:05	GLASSER Jerry	TABOR Ron	HABU	2.3	
23/10/85	968	10:15	MATTHEWS Joe	OSTERHELD Curt	FCF	2.3	
24/10/85	958	09:12	GLASSER Jerry	TABOR Ron	HABU	2.4	
28/10/85	968	10:30	DEAL Duane	VELTRI Tom	HABU	2.4	
30/10/85	968	18:15	CUNNINGHAM Nevin	TABOR Ron	N-HABU	2.3	
01/11/85	968	10:00	DEAL Duane	VELTRI Tom	HABU	2.3	
05/11/85	958	09:30	CUNNINGHAM Nevin	TABOR Ron	HABU	2.3	
06/11/85	968	09:32	DEAL Duane	VELTRI Tom	HABU	5.8	
07/11/85	958	10:15	CUNNINGHAM Nevin	TABOR Ron	HABU	2.5	
12/11/85	958	19:00	CUNNINGHAM Nevin	TABOR Ron	N-HABU	2.3	
14/11/85	958	10:30	DEAL Duane	VELTRI Tom	HABU	3.8	
19/11/85	968	11:00	SHUL Brian	WATSON Walter	HABU	1	A
21/11/85	958	10:30	DEAL Duane	VELTRI Tom	HABU	2.3	
23/11/85	968	12:15	SHUL Brian	WATSON Walter	HABU	2.3	
26/11/85	958	13:30	DEAL Duane	VELTRI Tom	HABU	2.2	
27/11/85	958	11:30	SHUL Brian	WATSON Walter	HABU	2.4	
29/11/85	958	09:10	DEAL Duane	VELTRI Tom	HABU	2.3	
02/12/85	958	17:00	SHUL Brian	WATSON Walter	N-HABU	2.4	
04/12/85	968	09:30	DEAL Duane	VELTRI Tom	HABU	2.3	
07/12/85	968	11:30	SHUL Brian	WATSON Walter	HABU	2.2	
09/12/85	958	09:32	SHUL Brian	WATSON Walter	HABU	5.9	
11/12/85	968	18:15	SMITH Bernie	WHALEN Denny	N-HABU	2.3	
13/12/85	968	09:03	SHUL Brian	WATSON Walter	HABU	2.3	
17/12/85	958		SMITH Bernie	WHALEN Denny	N-HABU		A
17/12/85	958	21:35	SMITH Bernie	WHALEN Denny	N-HABU	2.3	
19/12/85	968	12:00	SHUL Brian	WATSON Walter	HABU	2.3	
20/12/85	958	09:45	SMITH Bernie	WHALEN Denny	HABU	3.7	
23/12/85	958	09:35	SHUL Brian	WATSON Walter	HABU	0.8	A
23/12/85	958	13:20	SHUL Brian	WATSON Walter	HABU	2.3	
27/12/85	958	13:10	SMITH Bernie	WHALEN Denny	HABU	2.3	
30/12/85	958	12:30	SMITH Bernie	WHALEN Denny	HABU	2.3	
02/01/86	968	18:55	BOUDREAUX Stormy	ROSS Ted	N-HABU	2.3	
07/01/86	958	12:00	SMITH Bernie	WHALEN Denny	HABU	2.3	
09/01/86	968	09:00	BOUDREAUX Stormy	ROSS Ted	HABU	2.4	
10/01/86	968	11:00	SMITH Bernie	WHALEN Denny	HABU	3.8	
13/01/86	958	11:15	BOUDREAUX Stormy	ROSS Ted	HABU	2.3	
15/01/86	958	09:45	SMITH Bernie	WHALEN Denny	HABU	2.3	
16/01/86	968	09:11	BOUDREAUX Stormy	ROSS Ted	HABU	2.3	
21/01/86	958	17:35	BOUDREAUX Stormy	ROSS Ted	N-HABU	2.4	
22/01/86	968	10:58	SMITH Mike	SOIFER Douglas	ACFAM	2.5	
23/01/86	958	10:00	BOUDREAUX Stormy	ROSS Ted	HABU	4	
25/01/86	968	10:20	SMITH Mike	SOIFER Douglas	HABU	3.2	
27/01/86	958	19:00	BOUDREAUX Stormy	ROSS Ted	N-HABU	2.4	
29/01/86	958	13:30	SMITH Mike	SOIFER Douglas	HABU	2.4	
03/02/86	958	17:55	BOUDREAUX Stormy	ROSS Ted	N-HABU	2.3	
05/02/86	968		SMITH Mike	SOIFER Douglas	HABU		A
06/02/86	968	09:15	SMITH Mike	SOIFER Douglas	HABU	2.3	
07/02/86	958	10:45	SMITH Mike	SOIFER Douglas	HABU	2.3	
11/02/86	958	10:00	MADISON Jack	ORCUTT Bill	HABU	2.4	
12/02/86	958	10:50	SMITH Mike	SOIFER Douglas	HABU	3.9	
14/02/86	968	10:30	MADISON Jack	ORCUTT Bill	HABU	2.3	
17/02/86	958	09:10	SMITH Mike	SOIFER Douglas	HABU	2.3	
20/02/86	968	13:00	MADISON Jack	ORCUTT Bill	HABU	2.3	
21/02/86	958	10:30	SMITH Mike	SOIFER Douglas	HABU	3.9	
24/02/86	958	10:10	MADISON Jack	ORCUTT Bill	HABU	2.5	
26/02/86	968	11:00	SMITH Mike	SOIFER Douglas	HABU	4	
27/02/86	968	13:00	MADISON Jack	ORCUTT Bill	HABU	2.3	
03/03/86	968	10:16	NOLL Duane	VELTRI Tom	HABU	2.3	
04/03/86	958	10:00	MADISON Jack	ORCUTT Bill	HABU	3.9	
06/03/86	968	18:30	NOLL Duane	VELTRI Tom	N-HABU	2.4	
10/03/86	958	19:00	NOLL Duane	VELTRI Tom	N-HABU	2.3	
12/03/86	968	11:30	MADISON Jack	ORCUTT Bill	HABU	2.4	
17/03/86	958	11:00	MADISON Jack	ORCUTT Bill	HABU	3.9	
18/03/86	968	10:30	NOLL Duane	VELTRI Tom	HABU	2.3	
21/03/86	958	10:30	MADISON Jack	ORCUTT Bill	HABU	1.8	A
22/03/86	958	09:30	MADISON Jack	ORCUTT Bill	HABU	2.2	
24/03/86	968	19:15	YEILDING Ed	LEE Steve	N-HABU	2.3	
26/03/86	968	10:00	NOLL Duane	VELTRI Tom	HABU	2.3	
27/03/86	968	09:35	YEILDING Ed	LEE Steve	HABU	2.3	
28/03/86	958	09:15	NOLL Duane	VELTRI Tom	HABU	2.3	
01/04/86	968	11:30	YEILDING Ed	LEE Steve	HABU	2.3	
02/04/86	968		NOLL Duane	VELTRI Tom	HABU		A
04/04/86	967	06:15	DYCKMAN Rod	BERGAM Tom	FERRY IN-H	6.6	
05/04/86	958		NOLL Duane	VELTRI Tom	H-FERRY OUT		A
06/04/86	958	10:00	NOLL Duane	VELTRI Tom	H-FERRY OUT		
08/04/86	968	10:00	YEILDING Ed	LEE Steve	HABU	3.7	
11/04/86	968	10:00	DYCKMAN Rod	BERGAM Tom	HABU	4.7	
15/04/86	967	09:45	YEILDING Ed	LEE Steve	HABU	2.2	
16/04/86	967	19:35	DYCKMAN Rod	BERGAM Tom	N-HABU	2.3	
18/04/86	968	11:45	YEILDING Ed	LEE Steve	HABU	2.3	
21/04/86	967	19:30	DYCKMAN Rod	BERGAM Tom	N-HABU	2.3	
23/04/86	968	12:00	YEILDING Ed	LEE Steve	HABU	2.2	
25/04/86	968	11:15	DYCKMAN Rod	BERGAM Tom	HABU	2.3	
29/04/86	967	13:05	YEILDING Ed	LEE Steve	HABU	2.3	
01/05/86	968	09:30	DYCKMAN Rod	BERGAM Tom	HABU	2.4	
07/05/86	968	10:06	MATTHEWS Joe	OSTERHELD Curt	HABU	3.7	
08/05/86	967	15:00	DYCKMAN Rod	BERGAM Tom	HABU	2.2	
09/05/86	968	11:00	MATTHEWS Joe	OSTERHELD Curt	HABU	2.3	
12/05/86	968	19:15	MATTHEWS Joe	OSTERHELD Curt	N-HABU	2.3	
14/05/86	968	09:45	MATTHEWS Joe	OSTERHELD Curt	HABU	2.3	
16/05/86	968	11:30	DYCKMAN Rod	TABOR Ron	HABU	3.6	
19/05/86	967		MATTHEWS Joe	OSTERHELD Curt	HABU		A
20/05/86	968	09:15	MATTHEWS Joe	OSTERHELD Curt	HABU	2.4	
21/05/86	967	10:15	DYCKMAN Rod	TABOR Ron	HABU	2.3	
22/05/86	967	09:15	MATTHEWS Joe	OSTERHELD Curt	HABU	2.3	
27/05/86	968	19:44	MATTHEWS Joe	OSTERHELD Curt	N-HABU	0.4	A
27/05/86	968	22:21	MATTHEWS Joe	OSTERHELD Curt	N-HABU	2.3	
28/05/86	967	13:00	HOUSE Dan	BOZEK Blair	CRFAM	2.4	
30/05/86	967	11:00	HOUSE Dan	BOZEK Blair	HABU	4	
02/06/86	967	09:58	MATTHEWS Joe	OSTERHELD Curt	HABU	2.3	
03/06/86	968	11:28	HOUSE Dan	BOZEK Blair	HABU	2.4	
05/06/86	967	19:25	MATTHEWS Joe	OSTERHELD Curt	N-HABU	2.3	
09/06/86	968	11:00	HOUSE Dan	BOZEK Blair	HABU	3.9	
12/06/86	967	09:30	MATTHEWS Joe	OSTERHELD Curt	HABU	2.3	
13/06/86	968	11:00	HOUSE Dan	BOZEK Blair	HABU	1.9	A
16/06/86	967	10:00	HOUSE Dan	BOZEK Blair	HABU	2.2	
17/06/86	968	09:15	JIGGENS Jim	ROSS Ted	HABU	2.4	
18/06/86	968	12:00	HOUSE Dan	BOZEK Blair	HABU	2.1	
20/06/86	968	09:45	JIGGENS Jim	ROSS Ted	HABU	2.4	
23/06/86	967	11:57	HOUSE Dan	BOZEK Blair	HABU	2.2	
25/06/86	967	19:30	JIGGENS Jim	ROSS Ted	N-HABU	2.2	
27/06/86	968	12:00	HOUSE Dan	BOZEK Blair	FCF	2.6	
02/07/86	968	09:35	HOUSE Dan	BOZEK Blair	HABU	1.9	A
03/07/86	967	10:57	JIGGENS Jim	ROSS Ted	HABU	0.7	A
03/07/86	967	15:42	JIGGENS Jim	ROSS Ted	HABU	2.2	
07/07/86	967	20:15	SHUL Brian	WATSON Walter	N-HABU	2.3	
09/07/86	968	10:17	JIGGENS Jim	ROSS Ted	HABU	2.3	
11/07/86	968	09:43	SHUL Brian	WATSON Walter	HABU	2.3	
15/07/86	967	09:43	JIGGENS Jim	ROSS Ted	HABU	2.4	
17/07/86	968	11:59	SHUL Brian	WATSON Walter	HABU	2.3	

Date	*Instal. No.*	*T.O. Time*	*Pilot Name*	*RSO Name*	*Mission*	*Duration*	*Remarks*
18/07/86	967	09:59	JIGGENS Jim	ROSS Ted	HABU	2.3	
21/07/86	968	19:27	JIGGENS Jim	ROSS Ted	N-HABU	2.4	
24/07/86	967	10:07	SHUL Brian	WATSON Walter	HABU	2.3	
28/07/86	968	10:42	SMITH Mike	SOIFER Douglas	HABU	2.3	
30/07/86	967	11:25	SHUL Brain	WATSON Walter	HABU	2.4	
01/08/86	968	09:26	SMITH Mike	SOIFER Douglas	HABU	2.3	
04/08/86	968	11:23	SHUL Brian	WATSON Walter	HABU	2.3	
05/08/86	968	19:20	SMITH Mike	SOIFER Douglas	N-HABU	2.3	
08/08/86	968	09:40	SHUL Brian	WATSON Walter	HABU	2.2	
11/08/86	968	19:15	SMITH Mike	SOIFER Douglas	N-HABU	2.4	
13/08/86	967	11:09	SHUL Brian	WATSON Walter	HABU	2.3	
14/08/86	968	10:00	SMITH Mike	SOIFER Douglas	HABU	2.3	
18/08/86	967	10:53	NOLL Duane	VELTRI Tom	HABU	2.4	
20/08/86	968	19:25	NOLL Duane	VELTRI Tom	N-HABU	2.2	
22/08/86	967	10:25	SMITH Mike	SOIFER Douglas	HABU	2.3	
28/08/86	967	09:26	NOLL Duane	VELTRI Tom	HABU	2.3	
29/08/86	967	10:40	SMITH Mike	SOIFER Douglas	HABU	2.3	
01/09/86	968	11:00	SMITH Mike	SOIFER Douglas	HABU	2.3	
04/09/86	967	19:30	NOLL Duane	VELTRI Tom	N-HABU	2.3	
06/09/86	967	09:30	NOLL Duane	VELTRI Tom	HABU	2.2	
08/09/86	968	11:25	MADISON Jack	LEE Steve	HABU	2.3	
10/09/86	968	10:00	NOLL Duane	VELTRI Tom	HABU	2.2	
11/09/86	967	19:30	MADISON Jack	LEE Steve	N-HABU	0.5	A
11/09/86	968	21:45	MADISON Jack	LEE Steve	N-HABU	2.2	
13/09/86	967	09:45	NOLL Duane	VELTRI Tom	HABU	2.2	
15/09/86	968	20:04	NOLL Duane	VELTRI Tom	N-HABU	2.3	
17/09/86	967	07:00	NOLL Duane	VELTRI Tom	HABU	2.4	
18/09/86	967	05:55	MADISON Jack	LEE Steve	HABU	2.7	
24/09/86	967	10:00	NOLL Duane	VELTRI Tom	HABU	3.2	
27/09/86	967	10:00	MADISON Jack	LEE Steve	HABU	4.5	
01/10/86	968	10:18	DANIELSON Tom	GUDMUNDSON Stan	ACFAM	2.3	
02/10/86	967	12:30	MADISON Jack	LEE Steve	HABU	3.5	
06/10/86	968	10:30	DANIELSON Tom	GUDMUNDSON Stan	HABU	2.3	
08/10/86	967	18:30	DANIELSON Tom	GUDMUNDSON Stan	N-HABU	2.3	
10/10/86	968	09:45	MADISON Jack	LEE Steve	HABU	2.3	
14/10/86	967	18:20	MADISON Jack	LEE Steve	N-HABU	2.5	
16/10/86	968	09:58	DANIELSON Tom	GUDMUNDSON Stan	HABU	2.2	
20/10/86	968	18:40	DANIELSON Tom	GUDMUNDSON Stan	N-HABU	2.3	
22/10/86	967	11:30	SMITH Bernie	ORCUTT Bill	HABU	3.2	
24/10/86	968	10:50	DANIELSON Tom	GUDMUNDSON Stan	HABU	2.3	
27/10/86	968	09:15	SMITH Bernie	ORCUTT Bill	HABU	2.2	
28/10/86	967	11:10	SMITH Bernie	ORCUTT Bill	HABU	2.2	
30/10/86	968	09:10	SMITH Bernie	ORCUTT Bill	HABU	3.7	
03/11/86	968	10:58	SMITH Bernie	ORCUTT Bill	HABU	2.2	
07/11/86	967	12:10	DANIELSON Tom	GUDMUNDSON Stan	HABU	4.5	
12/11/86	968	17:50	MATTHEWS Joe	MORGAN John	N-HABU	2.3	
14/11/86	968	10:15	NOLL Duane	VELTRI Tom	HABU	3.9	
17/11/86	967	12:10	MATTHEWS Joe	MORGAN John	HABU	2.2	
18/11/86	968	19:40	NOLL Duane	VELTRI Tom	N-HABU	2.3	
20/11/86	968	09:50	MATTHEWS Joe	MORGAN John	HABU	2.2	
21/11/86	967	10:30	NOLL Duane	VELTRI Tom	HABU	3.9	
24/11/86	968	10:05	MATTHEWS Joe	MORGAN John	HABU	3.5	
25/11/86	967	12:10	NOLL Duane	VELTRI Tom	HABU	2.2	
01/12/86	968	09:10	DYCKMAN Rod	BERGAM Tom	HABU	2.3	
02/12/86	967	10:01	PAPPAS Terry	MANZI John	CRFAM	2.5	
03/12/86	968	18:00	DYCKMAN Tod	BERGAM Tom	N-HABU	2.3	
05/12/86	968	09:36	PAPPAS Terry	MANZI John	HABU	2.4	
08/12/86	968	09:50	DYCKMAN Rod	BERGAM Tom	HABU	2.4	
10/12/86	967	09:10	DYCKMAN Rod	BERGAM Tom	HABU	5.7	
11/12/86	968	17:45	PAPPAS Terry	MANZI John	N-HABU	2.4	
15/12/86	967	10:35	PAPPAS Terry	MANZI John	HABU	2.4	
16/12/86	968	09:20	DYCKMAN Rod	BERGAM Tom	HABU	2.4	
18/12/86	967		PAPPAS Terry	MANZI John	HABU		A
18/12/86	967	12:50	PAPPAS Terry	MANZI John	HABU	2.4	
22/12/86	967	17:40	YEILDING Ed	OSTERHELD Curt	N-HABU	2.2	
23/12/86	968	13:00	PAPPAS Terry	MANZI John	HABU	2.3	
29/12/86	967	10:45	YEILDING Ed	OSTERHELD Curt	HABU	3.9	
02/01/87	967	09:35	PAPPAS Terry	MANZI John	HABU	2.8	
05/01/87	968	09:59	YEILDING Ed	OSTERHELD Curt	HABU	2.2	
06/01/87	967	18:00	PAPPAS Terry	MANZI John	N-HABU	2.3	
08/01/87	968	10:21	YEILDING Ed	OSTERHELD Curt	HABU	3.3	
12/01/87	967		HOUSE Dan	BOZEK Blair	N-HABU		
13/01/87	967		HOUSE Dan	BOZEK Blair	N-HABU		
14/01/87	967	10:45	HOUSE Dan	BOZEK Blair	HABU	2.4	
15/01/87	968	11:00	YEILDING Ed	OSTERHELD Curt	HABU	1.9	A
16/01/87	967	11:00	HOUSE Dan	BOZEK Blair	HABU	2.3	
20/01/87	968	18:40	YEILDING Ed	OSTERHELD Curt	N-HABU	2.3	
21/01/87	967	14:50	HOUSE Dan	BOZEK Blair	HABU	2.4	
23/01/87	967	10:20	YEILDING Ed	OSTERHELD Curt	HABU	2.3	
26/01/87	968	11:35	HOUSE Dan	BOZEK Blair	HABU	2.3	
27/01/87	967	18:05	YEILDING Ed	OSTERHELD Curt	N-HABU	2.3	
29/01/87	967	13:07	HOUSE Dan	BOZEK Blair	HABU	2.4	
02/02/87	968		HOUSE Dan	BOZEK Blair	HABU		A
02/02/87	968	09:51	HOUSE Dan	BOZEK Blair	HABU	2.3	
03/02/87	967		SHUL Brian	WATSON Walter	HABU		
04/02/87	967		SHUL Brian	WATSON Walter	HABU		
05/02/87	967	10:20	SHUL Brian	WATSON Walter	HABU	3.8	
06/02/87	968	09:54	HOUSE Dan	BOZEK Blair	HABU	2.3	
07/02/87	968	10:05	SHUL Brian	WATSON Walter	HABU	2.2	
09/02/87	967	19:07	HOUSE Dan	BOZEK Blair	N-HABU	2.4	
11/02/87	967	12:11	SHUL Brian	WATSON Walter	HABU	2.3	
13/02/87	968	09:50	HOUSE Dan	BOZEK Blair	HABU	2.4	
17/02/87	967	09:10	SHUL Brian	WATSON Walter	HABU	2.3	
18/02/87	968	10:35	HOUSE Dan	BOZEK Blair	HABU	2.3	
19/02/87	967	11:55	SHUL Brian	WATSON Walter	HABU	3.2	
24/02/87	968	19:25	SMITH Mike	SOIFER Douglas	N-HABU	2.4	
26/02/87	968	09:35	SHUL Brian	WATSON Walter	HABU	2.3	
02/03/87	968	09:05	SMITH Mike	SOIFER Douglas	HABU	2.3	

Date	*Instal. No.*	*T.O. Time*	*Pilot Name*	*RSO Name*	*Mission*	*Duration*	*Remarks*
04/03/87	968	10:20	SHUL Brian	WATSON Walter	HABU	2.3	
05/03/87	967	10:28	SMITH Mike	SOIFER Douglas	FCF	1.1	
07/03/87	967	09:25	SHUL Brian	WATSON Walter	HABU	2.6	
10/03/87	967	19:15	SMITH Mike	SOIFER Douglas	N-HABU	2.4	
12/03/87	967	11:40	SHUL Brian	WATSON Walter	HABU	2.8	
17/03/87	967	18:50	NOLL Duane	VELTRI Tom	N-HABU	2.2	
20/03/87	968	10:45	SMITH Mike	SOIFER Douglas	HABU	1.8	A
20/03/87	968	15:56	SMITH Mike	SOIFER Douglas	HABU	0.5	A
21/03/87	967	10:00	NOLL Duane	VELTRI Tom	HABU	2.2	
23/03/87	967	18:50	SMITH Mike	SOIFER Douglas	N-HABU	2.3	
25/03/87	968		SMITH Mike	SOIFER Douglas	HABU		A
26/03/87	967	10:37	SMITH Mike	SOIFER Douglas	HABU	3.3	
27/03/87	968	09:50	NOLL Duane	VELTRI Tom	HABU	2.3	
01/04/87	967	09:45	SMITH Mike	SOIFER Douglas	HABU	2.3	
02/04/87	968	10:35	NOLL Duane	VELTRI Tom	HABU	2.3	
04/04/87	967	12:36	NOLL Duane	VELTRI Tom	HABU	4.2	
06/04/87	967	12:00	McKENDREE Mac	SHELHORSE Randy	CRFAM	2.5	
07/04/87	968	10:00	McKENDREE Mac	SHELHORSE Randy	HABU	2.3	
09/04/87	967	18:50	NOLL Duane	VELTRI Tom	N-HABU	2.3	
14/04/87	967		McKENDREE Mac	SHELHORSE Randy	HABU		
16/04/87	967	11:00	McKENDREE Mac	SHELHORSE Randy	HABU	4	
17/04/87	968	12:00	NOLL Duane	VELTRI Tom	HABU	2.2	
20/04/87	967	19:00	McKENDREE Mac	SHELHORSE Randy	N-HABU	2.3	
23/04/87	968	09:50	NOLL Duane	VELTRI Tom	HABU	2.3	
27/04/87	967	19:00	McKENDREE Mac	SHELHORSE Randy	N-HABU	2.4	
29/04/87	968	10:00	DANIELSON Tom	GUDMUNDSON Stan	HABU	2.3	
02/05/87	967	11:09	McKENDREE Mac	SHELHORSE Randy	HABU	2.1	
05/05/87	967		DANIELSON Tom	GUDMUNDSON Stan	HABU		A
05/05/87	967	12:11	DANIELSON Tom	GUDMUNDSON Stan	HABU	2.2	
07/05/87	968	10:45	McKENDREE Mac	SHELHORSE Randy	HABU	3.7	
11/05/87	968	09:30	DANIELSON Tom	GUDMUNDSON Stan	HABU	3.3	
13/05/87	975	11:30	YEILDING Ed	OSTERHELD Curt	FERRY IN-H	6.9	
14/05/87	968	08:00	McKENDREE Mac	SHELHORSE Randy	H-FERRY OUT		
18/05/87	967	10:45	DANIELSON Tom	GUDMUNDSON Stan	HABU	2	
20/05/87	967	12:00	YEILDING Ed	OSTERHELD Curt	HABU	3.5	
22/05/87	967	09:45	DANIELSON Tom	GUDMUNDSON Stan	HABU	2.1	
26/05/87	975	19:43	YEILDING Ed	OSTERHELD Curt	N-HABU	2.1	
28/05/87	967	09:15	DANIELSON Tom	GUDMUNDSON Stan	HABU	2.2	
01/06/87	975	11:00	YEILDING Ed	OSTERHELD Curt	HABU	2.1	
02/06/87	967	19:36	DANIELSON Tom	GUDMUNDSON Stan	N-HABU	2.1	
04/06/87	975	11:05	YEILDING Ed	OSTERHELD Curt	HABU	3.6	
08/06/87	975	19:20	SMITH Mike	SOIFER Doug	N-HABU	2.1	
12/06/87	967	10:30	YEILDING Ed	OSTERHELD Curt	HABU	2.2	
16/06/87	975	12:20	SMITH Mike	SOIFER Doug	HABU	1.6	A
17/06/87	967		YEILDING Ed	OSTERHELD Curt	HABU		A
17/06/87	967	11:54	YEILDING Ed	OSTERHELD Curt	HABU	4.2	
22/06/87	967		SMITH Mike	SOIFER Doug	N-HABU		A
22/06/87	967	21:18	SMITH Mike	SOIFER Doug	N-HABU	2.2	
24/06/87	975	11:55	YEILDING Ed	OSTERHELD Curt	HABU	3.2	
25/06/87	967	11:15	SMITH Mike	SOIFER Doug	HABU	2.2	
29/06/87	967	09:57	SMITH Mike	SOIFER Doug	HABU	2.2	
30/06/87	975		BROWN Larry	CARTER Keith	CRFAM		A
30/06/87	975	16:24	BROWN Larry	CARTER Keith	CRFAM	2.4	
01/07/87	967	13:00	BROWN Larry	CARTER Keith	HABU	2.1	
06/07/87	975	19:10	SMITH Mike	SOIFER Doug	N-HABU	2.1	
08/07/87	967	10:36	BROWN Larry	CARTER Keith	HABU	2.2	
10/07/87	975	09:32	SMITH Mike	SOIFER Doug	HABU	2.2	
13/07/87	975	09:20	BROWN Larry	CARTER Keith	HABU	2.2	
16/07/87	967	10:35	SMITH Mike	SOIFER Doug	HABU	2.5	
17/07/87	967	10:34	BROWN Larry	CARTER Keith	HABU	2.2	
20/07/87	975	09:30	PAPPAS Terry	MANZI John	HABU	2.4	
22/07/87	975	11:00	YEILDING Ed	OSTERHELD Curt	HABU	4.3	
22/07/87	967	10:16	SMITH Mike	SOIFER Doug	HABU	11.2	32
28/07/87	975	13:35	BROWN Larry	CARTER Keith	HABU	2.1	
30/07/87	967	18:52	PAPPAS Terry	MANZI John	N-HABU	2.3	
03/08/87	967	10:05	BROWN Larry	CARTER Keith	HABU	2.2	
04/08/87	975	18:50	PAPPAS Terry	MANZI John	N-HABU	1.5	A
06/08/87	975	10:45	BROWN Larry	CARTER Keith	HABU	2.1	
09/08/87	975	11:30	PAPPAS Terry	MANZI John	HABU	11.1	33
09/08/87	967	12:19	BROWN Larry	CARTER Keith	HABU	4.4	
14/08/87	967	13:41	SMITH Bernie	BERGAM Tom	HABU	2.2	
18/08/87	967	11:52	PAPPAS Terry	MANZI John	HABU	0.4	A
18/08/87	967	16:01	PAPPAS Terry	MANZI John	HABU	2.2	
24/08/87	975	12:20	SMITH Bernie	BERGAM Tom	HABU	2.1	
27/08/87	967	09:22	PAPPAS Terry	MANZI John	HABU	2.1	
01/09/87	967	13:00	SMITH Barnie	BERGAM Tom	HABU	2.1	
03/09/87	967	10:06	HOUSE Dan	BOZEK Blair	HABU	2.1	
08/09/87	967	18:25	SMITH Barnie	BERGAM Tom	N-HABU	0.4	A
08/09/87	967	21:09	SMITH Barnie	BERGAM Tom	N-HABU	2.1	
09/09/87	975	15:19	HOUSE Dan	BOZEK Blair	HABU	2.2	
11/09/87	967	13:00	SMITH Barnie	BERGAM Tom	HABU-100	2.3	
15/09/87	975	10:00	HOUSE Dan	BOZEK Blair	HABU	2.2	
17/09/87	967	12:11	SMITH Barnie	BERGAM Tom	HABU	2.5	
21/09/87	967	10:45	HOUSE Dan	BOZEK Blair	HABU	3.3	
22/09/87	975	17:50	HOUSE Dan	BOZEK Blair	N-HABU	2.1	
22/09/87	967	12:00	GRZEBINIAK Steve	GREENWOOD Jim	CRWFAM	2.5	
24/09/87	975	10:34	GRZEBINIAK Steve	GREENWOOD Jim	HABU	3.8	
26/09/87	967	09:45	HOUSE Dan	BOZEK Blair	HABU	2.1	
29/09/87	975	10:15	GRZEBINIAK Steve	GREENWOOD Jim	HABU	2.1	
02/10/87	967	10:00	HOUSE Dan	BOZEK Blair	HABU	3.7	
05/10/87	967	17:20	GRZEBINIAK Steve	GREENWOOD Jim	N-HABU	2.1	
13/10/87	975	11:47	McKENDREE Mac	SHELHORSE Randy	HABU	1.8	A
15/10/87	967	11:19	GRZEBINIAK Steve	GREENWOOD Jim	HABU	3.2	
17/10/87	975	08:45	McKENDREE Mac	SHELHORSE Randy	HABU	2.1	
19/10/87	975		GRZEBINIAK Steve	GREENWOOD Jim	HABU		A
20/10/87	967	09:35	GRZEBINIAK Steve	GREENWOOD Jim	HABU	2.1	
23/10/87	975	13:00	McKENDREE Mac	SHELHORSE Randy	HABU	2.1	
26/10/87	975	12:05	HOUSE Dan	BOZEK Blair	HABU	2.5	

Date	Instal. No.	T.O. Time	Pilot Name	RSO Name	Mission	Duration	Remarks
26/10/87	967	11:00	McKENDREE Mac	SHELHORSE Randy	HABU	10.8	34
28/10/87	975	10:30	McKENDREE Mac	SHELHORSE Randy	HABU	3.6	
02/11/87	975	10:05	NOLL Duane	VELTRI Tom	HABU	3.7	
06/11/87	967	10:15	McKENDREE Mac	SHELHORSE Randy	HABU	1.9	A
11/11/87	967	11:20	NOLL Duane	VELTRI Tom	HABU	3.2	
14/11/87	975	09:05	McKENDREE Mac	SHELHORSE Randy	HABU	2.1	
16/11/87	967	09:30	NOLL Duane	VELTRI Tom	FCF	2	
19/11/87	974		MADISON Jack	BERGAM Tom	FERRY IN/HABU	6.4	
20/11/87	967	07:00	McKENDREE Mac	SHELHORSE Randy	HABU/FERRY OUT		
23/11/87	975	09:25	NOLL Duane	VELTRI Tom	HABU	2.1	
24/11/87	975	11:00	MADISON Jack	BERGAM Tom	HABU	3.7	
02/12/87	974	11:20	NOLL Duane	VELTRI Tom	HABU	2.1	
04/12/87	975	10:05	MADISON Jack	BERGAM Tom	HABU	4	
08/12/87	974	17:55	NOLL Duane	VELTRI Tom	N-HABU	1	A
09/12/87	975	12:00	NOLL Duane	VELTRI Tom	HABU	2.2	
10/12/87	975	11:39	MADISON Jack	BERGAM Tom	HABU	3.4	
15/12/87	974	13:26	DANIELSON Tom	GUDMUNDSON Stan	HABU	2.2	
16/12/87	975	12:30	MADISON Jack	BERGAM Tom	HABU	2.2	
21/12/87	974		DANIELSON Tom	GUDMUNDSON Stan	HABU		A
21/12/87	974		DANIELSON Tom	GUDMUNDSON Stan	HABU		A
22/12/87	975	11:30	DANIELSON Tom	GUDMUNDSON Stan	HABU	2.1	
29/12/87	974	09:55	MADISON Jack	BERGAM Tom	HABU	2.1	
04/01/88	975	17:40	DANIELSON Tom	GUDMUNDSON Stan	N-HABU	2.3	
06/01/88	974	10:55	BROWN Larry	CARTER Keith	HABU	2.1	
12/01/88	974	12:15	DANIELSON Tom	GUDMUNDSON Stan	HABU	2.1	
16/01/88	974	13:20	BROWN Larry	CARTER Keith	HABU	2.1	
21/01/88	974	09:35	DANIELSON Tom	GUDMUNDSON Stan	HABU	5.5	
22/01/88	975	11:10	SMITH Bernie	CARTER Keith	FCF	2.1	
25/01/88	975	11:25	SMITH Mike	SOIFER Doug	HABU	2	
28/01/88	975		SMITH Bernie	CARTER Keith	HABU		A
28/01/88	975		SMITH Bernie	CARTER Keith	HABU		A
29/01/88	974		SMITH Bernie	CARTER Keith	HABU		
30/01/88	974	15:00	SMITH Bernie	CARTER Keith	HABU	0.7	A
31/01/88	974	15:00	SMITH Bernie	CARTER Keith	HABU	3.2	
01/02/88	974	11:15	SMITH Mike	SOIFER Doug	HABU	2.1	
04/02/88	974	13:25	SMITH Bernie	CARTER Keith	HABU	2.2	
09/02/88	975	10:40	SMITH Mike	SOIFER Doug	HABU	2.1	
12/02/88	974	08:05	SMITH Bernie	CARTER Keith	HABU	5.2	
16/02/88	975	09:40	SMITH Mike	SOIFER Doug	HABU	2.1	
17/02/88	974	10:45	McCLEARY Tom	VARDAMAN Blue	CRFAM	2.2	
18/02/88	974	15:00	McCLEARY Tom	VARDAMAN Blue	HABU	3.3	
22/02/88	975	18:05	SMITH Mike	SOIFER Doug	N-HABU	2.2	
29/02/88	974	08:35	McCLEARY Tom	VARDAMAN Blue	HABU	5.3	
03/03/88	975	10:17	DYCKMAN Rod	WATSON Walt	HABU	2	
04/03/88	975	10:45	McCLEARY Tom	VARDAMAN Blue	HABU	3.8	
09/03/88	975	09:55	DYCKMAN Rod	WATSON Walt	HABU	2.1	
14/03/88	975	08:49	McCLEARY Tom	VARDAMAN Blue	HABU	3.7	
16/03/88	975	10:20	DYCKMAN Rod	WATSON Walt	HABU	2.2	
22/03/88	974	18:27	PAPPAS Terry	MANZI John	N-HABU	2.1	
29/03/88	974	12:04	HOUSE Dan	BOZEK Blair	HABU	2.1	
05/04/88	975	13:36	PAPPAS Terry	MANZI John	HABU	2.2	
07/04/88	974	08:53	HOUSE Dan	BOZEK Blair	HABU	3.4	
14/04/88	975	10:15	PAPPAS Terry	MANZI John	HABU	2.2	
15/04/88	974		HOUSE Dan	BOZEK Blair	HABU		A
15/04/88	975	09:51	HOUSE Dan	BOZEK Blair	HABU	5.2	
20/04/88	974	.18:35	GRZEBINIAK Steve	GREENWOOD Jim	N-HABU	2.1	
21/04/88	975	11:45	HOUSE Dan	BOZEK Blair	FCF	2.2	
28/04/88	974	14:00	GRZEBINIAK Steve	GREENWOOD Jim	HABU	2.4	
30/04/88	974	09:17	HOUSE Dan	BOZEK Blair	HABU	10.9	35
30/04/88	975		GRZEBINIAK Steve	GREENWOOD Jim	HABU-G/A		A
04/05/88	974	19:05	McKENDREE Mac	SHELHORSE Randy	N-HABU	2.2	
10/05/88	975	09:05	GRZEBINIAK Steve	GREENWOOD Jim	HABU	3.5	
14/05/88	974	09:50	McKENDREE Mac	SHELHORSE Randy	FCF	2	
18/05/88	975	10:30	GRZEBINIAK Steve	GREENWOOD Jim	FCF	2.3	
20/05/88	974	15:00	McKENDREE Mac	SHELHORSE Randy	HABU	1.5	A
21/05/88	974	10:00	GRZEBINIAK Steve	GREENWOOD Jim	HABU	2.2	
23/05/88	975	14:10	McKENDREE Mac	SHELHORSE Randy	HABU	2.2	
26/05/88	974	10:20	GRZEBINIAK Steve	GREENWOOD Jim	HABU	4.8	
27/05/88	975	12:25	McKENDREE Mac	SHELHORSE Randy	HABU	1.9	
02/06/88	974	13:10	PAPPAS Terry	MANZI John	FCF	2.1	
06/06/88	975	11:30	McKENDREE Mac	SHELHORSE Randy	HABU	2.3	
09/06/88	974	11:18	PAPPAS Terry	MANZI John	FCF	2.2	
14/06/88	975	09:50	McKENDREE Mac	SHELHORSE Randy	HABU	2.1	
16/06/88	974	11:00	PAPPAS Terry	MANZI John	FCF	2.1	
17/06/88	975	12:10	McCLEARY Tom	BERGAM Tom	HABU	1.9	
21/06/88	974	12:30	PAPPAS Terry	MANZI John	HABU	2.1	
22/06/88	975	09:09	McCLEARY Tom	BERGAM Tom	HABU	3.5	
28/06/88	974	10:00	McCLEARY Tom	BERGAM Tom	FCF	2.1	
30/06/88	975	07:06	PAPPAS Terry	MANZI John	HABU/FERRY OUT		
03/07/88	979	05:00	BROWN Larry	CARTER Keith	FERRY IN/HABU	6.3	
07/07/88	979	09:06	BROWN Larry	CARTER Keith	HABU	3.2	
08/07/88	974	12:00	CRITTENDEN Greg	FINAN Mike	FCF	2.1	
12/07/88	974	10:00	CRITTENDEN Greg	FINAN Mike	FCF	4.3	
15/07/88	979	10:00	CRITTENDEN Greg	FINAN Mike	FCF	2.3	
16/07/88	974		BROWN Larry	CARTER Keith	HABU		A
18/07/88	974	12:10	BROWN Larry	CARTER Keith	HABU	2.3	
20/07/88	974	10:13	CRITTENDEN Greg	FINAN Mike	FCF	1.5	A
21/07/88	979	10:55	BROWN Larry	CARTER Keith	HABU	4.2	LTO
28/07/88	974	09:35	CRITTENDEN Greg	FINAN Mike	HABU	2.2	
31/07/88	979	13:00	DYCKMAN Rod	MANZI John	HABU	2.1	
02/08/88	974	09:44	CRITTENDEN Greg	FINAN Mike	HABU	2.2	
04/08/88	979	11:00	CRITTENDEN Greg	FINAN Mike	HABU	1.9	
06/08/88	979	09:30	DYCKMAN Rod	MANZI John	HABU	4.2	
12/08/88	979	09:12	DYCKMAN Rod	MANZI John	HABU/FERRY OUT		
17/08/88	974	14:50	CRITTENDEN Greg	FINAN Mike	HABU	1.1	A
23/08/88	974	11:45	SMITH Mike	SOIFER Doug	HABU	2.2	
25/08/88	974	10:40	NOLL Duane	VELTRI Tom	HABU	2	
29/08/88	974	09:30	SMITH Mike	SOIFER Doug	HABU	2.3	
31/08/88	974	13:35	NOLL Duane	VELTRI Tom	HABU	2.1	
02/09/88	974	09:20	SMITH Mike	SOIFER Doug	HABU	3.3	
07/09/88	974	09:01	NOLL Duane	VELTRI Tom	FCF	1.9	
08/09/88	974	10:01	SMITH Mike	SOIFER Doug	FCF	2.2	
12/09/88	974	09:05	NOLL Duane	VELTRI Tom	HABU	4.7	
14/09/88	974	10:36	WATKINS Don	FOWLKES Bob	CRFAM	2.2	
16/09/88	974	09:07	WATKINS Don	FOWLKES Bob	HABU	3.3	
19/09/88	974	09:30	HOUSE Dan	BOZEK Blair	FCF	4	
20/09/88	974	09:30	WATKINS Don	VELTRI Tom	FCF	2.2	
27/09/88	974	11:45	WATKINS Don	FOWLKES Bob	FCF	1.9	A
29/09/88	974	10:31	HOUSE Dan	BOZEK Blair	FCF	2.2	
04/10/88	974	10:45	WATKINS Don	FOWLKES Bob	FCF	2.1	
12/10/88	974	09:05	HOUSE Dan	BOZEK Blair	FCF	2.1	
20/10/88	974	14:00	HOUSE Dan	BOZEK Blair	FCF	2.1	
27/10/88	974	18:15	HOUSE Dan	BOZEK Blair	N-FCF	2.2	
02/11/88	974	10:02	HOUSE Dan	BOZEK Blair	FCF	2.2	
08/11/88	974	09:32	McCLEARY Tom	BERGAM Tom	FCF	2.2	
15/11/88	974	17:50	McCLEARY Tom	BERGAM Tom	N-FCF	2.3	
21/11/88	974	11:00	McCLEARY Tom	BERGAM Tom	FCF	2.2	
29/11/88	974	17:45	McCLEARY Tom	BERGAM Tom	N-FCF	2.3	
07/12/88	974	10:06	BROWN Larry	CARTER Keith	FCF	0.6	A
08/12/88	974		BROWN Larry	CARTER Keith	FCF		A
15/12/88	974	10:00	BROWN Larry	CARTER Keith	FCF	2.1	
19/12/88	974	11:00	BROWN Larry	BERGAM Tom	FCF	4	
21/12/88	974	11:01	BROWN Larry	BERGAM Tom	FCF	2.7	
04/01/89	974	11:00	NOLL Duane	MANZI John	FCF	2.1	
19/01/89	974	08:01	NOLL Duane	MANZI John	FCF	2.7	
24/01/89	974		NOLL Duane	MANZI John	FCF		A
25/01/89	974	15:02	NOLL Duane	MANZI John	FCF	2.2	
30/01/89	974	18:30	NOLL Duane	MANZI John	N-FCF	2.5	
07/02/89	974	11:00	GRZEBINIAK Steve	GREENWOOD Jim	FCF	2.1	
17/02/89	974	12:49	GRZEBINIAK Steve	GREENWOOD Jim	FCF	2.6	
22/02/89	974	12:49	GRZEBINIAK Steve	GREENWOOD Jim	N-FCF	2.2	
28/02/89	974	11:30	GRZEBINIAK Steve	GREENWOOD Jim	FCF	2.2	
10/03/89	974	11:29	CRITTENDEN Greg	BERGAM Tom	FCF	1.2	
14/03/89	974	18:50	CRITTENDEN Greg	FINAN Mike	N-FCF	2	
16/03/89	974	09:30	CRITTENDEN Greg	FINAN Mike	FCF	2	
27/03/89	974	10:30	CRITTENDEN Greg	FINAN Mike	FCF	3.9	
31/03/89	974	10:00	HOUSE Dan	BOZEK Blair	HABU	3.3	
03/04/89	974	12:21	HOUSE Dan	BERGAM Tom	FCF	1.6	
10/04/89	974	08:46	HOUSE Dan	BOZEK Blair	HABU	3.2	
12/04/89	974	14:25	HOUSE Dan	BERGAM Tom	FCF	2.2	
14/04/89	974	09:46	HOUSE Dan	BOZEK Blair	HABU	3.5	
21/04/89	974	09:30	HOUSE Dan	BOZEK Blair	HABU		C,36
09/06/89	962	07:04	McKENDREE Mac	SHELHORSE Randy	FERRY IN/HABU	6.2	
15/06/89	962	08:45	McKENDREE Mac	SHELHORSE Randy	HABU	3	A
20/06/89	962	19:51	McKENDREE Mac	SHELHORSE Randy	N-HABU	5.4	A
22/06/89	962	10:00	McKENDREE Mac	SHELHORSE Randy	FCF	2.1	
23/06/89	962	14:00	McKENDREE Mac	SHELHORSE Randy	HABU	3.2	
27/06/89	962	08:00	McKENDREE Mac	SHELHORSE Randy	HABU	4.8	
29/06/89	962	09:30	McKENDREE Mac	SHELHORSE Randy	HABU	3.4	
06/07/89	962	08:45	McKENDREE Mac	SHELHORSE Randy	HABU	3.6	
11/07/89	962	09:15	McKENDREE Mac	SHELHORSE Randy	HABU	3.7	
13/07/89	962	09:30	McKENDREE Mac	SHELHORSE Randy	HABU	3.6	
17/07/89	962	07:00	McKENDREE Mac	SHELHORSE Randy	HABU	5.4	
24/07/89	962	10:11	McKENDREE Mac	SHELHORSE Randy	HABU	3.5	
28/07/89	962	08:07	McCLEARY Thomas	GUDMUNDSON Stan	FCF	4.2	
03/08/89	962	12:00	McCLEARY Thomas	GUDMUNDSON Stan	FCF	2.2	
04/08/89	962		McCLEARY Thomas	GUDMUNDSON Stan	HABU		
09/08/89	962	09:15	McCLEARY Thomas	GUDMUNDSON Stan	HABU	3.8	
11/08/89	962	10:00	McCLEARY Thomas	GUDMUNDSON Stan	HABU	3.8	
15/08/89	962	09:05	McCLEARY Thomas	GUDMUNDSON Stan	HABU	3.7	
21/08/89	962	09:48	CRITTENDEN Greg	FINAN Mike	HABU	3.7	
23/08/89	962	15:00	CRITTENDEN Greg	FINAN Mike	N-HABU	5.3	
28/08/89	962	11:02	CRITTENDEN Greg	GUDMUNDSON Stan	FCF	3.9	
01/09/89	962	08:59	CRITTENDEN Greg	FINAN Mike	HABU	3.6	
06/09/89	962		CRITTENDEN Greg	FINAN Mike	HABU		A
18/09/89	962		WATKINS Don	FOWLKES Bob	HABU		
19/09/89	962	09:05	WATKINS Don	FOWLKES Bob	HABU	3.3	A
22/09/89	962	11:00	SMITH Mike	FOWLKES Bob	RTB FERRY	2.3	
25/09/89	962	09:10	WATKINS Don	FOWLKES Bob	HABU	3.4	
05/10/89	962	12:30	SMITH Mike	FOWLKES Bob	FCF	1.6	
06/10/89	962	12:00	WATKINS Don	FOWLKES Bob	FCF	1.5	A
23/10/89	962	10:08	HOUSE Dan	BOZEK Blair	FCF	2.3	
26/10/89	962	18:09	HOUSE Dan	BOZEK Blair	Nite-FCF	2.3	
31/10/89	962	11:30	HOUSE Dan	BOZEK Blair	FCF	2.1	
02/11/89	962	09:00	HOUSE Dan	BOZEK Blair	FCF	0.6	A
03/11/89	962	10:30	HOUSE Dan	BOZEK Blair	FCF	1.9	
06/11/89	962	09:30	HOUSE Dan	BOZEK Blair	FCF	2.2	
07/11/89	962	10:00	HOUSE Dan	SHELHORSE Randy	FCF	1.1	
14/11/89	962	11:50	GRZEBINIAK Steve	GREENWOOD Jim	FCF	2.3	
17/11/89	962	09:15	GRZEBINIAK Steve	GREENWOOD Jim	FCF	1.9	
21/11/89	962	11:30	GRZEBINIAK Steve	GREENWOOD Jim	FCF	2.2	
28/11/89	962	11:30	GRZEBINIAK Steve	WALTON Charles	HIGH SPEED TAXI		
05/12/89	962		GRZEBINIAK Steve	GREENWOOD Jim	FCF		A
06/12/89	962	10:00	GRZEBINIAK Steve	GREENWOOD Jim	FCF/CREW PROFICIENCY	0.9	
14/12/89	962	11:00	GRZEBINIAK Steve	ADRIAN David	HIGH SPEED TAXI		
18/12/89	962	08:10	GRZEBINIAK Steve	GREENWOOD Jim	FCF	2.5	
18/01/90	962	10:28	GRZEBINIAK Steve	GREENWOOD Jim	FCF	3.7	
21/01/90	962	05:00	GRZEBINIAK Steve	GREENWOOD Jim	FERRY OUT		

THE HABU'S DEAD, LONG LIVE THE HABU

Appendix 1

A-12, YF-12 and SR-71 Check Flights

Check Ride Number	Category	Rank	Name
001	Plt	ADP	Lou Schalk
000	VIP	ADP	Kelly Johnson
002	Plt	ADP	Bill Park
003	Plt	ADP	Jim Eastham
004	Plt	ADP	Bob Gilliland
005	Plt	CIA	William L Skliar
006	Plt	CIA	Kenneth S Collins
007	Plt	CIA	Walter L Ray
008	Plt	CIA	Dennis B Sullivan
009	Plt	CIA	Alonzo J Walter
010	Eng	ADP	Larry Edgar
011	Eng	ADP	Hank Stockham
012	Eng	ADP	Torrey Larsen
013	Plt	ADP	Darrell Greenamyer
014	FCO	Hughes	Tony Byland
015	FCO	Hughes	Ray Scalise
016	Eng	ADP	R L Dick Miller
017	Plt	ADP	Art Peterson
018	FCO	Hughes	George Parsons
019	Plt	ADP	Bill Weaver
020	RSO	ADP	Jim Zwayer
021	FCO	Hughes	John Archer
022	Eng	ADP	Keith Beswick
023	RSO	ADP	George Andre
024	RSO	ADP	Steven A Belgeau
025	RSO	ADP	Ray Torick
026	Eng	ADP	Larry Bohanan
027	Eng	ADP	Glen Fulkerson
028	Plt	CIA	Jack J Layton
029	Plt	CIA	Mele Vojvodich
030	Plt	CIA	Jack C Weeks
031	RSO	ADP	Kenneth E Moeller
032	VIP	ADP	Rus Daniell
033	Plt	CIA	Francis J Murray
034	Plt	CIA	Russell J Scott
101	Plt	Col	Robert L Stephens
102	FCO	Lt Col	Daniel Andre
103	FCO	Maj	Noel T Warner
104	FCO	Capt	James P Cooney
105	Plt	Maj	Walter F Daniel
106	FCO	Capt	Sammel M Ursini
107	RSO	Maj	Kenneth D Hurley
108	Plt	Maj	Charles C Bock
109	Plt	Col	Vern Henderson
110	Plt	Lt Col	Jacqres G Beezley
111	Plt	Col	H A Templeton
112	Plt	Maj	Mervin L Evenson
113	Plt	Maj	Allen L Hichew
114	RSO	Capt	Tom W Schmittou
115	Plt	Maj	Robert G Sowers
116	RSO	Capt	Richard E Sheffield
117	RSO	Capt	Cosimo B Mallozzi
118	Plt	Lt Col	Ray Haupt
119	RSO	Lt Col	Cecil H Braeden
120	RSO	Capt	James W Fagg
121	RSO	Maj	William R Payne
122	Plt	Col	Frenchy D Bennett
123	VIP	Brig Gen	H B Manson
124	Plt	Lt Col	Joe Rogers
125		Lt Col	Ralph Richardson
126	Plt	Col	Robert J Holbury
127	Plt	Col	Hugh C Slater
128	Plt	Maj	Harold E Burgeson
129	Plt	Lt Col	B S Barrett
130	Plt	Lt Col	Roland L Perkim
131	RSO	Lt Col	Norman S Drake
132	Plt	Maj	Ben Bowles
133	RSO	Lt Col	Harold C Peterson
134	Plt	Maj	William J Campbell
135	RSO	Capt	Albert N Pennington
136	Plt	Col	Douglas T Nelson
137	RSO	Lt Col	Russel L Lewis
138	Plt	Maj	Patrick J Halloran
139	RSO	Capt	Mortimer J Jarvis
140	RSO	Capt	David P Dempster
141	Plt	Maj	Buddy L Brown
142	RSO	Capt	David J Jensen
143	Plt	Capt	Charles W Collins
144	RSO	Capt	Jean C Seagroves
145	Plt	Maj	John H Storrie
146	Plt	Maj	Jack Kennon
147	Plt	Capt	Franklin D Shelton
148	RSO	Capt	Lawrence L Boggess
149	Plt	Lt Col	William L Skliar
150	Plt	Maj	Jerome F O'Malley
151	RSO	Capt	Edward D Payne
152	Plt	Maj	Donald A Walbrecht
153	RSO	Capt	Phillip G Loignon
154	Plt	Capt	Earle M Boone
155	RSO	Capt	Dewain C Vick
156	Staf	Col	Russell K Weller
157	Plt	Maj	James L Watkins
158	Plt	Maj	Anthony P Bevacqua
159	Staf	Col	William P Hayes
160	RSO	Capt	Robert J Roetcisoender
161	RSO	Maj	William C Keller
162	RSO	Maj	Donald E Mathers

Check Ride Number	Category	Rank	Name
163	Plt	Capt	Robert C Spencer
164	Plt	Col	Harold E Confer
165	RSO	Capt	Clyde L Shoemaker
166	Plt	Maj	Brian K McCallom
167		Lt Col	James C Schever
168	RSO	Maj	Jerald L Crew
169	Plt	Maj	Larry S Devall
170	RSO	Capt	Ruel K Branham
171	RSO	Maj	Thomas A Casey
172	Plt	Maj	Roy L St Martin
173	RSO	Capt	Robert M Locke
174	Plt	Maj	George M Bull
175	RSO	Capt	John F Carnochan
176	Staf	Col	John B Boynton
177	Plt	Maj	Robert M Powell
178	RSO	Maj	Charles J McNeer
179	Plt	Maj	Charles E Daubs
180	Eng	Maj	William A Lusby
181	Eng	Civ	Robert W Sudderth
182	RSO	Capt	William J Kendrick
183	Staf	Col	Charles F Minter Sr
184	Eng	Civ	Richard Abrams
185	Plt	Capt	Bobby L Campbell
186	VIP	Gen	Bruce Holloway (CINC)
187	VIP	Lt Gen	Arthur C Agan
188	VIP	Lt Gen	William K Martin
189	Plt	Maj	Gabriel A Kardong
190	VIP	Lt Gen	Jack J Catton (15th AF/CC)
191	RSO	Capt	Gary Heidlebauch
192	RSO	Maj	Jon P Kraus
193	Plt	Maj	Lothar J Maier
194	Plt	Maj	William E Lawson III
195	RSO	Maj	James A Kogler
196	RSO	Maj	Gary L Coleman
197	RSO	Maj	Gilbert Martinez
198	RSO	Lt Col	Harold E Chapman
199	Plt	Capt	David E Fruehauf
200	VIP	Col	Benjamin N Bellis
201	RSO	Capt	Allen R Payne
202	Plt	Maj	James W Hudson
203	RSO	Capt	Norbet L Budzinske
204	RSO	Maj	Donn A Byrnes
205	RSO	Maj	Bruce Hartman
206	RSO	Maj	R W Weaver Jr
207	Plt	Lt Col	Harlon A Hain
208	RSO	Maj	Don Rhude
209	Plt	Maj	Richard C Gerard
210	Plt	Maj	Thomas B Estes
211	RSO	Maj	Charles G McLean
212	RSO	Maj	Ken G Moeller
213	Plt	Lt Col	Kenneth S Collins
214	Plt	Maj	James H Shelton Jr
215	Plt	Capt	Reverdy J Allender
216		Lt Col	Fred Trost
217	Plt	Lt Col	Dennis B Sullivan
218	Plt	Lt Col	Mel Vojvodich
219	Plt	Capt	Bruce E Wilcox
220	Plt	Maj	E L Payne (EAFB)
221	VIP	Senator	Barry Goldwater
222	Staf	Lt Col	Ronald J Layton
223	Staf	Col	James E Anderson
224	VIP	Brig Gen	Alton Slay
225	VIP	Col	William R Payne
226	Plt	Maj	Darrel W Cobb
227	RSO	Capt	Myron L Gantt
228	Plt	NASA	Fitzhugh L Fulton Jr
229	Plt	Maj	Thomas S Pugh
230	Plt	NASA	Donald L Mallick
231	RSO	Maj	Ronnie C Rice
232	Plt	Capt	Dennis K Bush
233	Plt	Capt	Randolph B Hertzog
234	Plt	Col	D B Sullivan
235	RSO	Maj	Ronald L Selberg
236	Staf	Lt Col	Roy W Owen Jr
237	RSO	Maj	Billy A Curtis
238	Plt	Maj	George H Sewell Jr
239	RSO	Capt	Reginald T Blackwell
240	VIP	Lt Gen	P K Carlton 15th AF/CC
241	RSO	Capt	George T Morgan
242	Plt	Capt	Robert J Cunningham
243	RSO	NASA	Victor W Horton
244	VIP	Col	Ross Spinkle
245	Plt	Capt	Monty T Judkin
246	VIP	Brig Gen	Lukeman
247	Plt	Maj	Caroll D Gunther
248	RSO	NASA	William R Young
249	RSO	Capt	Thomas R Allocca
250	Staf	Bri Gen	Edgar S Harris Jr
251	VIP	Congress-man	Robert Price
252	Plt	Capt	Carl A Haller
253	VIP	Maj Gen	Salvador E Felices
254			Cancelled
255	Plt	Maj	A H Bledsoe
256	RSO	Maj	Cletius C Rogers
257	Plt	Maj	James V Sullivan
258	RSO	Capt	Noel F Widdifield
259	RSO	Capt	John T Fuller
260	Plt	Capt	Leland B Ransom III
261	RSO	Maj	Mark H Gersten
262	Plt	Capt	Harold B Adams
263	RSO	Capt	William C Machorek
264	Plt	Capt	Robert C Helt
265	RSO	Capt	Larry A Elliott
266	Plt	Capt	Eldon W Joersz
267	Plt	Capt	James F Wilson
268	VIP	Maj Gen	George W McLaughlin
269	RSO	Capt	Bruce S Douglass
270	VIP	Sec of AF	John L McLucas

Check Ride Number	Category	Rank	Name
271	VIP	Lt Gen	William F Pitts (15th AF/CC)
272	VIP	Brig Gen	Don D Pittman (14th AD/CC)
273	Plt	Capt	Maury Rosenberg
274	RSO	Capt	Donald C Bulloch
275	VIP	Lt Col	Hal Rupard
276	VIP	Lt Col	Jackie G Reed
277	Plt	Lt Col/ AFLC	Tom Smith
278	Staf	Lt Col	Raphael S Samay
279	Plt	Capt	Joseph C Kinego
280	RSO	Capt	Roger L Jacks
281	VIP	Maj Gen	Ray B Sitton
282	VIP	Hon	Malcom R Currie
283	VIP	Hon	Walter B Laberge
284	Plt	Capt	Alan B Cirino
285	RSO	Capt	Bruce L Liebman
286	Plt	Capt	Justin J Murphy
287	VIP	Gen	Albert L Melton
288	RSO	Maj	John A Billingsley
289	VIP	Lt Gen	James M Keck (Vice CINC)
290	VIP	Maj Gen	Billy J Ellis
291	Plt	Capt	Richard H Graham
292	RSO	Capt	Donald R Emmons
293	VIP	Maj Gen	Herbert J Gavin
294	Plt	Capt	Thomas M Alison
295	Plt	Maj/ AFLC	Robert L Riedenauer
296	RSO	Maj/ AFLC	William J Frazier
297	RSO	Maj	Joseph T Vida
298	VIP	Col	Merlyn H Dethlefsen
299	VIP	Lt Gen	Bryan M Shotts (15th AF/CC)
300	VIP	Lt Gen	Andrew B Anderson Jr
301	VIP	Maj Gen	John W Burkhart
302	Staf	Col	Robert D Beckel
303	VIP	Maj Gen	Otis Moore
304	Staf	Col	Richard J Bower
305	Plt	Capt	William G Gilmore
306	Plt	Maj	Robert W Crowder
307	RSO	Capt	John G Morgan
308	VIP	Gen	Russ E Dougherty (CINC)
309	Plt	Capt	Adelbert W Carpenter
310	VIP	Lt Gen	John W Roberts
311	RSO	Capt	John E Murphy
312	VIP	Brig Gen	Gerald E Cooke
313	VIP	Mr	James W Plummer
314	RSO	Capt	William C Keller
315	VIP	Lt Gen	Robert E Hails
316	Staf	Col	Lyman M Kidder
317	VIP	Hon	James B Connor
318	Plt	Maj	John J Veth
319	Plt	Maj	William G Groninger
320	RSO	Capt	Charles T Sober Jr
321	Plt	Maj	Bredette Thomas
322	VIP	Brig Gen	Bill V Brown (14th AD/CC)
323	RSO	Capt	Jay Reid
324	VIP	Maj Gen	Earl G Peck
325	Staf	Col	John W Fenimore
326	Plt	Capt	Thomas J Keck
327	RSO	Capt	Timothy J Shaw
328	Plt	NASA	John Manke
329	Plt	NASA	Bill Dana
330	Plt	NASA	Gary E Krier
331	Plt	NASA	Einar K Enevoldson
332	Plt	NASA	Thomas C McMurtry
333	Plt	Maj	David M Peters
334	RSO	Capt	Michael L Stockton
335	VIP	Col	Ted H Shadburn
336	RSO	Capt	Edgar J Bethart Jr
337	Plt	Maj	Lee M Shelton III
338	Staf	Col	Andrew G Terry
339	Staf	Col	David G Young
340	VIP	Lt Gen	Robert C Mathis
341	RSO	Maj	Barry C MacKean
342	Plt	Lt Col/ AFLC	Calvin F Jewett
343	Plt	Capt	Richard A Young
344			Cancelled
345	RSO	Capt	Russell L Szczepanik
346	VIP	Reverend	Theodore M Hesburgh
347	VIP	Lt Gen	James P Mullins (15th AF/CC)
348	Plt	NASA	Stephen D Ishmael
349	Plt	NASA	Michael R Swann
350	VIP	Bri Gen	John A Brashear (14th AD/CC)
351	Plt	Capt	Calvin J Augustin
352	RSO	Maj	Frank K Kelly
353	VIP	Col	Joseph S Stanton
354	VIP	Senator	Howard W Cannon
355	Plt	Capt	Gilbert M Bertelson
356	RSO	Capt	Frank W Stampf
357	VIP	Civ	Frank A Fishburne
358	Plt	Capt	Richard W Judson
359			Cancelled
360	VIP	Lt Gen	Lloyd R Leavitt Jr
361	Plt	Maj	Nevin N Cunningham
362	RSO	Capt	Gene R Quist
363			Cancelled
364	Plt	Capt	Dennis R Berg
365	RSO	Maj/ AFLC	Bill Flanagan
366	VIP	Civ	Jim Hartz
367	RSO	Capt	E D McKim
368	Plt	Maj	Gerald T Glasser

Check Ride Number	Category	Rank	Name
369			Cancelled
370	RSO	Capt	David M Hornbaker
371	VIP	Civ	Robert R Ropelewske
372	Plt	Capt	Richard S McCrary
373	RSO	Capt	David A Lawrence
374	Plt	Maj	Bernard J Smith
375	VIP	Maj Gen	John T Chain Jr
376	RSO	Maj	Dennis W Whalen
377	VIP	Brig Gen	Monroe W Hatch (14th AD/CC)
378	Plt	Capt	Gary I Luloff
379	VIP	Gen	Bennie L Davis (CINC)
380	RSO	Capt	Robert L Coats
381	VIP	Lt Gen	John J Murphy
382	VIP	Congress-man	Robert K Dornan
383	Plt	Maj	Leslie R Dyer
384	RSO	Capt	Daniel Greenwood
385	VIP	Lt Gen	George D Miller (Vice CINC)
386	VIP	Maj Gen	Louis C Buckman (SAC/DO)
387	Staf	Col	Lonnie L Liss
388	Plt	Capt	William Burk
389	Plt	Maj/ AFLC	Thomas V Tilden
390	VIP	Gen	Lew Allen (CS/Air Force)
391	RSO	Capt	Thomas J Henichek
392	VIP	Brig Gen	Jesse S Hocker (14th AD/CC)
393	Plt	Capt	James M Jiggins
394	RSO	Capt	Joseph J McCue
395	VIP	Sec of AF	Edward 'Pete' Aldridge
396	VIP	Lt Gen	Andrew P Iosue
397	Plt	Maj	Robert F Behler
398	RSO	Capt	Ronald D Tabor
399	VIP	Congress-man	'Bill' C W Young
400	Plt	Maj	Lionel P Boudreax
401	RSO	Capt	Walter F Newgreen
402	VIP	Lt Gen	Lawrence A Skantze
403	Plt	Maj	Joseph E Matthews
404	RSO	Capt	Edward W Ross
405	VIP	Brig Gen	Charles Yeager
406	RSO	Capt	Douglas C Osterheld
407	Staf	Col	George V Freese
408	Staf	Col	David H Pinsky
409	Plt	Capt	Jack E Madison
410	VIP	Lt Gen	James E Light (15th AF/CC)
411	RSO	Maj	William D Orcutt
412	Plt	Capt	Ed Yeilding
413	RSO	Capt	Stephen M Lee
414	Plt	Maj	Brian Shul
415	RSO	Maj	Walter L Watson
416	Plt	Capt	Duane W Deal
417	RSO	Capt	Thomas F Veltri
418	Plt	Maj	Duane M Noll
419	RSO	Capt	Charles A Morgan
420	VIP	Congress-man	Bob Stump
421	Plt	Maj	William R Dyckman
422	RSO	Maj	Thomas E Bergam
423	Staf	Brig Gen	John Farrington (14th AD/CC)
424	Plt	Maj	Michael L Smith
425	RSO	Capt	Douglas B Soifer
426	Staf	Col	Robert B McConnell
427	Staf	Maj Gen	Alexander Davidson (AF/XO)
428	RSO	Maj	Phillip L Soucy
429	VIP	Congress-man	Beverly Byron
430	Plt	Maj	Dan E House
431	RSO	Capt	Blair L Bozek
432	VIP	Gen	Larry D Welch (CINC)
433	Plt	Maj	Thomas J Danielson
434	VIP	Congress-man	Robert E Badham
435	RSO	Maj	Stanley J Gudmundson
436	Plt	Maj	Terry D Pappas
437	RSO	Capt	John D Manzi
438	Staf	Col	James Sarvada
439	VIP	Maj Gen	Hansford T Johnson SAC/DO
440	Plt	Maj	Warren C Mckendree
441	RSO	Maj	Randy F Shelhorse
442	VIP	Congress-man	Larry J Hopkins
443	Plt	Maj	Larry Brown
444	RSO	Maj	Keith E Carter
445	Plt	Capt	Steven Grzebiniak
446	RSO	Capt	James F Greenwood
447	Plt	Maj	Thomas R McCleary
448	RSO	Capt	Hunter W Vardaman
449	VIP	Lt Gen	Kenneth L Peek (Vice CINC)
450	Staf	Brig Gen	Howell M Estes (14th AD/C)
451	Staf	Col	Donald R Schreiber
452	Plt	Capt	Gregory N Crittenden
453	RSO	Maj/ AFLC	Tom Fuhrman
454	RSO	Maj	Michael J Finan
455	Plt	Maj	Donald T Watkins
456	RSO	Capt	Robert E Fowlkes
457	Plt	Capt	Ben Snyder
458	RSO	Capt	Briggs Shade
459	Staf	Brig Gen	Kenneth F Keller (14th AD/CC)

Check Ride Number	Category	Rank	Name
460	VIP	Lt Gen	Ellie G Shuler Jr (8AF/CC)
461			Cancelled
462	Plt	Maj/AFLC	Jim Halsell
463	Staf	Maj Gen	John L Borling
464	Plt	NASA	Roger Smith
465	FE	NASA	Marta Bohn-Meyer
466	FE	NASA	Robert E Meyer

Note the jump in check ride numbers from 034 to 101. This is due to the allocation of numbers 000 to 100 to the Oxcart programme, which were not taken up prior to its termination. The Senior Crown programme was allocated the numbers 101 onwards.

Appendix 2

Typical flight log of an early SR-71 Pilot†

Date	Duration	Serial No	Date	Duration	Serial No	Date	Duration	Serial No
23 Sept 66	2.00	957	8 June 67	0.40	A	24 Jan 68	4.25	980
28 Sept 66	2.40	957	13 June 67	3.55	A	6 Feb 68	4.25	980
30 Sept 66	3.50	957	19 June 67	3.10	A	28 Feb 68	4.50	978
6 Oct 66	3.25	957 (N)	22 June 67	4.30	A	7 Mar 68	1.45	964
14 Oct 66	3.05	957	26 June 67	2.50	A	11 Mar 68	1.45	956 (N)
21 Oct 66	0.55	958	3 July 67	2.50	A	15 Mar 68	3.20	980
28 Oct 66	3.00	958 (N)	11 July 67	3.10	A	21 Mar 68	1.00	973
1 Nov 66	2.55	958	17 July 67	2.10	A	1 Apr 68	3.25	969
4 Nov 66	0.45	958	28 July 67	2.30	B	9 Apr 68	5.05	968
7 Nov 66	0.45	958	14 Aug 67	2.30	B	26 Apr 68	5.00	970
7 Nov 66	4.40	958 (N)	16 Aug 67	3.05	A	2 May 68	4.25	972
10 Nov 66	4.45	A *	18 Aug 67	3.00	A	6 May 68	2.30	956 (N)
18 Nov 66	4.30	A (N)	22 Aug 67	3.05	971	8 May 68	0.50	956 (N)
21 Nov 66	Became a/c Comm		30 Aug 67	1.20	979 (D)	Deployed in tanker to Kadena		
7 Dec 66	1.30	A (N)	6 Sept 67	4.10	974 (N)	19 May 68	1.40	976
5 Jan 67	1.10	A	12 Sept 67	1.55	979	25 May 68	5.15	978 (O)
25 Jan 67	2.45	A	20 Sept 67	2.40	976	26 May 68	1.50	978
3 Feb 67	1.10	A	29 Sept 67	2.40	957	8 June 68	2.20	978
23 Feb 67	4.20	A	2 Oct 67	6.10	963	18 June 68	4.05	974 (O)
28 Feb 67	2.50	A	9 Oct 67	1.45	965 (N)	30 June 68	5.20	978 (O)
15 Mar 67	3.00	A	12 Oct 67	2.40	956	8 July 68	1.30	976
17 Mar 67	2.20	A	17 Oct 67	3.05	958	15 July 68	1.35	974
21 Mar 67	3.05	A	23 Oct 67	4.25	973	23 July 68	5.05	978 (O)
27 Mar 67	3.05	A	2 Nov 67	3.15	975	1 Aug 68	2.30	978
3 Apr 67	6.25	A	7 Nov 67	1.35	963	Redeployed to USA in tanker		
24 Apr 67	2.05	B	24 Nov 67	2.35	973	8 Aug 68	4.50	971
28 Apr 67	3.05	A	30 Nov 67	3.25	969	22 Aug 68	1.20	971
1 May 67	1.30	A	12 Dec 67	2.40	970	29 Aug 68	1.15	973
4 May 67	2.50	A	15 Dec 67	1.15	976	12 Sept 68	4.30	964
11 May 67	4.30	A	27 Dec 67	4.25	978	16 Sept 68	4.30	964
18 May 67	4.35	A	5 Jan 68	2.50	980	25 Sept 68	5.10	959 (M)
24 May 67	2.45	A	9 Jan 68	1.45	980			
6 June 67	4.45	956	12 Jan 68	2.45	970	27 Sept 73	2.55	956

Total SR-71 Flight Time 287 Hours 25 minutes

B = SR-71 B A = SR-71 A N = Night Sortie * = Check Ride D = Delivery O = Operational flight (all of these were conducted over North Vietnam) † = Maj Don Walbrecht
Don Walbrecht accumulated 3300 hrs in 12 years of AF flying prior to joining *Senior Crown*.

Appendix 3 – A-12

Tail No: LAC No:	First Flt Date: Last Flt Date:	No. of Flts Total Hrs:	Remarks:
60-6924 121	26 April 1962 ?	322 Flts 418.2 hrs	Prototype. Towed from Plant 42, Palmdale storage area to display area.
60-6925 122	? ?	161 Flts 177.9 hrs	Used for ground tests prior to first flight. Transported from Plant 42, Palmdale to USS *Intrepid*, NY, for display. Due to vandalism the aircraft is to be repaired by Lockheed and moved for display at CIA HQ Langley, VA.
60-6926 123	? 24 May 1963	79 Flts 135.3 hrs	Second A-12 to fly. Lost during training/test flight after aircraft stalled due to inaccurate data being displayed to pilot. Pilot Ken Collins ejected safely.
60-6027 124	? ?	614 Flts 1076.4 hrs	Only two-seat pilot trainer To be trucked to California Museum of Science, Los Angeles for display.
60-6928 125	? 5 Jan 1967	202 Flts 334.9 hrs	Lost during training/test flight. Pilot Walter L Ray successfully ejected but was killed after he failed to separate from his ejection seat.
60-6929 126	? 28 Dec 1967	105 Flts 169.2 hrs	Lost seconds after take-off from Groom Dry Lake following incorrect installation of SAS. Pilot Mel Vojvodich ejected safely.
60-2930 127	? ?	258 Flts 499.2 hrs	Deployed to Kadena from 24 May 1967 until June 1968 in support of operation *Black Shield*. Was stored at Plant 42, Palmdale. Trucked to Space and Rocket Center Museum, Huntsville AL, for display.
60-2931 128	? ?	232 Flts 453.0 hrs	Was stored at Plant 42, Palmdale. Transported by C-5 on 27 October 1991 to Minneapolis Air National Guard for display.
60-6932 129	? 5 June 1968	268 Flts 409.9 hrs	Deployed to Kadena from 26 May 1967, in support of operation *Black Shield*. Lost off the Philippine Islands during an FCF prior to its scheduled return to USA. Pilot Jack Weeks was killed.
60-6933 130	27 Nov 1963 August 1965	217 Flts 406.3 hrs	Was stored at Plant 42, Palmdale. Trucked to San Diego Aerospace Museum, CA, for display.
60-6937 131	? ?	177 Flts 345.8 hrs	Deployed to Kadena from 22 May 1967 until June 1968, in support of operation *Black Shield*. Was stored at Plant 42, Palmdal. Disposition to be determined.
60-6938 132	? ?	197 Flts 369.9 hrs	Was stored at Plant 42, Palmdale. Trucked to USS *Alabama*, located at Mobile, AL, for display.
60-6939 133	? 9 July 1964	10 Flts 8.3 hrs	Lost whilst on approach into Groom Dry Lake during test flight due to complete hydraulic failure. Pilot Lockheed Test Pilot Bill Park ejected safely.
60-6940 134	? ?	80 Flts 123.9 hrs	One of two A-12s converted for project *Tagboard* – the carriage of D-21 drones. Trucked to the Museum of Flight, Seattle, WA, for display, where it is the sole surviving example of its type.

Tail No: LAC No:	First Flt Date: Last Flt Date:	No. of Flts Total Hrs:	Remarks:
60-6941 135	? 30 July 1966	95 Flts 152.7 hrs	One of two A-12s converted for project *Tagboard* – the carriage of D-21 drones. Lost during tests off the coast of California. Pilot Bill Park and Launch Control Engineer Ray Torick, both Lockheed employees ejected safely, however Ray Torick tragically drowned in the subsequent feet-wet landing.

Appendix 3A – YF-12A

Tail No: LAC No:	First Flt Date: Last Flt Date:	First Crew Total Hrs:	Remarks:
60-6934 1001	8 Aug 1963 14 Aug 1966 (as YF-12)	Jim Eastham 180.9 hrs	Prototype YF-12 was used by Col Robert L Stephens and his FCO Lt Col Daniel Andre to establish a new speed and altitude record, however due to technical problems, these records were obtained in 936. Aircraft was transformed into SR-71C serial 64-17981.
60-6935 1002	26 Nov 1963 7 Nov 1979	Lou Schalk 534.7 hrs	After initial YF-12 test programme the aircraft was placed in storage at Edwards. It was later made available to NASA and flew again on 11 December 1969. On completion of this programme it was delivered to Wright-Patterson Air Force museum, where it remains as the sole YF-12.
60-6936 1003	13 March 1964 24 July 1971	Bob Gilliland 439.8 hrs	This aircraft was used to obtain all world absolute speed and altitude records of 1 May 1965. After a brief period of retirement the aircraft was made available to a joint Air Force, NASA and ADP test programme but was lost on 24 June 1971. Lt Col Jack Layton and Maj Billy Curtis ejected safely.

Appendix 3B – SR-71

USAF No: LADC No:	First Flt Date: Last Flt Date:	Crew First Flt: Total Flt Time:	Remarks:
17950 2001	23 Dec 1964 10 Jan 1967	Bob Gilliland: ?	Lost during anti-skid brake system evaluation at Edwards AFB. Pilot Art Peterson survived.
17951 2002	5 March 1965 22 Dec 1978	Gilliland/Zwayer 796.7 hrs	Operated by NASA from 16 July 1971 and known as YF-12C, serialled 60-6937. Removed from Palmdale storage and trucked to Pima Museum, Tucson, AZ for display.
17952 2003	24 March 1965 25 Jan 1966	? ?	Lost during test flight from Edwards AFB. Pilot Bill Weaver survived, RSO Jim Zwayer killed, incident occurred near Tucumcari, NM.
17953 2004	4 June 1965 18 Dec 1969	Weaver/Andre ?	Lost during test flight from Edwards AFB. Pilot Lt Col Joe Rogers, RSO Lt Col Gary Heidelbaugh ejected safely, incident occurred near Shoshone, CA.
17954 2005	20 July 1965 11 April 1969	Weaver/Andre ?	Lost on runway at Edwards AFB during take-off. Pilot Lt Col Bill Skliar, RSO Maj Noel Warner escaped without injury.

USAF No: LADC No:	First Flt Date: Last Flt Date:	Crew First Flt: Total Flt Time:	Remarks:
17955 2006	17 Aug 1965 24 Jan 1985	Weaver/Andre ?	Operated extensively by AFLC from Plant 42, Palmdale as the dedicated SR-71 test aircraft. This aircraft is on display at Edwards AFB, CA.
17956 2007	18 Nov 1965 Still Flying	Gilliland/Belgau 3760.0 hrs	One of two SR-71B two-seat pilot trainers. It is currently on loan to NASA at the Ames Research Center Hugh L Dryden Flight Research Facility, Edwards, CA. Renumbered NASA 831.
17957 2008	18 Dec 1965 11 Jan 1968	Gilliland/Eastham ?	One of two SR-71B two-seat pilot trainers. It was lost following fuel cavitation whilst on approach to Beale AFB. IP Lt Col Robert G Sowers, Student Capt, David E Fruehauf ejected safely.
17958 2009	15 Dec 1965 23 Feb 1990	Weaver/Andre 2288.9 hrs	Used on 27/28 July 1979 by Capt Eldon W Joersz and RSO Maj George T Morgan Jr to establish speed run over 15/25 kilometre course of 2193.167 mph. Flown to Robbins AFB, GA for display.
17959 2010	19 Jan 1966 29 Oct 1976	Weaver/Andre 866.1 hrs	Underwent 'Big Tail' modification to increase and enhance sensor capacity/capability. Trucked to Air Force Armament, Eglin AFB, FL, for display.
17960 2011	9 Feb 1966 27 Feb 1990	Weaver/Andre 2669.6 hrs	This aircraft has flown 342 combat missions, more than any other SR-71. Flown to Castle AFB, CA, for display.
17961 2012	13 April 1966 2 Feb 1977	Weaver/Andre 1601.0 hrs	This aircraft was delivered to Chicago, IL for display
17962 2013	29 April 1966 14 Feb 1990	Weaver/Belgau 2835.9 hrs	Although no funds made available for upkeep, this is one of three aircraft in storage at Site 2, Palmdale, and still owned by the USAF.
17963 2014	9 June 1966 28 Oct 1976	Weaver/Belgau 1604.4 hrs	Towed to current display area at Beale AFB, CA.
17964 2015	11 May 1966 20 March 1990	Weaver/Belgau 3373.1 hrs	Flown to Offutt AFB, NE, for display.
17965 2016	10 June 1966 25 Oct 1976	Weaver/Moeller ?	Lost during night training sortie, following INS platform failure. Pilot St Martin, RSO Carnochan ejected safely. Incident occurred near Lovelock, NV.
17966 2017	1 July 1966 13 April 1967	Gilliland/Belgau ?	Lost after night refuellinig, subsonic high-speed stall. Pilot Boone and RSO Sheffield both ejected safely. Incident occurred near Las Vegas, NM
17967 2018	3 Aug 1966 14 Feb 1990	Weaver/Andre 236.8 hrs	Although no funds made available for upkeep, this is one of three aircraft in storage at Site 2, Palmdale, and is still owned by the USAF.
17968 2019	3 Aug 1966 12 Feb 1990	Weaver/Andre 2279.0 hrs	Although no funds made available for up keep, this is one of three aircraft in storage at Site 2, Palmdale, and is still owned by the USAF.
17969 2020	18 Oct 1966 10 May 1970	Weaver/Belgau ?	Lost after refuelling, subsonic high-speed stall. Pilot Lawson, RSO Martinez ejected safely. Incident occurred near Korat RTAFB.
17970 2021	21 Oct 1966 17 June 1970	Weaver/Belgau ?	Lost following mid-air collision between KC-135Q tanker. Tanker able to limp back to Beale AFB. Pilot Buddy Brown, RSO Mort Jarvis both ejected safely. Incident occurred 20 miles east of EL Paso NM.

USAF No: LADC No:	First Flt Date: Last Flt Date:	Crew First Flt: Total Flt Time:	Remarks:
17971 2022	17 Nov 1966 Still Flying	Weaver/Moeller 3512.5 hrs	One of two SR-71As loaned to NASA and flown from the Ames Research Center Hugh L Dryden Flight Research Facility, Edwards. Renumbered NASA 832.
17972 2023	12 Dec 1966 6 March 1990	Weaver/Belgau 2801.1 hrs	Flown on 1 Sep 1974 Maj James Sullivan, RSO Maj Noel Widdifield, from New York to London in record time of 1 hr 54 min 56.4 sec. Flown on 6 March 1990 by Lt Col Ed Yeilding RSO Lt Col Joseph T Vida from Los Angeles to Washington DC in 1 hr 4 min 20 sec, West to East coast in 1 hr 7 min 54 sec. It is now on display at the Smithsonian Institute, Dulles Airport.
17973 2024	8 Feb 1967 21 July 1987	Weaver/Greenamyer 1729.9 hrs	Damaged whilst being demonstrated at the RAF Mildenhall display May 1987 by Maj Jim Jiggens. Aircraft was towed to its display site at Palmdale Airport.
17974 2025	16 Feb 1967 21 April 1989	Weaver/Belgau ?	One of three aircraft used on the first operational deployment to Kadena AB, Okinawa. Lost in 1989 whilst out-bound from Kadena on an ops sortie following engine explosion and complete hydraulic failure. Pilot Maj Dan E House, RSO Capt Blair L Bozek both ejected safely.
17975 2026	13 April 1967 28 Feb 1990	Greenamyer/Belgau 2854.0 hrs	Flown from Beale AFB to March AFB, where it is on display.
17976 2027	? May 1967 27 March 1990	Gilliland/Belgau 2985.7 hrs	One of three aircraft used on the first operational deployment to Kadena AB, Okinawa. 976 was flown by Maj Jerome F O'Malley and RSO, Capt Edward D Payne on 9 March 1968, on the first-ever SR-71 operational sortie. Flown to the Air Force Museum at Wright-Patterson AFB.
17977 2028	6 Jan 1967 10 Oct 1968	Gilliland/Greenamyer ?	Lost at the end of the runway of Beale AFB, following a wheel explosion and runway abort. Pilot Maj Gabriel A Kardong rode the aircraft to a standstill, RSO Capt James A Kogler ejected – both survived.
17978 2029	5 July 1967 20 July 1972	Weaver/Belgau ?	One of three aircraft used on the first operational deployment to Kadena AB, Okinawa. Lost four years later after a landing incident at Kadena AB, Okinawa. Pilot Capt Dennis K Bush, RSO Jimmy Fagg, both escaped unhurt.
17979 2030	10 Aug 1967 6 March 1990	Greenamyer/Belgau 3321.7 hrs	This aircraft flew the first three of nine sorties from the eastern seaboard of the USA to the Middle East and back, during the 1973, Yom Kippur War. The aircraft was flown to Lackland AFB, TX, for display.
17980 2031	25 Sep 1967 5 Feb 1990	Gilliland/Belgau 2255.6 hrs	One of two SR-71As loaned to NASA and flown from the Ames Research Center, Hugh L Dryden Flight Research Facility, Edwards CA. Renumbered NASA 844.
17981 2000	14 March 1969 11 April 1976	Gilliland/Belgau 556.4 hrs*	Designated SR-71C, this hybrid consists of the forward fuselage from a static test specimen matted to the wing and rear section of YF-12A, 60-6934. It was trucked to Hill AFB, Utah, for display.

* This figure does not include 180.9 hrs accumulated on the aircraft as YF-12A serial 60-6934.

Appendix 4

Commanders and Awards

9th STRATEGIC RECONNAISSANCE WING COMMANDERS

NAME	FROM	TO
Col Douglas T Nelson	Jan 1966	Dec 1966
Col William R Hayes	Jan 1967	Jun 1969
Col Charles E Minter	Jun 1969	Jun 1970
Col Harold E Confer	Jul 1970	May 1972
Col Jerome F O'Malley	May 1972	May 1973
Col Patrick J Halloran	May 1973	Jun 1975
Col John H Storrie	Jul 1975	Sep 1977
Col Lyman M Kidder	Sep 1977	Jan 1979
Col Dale Shelton	Feb 1979	Jul 1980
Col David Young	Jul 1980	Jul 1982
Col Thomas S Pugh	Jul 1982	Jul 1983
Col Hector Freese	Aug 1983	Jan 1985
Col David H Pinsky	Jan 1985	Jul 1987
Col Richard H Graham	Jul 1987	Nov 1988
Col James Savarda	Dec 1988	Jun 1990
Col Thomas J Keck	Jun 1990	Nov 1991
Col Richard Young	Nov 1991	*1

9th SRW VICE WING COMMANDERS

NAME	FROM	TO
Col Marvin L Speer	Jan 1966	Dec 1966
Col Charles F Minter	Dec 1966	Jun 1969
Col Harold E Confer	Jun 1969	Jun 1970
Col James E Anderson	Jul 1970	Dec 1971
Col Dennis B Sullivan	Dec 1971	Jul 1972
Col Patrick J Halloran	Jul 1972	Jun 1973
Col Donald A Walbrecht	Jun 1973	May 1974
Col John H Storrie	Jun 1974	Jun 1975
Col Robert D Beckel	Jun 1975	Sep 1976
Col Lyman M Kidder	Oct 1976	Sep 1977
Col William E Lawson III	Sep 1977	Jan 1979
Col David G Young	Feb 1979	Jul 1980
Col Thomas S Pugh	Jul 1980	Jul 1982
Col Lonnie S Liss	Jul 1982	Jan 1983
Col David H Pinsky	Jan 1983	Jan 1985
Col Robert B McConnell	Jan 1985	Aug 1987
Col Donald R Schreiber	Aug 1987	Aug 1989
Col Tom Atkinson	Aug 1989	Jun 1990
Col Rich Salsbury	Jun 1990	Jul 1991
Col Rich Young	Jul 1991	Nov 1991
Col Tieman	Nov 1991	*2

1st STRATEGIC RECONNAISSANCE SQUADRON COMMANDERS

NAME	FROM	TO
Lt Col William R Griner	Jan 1966	Mar 1966
Lt Col Harold E Confer	Apr 1966	Oct 1966
Lt Col Raymond Haupt	Nov 1966	Jul 1967
Lt Col Alan L Hichew	Jul 1967	Sep 1968
Lt Col Patrick J Halloran	Sep 1968	Nov 1969
Lt Col James L Watkins	Dec 1969	Mar 1971
Lt Col Harlon A Hain	Apr 1971	Jul 1971
Lt Col Larry S DeVall	Jul 1971	Jan 1972
Lt Col Kenneth S Collins	Jan 1972	Jun 1972
Lt Col George M Bull	Jun 1972	Jul 1973
Lt Col Brian K McCallum	Jul 1973	Jan 1974
Lt Col James H Shelton Jr	Jan 1974	Aug 1975
Lt Col Raphael S Samay	Aug 1975	Jun 1977
Lt Col Adolphus H Bledsoe	Jul 1977	Dec 1978
Lt Col Randolph B Hertzog	Dec 1978	Dec 1979
Lt Col Richard H Graham	Jan 1980	Jul 1981
Lt Col Eldon W Joersz	Aug 1981	Jul 1983
Lt Col Alan B Cirino	Jul 1983	Aug 1985
Lt Col Joseph Kinego	Aug 1985	
Lt Col William D Orcutt	*3	
Lt Col William R Dyckman		

99th STRATEGIC RECONNAISSANCE SQUADRON COMMANDERS

NAME	FROM	TO
Lt Col John B Boynton	Jun 1966	Dec 1967
Lt Col Robert G Sowers	Jan 1967	Mar 1968
Lt Col John C Kennon	Apr 1968	Nov 1969
Lt Col Harlon A Hain	Nov 1969	Mar 1971

9th STRATEGIC RECONNAISSANCE WING AWARDS DURING SR-71 OPERATIONS

PRESIDENTIAL UNIT CITATION	31 Mar 1968	31 Dec 1968
AIR FORCE OUTSTANDING UNIT AWARD	1 Jul 1970	30 Jun 1971
AIR FORCE OUTSTANDING UNIT AWARD, WITH 'VALOR'	1 Jul 1972	30 Jun 1973
AIR FORCE OUTSTANDING UNIT AWARD	1 Jul 1974	30 Jun 1975
AIR FORCE OUTSTANDING UNIT AWARD	1 Jul 1975	30 Jun 1977
AIR FORCE OUTSTANDING UNIT AWARD	1 Jul 1981	30 Jun 1982
AIR FORCE OUTSTANDING UNIT AWARD	1 Jul 1983	30 Jun 1984
AIR FORCE OUTSTANDING UNIT AWARD	1 Jul 1985	30 Jun 1986
AIR FORCE OUTSTANDING UNIT AWARD	1 Jul 1986	30 Jun 1987

OL-8 was also awarded the:
REPUBLIC OF VIETNAM GALLANTRY CROSS & PALM
31 DECEMBER 1970

*1 Col Young Nov 1991-Jun 1993; Col Larry Tieman to Jul 1994: Gen John Rutledge to Sep 1995; Gen Bob Behler, present.
*2 Col Tieman Nov 1991-Jun 1993; Col Carpenter to Jan 1995; Col George Lafferty to Aug 1995; Col Dale Smith, present.
*3 Lt Col Kinego Aug 1985-Aug 1987; Lt Col Orcutt Aug 1987-Nov 1988; Lt Col Dyckman Nov 1988-Jun 1990.

Appendix 5

AIR FORCE LOGISTICS COMMAND
SR-71 CREW HISTORY

PILOTS	FROM	TO
Merv Evenson	Jan 1970	Jul 1974
Dick Gerard	Jan 1971	Jul 1973
Tom Pugh	Jul 1973	Jul 1978
T Smith	Oct 1973	Jul 1975
B Riedenauer	Nov 1973	Nov 1978
Jim Sullivan	Jul 1978	Aug 1980
Cal Jewett	Jul 1978	Jul 1982
Bob Helt	Jul 1980	Jul 1984
Tom Tilden	Feb 1982	Jul 1989
BC Thomas	Jul 1984	Dec 1987
Ed Yeilding	Jan 1988	Jan 1990
J Halsell	Feb 1989	Jan 1990

RSO	FROM	TO
Red McNeer	Jan 1970	Jul 1971
Ron Selberg	Jan 1971	Aug 1974
Coz Mallozzi	Jul 1971	Jul 1974
B Frazier	Jul 1974	Jul 1980
John Carnochan	Aug 1974	Feb 1978
George Morgan	Jan 1978	Jul 1985
Bob Flanagan	Jan 1980	Aug 1985
Joe Vida	Jan 1981	Jan 1990
P Soucy	Jul 1985	Dec 1987
Tom Fuhrman	Dec 1987	Jan 1990

Appendix 6

CHRONOLOGY OF SIGNIFICANT EVENTS

Year	Date	Event
1957	24 Dec	Christmas Eve, First J58 Engine Run
1959	29 Aug	US Accepts A-12 Design
1960	30 Jan	CIA Approves *Oxcart* Project
1962	26 Apr	First flight of A-12, Pilot Lou Schalk
1962	4 Jun	SR-71 Mock-up Reviewed by Air Force
1962	30 Jul	J58 Completes Pre-flight Rating Test
1962	28 Dec	Lockheed Contracted to Build 6 Production SR-71 Aircraft
1963	31 Jan	First J58 Air Tested
1963	24 May	First A-12 lost in Accident
1963	7 Aug	First Flight YF-12 Pilot J Eastham
1964	29 Feb	Existence of *Oxcart*, A-12 Announced
1964	25 Jul	President Johnson, First Public Announcement of Mach aircraft, Twists Letters RS-71 and says SR-71. Designation Sticks.
1964	29 Oct	SR-71 Prototype to Palmdale
1964	7 Dec	SR-71s to be Based at Beale AFB, Announced
1964	18 Dec	First Engine Run of SR-71 Prototype
1964	21 Dec	SR-71 Taxy Tests
1964	22 Dec	First Flight of SR-71, Palmdale, Pilot Bob Gilliland
1964	22 Dec	First Flight M-12/D-21, Groom Dry Lake, Nevada
1965	3 Mar	First Flight of YF-12C
1965	1 May	YF-12 Sets Nine Speed and Altitude Records
1965	1 Jun	SR-71/YF-12 Test Force Formed Edwards AFB
1965	7 Jul	First Two T-38 Companion Trainers Delivered to Beale AFB
1965	2 Nov	SR-71B Maiden Flight from Palmdale, Pilot B. Gilliland and Bill Weaver
1966	6 Jan	First SR-71 Delivered to USAF. Crew Ray Haupt and Charlie Bock
1966	7 Jan	SR-71B Arrives at Beale AFB. Crew, Ray Haupt, Doug Nelson
1966	25 Jan	First SR-71A Lost in Accident
1966	10 May	First SR-71A Delivered to Beale AFB
1966	25 Jun	Nine Strategic Recon Wing formed at Beale AFB
1966	3 Jul	First Launch Attempt D-21 Drone from M-12
1966	30 Jul	A-12/D-21 Programme Ends
1967	17 Apr	SR-71 Flies 14,000 Miles, Mach 3, Wins FAI Gold Medal (Silverfox) Stephens
1967	31 May	First A-12 Operational Sortie
1968	11 Jan	SR-71B Lost, Beale AFB
1968	26 Jan	First overflight of North Korea by an A-12

Year	Date	Event
1968	21 Mar	First SR-71 Operational Sortie over SE Asia
1968	26 Jul	First confirmed firings of two SA-2s at an SR-71
1968	1 Nov	9 SRW receives AF Outstanding Unit Award
1969	14 Mar	First Flight of SR-71C
1969	13 Apr	9 SRW loses its first SR-71A
1969	11 Dec	YF-12 NASA/USAF Test Programme Begins
1970	16 Jan	SR-71/YF-12 Test Force Redesignated 4786 Test Squadron
1971	1 Apr	99 SRS Deactivated as an SR-71 unit
1971	26 Apr	SR-71A completes 15,000 miles non-stop around US, Time 10 hours, 30 minutes
1973	12 Oct	SR-71A First recon flights over Mid-east,Yom Kippur War
1974	1 Sep	New York to London record 1 hour 56 minutes Pilot J Sullivan, RSO N Widdefield
1974	13 Sep	SR-71 London to Los Angeles record 3 hrs 47 mins. Pilot Buck Adams, RSO Bill Machorek
1976	27 Jul	Speed Record, 2092 mph, Pilot Bledsoe and J Fuller
1976	28 Jul	Speed Record, 2193 mph, Pilot E Joersz and G Morgan
1976	28 Jul	Altitude Record, 85,068 ft, Pilot R Helt and RSO L Elliot
1978	16 Nov	First SR-71 overflight of Cuba
1979	31 Mar	DET 4, 9 SRW formed at RAF Mildenhall
1979	31 Oct	NASA Flight Test Programme Ended
1979	7 Nov	YF-12 lands at Wright-Patterson AFB for AF Museum
1981	1 Aug	4029 SRTS Formed to Train SR-71 Crews
1981	26 Aug	North Korea launches two SA-2s at SR-71 flight conducted over DMZ
1984	7 Nov	First SR-71 Sortie over Nicaragua
1986	13 Apr	2 SR-71s conduct Post Strike Recon over Libya after Operation *Eldorado Canyon*
1987	22 Jul	First operational mission into e Gulf by an SR-71
1989	1 Oct	USAF operations suspended (except for minimum proficiency sorties) while awaiting budget outcome
1989	22 Nov	All USAF operations terminated
1990	26 Jan	SR-71 is decommissioned in ceremony at Beale AFB
1990	16 Mar	West-East Coast 1 hour 7 minutes Kansas City-Washington DC 29 minutes 57 secs St Louis Cincinnati 8 min 32 secs (Yeilding and JT Vida)

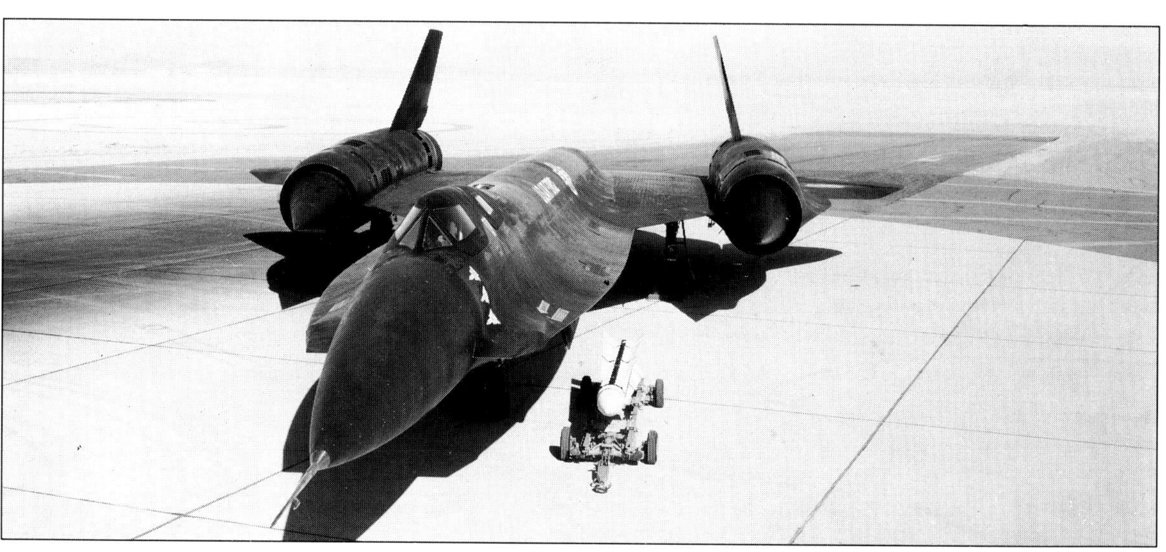

Appendix 7

The YF-12 History

Although the YF-12 was never deployed operationally, a book of this type would be incomplete without an outline of the part played by the aircraft in the overall development of the A-12 and SR-71.

During the late 1950s a specification was drawn up to provide a fire control and missile system for the North American F-108 interceptor. The aeroplane was to be Mach 3 capable, and its ASG-18 pulse-Doppler radar system, developed in parallel with the Hughes GAR-9 missile, would possess a look-down/shoot-down capability for head-on attacks.

As tests undertaken by Hughes engineers continued, a decision was made to cancel the F-108 on 23 September 1959. Despite this body blow, DoD officials decided that the outstanding FCS and 818 lb (372 kg), GAR-9 missile development should continue on a 'stand alone' basis.

On 16/17 March 1960 Kelly Johnson discussed with Gen Hal Estes and Dr Courtland Perkins, the Air Force Secretary for Research and Development, plans to build an interceptor version of the A-12. Johnson's ideas were keenly received and subsequently forwarded to Gen Martin Demler at Wright-Patterson AFB for further discussions and analysis. Soon after, Gen Demler directed Johnson to equip an A-12 varient with the Hughes ASG-18 FCS and GAR-9 missile system. Lockheed was contracted to build three test aircraft for the project, which subsequently bore the article numbers 1001, 1002, and 1003, and were serialled 60-6934, 60-6935 and 60-6936 respectively.

Hughes' chief pilot, James D Eastham, had flown every sortie relating to the missile and radar system on the B-58, and early in 1962 he was invited by his friend Lou Schalk to join the *Oxcart* programme. Jim possessed unparalleled knowledge in the field of flight testing missile and radar systems and was therefore the ideal test pilot/engineer to evaluate the YF-12A.

On 7 August 1963, Jim Eastham climbed aboard 60-6934 for a first flight which he later modestly characterized as a typical production test flight; throughout the sortie he was chased by Lou Schalk flying an F-104.

As much of the envelope expansion had already been achieved in the A-12, early YF-12 flight time was spent integrating the FCS and ANS into the aeroplane. On 3 February 1964, Jim Eastham and Flight Test Engineer (FTE) John Wallace took 60-6936 on the very first sustained heat soak of a 'Blackbird'. The test card called for the flight to cruise at Mach 3.16 for precisely 10 minutes. The test procedure was followed to the letter, however on recovery back at Groom Dry Lake, an inspection revealed that due to an error in the pitot static system, the pilot had exceeded Mach 3.2. Considerably higher stagnation temperatures incinerated practically all of the electrical wiring.

During President Lyndon B Johnson's announcement concerning the existence of the 'A-11' programme, YF-12s 60-6934 and 60-6935 were positioned from Groom Dry Lake to Edwards AFB, by Lou Schalk and Bill Park, thereby lending credibility to the President's 'political brag', and diverting attention away from Area 51 and the Agency's A-12 programme.

Having been rewired, 936 was airborne again on 28 April, crewed by Jim and John at cruising speeds in excess of Mach 3 for 30 minutes. On this occasion all systems functioned as advertised. The aircraft was later delivered to Edwards, where it conducted further test flights with its 'stablemates'.

With much of the 'pick and shovel work' completed in the B-58, the ASG and GAR-9 missile (the latter redesignated AIM-47) were quickly integrated into the YF-12, where the system transcended its predicted performance figures. The FCS was located in one of four main fuselage chine bays; the other three bays each housed an AIM-47. In all, approximately 12 live missile firings were made from the YF-12, eight of which were made by Jim Eastham. The remainder were launched by US Air Force crews. During such flights, the YF-12 maintained Mach 3.2 while cruising in excess of 80,000 ft (24,390 m), the ASG-18 radar aquired its Boeing JQB-47 remotely flown drone, flying as low as 1500 ft (457 m) over the sea.

Positioned for a head-on attack, the YF-12 consistantly destroyed its target with a single missile from 120 miles range. It was calculated that Aerospace Defense Command (ADC) would require 93 F-12B interceptors to provide a defensive screen that could protect the entire United States.

Incredibly, Secretary of Defense. Robert McNamara cancelled the programme and directed Lockheed to destroy all related tooling. A unique, money-saving opportunity of producing tri-sonic, stand-off interceptors and bombers, utilising the same aft body, was therefore lost forever. After the programme was completed all three YF-12s were placed in storage at Edwards.

Following the loss of SR-71B 957 on 11 January 1969, YF-12A serial 934 was removed from storage. Its fuselage forebody was removed and the rear of the aircraft was 'grafted' to the front fuselage of a static test specimen. This created a second, two seat-trainer. Nicknamed 'The Bastard', and given the serial number 64-17981, this so-called SR-71C, first flew on 14 March 1969.

Both 935 and 936 were subsequently used during a series of tests in a combined Air Force, NASA and ADP programme, and 936 was lost at Edwards AFB due to an engine-fire.

***Left* This YF-12 displays three white AIM-47 missiles on the left side of its cockpit, indicating the aircraft's participation in three launches of the 818-lb missile, which is also shown on its 'dolly' (*Lockheed*)**

U.S.AIR FORCE

DRAG CHUTE
CAUTION–MIN INFLIGHT AIRSPEED 150 KNOTS EAS
UHF
FUEL

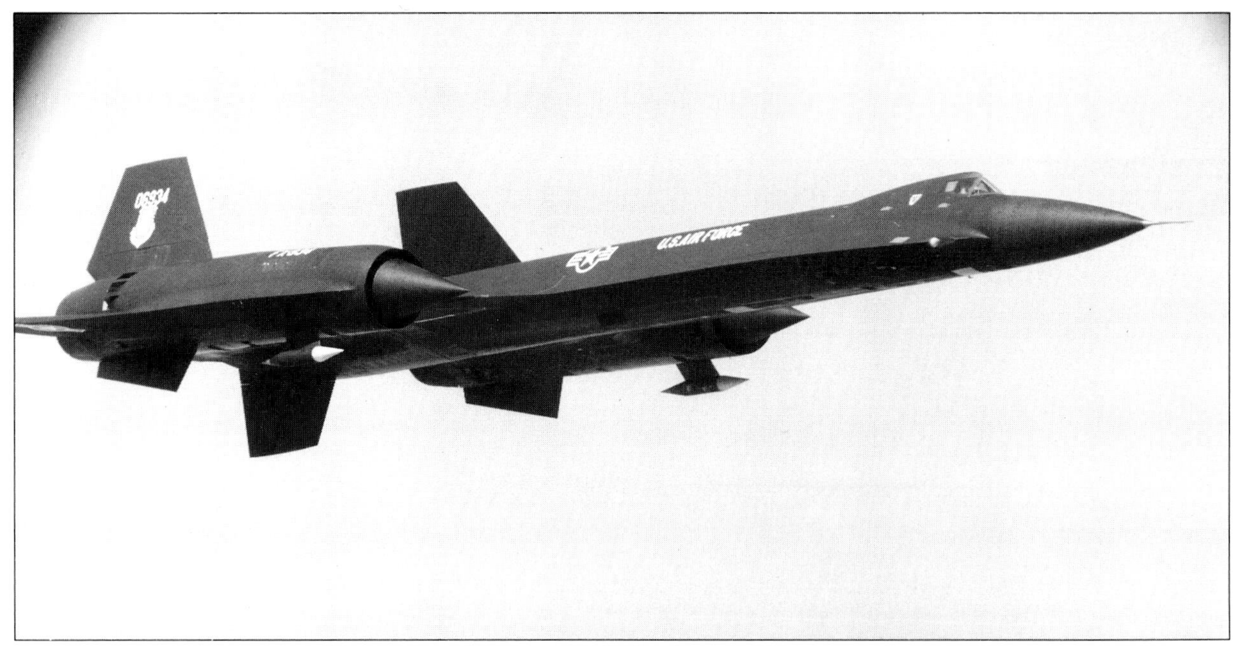

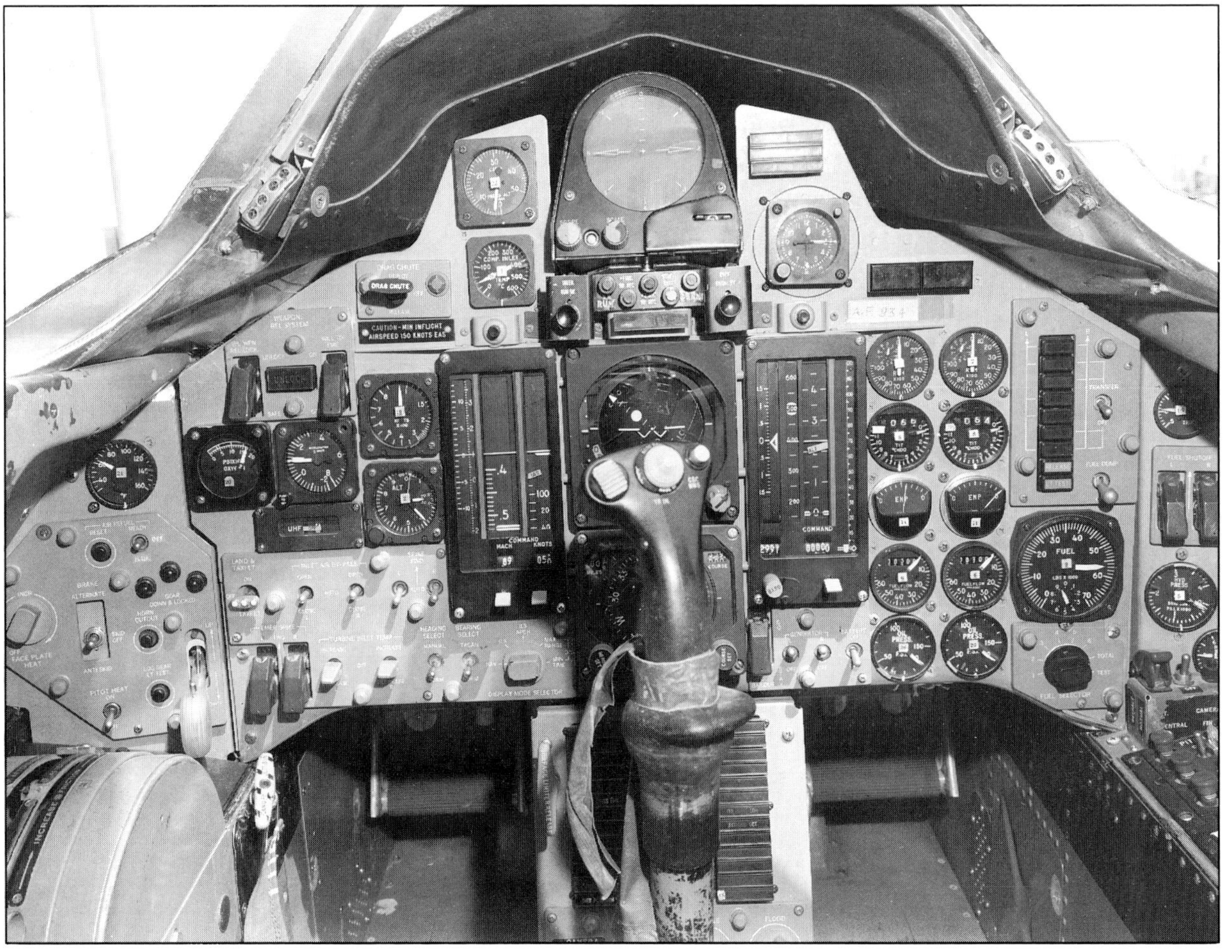

Above left YF-12 prototype 934 makes a high-speed low altitude pass. The streamlined pods located under each engine nacelle housed cameras to monitor AIM-47 missile launches (*Lockheed*)

Above and left This sequence of views, photographed by Lockheed technicians on 4 April 1964, clearly shows the overall layout of the YF-12 cockpit, including both consoles (*Lockheed*)

Appendix 8

Record Breakers

Countries and individuals have often, in the cause of 'national pride', tenaciously pursued various world speed, altitude and distance records. The *Oxcart* and *Senior Crown* programmes went beyond blind nationalism, with security considerations preceding banner headlines. It is perhaps worth bearing in mind that the records set out below, verified and authenticated by the Federation Aeronautique Internationale (FAI), were certainly not demonstrations of the aeroplane's absolute capabilities. As alluded to earlier in these pages, on 20 November 1965 an A-12 attained speeds in excess of Mach 3.2 and a sustained altitude capability above 90,000 ft. With the passage of time, several SR-71 records were later broken by a highly modified, stripped-down Soviet MiG-25. The inability of that country to subsequently build an operational aircraft that represented a serious threat to SR-71 operations, is indicative of the 'research only' status of that particular jet.

Date: 1 May 1965. Record: Absolute Altitude, 80,257.86 ft (24,390 m)
Crew: Pilot, Col Robert L 'Fox' Stephens. FCO, Lt Col Daniel Andre
Aircraft: YF-12A 60–6936

Date: 1 May 1965. Record: Absolute Speed over a straight course, 2070.101 mph
Crew: Pilot, Col Robert L 'Fox' Stephens. FCO, Lt Col Daniel Andre.
Aircraft: YF-12A 60–6936

Date: 1 May 1965. Record: Absolute Speed over a 500 km closed course 1688.889 mph
Crew: Pilot, Lt Col Walter F Daniel. FCO, Maj James P Cooney
Aircraft: YF-12A 60–6936

Date: 1 May 1965. Record: Absolute Speed over a 1000 km closed course 1643.041 mph
Crew: Pilot, Lt Col Walter F Daniel. FCO, Maj Noel T Warner
Aircraft: YF-12A 60–6936

Date: 27/28 July 1976. Record: Altitude in Horizontal Flight, 85,068.997 ft (25,929.031 m)
Crew: Pilot, Capt Robert C Helt. RSO Maj Larry A Elliott
Aircraft: SR-71A, ?

Date: 27/28 July 1976. Record: Speed Over Straight Course (15/25 km), 2193.167 mph (3529.56 kmh)
Crew: Pilot, Capt Eldon W Joersz. RSO Maj George T Morgan
Aircraft: SR-71A, ?

Date: 27/28 July 1976. Record: Speed Over a Closed Course (1000 km), 2092.294 mph (3367.221 km/h)
Crew: Pilot, Maj Adolphus H Bledsoe Jr. RSO Maj John T Fuller
Aircraft: SR-71A, ?

Date: 1 September 1974. Record: Speed Over a Recognised Course – New York to London
Crew: Pilot Maj James V Sullivan. RSO Maj Noel F Widdifield
Distance: 3490 miles. Time 1 hr 54 mins 56.4 sec.
Aircraft: SR-71A 64–17972

Date: 13 September 1974. Record: Speed Over a Recognised Course - London to Los Angeles
Crew: Pilot Capt Harold B Adams. RSO Capt William C Machorek
Distance: 5645 miles. Time 3 hrs 47 mins 35.8 sec
Aircraft: SR-71A 64–17972

Date: 6 March 1990. Record: Speed Over A Recognised Course – Los Angeles to East Coast
Crew: Pilot Lt Col Ed Yeilding. RSO Lt Col Joseph T Vida
Coast to Coast (2086 miles). Time 1 hr 07 mins 53.69 secs, average speed 2124.5 mph
Los Angeles to Washington DC (1998 miles). Time 1 hr 4 mins 19.89 secs, average speed 2144.83 mph
St Louis to Cincinnati (311.44 miles). Time 8 mins 31.97 secs, average speed 2189.94 mph
Kansas City to Washington DC (942.08 miles). Time 25 mins 58.53 secs, average speed 2176.08 mph
Aircraft: SR-71A 64–17972

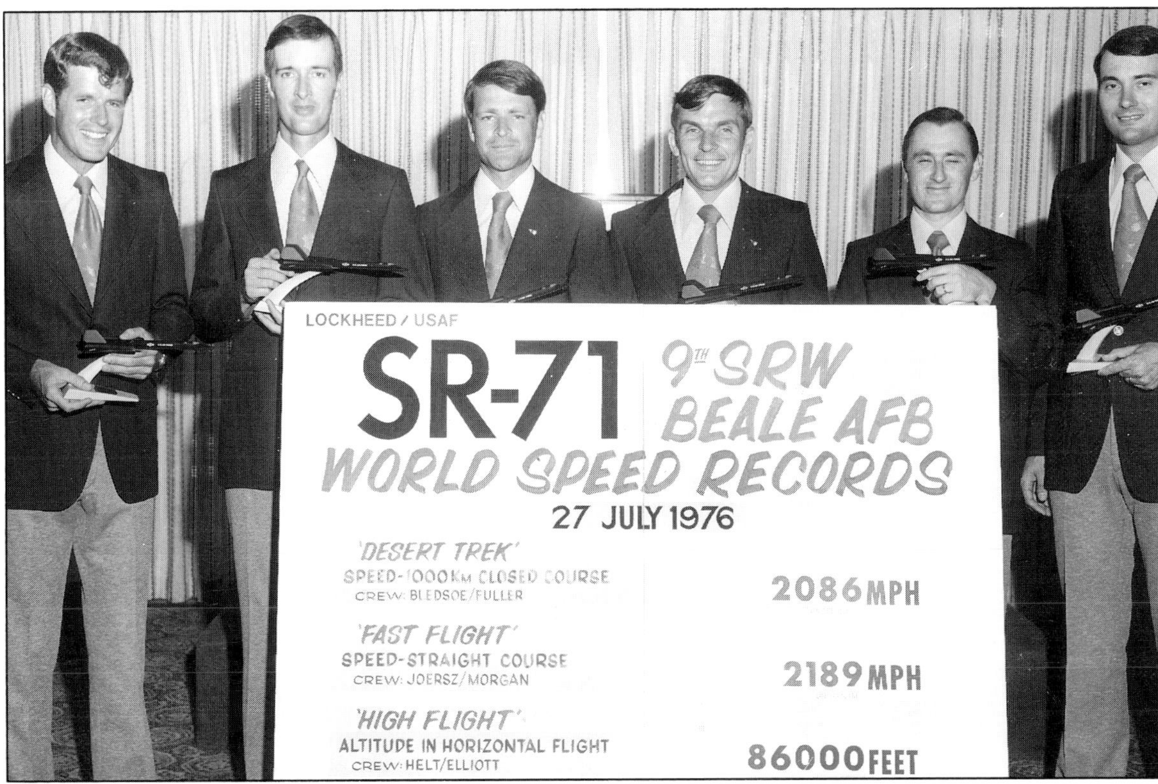

(Left to right) John Fuller, Pat Bledsoe, 'G T' Morgan, Al Joersz, Larry Elliott, Bob Helt (*USAF*)

Appendix 9

Senior Crown Statistics

Total Flight Time	53,490 hrs	
Total Mach 3+ time	11,675 hrs	
Sorties Flown	**Operational**	**Total**
Beale	238	12,252#
Kadena	2410	3943
Mildenhall	894	1058
Griffiss/ Seymour Johnson	9	41
Grand Total	3551	17294
Total Hours	11,008	53,234.8
Total Mach 3+ time	2752	11,675 hrs
# Includes Palmdale		
Total Crew Members		284
(Includes NASA, Test Force and crews to check out in the SR-71)		
Total VIPs/Staff		105
Total number of people to have flown in A-12, YF-12 and SR-71		389
Total Air Refuellings		25,862

On 31 August 1981 Kelly Johnson stated that over 1000 SA-2s had been fired at SR-71s, all missed their intended target.

Highest flight hours on type: JT Vida (RSO). 1392.7 hrs

Highest pilot flight hours on type: BC Thomas. 1217.3 hrs

First crewmember to reach 1000 hrs on type, Bob Powell

First sortie Jerry O'Malley/Ed Payne 21 March 1968

300 hr Club	163
600 hr Club	69
900 hr Club	18
1000 hr Club	8

SR-71 with the most combat missions – serial 64–17960 with 342 missions

Appendix 10

A-12, YF-12 and SR-71 losses

1963	24 May	A-12, 60-6926, article 123, pilot Ken Collins survived.
1964	9 Jul	A-12, 60-6939, article 133, pilot Bill Park survived.
1966	25 Jan	SR-71A, 64-17952, article 2003, pilot Bill Weaver survived, RSO Jim Zwayer killed.
1966	30 Jul	M-12, 60-6941, article 135, pilot Bill Park survived, LCO Ray Torick killed.
1967	5 Jan	A-12, 60-6928, article 125, pilot Walt Ray killed.
1967	10 Jan	SR-71A, 64-17950, article 2001, pilot Art Peterson survived, back seat was unoccupied.
1967	13 Apr	SR-71A, 64-17966, article 2017, pilot Earle Boone and RSO 'Butch' Sheffield both survived.
1967	25 Oct	SR-71A, 64-17965, article 2016, pilot Roy StMartin and RSO John Carnochan both survived.
1967	28 Dec	A-12, 60-6929, article 126, pilot Mel Vojvodich survived.
1968	11 Jan	SR-71B, 64-17957, article 2008, Instructor Pilot 'Gray' Sowers and student John Fruehauf both survived.
1968	5 Jun	A-12, 60-6932, article 129, pilot Jack Weeks killed.
1968	10 Oct	SR-71A, 64-17977, article 2028, pilot 'Abe' Kardong and RSO Jim Kogler both survived.
1969	11 Apr	SR-71A, 64-17954, article 2005, pilot Bill Skliar and RSO Noel Warner both survived.
1969	18 Dec	SR-71A, 64-17953, article 2004, pilot Joe Rogers and RSO Garry Heidlebaugh both survived.
1970	10 May	SR-71A, 64-17969, article 2020, pilot Willie Lawson and RSO 'Gil' Martinez both survived.
1970	17 Jun	SR-71A, 64-17970, article 2021, pilot Buddy Brown and RSO 'Mort' Jarvis both survived.
1971	24 Jun	YF-12A, 60-6936, article 1003, pilot Jack Layton and FCO Billy Curtis both survived.
1972	20 Jul	SR-71A, 64-17978, article 2029, pilot Denny Bush and RSO Jimmy Fagg both survived.
1989	21 Apr	SR-71A, 64-17974, article 2025, pilot Dan House and RSO Blair Bozek both survived.

Three classic designs from Kelly Johnson – an F-104, a YF-12 and an SR-71. The Starfighter was flown by John Manke, whilst Fitz-Fulton and Vic Horton crewed the YF-12, and Don Mallick and Ray Young flew SR-71A 951, which was then referred to as a YF-12C (*NASA*)

Appendix 11

NASA Flight Activity

Throughout the summer of 1967, a small team of NASA engineers worked under the leadership of Gene Matranga on various stability and control aspects of the SR-71 at Edwards AFB. This work helped speed up the aeroplane's service introduction, and led to the establishment of a close working relationship between the Air Force and NASA.

The Office of Advanced Research Technology was anxious to exploit the lessons and technologies learned during the development of the SR-71 and their possible applications to future commercial supersonic transports (SST). NASA requested an instrumented SR-71 as a test-bed from which to conduct such research. Unable to initially accommodate such a request, the Air Force offered NASA the two remaining YF-12s then in storage at Edwards. On 5 June 1969 a memorandum of understanding was signed between Air Defense Command (ADC) and NASA, in which the latter undertook to pay for operational expenses and ADC would supply maintenance and logistic support.

Langley AFB engineers were interested in conducting aerodynamic experiments and testing advanced strutures. Research engineers at Lewis Research Establishment would study propulsion, while Ames wanted to concentrate on inlet aerodynamics and the correlation of wind-tunnel and flight data. It was hoped that the structured experimental programme would solve many of the problems 'worked around' in the name of deployment expediency, enabling any future commercial SST venture to avoid expensive mistakes.

Three months work was needed to ready the two airframes (YF-12s, 60-6935 and 69-6936) for flight. On 11 December 1969 the two phase joint NASA/US Air Force test programme got underway when 60-6936 climbed away from Edwards with Col Joe Rogers in the front seat, and Maj Garry Heidelbraugh in the FCO position.

Phase one was controlled by the Air Force and consisted of developing procedures and establishing limitations for command and control, and working out possible bomber penetration tactics against interceptors with the YF-12s capabilities. This phase of the programme was terminated earlier than expected when, during the closing stages of its 63rd flight on 24 June 1971, a fire broke out on board 60-6936 whilst on approach to the Edwards traffic pattern. Flames quickly enveloped the entire aircraft and both Lt Col Jack Layton and systems operator Maj Bill Curtis were forced to eject from the stricken aeroplane. 6936 ended its career crashing into the middle of the dry lakebed.

In contrast 6935 became quite a workhorse in the NASA programme, conducting 22 flights during which measurements were corrolated against the effects of thermal heating and flight-loads – external factors which together changed the aircraft's shape and load distribution pattern. On 22 June 1970 6935 was grounded for nine months, during which time instrumentation changes took place. Once these were completed NASA pilot Don Mallick and test engineer Vic Horton flew an FCF on 22 March 1971, after which the folding ventral fin was removed and four further flights were conducted to assess the aeroplane's directional stability up to Mach 2.8.

The NASA test programme was bolstered on 16 July 1971 with the arrival of SR-71A article 2002, serial 64–17951. Its first NASA test flight was undertaken on 24 May 1972 by Fitz Fulton and test engineer Vic Horton. Redesignated a YF-12C for political reasons, the aircraft was also re-serialled 60–6937 at the same time.

Aircraft 60–6937 was retired from the programme after its 88th flight with NASA on 28 September 1978, transiting from Edwards to Palmdale on 22 December that same year. YF-12 number 60–6935 continued operating until the flight programme ceased after its 145th NASA flight, flown by Fitz Fulton and Vic Horton on 31 October 1979. A week later on 7 November, Col J Sullivan and Col R Uppstrom ferried the aircraft to the Air Force museum at Wright-Patterson AFB, Ohio, where the sole example of the YF-12 is on permanent display.

In early 1990, NASA elected to continue flying the SR-71 as a supersonic test platform. The Department of Defense bailed NASA two SR-71As, numbers 64–17971 and 64–17980, and one SR-71B, (trainer), number 64–17956. However, prior to the SR-71B being bailed to NASA, the Air Force flew three additional training sorties on the B-model in order to check-out a NASA instructor pilot. The missions flown were as follows:

Date	Pilot	IP	Time	Mach	Altitude
1 Jul 91	Steve Ishmael	Rod Dyckman	1:00	3:10	76,000 ft
10 Jul 91	Rod Dyckman	Steve Ishmael	1:25	3:23	80,800 ft
25 Jul 91	Rod Dyckman	Steve Ishmael	1:35	3:09	74,000 ft

On 25 July 1991, SR-71B, serial 64–17956 was officially delivered to NASA Dryden, located at Edwards Air Force Base, California. The following check outs were conducted as listed below:

14 Aug 91	Rogers Smith	Steve Ishmael	1:18	3.13	75,000 ft
26 Aug 91	Rogers Smith	Steve Ishmael	2:31	3.10	76,000 ft

Appendix 11 NASA Flight Activity continued.

23 Sep 91	Rogers Smith	Steve Ishmael	3:00	3.18	78,700 ft
4 Oct 91	Steve Ishmael	Marta Meyer	1:27	3.23	81,450 ft
9 Oct 91	Rogers Smith	Robert E Meyer	1:26	3.23	81,450 ft

To coincide with NASA's aircraft numbering system, all aircraft assigned to the Dryden Flight Research Center start with an 800 series number.

USAF Serial Number	NASA Number
64–17956	831
64–17971	832
64–17980	844

This change in the tail numbers greatly dismayed those who had flown the trio of SR-71s over the past 25 years. Since those aircraft were no longer Air Force assets they needed NASA nomenclature. However, the fact remained that 956 was still 956, no matter what NASA and the FAA named it! USAF Instructor Pilot Rod Dyckman was called to Edwards to check out Steve Ishmael so as to allow NASA to benefit from SAC's many years of operations, particularly in regard to emergency procedures and inlet disturbances.

On 1 July 1991, Ishmael got his initial 'ride' with Dyckman on a one hour flight which took the newly-designated 831 to Mach 3.1 and 76,000 ft. After two more flights in July, Steve was checked out as an instructor pilot. He then checked out Rogers Smith during August/September. Marta Bohn-Meyer became the first official female SR-71 crewmember in October 1991 (although Congresswoman Beverly Byron had been the first female VIP guest-rider in 1985). Marta and her husband Robert were the two NASA RSOs (Research Systems Operator-Engineers) who would carry out research flights with pilots Ishmael and Smith on 11 of the first 21 sorties performed up to 6 October 1992. The first 19 flights of the programme were undertaken in 831 (956), and the last two were in 844 (980). The 21 short flights varied in length from one hour to just under four hours, with the average usually being around one hour and 50 minutes.

On the following page is a complete record of NASA's SR-71 flight activity to date, and the 1995 return of the SR-71 to the USAF.

1 Experiment using the SR-71 as a target to check radars that were modified for use on an "Aegis" type Navy ship. This flight was the first time the SR-71B trainer had flown east of the Mississippi. The collection track was over the Atlantic Ocean east of the Virginia coast.
2. Evaluation of two ultraviolet spectrometers for multi-spectral (IR-UV) imagery. This was the initial experiment (using a Winkler Nose) to check UV (looking up).
3. JPL experiment in nose with UV sensor (looking up).
4. First time the SR-71 flew with JP-8 Fuel. Initial "boom" experiment for "Glove".
5. Boom experiment (SR-71, XL-16, F-18, F-15). XL-16 flew close formation witht the SR-71 at MACH 1.8, flying in and out of the SR-71 shock wave. XL-16 flew to within 50 feet of the SR.
6. Initial OADS "Optical Air Data System" flight (nose mounted). Initial flight with TM telemetry package on board.
7. OADS flight no. 2. OADS had to be shut down during descent due to overheating. Overheating was caused from radiated heat from the TEOC window into the OADS system. The organic cooling system within the OADS could not cool the lasers enough to continue operation.
8. This flight terminated early due to compressor stalls and engine inlet un-starts. The return leg was subsonic.
9. LEO "Low Earth Orbit" experiment flown for Motorola. The LEO component used the "L" and "S" band frequency range. Collection track was south of Chandler, Arizona. The SR-71 collected a total of 16 minutes of data for both missions. The SR-71 was "hot refueled", the right engine and all electronic equipment were shut down during the ground refueling.
10. NASA flight #44 was an orientation/familiarization flight for General Jack Daily, Deputy Director for NASA (Gen Daily received a MACH 3 + pen).

NASA Flights & 1995/96 USAF

LOG OF SR-71A, #971

Date	*Location*	*Pilot Name*	*Rso Name*	*Fight Duration*	*Max Mach*	*Max Altitude*	*Remarks*
12-/01/95	E	I	BM	0.2	0.39	3,200	Ferry to Palmdale
26/04/95	E	SC	BM	1.4	0.96	29,000	FCF
23/05/95	PMD	SC	M	2.5	3.23	81,000	
02/06/95	PMD	SC	BM				
26/06/95	PMD	SC	M	1.3	3.21	77,800	
06/07/95	PMD	SC	BM	4.3	3.20	79,100	
12/07/95	PMD	SC	M	4.1	3.06	77,500	
17/10/95	PMD	SC	BM	1.2	3.05	76,000	
01/02/96	PMD			2.7	3.05	77,200	Participated in Red Flag
08/02/96				0.6	0.90	20,000	
27/02/96				2.6	3.00	75,000	
01/03/96				2.3	3.19	78,400	
10/04/96				2.5	3.02	77,000	
14/06/96		SC	BOZEK	4.0	3.05	78,6000	ASARS/Data Link Test

LOG OF SR-71A, #967

Date	*Location*	*Pilot Name*	*Rso Name*	*Fight Duration*	*Max Mach*	*Max Altitude*	*Remarks*
28/08/95	PMD	SC	M	1.4	0.95	26,000	FCF
06/09/95	PMD	S	BM	1.5	0.92	24,000	FCF
13/09/95	PMD	S	BM	1.4	0.93	23,500	FCF
06/10/95	PMD	S	M	1.6	3.01	70,200	FCF
25/10/95	PMD	SC	M	2.5	3.23	79,000	FCF divert into Nellis
15/12/95	PMD	S	BM	2.3	3.15	74,100	FCF
09/01/96	PMD	S	M	2.3	3.15	74,100	FCF
12/01/96	PMD	S	BM	1.9	3.22	78,300	Final FCF
30/01/96	PMD			2.6	3.02	76,500	USAF flight & position to E
09/02/96	E			2.9	3.15	79,700	First Flight of data link randome
15/02/96	E			3.1	3.01	72,700	
16/04/96	E	LULOFF	FINAN	2.5	3.02	76,000	
09/05/96	E	LULOFF	GREENWOOD	2.3	???	???	ASARS/Data Link Test

LOG OF SR-71B, #956 (NASA 831)

Date	*Location*	*Pilot Name*	*IP/Rso Name*	*Fight Duration*	*Max Mach*	*Max Altitude*	*Remarks*
01/07/91	PMD	I	DYCKMAN	1.0	3.10	71,400	FCF
10/07/91	PMD	I	DYCKMAN	1.4	3.23	80,800 FCF	
25/07/91	PMD	I	DYCKMAN	1.6	3.09	74,500	DELIVERY TO NASA
14/08/91	E	S	I	1.3	3.06	75,500	FIRST NASA FLIGHT
29/10/91	E	I	BM	1.7	3.20	79,500	
1/11/91	E	S	M	2.1	3.25	81,500	
07/11/91	E	I	BM	3.3	3.21	81,500	
14/11/91	E	I	M	3.8	3.21	81,800	
28/01/92	E	I	M	1.8	3.26	77,400	
26/02/92	E	S	BM	1.5	3.26	81,100	
10/03/92	E	I	M	1.4	3.12	78,000	
22/04/92	E	S	I	1.7	3.22	81,800	OPERATION
20/05/92	E	S	I	1.6	3.21	83,500	CREW PROFICIENCY
04/06/92	E	I	McMURTRY	1.5	3.23	83,000	OPERATIONAL
26/06/92	E	I	BARTHELEMY	1.4	3.23	82,160	
24/10/92	E	I	BM	1.3	3.20	78,600	FCF
24/11/92	E	S	M	1.8	3.26	80,500	CREW PROFICIENCY & TANKER
08/12/92	E	I	BM (1)	5.2	3.09	76,500	WITH KC10
20/01/93	E	S	M	3.0	3.22	80,000	INLET TEST & CREW PROFICIENCY
14/04/93	E	S	BM	1.4	3.23	81,500	FCF/CREW PROFICIENCY
09/11/93	E	I	BM	1.9	3.07	75,850	FCF/CREW PROFICIENCY
18/02/94	E	I	M	1.7	3.20	81,200	FCF/CREW PROFICIENCY
25/02/94	E	I	GEN DAILY	1.6	3.17	82,100	
04/03/98	E	S	BM	1.5	3.23	80,800	FCF
24/08/94	E	S	M	1.3	3.23	79,300	FCF
06/10/94	E	I	M	1.7	3.22	83,600	CREW PROFICIENCY
18/10/94	E	SC	I	1.6	3.22	84,700	FIRST FLIGHT FOR ED
17/11/94	E	I	FULLERTON	2.8	3.23	82,300	CREW PROFICIENCY
08/12/94	E	I	S	2.5	3.23	82,500	CREW PROFICIENCY
20/01/95	E	SC	I	1.9	3.05	75,400	CREW PROFICIENCY
22/02/95	E	SC	S	2.3	3.11	77,000	CREW PROFICIENCY
18/05/95	E	SC	M	1.7	3.22	80,800	CREW PROFICIENCY
31/05/95	E	SC	BM	1.3	3.22	81,290	CREW PROFICIENCY
27/06/95	E	LULOFF	S	3.1	3.23	78,245	FIRST AF TNG FLT
15/07/95	E	LULOFF	S	3.1	3.03	75,100	SECOND TNG FLT
20/07/95	E	S	SC	3.1	3.04	76,200	
28/07/95	E	McCLEARY	S	2.8	3.15	76,650	AF-FIRST FLIGHT FOR TOM
02/08/95	E	McCLEARY	S	4.0	3.05	77,450	
11/08/95	E	McCLEARY	SC	2.8	3.15	78,000	
17/08/95	E	SC	BM	1.5	3.20	80,500	CREW PROFICIENCY
24/08/95	E	LULOFF	S	3.0	3.04	75,850	AF-NIGHT QUAL FOR LULOFF
29/08/95	E	McCLEARY	BOZEK	2.8	3.15	76,500	AF CREW RE QUALIFICATION
31/08/95	E	S	M	2.2	3.24	79,800	CREW PROFICIENCY
27/09/95	E	S	SC	1.4	3.21	80,300	FCF
30/10/95	E	McCLEARY	SC	1.5	3.05	74,500	AF RE ACTIVATION
09/11/95	E	LULOFF	S	2.2	3.18	80,000	AFA RE ACTIVATION
16/11/95	E	McCLEARY	SC	2.	3.02	77,050	NIGHT QUAL McCLEARY
22/11/95	E	WATKINS	SC	2.9	3.22	78,950	FIRST FLIGHT FOR DON
11/12/95	E	WATKINS	SC	2.9	3.21	80,250	
18/01/96	E	McCLEARY	SC	2.4	3.02	77,700	
01/02/96	E	SC	M	1.5	3.21	80,150	CREW PROFICIENCY
06/02/96	E	LULOFF	S	2.4	3.17	75,300	
16/02/96	E	SC	BM	1.5	1.50	48,000	CREW PROFICIENCY
20/03/96	E	SC	BM	1.4	3.09	79,000	FCF
29/03/96	E	S	M	2.3	3.22	80,000	CREW PROFICIENCY
04/04/96	E	SC	BM	2.1	3.04	76,400	CREW PROFICIENCY
10/04/96	E	S	M	2.5	3.22	80,100	CREW PROFICIENCY
25/04/96	E	SC	M	2.7	3.26	82,200	CREW PROFICIENCY
16/05/96	E	S	BM	2.9	3.01	74,000	CREW PROFICIENCY
05/06/96	E	SC	M	1.3	3.04	78,600	CREW PROFICIENCY
22/08/96	E	SC	BM	1.4	3.23	80,800	CREW PROFICIENCY

LOG OF SR-71A, #980 (NASA 844)

Date	*Location*	*Pilot Name*	*Rso Name*	*Fight Duration*	*Max Mach*	*Max Altitude*	*Remarks*
24/09/92	E	I	BM	1.7	3.25	76,680	OSC EXPERIMENT
06/10/92	E	S	M	1.5	3.26	80,000	OSC EXPERIMENT
09/03/93	E	I	BM (2)	1.5	3.17	82,350	UV CCD
16/03/93	E	S	M (3)	1.7	3.24	84,050	UV CCD
15/07/93	E	I	M (4)	3.0	3.23	81,800 UVS	(NEAR ULTRA VIOLET SPECTRMETER)
28/07/93	E	S	BM (5)	1.5	1.85	48,500	NUVS & SONIC BOOM TESTS
03/08/93	E	I	M (6)	1.7	3.23	83,950	UV SPECTROMETER & HANDLING QUALITIES
17/09/93	E	S	I (7)	1.7	3.00	76,070	HANDLING QUALITIES
01/10/93	E	I	BM (8)	1.7	3.17	76,500	NUVS
06/10/93	E	S	M (9)	1.7	3.03	73,025	NUVS
13/10/93	E	I	BM	1.8	3.23	83,700	NUVS
20/10/93	E	S	M	1.5	3.05	75,635	NUVS
08/12/93	E	I	M	1.5	3.21	77,375	NUVS
22/12/93	E	I	BM (10)	1.4	3.11	76,000	NUVS & LEOEX (LOW EARTH ORBIT EXPERIMENT)
22/12/93	E	I	BM (10)	1.5	3.11	76,150	NUVS & LEOEX
25/01/94	E	S	M	1.5	3.04	77,600	NUVS & LEOEX
25/01/94	E	S	M	1.4	3.04	77,600	DYNAMIC AURORAL VIEWING EXPERIMENT (DAVE)
07/07/94	E	I	M	1.3	3.16	77,750	DAVE
13/07/94	E	S	M	1.4	3.18	77,700	NUVS & DAVE
21/07/94	E	S	BM	1.3	3.19	80,300	NUVS & DAVE
31/08/94	E	S	BM	1.4	3.05	75,700	NUVS & DAVE
25/10/94	E	S	BM	1.4	3.21	80,000	NUVS & DAVE
15/02/95	E	S	M	1.5	1.27	31,500	SONIC BOOM WITH F-16XL CHASE
16/03/95	E	SC	BM	1.4	1.26	34,100	SONIC BOOM WITH F-16XL & AMES Y03A
22/03/95	E	I	M	1.5	1.28	33,000	SONIC BOOM WITH F-16XL & AMES Y03A
24/03/95	E	SC	BM	1.6	1.63	48,000	SONIC BOOM WITH F-16XL & AMES Y03A
29/03/95	E	SC	M	2.2	1.56	48,200	SONIC BOOM WITH F-16XL & AMES Y03A & F-18
05/04/95	E	S	BM	2.2	1.54	47,600	SONIC BOOM WITH F-16XL & AMES Y03A & F-18
12/04/95	E	I	BM	2.0	1.28	44,300	SONIC BOOM WITH F-16XL & AMES Y03A & F-18
20/04/95	E	SC	M	2.0	1.35	44,300	SONIC BOOM WITH F-16XL & AMES Y03A & F-18
25/05/95	E	S	BM	1.7	1.92	49,00	SONIC BOOM WITH Y-01A LANDED PMD AEROSPIKE
14/03/96	PMD	SC	BM	0.8	0.98	26,650	LOW FCF & RETURN TO DFRC
22/03/96	E	SC	BM	2.4	3.22	80,400	HIGH HOT FCF
12/07/96	E	SC	M	3.1	2.15	60,000	FIRST LASER POD OFF FLIGHT

Key
E = Edwards
I = Ishmael
S = Smith
BM = Bohn-Meyer
M = Meyer

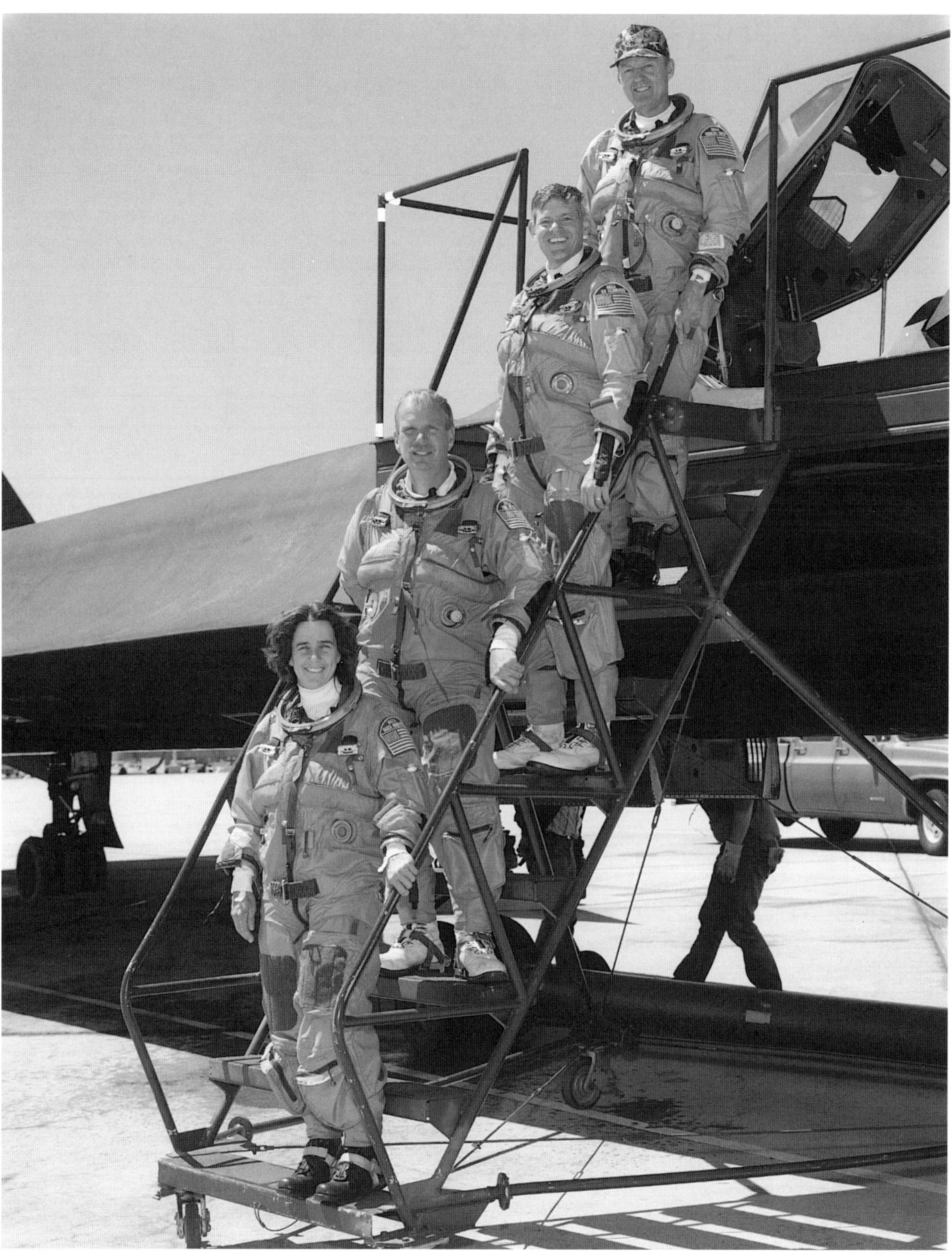

The current NASA team; top to bottom, Rogers Smith, Ed Schneider, Bob Meyer and Marta Bohn-Meyer *(NASA)*

Appendix 12

Edwards and Palmdale Test Crews

1965	Harold Burgeson	Pilot		
1966	Frenchy Bennett	Pilot	Bill Payne	RSO
	Joe Rogers	Pilot	Norm Drake	RSO
	B S Barett	Pilot	Hal Peterson	RSO
	Roland Perkim	Pilot	Jim Schever	RSO
	Ben Bowles	Pilot	John Carnochan	RSO
	Doug Nelson	Pilot		
1967			Bill Lusby	Engineer
			Bob Sudderth	Engineer
			Gary Heidlebaugh	RSO
			Dick Abrams	Engineer
1968	Dick Gerard	Pilot	Harold Chapman	RSO
	Charles McLean	Unk	Donn Byrnes	RSO
	Jim Sheltandr	Pilot	Bruce Hartman	RSO
	Rev Allender	Pilot	R W Weaver	RSO
	Fred Trost	Pilot	Don Rhude	RSO
			Ken Moeller	RSO
1969	Bruce Wilcox	Pilot		
	E L Payne	Pilot		
1970	Fitzhugh Fulton	Pilot (NASA)	Roland Selberg	RSO
	Don Mallick	Pilot (NASA)	Billy Curtis	RSO
1971			Vic Harton	RSO (NASA)

Appendix 13

Beale Staff Pilots and RSOs – 1965–1989

1965	Ray Haupt***	Chief of Flight Standardization and Director of Operations Chief Pilot
	Doug Nelson**	Wing Commander – Pilot
1966	Russ Lewis**	Director of Intelligence – Senior RSO
1967	Bill Hayes*	Wing Commander – Pilot
	Russ Weller	Director of Operations – Pilot
	Don Mathers*	Navigation Staff Planner – RSO
	Hal Confer**	Director of Operations and Wing Commander – Pilot
	Tom Casey**	Navigation Staff Officer – RSO
	John Boynton	Assistant Director of Operations – Pilot
	Charlie Minter*	Vice Commander and Wing Commander – Pilot
1968	Harlon Hain**	Squadron Commander and Director of Operations – Pilot
	Ken Collins***	Director of Operations – Pilot (1963 in A-12)
	Denny Sullivan***	Director of Operations – Pilot (1965 in A-12)
1969	Jim Anderson	Vice Commander – Pilot
1970	Roy Owen	Assisant Director of Operations – Pilot
1972	Ed Harris	14th Air Division Commander – Pilot
1974	Rafe Samay*	Squadron Commander and Assistant Director of Operations Staff Pilot
1975	Bob Beckel	Vice Commander – Pilot
	Richard Bower	Unknown
1976	Lyman Kidder	Vice Commander and Wing Commander – Pilot

Appendix 13 Beale staff pilots

1977	John Fenimore	Director of Operations – Pilot
1978	Andrew Terry	Director of Operations – Pilot
	David Young	Wing Commander – Pilot
1982	Lonnie Liss	Vice Commander – Pilot
1983	Hector Freese	Wing Commander – Pilot
	David Pinsky	Vice Commander and Wing Commander – Pilot
1985	John Farrington	14th Air Division Commander – Pilot
	Bob McConnell	Vice Commander – Pilot
	Alexander Davidson	HQ SAC
1986	James Sarvada	Wing Commander – Pilot
1987	Howell Estes	14th Air Division Commander – Pilot
	Don Schreiber	Vice Commander – Pilot
1988	Ken Keller	15th Air Force Vice Commander – Pilot
1989	John Borling	HQ SAC

* Designates those with more than one flight
** Fully checked out as Pilot or RSO
*** High Timers

Appendix 14

SR-71 Crewmembers by Order of Checkout

	Pilots	RSOs
1965	Al Hichew	Tom Schmittou
	Gray Sowers	Butch Sheffield
	John Storrie	Cos Mallozzi
	Ray Haupt	-----------
1966	Jack Kennon (at Edwards)	Cec Braeden
	Ben Bowles (at Edwards)	Jimmy Fagg
	Pete Collins	Connie Seagroves
	Bill Campbell	Al Pennington
	Pat Halloran	Mort Jarvis
	Buddy Brown	Dave Jensen
	Dale Shelton	Larry Boggess
	Jerry O'Malley	Ed Payne
	Don Walbrecht	Phil Loignon
	Earle Boone	Dewain Vick
1967	Jim Watkins	Dave Dempster
	Tony Bevacqua	Jerry Crew
	Larry DeVall	Clyde Shoemaker
	Bob Spencer	Keith Branham
	Brian McCallum	Bob Locke
	Roy St Martin	Jim Carnochan
	George Bull	Bill McNeer
	Bob Powell	Bill Kendrick
	Charlie Daubs	Bob Roetcisoender
	Bobby Campbell	Jon Kraus
	Abe Kardong	Jim Kogler
	Nick Maier	Gary Coleman
1968	Willy Lawson	Gil Martinez
	Dave Fruehauf	Al Payne
	Jim Hudson	Norb Budzinske
	Harlan Hain	(Sheffield)
	Tom Estes	(Vick)
	Jim Shelton	(Schmittou)
1969	Darrel Cobb	Myron Gantt
1970	Tom Pugh	Ronnie Rice
	Denny Bush	(Loignon)
	Randy Hertzog	(Carnochan)
	Caroll Gunther	Carl Haller
	George Sewell	Reggie Blackwell
1971	Robert Cunningham	G T Morgan
	Ty Judkin	(Shoemaker)
	Caroll Gunter	Tom Allocca
	Carl Haller	John Fuller
1972	Pat Bledsoe	Cleet Rogers
	Jim Sullivan	Noel Widdifield
	Lee Ransom	Mark Gersten
	Buck Adams	Bill Machorek
1973	Bob Helt	Larry Elliott
	Eldon Joersz	(Fuller)
	Jim Wilson	Bruce Douglas
	Maury Rosenberg	Don Bulloch
1974	Joe Kinego	Roger Jacks
	Al Cirino	Bruce Liebman
	Jay Murphy	John Billingsley
	Rich Graham	Don Emmons
1975	Tom Alison	Joe Vida
1976	Bob Crowder	John Morgan
	Al 'Buz' Carpenter	John Murphy
	John Veth	Bob Keller
1977	Bill Groninger	Charles Sober
	BC Thomas	Jay Reid
	Tom Keck	Tim Shaw
	Dave Peters	Ed Bethart
1978	Lee Shelton	Barry MacKean
	Rich Young	Russ Szczepanik
1980	Gil Bertelson	Frank Stampf
	Rich Judson	Frank Kelly
	Nevin Cunningham	Gene Quist
	Gerry Glasser	Dave Hornbaker
	Maury Rosenberg	ED Mckim
1981	Richard McCrary	Dave Lawrence
	Bernie Smith	Dennis Whalen
	Gary Luloff	Robert Coats

1982	Les Dyer	Dan Greenwood	1985	Bill Dykeman	Tom Bergam
	Bill Burk	Tom Henichek		Mike Smith	Doug Soifer
	Jim Jiggins	Joe McCue		-------	Phil Soucy
	Bob Behler	Ron Tabor		Dan House	Blair Bozek
1983	Stormy Boudreaux	Walt Newgreen	1986	Tom Danielson	Stan Gudmundson
	Joe Matthews	Ed Ross		Terry Pappas	John Manzi
	-------	Doug Osterheld		Warren McKendree	Randy Shelhorse
	Jack Madison	Bill Orcutt		Larry Brown	Keith Carter
	Ed Yeilding	Steve Lee	1987	Steve Grzebiniak	Jim Greenwood
1984	Brian Shul	Walt Watson		Tom McCleary	Hunter Vardaman
	Duane Deal	Tom Veltri		Greg Crittenden	Mike Finan
	Duane Noll	Chuck Morgan	1988	Don Watkins	Bob Fowlkes
				Ben Snyder	Briggs Shade

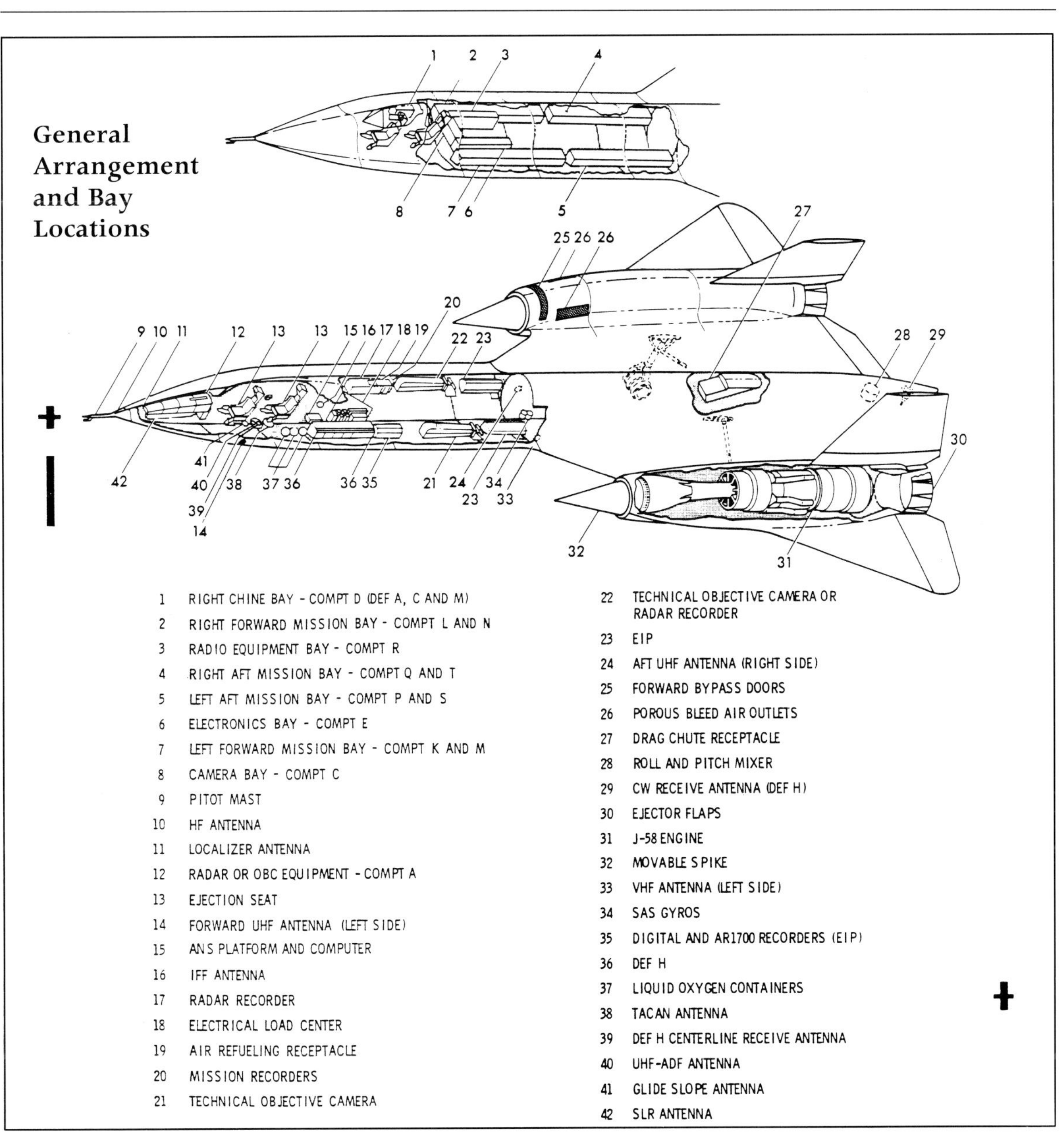

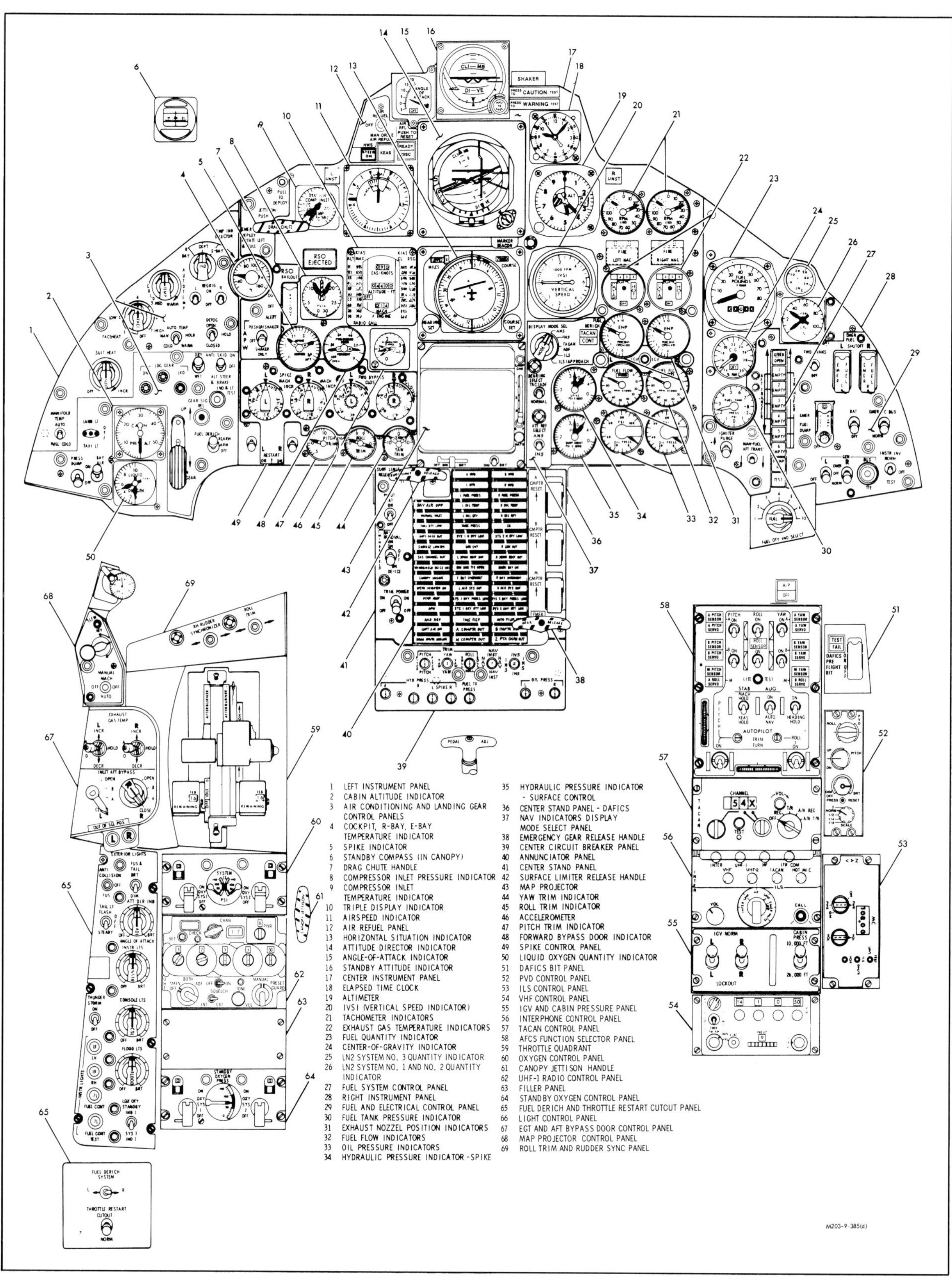
1 LEFT INSTRUMENT PANEL
2 CABIN ALTITUDE INDICATOR
3 AIR CONDITIONING AND LANDING GEAR CONTROL PANELS
4 COCKPIT, R-BAY, E-BAY TEMPERATURE INDICATOR
5 SPIKE INDICATOR
6 STANDBY COMPASS (IN CANOPY)
7 DRAG CHUTE HANDLE
8 COMPRESSOR INLET PRESSURE INDICATOR
9 COMPRESSOR INLET TEMPERATURE INDICATOR
10 TRIPLE DISPLAY INDICATOR
11 AIRSPEED INDICATOR
12 AIR REFUEL PANEL
13 HORIZONTAL SITUATION INDICATOR
14 ATTITUDE DIRECTOR INDICATOR
15 ANGLE-OF-ATTACK INDICATOR
16 STANDBY ATTITUDE INDICATOR
17 CENTER INSTRUMENT PANEL
18 ELAPSED TIME CLOCK
19 ALTIMETER
20 IVSI (VERTICAL SPEED INDICATOR)
21 TACHOMETER INDICATORS
22 EXHAUST GAS TEMPERATURE INDICATORS
23 FUEL QUANTITY INDICATOR
24 CENTER-OF-GRAVITY INDICATOR
25 LN2 SYSTEM NO. 3 QUANTITY INDICATOR
26 LN2 SYSTEM NO. 1 AND NO. 2 QUANTITY INDICATOR
27 FUEL SYSTEM CONTROL PANEL
28 RIGHT INSTRUMENT PANEL
29 FUEL AND ELECTRICAL CONTROL PANEL
30 FUEL TANK PRESSURE INDICATOR
31 EXHAUST NOZZEL POSITION INDICATORS
32 FUEL FLOW INDICATORS
33 OIL PRESSURE INDICATORS
34 HYDRAULIC PRESSURE INDICATOR - SPIKE
35 HYDRAULIC PRESSURE INDICATOR - SURFACE CONTROL
36 CENTER STAND PANEL - DAFICS
37 NAV INDICATORS DISPLAY MODE SELECT PANEL
38 EMERGENCY GEAR RELEASE HANDLE
39 CENTER CIRCUIT BREAKER PANEL
40 ANNUNCIATOR PANEL
41 CENTER STAND PANEL
42 SURFACE LIMITER RELEASE HANDLE
43 MAP PROJECTOR
44 YAW TRIM INDICATOR
45 ROLL TRIM INDICATOR
46 ACCELEROMETER
47 PITCH TRIM INDICATOR
48 FORWARD BYPASS DOOR INDICATOR
49 SPIKE CONTROL PANEL
50 LIQUID OXYGEN QUANTITY INDICATOR
51 DAFICS BIT PANEL
52 PVD CONTROL PANEL
53 ILS CONTROL PANEL
54 VHF CONTROL PANEL
55 IGV AND CABIN PRESSURE PANEL
56 INTERPHONE CONTROL PANEL
57 TACAN CONTROL PANEL
58 AFCS FUNCTION SELECTOR PANEL
59 THROTTLE QUADRANT
60 OXYGEN CONTROL PANEL
61 CANOPY JETTISON HANDLE
62 UHF-1 RADIO CONTROL PANEL
63 FILLER PANEL
64 STANDBY OXYGEN CONTROL PANEL
65 FUEL DERICH AND THROTTLE RESTART CUTOUT PANEL
66 LIGHT CONTROL PANEL
67 EGT AND AFT BYPASS DOOR CONTROL PANEL
68 MAP PROJECTOR CONTROL PANEL
69 ROLL TRIM AND RUDDER SYNC PANEL
M203-9-385(d)

SR-71A Forward cockpit instrument panel and side consoles

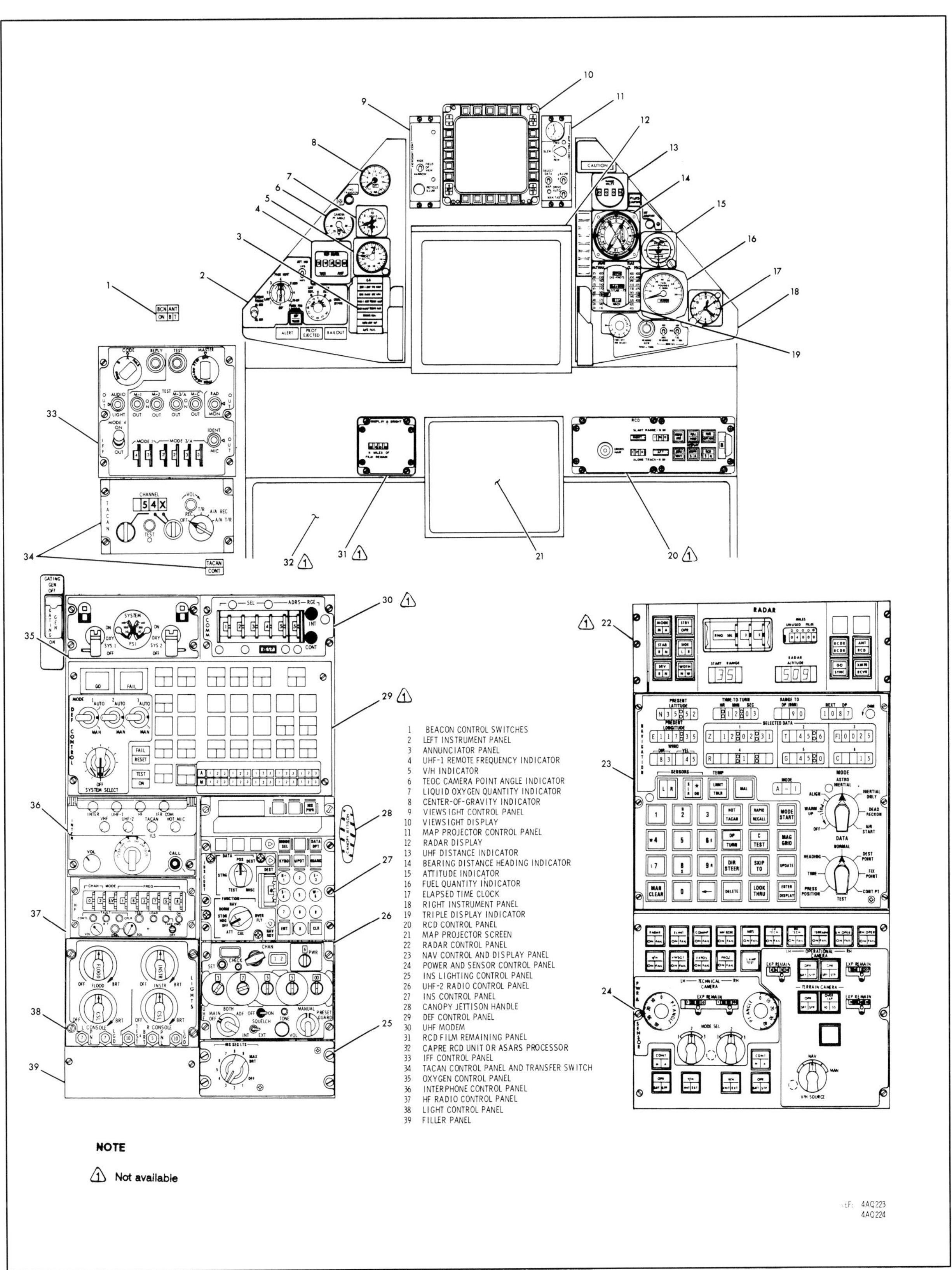
1 BEACON CONTROL SWITCHES
2 LEFT INSTRUMENT PANEL
3 ANNUNCIATOR PANEL
4 UHF-1 REMOTE FREQUENCY INDICATOR
5 V/H INDICATOR
6 TEOC CAMERA POINT ANGLE INDICATOR
7 LIQUID OXYGEN QUANTITY INDICATOR
8 CENTER-OF-GRAVITY INDICATOR
9 VIEWSIGHT CONTROL PANEL
10 VIEWSIGHT DISPLAY
11 MAP PROJECTOR CONTROL PANEL
12 RADAR DISPLAY
13 UHF DISTANCE INDICATOR
14 BEARING DISTANCE HEADING INDICATOR
15 ATTITUDE INDICATOR
16 FUEL QUANTITY INDICATOR
17 ELAPSED TIME CLOCK
18 RIGHT INSTRUMENT PANEL
19 TRIPLE DISPLAY INDICATOR
20 RCD CONTROL PANEL
21 MAP PROJECTOR SCREEN
22 RADAR CONTROL PANEL
23 NAV CONTROL AND DISPLAY PANEL
24 POWER AND SENSOR CONTROL PANEL
25 INS LIGHTING CONTROL PANEL
26 UHF-2 RADIO CONTROL PANEL
27 INS CONTROL PANEL
28 CANOPY JETTISON HANDLE
29 DEF CONTROL PANEL
30 UHF MODEM
31 RCD FILM REMAINING PANEL
32 CAPRE RCD UNIT OR ASARS PROCESSOR
33 IFF CONTROL PANEL
34 TACAN CONTROL PANEL AND TRANSFER SWITCH
35 OXYGEN CONTROL PANEL
36 INTERPHONE CONTROL PANEL
37 HF RADIO CONTROL PANEL
38 LIGHT CONTROL PANEL
39 FILLER PANEL
NOTE
1 Not available
4AQ223
4AQ224

SR-71A Aft cockpit instrument panel and side consoles

Lockheed SR-71A

1 Pitot tube
2 Air data probe
3 Radar warning antennae
4 Nose mission equipment bay
5 Panoramic camera aperture
6 Detachable nose cone joint frame
7 Cockpit front pressue bulkhead
8 Rudder pedals
9 Control column
10 Instrument panel
11 Instrument panel shroud
12 Knife-edged windscreen panels
13 Upward hinged cockpit canopy covers
14 Ejection seat headrest
15 Canopy actuator
16 Pilot's Lockheed 'zero-zero' ejection seat
17 Engine throttle levers
18 Side console panel
19 Fuselage chine close-pitched frame construction
20 Liquid oxygen converters (2)
21 Side console panel
22 Reconnaissance Systems Officer's (RSO) instrument display
23 Cockpit rear pressure bulkhead
24 RSO's Lockheed 'zero-zero' ejection seat
25 Canopy hinge point
26 SR-71B dual control trainer variant, nose profile
27 Raised instructor's rear cockpit
28 Astro navigation star tracker
29 Navigation and communications systems electronic equipment
30 Nosewheel bay
31 Nose undercarriage pivot fixing
32 Landing and taxying lamps
33 Twin nosewheels (forward retracting)
34 Hydraulic retraction jack
35 Cockpit environmental system equipment bay
36 Air refuelling receptacle (open)
37 Fuselage upper longeron
38 Forward fuselage frame construction
39 Forward fuselage integral fuel tanks
40 Palletised, interchange-able reconnaissance equipment packs
41 Fuselage chine member
42 Forward/centre fuselage joint ring frame
43 Centre fuselage integral fuel tanks; total system capacity 12,200 US gal (46,182 l)
44 Beta B.120 titanium alloy skin panelling
45 Corrugated wing skin panelling
46 Starboard main under carriage, stowed position
47 Intake centre-body bleed air louvres
48 By-pass duct suction relief louvres
49 Starboard engine air intake
50 Movable intake conical centre-body
51 Centre-body retracted (high speed) position
52 Boundary layer bleed air holes
53 Automatic intake control system air data probe
54 Diffuser chamber
55 Variable inlet guide vanes
56 Hinged engine cowling/outer wing panel
57 Pratt & Whitney JT11D-20B (J58) single spool turbo-ramjet engine
58 Engine accessory equipment
59 By-pass duct suction relief doors
60 Compressor bleed air by-pass ducts
61 Afterburner fuel manifold
62 Tailfin fixed root section
63 Starboard outer wing panel
64 Under-cambered leading edge
65 Outboard, roll control, elevon
66 All-moving starboard fin
67 Continuously operating afterburning duct
68 Afterburner nozzle

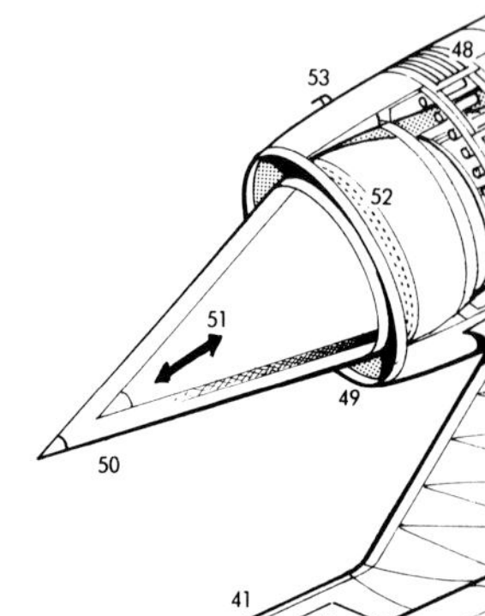

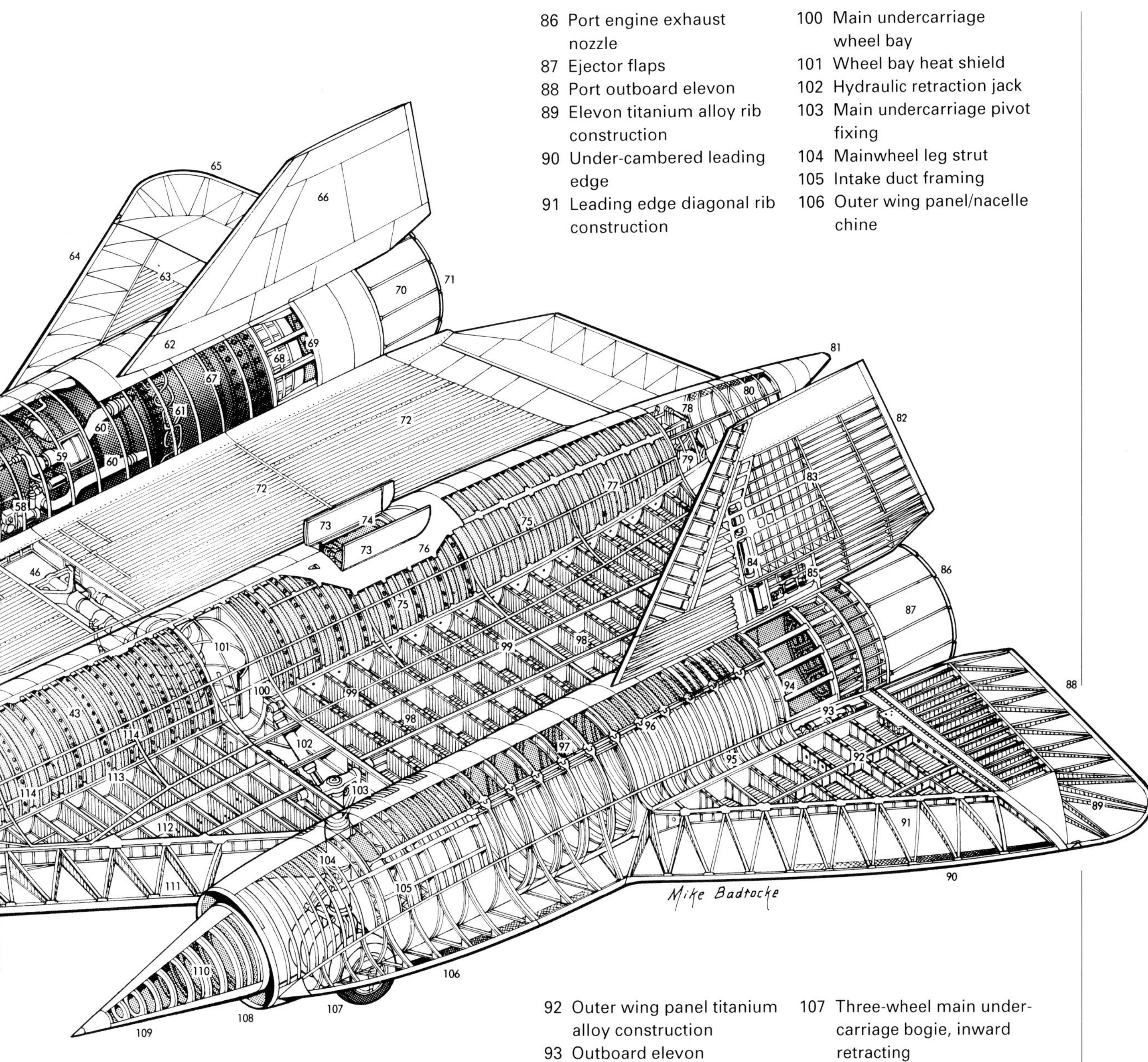

69 Engine bay tertiary air flats
70 Exhaust nozzle ejector flaps
71 Variable area exhaust nozzle
72 Starboard wing integral fuel tank bays
73 Brake parachute doors, open
74 Ribbon parachute stowage
75 Aft fuselage integral fuel tanks
76 Skin doubler
77 Aft fuselage frame construction
78 Elevon mixer unit
79 Inboard elevon torque control shaft
80 Tailcone
81 Fuel vent
82 Port all-moving fin
83 Fin rib construction
84 Torque shaft hinge mounting
85 Fin hydraulic actuator
86 Port engine exhaust nozzle
87 Ejector flaps
88 Port outboard elevon
89 Elevon titanium alloy rib construction
90 Under-cambered leading edge
91 Leading edge diagonal rib construction
92 Outer wing panel titanium alloy construction
93 Outboard elevon hydraulic actuator
94 Engine bay tertiary air flaps
95 Engine nacelle/outer wing panel integral construction
96 Engine cowling/wing panel hinge axis
97 Port nacelle ring frame construction
98 Inboard wing panel integral fuel tank bays
99 Multi-spar titanium alloy wing construction
100 Main undercarriage wheel bay
101 Wheel bay heat shield
102 Hydraulic retraction jack
103 Main undercarriage pivot fixing
104 Mainwheel leg strut
105 Intake duct framing
106 Outer wing panel/nacelle chine
107 Three-wheel main under-carriage bogie, inward retracting
108 Port engine air intake
109 Movable conical intake centre-body
110 Centre-body frame construction
111 Inboard leading edge diagonal rib construction
112 Inner wing panel integral fuel tank
113 Wing root/fuselage attachment root rib
114 Close-pitched fuselage titanium alloy frames
115 Wing/fuselage chine blended fairing panels

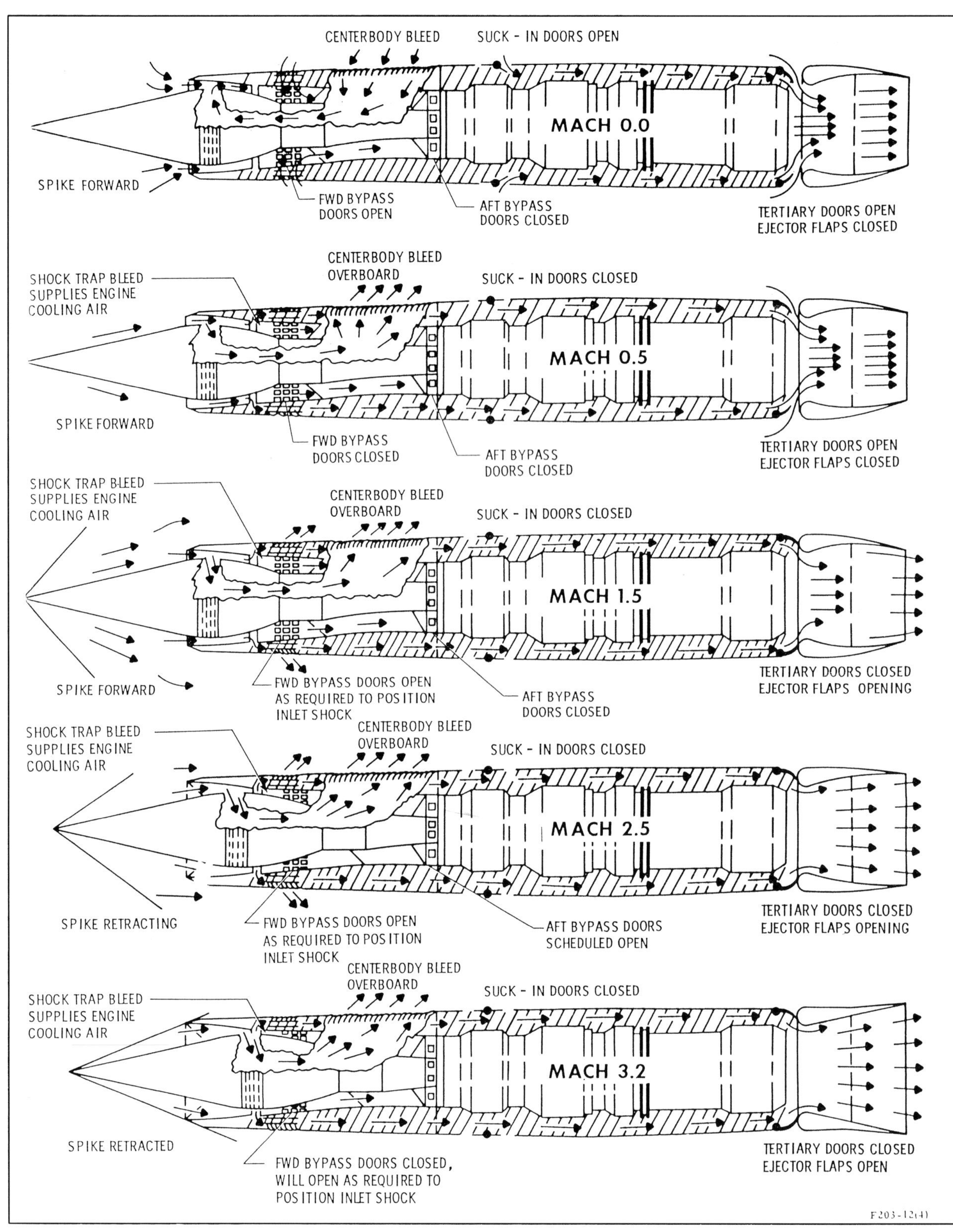

Lockheed SR-71A Inlet airflow diagram

Index